North of Everything

English-Canadian Cinema Since 1980

North of
everything

English-Canadian Cinema
since 1980

EDITED BY

William Beard

AND

Jerry White

University of Alberta Press

PUBLISHED BY
The University of Alberta Press
Ring House 2
Edmonton, Alberta T6G 2E1

Volume copyright © 2002 The University of Alberta Press.
Copyright for the individual chapters is retained by the rights holders.

NATIONAL LIBRARY OF CANADA CATALOGUING IN PUBLICATION DATA

Main entry under title:

North of everything

Includes bibliographical references.
ISBN 0-88864-398-5 (bound) – ISBN 0-88864-390-X (pbk.)

1. Motion pictures–Canada–History. I. Beard, William, 1946- II.
White, Jerry, 1971-
PN1993.5.C3N67 2002   791.43'0971   C2002-910362-2

The University of Alberta Press acknowledges the financial support of the Government of Canada through the Book Publishing Industry Development Program for its publishing activities. The Press also gratefully acknowledges the support received for its program from the Canada Council for the Arts.

Printed and bound in Canada by Houghton Boston, Saskatoon, Saskatchewan.
∞ Printed on acid-free paper.
Proofreading assistance by Tara Taylor.
Book design by Bruce Timothy Keith.
Cover design by Gregory Brown.

Contents

SECTION THREE
Aboriginal Voices

SECTION FOUR
The Avant Garde

Contributors

CHARLES R. ACLAND teaches media and cultural theory in the Department of Communication Studies, Concordia University. His books include *Youth, Murder, Spectacle: The Cultural Politics of "Youth in Crisis"* (1995) and a co-edited collection, with William J. Buxton, *Harold Innis in the New Century: Reflections and Refractions* (1999).

BLAINE ALLAN is an Associate Professor in the Department of Film Studies, Queen's University. He is co-editor of *Responses* (1992), is author of a reference guide on Nicholas Ray (1984), and has appeared in journals including *Canadian Journal of Film Studies, Historical Journal of Film, Radio, and Television,* and *Film Quarterly.*

KAY ARMATAGE is Associate Professor of Women's Studies and Cinema Studies, University of Toronto, and programmer for the Toronto International Film Festival. She co-edited *Gendering the Nation: Canadian Women's Cinema* (1999) and edited *Equity and How to Get It* (1999). Her book on Nell Shipman will be published in 2002.

KASS BANNING is a lecturer at Innis College, University of Toronto, and is a co-editor of *Gendering the Nation: Canadian Women's Cinema* (1999). She is at work on a manuscript entitled *Configurations of Race and Nation in Recent Canadian Film.*

WILLIAM BEARD is Professor of Film/Media Studies at the University of Alberta, where he is co-ordinator of the Film/Media Studies program. He is author of *Persistence of Double Vision: Essays on Clint Eastwood* (2000) and *The Artist as Monster: The Cinema of David Cronenberg* (2001).

LYNNE BELL is Professor of Visual Culture, University of Saskatchewan. She curated the exhibition *Urban Fictions* (1997), is currently co-editing with Lori Blondeau *High Tech Storytellers: An Interdisciplinary Indigenous Art Project* (2002), and is working on a collaborative SSHRC-funded study *Decolonizing Education in Canadian Universities: An Interdisciplinary Indigenous Research Project.*

MARIA DE ROSA is President of Communications MDR, a consulting practice based in Montréal specializing in policy analysis, program development, and strategic planning for the cultural industries of film, television, and publishing. She is also a freelance writer for print media and has a television documentary to her credit.

SETH FELDMAN has published widely on Canadian cinema and is a founder and past president of the Film Studies Association of Canada. He is a former Dean of Fine Arts at York University and the author of twenty-three radio documentaries for the CBC program *Ideas.*

NOREEN GOLFMAN teaches film and Canadian literature in the English department at Memorial University of Newfoundland. A former president of ACCUTE, she has also written on film for *Canadian Forum,* has been a fiction panellist on CBC Radio's *This Morning,* and is founding director of the St. John's International Women's Film Festival.

STEVE GRAVESTOCK is the Programming Coordinator at the Toronto International Film Festival. He is currently editing *Interviews: Louis Malle* for the University of Mississippi Press and is a contributor to *Cinema Scope* (where he is a contributing editor), *Take One,* and *Festival Magazine.*

D.B. JONES is a Professor of Film at Drexel University. He is author of *Movies and Memoranda: An Interpretive History of the National Film Board of Canada* (1981) and *The Best Butler in the Business: Tom Daly of the National Film Board* (1997).

JACQUELINE LEVITIN is an Associate Professor of Women's Studies and of Film in the School for the Contemporary Arts at Simon Fraser University in Vancouver. She is also a filmmaker of both documentary and fiction films. Her current project is on women, health, and housing in Vancouver's downtown eastside.

ANDRÉ LOISELLE teaches Film Studies at Carleton University. He is author of a book on Anne Claire Poirier's film, *Mourir à tue-tête* (2000) and co-editor with Brian McIlroy of the book *Auteur/Provocateur: The Films of Denys Arcand* (1995).

SUSAN LORD is Associate Professor in the Department of Film Studies at Queen's University. Her articles have been published in *Gendering the Nation: Canadian Women's Cinema* (1999), *Women Filmmakers: Refocussing* (2002), *Public,* and *CineAction.* She is currently completing a manuscript on Anne Wheeler and has begun a research project on the late Cuban filmmaker Sara Gómez.

BRIAN McILROY is Professor of Film Studies at the University of British Columbia. He was co-editor with André Loiselle of *Auteur/Provocateur: The Films of Denys Arcand* (1995). His most recent book is *Shooting to Kill: Filmmaking and the "Troubles" in Northern Ireland* (1998, 2001).

LAURA U. MARKS, a theorist and programmer of experimental media, is author of *The Skin of the Film: Intercultural Cinema, Embodiment, and the Senses* (1999) and the forthcoming *Touch: Sensuous Theory and Multisensory Media.* She is Associate Professor of Film Studies at Carleton University.

LEE PARPART is a PhD candidate in Social and Political Thought at York University in Toronto. A former video columnist with the *Globe and Mail,* she has taught film studies at York University and the University of Toronto, and has contributed essays to *Gendering the Nation* (1999), *Canadian Journal of Film Studies, Masculinity: Bodies, Movies, Cultures* (2001), and *POV.*

GEOFF PEVERE is a writer, broadcaster, and hoser of long standing. When not converting whale blubber into aftershave, he writes about movies for the *Toronto Star.* He is co-author of *Mondo Canuck* (1996) and a former programmer for the Toronto International Film Festival.

CHRISTINE RAMSAY is a Professor in the Department of Media Production and Studies at the University of Regina and president of the Film Studies Association of Canada. She has published on Canadian cinema and gender in such journals as *Canadian Journal of Film Studies* and *PostScript,* and has a forthcoming article in *Canada's Ten Best Features.*

CHRIS ROBINSON is the artistic director of the Ottawa International Animation Festival, founder and director of the Ottawa International Student Animation Festival, and editor of *ASIFA News*. He has curated film programs and served on festival juries throughout the world, writes a monthly column for Animation World Network, and is currently writing a book on animation in Estonia, due out in 2003.

WAYNE ROTHSCHILD is a former editor of *Wide Angle* and has also published in *Cinémas*. He currently teaches film studies at the University of Alberta and is active in a number of political organizations at the University and in Edmonton.

CATHERINE RUSSELL is Associate Professor of Film Studies at Concordia University in Montréal. She is the author of *Narrative Mortality: Death, Closure and New Wave Cinemas* (1995) and *Experimental Ethnography: The Work of Film in the Age of Video* (1999).

STEVEN SHAVIRO teaches in the Cinema Studies Program at the University of Washington. He is the author of *The Cinematic Body* (1993), *Doom Patrols: A Theoretical Fiction About Postmodernism* (1997), and numerous articles on digital culture and on contemporary North American film.

JASON SILVERMAN is the artistic director of the Taos Talking Pictures Festival and curatorial assistant at the Telluride Film Festival. He has written extensively on film and mass media, is a contributing writer at *Wired News,* and contributed to *Critical Guide to Contemporary Directors: North America* (2000).

MONQIUE TSCHOFEN is Assistant Professor of English at Ryerson University. She is currently finishing a book on Kristjana Gunnars and editing an anthology on Atom Egoyan, both for Guernica Press, and has published in *Canadian Review of Comparative Literature*.

GENE WALZ is Provost of University College and Professor of Film Studies at the University of Manitoba. He has published extensively on Canadian film, including *Canada's Best Features* (forthcoming), an anthology of fifteen essays which he edited, and *Cartoon Charlie*, winner of two awards.

THOMAS WAUGH teaches Film Studies at Concordia University, where he has developed curricula on HIV/AIDS and sexuality/queer studies. His books include *The Fruit Machine: Twenty Years of Writings on Queer Cinema* (2000) and *Hard to Imagine: Gay Male Eroticism in Photography and Film from Their Beginnings to Stonewall* (1996).

JERRY WHITE is Assistant Professor of Film/Media Studies at the University of Alberta. He has worked for the Philadelphia, Edmonton, Taos, and Telluride film festivals, and is president of the Canadian Association for Irish Studies.

JANICE WILLIAMSON, a Professor in the Department of English at the University of Alberta, has published five books, most recently *Crybaby!* At present, she is at play with "Hexagrams For My Chinese Daughter," a creative documentary memoir about the adoption of her beloved child.

ROBIN WOOD is retired from York University's Atkinson College, author of many seminal works of film criticism (including *Hitchcock's Films Revisited*), and on the editorial collective of *CineAction*. His most recent books are *Sexual Politics and Narrative Film* (1998) and *Wings of the Dove* (1999).

LYSANDRA WOODS is a former film critic for the Edmonton weekly *See* and contributed to *Critical Guide to Contemporary Directors: North America* (2000). She has taught Film Studies at the University of Alberta and is currently a graduate student in Cinema Studies at Concordia University.

MICHAEL ZRYD teaches Film Studies at the University of Western Ontario and writes primarily on experimental/avant-garde cinema and documentary film. He has published in *Canadian Journal of Film Studies, The Moving Image, Public, Film Quarterly*, and *Shipwreck* (2001).

Foreword

Seth Feldman

BILL BEARD AND JERRY WHITE HAVE SOMEHOW REMEMBERED *Canadian Film Reader* and *Take Two*, the long-out-of-print 1976 and 1984 anthologies on Canadian cinema in which I had a hand. This led to their asking me to write the Foreword to their overdue and much-needed collection of writing on the last twenty years of Canadian cinema. I am delighted to do so just as I am delighted they have undertaken this thankless project. The editors have also done the field a service in spotlighting so many of the recently emerging and even not so recently emerging commentators who make Canadian film studies at least as lively an experience as the films themselves

So much for the jacket blurb. Looking at the articles contained herein, I would like to disabuse the reader of the notion that Beard and White's collection is in any way a continuation of the early days of writing on Canadian cinema or of a cinema milieu that is today unrecognizable. When Joyce Nelson and I edited *Canadian Film Reader* a quarter century ago, we were simply trying to make the point that there was a body of films that could, with much work, be construed as the beginnings of a national cinema. The Film Studies Association of Canada, conceived the same year as the anthology, would undertake the making of that case. Its members sought out the elusive prints and even more elusive scholarly writing. They invented Canadian cinema courses and, several convocations later, found they had reproduced themselves.

On its part, *Take Two* was compiled in conjunction with the first Perspective Canada. That was an event at which the Toronto International Film Festival (then the Festival of Festivals) suggested that there were not only enough films to talk about but enough good Canadian cinema that our work could be screened, without undue embarrassment, alongside the world's best. The Festival has made this case every September since—as has virtually every cinema event in this country.

Today, we may congratulate ourselves on our early and mostly unfounded hubris. We looked at the cinemas of Europe, Japan, and even the developing world as models for what Canada could be. Perhaps we could be forgiven for seeing Cuban cinema as identical to Cuba itself, the New German cinema as defining the new Germany. It was too early (at least in English Canada) to document the exact relationship between Québec cinema and the politics of Québec nationalism—but there was no doubt that the link was a strong one. And with this in mind, we were sure that a vibrant Canadian cinema (in conjunction with the rapid rise of CanLit and Canadian music) would provide the long-elusive national identity.

The consequence of this logic was very much apparent in the writings selected for those earlier anthologies. Many of the authors Joyce Nelson and I included lived in a state of outrage at the lack of a national cinema; the pieces they contributed were righteous and welcome polemics. It was a moment permeated with a sense of beginning, and we forgave much. An auteur was anyone who had completed two features, at least one of them watchable. Documentary filmmaking was never more than two reels away from sparking revolution. And both forms were about to be swept aside by the avant-garde practices that Bruce Elder would describe not long after as "the cinema we need."

A quarter century ago, we wrote about a largely imagined cinema; now we write about one that is all too real. After all the fuss, Canada is still the home of a truly marginal cinema. Although the margin is larger, the features we make are shot, on average, in three weeks and on about one-tenth the budget of their Hollywood competition. Once made, they continue to be treated as foreign films when—if—they appear on Canadian screens, usually at art houses and usually for short runs. Television, depending upon whom you believe, has either helped by making these films more widely available or has served as yet another reminder that Canadians enjoy a minimal presence in their own movie theatres. Sympathetic critics hype our films and pretend their creators are on par with the Hollywood celebs who glide effortlessly across the entertainment pages. In the privacy of their own homes, consenting adults snicker at the production values and general lack of glam in Canadian film. The political right begrudges every cent of public funding that goes into filmmaking while the left protests any profit that comes out of it. Every year, around the time of the Genies, there is no shortage of reminders that relatively few paying customers have actually seen the films being celebrated.

Not surprisingly, since the 1970s and early 1980s, most Canadians lost whatever expectation they may have had that film would serve as a nation-building tool. In fact, just the opposite has happened. The Americans studios didn't leave our movie theatres. Instead, their elaborate shoots invaded our streets to compete for public funding against our far more humble "local" productions. Questions of what was and wasn't Canadian about a film have long since been settled by a perfectly logical and highly malleable point system. The very idea that any nation could sustain an independent national cinema is now treated with some nostalgia. Who would have guessed that Canadianization was the model for what our idealized cinema/nations would become, that other nations' cineplexes would come so closely to resemble our own? Nor is there any indication, no matter how intense the outrage and struggle, that this is going to change. American cultural hegemony is like "late capitalism" in that it just keeps getting later.

The result of these several setbacks is our more pragmatic view not of the Canadian identity we want or need but rather of the best one we are going to get. Outside of a somewhat ironic beer commercial, there is, in this second year of the new century, not much interest in what it means to be Canadian. In their daily lives, most individual English Canadians are sufficiently secure in their regionalism and ethnicity to accept Canada as a nationless state. Ottawa offers its citizens—or, more properly, its subscribers—a state apparatus that, at least according to UN standards (and certainly in comparison to the Americans), serves us well. Put a bit more optimistically, the nationless Canadian state serves us well enough that we might ask if we really want to live in a nation that, like the United States, has placed the national fantasy at the nexus of daily life.

By the same token, we might wonder how important a role we would like for the fantasy industry in our industrial strategy. The Americans have discovered there is a price to be paid for being Hollywood's company town. Public discourse becomes an entertainment composed of predictable events and an even more predictable set of characters. History is sold as a happy ending just over the horizon.

There might be some wisdom to a nationless state's limiting film expression to a set of policies, goals that might be summarized as follows:

First, that we have the means to discuss issues of national importance through the use of moving-image technologies.

Secondly, that we use our mixed economy to provide the means by which the artists and craftspeople who work with the moving image can pursue their vocations.

Thirdly, that we have as a goal a contribution to the international dialogue that takes place through the moving image or at least that part of the moving image that remains outside the Hollywood sphere.

As the contents of this volume demonstrate, Canada has, by these measures, enjoyed a degree of success that would not have disappointed the polemicists of a quarter century ago. After some billions of dollars of trial and error, there is a reasonable expectation that our documentaries and fiction films on the large and small screen will, from time to time, reflect if not inspire a national agenda. There are a handful of internationally recognized Canadian film artists, people secure enough to survive a failed project, people who can do their work in this country. Avant-garde filmmaking is stronger in Canada than it is in most places. Those who do not necessarily aspire to artistic control enjoy careers in an industry that is likely to flourish as long as the Canadian dollar is not replaced by hard currency. They are, by all accounts, extremely good at what they do. And we do well on that alternative international circuit, the trade in cinema that is not Hollywood. Canada is at the festivals; cinematheques offer us retrospectives. Not all the writing on Canadian cinema takes place within the borders of Canada.

One price we have paid for this pragmatic success is demonstrated by the organization of this collection. Were we a nation capable of being scandalized, some readers would react in just that way to the exclusion of Québec or even, as Beard and White suggest in their Introduction, its *de facto* independence in a hypothetical second volume. My Canada includes the wish that it were otherwise but, frankly speaking, the absence of Québec is as much a part of contemporary Canadian cinema as is the presence of the films discussed here. Nor, despite the Herculean efforts of a few individuals, has a bilingual cinema ever really been a national priority. The National Film Board and the CBC have never been very successful in carrying their own products across the linguistic divide. Private filmmakers are more likely to collaborate with foreign investors who speak their own language. And neither of these logistical factors is as important as the schism dividing the very nature of the two cinemas: Québec's pursuit of the localized and self-referential versus Canada's ethos of the cross-regional and multicultural.

To a small and perhaps unintentional extent, Québec has been replaced here by a welcome emphasis on Native filmmaking. The editors are entirely correct in their assertion that not only have these filmmakers come of age but their films have grown into a coherent body of work. But there is another reason for a more general interest in Native expression. First Nations are for most Anglophone Canadians the vicarious thrill of a deserving nationalism. They are the non-threatening distinct society, a people linked to the land whose singular case we can all affirm with some guilt but minimal real cost. Whether or not First Nations peoples see themselves this way is irrelevant to this particular corner of the national project (having seen some of the Native films described in this volume, I think they are far less sombre about their identity than we are). What is more important is that what remains of Canadian nationalism is subsumed in the gesture of finding other nations.

Another price we have paid is represented here by the exclusion of a section on documentary filmmaking–although documentary and animation survive as healthy subtexts in the volume. Documentaries worthy of critical attention have indeed been made in this country during the last twenty years. Canada is still known for its work in the genre–and that, of course, is the problem. Documentaries represent the excellence that John Grierson foisted upon us, what someone else made us do before we were smart enough to think for ourselves. Documentary is, by virtue of this historical placement, too often perceived by Canadians as our colonial expression–and indeed, at the Academy Awards, prize Canadian documentaries are treated as a quaint but well-crafted contribution from the developing world. Directors, craftspeople, whole companies try to move on from doing documentaries to the worlds of feature films and television drama. Their ability to do so is seen as a measure of their success.

All of this is reflected in an institutionalized contempt for documentary filmmaking. The National Film Board has already celebrated the fiftieth anniversary of calls for its dissolution and (at least) the thirtieth anniversary of its progressive underfunding. Our largest pots of film-development subsidy are proud to shut the genre out just as our theorists are wont to remind us that the pursuit of truth is naïve, hopeless, and decidedly modernist. Or it may be just that documentaries thrive in times of strife and that, in these last two decades of economic boom, it has become harder to notice them. Conversely, with the recent collapse of the high-tech boom, we may be able to look forward to a documentary renaissance–perhaps one whose fruits may be considered in the next volume of this work.

Beard and White are to be commended for including in this volume a section on the Canadian avant garde. Canada has, from Norman McLaren's arrival, always had room for at least one extraordinary experimental filmmaker. What is surprising is that we now have so many. There are no Academy Awards for the avant garde, no junkets to Cannes, only grudging and confused mention in the entertainment section. Nevertheless, our arts councils have, by and large, succeeded in making it possible for these filmmakers to develop as artists. Many of our film schools–despite the temptation to redefine experimental film as digital effects–continue to incubate the genre in its richest form. The results are the major figures discussed here and the far longer list of avant garde film and video artists to whom the editors make their apologies in their Introduction. A second outcome is a kind of safety-net cinema, an assurance provided by the avant garde that the moving image can be a product of conscious intent transcending the logistics of production and the geopolitical whims that spawn them.

Acknowledgements

SOME OF THIS MATERIAL has been previously published elsewhere. Lynne Bell and Janice Williamson's "In the Hands of the People: A Conversation with Marjorie Beaucage" originally appeared as "On Crossing Lines and Going Between: An Interview with Marjorie Beaucage" in *Tessera* 22 (1997), but the authors have added the introduction for this volume. Laura U. Marks' essay originally appeared, in a different form, in *Lux: A Decade of Artists' Film and Video*, Steve Reinke and Tom Taylor, eds. (Toronto: YYZ and Pleasure Dome, 2000). Jerry White's essay on Alanis Obomsawin originally appeared in *CineAction!* 49 (1999). Robin Wood's essay on William MacGillivray also originally appeared in *CineAction!* 17 (1989), although here we reprint a revised version that appeared in his book *Sexual Politics and Narrative Film* (New York: Columbia University Press, 1998) it is used by permission. Many thanks to the publishers, editors, and, in the case of *CineAction!*, editorial collectives for their kind permission to reprint.

Introduction

"ENGLISH-CANADIAN CINEMA SINCE 1980"—WHY? Why since 1980 (and not some other date), why English-Canadian (and not, especially, French-Canadian), and why cinema (and not television, multimedia, or other manifestations of moving-image culture)? These are all questions to be asked about the present volume, and ones which we did some thinking about before setting out on our work. In 1977, early in the history of film studies in English Canada, there appeared Peter Harcourt's overview of Canadian "national cinema," *Movies and Mythologies*, and Seth Feldman and Joyce Nelson's *Canadian Film Reader*, a survey of Canadian film in the form of an anthology of essays on specific subjects. In the succeeding decade, more books of this kind arrived: Pierre Véronneau and Piers Handling's *Self-Portrait* (1980) and Feldman's *Take Two* (1984), as well as Douglas Fetherling's *Documents in Canadian Film* (1988) and David Clandfield's single-authored, very short, but very complete survey *Canadian Film* (1987). Whatever their inevitable omissions or other limiting consequences of editorial/authorial choice, they performed a useful function for both scholars and pedagogues: the function of trying to bring as broad a spectrum of the phenomenon of Canadian film as was practicable into one volume.

Since that time, around a decade and a half ago, the currents of book-form scholarship on the subject have taken rather different channels. A parallel tradition of historical, institutional, and socio-industrial scholarship began early in the 1980s and has flourished right through the 1990s. There have been several books about the foundation and subsequent history of the National Film Board and some of its powerful individual figures (notably D.B. Jones' *Movies and Memoranda* and *Tom Daly: The Best Butler in the Business*, Gary Evans' *John Grierson and the National Film Board* and *In the National Interest*, and Joyce Nelson's *The Colonized Eye*), a detailed study of the early history of Canadian cinema (Peter Morris' *Embattled Shadows*), and a substantial literature about the industrial and political base of Canadian film production, distribution, and exhibition (books by Manjunath Pendakur, Ted Magder, and Michael Dorland). The title and bulk of Bruce Elder's *Image and Identity: Reflections on Canadian Film and Culture* seem to promise a substantial general consideration of the subject, but in fact his book concentrates mostly on avant-garde cinema. The recently published anthology *Gendering the Nation* (edited by Kay Armatage, Kass Banning, Brenda Longfellow, and Janine Marchessault) is again a substantial contribution but restricts itself to women's cinema; two other anthologies reportedly in press—*Canada's Best Features* (edited by Gordon Collier and Gene Walz) and *Canada's Unknown Cinemas* (edited by Chris Faulkner and William O'Farrell)—also have narrower organizing principles. Our Alberta colleague Chris Gittings' newly published *Canadian National Cinemas: Ideology, Difference, and Representation*, an instalment in the Routledge National Cinema series, is a wide-ranging study, taking the whole history of film in Canada as its field; but it has a theoretical approach, and also a topic (the construction of nation). Ironically, the only general study of English-Canadian cinema in the last decade has been done in French: Pierre Vérroneau's valuable 1991 anthology *À la recherche d'une identité: Renaissance du cinéma d'auteur canadien-anglais*, published by the Cinémathèque Québécoise.

What we have endeavoured to do is to move back to a similarly general vantage point and to cover a broad field: to do something akin to the work *The Canadian Film Reader*, *Self Portrait*, and *Take Two* were doing twenty-odd years ago. Of course, our range of subjects and our predispositions are somewhat different, but we hope we have provided something comparable for this moment. Setting a starting point of 1980 is arbitrary to an extent, but it does serve the functions of not overlapping very much with the material covered in *Take Two*, enabling a concentration on work which has so far not received this kind of attention, and helping to restrict the subject to at least somewhat manageable dimensions.

Part of this manageability has entailed the omission of Québec or Francophone-Canadian cinema. This exclusion will undoubtedly raise some eyebrows among our readers, but it has led us towards a consideration of some crucial issues in both cultural studies throughout Canada and in film historiography. Of course we do not hope to offer definitive answers to these ongoing questions. We do, however, want readers to know that our editorial decisions are related to sometimes-impassioned arguments in Canadian intellectual life.

Previous works dealing with Canadian cinema have tended to sidestep the often contentious discussions around the meaning of "nation" and "national cinema" that have gripped the humanities and social sciences in the last two decades. Sometimes their strategies have taken the form of including Québec cinema as part of a larger Canadian cinema, sometimes that of providing thematic or institutional essays that deal with films in both French and English, and sometimes through creating books that have a section on Québec cinema alongside, say, sections on experimental cinema and documentary cinema. While the attempt to bring Québec cinema to as wide an audience as possible is entirely worthy, we are opting for a very different path. Part of this is because of our skepticism towards the rhetoric of Trudeau-era federalism. The idea that there is a coherent Canadian national self, composed of both English and French elements, seems to us somewhat naïve. Nor is it an idea that is really shared by very many people in Canada. A defining characteristic of contemporary Québec is the pronounced national consciousness that generally exists among *both* federalist and separatist Francophones and that defines political and cultural life there. At the same time, while there are still pockets of Francophone life in the far north, western Canada, and the Maritimes (and we should exclude the unique case of Acadia from this formulation), it is certainly rare to encounter a Canadian Anglophone outside the federal government or the province of Québec who would regard the French language as an organic part of his or her day-to-day existence as a Canadian. This reality, of course, leads us to the "two nations" and "many nations" theories of Canadian nationhood, theories that are, we feel, more reflective of the cultural reality in both English Canada and Québec. We, then, are adopting a "two national cinemas" theory of Canadian cinema, a position that seems to us the most organic way of writing film history.

We are not alone in this position. In his introduction to the 1978 collection *Les cinémas canadiens*, Pierre Véronneau wrote that "[l]e titre peut surprendre. En existe-t-il donc plusieurs? Je pense que oui."[1] We think so too, and this book is about one of those cinemas. And while Véronneau's schema differs slightly from our own, it is very close to the approach we would advocate, much closer than a lot of contemporary work on cinema in Canada and Québec. Similarly, Tom Waugh, in his Martin Walsh Lecture at the 1998 Film Studies Association of Canada conference, sought to construct a canon of queer Canadian cinema. He made it clear in that lecture that he did not include Québec as part of this, writing that "I am referring to cinema exclusively made in English, since one premise of this research, always open to challenge, is the lingering cultural chasm between our two founding cinemas that has been so often erased at its peril by Ontario film studies."[2] Similarly, Bill Marshall, in his recent book *Québec National Cinema*, has written of the frustration he experienced communicating the nuances of this situation:

> [T]he idea of this book was rejected by another publisher's series on national cinemas on the grounds that Québec "is not a nation," whereas "Canada is" (in the singular). n Canada and Québec, this represents a loaded political statement which immediately takes sides in the ongoing controversy about Quebec's status. My argument [is] that Québec certainly is a nation and has a national cinema, and that these terms are still useful ....[3]

We side wholeheartedly with these scholars. Québec has its own national cinema, complete with commercial, avant-garde, semi-independent, and documentary sectors, and would, in a perfect world, be the subject of a book in English as large as the one you hold in your hands. So we very much want to separate the nation-state from the national cinema; you don't need to have your own currency or issue stamps to have a national cinema. Scottish cinema or Welsh cinema could, arguably, be part of a larger study of "British Cinema"; but such endeavours too often ignore the cultural, historical, and linguistic differences that define these places and the films that come from them.

This does not mean that we think English-Canadian and Québec cinema should be studied only in isolation. They have clearly had an appreciable influence on one another. But English-Canadian cinema has certainly been influenced less by Québec cinema than by American cinema, and possibly even less than by Australian cinema; while Québec cinema has been far more influenced by the French New Wave than by English-Canadian cinema. To collapse both English-Canadian and Québec cinema into a giant "Canadian cinema" obscures such details, and we think that film history, especially in English Canada, has been encumbered and complicated even more than is necessary, by that tendency.

All this said, we are including aboriginal cinema as part of the book, and we acknowledge that this is something of a cheat. Again, in a perfect world, North American aboriginal cinema would have its own book, one that ignored the political borders between the United States, Canada, and Mexico, and dealt with such figures and institutions as Zack Kunuk (Inuit), Gil Cardinal (Metis), Loretta Todd (Cree), Alanis Obomsawin (Abenaki), Zachary Longboy (Dene), Victor Nayasava (Hopi), Gary Farmer (Cayuga), the Inuit Broadcast Corporation, the Aboriginal Peoples Television Network, and the Chiapas Media Project. For the time being, we include a short section on aboriginal cinema, largely because we feel this work is important and needs to be seen and discussed much more than it is (and this is a problem that does not plague Québec cinema in the same way). We also include it because, abandoning our transnational idealism for a moment, we feel the situation in Canada for aboriginal filmmakers is very different from the situation in the United States or Mexico. Much of this difference has been the result of *Canadian* governmental agencies (such as the NFB), and a lot of the important work has happened in English. Indeed, we decided not to include an essay on Inuit video and broadcast, which is some of the most dynamic, exciting work on the post-1980 North American media-arts scene, because it is mostly in Inuktitut and that linguistic identity is central to the meaning of the work. In other cases, though, we are willing to stretch our model of national cinema a bit.

Next comes the question, Why not television? Twenty years ago, the spheres of film and television were reasonably distinctly delimited. That is not the case now. From NFB documentaries, whose only real life is on television, to the work of fiction filmmakers, whose theatrical projects are not intuitively separable from their work in TV features or episodes or miniseries, through the whole field of animation, all the way to avant-garde video artists whose work is, so to speak, on the far side of television (in art galleries, for example), the category of "cinema" in its very broadest sense is clearly not divisible into "film" and "television" in any pragmatically responsible way. And yet with this question we have once again been driven to make a rough-and-ready decision as to what to include and what to leave out—and once again it has been a decision made for practical reasons as well as for intellectual ones. Clearly the field of Canadian television altogether is big enough to sustain a large book itself, one that would not cover that field any more comprehensively than the present volume does its field of focus (the same could probably also be said even about distinct areas of work *in* television, such as documentary, fiction, or animation). So although a good deal of material that really should be categorized as "work for television" rather than strictly "cinema" finds its way into this anthology, we have left it mostly to slide in through the back door rather than inviting it in through the front entrance.

Devoted followers of Canadian cinema may notice the relatively small amount of attention given to documentary, especially in comparison to the space devoted to feature-length fiction. We might have justified the inclusion of individual essays on filmmakers such as Peter Mettler, Nettie Wild, or Peter Lynch, all of whose work departs dramatically from the principal NFB model of documentary towards a more hybridized model of fictional, documentary, and non-narrative modes. But for whatever reason, the trend of scholarship over the past two decades has been to shift attention away from documentary and towards narrative cinema. This narrative cinema was simultaneously proliferating in many directions, and in particular was moving away from the model of a "realist" or "documentary" kind of Canadian fiction film that was dominant during the 1960s and '70s. One effect of this movement is that our book has more essays on narrative cinema than on documentary cinema, and its proportions in this regard are different from its ancestor books.

Arguably in contrast to documentary, the Canadian avant garde experienced a very exciting renewal in the 1980s and '90s. Some figures have been omitted simply because of that age-old problem of the avant garde: the unavailability of the films. Is there really much sense in including an essay on avant-garde and aboriginal filmmaker Thirza Cuthand when so few people have, or indeed, can, see her unsettling, fragmented diary videos? At the same time, though, we genuinely regret not including essays on Cuthand, or on Sara Diamond (or the very dynamic media-arts operation she runs at the Banff Centre for the Arts), Bruce Elder, Donigan Cumming, Cathy Sisler, and many others.

We have the same sense of gentle regret about the aboriginal section, which could easily have been much bigger. This section is geographically oriented in the west, not only because of our shared affiliation with the University of Alberta but also because of our contention that, except for the Arctic, this is where the most exciting work in aboriginal film and video is being done. Part of this, no doubt, is because of the presence of the NFB's Studio One in Edmonton. This was a path-breaking attempt to create a viable aboriginal cinema in Canada, and we are especially pleased to offer an insider's account of the formation and operation of that studio. That account, readers will notice, is quite clearly written *from* the inside: its author, Maria de Rosa, is a long-time NFB consultant and is writing its history from that point of view, rather than from that of an independent scholar. Still, we felt her comprehensive access and knowledge of NFB operational detail would offer those interested in aboriginal cinema a look inside an institution we consider very important indeed. Of course, we also regret that we left out full discussions of veterans like Gary Farmer or up-and-comers like Clint Star, or sustained consideration of the path-breaking Aboriginal Peoples Television Network. So much cinema, so little space!

We have solicited the essays, and organized the book, in four major sections: Institutions/Policies/Histories/Forms, Feature Filmmakers and a Few Others, Aboriginal Voices, and the Avant Garde. The first section is rather hefty in heterogeneous subject matters and without an accompanying bulk in actual numbers of essays, and there are many, many topics that might have been included under its multiform title—and arguably should have been in any volume attempting to be comprehensive. On the other hand, as we have already noted, one area of recent scholarship on Canadian cinema that is reasonably well served is that of institutions. Charles Acland's essay on exhibition practices is a lonely example here of an essay on purely industrial matters, and it incisively addresses questions that are crucial to the existence of a viable theatrical film industry in this country; but behind it lies an already fairly well-mined field of scholarly work (e.g., Pendakur, Magder, Dorland), many of whose points are now sharpened or refocussed by the present essay. Region (Noreen Golfman on Newfoundland film) and ethnicity (Kass Banning on Afro- and Caribbean-Canadian film) get included here, and we are grateful to have this representation, even if there are other regions (e.g., the West Coast) and ethnicities (e.g., Italian-Canadian) that have just as much right to be admitted but have not been for a variety of reasons, good and bad. Similarly, animation appears here because, first, it is too important to English-Canadian filmmaking since 1980 to be excluded, even if it raises the issue of television origins perhaps more pointedly than any other kind of work; and, second, we were not willing to devote an entire section to it. Lastly, Geoff Pevere's essay is completely *hors concours* as to category, but as it quirkily confronts an important quality of "weirdness" in English-Canadian feature filmmaking that isn't directly addressed anywhere else, this seemed the place for it.

The Feature Filmmakers and a Few Others section is the longest and most varied. As the title suggests, it contains authorially related essays on a substantial number of filmmakers who have done all or most of their work in theatrical feature-fiction film, or are at least primarily known for such work, as well as on a few filmmakers whose work does not fit that description so comfortably or at all. The former category includes most of the names one would expect (Cronenberg, Egoyan, Greyson, McDonald, Rozema, Wheeler, etc.) as well as some that one might not, and the latter category includes Janice Cole, Holly Dale, and Ron Mann, whose primary work has been in documentary but who have worked in film and had at least some theatrical exhibition. Some filmmakers with only one or two directorial credits—Don McKellar or François Girard (only one and a half or two in English, at any rate)—are here; others—Thom Fitzgerald, Lynn Stopkewich, Mina Shum, John Paizs, and Gary Burns—aren't. These were basically judgement calls. Deepa Mehta has recently said that she doesn't consider herself a Canadian filmmaker but rather an Indian one. But she does (as Jacqueline Levitin's essay points out) exemplify a transnational identity whose importance to ideas not only of nation but specifically of Canadian national cinema is highly instructive. Also, if CanLit can claim Malcolm Lowry and Brian Moore, we can claim Deepa Mehta. Cole/Dale and Mann are here for the aforementioned length and format reasons, but also because we don't have a real documentary section and thus practitioners of documentary find themselves spread into every section of the book. At the same time, the sheer variety of the contents of this section–and of the book as a whole, for that matter–reflects the impressive diversity of activity in English-Canadian film over the past two decades.

The last twenty years have seen the full emergence of an aboriginal cinema in Canada, a birth that has led to what could be described as a third national cinema (which makes for a nice pun on the concept of Third Cinema). As we noted earlier, aboriginal cinema could well have its own book, although it is also closely tied to English-Canadian cinema through both a linguistic orientation (much, although certainly not all, of the relevant work is in English) and an English-Canadian institutional attachment (although Alanis Obomsawin is a staff director at the NFB's Montréal headquarters, the aboriginal production program Studio One was based in Edmonton). We include here interviews with and essays on a variety of filmmakers, although each has a base in documentary and each sees his or her work in film and video as part of a larger project of cultural recovery or connection. This is quite common in aboriginal media around the world, both throughout the Americas and in Australia/New Zealand. Mediamakers in all of these regions are wrestling with how to integrate film, broadcast, and video–media that have traditionally excluded them–in ways that both rectify this exclusion and are organic to their own indigenous cultural traditions, which are often orally based. The result, as some commentators like Faye Ginsburg at NYU have observed, is films and videos that often do not look much like the technically polished, narrative cinema of their dominant cultures.[4] This is to a certain extent true of the work discussed in the aboriginal section, which is in many ways closer to work being done by aboriginal mediamakers in the southwest United States, in Oceania, or in the Arctic than it is to the mainstream of documentary work being done in Canada. That said, the Canadian connection is important, and so we lead the section off with Maria de Rosa's history of the NFB's Studio One, an institution that has no equivalent in either the US or Mexico.

The section on the avant garde tracks a period in which the very idea of an avant garde, in the US, Canada, and Europe, was being re-evaluated. These essays, we believe, reverse the tendency in avant-garde film history to focus on single, genius artists visionarily pursuing their muse, turning their attention instead towards the complex, sometimes contradictory social and political forces that help to shape experimental film and video.

While the majority of the essays in the book were written by academics, a number of our contributors come from the worlds of film festivals and journalism. There is, then, a certain variance of tone in the anthology that we should like to say entirely pleases us. Critical writing is too often constrained by a desire to be "scholarly" and a fear of being "popular" or, even worse, "journalistic," an attitude that illustrates a binarism and acceptance of conventional definitions of low and high that would be unthinkable if they formed a scholar's view of cinema itself (the distinction between low and high art has become pleasantly blurry over the last few decades, and yet the boundary between low and high critical work is too often puzzlingly intact). We think that readers will benefit from a heterogeneity of critical styles and a diversity of critical perspective.

Lastly, a quick word about the book's title. On the one hand it points to, say, *North of 60*. On the other, it points to Jane Tompkins' book on the Western, *West of Everything*, whose title in turn quotes another source, Louis L'Amour's novel *Hondo*. There, "west of everything" is a metaphor for "dead." If death is what's west of everything, what's north of everything? That is a question for those of us who are trying to understand and place Canadian cinema.

Notes

1   Pierre Vérroneau, introduction to *Les cinémas canadiens* (Paris: Pierre Cherminier Editeur/ Montréal: Cinémathèque Québécois, 1975), 1.

2   Tom Waugh, "Cinemas, Nations, Masculinities: The Martin Walsh Memorial Lecture (1998)," *Canadian Journal of Film Studies* 8, no. 1 (Spring 1999): 11.

3   Bill Marshall, *Québec National Cinema* (Montréal/Kingston: McGill-Queen's University Press, 2000), x.

4   Faye Ginsburg, "Mediating Culture: Indigenous Media, Ethnographic Film, and the Production of Identity," in *Fields of Vision: Essays in Film Studies, Visual Anthropology and Photography,* Leslie Devereaux and Roger Hillman, eds. (Berkeley: University of California Press, 1995), 259.

Institutions
Politics
Histories
Forms

Screen Space, Screen Time, and Canadian Film Exhibition

Charles R. Acland

OPEN A NEWSPAPER AND TURN TO THE MOVIE LISTINGS. Can you spot any Canadian films currently showing in your area? Chances are you will spot a couple—if not at the venue closest to you, then somewhere—but most of the listings will be films from our southern neighbour. This simple exercise has introduced you to one of the most troublesome dimensions of Canadian cinema culture: the dominance of US film in Canadian theatres.

The long history of this US presence is perhaps the most visible manifestation of cultural absence in Canadian film.[1] Our cinema, missing in action from traditional commercial exhibition channels, occupies only two to three percent of the theatrical market.[2] Even in Québec, domestic film captures only four percent of box office revenue.[3] Two international media giants, Viacom and Universal, are the parent corporations for our two main chains, Famous Players and Cineplex Odeon, respectively. The resulting industrial structure has meant that Canada is treated as an extension of the US domestic market for film. Every Monday, when the weekend box office numbers appear in US newspapers, hidden in those figures is the box office of another country: Canada. US domination of Canadian movie theatres is often cited as a symptom of the "Americanization" of Canadian culture.[4]

This assessment of cultural imperialism is hardly the exclusive domain of political economists. Rather, journalists, editorialists, policymakers, and government representatives repeat and extend the argument. A striking feature of Canadian film is the frequency with which popular periodicals report on its absence, invariably citing the "colonization" of theatres as evidence. One article about the Toronto Film Festival reported on the uncertain future of Canadian film, especially when compared to the international success of Canadian television.[5] *Globe and Mail* reporter Robert Everett-Green captured this thinking in the headline "Not Coming to a Theatre Near You."[6] The pervasiveness of this assessment leads me to suggest that it forms a part of our contemporary common sense: Canadian film's absence has an unusual presence in the popular imaginary.

These examples are more than descriptions of the status of our film culture. They represent an agreement about its meagre existence; they are judgements and evaluations reflecting a particular history of film culture and criticism. But what falls away from this observation's purview?

That is, what aspect of Canadian cinematic life does the argument about industrial control, absent Canadian film, and Americanization de-emphasize? I propose that while the economic argument is indispensable, it cannot account for all facets of cultural existence, nor is it designed to. For example, the political-economic approach leaves little room to consider the experience and enjoyment of Canadian audiences who frequent US productions in our cinemas. Our over-confidence in the political-economic explanation has tended to reduce attention to the multifarious pleasures, conditions, and operations of a travelling US cinema, seeing it as an economic and ideological invasion only. True enough, Canadian distributors, producers, and filmmakers struggle for minor accomplishments in the context of the overwhelming presence of US film. This, however, cannot be taken as equivalent to the struggles and experiences of Canadian audiences who must live and negotiate the existing popular cultural scene. For this reason, and for the more general reason that exhibition sites have been under-researched in Canadian film studies, this chapter begins with a characterization of the current landscape of motion-picture theatres and then presents a counter-argument to the measures used to identify US dominance of our screens, offering a reading of the practice of Canadian cinema-going.

The Changing Face of Canadian Exhibition

To begin, it is worth remembering that not so long ago many people felt cinema-going was not only in a state of decline but headed for oblivion. Cries about the "death of the cinema" continue today, and many agree that home video, pay-per-view, the increasing size of the television screen, the improving quality of its sound and image, and the competing entertainment options offered by computer-related technology spell the certain demise of the century-old activity of public moving-image consumption. Why take the added time and expense of going out to a film when the options at home are wider, cheaper, and more convenient?

Table 1: Motion picture theatres and admissions

	THEATRES			SCREENS			
Year	Indoor	Drive-ins	Total	Indoor	Drive-ins	Total	Admissions
1953							252,000
1963							97,882
1964							101,728
1988–89	657	132	789	1490	175	1665	78,868
1989–90	650	123	773	1555	168	1723	82,018
1990–91	633	109	742	1565	148	1713	78,934
1991–92	620	103	723	1611	143	1754	71,625
1992–93	598	88	686	1613	129	1742	73,727
1993–94	581	83	664	1601	126	1727	78,812
1994–95	582	77	659	1682	126	1808	83,766
1995–96	584	74	658	1773	119	1892	87,304
1996–97	588	68	656	1877	112	1989	91,327
1997–98	617	71	688	2186	115	2301	99,894

Note: Information derived from *Quick Canadian Facts, 1966–1967*; *Film Canada Yearbook, 1994*, Patricia Thompson, ed; Statistics Canada, "Film and Video, 1992-93, Culture Statistics"; and Statistics Canada, "Movie Theatres and Drive-ins, 1997-98, Culture Statistics."

Table 2: Employment and profit (as a percent of total revenue)

	THEATRES			DRIVE-INS		
	Full-time	*Part-time*	*Profit*	*Full-time*	*Part-time*	*Profit*
1993–94	1305	8323	10.7	133	762	9.8
1994–95	1155	7722	11	173	784	9.6
1995–96	997	8132	10.6	163	782	12.3
1996–97	1251	7981	10.2	132	777	12
1997–98	1274	9168	11.9	102	727	13.6

Note: Figures from Statistics Canada, "Movie Theatres and Drive-ins, 1997–98, Culture Statistics."

In actuality, attendance figures do not support the argument of demise. After years of decline, attendance stabilized in the late 1960s and has made gains over the last few years, with box-office revenue increasing and breaking annual records frequently since 1989 (largely a consequence of rising ticket prices). North American admissions for 1997 were the highest since 1966.[7] As shown in Table 1, Statistics Canada reports that 1997–98 marked a nearly two-decade record of attendance at indoor—"hardtop"—theatres and drive-ins, just shy of 100 million. Considering only "hardtop" admissions, 97.7 million is a 36-year record. Nonetheless, we can be confident that Canadian attendance will never match its peak year of 1952–53, which Statistics Canada recorded at 256 million admissions.[8]

The argument about the death of cinema-going fails to consider that more money is made at theatres than ever before. Notice, too, in Table 1 that there are comparatively more screens and a smaller number of theatres. This signals the increasing number of screens per site, meaning there are fewer locations to which one can travel to see a film but an increasing number of auditoria at a given location. The rising number of screens presents audiences with either a variety of films or a wider range of start times when a single film is playing on several screens at a given theatre. The concentration of screens at fewer sites parallels a downsizing of both full-time and part-time staff, as seen in Table 2. This trend has translated into increasing profit margins over the last five years as well as growing box office revenue. Indeed, large theatres account for 94 percent of the exhibition sector's $83 million in profit. Statistics Canada notes that this income may be due to the extra concession offerings at megaplex locations.[9]

Historically, exhibitors have actively reworked their operations to fit the changing context of leisure. Whether we think of the construction of opulent movie palaces of the 1920s and 1930s or of the widescreen, Cinerama, and 3-D experiments of the 1950s, the site of cinema-going has repeatedly been altered to offer a distinct cultural engagement. Our era is no different, as we see exhibitors reconfiguring their businesses to accommodate the reality of home-entertainment technologies. The last two decades have seen substantial efforts to construct massive media corporations, largely through mergers and acquisitions. Consequently, it is not uncommon to see corporations involved in broadcasting, film and television production, merchandising, home video, cable, film distribution and exhibition, and web-based services. In place of an imagined fractious relationship between, say, television and film, we must consider the synergies, or economic fit, between those aspects of the cultural industry, and to think about how such synergy might influence the redesign of movie theatres.

As in many other countries, movie audiences in Canada face a new landscape of cinemas. Famous Players and Cineplex Odeon dominate cinema exhibition, and their prominence is worth noting. They represent a long-standing presence, with Famous Players forming in 1920 and Cineplex Odeon appearing in 1984. The latter is a product of Garth Drabinsky's Cineplex, which began in 1979 with Toronto's eighteen-screen multiplex in the Eaton's Centre; Cineplex eventually bought the Odeon chain, founded in 1941. Such enduring presence has allowed the exhibitors to develop connections with major distributors: Famous Players has had ongoing understandings with Buena Vista, MGM, Warner Brothers, and Paramount, while Cineplex Odeon has relationships with Columbia, Fox, and Universal.[10] These agreements are not guaranteed, of course, and indeed, the divisions today are not as evident as they were in the past.

A fundamental consequence of the exhibitors' might is the high concentration of chain-owned theatres in Canada, in contrast to the numerous chains in the US. The proposed merger in late 1997 between three major theatre chains (Regal, Act III, and UATC)—a merger that ultimately did not succeed—caused shock waves in the US industry as it would have given the merged entity more than nineteen percent of US screens.[11] In Canada, Famous Players and Cineplex Odeon control approximately 30 percent and 43 percent of screens respectively.[12] Some estimates claim that these two chains account for as much as 80 percent of the theatrical grosses of a film,[13] and by 1999, Famous Players held an incredible 47-percent share of the Canadian market.[14] This kind of concentration, unheard of in the US, has been a fact of the Canadian scene for decades. The remaining twenty-odd percent of screens consists of chains defined

Table 3: Canada's top 21 chains (screens and provinces of operation, as of May 1999)

Cineplex Odeon (Alberta, BC, Manitoba, Ontario, Québec, Sask.) 800

Famous Players (Alberta, BC, Manitoba, NB, NS, Ontario, Québec, Sask.) 659

Empire Theatres (NB, NF, NS, PEI) 116

Landmark Cinemas (Alberta, BC, Manitoba, Sask., Yukon) 95

Guzzo (Québec)   80

Caprice Showcase (BC)   54

AMC (Ontario)   44

Stinson (Ontario)   39

Magic Lantern Theatres (Alberta, NWT, Sask.)   34

Galaxy Entertainment (Ontario)   34

Tarrant Enterprises (Ontario) 29

Cinema City (Alberta, Manitoba)   28

May Theatres (Alberta, Sask.)   26

Cinemark (Alberta)   24

Premier Operating (Ontario) 19

Golden Theatres (Ontario)   15

Alliance Atlantis Cinemas (BC, Ontario)   11

Harris Road Entertainment Group (BC, Manitoba) 9

A Theatre Near You (BC)   8

The Movie Mill (Alberta)   7

Festival Cinemas (Ontario)   6

Note: Figures from "Canadian Giants of Exhibition," *Boxoffice Online*.

primarily by province, such as Québec's Guzzo, Ontario's Stinson, the western provinces' Land-mark, and Newfoundland and the Maritimes' Empire.[15] But even these smaller chains, at times, strike arrangements with the majors; for example, Guzzo and Empire have had Cineplex Odeon bid for films for them.

Since 1994, the two titans have been investing substantially in the construction of new the-atres and the refurbishment of existing theatres, introducing new technology, expanded conces-sions, additional leisure activities like playrooms and high-tech arcades, and innovative design and decor. Some regional chains, like Empire and Guzzo, have been refurbishing and building multiplex cinemas, and a new chain, Galaxy Entertainment, is supposed to develop an exhibition circuit in smaller cities and towns, starting with Ontario.[16] But nothing compares to the extent of investment from the two national chains, especially in their new megaplex cinemas. With 475 screens at 107 locations in 1996, Famous Players' expansion brought its total to 771 screens at 111 locations in 1999.[17] With 981 screens in the US and 621 in Canada, Cineplex Odeon added 487 screens to the chain by 1999, 40 percent of them in the Canadian market.[18] For Cineplex Odeon, consolidation at an international level had several industry-shaking illustrations. A merger between Cineplex Odeon and Cinemark USA in March 1995 made Cineplex Odeon the largest chain in the world at the time, with 2800 screens.[19] In September 1997, Cineplex Odeon announced a merger with Sony's Loews Theatres, creating a chain immediately consisting of 460 theatres, accounting for 2600 screens.[20] The day after the announcement, Canadian Heritage Minister Sheila Copps insisted that, for this deal to be approved, the new corporation must make a commitment to screen more Canadian films.[21] Cineplex Odeon might have to divest its distribution arm, Cineplex Odeon Films.[22] Indeed, following Investment Canada's approval of the Loews–Cineplex Odeon merger, the restrictions on foreign ownership of distribution re-quired that Cineplex Odeon Films be sold.[23] Part of the merger plans, as they went before the US Securities and Exchange Commission, was to close theatres that were unnecessarily in competi-tion with one another or were not performing well.[24] By 1998, the merger created the exhibition giant Loews Cineplex Entertainment, then with 2900 screens in 450 locations throughout North America and Europe,[25] and with a full 13 percent of North American market share.[26] By May of that year, the new corporation sacked almost all of the top executives at Cineplex Odeon in Toronto.[27]

The corporate restructuring and building boom of the mid 1990s is arguably the most exten-sive and concentrated in the history of Canadian cinema. It is instructive to remember that the late 1980s were also a time of expansion. *Variety* declared "Famous Players hypes expansion" in June 1986; its plan was to add between 50 and 60 screens over 5 years.[28] In 1986, Famous Players (then controlled by Gulf and Western) owned only 74 of its 469 screens and leased the rest.[29] When it was going public, it planned continued screen expansion of 25 percent over 3 years.[30] Adding to its on-site offerings, in 1988 Famous Players announced expansion plans, including the introduction of lobby kiosks to sell movie merchandise.[31] At that time, *Variety* quoted CEO Walter Senior as saying that the 3-year, $50,000,000 plan was "the largest single construction project in the history of Canadian motion picture exhibition."[32]

The spark to its growth plans during the 1980s was a renewed interest in cinema-going. Famous Players announced a sudden 16.2-percent increase in admissions and 13.3-percent in-crease in box office for the 15-week summer of 1986.[33] Explaining these changes, *Playback* quoted the then-incoming Senior as saying "A successful theatre must be a part of the community it serves," and that "modern-day moviegoers want an experience that takes them as far out of their living rooms as they can be. They want to become immersed in the public experience of motion pictures ...."[34] Here we see the idea that cinemas are about community life and relate to other sites of cultural consumption. The sense that people escape to an immersive experience when they go to the cinema guides many exhibitors' decisions, especially in the agreement that sites might be perceived as "total" entertainment locations. Thus, we witness one industry "solution" to the changing entertainment context in which cinema-going must operate: not the death of the cinema, but the reconfiguration of cinema-going.

Such thinking was not unique to Famous Players. Cineplex Odeon planned a greater expansion of 200 screens from 1986 to 1988, proposing to get rid of its small "airline-type" screens, and 300 in the US.[35] This came after CEO Garth Drabinsky criticized theatre operators for "a lack of inspiration, a lack of creativity, in the way that theatres are being built and the way theatres are being managed and maintained."[36] These plans were buoyed by the merger with MCA and the purchase of 97 screens from RKO Century Warner Theatres, both in 1986.[37] Cineplex Odeon then re-bought 56 theatres it had sold in 1988, then bought 4 more, all in the US.[38] Table 4 shows Cineplex Odeon's Canadian purchasing, new building, and closing activity for the latter half of the 1980s.

In the familiar dialectic of urban environments, closing and divestment accompanies building and investment. At one point in 1997, Famous Players stated that its expansion plans included closing 75 screens.[39] A decade earlier, in September 1987, *Variety* reported a protest against the closing of the Regency Theatre in Toronto, a repertory house owned by Cineplex Odeon, even though it was bringing in more than the average screen. The protest included appearances by Tony Randall, Isaac Asimov, Betty Comden, and Adolph Green, and the reading of letters from Lillian Gish, Arthur Penn, Kim Hunter, and Myrna Loy.[40] In 1988, Cineplex Odeon began to retreat from "secondary markets" of 50,000 to 100,000 people by selling 57 multiplexes across Canada.[41] In 1990, Cineplex was still selling off screens in suburban and smaller markets in the US, with a number going to Carmike and Plitt, as part of a strategy to focus on urban locations.[42]

By 1990, the openings and closings left Famous Players with 506 screens and Cineplex Odeon with 563 in Canada.[43] Exhibitors continued to revise their operations through the decade. In a move toward consolidating Canadian exhibition, Cineplex Odeon bought 152 screens at 55 sites in western Canada from Carena Development in early 1990.[44] "New attempts to woo customers" describes Cineplex Odeon being saved by blockbuster movies and by expanding concession snacks (what it called "Project Popcorn"), noting a growing interest in location-based entertainment.[45]

Table 4: Theatre activity for Cineplex Odeon in Canada (sites/screens)

	Purchases/Acquired	New builds	Closings/Disposals
1985	10/25	8/38	8/10
1986	12/24	5/27	33/44
1987	5/7	8/37	20/27
1988	4/9	9/25	12/24
1989 (est.)	n/a	11/56	23/51

Note: Figures from "Cineplex Theater Activity."

Another notable change has been US exhibitors moving their operations northward. Cinemark opened discount screens in Edmonton and Winnipeg, and now continues to operate in Alberta only.[46] Smaller regional chains Golden Theatres and A Theatre Near You are both US-based. But the most rapid and aggressive change has been the construction of a handful of AMC megaplexes in Toronto and Montréal, beachheads for the Kansas City exhibitor in Canada. These are among the grandest complexes in the country, moving AMC overnight from no screens to a position among the top ten largest chains.

Aside from general efforts to increase competitiveness by adding to the size of operations through building and mergers, economic rationales for the expansion varied from changing de-mographics to the accommodation of distribution strategies. For example, an increase in the number of films released theatrically (from 411 in 1994 to 471 in 1996) required additional space for film presentations and releasing. About 150 films each year get a wide release, which calls for simultaneous access to hundreds of screens for the opening weekend.[47] While the economic forces propelling the boom were a matter of debate, the "improvement" of the movie-going ex-perience was a major rationale for the wave of investments, as ample press coverage repeatedly noted. Indeed, there appeared to be an industry-wide agreement that movie-going required im-provement and that a re-design of the movie-going site was the way to do it. In *Variety*, a fasci-nating debate ran in the background of this continent-wide theatre expansion. It seemed no con-sensus existed as to whether North America was over-screened or under-screened, although some sources indicate that Canada has traditionally been seen as under-screened.[48] There did seem to be an agreement that the continent was in some way inadequately screened: its screens were in the wrong locations and were equipped with archaic technology and design.

The re-design of theatres has been prominent, revealing a trend over the last fifteen years away from generic, placeless auditoria toward unique, branded locations. When Cineplex Odeon opened its four-theatre complex on the lower-level concourse of the Chateau Faubourg in De-cember 1986, it was the chain's first new theatre in Montréal in five years. *Variety* quoted the cor-poration as saying that the Faubourg Cinema's design was a contemporary take on art deco, in-tended to be "reminiscent of the splendour of the movie palaces of the 1920s and 1930s."[49] These halls were seen as an early sign that the tiny multiplex cinemas were about to become a thing of the past. As Douglas Gomery puts it, Cineplex Odeon shifted in the mid 1980s from "drab 'cookie-cutter' multiplexes" to "vast complexes of whimsical, postmodern 'picture palaces' ...."[50] The expansion and design enterprises abounded. In 1987, *Playback* presented a front-page an-nouncement of Cineplex Odeon's intentions of building a theatre, hotel, and shopping complex in Toronto, potentially becoming a permanent site for the Festival of Festivals.[51] It opened its "art house," the nine-screen Carlton, in May 1988 after renovations.[52] In 1991, Carleton Cinemas in Toronto received a liquor licence for beer and wine, the first such licence in Ontario; previously, Québec had been the only province with licensed cinemas.[53] This was part of Cineplex Odeon's overall sense that theatres need to be "desirable" and must "fit into their environment, rather than all being branded with a specific Cineplex style."[54]

Pricing was another method used to demarcate the special qualities of the service. Famous Players raised its ticket prices from $6 to $6.50 just before Christmas 1987.[55] Prices went to $7, and to $7.25 in BC, in May 1989.[56] Cineplex Odeon followed suit with $7 admissions.[57] Then, over that winter, Famous Players cut Monday to Thursday admissions to $5 or $4, depending on the market, a strategy to spread the glut of audiences appearing for $3 Tuesday over weekday evenings.[58] This innovation in pricing shows the industry recognizes the temporal distinctions in cinema-going. When Cineplex Odeon raised prices in Manhattan to $7 US, other exhibitors reportedly reacted with "shock," suggesting how bold and unconventional this tactic was.[59] Cineplex Odeon used the opening of new cinema complexes to increase admissions to $7.50 for weekends in the summer of 1989, with matching increases in Canada.[60] On 14 December 1990, Cineplex Odeon bumped prices up to $8, saying this figure included GST. The tax, however, did not come into effect until 1 January, so for two weeks, over the busy Christmas movie-going season, Cineplex Odeon collected and pocketed the extra 50 cents. Increases in admission prices have occasionally been attributed to the expense of upgrading cinema sites to make them "an attractive place of entertainment for families and teenagers."[61] With regular adult admissions now at $10-plus, it appears that price hikes have been a way to mark the upscaling of cinema-going and to signal exclusivity and prestige.

Continuing to examine and celebrate the expansion of theatres, the 1997 ShowCanada convention reflected an industry-wide focus on family audiences. One innovation exhibitors discussed was the introduction of 6000-foot reels, replacing the standard 2500-foot reels, expected to reduce on the labour needed for projection.[62] Another was the recent switch from acetate-based film to polyester, which had the advantage of durability but caused projection problems.[63] *Playback* noted that the "Service: Disney Style" seminar was the talk of the meeting. While the article describes no special connection to motion-picture exhibition, the seminar is evidence of the continuing power of Disney as a model for out-of-home leisure, the primary focus of which is customer service. Or, as the presentation put it, "Success in any business is 10 percent product and 90 percent service."[64] As part of its plans for the new megaplexes, Famous Players sent managers to Disney University, where they received training in the Disney approach to service and entertainment.[65]

Some commented that the Canadian strategy was slightly inappropriate and might be based upon a misinterpretation of the direction of the industry. *Variety* reported that distributors generally consider Canada under-screened, especially when compared to the US, and therefore warranting additional screens, but that the recent construction of theatres with eight to twelve screens is not in sync with the massive sites being built elsewhere.[66] Extraordinary growth in some areas meant that chains created congested cinema-going markets. Ottawa, for instance, saw its screen tally go from 69 at the end of 1997 to 111 at the close of 1998.

With fewer sites, more screens, and greater profitability, most assessments would mark the Canadian exhibition industry as a healthy, stable part of the cultural scene. Yet it has historically been treated as a problem, as too American in its ownership and film-booking. The restructuring and investment described above did not change this in the slightest, making the growth in exhibition yet another phase in the international, and primarily American, orientation of Canadian popular cinema. Where people go to the cinema, the relative choice of films and show times afforded by multiple screen, and the extra-filmic practices one now expects—all are evident developments of the post-1986 period. Upscaling did not break the barriers to Canadian film at those sites. But what can we read and learn by looking at the structure of these sites? Here, I think it is important to ask about popular film in Canada and to understand that this question is distinct from concerns about Canadian film. In what follows, I wish to address the ways in which the condition of internationalized Canadian popular cinema-going is conceptualized.

The 90-Something-Percent Solution
Screen time and the Canadian popular

So abundant are references to screen time—in particular, the percentage of screen time for Canadian film in commercial theatres—that it appears to have the status as a standardized rhetorical trope in the construction of arguments about Canadian cinema, whether for policymakers, industry agencies, or critics. In fact, figures enumerating non-Canadian film, typically between 95 and 98 percent, are so common that they frequently appear without citation; they are taken as part of the general knowledge about film in Canada. A 1994 report by Secor Group provides the figures for many, although their numbers are themselves taken from another report, "European Cinema Yearbook, A Statistical Analysis, 1993." This comparison of market share for theatrically released films based on country of origin puts Canada (excluding Québec) at 96 percent US, 2 percent other countries, and 2 percent domestic; Québec's breakdown is 83 percent US, 14 percent other countries, and 3 percent domestic.[67] While it is unclear if this measure of market share is a ratio of films (a version of screen time) or of revenue from those films (a measure of financial success), the figures Secor Group presents have been referred to by others as screen time. Table 5 shows Statistics Canada's charting of market share, here referring not to screen time but to revenue.

Take One publishes a valuable annual survey of screen time for Canadian films in the Greater Toronto Area. Its major liability, of course, is its restriction to screen time for Canadian films in the Greater Toronto Area. Its tabulation for 1997 was 1.45 percent and for 1998, 1.7 percent, significantly lower than the usual figures cited.[68] Regardless, screen time is taken as shorthand evidence of the agreed-upon "problem" or "failure" of Canadian film: that is, the lack of channels moving from producer to distributor to exhibitor. For example, "The Road to Success," a government report on Canadian film, begins with box office revenue as a mark of the dismal state of Canadian film and ends with the goal of increasing screen time from two to ten percent by 2004 as one of its majority recommendations.[69]

What exactly does screen time measure? It is not a site of obvious evidence. Indeed, all statistical figures must be made to mean. Such data are key aspects of how we make cases and claims about cultural life. Ultimately, we need to pay attention to the measures we deploy, often without devoting any special attention to the variety of ways in which they might be read. Figures are not arguments; they serve arguments and become evidence. I would hazard that the more obvious the claim to evidence, the more surely we are in the presence of ideological settlement—and there has been a certain settlement around screen time, one that needs to be shaken loose just a bit.

Table 5: Canadian share of theatrical market (percent of distribution revenue)

1992–93	5.2
1991–92	6.4
1990–91	5.8
1989–90	4.3
1988–89	4.9

Note: Figures from Statistics Canada, "Film and Video, 1992–93, Culture Statistics."

Screen time represents only one narrowly defined dimension of distribution and exhibition. Screen time is not the actual running time of films, nor is it the number of showings. It does not tell us if the venue seats 50 or 500; it does not tell us if anyone is actually in the seats, let alone the financial or critical evaluations of the film. It does not tell us what percentage of the number of films distributed in a year are Canadian, nor how many produced films actually got distribution. Taking screen time as a mark of the status of a national cinema assumes one thing: that visibility in commercial theatres matters. Or, conversely, that films' absence from theatres is an indicator of the inaccessibility of Canadian films to Canadians and acts as a barrier to a popular film culture. More generously, there is a sense that merely having films available at a location is an important first step to their appreciation. In our context, this is a problematic assumption. In light of an ongoing reconfiguration of the relation between public and domestic forms of consumption, and the increasing selectivity of cinema-going, motion-picture theatres should no longer be treated as the exclusive, or even the primary, site at which a national cinema is engaged.

On its own terms, screen time is conceptually complex, trying to capture an intersection between the spatial and temporal dimensions of cultural life. In its articulation of the space of the screen and the temporality of its occupation, screen time transforms auditoria into raw material, like a mineral to be mined. Importantly, in any finite period, screens are a scarce resource: there are only so many screens, so many evenings. This approach is well suited to an economic impulse for distributors, such that the objective of occupying this scarce resource with your own films means they cannot be occupied with your competitor's, which is part of the logic of block booking.

Here is a quick illustration of how to think about screen time. Every screen has a maximum of 52 weeks that a film could be booked over the course of a year. If a film shows for one week, that's just under two percent of the total; screen time for that film is roughly two percent. In fact, here, screen time is more accurately screen weeks. If a film plays for 2 weeks on 2 different screens, screen time is 4 weeks, a little over 3.8 percent of a total of 104 weeks possible. This measure assumes the standardized practices of exhibitors in which one film is booked on one screen for a unit-multiple of a week. Special showings and sneak previews do not count because they are usually single-evening screenings. Most certainly, the measure is confounded when two films are booked for a single screen, which reduces the number of showings, although the screens available seem suddenly to have doubled. Moreover, tabulations of screen time do not typically include parallel and non-theatrical venues (libraries, festivals, galleries).[70]

As the tally goes, there is a list of the films and the weeks they are booked for, matched up with a list of the screens possible. At times, the number is not screens but an amalgamation with prints shipped, or a percent of total film titles, as in Cineplex Odeon's claim that Canadian film hit six percent of its titles in 1995.[71] Despite the apparent simplicity just described, screen time is easily confused and conflated with other measures. Distributors use it as a measure of market share, but this figure need not correspond with revenue, as is sometimes mistakenly assumed. For instance, the publication of Statistics Canada's film and video distribution survey in July 1996 remarked that for 1994–95, Canadian film accounted for eighteen percent of the revenue earned by film distributors from theatres.[72] A minor flurry of letters to the editor of the *Globe and Mail* challenged this as an inflated figure, including one on 30 July 1996 from Dan Johnson, president of the Canadian Association of Film Distributors and Exporters and from industry analyst Paul Audley on 10 September 1996.[73] Interestingly, from my point of view, Audley used the number of Canadian films in cinemas as evidence that the StatsCan figure was inaccurate; in other words, he used screen time to challenge a different measure, a percent of distributors' revenue. He wrote, "Anyone who reads the movie ads in their newspaper will know that Canadian films do not account for just under one in five movies shown." This, of course, was not what the StatsCan figure was saying. Audley continued by quoting Québec government figures that Canadian film in that province accounts for 4.6 percent of box office, again comparing a figure expressed in relation to total box office with one that is expressed in relation to total revenues for distributors. The point here is not to say that StatsCan's numbers are right, nor to create a more positive outlook on the state of Canadian theatrical performance, which in part was what Audley was quite rightly protesting. Instead, it is merely to show that, first, the foremost analysts of Canadian culture industries can conflate measures and, second, the way screen time appears as a sort of wild card, trumping other measures.

When we are in the presence of this kind of "obviousness," my instinct is to be suspicious. The regularity with which this statistical figure appears is itself a stamp of a particular critical common sense; it harbours an already agreed-upon analysis, that is, that screen time carries with it its own presumed implication. Such instances of taken-for-granted assumptions, after Antonio Gramsci, are precisely the fields upon which cultural hegemony operates. Contrary to the presumed ideological neutrality of statistics, figures are made to mean; they do not float around outside historical circumstances, despite their pretences to objective reality. The suggestion here is that one site for understanding Canadian critical discourse is to examine the fixity between the figures measuring screen time and their interpretation.

To do so, here is a snapshot of the box office for the week ending 16 January 1998, published in *Variety*, 19–25 January 1998. I use this period because I have fairly reliable information for it on the number of screens in Canada, which is continually in flux. The StatsCan figure of around 1877 screens for 1996/97 supports an article in the *Globe and Mail*, published on 17 January, noting that screens were between 1800 and 1900. To be conservative with the calculations, I will use the latter figure. Choosing January additionally eliminates drive-in screens.

Table 6: Canadian box office
(week ending 16 January 1998)

		Distributor	Week's box office	Weeks in release	Screens	Screen average
1	*Titanic*	Paramount	$3,991,523	4	335	$11,914
2	*Good Will Hunting*	Alliance	$1,164,986	2	163	$7,147
3	*Tomorrow Never Dies*	MGM	$1,093,994	4	269	$4,066
4	*As Good As It Gets*	Sony	$970,444	3	127	$7,641
5	*Jackie Brown*	Alliance	$471,921	3	120	$3,932
6	*Firestorm*	Fox	$393,438	1	117	$3,362
7	*Amistad*	DreamWorks	$291,466	5	81	$3,598
8	*Les Boys*	C/FP	$267,695	5	55	$4,867
9	*Mouse Hunt*	DreamWorks	$263,536	4	118	$2,233
10	*Scream 2*	Alliance	$231,072	5	148	$1,561

Note: Figures from "[*Variety*] International Box Office."

Adding up the Screens column in Table 6, the top ten films were in 1533 of the 1900 possible screens in Canada. That's 80.68 percent: not for international movies, necessarily, nor for US movies, although this is primarily what they were; it is screen time for the ten biggest revenue-generating films for that week. As a point of comparison, the top ten films for that same week were in 85.5 percent of available US screens, generating 82.2 percent of revenue for that week,[74] not substantially different from the Canadian figure. Instead of the small space for Canadian film, this points to the need to understand the formation of a dominant core of films, small in number, that characterizes the landscape of a shifting current cinema. The one domestic film to make it into the top ten is the Québécois film *Les Boys*. Its 55 screens gave it 2.9 percent of screens. Thus, a single film for this particular week accounts for a good proportion of the total screen time for Canadian film we might expect, given the often-quoted rate of three to five percent. The average box office per screen, in the final column, is an exceptionally important measure for exhibitors, for it tells them how lucrative a film can be in each auditorium, rather than cumulatively. Using this measure, *Les Boys* was ranked third for that week, pulling in an average of $4,867, just beating out the James Bond film's $4,066.

What share do Canadian distributors have of this take? Adding up the films distributed by Alliance and C/FP, we get 25.58 percent of screens, even though, of the four films *Good Will Hunting*, *Scream 2*, *Jackie Brown*, and *Les Boys*, only the latter is of domestic origin. This share gives credence to Statistics Canada's encouragement for the distribution sector. Although Statistics Canada's figures for 1997–98 recorded the continuing supremacy of international products in Canada, distributors' exports hit their highest levels, with $101.2 million in sales. International sales of non-Canadian products by Canadian distributors increase this amount by another $30.9 million. Further demonstrating the global nature of the Canadian industry, international sales of Canadian product made up 57 percent of distribution revenue. Overall profit margin was a more-than-respectable eighteen percent for 1997–98.[75] The entire film and video distribution sector equally demonstrated its strongest year, with $1.8 billion in revenue, a figure representing a 13-percent increase over 1994–95 and a dramatic 400-percent increase over 1991–92.

Beyond the relatively vigorous character of one segment of the industry—distribution—this screen-time illustration also reflects prevailing releasing strategies, especially the logic of saturation openings. It follows, then, to wonder about the kinds of cinema-going this strategy affords audiences. What does this produce? What kinds of negotiations and practices does it facilitate?

Table 7: Screen-time calculations for Canadian box office (week ending 16 January 1998)

* Approximate number of screens in Canada, January 1998: 1900
* Top 10 films: 1533 of the 1900 possible screens in Canada, or 80.68 percent
* US top 10 films: 19654 of 23000 possible screens, or 85.5 percent
* US top 10 films, revenue: $106,615,516 of $129,704,222, or 82.2 percent
* Screen time for domestic film in top 10 : *Les Boys* on 55 screens of 1900 possible, or 2.9 percent
* Screen time for Canadian distributors: Alliance and C/FP on 486 screens of 1900 possible, or 25.58 percent

Here, the interest is to understand what sorts of modes of consumption are stimulated by the qualities of this formation, of these determinants. As Pierre Bourdieu argues, cultural life has as much to do with the structures of engagement and consumption as it does with the actual texts themselves.[76] Such *dispositions*, he continues, toward cultural forms and practices importantly become a way through which distinctions are made among populations, forming correlations of class power. Most generally, the statistical presence of "hit" films offers a portrait of the role of international cultural forms in the everyday life of Canada. We should ask what dispositions of cinema-going are developed and seen as appropriate to a context not only of international films but of relatively few, massively visible, motion pictures. Simply put, cinema-going is about the practices of congregation and sociability, both foundational aspects of community. To take absence or lack as its primary characteristic is to reassert a judgement that existing cultural life is inauthentic or, worse, diseased. For what screen time reveals is not absence: *it is the presence of simultaneity and currency in Canadian cinema culture.* This is the sense of event made possible by the day and date co-ordination of the appearance of new films in both major and minor centres across the continent. Currency is implied in the "newness" of the texts accounted for. In the above illustration, the ten films occupying a solid majority of screens are no more than five weeks old. We might conclude, then, that the role of cinema-going in contemporary life is, in part, made up of a special set of dispositions and strategies developed to accommodate the determination of this simultaneity and currency. Cinema-going in Canada emphasizes a familiarity with and negotiation of international, and novel, cinema events. Simultaneity of the current cinema expands a long-standing disposition in popular Canadian life, that the motion-picture theatre is a location at which one vector of global cultural traffic is encountered. Seen in this fashion, cinema-going in Canada is partly participation in cinematic cosmopolitanism, displaying the degrees of immersion into international cultural life.

This argument is not intended to reveal the inaccuracies of statistics when deployed in cultural arguments, nor is it to flip the conclusion of "failure" into one of "success." Instead, the intention has been to open up debate around one key set of assumptions in the expectation that the results will offer an expanded analysis of the role of popular cinema in Canada. In the context of the formation of a new place for cinema-going in cultural life, as I discussed earlier, it is time to challenge a policy view that seems to rally single-mindedly around the expressly selective practice of cinema-going as the measure of our national cinema.

The experience of movie-going in Canada can be frustrating. Although it offers a view to an exhilarating world movie culture, movie-going essentially takes you away from your national home. A seat in a Canadian movie theatre is essentially a seat on international territory; it offers the experience of being "anywhere"—of cosmopolitan connection to other world movie audiences. Movie-going, however, does not offer an experience of national spectatorship in the conventional sense; the idea of Canadians watching images of Canada in commercial theatres is rarely realized. Canadians expect this, if only through a tacit agreement that US culture is currently a brand of "degree zero" cultural specificity, finding itself at home in virtually any location. Canadians live with a near-total integration with US cinema culture, involving not only the films and the industrial structures producing and distributing them, but also the movie magazines, the TV shows about movies, the advertising, the Hollywood press junkets, the star interviews, the awards ceremonies, the popular criticism, the scholarly analyses, and so on. Taking a single example, newspaper advertisements for *The Insider* (Mann, 1999) declared, "Only one motion picture has been rousing, stirring and uplifting critics and audiences all across Canada," followed by quotes from *Good Morning America, Newsweek, Time, Rolling Stone,* and Roger Ebert.[77] Not one of these is a Canadian voice; and yet, Canadian audiences do access all of these sources to gauge cinema-going choices. This absurd insensitivity to national difference is, at the same time, a speck of evidence demonstrating internationalist, or at least continentalist, orientation. Hence, it is important to recognize that the entwinement of the two cinema cultures includes a range of texts and practices, beyond the films themselves.

To summarize, while this chapter has focussed upon industrial structure and practices, it has been my intention to point out the variability in the conclusions one might draw from economic data. In particular, the data suggest that cinema-going is a practice, shaped by activities of exhibitors and distributors, that this practice has a structured relationship with other sites of audio-visual consumption, and that there has been a too-rapid agreement that access to Canadian films through theatrical exhibition will build a currently underdeveloped Canadian popular film culture. Instead, I submit that policymakers and scholars alike have given scant attention to the entwinement of US and Canadian film cultures, especially where exhibition is concerned. Doing so reveals that, for Canadians, cinema-going is solidly a practice involving a sense of the new and the international. The crucial efforts to continue to support Canadian filmmaking and Canadian access to it must take this practice into consideration, and imagine other ways in which the health of our national cinema culture might be measured and assessed.

Notes

1 Manjunath Pendakur characterizes the demise of Allen Theatres circuit in 1923 and the rise of Famous Players as a significant part of the roots of Canada's dependent relationship to the US in film. See *Canadian Dreams and American Control: The Political Economy of the Canadian Film Industry* (Toronto: Garamond, 1990), 51–78.

2 Canadian Heritage, *The Road to Success: Report of the Feature Film Advisory Committee* (Ottawa: Canadian Heritage, 1999), 3.

3 *Road to Success,* 3.

4 For a complete rendering of the political economic approach to Canadian culture see Pendakur, *Canadian Dreams and American Control*; Susan M. Crean, *Who's Afraid of Canadian Culture?* (Toronto: General, 1976); and Dallas Smythe, *Dependency Road: Communications, Capitalism, Consciousness and Canada* (Norwood, NJ: Ablex, 1981). For a critical re-examination of this history, see Michael Dorland, *So Close to the State/s: The Emergence of Canadian Feature Film Policy* (Toronto: University of Toronto Press, 1998) and Ted Magder, *Canada's Hollywood: The Canadian State and Feature Films* (Toronto: University of Toronto Press, 1993).

5 "Doubt Clouds Canada's Film Future," *Calgary Herald,* 9 September 1997, C3.

6 Robert Everett-Green, "Not Coming to a Theatre Near You," *Globe and Mail,* 17 January 1997, C2.

7 Leonard Klady, "H'wood's B.O. blast: '97 admissions highest in three decades," *Variety,* 5–11 January 1998.

8 Harvey Enchin, "Canadians Going Back to the Movies," *Globe and Mail,* 11 July 1996, B1. This peak was a full six years after the same turning point in the US in 1946.

9 This argument runs counter to a growing industry feeling that megaplexes have not been as successful as they were expected to be, as evidenced by Loews Cineplex's financial troubles in 2000. For a full discussion of the megaplex, see Charles R. Acland "Cinema-going and the Rise of the Megaplex," *Television and New Media* 1, no. 4 (2000): 375–402.

10 Christine James, "The Great Divide," www.boxoffice.com/showcanada99/daily99story4.htm, accessed 3 November 1999.

11 Martin Peers, "Exhibs vexed by Wall St. hex on plex," *Variety,* 26 January–1 February 1998, 83.

12 Similar tendencies toward oligopoly have been evident in other aspects of the audio-visual business. In 1993, *Variety* noted that Canadian video retail was only twenty percent chain-controlled, but that many were about to expand dramatically; see Brendan Kelly, "Major Video Chains Prepare for a Boom," *Variety*, 22 November 1993, 54. Consolidation in video distribution, however, was unambiguous, with Astral and Video One accounting for almost 80 percent of the market. See Carolyn Leitch, "Astral Considering Acquisitions: Company May Buy Small Video Distributors to Consolidate Market," *Globe and Mail*, 31 January 1997, B8.

13 Karen Mazurkewich, "Film grosses far below target," *Playback*, 19 August 1991, 16.

14 Shlomo Schwartzberg, "Major Players," www.boxoffice.com/showcanada99/daily99story4.html, accessed 3 November 1999.

15 These smaller chains, especially when operating in close markets to Famous Players and Cineplex Odeon, have complained about limited access to the most lucrative films, a clear result of the buying might of the two dominant chains. Québec's Guzzo, for example, has brought a lawsuit against the two, claiming they have actively denied them access to first-run films. Shlomo Schwartzberg, "Guzzo's Gusto," www.boxoffice.com/showcanada99/daily99story4.html, accessed 3 November 1999.

16 Three of the partners involved have ties to other distribution and exhibition companies. Ellis Jacob is an executive at Cineplex Odeon, Robert Lantos was chair of Alliance Communication and now heads Serendipity, and Victor Loewy is head of Alliance Atlantis Motion Picture Group, which has started its own chain, Alliance Atlantis Cinemas, with Famous Players. Gayle MacDonald, "Onex partners launch cinema chain to show flicks to the sticks," *Globe and Mail*, 15 September 1999, B1.

17 Leo Rice-Barker, "Industry Banks on New Technology, Expanded Slates," *Playback*, 6 May 1996, 19; Brendan Kelly, "Bigger, Better Plexes: With eight decades in business, circuit is on expansion course," *Variety*, 29 November–5 December 1999, 35. It is worth noting that although Famous Players does not have any screens in the US, unlike its competitor Cineplex Odeon, its parent corporation Viacom owns National Amusements, one of the largest US chains.

18 Rice-Barker, "Industry Banks on New Technology," 19.

19 Martin Peers, "Cinemark, Cineplex merge ops," *Variety*, 6–12 March 1995, 22.

20 Harvey Enchin, "Deal Creates Box Office Giant," *Globe and Mail*, 1 October 1997.

21 Shawn McCarthy, "Ottawa Eyes Cineplex Merger," *Globe and Mail*, 2 October 1997, A14–15.

22 Shawn McCarthy, "Cineplex Deal May Hinge on Sale of Unit," 3 October 1997, B20.

23 Andy Hoffman, "Cineplex deal raises multiplex of scenarios," *Playback*, 12 January 1998, 1.

24 Bruce Orwall, "Theatre closings possible in Cineplex–Sony merger: Draft document filed with SEC also foresees expansion," *Globe and Mail*, 4 February 1998, B12.

25 "Loews Cineplex Entertainment Announces Financial Results for Second Quarter," www.newswire.ca/release/October1998/08/c2008.htm, accessed 8 May 2000.

26 Harvey Enchin, "Theatre deal highlights market fragmentation," *Globe and Mail*, 3 October 1997, B20.

27 Gayle MacDonald and John Partridge, "Cineplex executives let go," *Globe and Mail*, 2 May 1998.

28 Sid Adilman, "Famous Players hypes expansion after losing 3 Imperial screens," *Variety*, 11 June 1986.

29 Adilman, "Famous Players hypes expansion," 7.

30 "Famous Players is going public," *Variety*, 25 November 1987.

31 Christopher Harris, "Famous Players makes an expansive move," *Playback*, 30 May 1988, 3.

32 "Famous Players sets $C50-million Toronto expansion," *Variety*, 18 May 1988, 39.

33 "Summer b.o. surge posed in Canada by Famous Players," *Variety*, 15 October 1986, 34.

34 "Cinemas need a personal touch," *Playback*, 10 November 1986, 1.

35 Sid Adilman, "Cineplex Odeon Circuit to add 200 Canadian Screens thru '88," *Variety*, 2 July 1986.

36 Morry Roth, "Cineplex boss details Chi plans; aims for 400 new U.S. screens," *Variety*, 2 April 1986, 37.

37 Jim Robbins, "Drabinsky Confirms Cineplex buy of RKO Century Warner; To add 38 N.Y.-area screens," *Variety*, 6 August 1986.

38 Christopher Harris, "More buys for Cineplex," *Playback*, 4 September 1989, 4.

39 Allison Vale, "Boffo Screen Build," *Playback,* 5 May 1997, 28.

40 Jim Robbins, "Emotional crowd protests close of Regency; Cineplex Odeon mum," *Variety*, 9 September 1987.

41 Will Tusher, "Cineplex Odeon agrees to sell 57 Canadian multiplexes in fall," *Variety*, 17 August 1988, 6.

42 Brian Milner, "Cineplex to Stick to Film Exhibiting," *Globe and Mail,* 16 June 1990, B5.

43 "Briefing: Film exhibition," *Variety*, 19 November 1990, 58.

44 "CO completes buy of 152 screens in western Canada," *Variety*, 7 February 1990, 24.

45 Jen Mitchell, "New attempts to woo customers," *Playback,* 5 December 1994, 27.

46 Leonard Klady, "B.O. tastes Yank-flavored," *Variety,* 2–8 September 1996, 42.

47 Christopher Harris, "Faith in Popcorn," *Globe and Mail,* 10 May 1997, C3.

48 Harris, "Faith in Popcorn," C3.

49 "Cineplex readies Montréal fourplex," *Variety,* 26 November 1986, 7.

50 Douglas Gomery, "Building a Movie Theatre Giant: The Rise of Cineplex Odeon," in *Hollywood in the Age of Television*, Tino Balio, ed. (Boston: Unwin Hyman, 1990), 377.

51 "Cineplex empire builds," *Playback*, 10 August 1987, 1.

52 "Cineplex Odeon art house re-opens with benefit fest," *Playback*, 2 May 1988, 3.

53 "Toronto CO multiplex gets liquor license," *Variety,* 17 June 1991, 36.

54 Karen Murray, "Designing theaters around environment," *Variety*, 25–31 July 1994, 40.

55 "Hold the popcorn," *Playback*, 14 December 1987, 3.

56 "Famous Players ups Canadian admission to $C7," *Variety*, 17–23 May 1989, 14.

57 "Cineplex Odeon ups Canada tickets to $C7," *Variety,* 31 May–7 June 1989, 5.

58 "It's a Famous idea to drop movie prices," *Playback*, 7 March 1988, 1; and "Famous Players theater chain lowers ticket prices in Canada," *Variety*, 9 March 1988, 7.

59 "Shock to silence: Exhibitors react to Drabinsky's move," *Variety*, 25 November 1987.

60 "At $7.50 top, CO turns up b.o. heat," *Variety* 14–20 June 1990, 7; and "Cineplex Odeon hikes Canadian admissions," *Variety*, 30 May 1989, 13.

61 Enchin, "Canadians Going Back to the Movies," B1.

62 Mary Ellen Armstrong, "Expansion and Change," *Playback*, 19 May 1997.

63 Pamela Swedko, "Theatre Executives gather for ShowCanada confab," *Playback,* 5 May 1997, 26.

64 Mary Ellen Armstrong, "Service, Disney Style," *Playback*, 19 May 1997, 8.

65 Vale, "Boffo Screen Build," 1.

66 Klady, "B.O. tastes Yank-flavored," 42.

67 Secor Group, "Canadian Government Intervention in the Film and Video Industry," 19 October 1994, 24.

68 Wyndham Wise, "*Take One's* 1998 Survey of Canadian Films in the GTA," *Take One,* Winter 1999, 51.

69 *Road to Success,* 5.

70 For an argument about the importance of these non-theatrical venues in Canadian film culture, see the discussion of "expo-mentality" in Charles R. Acland, "Popular Film in Canada: Revisiting the Absent Audience," in *A Passion for Identity: An Introduction to Canadian Studies,* third edition, David Taras and Beverly Rasporich, eds. (Toronto: Nelson, 1989), 281–96.

71 Robert Everett-Green, "Canadian film by the numbers," *Globe and Mail,* 18 January 1997, C2.

72 Statistics Canada, "Film and Video Distribution Survey, 1994–95."

73 Dan Johnson, letter to the editor, *Globe and Mail,* 30 July 1996; Paul Audley, letter to the editor, *Globe and Mail,* 10 September 1996.

74 From figures provided in *Variety's* "Box Office," 19–25 January 1998.

75 Statistics Canada, "Film and Video Distribution and Wholesaling Survey."

76 Pierre Bourdieu, *Distinction: A Social Critique of the Judgement of Taste,* Richard Nice, trans. (Cambridge: Harvard University Press, 1984).

77 Advertisement for *The Insider* (1999) in *Montréal Gazette,* 12 November 1999.

Brave New Film Board
D.B. Jones

ON 10 MAY 2000, I DROVE UP TO MONTRÉAL for what would be a mere two-day visit at the National Film Board (NFB). The editors of this anthology had invited me to write on the Board's English-language production since 1980. I hadn't kept up with the Film Board since publishing a history of it in 1982; my later book on Tom Daly focussed on him, not the Board, and he had retired in 1984. I saw this invitation as an opportunity to catch up on the Film Board's work. The NFB's publicity department agreed to send me videotapes of whatever films I or they thought I should see. By the time of my visit, I had already seen about one hundred titles new to me, and I would watch about another hundred and fifty after the trip.

Although my essay would explore how English production over the past twenty years stood up aesthetically, against a broadly defined interpretation of NFB founder John Grierson's documentary idea, and would not study the organization itself, I wanted to step inside the Film Board's doors once again in order to get at least a rudimentary first-hand impression of its current pulse and to speak with whatever administrative and creative personnel were available and willing. The organizational character of the NFB had been closely tied to the quality of its films. And I had reason to believe that character might have changed. Through snippets of news that now and then made their way down south, I was aware that in the mid 1990s the Film Board had undergone some kind of a traumatic restructuring. Most of its filmmakers had left—forced out, through early retirement, in disgust, or combinations thereof—and, I was told, the Film Board was but a shell of its former self.

The next morning, as I approached the NFB's headquarters on Côte-de-Liesse Road, I noticed a huge vertical banner hanging on the side of the building's east wing and exclaiming, "Images of our lives! Images de nos vies!" The banner looked over a nearly empty parking lot. I drove past the main entrance and pulled into a lot on the west side of the building. It too was nearly empty. Inside, the labyrinthine hallways were freshly painted, cleaner than I remembered them, but also empty. I headed for the cafeteria, which in the 1970s, when I did most of my earlier research, was my base of operations. Every morning, until about nine o'clock, it would fill up with filmmakers, cameramen, editors, technicians, administrative staff. It would fill again at lunchtime. One could sit at almost any table and join any discussion. It was here that one day in 1974 Michael Rubbo and various interested filmmakers vigorously debated whether the heated argument between Rubbo and media mogul Geoff Stirling should remain in the rough cut of a documentary on Cuba that had just been screened. Donald Brittain might stagger in for coffee and conversation after completing yet another cut of what would become *Volcano*. Kathleen Shannon used to sit here, listen, and decide to prove that women could make films without men. On any given day, one might hear Tony Ianzelo and Boyce Richardson fielding responses to their films on China, a director pitching an idea to a producer, cameramen kvetching about a temperamental director, or competitive jealousies and professional resentments surfacing in one way or another.

I had the cafeteria to myself this morning.

ॐ ॐ ॐ

The banner exclaiming "Images of our lives!" reminded me of a film I had already seen: *The Image Makers: The National Film Board: The First Forty Years*. It was released in 1980, the precise transition point from the earlier period to the one I had agreed to survey. Directed by Albert Kish, the film mentions early on the sheer bulk of the Film Board's achievement: 10,000 titles ("the collected memory of a nation"), audiences of over a billion a year, nearly 2000 international awards. It then samples this collected memory, covering major trends from the wartime propaganda films to the dissident and counter-cultural films of the 1960s and '70s. The film is deftly edited, the clips linked through visual associations. And, by giving unusual emphasis to the Film Board's founder and founding purpose, *The Image Makers* provides an apt perspective from which to consider the Film Board's subsequent work. At the beginning of the film, over footage of the abandoned Ottawa sawmill in which the Film Board was first housed, is a scratchy recording of John Grierson recalling that

> the Film Board was a *deliberate* creation to do a *deliberate* work. It was there to bring Canada alive to itself and to the rest of the world. It was there to declare the *excellences* of Canada to Canadians and to the rest of the world. It was there to *evoke* the *strengths* of Canada, the imagination of Canadians in respect of creating their present and their future.

The film concludes with an exact replay of this admonition.

Like most of Grierson's remembered phrases (e.g., documentary is "the creative treatment of actuality"; "tell a lie today so that it comes true tomorrow"; art is "not a mirror but a hammer"), this passage is compact, complex, and ambiguous. Nevertheless, it can be given a brief—and I hope reasonably non-controversial—interpretation that will enable it to serve as a kind of template by which to identify changes, if any, in the Film Board aesthetic over the past twenty years.

For Grierson, declaring Canada's excellences and evoking its strengths meant, at the least, showing it off in its variety. The Film Board was "to see Canada and see it whole." Its original mandate, which Grierson wrote, was "to help Canadians in all parts of Canada to understand the ways of living and the problems of Canadians in other parts."

This image-making would be primarily in documentary, even if drama and animation would have a place in the Film Board production from the beginning. But although he was an avowed propagandist, Grierson's notion of documentary was at its core a sophisticated aesthetic concept. Documentary filmmakers must be poets "or stay forever journalists." There must be a sense of purpose in a film, and for that "there must be the power of poetry or prophecy [or, failing that] at least the sociological sense implicit in poetry and prophecy." In this statement, Grierson establishes as documentary's goals the classical values of the True, the Beautiful, and the Good. The main difference between documentary and the other arts was its material: actuality, whether the footage be original or archival.

Because the establishment of the NFB preceded the outbreak of World War Two by only months, the NFB under Grierson's direction didn't come close to tapping the full aesthetic possibilities of his documentary idea. Grierson himself suppressed it in the interests of Allied propaganda. But he had created an organization strong enough—politically, constitutionally, and philosophically—to develop on its own long after he departed at the end of the war. And it was not until the Film Board changed in ways Grierson opposed that filmmakers began to explore the aesthetic possibilities in his documentary idea much more probingly than he ever did. Grierson had insisted that filmmakers be hired on three-month contracts to avoid organizational stagnation, but by 1950 filmmakers had won the security of civil-servant status. In the late 1960s, Grierson raged against what he perceived as a self-centred, irresponsible attitude in the Film Board's creative people. But the establishment of job security had given filmmakers, many of whom retained the fervent sense of public duty that Grierson inculcated, the freedom to explore sensitive subjects, take controversial stands, and experiment technically and artistically, often in defiance of Film Board management.

The best films from what has come to be considered the Film Board's "golden era" embodied Grierson's original ideal in full balance. Documentaries like *City of Gold* (1957), *Circle of the Sun* (1961), *Lonely Boy* (1961), *Memorandum* (1965), *Cree Hunters of Mistassini* (1974), and *Sad Song of Yellow Skin* (1974)—many others could be mentioned—make social comment, are beautifully crafted, and respect the actuality of unscripted, minimally contrived photographic images. These films presented a rounded treatment of their subjects, and while they did not flinch from the unpleasant or horrific where appropriate, neither did they wallow in despair, or denounce, or whine. Their craftsmanship was an aspect of their affirmation, their technique evidence of their sincerity. From around 1955 on, the Film Board set the international standard for documentary film.

It still held this place of prominence in the early 1980s, producing films that embodied Grierson's tripartite documentary idea and yet reflected distinctive styles of individual filmmakers. In his affectionate and moving *Daisy: The Story of a Facelift* (1982), Michael Rubbo, who had pioneered the participatory documentary at the Film Board, added a new permutation to the genre. In this film, he interacts not only with his subjects but also with the audience, challenging us to watch a facelift operation but warning us when we might want to turn away. Donald Winkler's masterful *F.R. Scott: Rhyme and Reason* (1982) represents the unusual symmetry and commonality between Scott's dual pursuits with a fine balance of its own, gracefully weaving back and forth between scenes emphasizing Scott's legal triumphs and scenes explicating, visually and light-handedly, his poems. In the enigmatic, mesmerizing *Boulevard of Broken Dreams* (1987), Derek May and his co-director and cameraman Albert van der Wildt manage to present a documentary subject (the Canadian visit of a unique Dutch theatrical troupe) coherently and interestingly while deliberately ignoring the usual documentary expectations of a clear narrative line and explanatory information. In his epic *The Champions* (1986), Donald Brittain uses archival footage and his inimitable narration style to create an affectionate, ultimately sad chronicle of the long rivalry between the cool federalist Pierre Trudeau and the passionate separatist René Lévesque.

And in 1982, Colin Low (as director) and Tom Daly (as producer and editor) collaborated on what would be Daly's last major NFB project, the quietly seductive, deeply spiritual, and superbly crafted documentary *Standing Alone*. Low and Daly had collaborated similarly on *Circle of the Sun* (1961). The later film visits the subject of the earlier film, Pete Standing Alone, a Blood Indian, and finds him belatedly interested in his heritage. "I didn't always appreciate why the Sun Dance survives," he says, "when everything else changes." The film explores at a deceptively leisurely pace the flux of Pete's life: his attempt to instill in his children an appreciation of their heritage; his business ventures; a failed but principled foray into politics; his daughter's participation in a blockade; his serene adaptation to contemporary reality. The film is structured such that everything we see and hear seems to represent Pete's point of view or his thoughts, even though he is in most of the scenes. The persistence of the Sun Dance and the ineluctability of change are resolved in the film's final images, a few shots at sunset of a man sitting outside the circle of the dance, bouncing a diaper-clad baby on his knee to the rhythm of the drums.

Each of these five documentaries exemplifies the possibilities inherent in Grierson's aesthetic. They are extremely well crafted, and each constitutes a whole in which the parts easily fit without Procrustean manipulation. Each uses the standard materials of documentary—"actuality," in Grierson's term—and tries to build its "truth" from them. Three of the films—arguably all five—touch upon an issue of concern to Canadians, and, *mutatis mutandis,* to most people. They reflect Canadian reality yet set high the bar: Pete's serenity, Scott's service, Daisy's courage, the heroic ambition of Trudeau and Lévesque, the existential honesty embodied in *Boulevard of Broken Dreams*. In short, they have aspects of poetry, prophecy, and social concern. It is in this way that they declare the excellences and evoke the strengths of Canada. And each film is so distinctive from the others, and so representative of its maker's (or makers') style and interests, that together they show that Grierson's complex aesthetic could accommodate, and his institutional creation encourage, rich and distinctive artistic voices in documentary, even into the Film Board's fifth decade.

But the films also mark a crest for the full-bodied interpretation of the Grierson aesthetic at the Film Board. It would be challenged and displaced by a new generation—and gender—of filmmakers who had no interest in declaring Canada's excellences or in evoking her strengths and who were not excited by a conception of documentary that emphasized meticulous craftsmanship and wholeness of vision. Of the three Kantian values in Grierson's documentary idea, they valued one far over the others: the Good or, as they interpreted it, social advocacy. It's not that they cared little for truth. They were sure they possessed it. Truth was not something to be wrested from actuality material; actuality was to be used to illustrate or accompany a verbalized idea of the world. As for art, they were impatient with the craftsmanship and toil needed to create it.

This attitude was nothing new at the Film Board. Encouraged by Grierson himself, it had been present since the beginning of the documentary movement as a check against any tendency for documentarians to drift into making art for art's sake, something Grierson abhorred. "Bang them out and no misses" was Grierson's bottom-line wartime aesthetic. Later, films from the radical wing of French Production and Challenge for Change often brought social advocacy to the forefront at the expense of documentary truth and art. What changed after 1980 was that the use of documentary to advocate a cause at the expense of art or truth-seeking would dominate the Film Board's program. Instead of absorbing the adversarial impulse into a larger whole, the films would be more directly expressive of the fears, resentments, and desires of the time.

Two films from the early 1980s mark this shift in the predominant Film Board interpretation of the documentary idea. Terri (later Terre) Nash's *If You Love This Planet* (1982) is built around a lecture by Dr. Helen Caldicott on the horrors of nuclear war and the idiocy of the arms race. Intercut with the lecture is footage from the aftermath of Hiroshima and Nagasaki, and clips from *Jap Zero*, a 1943 U.S. War Department film featuring a young Ronald Reagan. After a shot of a nuclear blast, the film cuts to a clip from *Jap Zero*, where Lt. Jimmy Saunders, the character played by Reagan, is made to seem to refer to the 1945 atomic blast when he says, "It was a helluva explosion … and I guess that's all, sir." Later Caldicott says of the arms race that "the mentality is about at a level of a nine-year-old boy," and again the film cuts to Reagan in *Jap Zero*. When not mocking Reagan, *If You Love This Planet* reeks of doom. Dr. Caldicott cites a scientist who doubts the world will make it to 1990.

In *Not a Love Story* (1981), director Bonnie Sherr Klein tours the underworld of the pornography business, with exotic dancer Linda Lee (later Lindalee) Tracey as her guide. Interspersed with various scenes of pornographic display and production are interviews with prominent feminists, denunciations of patriarchy, and condemnations of *Hustler* publisher Larry Flynt. Its strongest scenes are disturbing and funny at the same time. In a photographic session for a men's magazine "spread" shot, featuring Tracey herself, the female photographer calls to her crew, "We need more pussy juice." Soon Tracey's private parts glisten for an international audience of millions while Tracey provides a running commentary on the absurdity of it all. In a peep show in Manhattan, men pay by the minute to ogle at naked women through small shuttered windows; when time is up and the shutters descend, each customer scrunches down to grab every last possible glimpse, squinting through the final millimetres of open window.

Both films were smash hits with activist audiences and catalysts for political movements. *If You Love This Planet* won an Academy Award in 1983 and was used in the anti-nuclear movement. *Not a Love Story* was shown widely in colleges and community venues. It served as briefing material for a federal standing committee, an educational tool for police, and ammunition in a 1983 nation-wide protest against allowing *Playboy* on pay television.[1]

But the argument in *If You Love This Planet* is simplistic and tendentious. The cuts to Reagan are used dishonestly, since a character in a 1943 film could not have been referring to an atomic blast. *Not a Love Story* reeks of resentment, a pervasive implication that the degradation the film shows is all the fault of men. And Klein does not trust her audience to judge her material for themselves. She uses the reaction shot as moral arbiter, again and again cutting to shots of herself to show how she feels, and how we should feel, about each event or interviewee. As the centrefold photographer talks about her work, successive cutaways show Klein first appalled, then quizzical, and lastly disapproving. When Kate Millet discourses on patriarchy, Klein is rapt. And so on.

Yet the two films share qualities that, in determining their significance, trump their shortcomings. They were bold. They were powerful. And they clinched a role at the NFB not just for women filmmakers but for a feminist point of view. Both films were the product of Studio D, a unit established in 1976 to make films for and about women as well as to advance women filmmakers at the Board. Through the 1980s and early 1990s, Studio D would be the Film Board's pace-setting, most purposeful unit, although the purpose was not to make films in the round but to promulgate a cause. A 1989 retrospective of its work, *Studio D: 15th Anniversary*, opens with the studio's founder Kathleen Shannon stating in hushed, sacerdotal tones Studio D's creed:

> Studio D began as an opportunity for women to take *our* place in making films that reflect, and reflect on, our lives. As women, we looked into our *own* experience, named things as *we* saw them, and started to speak our truth in public places. Films give us a chance to hear *each other*, and old stereotypes dissolve. We found we are a part of a continuous and world-wide *history* of women's thinking and analysis, protest and creativity, skills and commitment. All subjects of the *world* belong to women, and our perspectives on them will play a vital part in achieving our *goals*: the liberation of *all* human beings from all oppressions, and our right to global peace. As we honour women's wisdom, so long silenced, new vision is birthed, and hope begins to find a place to grow.

This statement reflects the ambitiousness of Studio D's project. The excellences it would declare and strengths it would evoke were women's, not Canada's. It not only presumed to give voice to a neglected group of people—the half of the world's population that are women—it also intended, thereby, to save the world from destruction. Its films tended to reflect one or the other, and often both, of these aims. *Not a Love Story* turned inward, focussing on the victimization of women and seeking their liberation. *If You Love This Planet* looked outward, hoping to save not just women but the whole world. But while both tendencies were most clearly manifested in Studio D films, they were operating elsewhere in the Film Board, not just in Studio D. Many of the Film Board's most important films of the 1980s and early 1990s embodied primarily one or the other tendency, even when women or war was not the main or only focus.

But there are two areas in which the statement does not reflect ambition. There is no ambition to discover the truth, for it is already known. And the credo expresses no interest in the art of documentary. It was enough "to speak our truth." And that's what Studio D films, along with other films following the same general tendency, typically did. The truth was *their* truth, and they *spoke* it. Compared to the NFB's golden era, when truth was something to be forged from actuality material, the dominant rhetorical strategy of the films from the early 1980s on was essentially one of declaration and dogma. Aesthetically, the films marked a reversion to the NFB of World War Two, when Grierson subordinated his richer notions of documentary art to the task at hand, which was to defeat fascism. In its zeal to defeat patriarchy and abolish war, Studio D and its like-minded colleagues made films that, like those of Grierson's wartime NFB, resembled tracts. In both eras, the word overwhelmed the image, then through stentorian voice-of-god narration, now through softer, usually voice-of-goddess narration, talking heads, or both.

Margaret Wescott's 130-minute *Behind the Veil: Nuns* (1984) recapitulates in itself the transition from a documentary approach that seeks knowledge from actuality to one that advocates an unquestioned political position. The film begins as a seemingly straightforward exploration of how the life of Catholic nuns has evolved over the years, but about 30 minutes in launches into a litany of complaints against the suppression of women by the Church patriarchy, finally morphing into a plea for world peace. The film gives its audience no room to breathe, alternating stretches of wall-to-wall narration over slide-lecture photography and interviews with activist nuns. Over a scene of anti-war nuns protesting at the Pentagon, the narrator salutes "[this] cluster of non-violent spiritual beings ... these thinking women" and invites the audience "to join with them in making a new world of equality, love, and peace."

While *Behind the Veil* expresses in equal measure female victimization and an impulse to save the world, films from or influenced by Studio D tended to emphasize one or the other. But whether through narration or talking head, or both, most of them privileged the word over the image, using the visual track primarily as a delivery mechanism for verbalized ideas. Whatever the merit of its particular position on its issues, the persuasiveness of film after film is eroded by incongruity, obduracy, or confusion in its argument.

Speaking Our Peace (1985), by Bonnie Sherr Klein and Terre Nash, extols the effort of women's groups to protest the arms race. It has more actuality footage than *Behind the Veil*, but much of it is of gratingly self-righteous demonstrations, and it relies heavily on interviews with prominent Canadian women uttering inanities, such as writer Margaret Laurence exclaiming that "If peace is subversive, in God's name, what is war!?" The basic strategy in each of Donna Read's three films on women's spirituality and its pacifist nature—*Goddess Remembered* (1989), *The Burning Times* (1990), and *Full Circle* (1992)—is to interweave the musings of feminist discussion groups with an illustrated lecture espousing the director's unquestioned thesis. A narration excerpt from *Goddess Remembered* conveys the tone of the series:

> All over the Western world, waves of conquerors descended on the peaceful, goddess-worshipping cultures. And at Delphi, too, the gentle temple became a male-dominated hive of exploitation, with the gentle voice of the priestess buried under layers of hierarchy.

Shelley Saywell's *Rape: A Crime of War* (1996) argues that rape should be considered a war crime because it "is all part of the aggressive nature of war." But if rape is just part of the aggressive nature of war, then rape is a war crime only if war itself is a crime, a position the film does not take. Largely through lecture material, Terre Nash's *Who's Counting: Marylin Waring on Sex, Lies and Global Economics* (1995) ties women's issues to war and economics. Waring points out that an American homemaker is called "economically inactive" while her husband, whose job is to sit in a missile silo all day long and, if ordered, launch a nuclear missile, is considered a contributor to the nation's growth, wealth, and productivity. The economic measurements used by the United Nations recognize only market transactions and place no value on peace or reproduction. Waring's sympathy for the Third World and her denunciation of Western hegemony are rendered suspect by the film's last scene, at Waring's beautiful New Zealand farm, leaving us to wonder through what economic system she acquired this edenic property and where the Maoris who once lived there live now.

The NFB's most ambitious set of anti-war films were three series made outside of Studio D and featuring historian and journalist Gwynne Dyer. He is the on-camera narrator of the seven-part *War* (1983) and the three-part *Defence of Canada* (1986), and he narrates off-camera the three-part *Protection Force* (1995) on the Canadian peacekeeping forces in the former Yugoslavia. Although he does not direct the films, he controls their tone and vision. There are no developed scenes in the first two series, and their uninspired footage is smothered by Dwyer's preening self-importance. He pops up on location for no apparent cinematic purpose; he is merely lecturing, not participating à la Rubbo or even reacting à la Klein. And his narration has a tendency to engage in sleight-of-tongue. "If you prepare for war, sooner or later you will get it," he says, without addressing what happens if you do not prepare for it. "If you believe that there is no so-lution to your problems except war, people are going to die," he warns, apparently unaware that often the problem for which there seems to be no other solution is that people are already dying. "Armed forces require enemies to justify their existence," he remarks, without suggesting a better reason. While we are spared Dyer's pointless visual presence in Garth Pritchard's generally more engaging *Protection Force* series, talking heads replace him sometimes just as wearisomely. The death of Corporal Isfeld, the subject of the otherwise compelling *The Price of Duty*, is recounted in a seven-minute tight close-up relieved by only a cutaway or two.

The films that focussed primarily inward, on the problems of female identity and empower-ment, likewise tended to suffer from crudely fashioned argument and insipid verbal content, of-ten to proclaim victimization. Gail Singer's *Abortion: Stories from North and South* (1984) includes some absorbing actuality footage—Buddhist monks blessing an abortion clinic in Thailand, an Irish woman clandestinely arranging a trip to England for an abortion—but this material is swamped by long stretches of narrated pronouncements often expressed in insensitive language. "Large families and attempted abortions took their toll," the narrator laments, apparently unable to imagine or acknowledge, however allusively, that for those on the equally passionate other side of the issue completed abortions also take a toll.

Forbidden Love: The Unashamed Stories of Lesbian Lives (1992), by Aerlyn Weissman and Lynne Fernie, is built around interviews with ten mostly middle-aged or older lesbians recalling their youth when lesbian behaviour was suppressed. The slow-moving film springs to life whenever it cuts to a skilfully rendered, steamy fictionalized story of lesbian epiphany done in a style meant to reflect 1950s lesbian literature. Oddly, though, the film endorses for lesbians behaviour it con-demns in men. One interviewee talks acceptingly about aggressive butch territoriality, and oth-ers revel in past affairs. A clip from an early NFB film is disparaged for extolling feminine beauty, but the two women in the lovingly directed fictional romance are very attractive, and the story validates quickie, casual sex.

In some of these films, the cry of victimhood assumes an angry ideological tone. *Sisters in the Struggle* (1991) is constructed almost entirely from interviews with members of the Black Women's Collective in Toronto, several of whom are immigrants from the Caribbean, all of them complaining about racist Canada. A woman asserts her need to fight "racism, sexism, ho-mophobia, you know, elitism, ageism, the whole thing." "On top of everything else, they're fuckin' shooting us down, too," reports another. In a neglect of craftsmanship that verges on moral lapse, the filmmakers allow a labour activist to sound embarrassingly inarticulate as she states her simple point in five similar and easily condensed ways:

> I think black women have *always* worked. I mean, uh, black women have always *worked*, I mean in the West Indies, I'm talkin' about immigrant black women, I mean, women have always *worked*. You had an extended family to care for the, for the child, or the chil-dren, and women have always gone out and *worked*. It's not a choice of black women. You have to work to make ends *meet*, I mean, there's no choice, and I often *wonder*, uh, how black women survive in this country.

But it can be the exercise of craftsmanship, not its absence, that seems, intentionally or not, to turn victimization into a positive identity or all-encompassing explanation for one's failures. In Beverly Shaffer's *To a Safer Place* (1987), Shirley Turcotte, sexually abused in her childhood by her father, embarks on a project to visit and confront family members and ex-neighbours. Ostensibly her purpose is to lift the burden of guilt and fear that has haunted her, but it seems as if on some level Turcotte takes pride in her scars of abuse. The filmmaker has Turcotte reveal the most sensationalistic details of it in coy, scripted-sounding asides. Glynis Whiting's *The Sterilization of Lelani Muir* (1990) is a well-made film constructed around Muir's suit against the Province of Alberta for sterilizing her at age fourteen. As Muir enters the courthouse, a reporter asks her how her life would have been had she never been sterilized. A lot better, she says. In a news conference after she has been awarded $750,000 in compensation, Muir says that no amount of money could make up for what happened to her; the hurt will be there until the day she dies. But in an effort to make us feel Muir's pain, the film has shown her life as so feckless that we are left to wonder how much different her life would have been had she not been victimized.

In Dionne Brand's *Long Time Comin'* (1993), a talented painter who repeatedly insists on defining herself as a black, lesbian artist complains that her work has been marginalized. *Them That's Not* (1993), by Cristene Browne, surveys and seems to endorse the demands of several mothers on welfare who share a resentment for the welfare system and a demand for more money. The film ends with a veiled if laughable threat, sanctimoniously uttered, of a revolution "without the violence, hopefully." *When Women Kill* (1994), by Barbara Doran, absolves three women who had killed their husbands or lovers of responsibility for their actions. Women kill when men make them do it. Each woman recalls her lethal action as if it were an out-of-body experience: the car went into reverse by mistake, "I turned around and he was bleeding," "the knife went that way."

Attention to victims, as individuals or in classes, is nothing new to the Film Board. The Griersonian documentary itself has been broadly excoriated for it, most expressively in Brian Winston's disgust at its condescending focus on "the halt and the lame." Challenge for Change was established to make films on behalf of the disadvantaged. But for Grierson and successive leadership at the Board, neither the assignment of blame for one's degradation entirely on others nor an acceptance of degradation, by either the subject or the filmmaker, was ever a sanctioned option. The intended prototype for Challenge for Change, *The Things I Cannot Change* (1966), was roundly criticized within the Film Board itself for the defeatism of its subject and the film's tacit acceptance of it, and most subsequent Challenge for Change films focussed on the amelioration or transformation of unacceptable conditions.

One shift in attitude regarding victimization can be seen clearly in a comparison between two NFB films on obesity made 25 years apart: William Weintraub's *A Matter of Fat* (1969) and Jeff McKay's *Fat Chance: The New Prejudice* (1994). Both films are excellently made, are similarly structured, and feature likeable subjects. But while *A Matter of Fat* chronicles Gilles Lorrain's campaign to lose weight, *Fat Chance* traces Rick Zakowich's decision to stay fat. At a conference aimed at building the self-esteem of overweight people, Zakowich hears an expert assert that rage is good: "There shouldn't be any unbroken windows left at a diet clinic." A woman who specializes in taking nude photos of fat people recounts to an increasingly rapt Zakowich how, after being humiliated by someone who called her a "fat ass," she resolved that no one was *ever* going to have that kind of power over me again, and that I *deserved* to have a good life, and—*goddammit!*—I was going to do *whatever it took*. I was going to make *whatever kind of world* I needed to make .... I took down all the artwork in my apartment that was of thin people—a lot of Erte things and art nouveau things—they all went. Only representations of fat people went up there .... And now I only sleep with fat lovers.

On a radio show back in Winnipeg, Rick maintains that one can be both obese and healthy. About 95 percent of diets don't work. "Don't fall into the trap that's been set for us," he urges. But for the Film Board of 1969, obesity itself was the trap. Being fat is not all Gilles Lorrain's fault, the narrator of *A Matter of Fat* says, but that doesn't help him lose weight. "Nature may have been unfair to him, but if he wants to fight it, he still has only two weapons: more exercise and less food." For Lorrain, it is, so to speak, the five percent that inspires him, not the ninety-five percent that discourages him. Undergoing a seven-month ordeal of exercise and a near-starvation diet, he loses one hundred forty pounds. At a party given in his honour, he looks exceedingly happy. We sense that even if he eventually regains the weight—the credits report that he has kept the weight off for a year so far—these days of happiness are worth the ordeal.

A Griersonian impatience with avoidance of responsibility surfaces late in Norma Bailey's *The True Story of Linda M.* (1995). Linda hates being an alcoholic and a drug addict, but she doesn't do anything about it. Over and over, she laments her abused and loveless childhood. When she complains about her problems to her son Jason, who is in dire trouble for a serious felony, it is he who maturely suggests she ought to think about her two younger children rather than wallow in self-pity. Even the director becomes exasperated, urging Linda to say to herself, "Fine, I was abused, I'm going to go on from here," but the film leaves us doubting that Linda is ready for that.

The effect of ideology on a film's tone can be seen clearly in a comparison between two films that bear several resemblances: *Older Stronger Wiser* and *Black Mother Black Daughter*. The films were both made in 1989, are the same length (28 minutes), and even share an aversion to punctuation. The director of the former film, Claire Prieto, co-directed (with Sylvia Hamilton) the latter one. The main apparent difference in the films' production circumstances is that *Older Stronger Wiser* was a Studio D film, while *Black Mother Black Daughter* hailed from the Atlantic Centre. They begin on an almost identical note of accusation. Of the five black women who are its subjects, *Older Stronger Wiser* complains that the "the rich record of their lives has been hidden from us." *Black Mother Black Daughter* gripes about a heritage having been "stolen from us." But in the Studio D film, interest in the women is subverted by seemingly forced partisan content. A farming woman says we could feed the world if it weren't for the multinationals. Experience as an underdog led another to become a union activist. Another runs a Third World bookstore. The Atlantic Centre film, by contrast, lets us get to know women of a small black community in Nova Scotia as people rather than spokespersons for political aims. When one of the filmmakers says at the end of the film that she wants her own daughters "to be touched and moved by the example of their lives," we believe they will be, for we have been touched and moved ourselves.

The personal film may seem to have offered films on identity a way of avoiding domination by anger or ideology, but it could lead to confusions of its own. In her *Return Home* (1992), Chinese-Canadian Michelle Wong visits her aging grandparents in a remote part of Alberta, interviews them at length, and reports that the experience of making the film changed her. She had never appreciated her grandparents, she says—leaving us to wonder why she took a film crew out there in the first place—and concludes that it is OK to live in both cultures. In *Domino* (1994), Shanti Thakur, whose father is of Indian and mother of Danish origin, interweaves several portraits of young men and women of mixed race. Thakur concludes that people in her situation should try to take the best from both cultures, maintaining a delicate balance of loyalties. This leaves us to speculate on what would happen if someone like the director were to marry one of her subjects—the Chinese-Black man, for example. Would their children have to delicately balance *four* cultures? Wouldn't it be simpler just to become a Canadian? This is the conclusion in Michael Fukushima's *Minoru: memory of exile* (1992), in which, using gorgeous animation, family photos, and his father's own voice, Fukushima tells the story of his father's family's wrenching dislocation from Vancouver during World War Two, when his father himself was just a small boy. To his father, it was all part of childhood, and he seems grateful for having had the chance "to be a Canadian ... to start over, to have justice, in a way." The filmmaker describes his own Canadianness as "complete, totally natural, immutable. My father affirmed his in the face of hatred and oppression. I am a Canadian because he struggled to remain a Canadian."

Alanis Obomsawin is one NFB filmmaker of this era who produced a body of work that, although expressing a clearly partisan point of view and lacking interest in artistic breakthroughs, consistently manages to avoid crude tendentiousness and over-reliance on words. She uses more actuality footage than the typical NFB advocacy film, and she does not insist that her sufferers are without responsibility or their enemies lacking in humanity. Her films are both personal and self-effacing, and they are engaged in a Griersonian way. Her *Richard Cardinal: Cry from the Diary of a Métis Child* (1986) finds the cause of her subject's suffering outside the subject himself, but it proceeds from there in a traditionally Griersonian direction. Cardinal's diary, discovered after he hanged himself, recounts a history of abuse, neglect, and hopelessness. Obomsawin blames—calmly, gently—a system that too readily makes aboriginal and Métis children wards of the state. "The answer," Obomsawin concludes, "lies in a return to traditional values in caring for our children and remembering that every child has many mothers." Her 1988 *No Address*, on problems of homeless Indians in Montréal, is similarly purposive. The subjects of her film are honest about the reasons for their degraded condition, which include alcoholism and drug addiction. They and the film focus on self-help measures that the aboriginal community is taking on behalf of its homeless. *Kanehsatake: 270 Years of Resistance* (1993), an account of the 78-day stand-off in 1990 between the Mohawks of the Kanehsatake reserve and the Canadian army at Oka, Québec, is strong documentary cinema constructed from often-tense actuality footage. It embodies a point of view but won't endorse the demonization of those who oppose it. There is a lot of macho posturing among the Mohawks—the men are called "warriors"—but Obomsawin subtly undermines the more belligerent tendencies of the rebels with an interesting scene depicting a man whose job it is to help the "warriors" overcome their anger.

Obomsawin's films were not alone in resisting the oversimplification of issue and technique that was the dominant trend for most of the 1980s and early 1990s. *To a Safer Place*, if overly contrived, was not dull. *Black Mother Black Daughter* transcended complaint. *Fat Chance* made good use of observational technique, and it developed rather than asserted its argument. More films than can be mentioned were interestingly made and had something to say. *Manufacturing Consent: Noam Chomsky on the Media* (1992), by Mark Achbar and Peter Wintonick, is skilfully held together by a composite "narration" constructed from Chomsky's lectures, talks, debates, television appearances, and interviews. It uses talking heads, but provocatively. In his intriguing *After the Axe* (1981), Sturla Gunnarsson creates a composite fictional character, a recently fired middle-aged executive, who in his effort to find a new job interacts with real people whose lines apparently are not scripted. His *Final Offer* (1985) is a closely observed, direct-cinema account of a Canadian labour leader's nervy defiance of his union's international leadership.

Irene Angelico's *Dark Lullabies* (1985) offered a then-fresh perspective on the Holocaust, that of a survivor's daughter. Paul Cowan's *The Kid Who Couldn't Miss* (1982) combines archival footage, interviews, and extensive excerpts from a stage play to debunk the reputation of Canada's most decorated military hero, Billy Bishop. In his *In My Own Time* (1995), Joseph Viszmeg chronicles his bout with cancer and his attempt to come to terms with it. Michael Rubbo made a pair of absorbing personal-encounter films with Canada's most prominent author, *Margaret Atwood: Once in August* (1985) and *Atwood and Family* (1986). Kent Martin's *Donald Brittain: Filmmaker* (1992) is an affectionate, uncritical, but informative career portrait. Albert Kish's *Notman's World* (1989) is a visually elegant biography of a Canadian photographer whose career seems to have encapsulated major technological developments of the nineteenth century. Donald Winkler made several illuminating portraits of Canadian literary figures, and his *Breaking a Leg: Robert Lepage and the Echo Project* (1992) is an absorbing account of a promising but minimally successful avant-garde production by a theatrical wunderkind.

But many of these films deviated only in degree from the NFB's increasing reliance on the talking-head interview or some variation of it. It is as if filmmakers were losing confidence in their ability to draw "truth" out of actuality. This was happening not only at the Film Board—the talking head had become the scourge of American independent and public-television documentary—but the Film Board, for years the leading innovator in documentary art, had farther to fall. In the 1970s, Guy Glover decried the emerging use of the talking head as if "simple quotation were the only guarantee of veracity ... to use terribly simple means ... underplaying everything to the point where it becomes kind of mousy ... sanctimonious ...."[2]

The gradual replacement of 16-mm film by video also encouraged its use. Mark Zannis, a Film Board producer, remembers that the camera department used to set standards for the directors. The head of the department would screen rushes with the cameraman and director. The concern was with visual quality, and talking-head material was discouraged:

> In film, we also tended to limit interviews due to concern for the cost of stock. I remember that people felt they needed to excuse themselves if they came back with lots of interviews ....
>
> In video there is no such pressure to conserve stock. In fact, that becomes an excuse for shooting more .... The easiest thing to shoot is the straight talking head .... One can also go non-stop for longer periods, and it is cheap to put on a new tape. In the end, there is a lot of videotape of talking heads and this may be the incentive to use so much of it in the final production.
>
> Talking heads are also a feature of television ... a more information-based medium [that is less concerned about visual quality than about content].[3]

The loss in visual vitality entailed by the triumph of the talking head is brilliantly displayed in a subtle film that turns the loss into strength. *The Summer of '67*, made in 1994 by Albert Kish and Donald Winkler, interviews several now-middle-aged men and women who, as teenagers, had appeared in two 1967 NFB films on the rebellious youth culture of that era, *Flowers on a One-Way Street* and *Christopher's Movie Matinee*. The two older films were shot in 16 mm; all the new shooting is in video. *Christopher's Movie Matinee*, maligned at the time for being undisciplined and not very cinematic, contains scenes that now seem gorgeous. In a scene from the new film, Larry Frolick sits at a monitor watching a clip from *Christopher's Movie Matinee* in which his teenage self and young Doreen Foster are in a small grassy area away from the film crew, tenderly embracing each other and exchanging whispers. A train is racing past behind them, filling the top third of the frame, blocking off the sky. The high sun is a bit behind the couple and the train, bathing the couple in light while casting what we see of the train in shadow. In the next scene—we are still in *Christopher's Movie Matinee*—Doreen upbraids the cameraman, Martin Duckworth, for filming that private, personal moment. Duckworth replies, "It's only the personal things that are worth filming, really." The middle-aged Frolick—in talking-head video—starts to expand inanely upon Duckworth's remark, but he seems preoccupied. Suddenly he blurts out, "I sure can remember the smell of the sunlight on her hair, though." Then he is speechless, looking upward, as if jolted by a sudden and profound sense of loss. While neither we nor the filmmakers nor even Frolick may know if the felt loss is for something objectively wondrous about the times or simply for vanished youth, the film itself embodies a parallel lament for the loss of the cinematic energy of NFB past. And yet without the talking-head video footage, and the filmmakers' clever use of it, none of this could have been communicated.

Another film that turned talk into art was a dramatic feature. Fiction had been an occasional component of the NFB's program since the beginning, but it enjoyed a little boom in the 1980s and early 1990s. After Giles Walker won an Oscar nomination for his gritty *Bravery in the Field* (1979) and John Smith won a nomination for his portrayal of pioneer-days hardship in *First Winter* (1981), the emboldened Film Board established an Alternative Drama Program dedicated, in Smith's words, to "making fiction truthfully."[4] Smith and Walker collaborated on the Program's first project, *The Masculine Mystique* (1984), a limp comedy about four men befuddled by feminism. Smith went on to make several hard-edged docudramas. His *Sitting in Limbo* (1986) follows the life of a poor young couple in Montréal. It has the feel of authenticity and introduces likeable minor characters, but it lacks development, simply showing one screw-up after another by the male partner. *Train of Dreams* (1987) depicts a similarly self-defeating loser but has more cinematic impact. *The Boys of St. Vincent* (1992) is a meticulously scripted, shrewdly cast, and effectively directed two-part, three-hour depiction of a tyrannical and pederastic young priest who is finally brought to justice.

Walker, in contrast, moved into progressively farcical comedy with *90 Days* (1985) and *The Last Straw* (1987), films that build on two characters from *The Masculine Mystique*. Other filmmakers produced the occasional conventional drama. A short film, *The Painted Door* (1984), by Bruce Pittman, based on a story by Sinclair Ross, depicts a sexually starved woman's betrayal of her husband during an unusually vicious winter night and her horrifying manner of discovering that her husband had found out. Aaron Kim Johnston's *For the Moment* (1993), a story about a married woman's affair with an Australian officer who is undergoing flight training on a nearby base, overcomes its melodramatic clichés with likeable and believable characters.

The more interesting dramas, if not the more pleasurable or entertaining, were, like Smith's work, experiments in "making fiction truthfully," in giving fictional films an action or archival documentary look. Paul Cowan's informative *Democracy on Trial: The Morgentaler Affair* (1984) combines newsreel footage with recreated scenes carefully based on interviews and official transcripts. Dr. Morgentaler plays himself in recreated scenes. Cowan's *Justice Denied* (1989) is a stark docudrama about Donald Mitchell, a Micmac who at age seventeen was convicted and served eleven years in maximum security for a crime he did not commit. In *Canada's Sweetheart: The Saga of Hal C. Banks* (1985) and the 307-minute *King Chronicle* (1988), Donald Brittain scripted snippets of activity to function as if it were archival footage, material on which to exercise his gift of commentary.

But like *The Summer of '67*, the Film Board's most impressive fiction film from this era embraces video-era documentary style and uses it to creative advantage. Cynthia Scott's *The Company of Strangers* (1990) tells the story of seven elderly women who, on some kind of vaguely explained outing, get lost and wind up stranded for several days in an abandoned house. Most of the film consists of scenes involving two women talking, often while engaged in some minor activity such as slicing an apple, administering a poultice, or watching birds. But gradually, against all expectations, the film becomes compelling. The women are confronting disappointments in their lives and their fears of death. And the director sneaks in some interesting cinema. About forty minutes into the film, a very brief sequence of still photos from the earlier years of one of the women is injected into a scene, and it is at first jarring. But the device is repeated for each woman and contributes to a sense of a fleeting, receding remembrance of things past. In a simple but lovely shot, two women are looking up at the moon, its bluish light falling warmly on them. "All is well with the world—we hope," says one. "Uh-huh" is as committal as the other chooses to be.

Perhaps it is just a coincidence that two of the emotionally most subtle NFB films of the early 1990s embrace and turn to their advantage the Film Board's cinematic decline. Doom seemed to hover over the Board in the early 1990s. From its inception, the Film Board faced periodic challenges from an envious private sector and a politically sensitive, often suspicious government, and it had gotten in the habit of expecting attacks—but expecting to repel them. Since the early 1980s, the Film Board had been the object of numerous government reviews gradually chipping away at its mandate. The reports were often inconsistent and some were not acted upon, a point made in a document that would indeed be acted upon, the 1996 report of the Mandate Review Committee, "Making Our Voices Heard," a government-initiated review of the Canadian Broadcasting Corporation, Telefilm Canada, and the National Film Board.

The review, whose report is also known as the Juneau Report after its Chairman, Pierre Juneau, was initiated in 1994 in tandem with an announcement of severe cuts in the examined institutions' budgets. The NFB's budget would be cut from its 1994–95 appropriation of $82 million to $56 million for fiscal year 1997–98. The purpose of the Juneau Report was to suggest how each of the three targeted institutions might redefine its mandate and restructure its operations in order to survive.

In the view of Juneau's committee, the main problem facing the three institutions was a decline in their public image. To survive, they "must be perceived by all Canadians, and by the Canadian government, as indispensable public services."[5] The institutions had a crucial role to play in Canada if they were up to it. Canada was facing "issues of civic understanding, of tolerance and acceptance, of diverse cultural development, of national pride and confidence, and of our reputation in the world."[6] For Canada to remain a stable democracy presupposes respect and understanding, a sharing of views and a common political language. Citizens need to appreciate one another and to enjoy what they have in common. They need to join in shared celebration of heroes and accomplishments, and to accept and respect the differences that exist. Understanding and tolerance are basic values that societies must work on constantly...[7]

In its section on the Film Board, the report states that two things have made the Film Board unique: it has allowed filmmakers to work free from the constraints of the commercial marketplace and it has provided fresh, iconoclastic perspectives "on the rhythms of daily life." The Film Board "has a repository of skills, experience, a willingness to experiment, and a tradition of excellence that, under the right conditions, will enable it to play an indispensable public service role once again."[8] Although the report ostensibly defends the quality of NFB films, it slips a criticism of them into a paragraph on audience reach, suggesting that disappointing distribution figures raise the question "of whether NFB productions have lost some of their ability to strike an emotional or intellectual chord with the Canadian public."[9]

The report highlights five structural problems. The changing audio-visual environment in Canada had relegated the once-dominating NFB to the status of just another production organization. The Film Board had become grossly inefficient, devoting far too many resources to administration, resulting in a cost of $1,187,000 per hour of finished NFB film. The Board's films weren't seen widely enough. It was overly centralized, with 75 percent of its budget allocated to its Montréal operations. Finally, the Film Board's "inflexible and outmoded staffing practices" not only contributed to inflated production costs but also limited the use of outside talent, rendering the Film Board (in the perception of the outside film community) a closed shop. The Committee made several major recommendations. The Film Board should replace its permanent production staff with freelancers. It should spread production resources more equitably across the country. It should explore a variety of "pathways" for reaching larger audiences but make a special effort to use television. The Board should continue making documentaries, animation, and features that aren't adequately supplied by the Canadian audio-visual market.

The Committee's analysis and most of its recommendations were accepted with a readiness that dismayed NFB filmmakers. In its 12 February 1996 response, "The National Film Board of Canada in the Year 2000: The Transformation Plan," Film Board management proposed an almost complete elimination of staff filmmaking positions. It would phase out its laboratory and severely scale back other technical services. The studio system would be scrapped, and English production would be reorganized into two programs, Documentary and Animation/Children/Multi-Media. Executive producers and producers would have three- to five-year contracts. Feature-length dramas were deemed too expensive for the pared-down Board. For Documentary, there would be three executive producers: one for Québec and the Maritimes, one for Ontario, and one for the West. Animation/Children/Multi-Media would have two executive producers, one for East and one for West. Twelve producers would be spread equally among the three branches of the documentary program. Film Board management stated that by doing this it could maintain its current production level of about 85 titles per year.

The Transformation Plan asserted an aggressive commitment to diversity, declaring that "it matters who makes a production" and that therefore the Film Board's creative personnel should be drawn "from all segments of the society and from all regions of the country."[10] Dedicated

structures and funding would be developed for "groups considered underrepresented in the production milieu—women, aboriginal people, people with disabilities and people of colour." In
boldface type, the Plan states, "There is no dispute that the Board should aim to have a
workforce reasonably reflective of the society as a whole."[11]

Over the protests of filmmakers—who were upset at the cuts in personnel and facilities, not at
the refashioned mandate—the Board of Governors approved the Transformation Plan, and management swiftly implemented it. Almost overnight, the organization was dramatically transformed. Studios were disbanded. The film lab and sound stage were closed. Technical services
were drastically curtailed. In English production, only six staff filmmakers were retained—three
in documentary, three in animation—and they would not be replaced when they retired.

⚲ ⚲ ⚲

After my lonely morning coffee in the Film Board cafeteria, I had an opportunity to talk with
Barbara Janes, Director-General of English production; Sally Bochner, Executive Producer for
Documentary East; and the three remaining staff documentary directors. I wanted to hear their
views on how the cuts and structural changes at the Film Board had affected its filmmaking.

For Barbara Janes, the major effect of the downsizing was on the culture of filmmaking: "Not
every documentary had to cost a half million dollars." What has affected the Film Board documentary more than the cuts, in her view, is television. With the advent of multiple channels, almost every NFB film gets shown on television. But "If you're going to be on TV, you have to
catch the audience's attention immediately." Younger audiences and younger filmmakers, having
grown up with MTV and computer games, are impatient with probing, issue-oriented documentaries. "I'm starting to see a trend," Janes says. "A lot of younger filmmakers are interested in
making documentaries more 'in breadth' than 'in depth.' They want to explore the breadth of a
subject rather than drilling down with a very precise focus."

"We learned to lighten up," Janes adds. "It's OK to laugh. There was a 'house earnestness'
about our films."

Since diversity seemed to be the highest thematic priority in the Juneau Report and the Film
Board's Transformation Plan, I was curious about the effect of closing Studio D entailed by the
dismantling of the unit system of production. For all its rebarbative aesthetics, Studio D had
blasted a hole in the wall of white male domination of Film Board production, and the breach
had been wide enough to allow other groups through as well. Wouldn't its closing amount to a
setback to diversity?

Janes had been a member of Studio D earlier in her career. In her view, Studio D was
no longer needed. Women were "already directing almost half the films, most of them *outside*
Studio D. So we didn't *need* a dedicated studio." Janes says that the people who wanted to keep
Studio D "wanted to do so for reasons of ideology. But if you're going to base it on feminist ideology, it's a political thing. We can't define the NFB in terms of 'isms'. Studio D had been in existence for twenty years. In that time, society changed a lot. But Studio D kept the mindset of 1975,
fighting battles already won."

"We're putting our emphasis on cultural diversity. We looked around, and we were an all-
white organization. We had to change that. But this time, we didn't create a dedicated studio.

We hired three producers—two Black Canadians and a Chinese Canadian—in the Documentary program." To encourage aboriginal production, the NFB allocated $1 million a year for aboriginal films that can go through any of the regional offices.

When I mentioned to Sally Bochner my widely shared perception that the NFB has not been a leader in documentary over the past ten years or so, she confidently retorted, "But we will be in the next five!" The cutbacks in staff and facilities were brutal, she acknowledged. "It was very hard and painful to wave good-bye to people who had been here for twenty or thirty years. But we had no other way of rejuvenation. Now we're working with a variety of filmmakers, accomplished filmmakers, new filmmakers, filmmakers of colour."

"It's quite energizing. People want to work with us. I can cherry-pick among projects."

"Documentary has had a rebirth. Filmmakers can come here and don't have to make a film to fit a mould. They can still take the time—relative to everybody else—and make a high-end documentary."

ᠵ ᠵ ᠵ

If the Film Board documentary is experiencing a rebirth, it has not been an easy one, and the outcome is still not clearly defined. Institutional culture does not change overnight, and many films dated in the late 1990s were initiated before the overhaul. Yet there do seem to be indications that the NFB documentary is struggling to achieve a fresh orientation consistent with its founding mission.

The commitment to "isms" that Barbara Janes identified as a flaw in Studio D shows up in a few NFB films completed shortly after the approval of the Transformation Plan. Margaret Wescott's *Stolen Moments* (1997), for instance, applauds behaviour in lesbians that feminists typically have condemned in heterosexuals and contains outbursts of numbing stridency. Its ideological self-centredness is starkly exhibited in a tale about a Dutch woman, Maria van Antwerpen, who, posing as a man, married. When her bride discovers the truth three years later—why it took so long is not addressed—Maria is banished. The film expresses deep compassion for Maria but no concern at all for the humiliated bride. In vintage high Studio D dudgeon, an expatriate poet rages about being "invisible as a *fat, black, lesbian, activist, almost blind* woman ... in a *racist, sexist, homophobic, classist, antisemitic, ageist world*!"

Generally, though, the newer films with a feminist slant exhibit cracks in the old orthodoxy. In Teresa MacInnes' *The Other Side of the Picture* (1998), a plea for gender parity in museum acquisitions, the director's assertion that women paint differently from men collides with a demonstration of the audience's inability to discern a difference. In *"You Can't Beat a Woman!" another film about violence against women* (1997), Gail Singer wields a far softer ideological edge than she had employed in her 1984 film on abortion. Here she "lightens up" on a heavy subject, frequently mocking her own film so as not to come off as too sombre. Although the tone and content are annoyingly in conflict, there is some powerful filmmaking in this sprawling film. Lois Siegel's *Baseball Girls* (1995) is an enjoyable survey of women's participation in baseball and softball that manages to show triumphs without trumpeting them and injustices without fulminating against them. The best of its superb archival footage is a shot in which a field full of synchronized umpires in training practise giving the "out" sign. In *Packing Heat* (1996), director Wendy Rowland weaves together portraits of several women in Canada and the United States who have opposing attitudes toward guns. Although the film comes down on the anti-gun side, it tries to avoid the expected ideological associations.

As if in overreaction to the pious indignation of *Not a Love Story*, several recent films adopt a light, aren't-we-sassy attitude toward sex. In Ann Kennard's *The Powder Room* (1996), women talk frankly among themselves about their favourite forms of it. In Barbara Doran's *The Perfect Hero* (1999), an author of romance novels reads a graphic passage from one of her books. The aforementioned *Stolen Moments* stages a romantic scene in which a woman slides her hand down to her partner's partly exposed crotch. Clint Alberta's *Deep Inside Clint Star* (1998) features much smirking talk about penis size, masturbation, and whorehouses. Donald McWilliams' *The Passerby* (1995) includes a pointless digression, in stand-up talking head, about a mythical whale with a four-foot erection. In Rosemary House's *Rain, Drizzle, and Fog* (1998), the director's attempt to convey her love for her weather-challenged hometown of St. John's, Newfoundland gets sidetracked by a long interview with a local actor who recounts in detail the dilemma masturbation posed for him as a young Catholic.

By contrast, films that serve the Film Board's new mandate on diversity have retained a fair measure of the "house earnestness" that management sometimes regards as a burden. This is especially true of films on aboriginal subjects (*Deep Inside Clint Star* notwithstanding), which try to redress injustice with positive citizenship. In *Power: One River, Two Nations* (1996), Magnus Isacsson chronicles the five-year battle by the Cree to prevent Hydro-Québec from building a huge dam on the Great Whale River. The film explores the interesting irony that aboriginal tribes, so often at odds with the federal government, fear an independent Québec far more. In John Walker's *Place of the Boss* (1996), the Mushuau Innu lament the loss of their culture and religion that ensued when, after a poor hunting season in the 1960s, they were lured into abandoning their hunter-gatherer way of life and settling on the coast of northern Labrador. Daniel Prouty's *First Nation Blue* (1996) is an appealing, low-key film about an arrangement whereby many of the cops policing reserves are Indians themselves, and even the white police are required to live in the area and know the community. *Circles* (1997), by Shanti Thakur, is a leisurely, talky, but absorbing look at a form of community-based criminal justice that has roots in aboriginal culture.

Of Alanis Obomsawin's several follow-up films on the Oka stand-off, *Spudwrench: Kahnawake Man* (1997), a portrait of a Mohawk high-steel worker who was severely beaten during the stand-off, is the most rounded. The film's gentle pace is a stylistic analogue to its mood of serenity. Obomsawin's interviewing voice is soft and lilting. Small touches of seemingly off-the-point cutaway shots reinforce this mood: a girl on a porch swing, a man harvesting potatoes from his garden. The most striking thing about the confrontation, as Obomsawin depicts it in a flashback, is that despite the tension and hostilities, neither side really wants to hurt the other.

Even though it relies heavily on interviews, the most disarming recent film on an aboriginal subject is Christine Welsh's *The Story of the Coast Salish Knitters* (2000). The proud, tough knitters recall past injustices—they've won control of their craft—as simply the way things were. A woman who makes sweaters to order does it "because I love to knit, and I guess I like to make people happy in what they wear, and I'm proud to have my sweaters all over the world."

The struggle between bitterness and gratitude is evident in films with Asian-Canadian subjects as well. *Desperately Seeking Helen* (1998) concerns director Eisha Marjara's quest for an identity, complicated by her problematic relationship with her mother. Marjara verges on self-pity and often seems self-absorbed, but she also can be brutally honest about herself. In *Unwanted*

Soldiers (1999), Jari Osborne mixes archival footage with interviews to tell the story of her father's prideful service in a Chinese-Canadian military unit assembled in World War Two to infiltrate Japanese-held territory in Southeast Asia. Osborne seems to resent the severe discrimination Chinese-Canadians once suffered more than her father did. *Western Eyes* (2000), by Ann Shin, follows two young women who want operations on their eyes to make them look more Caucasian. The girls and the film seem unable to decide whether to place the blame for their unhappiness on Western culture or themselves. *Sunrise Over Tiananmen Square* (1998), by Shui Bo Wang, is a fascinating account, illustrated with imaginatively filmed old photos, archival footage, animation, painting, and drawing, of the director's Chinese childhood, youthful Maoist zeal, art training, disillusionment at Tiananmen Square, and emigration. The film ends on an ambivalent note about the country that took him in: "I left China for North America, where I hoped there would be no violence, no hatred, and of course no homeless. I was very sad, and hope that one day I can return home."

Recent NFB films on black subjects are impressively modulated in tone, following the lead of *Black Mother Black Daughter* rather than *Older Stronger Wiser*. Selwyn Jacob's *The Road Taken* (1996) balances honest resentment at policies that once limited black advancement in the railroad industry with matter-of-fact wisdom about coping with injustice. *Black, Bold & Beautiful* (1998), by Nadine Valcine, complains about the dominance of a "white" standard of beauty, but instead of capitulating to resentment, the film sings the praises of black hair in its variety of manifestations: afros, cornrows, dreadlocks—even straightened hair. Meilan Lam's *Show Girls* (1998) features three extremely likeable women who had been dancers in the heyday of Montréal's jazz scene. The film incorporates some superb archival material illustrating the racism of the time. The women aren't bitter. One of them, now a saleslady, says simply that people will be nice to you if you are nice to them. Grant Greschuk's *Jeni LeGon: Living in a Great Big Way* (1999) is a portrait of a legendary figure in African-American entertainment. LeGon is now an octogenarian living and teaching in Vancouver. Although regretting the prejudice that relegated her to subordinate roles in Hollywood films, she doesn't rage about it. The film's highlight is footage of LeGon tap dancing. Her joyous exuberance when dancing should make even the most hardened of viewers regret the racism that kept us from having more such material.

Lesley Ann Patten's *Loyalties* (1999) follows two residents of Halifax, one black (Carmelita) and one white (Ruth), who discover a common South Carolina heritage and subsequently go on a pilgrimage together to Charleston. The film is honest, sensitive, and hopeful. Carmelita is delighted to discover records of a slave woman who might be related to Carmelita's family, but she senses—and resents—that Ruth, despite her guilt at the wealth of her ancestors, also feels a bit proud of it. Back in Nova Scotia, Ruth invites Carmelita's family to her daughter's wedding. When it comes out that Ruth's ancestors were slave owners, there is awkward silence. The film ends with both women hoping for a broader racial reconciliation but without any false complacency about its likelihood.

The Film Board's new emphasis on diversity includes the disabled. In *Just a Wedding* (1999), Beverly Shaffer revisits the main character of her 1977 Oscar-winning *I'll Find a Way*, the brave and confident Nadia DeFranco, who has spina bifida. DeFranco is now grown up and getting married. It is a visually rich, fast-moving film diminished by the obviousness of its set-ups in supposedly spontaneous discussions and encounters. *Working Like Crazy* (1999), by Gwynne Basen and Laura Sky, is about mental patients who have started their own business, but the film tends to undercut its championship of independence for the mentally ill. Like the men in *Fat Chance*, the "psychiatric survivors," as one person terms them, castigate the system that has tried to help them. One woman complains of her family that "they see this ... girl who's, like, setting things on *fire*, and they think, oh, something must be seriously *wrong* ...."

The Film Board's concern for minorities occasionally extends beyond Canada's borders. Nettie Wild's *A Place Called Chiapas: Eight Months Inside the Zapatista Uprising* (1998), however, is little more than extended reportage, travelogue-y in tone ("It's the Day of the Dead in the graveyard of La Realidad, and our last week in Mexico"). John Paskievich's *The Gypsies of Svinia* (1998) is an earnest and sympathetic look at the plight of a community of Gypsies loathed by their Slovakian neighbours, but it undermines its case by depicting the Gypsies as lazy, unhygienic, drunken, thieving, quarrelling, oversexed complainers.

It might seem the NFB's emphasis on diversity—especially its claim in the Transformation Plan that it matters who makes a production—marks a departure from Grierson's documentary idea, but that is not the case. The Film Board's original mandate was to make films "designed to help Canadians in all parts of Canada to understand the ways of living and the problems of Canadians in other parts." But it wasn't just diverse geographic content that mattered. Grierson criss-crossed Canada in search of the best talent for the Film Board; he wanted to staff the organization with filmmakers from across the country. The regionalization of production that was initiated decades later and has finally been achieved was a natural development of that idea. Ethnic diversity was similarly inchoate in the original idea. Anglophone Canadians dominated, but there was a tiny French program during the war that in the early 1960s grew into a separate unit staffed almost entirely by Francophone filmmakers. Aboriginal subjects were part of the program early on; beginning with Challenge for Change, films on aboriginal subjects were often made by or with the involvement of aboriginals. The establishment of Studio D was a logical further step. The recent hiring of minority producers and the programming of more films on minority subjects are simply extensions of Grierson's original concept for the Film Board.

What is new is that the Film Board's commitment to diversity now dominates its English production program. But unlike the angry, separatist thrust of Studio D, the predominant sentiment now seems to be a desire for inclusion. There is a nice balance in most of the diversity-serving films between pride in one's heritage and appreciation for the chance to be a Canadian.

But one group tends to fall outside this umbrella of concern: white, English-speaking, Canadian males. Perhaps it is assumed that they have no problems, questions, or contributions related to the issues of diversity and multiculturalism. They are neither maligned nor praised, but they are often depicted, or present themselves, as eccentric, effete, or spiritually ailing. *The Passerby*, Donald McWilliams' aforementioned meditation on the meaning of time and images, is at times engrossing but ultimately diffuse and elusive. John L'Ecuyer's *Confessions of a Rabid Dog* (1997), a recovering addict's confessional, combines some embarrassing faux-Beat stream-of-consciousness narration with scenes that probe deeply into what addiction is like. George Ungar's *The Champagne Safari* (1995) is structured around recently discovered footage of a pointless and truncated expedition across the Canadian Rockies by a delusional multimillionaire. John Kramer's *The Man Who Might Have Been: An Inquiry into the Life and Death of Herbert Norman* (1998) is an interesting speculation on why an unusually talented diplomat committed suicide. John Brett's *One Man's Paradise* (1997) pays homage to an ebullient Nova Scotia fisherman who believes in ghosts and yodels while doctors perform surgery on his hernia. Peter Lynch's entertaining *Project Grizzly* (1996) follows an obsessive inventor's bungled attempt to encounter a grizzly while wearing a specially designed armoured suit. Even Peter Wintonick's entertaining and impressively comprehensive *Cinéma Vérité: Defining the Moment* (1999), which sketches the history of *cinéma vérité* from its early days at the NFB and elsewhere to the present, seems compelled to assume a tone of jocular self-mockery—as if to explore in depth some of the important issues raised by what they regard as the triumph of *cinéma vérité* would be too ponderous.

Yet it is in one of these films, of all places, that the diversity agenda gets most firmly articulated in a new interpretation of Grierson's call to declare Canada's excellences and evoke her strengths. The unlikely film is Paul Jay's *Hitman Hart: Wrestling with Shadows* (1998). It chronicles the fall of Bret Hart, beloved Canadian wrestler, who takes seriously the "good versus evil" theme in professional wrestling and is unable or unwilling to separate his ring persona from his personal life. When he refuses to compromise his image as a good guy, he is nearly ruined by the leading entrepreneur of modern wrestling, the cynical Vince McMahon. Hart's personal struggle assumes international dimensions. In Pittsburgh, he calls the United States "*one big giant toilet bowl.*" To a frenzied crowd in Canada, he states his creed:

> For me, Canada's a country where we still take care of the sick and the old, where we still have health care. We got gun control, we don't shoot each other and kill each other on every street corner. Canada isn't riddled with racial prejudice and hatred. Across Canada we all care for each other. And I am *proud* to be *Canadian*, and am proud to be your hero!

And the film as a whole, through Hart's struggle to maintain his wholesome persona, affirms something harder to stand up for in an ironic, "lightened up" culture than mere diversity. It lauds values of nobility, honour, fidelity. It does so through a kind of reversal of irony, turning irony on its head, locating the value in the ironized situation itself. We don't dismiss it out of hand when a pair of commentators liken Bret Hart to Hamlet, "a good man in a bad world."

So it is here, in this entertaining film about an institution that no one but a wrestler who is a bit naïve can take seriously, that a new interpretation of Grierson's statement of purpose for the NFB comes closest to articulation. It is one that declares Canada's excellences to be, first, that it is not the United States; second (and centrally), that it is tolerant and caring; and third, that there are values beyond diversity.

It would be expected that films on minorities embody tolerance as a value, that it would pervade such films as *First Nation Blue*, *The Story of the Coast Salish Knitters*, *The Road Taken*, *Spudwrench*, *Show Girls*, *Jeni LeGon*, *Loyalties*, and *Unwanted Soldiers*. What is refreshing and hopeful is that the tolerance is urged in both directions. There is a forgiving, accepting tone to these films, a sense that while Canada's social fabric has many flaws, it is nevertheless a rare and lovely tapestry which in an imperfect world deserves the gratitude and protection of persons fortunate enough to be Canadians.

This tolerance on which a new interpretation of Griersonian purposiveness may be centring is an active tolerance, not a passive one. It goes beyond the tolerance of, say, Robin Benger's *East Side Showdown* (1998), a nicely balanced, well-crafted depiction of a fight between residents and street people for control of a Toronto neighbourhood, or Barry Greenwald's crisply photographed, skillfully cross-cut, suspenseful *High Risk Offender* (1998), an account of seven parolees considered to be strong risks to commit crime again. These films are determinedly non-judgemental, their rhetorical stance one of simply presenting an account of reality without comment.

More interesting is the active tolerance that asserts other values. *Tokyo Girls* (2000), by Penelope Buitenhuis, is accomplished reportage that grows into a film about self-knowledge. It follows several Canadian women who went to Japan to work as hostesses. It neither condemns nor extols the women, but it likes them. A French-Canadian hostess says she was surprised to discover that she enjoyed using her femininity. In a voice-over, she says, "It's strange for a Canadian to use just your charm and your smile," but near the end of the film she confesses, "In fact, I detest the job of hostess." Jeff McKay's finely textured *And So To Bed* (1999), which explores different ways in which beds can be meaningful to people, serves the diversity agenda while provoking thought about something more than diversity. For a black immigrant, "being bedless is being homeless." For a Canadian of Hindu origin, sleep may be the real world. To an inmate who works in a prison mattress factory, the beds offer an "escape" from prison. A widow recently home from the hospital loves her bed: it is quiet; she can lie back on it, reminisce about her happy life and marriage, and fall asleep. "What more could I want?" she asks. Even Pierre Lasry's *Shylock*, a pained, modulated essay on the interpretation of the infamous Shakespearean character over the centuries, ends in an acceptance of Shakespeare as a flawed man but great writer who saw the good and evil in all of us.

An affirming tolerance becomes the overriding, controlling value of four of the very best recent NFB films. Perhaps not surprisingly, three of them have to do with the problem of Québec. Stéphane Drolet's *Referendum: Take Two* (1996) is an outwardly calm but urgent, tense documentary about the six days leading up to the 1995 Québec referendum. The film's central figure, writer Josh Freed, frets about the possibility of separation and earnestly seeks an understanding between the factions. Near the film's end, he engages the French-Canadian soundman in debate. When the soundman says quietly that "a people and a nation cannot exist freely without sovereignty," Freed responds that the two groups need each other. The soundman asks Freed what he hopes for. Freed hopes that in ten years "we can have the same conversation as peacefully as now, without the bitterness that I fear we'll see. I hope we'll always be civil like this. Good luck." The camera tilts down to catch them shaking hands.

Paul Jay's *Never-Endum Referendum* (1997) also explores the conflicts that ordinary Quebeckers, French and English, experience whenever separation seems possibly imminent. One scene is a group interview with a family of four. The mother dreads the next referendum; her Francophone husband will vote yes on separation. Then their two children, a boy and a girl, are invited into the interview. They both agree with their mother. When the boy says that he feels more Canadian than Québécois, the father frowns in disappointment. "I'm surrounded by federalists," he sighs. Josh Freed is in this film as well. He and the filmmaker/author Jacques Godbout agree that the dispute is essentially about culture. Godbout says that the rest is negotiable. Freed offers to start writing a proposal. Godbout says that the first words should be "We trust each other."

Catherine Annau's *Just Watch Me* (1999) is a series of interwoven portraits of thirty-something men and women who grew up under Trudeau's effort to make Canada a bilingual country. Although suffering from too much talking-head material and an annoying tendency to build a narrative line by cross-cutting directly between interviewees, it is a provocative debriefing on the effectiveness of bilingualism. A young aboriginal says that Trudeau's election made him think it possible that a Native Canadian could one day be Canada's prime minister. An English-Canadian from the prairies, whose parents bought into Trudeau's vision and sent their son to French school, calls bilingualism "a failed social experiment." He resents having worked hard to become bilingual only to have Québec try to split from Canada. He came to realize, he says, that the real achievement of Canada was the way it allowed people "from all over the world to come together rather than just two European groups." He got a job in the Northwest Territories and married an Inuit woman. If two cultures can't live together, the film may be hinting, perhaps several can.

Of all the recent films, however, the one that seems to embody most refreshingly this possible new aesthetic is Veronica Mannix's *Through a Blue Lens* (1999). The film portrays the work of a group of seven Vancouver policemen, called "the Odd Squad," who have developed a program for educating teenagers about the danger of drugs by showing them video footage of hopeless-seeming addicts. It turns out, though, that the cops spend as much time trying to help the addicts themselves. The film's structure reproduces the transformation of a typical Odd Squad cop's attitude from disgust to empathy and acceptance. The early images are raw and revolting. A young woman writhes in the middle of a heavily trafficked street. A woman in rags shows us a huge, festering cavity in her arm, the result of her paranoid bouts of picking at bugs she imagines to be crawling there. Later this woman shows a cop her family photo album. We see cops bringing Christmas presents to addicts. These men are manly and gentle at the same time. Their tolerance, while caring, is also doggedly expectant. The real payoff for the men is when they can visit one of their friends doing well in a detoxification centre. The film makes no grandiose claims for the effectiveness of the Odd Squad project, and it really doesn't have to. It is a film that praises social amelioration in a mood of tragic realism.

And so the Film Board seems to be relearning how to declare what is excellent in Canada and to appeal to her strengths. If there is a sometimes wearying uniformity in the vision, it is at least a positive vision. And it is expressed in a way that restores actuality to its traditional pride of place in documentary. While the talking head is still used frequently, its worst abuses appear to be a thing of the past. Hectoring narration has been abandoned. What truths the filmmakers think they have discovered emerge more from filmed reality than from received notions of it. In this their films resemble *Standing Alone, The Champions, Daisy, F.R. Scott*, and *Boulevard of Broken Dreams*. And they are well crafted. But the best of the new films, good, solid, and open-minded though they be, seem a bit pedestrian aesthetically. They are stylistically conventional. They typically offer little more than chronology for structure. There are no apparent technical innovations. They aren't expressions of distinctive documentary talents in the way that those earlier films were. Committed to diversity, they all look alike.

It is hard to predict how the art of the Film Board documentary might fare in the first decade of the new millennium. The Film Board apparently has been able to maintain a level of production equal to that before the transformation.[12] This is an admirable feat, and not one to be minimized: from 1940 on, the very quantity of the Film Board's output has been a necessary substratum for the acknowledged gems, just as in any flourishing art form. It is not for nothing that *The Image Makers* mentioned those 10,000 titles. But the efficiency that stabilized productivity was accomplished by eviscerating the Film Board. With no lab, few technicians, and no staff directors once the remaining ones retire, it seems unlikely that the Film Board will ever again provide the deep, broad creative community that spawned its classic work.

And without staff or facilities, what role will the NFB play in "its" films besides funding them? What credit will it deserve for a good film above and beyond having offered the filmmaker a larger budget with less interference than he or she would have had elsewhere? The Film Board still has producers, and perhaps through them some of the Film Board's accumulated filmmaking wisdom will be preserved, communicated, and enriched. But quite possibly what most accounts for recent Film Board successes is that, as Sally Bochner boasted, it can cherry-pick among projects. If that is the primary factor, then what justification is there for maintaining a still-large, still-expensive institution whose main production function is to dole out money? If the Film Board has maintained its pre-1995 production level, then it has reduced the cost per hour of its films from the $1,187,000 cited in the Juneau Report to somewhere in the neighbourhood of $700,000—still a high-seeming figure for projects done mainly in video, increasingly in digital video. Would not a much smaller organization, something like a panel of accomplished filmmakers meeting, say, quarterly to review proposals, be even more efficient? This is the kind of question that the Film Board's very successes in efficiency inevitably raise.

Efficiency may exact a cost of its own. Many—perhaps most—of the Film Board's documentary classics went over budget, past schedule, and against stylistic norms that would make for easy distribution. Most of them were made in a reasonably well-matched tension between management and filmmakers. When every filmmaker is a freelancer, the power relationship shifts inordinately to management. When management can cherry-pick among projects—and filmmakers—everything rides on the taste, judgement, and vision of management.

When I spoke with them, the three remaining staff documentary directors expressed mixed feelings about the new Film Board. They agreed that radical changes had been necessary and that in many ways the new production process is more efficient. They all say there is no other place in the world where they could make the films they do. But they also say, in one way or another, that something deeply valuable has been lost to the Board—its soul, in the words of one. They were dismayingly skittish about speaking for the record. One griped of "a closed door" separating the filmmaking process from the administration and cited the title "Director General" as "telling," but then added, "I love the joint."

Perhaps the unique concentration of tradition, talent, technical support, and job security that for most of half a century was the National Film Board of Canada will prove unnecessary in an age of regionalization, large festivals, multi-channel television, the Internet, widespread film culture, and the welfare state. The best NFB films of recent years have come through its offices across Canada, not just from Montréal. Perhaps the freelance filmmakers who get funding from the Film Board are absorbing tradition and being prodded to innovate through means that no longer require a central location. Perhaps they get it largely from other sources now that documentary expertise and practice have diffused geographically and institutionally throughout North America.

Who knows if or where new creative leadership at the Film Board will emerge. During my visit, I was invited to a screening of three new animation films. Although animation historically has constituted less than ten percent of the Film Board's program, it has played a vital role from the beginning. Grierson called scratch-on-film artist Norman McLaren, one of his first hires, the most important filmmaker at the Board. Guy Glover thought the McLaren-led animation program inspired documentary filmmakers to think about form.[13] For Tom Daly, McLaren set an example by his ability to "make something from nothing. McLaren never looked at what he didn't have. He made something out of what there was. And it was always first-rate."[14] McLaren's *Neighbours* (1952) was the first Film Board animated film to win an Oscar. The main and soon to be only NFB building at the Montréal Office is called the McLaren Building, and McLaren remains the Film Board's most famous filmmaker.

Animation has accounted for five of the Film Board's ten Oscars. By 2000, the NFB had received sixty-four Oscar nominations, twenty-six of them for animation films. Twelve of the nominations for animation films were received since 1980; two of the films—*Every Child* (1979) in 1980, *Bob's Birthday* (1994) in 1995—won the Oscar. Unlike the Board's recent documentary work, the animation films exhibit a wide range of distinctive styles. The nature of the art, of course, puts up fewer barriers to stylistic individuality than does documentary, constrained as documentary is by "actuality." Janet Perlman's *The Tender Tale of Cinderella Penguin* (1981) is a fairly straightforward rendition of the Cinderella story with all the characters as penguins. Ishu Patel's allusive and mystical *Paradise* (1984) recalls McLaren's *Pas de deux* (1968), although employing a completely different technique. Richard Condie's *The Big Snit* (1985) also recalls McLaren, but the McLaren of *Neighbours*, where the theme was the petty origin of hostility. Brad Caslor's energetic *Get a Job* (1985) is Disneyesque in technique. *George and Rosemary* (1987) uses rather simple drawings to tell a love story about a pair of lonely senior citizens. *Bob's Birthday*, by Alison Snowden and David Fine, is a cheeky, hilarious animated cartoon about a well-meaning woman's failed surprise party for her dyspeptic husband. Craig Welch's *How Wings Are Attached to the Backs of Angels* (1996), by contrast, is a surreal meditation on emotional sterility. Richard Condie's *La Salla* (1996), absurdist in tone, is about a man who thinks he is free but is being manipulated by a much larger version of himself.

In 2000, two 1999 NFB animation films received Oscar nominations. Torill Kove's *My Grandmother Ironed the King's Shirts*, a co-production between the NFB and Norway's Studio Magica, is an appealing story about a woman who irons the shirts of Norway's rumpled king but sabotages the Nazis when they invade. *When the Day Breaks*, by Wendy Tilby and Amanda Forbis, uses watercoloured animal figures in a haunting evocation of urban angst.

Clearly there was vitality in the animation program (technically now the Animation/Children's/Interactive program) in the year 2000. But at the time of my visit, I had not yet seen the recent films, and because of the generally dismal impression the seemingly empty building had made on me, I wasn't expecting much from the screening. To my surprise, the theatre filled up quickly. The walls were lined with people—Director General Barbara Janes among them—who arrived too late to get a seat. More people were trying to squeeze in until there was an announcement of a second showing for the overflow. Where did all these people come from? Throughout the Film Board's history, a stronger sense of community usually had existed among the NFB's animators than its documentary filmmakers. But Animation had suffered cuts along with the rest of the Film Board. Marcy Page, a producer for the Animation/Children's/Interactive program, suggested to me later that the solitary nature of animation creates a need for a sense of community. The freelance directors are encouraged to do their work on the premises. Whenever a film is finished, not only is anyone who worked on it interested in the result, but so are other animators and people associated with it. Animation also can transcend cultural and language barriers more easily than documentary, especially since the advent and triumph of the talking head. Hence the audience in the screening room included persons from both English and French animation, some administrators at the Board, and numerous filmmakers from the freelance community.

In the older days, there was usually an undercurrent of apprehension and competitiveness at these screenings, but an air of genuine good will seemed to pervade the screening room today. As with the recent documentary work, diversity was the common theme of the films. Janet Perlman's *Bully Dance* (2000) is an odd, abstract tapestry featuring a schoolyard of dark figures looking like bent cigars moving to a soundtrack woven from various African and Caribbean rhythms. The other two films were part of a multicultural series for children called *Talespinners* and were made by comparative beginners. Cilia Sawadago's boisterous, happy *Christopher Changes His Name* (2000) is about a black boy who doesn't like his name, changes it to "24," but reconsiders when he can't cash a birthday check. He learns to accept what he has been given, including his name. *From Far Away* (2000), by Shira Avni and Serne El-haj Daoud, is about an immigrant schoolgirl who does not yet understand the language of her new home, has to go to the bathroom, but doesn't know how to tell her teacher. It is a vibrantly drawn, boldly patterned, moving film.

If the films weren't scintillating, they were interesting, well made, good-natured, and engaging, especially the two from the *Talespinners* series. And if they don't equal *Through a Blue Lens*, the Québec-crisis films, or, say, *Loyalties* in gravitas, they have the same mood of positive tolerance of those films. Further, the two *Talespinners* films, though "multicultural" and slight in their stories, are universal in appeal. They don't shut you out but draw you in. And together the three films have something the documentaries, by comparison, lack: they are stylistically distinct from one another.

All three received warm applause, although it was not clear for what. The art? The entertainment? The diversity? And everyone seemed happy. The atmosphere was more congenial than I remember that of the predominately white, male Film Board to have been, but it also lacked that evident critical, competitive edge which contributed to the Film Board's excellence. Maybe I was getting a misleading impression. And was it by mere chance that the screening coincided with my visit? Still, the question arises: could animation once again inspire advances in documentary aesthetics at the Film Board? And what if it doesn't? Maybe advances in documentary are no longer possible; maybe documentary art has already crested as did the novel in the nineteenth century or theatre with Shakespeare. The Film Board of the last few years has produced numerous well-made, engaging documentaries that both reflect and shape positive aspects of Canadian life, films that promote acceptance of others among Canada's citizenry while affirming deeper values and evoking more fundamental strengths essential for a rich and vital humanistic culture. In an era in which Canada and other Western nations have committed themselves to the potentially fractious goal of diversity, maybe that is more than enough.

Notes

I appreciate the generous assistance of NFB personnel Shawn Goldwater, Pat Dillon, Rita Chiovitti, Nicole Périat, Christiane Talbot, and Bernard Lutz in researching this article.

1   Chris Sherbarth, "Why Not D? An historical look at the NFB's Woman's Studio," *Cinema Canada* 139 (March 1987): 9–13.

2   D.B. Jones, *Movies and Memoranda: An Interpretive History of the National Film Board of Canada* (Ottawa: Deneau, 1982), 168–69.

3   E-mail to the author, 11 July 2000.

4   "NFB's Alternative Drama Program," undated NFB press release.

5   Mandate Review Committee, CBC, NFB, Telefilm (Canada), *Making Our Voices Heard: Canadian Broadcasting and Film for the 21st Century* [aka "The Juneau Report"] (Ottawa: Minister of Supply and Services, 1996), 25.

6   The Juneau Report, 23.

7   The Juneau Report, 24.

8   The Juneau Report, 161.

9   The Juneau Report, 163.

10 National Film Board, *The National Film Board of Canada in the Year 2000: The Transformation Plan* (National Film Board, 12 February 1996), 4.

11 NFB, *Transformation Plan*, 5.

12 National Film Board, *Annual Report 1997–98* (Montréal: Communication Services, 1998), 9.

13 D.B. Jones, *The Best Butler in the Business: Tom Daly of the National Film Board of Canada* (Toronto: University of Toronto Press, 1996), 75–76.

14 Jones, *Best Butler*, 34.

Imagining Region

A Survey of Newfoundland Film
Noreen Golfman

At the Northwest Atlantic Fisheries Centre—
Fascinating tours.
And films showing—every two hours—
Ten Days, Forty-eight Hours,
Depicting the lives of offshore
Fishermen and their families.
— Mary Dalton, "St. John's Day 1987"

IT IS IMPOSSIBLE TO SPEAK OF THE PRODUCTION of contemporary film in Atlantic Canada without invoking the cultural conflicts embodied in Mary Dalton's poem of the late 1980s. In many ways, to live in this region of Canada in the millennium is to live in a postmodern laboratory, where the contradictory effects of social change and destabilization seem sudden and transparent—transparent, perhaps, because they seem sudden. The signifiers of this postmodern laboratory are as ubiquitous as the portable advertising marquees that dot the landscape of the region from Edmunston to Bonavista. These tacky black-plastic billboards line the highways and front confectionery stores, often announcing at once such seductive offerings as dried salt cod, worms, and *The Matrix*. If proof were needed that postmodernity had arrived, one need only paddle to the remotest outport community to rent one's own DVD of Keanu hurtling himself through space. The global media industries reach everywhere, making the challenge of producing homegrown images especially daunting. Indeed, home is changing at an alarming and exhilarating pace.

This chapter first attempts a modest understanding of recent film (largely dramatic feature) production in Atlantic Canada in view of, and in uneasy relation to, the slippery category of region. To speak of Atlantic Canada is to acknowledge not merely the three maritime provinces that helped form the political–economic foundation for Confederation in 1867, but also the province of Newfoundland, which rejected such a union until eighty years after that historical fact. The designation of Atlantic Canada thus conveniently defines the broad geographical field of four provincial sites while it erases the complex histories and cultural differences not only between Newfoundland and the Maritimes but also between each of the separate maritime provinces themselves. A brief chapter cannot do justice to an appreciation or history of the region's emergent image-producing industries without generalizing foolishly and thereby dissolving the distinctive characteristics that mark provincial identities; the result would be as phony as a screech-in.

In his terse 1987 survey of Canadian film, David Clanfield devotes a short section to "Regional Film," that being a term implicitly identified with work outside the image factories of Toronto and Montréal.[1] The work is too short and the centralizing assumptions too many for Clanfield to take up the problematic of "region," but his cursory definition merits consideration here. "A film shot on location with a strong sense of local colour does not constitute regional film-making," he writes. "But true regional film-making is represented by the work of local companies and directors committed to making films that dwell upon a particular region's pictorial qualities, social problems, and dilemmas."[2] Among other obviously striking weaknesses suggested by this statement, we can recognize an insidious association of region with central Canadian notions of rural life, a place of tourist potential ("pictorial qualities"), and economic deprivation ("social problems, and dilemmas"). This association is astonishingly naïve but unwittingly indicative of the continual play of the co-dependent grand narratives of Canadian cultural life. It is a tired formula, and as wise filmmakers all over Atlantic Canada well know, to remain within it is to be trapped in a perpetual self–other, centre–margin binary.

That said, it is true that some honest generalities can be broached. After 1867, the centre of political power shifted away from the east and toward the houses of Upper and Lower Canada, where they have remained ever since. The effect of this shift was a radical decline in the influence of the maritime provinces, although here again it is necessary to keep in mind the shifting relations of power *between* the eastern provinces, each with its own nexus of cultural tensions and historical forces at play. Certainly it is safe to describe the region as a whole as having been increasingly politically marginalized by and since Confederation, with Newfoundland's own status as the most marginalized of all provinces having emerged—sometimes as a boast, sometimes as a curse—since its own 1949 entry into the federation.

Partly because of that self-identifying distinctiveness and partly because more critical justice can be done to an analysis of one segment of this region's filmmaking history for the reasons described above, here I will concentrate on a recent history of filmmaking in Newfoundland.[3] The dialectical and unstable relations of subject and other, centre and margin, past and present, native and non-native, that inform much of this discussion also attend to the emerging cinema histories of the provinces of New Brunswick, Nova Scotia, and Prince Edward Island, but there are several reasons why Newfoundland can claim a few advantages as a field of study appropriate to this anthology.

First, the province's film industry is both new and thriving, affording an immediate opportunity to examine the articulation of film policy, collective strategy, and the intersection of public and private interests in the industry. Through an act of the Legislature, the province established the Newfoundland and Labrador Film Development Corporation in 1997, thereby formalizing public support for a local industry. This legislation necessarily included a budget for development and equity investment, and a tax-credit package that has become *de rigeur* in Canada today.[4] Second, a remarkable number of features have been produced or are in development in the province—remarkable for the short amount of time that public funds have been available through local government agencies. The features extend the overall high number of films in production in the last dozen years or so, from award-winning five-minute shorts to standard-length, made-for-television documentaries. In other words, the field of observation is relatively wide. Such a convenient critical mass of genres, approaches, and styles makes issues of representation interesting and complex, as local filmmakers in one way or another must come to terms with the vexing politics of identity. How they do so is largely the subject of my investigation.

Not surprisingly, Newfoundland's historically positioned marginality within Canada has helped to reinforce a tacit awareness of a local nationalist sensibility, one that informs an imagined community of Newfoundland even while it strengthens Canada as an equally imagined other and foreign nation.[5] It follows naturally from this point that, more so than at any time in its provincial history, Newfoundland is now exploiting its outsider status in the image-producing marketplace of the nation. Obvious evidence of this is the enormous popularity of the satirical comedy show *This Hour Has Twenty-Two Minutes*, and the resultant iconic status afforded its Newfoundland creators and performers. But, as others have pointed out, the invasive presence of the appealing aspects of this show—wit, irreverence, candour, observational acumen, mimicry— manifests a long-standing tradition of distinctive cultural expression.[6] The "secret nation" is no longer a secret anymore. As Stuart Hall notes so eloquently in relation to black popular culture, "marginality, though it remains peripheral to the broader mainstream, has never been such a productive space as it is now."[7]

Two dramatic features must form the foundational base for any extended study of Newfoundland film: *The Adventure of Faustus Bidgood* (1986) and *Secret Nation* (1992). Indeed, these two works already share canonical status as initiating gestures for a tradition of Newfoundland film, however young and inappropriate the term *tradition* is in this context. Here, tradition means a history of production, one largely centred in the city of St. John's, itself an entity distinctively separate from rural Newfoundland. That production history reaches back before the appearance of these two films, to the early days of the Newfoundland Independent Filmmakers Cooperative (NIFCO), a cell of experimental activity now more than twenty years old. In fact, both *Faustus* and *Secret Nation* trace their origins to NIFCO. Andy and Mike Jones, who co-wrote and directed the former, and Mike Jones, who directed the latter, are founding members of the Cooperative, and the crews and cast of both films are almost exclusively drawn from the NIFCO stable. As with other independent cooperative houses in the Atlantic region and other parts of Canada, NIFCO was a necessary site of creative activity, invented because it had to be in a vacuum of local film production.

In particular, the wandering plot lines of *Faustus* speak to the nature of NIFCO's insistent alternative status. The film is largely an expressionist dream of belonging and resistance, as the titular character endures the life-stifling oppressions of the government bureaucracy in which he toils. Like Herman Melville's "dead-wall" dreamer, Bartleby the Scrivener, Faustus (Andy Jones) spends his days meekly attending to dehumanizing tasks. He dutifully serves the provincial Department of Education, aptly constructed as a labyrinthine structure intent on reproducing the power relations of the ruling class. A combination of farcical elements propels the daydreaming Faustus into the role of president of the new People's Republic of Newfoundland, a role for which he is both unsuited and as appropriate as any other leader of any other nation-state.

Audiences familiar with the imaginative hyperbole of CODCO sketches will recognize in *Faustus* a similar manic intensity and an almost always subversive challenge to dominant ideology. You don't have to be a Newfoundlander to recognize the film's savage assault on the power élite, but it does help to appreciate the nuances of place and the specifics of history. In particular are the ways the various sectors of that élite, such as the press, education, and the church, collude at first with the British and then with the Canadian government to maintain control of the island's economy. In imagining a revolutionary coup, the film wills the overthrow of those controlling sectors, especially as embodied in the insipid leaders of government. Government here is provincial, formed by a collection of thieves and crooks, recognizable as composite types of Newfoundland premiers, past and present. But clearly these policy practitioners have borrowed their notions of government from the mainland and attempted to transplant them in the resistant Newfoundland soil. They serve a system imported from Canada, a spectacle of democratic sameness as uninspired as the modular work stations at which their bored servants work.

So it is that at the heart of *Faustus* beats a wild nihilism, a profound suspicion of political systems of any kind, and a contempt for the pretences of false collectives. The characters who resist the totalizing mandates of the Department of Education are routinely eccentric, anarchic, and bizarre. Faustus himself is the least likely candidate for ruler of the new republic because his outwardly passive manner renders him virtually invisible. He is the prototype of the government clerk, perfectly ineffectual and unquestioning. But as we see, beneath the broad brow of the civil servant resides a luridly vivid imagination, one that seamlessly transforms the world into a pornographic fantasy or a revolutionary coup. Andy Jones' naturally baffled countenance has always worked as a kind of mask of a fermenting inner life. In *Faustus* the mask is worn well as the perfect expression of an inscrutable confusion. Faustus' high-strung boss (CODCO's Robert Joy) also wears his own mask of intense composure, as he tries to hammer home his plan for a pernicious program of Total Education. But to maintain his performance as a controlling administrator, he is compelled to conceal the scandal of his former life as a flamenco dancer, the revelation of which would surely undo his credibility as manager and man.

Faustus is, above all, the exuberantly produced result of a ten-year exercise in fundraising. The 2000 guide to the Atlantic Film Festival described it as "Canada's only epic film comedy," an overarching description that says more about the protracted production history than this wonderfully sloppy film itself. As much as Newfoundland "belongs" to Canada, it might be said that *Faustus* is "Canada's only epic film comedy," but it would be fairer to admit that the film was forged as an assertion of independence *from* Canada, just as NIFCO itself grew out of a community suspicious of the benefits of confederation. The force of the film's critique is driven by a conviction that regulatory systems (of church and state) eradicate difference, which in the local case takes the form of eccentric behaviour, unconventional responses, creative expressions, and alternative sexuality, queer and otherwise. To pass as Canadian is, arguably, to stop being a Newfoundlander. The crisis this conflict generates is manifest in the strange disappearing act of the Newfoundland premier and in the psychologically damaged characters who float in and out of the system. But the interesting achievement of *Faustus* is that it refuses to structure its oppositions exclusively in such simple-minded terms. In many ways, Canada is irrelevant to the film's operations. Of more importance is the challenge of maintaining difference itself, defined broadly as a natural condition but easily denied in the interests of class and power, in the day-to-day demands of the regulated workplace and certainly in the levelling corridors of government.

It is difficult to overstate the cultural effects of the long-awaited completion and screening of *The Adventure of Faustus Bidgood* in 1986, a symbolic event that helped focus on the creation of a *bona fide* film industry itself.[8] After ten years of editing and fund-hustling, the film had acquired the status of a good-natured local joke, an unconsummated dream of revolutionary creativity. Children who had been featured early in the film as extras had grown up into young adults by the time the filmmakers returned to final shooting. The closing credits scrolled down through hundreds of contributors who had all, at some point or another, appeared in or helped with the production of the "epic." The triumph of the film's completion, because of and in spite of its inability to access large pots of public money for its production through the years, helped galvanize a sense of the legitimacy of community itself.

In this light, it might be said that *The Adventure of Faustus Bidgood* marked the birth of a secret nation. Mike Jones' 1992 film of that title picks up where *Faustus* leaves off, with a more naturalistic exploration of many of the themes that drive the earlier feature. In every way a more polished production, *Secret Nation* nonetheless struggles openly with its own attempt to find legitimacy for the community evoked in *Faustus*. It is audacious enough to take on the question of identity and difference directly, shrewdly grounding it in a strong narrative about the lost origins of that very community.[9] Cathy Jones (yes, a relation) plays Frieda Vokey, a PhD student in history at McGill who returns to St. John's where she is soon embroiled in the province's informing national myth, the mystery of Newfoundland's joining confederation in 1949. Her (re)search leads almost certainly, if not conclusively, to the discovery that the referenda confirming Newfoundland's choice of entry were rigged. Her extended quest opens her up to a cast of suspicious characters and conspiracy theorists, not to mention a rash of local personalities, as well as to her own inquiry into the nature of identity and well-being. At the end of the film she has produced a thesis fortuitously labelled "Secret Nation." To be sure, the thesis of this film itself enters the official history of Newfoundland, a history long concealed or avoided but now reclaimed as a necessary part of the past.

It is an imagined past, of course, and therefore dangerously close to being a symptom of nostalgia, not truth. But Jones and screenwriter Riche have scrupulously avoided the "politically regressive form of reactionary nostalgia" that David Morley offers as being widespread in mainstream film today.[10] Wisely, the film flirts with but refuses to indulge it. Frieda's father, Lester (Michael Wade), is a victim of this condition, however. He both knows and drinks too much. Memories of the suspicious occurrences surrounding the so-called Great Debate, which led to the referenda on confederation, haunt his addiction to alcohol. When not brooding by a bottle, he works slavishly for the premier, ironically played by Faustus himself—Andy Jones, that is—as Valentine Aylward, a clearly unfit leader in an emerging tradition of cinematic and real-life premiers. Frieda, who has been studying in an equally distinctive part of Canada, has the privilege of a more detached view of history and place. She can marry an academic's objectifying gaze to a local's sense of indignation, a guarded position that prevents her from slipping into self-pity or abject resignation.

Secret Nation undertakes an intimidating challenge: how to represent Newfoundland and Newfoundlanders cinematically? Whereas *The Adventure of Faustus Bidgood* deploys the liberating strategies of satire to convey a sense of the wacky, on-the-edge nature of place and character, *Secret Nation* binds itself to the constricting conventions of classical realism. That it does so might be understood as necessary to its project of reclaiming forgotten history or, more to the point, imagining a history that had never been told, what Benedict Anderson calls the "Biography of a Nation." The act of challenging the orthodoxy of confederation requires a narrative frame, one in which the characteristics of a separate identity would emerge "naturally," in the course of the telling. As Anderson describes the process,

[a]ll profound changes in consciousness, by their very nature, bring with them character-istic amnesias. Out of such oblivions, in specific historical circumstances, spring narra-tives.[11]

More so than any other work of literature or art since confederation, *Secret Nation* marked the official coming of age—the biography—of Newfoundland.[12] Awareness of being imbedded in secular time, serial time, with all its implications of continuity, yet of "forgetting" the experience of continuity—product of the ruptures of the late eighteenth century—engenders the need for a narrative of "identity."[13]

Thus, the biography is written from the historical present, the present itself being the point of origination. The nation's biography, unlike that of individuals, must be fashioned "up time." In other words, the present, which registers a change in consciousness, "begets" the past, and the early 1990s give birth to the truth—or lie—of confederation. Significantly, 1992, the year of *Secret Nation*'s release, marks the beginning of the cod-fishing moratorium, arguably the most devastat-ing federal policy ever to have been imposed on the whole of Newfoundland. The radical break from a four-centuries-old fishing tradition occasioned a radical shift in cultural consciousness—and, paradoxically, a strengthening of a separate national identity. Newfoundlanders came to recognize the moratorium as the unhappy but logical effects of confederation itself, a raw deal leading logically from the earlier bigger deal.

So it was that John Fitzgerald, an enthusiastic reviewer and historian, noted the following about *Secret Nation*:

Secret Nation gives a long-overdue intellectual tilt to what it means to be a Newfound-lander, something which has been lacking in 30-second enunciations of our identity by Labatt's Blue commercials. In fact, there is a rebellion here against the stereotyping of Newfoundland's history, culture, and identity, an incessant railing against the distillation of our essential characteristics—the "I winks, and you nods accordin' " routine—into a commodity for mainland audiences which leaves the impression that we are a beer-guz-zling crew of simpleton 'Newfies.' Frieda is outraged at the racist Newfie jokes which are prevalent in Canada—and Newfoundland. Bravo![14]

Notable here is the reviewer's identification as a Newfoundlander—the repeated use of the col-lective first-person pronoun—and his explicit opposition between real Newfoundlanders and others, whether condescending Canadians or unenlightened Newfoundlanders themselves. Con-fidently acknowledging the "essential characteristics" of "our identity," he understandably avoids describing specifically what these might be. Of course, as the film implies and the reviewer should know, Frieda's credentials as a doctoral candidate at a mainland university make her more Canadian, not more essentially a Newfoundlander; indeed, the film wishes to have it both ways. It viscously demonizes the academic world, particularly that of the local university, imag-ing it cheaply through the squandering excesses of one of Frieda's old friends, historian Dan Maddox (performed with salacious gusto by Ron Hynes). But it also wishes to enhance Frieda's credibility and thus the legitimacy of her quest by situating her solidly within that world itself—and a mainland version of it at that!

Here we arrive at the central paradox of defining national identity. The film's explicit chal-lenge to Canada, and, by extension, to the imperial masters of Britain, both forges the birth of

Newfoundland distinctiveness and reinforces the dominance of the controlling nation(s). The post-confederation birth of Newfoundland, as *Secret Nation* represents it, is possible only when confederation is understood to be the fix it was, a realization given cinematic expression almost fifty years after the event. To be sure, *Secret Nation* perfectly embodies the exigencies of cultural representation. As the largest and most expensive feature film to that date, it resisted the overt strategies of postmodernism in favour of a realism or naturalism that prefers the straight line of history, read backwards as it must be. The film opens with a stirring archival montage of down-town St. John's around the time of confederation, replete with images of prosperity, a plenitude of fish, and smiling children. The montage is meant to belie the myth of pre-confederation New-foundland as a desolate, dying place, a myth perpetuated by Smallwood and his Canadian allies. These images evoke what Fitzgerald calls "a bitter nostalgia," establishing a template of "truth" against which the false history of Newfoundland will be judged.[15] But in substituting one version of history for another, the film competes with its tendency to remain detached from absolute declarations, nostalgic indulgence, and the untrustworthy world of appearances. We do see here, however, how a contained and strategic nostalgia can be what John Durham Peters calls a "pro-ductive cultural agent."[16]

If Fitzgerald and others applauded the film's avoidance of tired Newfoundland stereotypes, especially as defined by Canadians, it also necessarily feeds them, in part through the cast of sec-ondary characters who animate the script, providing comic relief and local "colour." Perhaps the most memorable of these is Rick Mercer as Frieda's brother Chris, a prodigal son who, after a nomadic fling in New York City, settles into dispatching for the Crown taxi company, the con-temporary occupation of the street philosopher. In *Secret Nation*, Mercer exhibits for the first time away from the theatrical stage the talent that has since catapulted him into the pantheon of Canadian celebrity. Fitzgerald singles out one of Chris' side-splitting exchanges as evidence of a "quintessential" local wit; but, tellingly, such quintessence is realized explicitly in contradistinc-tion to (or parallel sympathy with?) another distinctive group within Canada:

> The phone rings. Chris answers:
> "Crown? Er, ah, *Bonn Swaw*."
> Chris (into microphone to the cabbies): "Byze, don't be usin' the word 'Frog'
> in the vee-hicles."[17]

As the saucy-wise Chris, he has the wit and wherewithal to mimic the voices in cabs all over town, offering words of wisdom to Frieda and the family from a hilariously ironic distance. Im-plicit in his character is what might be appreciated as the "essential characteristic" of being a Newfoundlander, an ability to comment on the specificity of place, being at once part of and apart from it. In him, and in a more serious expression in Frieda, we see how marginal status can be transformed into the grist of a "national" identity, even while it necessarily defines itself in op-position to an established other.

It is interesting to situate *Secret Nation* and its complex treatment of history as a revisioned construct next to *John and the Missus*, Gordon Pinsent's feature film of 1986, also the release date of *The Adventure of Faustus Bidgood*. Pinsent's film, directed in the straight-ahead conventions of realism, gives itself over almost completely to nostalgia, imagining a past of good-natured suffer-ing, depicting a couple of middle-aged Newfoundlanders enduring the imposition of Joey Smallwood's ignominious "Resettlement Program" of the early 1960s. As John Munn, Pinsent brings his well-admired chops to the screen, but the film must endure the overbearing weight of an idealized sense of outport life, a false utopia of serial sunshine and friendly breezes, and the grim nobility of Jackie Burroughs as the "Missus." More personal indulgence than enduring cinema, *John and the Missus* aims high at capturing some essentially abiding quality of forbearance in Newfoundland life, but its reach is inevitably weakened by its largely unexplored historical context. Unlike the anarchic power of *Faustus* or the complex probings of *Secret Nation*, *John and the Missus* tries too hard to represent an essential Newfoundland, assuming it knows what this might be in the first place. Failing to take a fierce grip on history, it never quite reveals or makes real what the present—in this case the mid 1980s—might itself be concealing.

A similar hazard plagues the unfortunately titled *No Apologies*, a 1990 feature film produced and directed by Newfoundlanders William MacGillivray and Ken Pittman respectively. The troubled family at the centre of the drama must carry the entire weight of national allegory. Here, too, the politics of history—the imminent collapse of the fishery and the province's dependence on seasonal work and (un)employment insurance, for instance—are drowned in a sea of sentimentality. Representation is unrelievedly grim and self-victimizing, a risky approach for a film that claims a stake on regional identity. *No Apologies* is, after all, more interesting for its failure to offer an acceptable or appealing register of regional distinctiveness. It is as trapped within the grand counter-narratives of nation and region as its own dysfunctional family, producing an exclusionary cultural fundamentalism. It would seem that audiences are looking for dramas that resist such oppositional structures.

The examples of *John and the Missus* and *No Apologies* can best be understood as the necessary markers of an emerging local industry. The same applies to now-forgotten features in all parts of Canada, more useful as training fields for a film community than notable as enduring works of art or even popular culture. In the region known as Atlantic Canada, the growth of the industry is now transparent enough to invite scrutiny of why some features rise and others slide into oblivion, and why filmmakers are making certain kinds of choices regarding the representation of place in view of such growth. A long-acknowledged major force of regional production is MacGillivray himself, a defiantly independent artist whose uneasy response to the traditional binaries of Canadian culture have fuelled his most interesting work. All of MacGillivray's films are worth examining in light of the challenge of representation and the politics of identity, among other aesthetic and thematic reasons. But, in particular, *Life Classes* (1987) and *Understanding Bliss* (1993) work from and through a frame of cultural containment to come up with a sense of the shifting and creative relations between the elements of identity.

In *Life Classes*, nothing is ever as we might expect. Non-professional actor Jacinta Cormier plays the central character, Mary Cameron, with an almost hypnotic intensity. Life takes Mary to Halifax and eventually home to Cape Breton where she renegotiates her sense of self, having had a radically transformative experience along the way. Jolted from complacency and compelled to confront the twin handicaps of gender and ruralness, Mary fashions a new future into which she can fit herself as an artist. *Life Classes* is audacious, provocative, and meditative, a testimony to the power of cinema to explore the complex and unstable signifiers of power. The film is less interested in fixing representative types than it is in probing the effects of cultural resistance and in animating the contradictory effects of postmodernity, as satellite dishes invade the rural spaces of an Atlantic Canada suddenly altered by new global technologies. The film shares with more recent features in the region, such as *The Bingo Robbers* (2000), an emancipatory willingness to get beyond the confining stereotypes of the urban–rural binary. The specificity of place no longer guarantees corruption any more than it promises nobility. In both films, home is where characters work out how they want to be in the world.

MacGillivray's *Understanding Bliss*, one of the first features in the region to be shot in digital video format, is equally intense about its dialectical approach to the challenge of identity. Here Peter (Bryan Hennessey), a Newfoundland university professor from a fishing family, is compelled to confront what he wants and needs to be. The narrative assumes the form of a romantic struggle with his girlfriend, Elizabeth (Catherine Grant), a Toronto-based professor who has dropped into Newfoundland to deliver a guest lecture. From imagining an idyllic retreat together to his roots, Peter gradually realizes the nexus of contradictions that disturb this romantic fantasy. Home is both the past and a present he no longer inhabits. With a foot in the worlds both of here and there, and of then and now, Peter is unsurprisingly shaky with a growing awareness of the complexity and burden of difference. As with home, difference changes all the time.

MacGillivray's uncompromising representation in these and his other films of the travails of exile status within one's own community speaks to a struggle over cultural hegemony. His doubly punning Picture Plant Productions, based in Halifax, echoes his Newfoundland roots, informing a consistent approach to the multiplicity and entanglements of so-called regional experience. One of MacGillivray's chief peeves has been the way the growing industry encourages token representations of place and experience. Examples abound, but it is commonplace that the seductive tax-credit packages now offered by provinces in the Atlantic region—lures for Hollywood appropriation—encourage distorted hybrids of place. When New Brunswick stands in for an anonymous German forest or the Nova Scotia coastline substitutes for Long Island, local filmmakers understandably wonder who benefits.[18] This is an old problem, at least as old as that of Toronto licence plates being replaced by Chicago or New York ones, but the challenge in the east is how to sustain homegrown product while labour and locale resources are taken up by foreign or partnered productions. The invitation to partnerships, made necessary and attractive in a global marketplace, is bound to affect the way stories are told.

Ever conscious of these hazards, Newfoundland filmmaker Ken Pittman has inclined toward European, rather than American, partnerships. *Misery Harbour* (1999), a recent feature co-production based on a hugely popular Norwegian adventure story, is a noble attempt to produce a narrative of shared interests and effects. The result may be less than smashing, but the effort to match narrative and historical interests marks a fruitful collaboration with like-minded partners. The Norwegian and Newfoundland crews traded experience and know-how, each nation, so to speak, ostensibly benefitting from the other's expertise and divergent ways of approaching their sets. Pittman has aggressively partnered with friendly collaborators, his SF fantasy *Anchor Zone* (1994) having been an ambitious attempt to represent, with Québec partners, a post-nuclear future, somewhere between hell and high water. Again, the result was less than glorious, but it is hard to deny the perceived benefits of training and the building of a community infrastructure. Notable as well is that these examples, while invisible from a theatrical marketplace perspective, have actively contributed to the formation of a tradition of cinematic practice while being faithful to the challenges of honestly representing place and identity. No one would accuse Pittman or MacGillivray of *mis*representation.

Two Newfoundland features require mention in the context of the difficulties of local signification: *The Divine Ryans* (1999) and *Extraordinary Visitor* (1998). Both comedies draw on a carnivalesque experience of St. John's. In the former, adapted for the screen by novelist Wayne Johnston, Jordan Harvey stars as Draper Doyle, a nine-year-old boy with prepubescent yearnings and a haunted imagination fed by a disturbed family. Set during the glorious 1966–67 hockey season, the film taps the town's familiar post-confederation relations with Canada, borrowing the larger nation's signifiers for local and often comic consumption. Yet a strong cast and a powerful narrative source do not necessarily guarantee a successful feature. *The Divine Ryans* was received as a mediocre, if sometimes charming, initiation story. Typical of critical reaction were *Globe and Mail* reviewer Rick Groen's politely sarcastic remarks: "The place is Newfoundland ... the goal is bittersweet comedy, the cute quotient keeps getting cranked up a bit too high and the result is the Cancon equivalent of clog dancing or tuba bands—accomplished in its own way but, ultimately, more precious than profound."[19] As a co-production with Imagex films, who scored much better with the generally acclaimed *Margaret's Museum* (1995), the *Divine Ryans* might be said to have suffered from a diffuse representation of place.[20] Halifax director Stephen Reynolds found himself on unfamiliar ground directing the likes of Pete Postlewaite, a talented character actor, and Mary Walsh, an inspired bit of casting; but that did not translate finally into more than a collection of discrete set pieces. *Extraordinary Visitor* (1998), on the other hand, drawn almost exclusively from Newfoundland sources, fared more sympathetically as an innovative satire, receiving nominations for and winning several international awards. Its comic premise rests on the "extraordinary" visit by John the Baptist to his urban namesake. The film dares to ask what would happen if St. John's were God's test site, the last place on earth to offer a possibility of redemption before the whole planet goes up in fire and brimstone. Working from his own script, director-writer John Doyle harnessed the talents of Andy Jones and Mary Walsh as suitable foils for St. John's (Raoul Bhaneja) inquisitive character. In spite of Johnston's writing talent, *The Divine Ryans* lacked the cinematic credibility of *Extraordinary Visitor*. Why this is so has much to do *Extraordinary Visitor*'s refusal to turn its characters into stage Newfoundlanders, thereby avoiding the spectacularization of place of which *The Divine Ryans* is ultimately guilty. It is safe to say that, had *The Divine Ryans* been made fifteen years ago, it might have achieved an entirely different niche in Canadian film history. With the recent increase in productions in the region, spectators are likely to become more discriminating in their preferences, refusing the kitsch that informs *The Divine Ryans*.

To this last list of injunctions one could add what is authentic; but, indeed, the term is now under such pressure, due to the enormity of change and destabilizing forces in the region, that we can no longer invoke it without qualification. When the term itself is contested, as it is implicitly in *Extraordinary Visitor*, we enter uncharted terrain. We need only examine the rapid emergence of short films from all over Atlantic Canada to recognize the power of this observation. At the risk of privileging Newfoundland over other production sites in the region, I should acknowledge the achievements of filmmakers Mary Lewis and Anita McGee, both younger challengers making refreshingly original works that draw directly from their relations with place.

McGee's most recent short, *New Neighbours*, is a brilliant mixed-media study of character, an essentially wordless dream of desire and history; as McGee herself describes the film, it is "about better sex next door."[21] It is as if McGee and her generation no longer need to agonize over the struggles of post-confederation experience; the struggles are innovatively both assumed and resisted. But *Seven Brides for Uncle Sam* (1997), McGee's first hour-long documentary on the cultural invasion by American officers during World War Two, plainly relied on the efforts of the early NIFCO creators, *Faustus*, and *Secret Nation* to prepare the way. *Seven Brides for Uncle Sam* captures the ambiguous relations between Newfoundland women and American men with a confident sense of the lines of history and the ambivalent boundaries of identity. It is an unsparing, moving portrait of the inevitable consequences of cultural change.

With director Mary Lewis, McGee produced *Clothesline Patch* (1999), a half-hour drama based on a short story by Newfoundland writer Donna Morrissey. A persuasive rendering of outport life in the 1960s, *Clothesline Patch* avoids the sentimentality of *No Apologies*, preferring to send up its gossipy, meddling subjects with humour drawn from an edgy script. Told from the point of view of a young girl entering puberty, the film playfully mocks the clichéd portraits of outport inhabitants in both searing and affectionate ways. As a filmmaker in her own right, perhaps no one better embodies the achievement of a maturing film culture than Mary Lewis. Her animated short *When Ponds Freeze Over* snagged every major festival prize in her category in 1998, a harbinger of strong work to come. Lewis' luminous short exuberantly captures a personal memory forged at the intersection of private girlhood and public life in Newfoundland. Its confident lyricism practically swaggers, as Lewis' images move through a circle of associative logic. Again, it is tempting to observe that films like these are made possible only in the wake of both a rapidly evolved inventory of local production and a complex historical moment, fifty years after Newfoundland's entry into confederation and the shift into a world exploring new media technologies.

I would be remiss if I did not finally mention the twin feature productions of *Violet* (2000) and *The Bingo Robbers* (2000), the first full-fledged dramas to have benefitted directly from the development and equity funds of the Newfoundland and Labrador Film Development Corporation. Both produced exclusively in St. John's, these recent works are particularly interesting for the way they deploy strategies of narrative and representation. Both have been largely written and produced by women; both turned to the same financial resources; both have taken the requisite steps of appearing in major festival exhibition space; both face major distribution challenges common to independent productions in Canada. But whereas *Violet* deliberately derives its conceit from a European model of romantic comedy, transforming St. John's into a virtually anonymous, universalized space of possibility, *The Bingo Robbers* is resolutely dependent on a recognition of specificity of place and cultural milieu. The results are thus radically different, as if each were starting at zero in the game and then testing time and critical reception to determine which strategy might pay off. This comparison is unfair, of course. The filmmakers are not competing with each other, and the success of each film has in many ways already been determined by the actual completion of the projects, the labour invested and harnessed, the local industrial infrastructure the films helped to reinforce. Then again, *Violet* and *The Bingo Robbers* might very well disappear into the dustbin of history, but it is worth observing how each film responded to an already evolving film culture and to the wider demands of the marketplace.

Violet, Rosemary House's first dramatic feature, extends the romantic view of her *Rain, Drizzle, and Fog* (1998), an openly personal documentary of her native city, into a fictional dream. Mary Walsh stars—yet again—as the title character, a restless middle-aged woman on the verge of a goosey breakdown. The film tracks the path of Violet's self-absorption, as her purposeful withdrawal from active life takes an often humorous toll on a pageant of friends and family. These characters, individuated as the kinds of eccentrics who have aged badly since *The Adventure of Faustus Bidgood*, orbit Violet and her property like a studied bunch of Fellini extras. Indeed, the film relies heavily on a history of Italian comedy for its spirited antics, invoking the crooning tunes of Dean Martin for its transitional sequences and exploiting the verdant backdrop of Newfoundland in midsummer to effect the sensibility of a leisurely Latin sensuality. The camera continually pans, tilts, and floats across the lush landscape of Violet's estate, more slowly than a tourist travelogue but comfortably enough to invite a wistful longing of place. You might think you were atop a Tuscan hill, not perched high over a capital city at the edge of the chilly north Atlantic. By the end of the film, Violet has come out of her fragile shell, shaken her family curse, and discovered true love, and the entire cast is ready to parade around the estate as if queuing up to take the waters with Claudia Cardinale.

Violet is at times beautiful and amusing, but its curious substitutions and geographical disguises and its diligent lightness inscribe it as a form of popular cinema, pitched at a global marketplace situated far from the grounds of its production. It is at once clever and conventional, a shrewd exercise in casting and tone, far from the edgy practice of the films described earlier in this chapter. As such, it turns its back on the local, drawing on its talent but refusing almost all other aspects of its existence.

Is there anything wrong with this decision? Is the achievement of *Violet* not in itself a sign of the healthy growth of the industry, an effect of which is the assimilation of Newfoundland culture into a commercial mainstream ethos, as the feature examples in Nova Scotia demonstrate? These questions do not necessarily presume Newfoundland foundationalism, but they do imply the hazards of moving away from history and specificity, hazards directly confronted in *Secret Nation*. If something called Newfoundland culture exists at all, it does so, as one social theorist argues, not as an immovable reality but as a "particular lens through which the world is experienced."[22] This apt metaphor underscores the consequences of looking through the world through other lenses. Perhaps if local filmmakers refused to shoot through a Newfoundland lens, Newfoundland itself would cease to exist. But, as I have attempted to show here, taking control of the construction of marginal space has given birth not only to many diverse and challenging works of cinema but also to the continuing invention of Newfoundland itself.

The Newfoundland imaged in *The Bingo Robbers* is distinct from that of *Violet*, both new and familiar. Amazingly, Mary Walsh does not appear in a single frame of the movie, although some of the original NIFCO crowd, whose influence is obvious, make cameo appearances. Notable is Mike Jones' off-screen role of Web Cast Author, in effect the production diarist. Jones maintained an on-(web)site chronicle of the shoot, an often humorous and self-indulgent record that cleverly appeared on the digital film's website (www.thebingorobbers.com). Andy Jones, who appears hilariously in one of the film's recurring foiled robbery scenes, is also credited as script consultant. Conceived, written, and directed by relative film newcomers Barry Newhook and Lois Brown, *The Bingo Robbers* draws heavily on a townie sensibility, exuberantly exploiting the small cruising strips of St. John's waterfront as the site of a restless journey. Nancy (Brown) and Vallis (Newhook) are a couple of brainy young misfits who live by night, all dressed up in mismatched Value Village finery with nowhere to go. Of course, there *is* nowhere to go. Every attempt to make a quick and crooked killing at corner store and bingo hall is met with comic impossibility. In St. John's, everyone knows or is related to everyone else. Robbery is an unfulfilled fantasy, prohibitive when the guy behind the counter recognizes you even in your ski mask.

The filmmakers chose digital format largely for economic reasons, but their preference suits their subjects. In the grainy, underlit field of videotape, St. John's acquires the stylized hue of a smoky punk bar. Nancy and Vallis are wannabe fall-outs from the middle class, suspicious of convention, authority, and the adult world in general. They are adults themselves, but they cling to their alternative status as fiercely as the town clings to the edge of the North American continent. *The Bingo Robbers* effectively turns the world of *Violet* inside out, exhibiting the chatty milieu that made a Mary Walsh possible in the first place. It reclaims the specificity of place as a vital breeding ground for language, story, and, by extension, community. In its spirited enthusiasm, its noir-inflected cinema of jump-cuts and digital pans, and its pulsating rhythms performed by well-known local band Fur-Packed Action, the film celebrates a younger generation's inheritance of and emergence into film culture.

The Bingo Robbers signals a significant turning point in the evolution of Newfoundland, and to speak more broadly, regional film. In technique and attitude, the film extends the search for and embrace of all that is valued in the local, an embrace that necessarily rejects all that is taken to be alien to its existence. Yet the film also acknowledges that such difference does not necessarily partake of a romantic or idealized existence. In place of sentimentality, *The Bingo Robbers* offers spontaneity, a way of being that is compulsive about maintaining distinctiveness both in spite and because of a larger world. The film's website perfectly captures this paradox in its marketing manifesto:

> This newly formed company is excited by the challenge of producing new work in film and video production. Today's market allows any filmmaker anywhere in the world to experiment in the medium of filmmaking while enjoying the benefits of all technologies without restriction. THE BINGO ROBBERS, a feature length film, is the company's first project. Written by Barry Newhook and Lois Brown, two directors of the company, the feature will be shot on video with the intent of transferring to film for distribution. For the film and video industry, this concept is in its infancy, making the development of beyond low budget filmmaking a reality. The company intends to develop global interest for this movie through the underground market by way of the Internet, festivals, video sales and distribution.[23]

In the postmodern moment of Newfoundland's film culture, steering one's cultural product in the *underground* of global media technologies radically challenges and reconfigures traditional concepts of space. Whether the cultural production of the region can sustain its distinctive energetic push through such space remains to be seen. The future looks interesting.

Notes

1 David Clanfield, *Canadian Film* (Toronto: Oxford University Press, 1987), 105.

2 Clanfield, *Canadian Film*, 105.

3 Since 1996, the official name of the province has been Newfoundland and Labrador. I speak here of Newfoundland film only, an acknowledgement of the island's controlling interests and production of what might be called a provincial industry.

4 For an incisive account of the so-called tax-shelter history in Canada and how it has helped determine the formation of a national industry see Ted Magder, *Canada's Hollywood: The Canadian State and Feature Films* (Toronto: University of Toronto Press, 1993). See also the website advertising Newfoundland's tax-credit package (www.newfilm.nf.net/programs/).

5 Indeed, many Newfoundlanders in conversation distinguish between the province and Canada, as if referring to two separate political and national spheres.

6 The comedy troupe known to many Canadians as CODCO served as the working laboratory for much of what has become identified today as Newfoundland humour. Original members Andy Jones, Cathy Jones, and Mary

Walsh remain at the core of the province's theatrical and comedy activities. See Helen Peters, ed., *The Plays of Codco* (Toronto: Peter Lang Publishing, 1993).

7   Stuart Hall, "What is this 'Black' in Black Popular Culture?", in *Critical Dialogues in Cultural Studies,* David Morley and Kuan-Hsing Chen, eds. (London: Routledge, 1996), 467. Perhaps no one realizes this more than the provincial officers who work for the Department of Culture, Tourism, and Recreation. For an excellent overview of arts policy and its implicit links to the emergence of cultural tourism see Ronald Rompkey, "The Idea of Newfoundland and Arts Policy Since Confederation" in *Newfoundland Studies* 14, no. 2 (Fall 1998): 266–81.

8   A series of memorable premier screenings took place at the LSPU Hall in downtown St. John's, a now-historic site of creative initiation. Perhaps fittingly, the Hall, as it is commonly known, was once the home of the Longshoremen's Protective Union.

9   Credit needs to be awarded here to screenwriter and award-winning novelist Ed Riche, whose recent project is the cinematic adaptation of his comic novel *Rare Birds* (New York: Doubleday, 1998), starring, oddly enough, Hollywood renegade William Hurt.

10 David Morley, "Bounded Realms: Household, Family, Community, and Nation," in *Home, Exile, Homeland: Film, Media, and the Politics of Place,* Hamid Naficy, ed. (New York and London: Routledge, 1999), 163.

11 Benedict Anderson, *Imagined Communities: Reflections on the Origins and Spread of Nationalism* (London: Verso, 1991), 204.

12 This statement is not meant to undermine the weighty dramatic tradition in which this subject has been extensively explored. See in particular the works of Thomas Cahill, playwright and television producer. The Centre for Newfoundland Studies at Memorial University is an excellent resource for this and related material.

13 Anderson, *Imagined Communities,* 205.

14 John Fitzgerald, "Newfoundland Politics and Confederation Revisited: Three New Works," *Newfoundland Studies* 9, no. (Spring 1993): 110.

15 Fitzgerald, "Newfoundland Politics," 110.

16 John Durham Peters, "Exile, Nomadism, and Diaspora: The Stakes of Mobility in the Western Canon," in *Home, Exile, Homeland,* Hamid Naficy, ed., 30.

17 Fitzgerald, "Newfoundland Politics," 111.

18 See my essay on the contradictions besieging *Love and Death on Long Island*: "Mixed Messages: Standing in for the Hamptons," *Canadian Forum,* November 1997, 28–29.

19 Rick Groen, "Stars made of pucks, and other cute things," *Globe and Mail,* 5 November 1999.

20 That said, it is worth reading what historian David Frank has to say about the skewed representation of mining history in *Margaret's Museum*: "One Hundred Years After: Film and History in Atlantic Canada," *Acadiensis* 26, no. 2 (Spring 1997): 112-136.

21 See the Kickham Productions website (www.kickham.com).

22 Jim Overton, *Making a World of Difference: Essays on Tourism, Culture, and Development in Newfoundland* (St. John's: ISER Books, 1996), 57.

23 See the website (www.thebingorobbers.com/makers.html).

English-Canadian Animation
1975–2000
Chris Robinson

ATTEMPTING TO DEFINE CANADIAN, let alone Canadian animation, is like trying to explain hockey to an American: frustrating and complicated, with a tendency to simplify ("you try to get the black round thing in the net"). If we accept Canadian sociologist Ian Angus' definition of social identity as "the feeling of belonging to a group, and of having this feeling in common with other members of that group" or Max Weber's concept of the nation as a human group that feels itself a unity to an external organization, then Canadian animation certainly doesn't subscribe easily to the concept of national identity.[1] Like the country itself, Canada's animation communities are spread far and wide across the landscape. Canadian animation is best defined as a patchwork of differing voices struggling to be heard through the shouts from the south.

Prior to the mid 1980s, the definition of Canadian animation was fairly straightforward. The National Film Board of Canada (NFB) was the calling card of Canadian animation, merging propaganda with artistic innovation. In those days, there was little activity beyond the NFB. As early as the 1940s, there were commercial houses like Graphic Visuals owned by former NFB animators Jim McKay and George Dunning; in the 1960s and 1970s, a variety of service studios existed in Vancouver, Ottawa, and Toronto to provide work for the graduates of Canada's new animation school, Sheridan College, which opened in 1967. In the late 1970s, Toronto's Nelvana Studios and Montréal's Cinar were small, fledgling companies. In Vancouver, Al Sens was quietly producing anti-industrial films, while Marv Newland was opening up his studio, International Rocketship. But while opportunities for government funding were more plentiful than they are today, there was little opportunity for animators in Canada unless they were among the privileged few able to find work with the NFB.

This situation has changed in the last ten to fifteen years. Animation has emerged from the margins of cultural expression into an accepted form of cultural and economic capital that has found a popular audience. In particular, "classical" American cel animation (such as that seen in Disney and Warner productions) has established itself as the norm in mainstream culture. Canadian animation has shifted from the production of government-funded personal or propaganda films to a market-driven industry that exists primarily to feed the global entertainment machine.

The National Film Board

Given the demise of the theatrical animated short film and the rise of low-quality, "limited" animation television productions, animation, to say nothing of Canadian animation, was not a booming industry in the 1970s. Nevertheless, this period saw a rise in the number of animators and small studios across the country. At the same time, the National Film Board embarked on one of its most successful periods to date.

In the mid 1970s, the NFB was at a crossroads. During the previous decade, the English studio had moved far from the innovations of Norman McLaren. Led by Don Arioli, Derek Lamb, Kaj Pindal, and others, the Film Board turned increasingly toward cel animation and government contracts. Small private studios were fighting the Board's exclusive government "cash cows," and soon the NFB was forced to make more personalized, cultural films. This period led to the creation of some of this country's finest animation. Under the direction of Lamb, an Englishman from Harvard, the NFB produced a series of acclaimed films including *Every Child* (Fedorenko, 1980), *Why Me?* (Perlman, 1978), *Special Delivery* (Weldon, 1978), and *The Sweater* (Cohen, 1979).

The Sweater, in particular, stands as one of Canada's finest cultural artifacts. In this beautifully painted film, Québec author Roch Carrier's childhood hockey memories emerge as astonishing commentaries of the state of language, nation, and religion. Although the film is set in the 1950s, it reflects the tensions of its time. During the late 1970s, Québec nationalism was peaking under René Lévesque and the Parti Québécois. The late 1970s also saw the Montréal Canadiens at their peak. On the verge of winning their fourth straight Stanley Cup, they were led by the inspired play of Guy Lafleur, who closely rivalled the popularity of Maurice Richard, hero of *The Sweater*. If ever a film addressed the inherent complexities and contradictions of Canada, it was *The Sweater*.

By 1982, clashes over creative direction and budget cuts led to Lamb's resignation. For more than a decade, the English studio dissipated under the stagnant direction of Doug McDonald, a lifetime bureaucrat with no animation experience. The Board continued to receive Oscar nominations (which, given the almost automatic annual selection, has rendered the honour valueless), but the films, while still technically innovative and well crafted, were mired down with political agendas.

In a telling article in the *Vancouver Province* about a dozen years ago, several animators went on record slamming the McDonald era. "Norman McLaren would be turning in his grave if he knew how the place was being run," said David Fine, who went on to success with Nelvana in the late 1990s with *Bob and Margaret*. The article described a situation in which conservative managers had "an unhealthy degree of control over the films being produced." Because of this atmosphere, the English studio lost not only David Fine but also Caroline Leaf, who transferred to the French animation studio and later left the NFB altogether.

During this time, the board desperately wanted a specialty channel and so clamped down on the films to ensure they were market-driven and followed a specific agenda. To make matters worse, McDonald toyed with the physical layout of the animation studio. "The NFB used to have this great open social area," said former NFB animator Ellen Besen. "When McDonald came in, it became his office. A windowless storage room became the new 'social' rendezvous for animators. The whole atmosphere of the studio changed ... Ideas used to be welcome. Dialogue existed between producers, executives, and filmmakers. Today, it is just producer-driven. They simply try to find a niche."[2]

This mindset dominated NFB productions until the late 1990s, when the situation appeared to have improved. Today, thanks to the guidance of producers David Verrall, Marcy Page, and Michael Fukushima, the English Animation Studio has produced a number of critically acclaimed films, including *How Wings Are Attached to the Backs of Angels* (Welch, 1997), *The Village of Idiots* (Fedorenko and Newlove, 1999*)*, *My Grandmother Ironed the King's Shirts* (Kove, 1999), and the astonishing *When the Day Breaks* (Tilby and Forbis, 1999).

Regionalization and Beyond

Due in part to the federal government's regionalization of culture in the early 1970s and the NFB's opening of regional studios, animation communities grew in Halifax, Winnipeg, and Vancouver.

Winnipeg

Rather than merely aping the NFB's head studio, the Vancouver and Winnipeg branches attempted to reflect the characteristics of their regions. The results were successful. In Winnipeg, NFB executive producer Mike Scott found Richard Condie, Brad Caslor, and Cordell Barker. From the late 1970s to about 1989, this Manitoban trio produced some of the funniest films in the history of animation, let alone Canadian animation: *Getting Started* (1982), *The Big Snit* (1985), *Get A Job* (1985), and *The Cat Came Back* (1988). *The Cat Came Back,* in particular, stands as a classic of twisted Canadian humour (the film is about a man trying to kill a cat), while *The Big Snit* remains a remarkable critique, rooted in Cold War paranoia, of the triviality of domestic squabbles. Ironically, the success of these distinctly Canadian films was based on their love for and appropriation of American cartoons, specifically those of Tex Avery and Bob Clampett. These classically drawn films are instantly recognizable by their exaggerated characters with balloonish noses and beady eyes. While this look is likely rooted in Kaj Pindal's character designs from *I Know an Old Lady Who Swallowed a Fly,* the Winnipeg trio took the design to new levels of absurdity. The style is also recognizable in later NFB films like *No Problem* (Welsh, 1992) and *Bob's Birthday* (Fine, Snowden, 1994)

But the Winnipeg scene today is nowhere near what it was. Condie's last work, the operatic *La Salla* (1996), despite its Oscar nod, is a poor film. Until the recent *Strange Invaders* (2001), Barker's output was reduced to commercials. Outside of the Red River College animation program, there appears to be little animation activity in Winnipeg today.

Vancouver

A vibrant, diverse animation community has emerged in British Columbia. A variety of established service and industry studios like Studio B, Delaney and Friends, Stanfield Animation, Bardel, Natterjack, Aka Cartoon, and International Rocketship exist alongside independent animators Richard Reeves, Scott Clark, Gail Noonan, Leslie Bishko, Marilyn Cherenko, Stephen Arthur, and Al Sens.

Al Sens is Vancouver's most important voice. He has made a healthy body of politically inspired work since 1959, including *The Twitch* (1973), *The Bureaucracy* (1975), *A Hard Day at the Office* (1978), *Dreamtime* (1999), and the recent *A Courtship for Our Time* (2001), and he owns the only animation stand in Vancouver outside the NFB. Virtually every Vancouver animation film has Sens' name in the credits, and most animators owe something to the man, who was quick to encourage young talent.

Before the NFB arrived, Vancouver produced a variety of service work. In 1968, Emily Carr School of Art and Design opened an animation department. One of the most important figures of this early period was Hugh Fouldes, who, in addition to making some of the first NFB films out west (*Citizen Harold*, 1971), set the tone at Emily Carr by encouraging independent animation. But the most famous figure to emerge from this period was undoubtedly Marv Newland. The Californian became infamous for his student film *Bambi Meets Godzilla* (1969) and freelanced for a variety of Canadian companies (Cinera, Crawley, Sesame Street) before setting up shop in Vancouver, where he worked with Al Sens, Wayne Morris, and other established animators. In 1975, Newland founded International Rocketship, producing commercials for an array of clients. Most notably, he used the commercial proceeds to invest in films by other animators. Newland's generosity and influence are unparalleled. The studio relied on commercial work to survive, but Newland fed the profits back into creating short independent films by Newland himself and by animators Danny Antonucci, J. Falconer, Dieter Muller, and others.

Newland made some marvellous, 1930s-inspired animations including *Sing Beast Sing* (1980) and *Black Hula* (1988). In 1990, he made the "porn animation" anthology film *Pink Komkommer* and in 1995 won the Grand Prix at the Annecy Animation Festival for his unique adaptation of Gary Larson's *Tales from The Far Side*. But, alas, good guys finish last. International Rocketship faced financial difficulties in the late 1990s, and Newland was forced to work as a hired gun on American TV shows like Will Vinton's *The PJs*.

Beyond his own work, Newland has nurtured a number of animators under the Rocketship banner. J. Falconer created the funny shorts *Dog Brain* (1988) and *Deadly Deposits* (1992), while Dieter Muller, undoubtedly one of the most unheralded animators in this country, made three miniature masterpieces: *Waddles* (1989), *Points* (1983), and *Dry Noodles* (1985). The most infamous of the Rocket crew is Danny Antonucci, whose gross-out film *Lupo the Butcher* (1988) turned the animation world on its head. Influenced by older animations, *Lupo the Butcher* is a dazzling, shocking short about a foul-mouthed Italian butcher who chops himself to bits. The film brought Antonucci a cult following and opened the doors for his MTV series *The Brothers Grunt*. In 1994, Antonucci opened Aka Cartoon. After the failure of *Brothers Grunt*, Antonucci hit the big time with the Cartoon Network series *Ed, Edd and Eddy*.

Aside from a variety of service studios—including Bardel Animation (founded in 1987 by Barry Ward), Studio B, Stanfield Animation, and Natterjack Animation—Vancouver is also the birthplace of one of the world's most innovative computer studios, Mainframe Entertainment. Mainframe hit the animation map with its computer-driven show *Reboot* (1994). The show was the first completely computer-animated television series and went on to great acclaim while opening the door for other computer-animated TV ventures, such as Nelvana's *Donkey Kong* and *Rolie Polie Olie*. In 1996, Mainframe created a second show, *Beast Wars*, and continues to set the standard for computer animation with shows like *Shadow Raiders*. Computer animation for TV was once unheard of, but today, with ongoing technological developments, computer animation has become not only an affordable option but almost a necessity in the television industry.

Ottawa

Ottawa has long been an active, if not particularly inspiring, location for animation. The innovative work in the 1970s came from the National Research Council, where Nestor Burtnyk and Marceli Wein became pioneers of computer animation development. In collaboration with French studio producer René Jodoin, NFB and the Council produced the acclaimed computer films *Metadata* (1971) and *Hunger* (1973), both directed by Hungarian artist Peter Fouldes.

Beyond that, there was little activity in Ottawa. Crawley Films, which had produced the TV-animation version of *The Wizard of Oz*, focussed on live-action films. In 1974, animator Vic Atkinson left Crawley to form Atkinson Film Arts with Bill Stevens. The studio produced a number of TV specials including *The Little Brown Burro* (1978).

Arguably the most significant happening in Ottawa during this period was the first Canadian International Animation Festival, which took place was in 1976. Founded by the Canadian Film Institute, the festival offered a week of screenings and panels. The Festival is still running and is now known at the Ottawa International Animation Festival (I am the current director).

Animation activity continued to evolve in Ottawa in the 1980s. After Atkinson left Film Arts, Stevens bought Crawley Films and merged the two studios. Throughout the decade, Crawley's animation produced children's specials, including *The Raccoons* and *Babar and Father Christmas,* and two televisions series, including *Dennis the Menace.* Other notable companies to emerge included Hinton Animation Studios (which took over *The Raccoons*) and KLA Visual Productions, a small operation run by the Atkinson family.

By the end of the 1980s, the Ottawa picture was not so rosy. While the animation festival had returned after turns in Hamilton and Toronto, the Hinton and Crawley studios ran into enormous debts and folded. Lacewood Animation Studios was formed in the late 1980s (by Sheldon Wiseman, the former head of Hinton) and continued to produce a flurry of mediocre television specials. Unfortunately, Lacewood went under, and Wiseman was locked out of the company's offices. Within a year, Toronto company Paragon Entertainment, which briefly took over Lacewood, went belly up. But Wiseman survived and today heads up Amberwood Productions.

Toronto

In Toronto, the animation community lived through a period of flux in the 1970s. Al Guest Studios, the biggest service studio, had just collapsed following a falling-out between Guest and Ralph Bakshi and Steve Krantz. Although Guest later made a 30-minute Inuit film (*Ukalik,* 1975), his tenure was at an end, as were the jobs of many Toronto animators. For a brief period, Cinera emerged as a saviour, but it accomplished little.

Fortunately, help came in the form of Nelvana. Today, Nelvana is one of the biggest animation companies in the world, but in 1971, it was five guys working in a dingy Toronto apartment. The three major players were artist Clive Smith, Patrick Loubert, and businessman Michael Hirsh; their first significant live-action/animation short was *Christmas Two Step* (1975), to which graduates from the animation course at Sheridan College had contributed. The film's success encouraged the trio to make a fully animated special, *Cosmic Christmas* (1977), which, thanks to the SF explosion of the time, became a massive international hit. More specials followed, including *The Devil and Daniel Mouse* (1978), *Intergalactic Thanksgiving* (1979), and a short animation for George Lucas' *Star Wars Holiday Special* (1977).

Things were looking up in Toronto. Thanks to Nelvana's success, Toronto's vastly talented but out-of-work animators found their calling. The road was now paved for Sheridan College, which soon emerged as the major animation school in the world. But Nelvana almost collapsed when it attempted to make a feature film. *Rock and Rule* (1983), like *Heavy Metal* (Potterton, 1976), merged a SF story with contemporary rock music, but it was a financial disaster for the studio and almost forced Nelvana into bankruptcy. Following the collapse, Nelvana turned strictly toward service work such as *The Care Bears* (1988) and *Babar* (1989). With the success of *Babar*, the studio turned to the production of children's programming and was off to the races.

Nelvana did not quite have a monopoly on the Toronto scene in the 1980s. Bob Fortier, a former Nelvana animator, opened up Animation House in 1983; and in 1987, Chris Wallace, Don Allen, and James Snelling formed TOPIX Computer Graphics and Animation (now known as Topix/Mad Dog).

Halifax

Until the mid 1990s, there wasn't much activity in Halifax. The major independent players were the Atlantic Filmmakers Co-operative and Ramona McDonald's Doomsday Studios. In the late 1970s, McDonald purchased an Oxberry camera from the CBC and, with her assistant Elaine Pain, began teaching people how to use it. One of the first people to make an animation short was James McSwain, a former actor, stage designer, and puppeteer. His first film was *Atomic Dragons* (1982), a collage piece. McDonald eventually left for Ottawa; McSwain went to Toronto in 1989 before returning to Halifax, where he continues to make short films.

The Animation Boom

Today, Nelvana and Cinar have established themselves as leaders in the mass production of children's television. While Canada boasts a variety of innovative commercial studios (Cuppa Coffee Animation, Head Gear, Mainframe Entertainment), software companies (Alias/Wavefront, Softimage, Side Effects), and special effects companies (C.O.R.E Digital), the animation landscape is dominated by a plenitude of service studios. As the market for animation has expanded, many service studios have turned toward original productions. But with few exceptions, most productions merely attempt to emulate the American norm.

Canada remains a pioneer and leader in computer animation. Softimage, Side Effects, C.O.R.E. Digital, Alias/Wavefront, Mainframe Entertainment, and most recently Nelvana have established themselves as prominent players in digital animation and special effects. In Montréal, a flurry of effects companies have started, including Hybride Technologies, Tube Images, Big Bang F/X Animation, Buzz Image Group, and Voodoo Arts. While most of the work is service oriented, Toronto's Alias/Wavefront, thanks in part to Chris Landreth, turned its tools to a pair of test shorts, *The End* (1996) and *Bingo* (1998), which became award-winning films. Landreth is one of the few computer animators to take the medium beyond technical experiments and into challenging, thoughtful critiques of human existence. His work at Alias/Wavefront combined stylish computer graphics with an intelligent, absurdist point of view to create two masterpieces of self-referential cinema. In April 2000, Landreth moved briefly to Nelvana to head up a new computer animation division; he left this position in 2001 and at the time of writing is in the early stages of a possible collaboration with the NFB.

While high-tech has dominated the animation landscape, there has also been a trend toward a more low-end, multi-media approach. This style encompasses live-action, photo-collage, cutout, and virtually every other technique. The pioneer of this trend is undoubtedly Toronto's Cuppa Coffee Animation. Founded in 1992 by Adam Shaheen and Bruce Alcock, Cuppa Coffee set the industry standard by selling bold, experimental graphics to advertisers and broadcasters. In just eight years, Cuppa Coffee has produced some landmark work, including commercials and promos for Much Music, Coca-Cola, Mazda, Bell Canada, and the Disney Channel; trailer films for the Ottawa 98 International Animation Festival and the Toronto Worldwide Short Film Festival; and two particularly creative children's shows, *Crashbox* and *Trevor*. Another Toronto-based company, Head Gear, was formed in 1997 by former Cuppa Coffee directors Julian Grey and Steve Angel. Head Gear specializes in the production of mixed-media techniques and has already made a handful of inspired spots for the Sundance Channel and Nestlé, as well as three very funny condom ads. C.O.R.E. Digital, primarily a computer-effects service house, ventured into proprietary production by co-producing the series *Angela Anaconda* in 1999. The show is a striking stylistic departure for television animation. Using a two-dimensional collage style with scanned photos, *Angela Anaconda* presents Angela and her not-so-perfect life with family, friends, teachers, and arch enemy Nanette Manoir.

The Educational Front

There has been much debate about the direction of colleges and universities. On the heels of the success of Sheridan College, various animation schools have sprung up all across the country. Vancouver Film School (founded in 1994), VanArts (founded in 1995), Seneca College, Capilano College, College-Interdec, and Algonquin College have met success with their animation or visual-arts programs and have become major recruiting sources for the likes of Nelvana, Cinar, and most of the American majors. Some commentators criticize training schools like Sheridan, Algonquin, and Vancouver Film School for simply mass-producing students as if they were factory workers. According to this critique, students are discouraged from conceptualizing or drawing freely, and instead are forced to adapt to an inflexible template that exists almost solely to meet the needs of major studios like Disney, Nelvana, and Warner Brothers.

At the same time, cutting-edge schools like Emily Carr and Concordia are producing work that is interesting but not risk-taking. Some of the most promising Emily Carr graduates include Sonia Bridge (*The Day Stashi Ran Out of Honey*, 1999) and Jakub Pistecky, whose film *Maly Milos* (Little Milosh, 1999) won the Best Canadian Student Film at the 1999 Ottawa International Student Animation Festival. *Milos* is a beautifully designed and well-told story but is decidedly mainstream, in the gothic tradition of Vincent Price and Tim Burton. Concordia has also produced a number of independent-oriented films over the years, but these films are rarely seen because of the school's ineffectiveness at self-promotion. Most recently, Anouck Prefontaine generated enthusiasm for her NFB-inspired film *Oh Lord* (1998).

Aside from Emily Carr and occasional individual films, Canadian student animation is not particularly inspiring. Many schools have started animation departments simply to cash in on the success of Sheridan and Vancouver Film School. But if the industry ever collapses, the students will be without work, lacking the proper training to evolve on their own.[3] As long as students are finding jobs and are content to accept a variety of unimaginative positions, it is doubtful that the quality of animation education will improve.

Independent Animation

Another area of concern in Canada, as it is throughout the world, is the state of independent animation. With government funding in decline, the NFB absorbing two decades of cuts, and the industry booming, it has become increasingly difficult for independent animators to make their films, let alone get them shown outside of a festival. Oddly enough, Canadian independent animation has arguably never been stronger. Cooperatives in Calgary, Halifax, and Ottawa in particular have, in the last decade, been key developers of Canadian film talent. For access to equipment and training at reasonable rates, many aspiring artists are turning to such institutions as an alternative to the increasing costs of post-secondary education. Additionally, while film schools tend to provide industrial training, co-ops afford an environment conducive to independent artists.

Calgary's Quickdraw Animation Society (QAS) was founded in 1984 and is a non-profit, artist-run centre committed to any type of animation. The co-op has nurtured animators such as Richard Reeves (*Linear Dreams,* 1997), Wayne Traudt (*Movements of the Body,* 1994), Carol Beecher (*Ask Me,* 1994), Kevin Kurytnik (*Abandon Bob Hope, All Ye Who Enter,* 1998), and Don Best (*Raw,* 1996), and has emerged as a leading producer of "alternative" animation in Canada.

While Halifax's Atlantic Filmmakers Co-Op is not animation-specific, a small group of animators has emerged from it, most notably Helen Hill, a former California Institute of the Arts student who until recently taught courses at the AFC and the Nova Scotia College of Art and Design. Hill has fashioned a deceptively pared-down body of works best described as quirky and unpretentious personal journeys into lands that are foreign and exotic yet strangely familiar. Hill's most recent film, *Mouseholes* (1999), is a moving, comic-poetic tribute to her grandfather that merges cut-out and live-action with actual interviews between the filmmaker and her grandfather, and snippets of dialogue from his funeral. Sadly, Hill is returning to her home in the US, and the future of Halifax independent animation will be in question without her enormous, influential presence.

An independent scene is slowly emerging in Ottawa thanks to the Independent Filmmakers Co-operative of Ottawa (IFCO). Brian McPhail has produced two deliriously demented films: *Stiffy* (1996; it toured in 1997 with the Spike and Mike Animation Festival and was then put into development as a TV series for the Comedy Network) and *Down a Dark Chimney* (1999). Calvin Climie is currently at work on a stop-motion film, and Dan Sokolowski, a noted experimental filmmaker and a major influence on the Ottawa filmmaking scene, continues to merge elements of animation and live-action into his picturesque landscape films.

South of Ottawa, in a town called Toronto, the animation scene remains primarily industry-dominated, but thanks to the efforts of Patrick Jenkins and others, there seems to be a revival in independent animation production through the re-formation of the Toronto Animated Image Society (TAIS). Most recently, veteran animator Arnie Lipsey screened his film *Almonds and Wine* at a variety of festivals. The Toronto scene in particular will be exciting to watch over the next few years as TAIS shifts from an information provider to a producer of independent short animated films.

Beyond cooperatives, a few animators have furnished careers primarily on their own with minimal government support. Gail Noonan has been making films in British Columbia since 1989 but has found festival success with recent films *Your Name in Cellulite* (1995) and *The Menopause Song* (1996). While *Menopause* lightly celebrates the joys of menstruation, *Your Name* is a damning comment of the mass media's perception of women's beauty. Noonan's latest film, *Lost and Found* (1999), is a tale about two children who encounter "homeless" people. Stephen Arthur, who has made experimental films since 1969, has a diverse background that includes feature-film scriptwriting and neurobiology. In recent years he has turned toward surreal, exploratory works. *Transfigured* (1998) brought movement and interaction to Canadian painter Jack Shadbolt's work, while Arthur's latest film, *Vision Point* (1999), is a photo-animated journey through western Canada.

In an attempt to bridge the gap between commercial and independent animators, a few companies have turned to producing independent short films. Montréal's Pascal Blais Productions, a commercial studio that has worked with the likes of Caroline Leaf and Cordell Barker, co-produced the short film *The Old Lady and the Pigeons* (Chomet, 1998). The film was met with re-sounding success at festivals around the world and brought a new respect to the Blais studios. More recently, Blais partnered with Russian animator Alexander Petrov to create a 22-minute IMAX animation based on Ernest Hemingway's *The Old Man and the Sea*. Aside from a variety of awards, including the Oscar, Petrov's adaptation has attracted thousands of spectators to this "independent" film. Whether studio-sponsored short films prove an adequate venue for independent animators remains to be seen, but they do provide an interesting option.

While the Canada Council has re-emerged as a strong supporter of Canadian artists, the government on the whole has shown more interest in backing industrial projects. In 1997, the Ontario government gave Sheridan College a $12-million grant to open a new-technology centre. This move was meant to benefit the Ontario industry, but most of the students will likely travel to the US to find more lucrative work. More disturbing still was the government's tax subsidy for the creation of Disney's studios in Toronto and Vancouver (both recently closed). The Ontario provincial government introduced a tax-credit system, but it encourages only the production of computer animation or special effects.

The major problem for Canadian animators remains distribution. Despite the emergence of Teletoon, an dedicated animation channel, and new opportunities in home video and the Internet, the festival circuit remains the leading source for viewing non-mainstream animation. The Ottawa International Animation Festival, now North America's largest animation festival, has managed, despite heavy government cuts, to remain a primary supporter of independent animation while carving out a place for the industry. In recent years, animation festivals have started in Vancouver and Halifax, and another animation festival has sprung up in Ottawa; all are devoted to student and emerging animators.

Until recently, two favourite topics of the Canadian media were the low Canadian dollar and the so-called brain drain, which has seen Canadian professionals from hockey players and actors to writers and doctors lured to the US by increased opportunities and a higher dollar. Animation in particular has been affected. Virtually every American studio houses Canadians. Some of the more prominent émigrés include John Kricfalusi (*Ren and Stimpy*) and Steve Williams (the digital guru behind *Jurassic Park*). When Disney announced it was opening studios in Vancouver and Toronto in 1995, it said the decision was based on the legendary reputation of Canadian animators. While there is some truth in that statement, the reality is that, in addition to tax subsidies, Disney hoped to take advantage of the Canadian dollar. In essence, Canada was serving as an animation sweatshop. The currency differential has evolved into a complex situation, since if the Canadian dollar rises to par with the US dollar, we will likely find that, despite our reputation for quality, most Canadian studios will be out of work. At the same time, as long as the dollar is low, Canadian studios will continue to offer primarily service work to American companies.

The Scandals

The year 2000, in which most of this article was written, was fraught with turmoil for Canadian animation. First, Disney announced it was closing its studios in Vancouver and Toronto; some 400 people were laid off. The official word came in March 2000, but insiders had known since late summer 1999. Publicly, Disney said it no longer felt pressure to meet production deadlines. In the end, no one cared. Nelvana and other studios picked up the jobless, and Disney walked away with minimal damage thanks to a tax break that eased any possible financial pains. Everybody won except the Canadian taxpayer.

On 29 May 2000, the *Globe and Mail* published a scathing portrait of Vancouver's animation industry. As if scripted by Dickens, an anonymous animator told of the long hours, mundane work, and fear of losing one's job: "Work is so desperate that people will do anything to stay on. People are working themselves to death." In typical Canadian fashion, there was minimal reaction to this article (the hockey playoffs were on), but one animator did say that "[i]t's possible that the industry's in a slump at the moment, but why make it look so awful and smell so bad?" Another responded that this was the first time the media had portrayed the industry in a negative light and that it was about time truths were told.

There is some legitimacy to that claim. For too long, we have heard about the wonders of the animation industry. It is akin to the Klondike Gold Rush of the 1800s, when desperate men from across the continent travelled to the far reaches of northern Canada in the hopes of finding gold. Some did; most did not. In animation, the rush is very much over, but the schools continue to churn out "factory workers"; where they go, nobody knows. One thing is certain: they are not going to animation studios. Animation schools continue to boast about their high job-placement rates, but the students are working briefly on projects before being displaced into unskilled jobs. The animation industry, at least in Canada, had become an illusion of prosperity, diversity, and opportunity; people were rapidly becoming disillusioned.

But things got worse. The biggest scandal since Canada held off the US attacks of 1812 occurred when the media learned not only that Cinar Animation was fudging its numbers to gain federal tax credits, but also that some $122 million was invested in a Bahamas investment fund without the board's knowledge. The controversies led to the drop of Cinar stock by 70 percent in a single day, the removal of Cinar from the market listings, and the resignation of the company's blissfully married founders, Micheline Charest and Ronald Weinberg.

The first scandal broke in the fall of 1999 when a Canadian politician accused Cinar of falsely crediting Canadians for the work of Americans in order to receive government subsidies. Over a five-year period in the mid 1990s, Cinar received more than $50 million in tax benefits. It was eventually determined that Hélène Charest, sister of Québec Liberal leader Jean Charest, was listed on more than 100 episodes she didn't write. Given the many loud whispers that this is common practice, one might think a less-obvious name could have been invented. Since this time, federal funding organization Telefilm Canada has stopped all transactions with Cinar (strangely, one Cinar board member is from Telefilm Canada), and Cinar is still negotiating with the federal tax department to repay the misused funds.

The second scandal arose less than six months later when an improper use of company funds was discovered. The stories initially reported that Senior Executive Vice-President Hasanain Panju had made offshore dealings without board knowledge, but the scapegoat soon changed when it was discovered that Weinberg had actually signed some of the transfers. This internal scandal has evolved into an intricate web of lawsuits and accusations that has seen Cinar banned from the Toronto Stock Exchange. Private investors are now thinking carefully before investing in the animation industry. As one observer tells it: "What if the production I invest in doesn't even get their funding because they don't qualify for government subsidies? My investment will have crashed without ever having left the ground."

For our purposes, the alleged misuse of tax credits is the bigger story. The Cinar scandal erupted during another government department screw-up, and opposition politicians began accusing the government of lazy tax policies. Fuelling matters was the presence of a Telefilm Canada executive on Cinar's board and Cinar's close relationship with the governing Liberals.

The scandal re-opened the issue of cultural funding and tax incentives to business, and prompted loud right-wing calls for a dismantling of tax subsidies to the Canadian film and television industry. As one insider pointed out, "With all the cuts to other public sectors—health, education, welfare, etc.—there is a public outcry over funding large wealthy companies. The film-funding institutions are having an even harder time justifying funding film production, when there are so many more popular worthy causes demanding attention." The right wing was not alone in its complaints. In the US, members of the Motion Picture Screen Cartoonists Union came out in full force in spring 2000 to complain about jobs being lost to Canadian companies because of generous tax subsidies. Many Canadians, of course, viewed these complaints with skepticism.

Montréal in particular has been hit hard by the scandals. Cinar has laid off many employees, and studio morale is low. With the exception of CineGroupe, Montréal studios were not hiring in 2000. That year saw Montréal lose a lot of talent to competitors like Nelvana and Funbag. But despite the scandals, the turn of the century marked one of the most successful periods in Canadian animation history. Cinar was expected to rise from this crisis stronger than before, and it seemed unlikely the rest of the industry would suffer because of the actions of one company. Nelvana and Cinar continue to produce a barrage of successful international children's entertainment, while Ottawa's Funbag Animation Studios, which recently expanded its operations to Halifax, is growing and soon will rival Nelvana and Cinar.

What is disturbing, especially in light of the Cinar scandal, is the trend towards public investment in private profit. Canadian taxpayers are funding educational institutions to train students for export. This fact makes the government ransacking of the NFB all the more frustrating. Regardless whether one thinks McLaren was a genius or an artsy wanker, the current success of the Canadian animation industry simply would not have happened if not for the NFB. The NFB has garnered awards from all over the world for its animation and attracted animators from around the globe to Canada (including Derek Lamb, Kaj Pindal, Gerald Potterton, Paul Driessen, Ishu Patel, Co Hoedeman, who, a cynic might add, all took advantage of a free ride), but it has done much more. The NFB, along with the National Research Council, laid the foundations for the Canadian computer-animation scene, now among the most respected in the world. Internationally, Cinar and Nelvana are two of the most sought-after co-production partners. Would this be the case without the NFB, who fostered co-production initiatives long before either company materialized? Would the Ottawa International Animation Festival be so prominent without the NFB? Of course not; but the modern mind suffers from a twentieth-century ailment known as historical amnesia, quickly forgetting the long-term investment made by the NFB. Thanks to the NFB, companies like Nelvana, Cinar, and Funbag benefit from Canada's status.

Perhaps more than any other country, Canada has shown there is room for both art and industry, and suggested both be embraced, in moderation. For more than forty years, Canada has been privy to an environment that has produced innovative, creative animation. Ironically, because of this success, animation has become a major industry in Canada, at the expense of independent work. For years there were no opportunities for Canadian animators; now they are abundant. But the boom can't go on forever, and it seems the current imbalance will eventually level out. Perhaps this will even lead to a yet richer and stronger animation community, if one believes the words of the philosopher Heraclitus, who said, "Opposition brings concord. Out of discord comes the greatest harmony."

Where is here? Canadian literary critic Northrop Frye once noted that this question pervades Canadian culture. It also applies to Canadian animation; but unlike other facets of Canadian culture (literature, music, painting) and very much like hockey, there was once a sense of where *here* was. Before 1972 and the historic series with the Russians, hockey was a Canadian game. Before the 1980s, Canadian animation was the National Film Board of Canada. Just as hockey is now flourishing as an international and increasingly Americanized business, so too is animation. Where once there was certainty, there were also limitations; where now there is uncertainty and fragmentation, there are possibilities. Like hockey, which is "re-invented at the drop of every puck," Canadian animation is reborn with every drawing, print-out, scan, cut-out, or scratch. Canada, perhaps the first postmodern country, is a constantly shifting space where here is also out there, anywhere.

Notes

Thanks to Heidi Bohme for her research assistance, with acknowledgments to Karen Mazurkewich, Ellen Besen, Marc Glassman, Tom McSorley, Marv Newland and Mark Freedman, Trish Stolte, Gene Walz, Leslie Bishko, Gordon Martin, Joan Kim, Kelly Neall, and Keith and Francine Daniels. Portions of this article appeared as "Whose Golden Age?: Canadian Animation in the 1990s" in *Animation World Magazine*, June 1998 and "Here is There is Anywhere: Canadian Animation at the Turn of the Century" in *Animation World Magazine*, August 2000. Unattributed quotations derive from personal communications with individuals in the animation field who requested anonymity.

1   Ian Angus, *A Border Within: National Identity, Cultural Plurality, and Wilderness* (Montréal: McGill-Queen's University Press, 1997), 11.

2   Interview with Ellen Besen, July 1998.

3   The government must assume the brunt of the blame for this situation. Its systematic dismantling of education funding has forced schools to find new sources of revenue. More often than not, these avenues involve corporate sponsorship and, with it, an industrial makeover of the institution's aims.

Shack-Wacky Animation
The Case of Manitoba
Gene Walz

IN 1972, A MINORITY GOVERNMENT WAS VOTED INTO OFFICE in the Canadian federal elections. One of the many deals made after the election was an agreement to disperse government-controlled cultural artifacts and agencies more equitably throughout the country. Thus, both policy and funding were established for the "regionalization" of museums, archives, committees, and, most notably, the production facilities of the National Film Board (NFB). That same year, the Pacific Regional Production Office of the NFB opened in Vancouver. Two years later, the Atlantic Production Office was launched in Halifax and the Prairie Production Office in Winnipeg, with a branch office soon established in Edmonton. With a Toronto office set up in 1975 and the Edmonton office achieving independence in 1980, the regionalization of the NFB was complete.[1]

Although this dispersal of government-sponsored filmmaking was seen by some inside the NFB as an easy and logical extension of its Challenge for Change program of the 1960s, regionalization did not meet with overwhelming approval. Some predicted it would kill the NFB, that the splitting of resources was not cost-effective and would lead to an inevitable demise in quality and output; others said it would significantly reduce the studio effect of the NFB's Montréal headquarters. The complaints about the regions themselves were numerous: no self-respecting filmmaker would want to work there (especially in Winnipeg!); films made there would dilute, parochialize, and amateurize the NFB's catalogue and reputation; filmmakers in the regions would be forced to reinvent the wheel continually.

Twenty-five years later, it is clear the Jeremiahs were mistaken. Regionalization has been an undeniable success—at least in the case of the Prairie Regional Production Office. Not only is the list of award-winning NFB films made in Winnipeg lengthy, but the Prairie Office's innovations, particularly in marketing, pushed the NFB in new directions.

Regionalization brought to the NFB gifted filmmakers and craftspeople who would otherwise not have worked in the business, and allowed these people to work on subjects of local, national, and international interest that would not have been filmed—or not in the same unique ways. Most importantly, the NFB became the linchpin in the creation of a community of professional filmmakers, many of whom have gone on to distinguished careers. Nowhere is this as evident as it is in animation.

A modest groundwork had already been laid for NFB animation when Jerry Krepakevitch and Mike Scott, the first Prairie Region executive producers, set up shop in Winnipeg in the mid 1970s, determined to make animated films and dramas rather than just the traditional NFB social and educational documentaries. There was also a discontinuous but not inestimable history of film animation in the city that stretched back to the early part of the twentieth century. Still, it was a surprise to many when the Prairie Region started to make animated movies. And it continues to amaze some people that three Winnipeg films have been nominated for Academy Awards for Best Animated Film, that two of these films have been listed among the top fifteen films of all time, and that an amusing documentary called *Cel-Mates* (directed by Derek Mazur, 1992) was made to celebrate the talents of three Winnipeg animators.[2]

Winnipeg, like Kansas City where Walt Disney got his start, is not as unlikely a place for animation as it might seem. As a major transportation centre, especially in the early decades of the twentieth century, it has been directly connected to the latest cultural developments yet isolated enough on the vast Canadian prairies to have to rely on its own resources. Among the most ethnically diverse communities on the continent, the city has long cultivated a "we'll-show-you" attitude in the arts, supporting the Royal Winnipeg Ballet, a diverse and long-standing theatre tradition, and a storied musical history which includes everything from the Guess Who and the Crash Test Dummies to a symphony orchestra and an annual musical festival featured in an NFB film in the 1940s. This attitude was literalized by James Freer, the first Canadian to make movies in Canada. In 1897, he began filming scenes and events on and near his farm in western Manitoba to take to England to encourage immigration.

More importantly for animation than for other arts and other kinds of film, Winnipeg is a centre of commerce, providing ready opportunities for advertising and promotional work in graphic design, illustration, and animation. When Eaton's, the once-supreme Canadian merchandising company now fatally diminished, expanded beyond Toronto in 1905, it enticed its graphic design firm, Brigden's, to open a branch plant in Winnipeg as well. A company of illustrators, photographers, and engravers whose chief responsibility was to produce semi-annual mail-order catalogues, Brigden's employed some of Canada's best artists, art teachers, cartoonists, and even a few animators. Later in the century, because of its size, isolation, and tough-sell mentality, Winnipeg became a favoured test market for multi-national corporations—with an attendant increase in specialty, narrow-cast advertising.

Winnipeg's Animation Archaeology

The oldest existing piece of animated film made in Winnipeg is ample proof of animation's commercial connection. In 1919, the Federated Budget Board (a precursor of the United Way appeals) commissioned a promotional film entitled *The Man Who Woke Up*. Written by William Ganson Rose and directed by J.A. Norling, this live-action silent film tells the story of a wealthy miser who refuses to give to charities. A visit to a hospital full of sick children (tuberculosis and the devastating 1918 influenza epidemic provide the background to the film, as do the lack of any formalized government-assistance programs for health emergencies) reunites the man with his lost, orphaned granddaughter. Back home, he falls asleep, and his dream is presented as a blue-tinted animated insert. "In cartoonology," as the National Film Archives' cataloguer quaintly describes it, the miser "sees the charities closed, the hospital closed, and awakens to the horrible realisation that if he does not give, these terrible things might become a reality." The characters in this dream sequence are drawn realistically rather than as surreal or comical figures, and the animation is convincing, if minimal.[3]

While the existing print of *The Man Who Woke Up* confirms Rose and Norling's place as the mysterious grandfathers of Winnipeg animation, they did have a predecessor. Jean Arsin, a local stringer for Fox Movietone News, which provided short news films for North American theatrical release, used his spare time to create animated movies. According to pioneer industrial filmmaker Francis J.S. (Frank) Holmes, Arsin made crude animated movies featuring articulated puppets around 1910 or 1911 in a tar-paper shack on a sandlot in the fabled north end of the city. Unfortunately, as with most movies of that era, no evidence of these early works now seems to exist.

The most ambitious animated movie ever made in Winnipeg has also disappeared. In 1926, Charles Lambley created a twenty- to twenty-five-minute film called *Romulus and Remus*, commissioned, oddly enough, by the Montréal Catholic Diocese. The film was noteworthy for its artwork. Frank Holmes, who assisted Lambley on the project, was impressed by the beautiful showcard cut-outs used for the characters and the cleverness of the movable neck, arm, and leg joints.

Holmes used the lessons he learned from Lambley to animate a portion of his own film, *Each Year They Come*, an amusing piece about waterfowl migration made for Ducks Unlimited in 1946. While his mentor Lambley's animation was European in subject matter and style, Holmes took his inspiration from American puppet and cel animation. Simple and colourful, yet more realistic than the comically individuated Donald and Daffy, Holmes' ducks sang and danced in the animated segment of this otherwise straightforward live-action film. The results were mixed; the blue-collar filmmaker never again tried to impose his kind of animation on a client's films. Like other kinds of films made across Canada in the first half of the twentieth century, animated films in Winnipeg were hit and miss. There was no continuity of production, no development of the art, and no sense that animation was actively cultivating an appreciative audience.[4]

This trend changed when two young graphic artists formed their own small production company to take advantage of new developments in the post-war economy. By the time nation-wide television came to Canada in the early 1950s, John Phillips and Harry Gutkin had completed several short promotional films, including a film about prairie co-ops called *What's Co-operation All About?* It was half live-action and half animated. Rudimentary in design and structure, the movie is significant mainly because it forced Phillips Gutkin and Associates (PGA) to invest in a now-historic animation stand. The stand and the experience they gained using it meant they were able to compete with Toronto for the lucrative national TV-commercial market.

Phillips and Gutkin's animation breakthrough was the account for Libby's Foods. Their ads began airing during the premiere of National Movie Night on CBC television in 1954. Their first commercial was, in trade parlance, a "sandwich": the opening and closing sequences involved animation of Libby's Quality-Control Cops while the middle part contained live-action shots of pitchmen and foods. Within a year, the company had to hire more employees. The company averaged fifteen to thirty commercials per month, most of them either "sandwiches" or limited animation spots in the quirky, spare UPA (United Productions of America) style that was very popular at that time. Their national account included Kellogg's Cereal, Kraft Foods, Chrysler Corporation, Simonize Wax, Blue Ribbon Tea, and the Bank of Canada. Most of these clients required exclusively Canadian ads; Kraft, Libby's, and Windsor Salt spots also appeared on American television.

Although the ads used minimal animation, the commitments were overwhelming. At its peak, PGA needed more than thirty animators working full-time to keep up with the pace.[5] This made it one of the largest animation houses in the country, with enough clout to forge a trans-Atlantic alliance with John Halas and Joy Batchelor, England's premier animators at the time. It might have been the first international co-production deal in Canadian film history.

In 1960, Harry Gutkin and John Halas worked out a plan to alternate production of a weekly animated television show between London and Winnipeg. Called *T. Eddy Bear*, the half-hour se-ries was to be based on a set of children's books that Gutkin had published and one of his PGA animators, Ray Darby, had created. Although the menagerie of circus animals was cute and the UPA-style animation colourful and inventive, the pilot program did not have enough drama or humour to engage much interest. The *T. Eddy Bear* project collapsed, the beginning of the end for PGA. By 1966, the modest "golden age" of Winnipeg animation was over.

Fortunately, the PGA animation stand was purchased by Kenn Perkins, who needed it to film *A Brief History of Astronomy* for Winnipeg's Museum of Man and Nature. Perkins quickly became the king of the K-tel commercials. It was at his animation shop that Cordell Barker, Brad Caslor, and others learned their craft. They swept floors and emptied wastebaskets there just to get a chance to see their own cels under the Bolex camera on the old animation stand. Perkins, still regularly cranking out Chicken Delight ads and now relying heavily on computer graphics, is the necessary link between animation's glorious past and its current ascendance.

Kids Watch the Darnedest Things

Winnipeg's animators would likely have been confined to strictly commercial projects were it not for a national decision to Canadianize the immensely popular American television show *Sesame Street*. The Canadian version of *Sesame Street* was a great boost for regional animation. Twenty minutes per day of the heavily urban, New York City-oriented show were excised by CBC television and replaced by Canadian-made content: French lessons instead of Spanish; "zeds" instead of "zees" in the alphabet; Canadian locations, folklore, cultural allusions, and eth-nic peoples rather than American. Throughout the 1970s and '80s, Winnipeg animators, both freelancers and in-house CBC employees, provided upwards of forty animation spots per year to *Sesame Street*. These spots varied in length from about twenty seconds to as long as two minutes, and each segment was broadcast twice a year.

Sesame Street animation is simple concept animation. Probably familiar to all parents, children, and daycare workers of the last three decades, the *Sesame Street* format places a premium on two dimensions and screen centre; on brevity, spareness, and clarity; and on ease of recognition. The spots have a clear throughline and rely on repetition rather than amplification or complication, caricature rather than characterization; they are anecdotal rather than incremental. But as Brad Caslor's one-minute story about the invention of snowshoes and Richard Condie's zany num-bers games illustrate, *Sesame Street* animation can still be charming and memorable. As zippy, witty, and captivating as good commercials (clearly their models), the animations frequently as-pire to classic moments from the golden age of American animation or even, occasionally, to cinematic haiku: brief, highly structured, but poignant vignettes.

Sesame Street's value to the Winnipeg animation community lies in the fact that it has allowed beginners like Jason Doll, Anita Lebeau, and Patrick Lowe a chance to test themselves and develop their craft. More experienced animators like Neil McInnes, Bill Stewart, and Andrew Schultz used it to perfect their squash-and-stretch techniques, and Dave Strang and Alan Pakarnyk use it to experiment with computer animation within a limited but demanding framework. More importantly, *Sesame Street* has meant that the Winnipeg community has been able to keep busy between other major commitments—such as contracts provided by the Prairie Production Office of the NFB.

The NFB Comes to Winnipeg

When the NFB arrived in 1974, three of Kenn Perkins' young animation assistants—Brad Caslor, Chris Hinton, and Richard Condie—were among the first local filmmakers recruited. Already somewhat experienced on *Sesame Street*, Caslor and Hinton tackled three manageable, one-minute animated histories as their initial NFB projects. *Fort Prince of Wales* and *Spense's Republic*, both by Caslor, are perfectly timed and expertly designed depictions of amusing moments in Manitoba's past: the surrender of a military bastion on Hudson Bay without a shot and the dissolution of a ranch-sized, private "empire." Hinton's *Lady Frances Simpson* is a much more frenetic and exaggerated account of the arrival of the province's first piano by canoe. Because of the massive exposure these three vignettes got filling unsold advertising slots on local television, they signalled in no uncertain terms the revival of Winnipeg animation.

Caslor and Hinton's second project was also determinedly regional. *Blowhard* (1978) is an amusing satire about a profiteering easterner who depletes the fire-breathing dragon population of a prairie region and exploits lax government regulations to heat his oversized castles. Made for the NFB's *Renewable Society* series, the film not only addressed the environmental concerns of the day but also gained some additional bite by capturing the western alienation that still simmers today. *Blowhard* and a few non-animation films served notice to NFB headquarters that the Prairie Production Office was an independent and even feisty operation.

A collector of American cartoons from the 1930s and '40s, Caslor used them as source materials on his next project, a solo venture, because Hinton moved out of province. *Get a Job* began as a short, animated training film for Canada Manpower. Originally inspired by Disney's how-to films—in which the unstoppable Goofy comically provides lessons in various sports and occupations—the film morphed into a music-filled compendium of classic animation characters, gags, and techniques (an homage especially to the squash-and-stretch antics of Bob Clampett and Tex Avery) and pop-culture allusions to everything from Elvis to the Andrew Sisters, soap operas, and even K-tel ads. Characterized by an undercurrent of bleak terror about the process of job-seeking and capped by a cynical ending in which the stumpy, adolescent Bob Dog gets a job offer by phone from his father, *Get a Job* is an energetic and clever postmodern pastiche rather than a cheery instructional film. Its seven-year gestation period pays off in every vivid frame but seems to have exhausted or intimidated the filmmaker. *Get a Job* won a Genie award for best animated film in Canada for 1986, but Caslor has since abandoned animation for film editing, a keen loss to the animation world. His body of work—dozens of TV commercials and *Sesame Street* inserts and four NFB films—has a professional's sense of pace and design, a mastery of American cel-animation techniques, and a uniquely personal cast of characters and tone. Even a truncated career such as Caslor's underlines the importance of regional cinema.

Winnipeg's Animation Superstars

A longer-lasting and more prolific animator, Richard Condie was already at work on an independent film called *Oh Sure* when the NFB arrived in Winnipeg. The NFB provided funding for this funny, slight, conventionally drawn riff on adolescent one-upmanship and then immediately financed *John Law and the Mississippi Bubble* (1978), a more mature yet still humorous examination of the introduction of paper money to France. Although these two early works did not demonstrate Condie's distinctive character design, his wavy-line style, or the full range of his sense of humour, they did establish two themes central to his subsequent work: arrested development and the weird fragility of life.

Condie's first major movie examines ten minutes in the afternoon of a restless pianist who can't settle down to practise for a concert. *Getting Started* (1982) is clearly based on personal experiences, but it is also delightfully universal. Alone in his vast parlour with a grand piano, a television, a friendly mouse, a ladybug, and a maddeningly ticking cuckoo clock, Eugene the pianist can barely get past two bars of Debussy before some self-generated distraction pulls him away. Although the film is remarkable for the precise and varied "camera positions" arranged by the cels' framing, *Getting Started* has the feel of a fly-on-the-wall documentary or a surveillance film in which an unsuspecting subject reveals his most adolescent idiosyncrasies.

As hilarious as the distractions are (Eugene puts a soda can on his nose and sings "Strangers in the Night" to a mouse, bashes himself with the clock's lead pendulum, and picks his ears), the film presents an undertone of melancholy. Behind the comedy are loneliness, isolation, and pain. This tone is mainly what distinguishes Condie from his Manitoba colleagues and elevates him to the higher ranks of the world's animators. As resourceful a comedian as he is, each of his movies contains a dark, serious, almost contemplative undercurrent. This depth is particularly evident in his most famous movie, *The Big Snit* (1985).

The Big Snit is the story of a middle-aged suburban couple who argue over a game of Scrabble. The wife accuses her husband of cheating at the game; he complains that she is constantly "shaking her eyes." She goes off to clean the bathtub with a vacuum cleaner while he turns on his favourite TV show, *Sawing for Teens*, and saws some furniture. Their cat packs a suitcase and leaves. Romantic memories reunite them just as the world ends in nuclear holocaust.

An absurdist examination of love and marriage more fanciful than Ionesco's plays and more profound than American sitcoms (yet with echoes of both), *The Big Snit* has been compared favourably to the best work of Woody Allen and Monty Python. With its fleeting critiques of television and society and an ending as blackly humorous as *Dr. Strangelove*, the film, despite its zaniness, possesses an underlying seriousness and melancholy that give it a dimension usually lacking in North American cartoons. A favourite of film festivals around the world, *The Big Snit* won more than a dozen awards, including an Oscar nomination.

With the success of *The Big Snit*, a brief instructional film that Condie made for Canada Customs, intended to warn air travellers of the dangers of smuggling, was released to a wider audience. Called *Pigbird* (1982), after the strange creature that is sneaked past airport customs officials only to release deadly bugs that quickly destroy the smuggler's house, neighbourhood, country, and ultimately the planet, the three-minute film is both ridiculous and apocalyptic. Like Brad Caslor's *Get a Job*, it transcends and perhaps even undermines its intended purpose.

Pigbird is a showcase of Condie's rich and distinctive sense of humour. He does not generate laughs in the usual cartoon ways, avoiding especially the squash-and-stretch gags of traditional cel animation. As the title character (a hybrid creature with the head and skin of a pig and the legs and body of a chicken) indicates, uniquely funny-looking characters are the centrepieces of his comedy. His comic worlds are dominated by middle-aged males with pin-heads, six wispy, stand-up hairs, beady eyes, oversize bulbous or tubular noses, and rounded, clattery buck teeth. Their exaggerated behaviour runs the gamut from slapstick and pratfalls to adolescent silliness, non sequiturs, and tastelessness. Nervous and isolated, they are the animated equivalents of the prairie geeks who populate the so-called prairie postmodern films released by the Winnipeg Film Group in the 1980s and '90s.

Condie, however, has less in common with his live-action Manitoban colleagues than with Vancouver's Marv Newland (although he is not quite as profane and anarchic), American underground favourite Bill Plympton (although he is not as surreal or meta-animatic), and especially Paul Driessen (although he is not as ironic and dark). Like these filmmakers, Condie has been a constant experimenter, refusing to repeat himself, regularly moving on to new challenges. In this regard, he has been the best filmmaker to exploit the resources of the NFB. He became the first person to produce animation in the 70-mm IMAX format, partitioning the 5-storey screen into smaller segments to present comic vignettes about life in Manitoba. His section of IMAX's *Heart Land* (1987) was the only one to paint a negative image of the province; the rest of the live-action film was a relentlessly upbeat, chamber-of-commerce portrait of the province's tourist attractions and trade opportunities.

After his *Heart Land* animation, Condie experimented with narrative and sound in the deliberately enigmatic *The Apprentice* (1991). A series of cryptic black-out sketches, the film tells the story of a tolerant medieval magician who allows his young, naïve knight to learn life's hard lessons on his own, when even the flowers laugh derisively at the knight's failures. *The Apprentice* makes unusual demands on its audience, especially after the clear and easy humour of *The Big Snit* and *Pigbird*. The story is strange and elliptical, and the soundtrack does not clarify its meaning. Dialogue is suggestive rather than decipherable, like a child's playful attempt at a weird universal "language" (it was concocted out of gargling noises sampled on a computer).

Condie took his computer experiments to their natural conclusion for *La Salla* (1996). Abandoning cels completely, he learned computer animation (Soft Image 3-D version 3.0) from scratch. *La Salla* retains his distinctively oddball character designs and *mise en scène* while continuing his other experiments with narrative, sound, and point of view. The story of *La Salla* is virtually non-existent, pared down to a random series of comic routines. A typically Condie-esque man-child, bulbous-nosed and self-absorbed, plays with a weird collection of toys in a small room. His attention is periodically drawn away from his toys (a mechanical fish, a strange 3-D combination of TV and etch-a-sketch, and a cannon that shoots toy cows instead of armaments) to the room's only door, as if something ominous is luring him away from his bizarre games. At the end, a giant, look-alike character peers into the room; the game-playing occupant is merely a toy in another character's game.

Similar to all his previous films in its contrast between enclosed, personal space and the external world, *La Salla* explores the dimensions of its setting rigorously. Because it is a staged performance rather than a series of drawn and painted cels, Condie could play with a moveable "camera" and with sources and intensities of illumination. As a result, light, shadows, foreground, and background are more pronounced, creating a sense of claustrophobia and menace perfectly in keeping with the film's dark themes.

More sophisticated in its manipulation of three-dimensional space than *Toy Story* and other computer-generated films from Pixar, and more complicated in its animation because of its wavy-line style, *La Salla* is also more varied in its comedic resourcefulness. Once again, conventional spoken dialogue is eschewed, here replaced by an operatic recitative sung by the main character. One of the film's typically oddball recitative lines occurs when the main character shoots a toy cow from his cannon. "Moments ago I had everything," he sings. "Now there's a cow in my nose."

A development on his earlier films in visual design and tonal texture, *La Salla* echoes *Getting Started* as a self-reflexive parable. Like the piano player, the man-child playing obsessively with his toys is not so terribly far away from the animation artist playing at his computer: trapped in a room, wishing to be elsewhere, and trying to make the best of it. Particularly resonant on the Canadian prairies, this unique brand of cabin-fever animation found a wider audience because of its rare mixture of comedy and paranoia, silliness and high art, wacky humour and aesthetic ambition. Condie himself hinted at the broad range of *La Salla's* appeal by describing it as a combination of *Genesis-2* and *Paradise Lost*. Nominated for an Academy Award, it lost out to a far less demanding piece of animation.

A film that Condie co-produced met with a similar close-but-no-cigar fate. Like Condie's films, Cordell Barker's *The Cat Came Back* (1988) was nominated for an Academy Award that went elsewhere; like *Get a Job* and *The Big Snit*, it too won a Genie for best animation. Based on a folk song popularized by Winnipeg children's performer Fred Penner, *The Cat Came Back* is a series of slapstick sketches of an escalating war between a destructive cat and the lonely man who tries to get rid of it. There is an obvious American influence—notably Chuck Jones' Roadrunner and Wile E. Coyote chase sequences, which this film cleverly reverses. But the film has a decidedly Canadian flavour, recalling the immensely popular sing-along films from the *Let's All Sing Together* series initiated by Norman McLaren at the NFB in the 1940s. And Condie's influence is unmistakable: from the subtly coloured backgrounds to the geeky character design and over-modulated soundtrack full of ripping noises and exasperated, guttural wails. Barker reused the characters in an NFB trailer and a British advertising campaign. Since then, he has been resourceful in exploiting commercial markets, creating memorable, award-winning ads for Nike, Bell Telephone, and Chlor-Tripolon cold medicines, and working regularly for Les Productions Pascal Blais, a Québec company with a growing reputation for animated ads and feature films.

In 2001 he took a break from advertising to complete *Strange Invaders*, a metaphoric comedy about the effects of a demanding and disruptive little creature on the lives of a complacent urban couple. As in *The Cat Came Back*, this comedy gets many of its laughs from the weird reactions of the couple and the persistence of their tormentor, but it is more resourceful, wider ranging, and often darker and more adult in its humour than its predecessor. With different character design, brilliant coloration, and rigorous pacing, *Strange Invaders* opens new areas for development in the comedy of victimization that Barker is refining. Its Oscar nomination (beaten again by a Pixar short) and growing list of animation festival awards attest to Barker's gift for tapping into cultural anxieties in uniquely funny and arresting ways.

Less well known than their comic-animation cohorts are two NFB animators whose work is abstract and poetic. Alan Pakarnyk and Réal Bérard give the Manitoba scene a breadth it might not otherwise have. Bérard is a local artist whose film work has been financed by the French division of the NFB. His *Jours de Plaine* is like a series of Monet paintings of the prairies, animated into a reverie on the wind and the landscape. Pakarnyk too is interested in the prairie landscape and its magnificent skies. In his short film *Carried Away* (1985), a man (Pakarnyk himself) appears in sepia-toned, live-action footage, slightly pixillated, wandering in a barren prairie gulch. A butterfly appears and is transformed into a pair of glasses; once the animator puts on these glasses, his world is enlivened with brightly coloured spheres and vividly swirling cloud formations. With its dreamy psychedelic imagery and electronic-music soundtrack, *Carried Away* is more in tune with contemporary popular culture (especially early rock videos) than Bérard or anyone else in Winnipeg. But both Pakarnyk and Bérard capture a sense of the non-urban prairie space that is rarely seen on film. Their work might therefore be truer to the spirit of NFB regionalization than that of their more famous fellow animators.

Manitoba Society of Independent Animators

While *Carried Away* was included on the popular NFB compilation video *Incredible Manitoba Animation*, Pakarnyk's earlier film, *Daydream* (1976), and subsequent film, *Adam's Dream* (1989), although similar in theme and imagery, were not made for the NFB. *Daydream* was financed independently and released by the Winnipeg Film Group (WFG), the other major source of animation in the province.

Founded in 1974 when a small group of would-be filmmakers was thrown together with others from across the country at a University of Manitoba film symposium, the WFG is one of Canada's most successful film co-ops. In the early years, the group had a Mickey Rooney "let's make a movie" spirit. Its guiding principles were not especially political or even contrarian; the unspoken motto seemed to be "Other people are making movies in their own hometowns; we should too!"

The first WFG film, *Rabbit Pie* (1976), a black-and-white comedy about a strange poet and a restaurant full of proliferating pies, was a group effort. But other early projects were experimental films (i.e., weird, different, or unique films with non-traditional but decipherable narratives) or documentaries conceived (rarely scripted) by one person and crewed by a small number of WFG members or friends. The films wore the marks of inexperience, low budgets, rudimentary equipment, and amateur acting as badges of honour. A second generation of filmmakers emerged in the 1980s (the so-called prairie po-mo school), many of them with film school or workshop training and a jaundiced eye for contemporary and old-fashioned popular culture.[6]

With Caslor and Condie among its originating members, the WFG supported animators from its inception. This support usually came in the form of assistance with distribution and exhibition rather than actual production. While the PGA animation stand was housed briefly in the WFG offices during the mid 1980s, the animators themselves functioned independently. They often assisted each other with inking and painting, as well as with advice on such matters as storytelling and sound, but not so much as to create a discernible WFG house style or distinctive prairie signature. Most are cel animators whose films have humorous dimensions; they have little else in common.

In the early years of the WFG, the animators were more experimental—in keeping with the spirit of the times. No one embodied the era better than Nancy Edell, whose *Blood Pudding* (1977) is a dark, surrealist fantasy full of bizarre, often erotic imagery and feminist themes. Even Neil McInnes, in many ways the most conventional animator of the lot, created some unusual works. *Boarding House* (1972), with its strange cast of characters, and *Transformer* (1980), with its mechanical monster, represent departures from the norm.

The most inspired of the early WFG animators was Ed Ackerman. His first film, *Sarah's Dream* (1980), is a clay-mation story made with the assistance of a group of senior citizens. Under his supervision, they chose a personal story—the simple tale of a Ukrainian woman's separation from her family's beloved cow when she emigrated to Canada—and used clay figures to animate it, albeit crudely. The voice-over narration, in an clearly contrived falsetto voice, contributes to the simple charm and emotional effectiveness of the movie. *Sarah's Dream* is like a Grandma Moses painting brought to life. That same year, Ackerman tried his hand at what he called Xerox animation. His film *5¢ a Copy* animated a weird set of photocopied images (faces, hands, and such), taken by pressing unlikely objects and body parts on a copy machine. They were accompanied by a lively rock-and-roll soundtrack.

For his next project, Ackerman invented "typewriter animation." After much experimenting, he chose a sound poem, *Primitti Too Taa* (1989), a series of evocative but nonsensical "words" arranged in pseudo-stanzas. Read aloud and animated in black and white using typewritten print, the "words" formed bizarre, abstract patterns, both simple and cluttered. The resulting film was so affecting that it was re-shot in 70-mm for production as an IMAX film.

Another talented animation artist in the early years of the WFG was John Paizs. Before spearheading the "prairie postmodern" movement of offbeat dramas that skewered suburban life, Paizs made three short cel-animation films of differing styles and affects. *The Dreamer* (1974) is an imitation Disney movie with full-blown backgrounds, symphonic music, and a cute elephant chased through a castle by a devillish monster in a whimsical parody of birthing. *Hoedown* (1977) and *The Nine to Five Crack* (1979) are much simpler graphically and indebted to the era's pop-culture combination of horror and irreverent humour. Although he complained that animation was too labour-intensive, Paizs brought the same painstaking work ethic and weird sense of humour to his live-action films.

Encouraged by these successes, animators in the province banded together to form an association called the Manitoba Society of Independent Animators (MSIA). For a few years in the late 1980s, MSIA had a paid coordinator, an impressive training program, an elaborate series of lightboards and workstations at the NFB, and a regular newsletter called *Peg-head*. But for all its energy and promise, MSIA's output was disappointing. Only two new filmmakers have emerged so far with completed, independent animated films: Paul Ulrich and Patrick Lowe.

Paul Ulrich's film *Silence of the Clams* (1994) won the Blizzard award for best animated film at the Manitoba Film Awards, and the lyrics for his second film *Love Means Never Asking You to Shave Your Legs* (1995) won a CBC radio prize. Both films are amusing rather than sophisticated examples of animation design and execution—charming if slight jibes at contemporary political correctness.

Patrick Lowe's films are deliberately naïve in form and content. *Going Ape* (1985) features Adam and Eve and a gorilla in a *Bambi Meets Godzilla*-style jape at evolution. In *Gerald the Genie* (1991), Lowe examines the age-old problem of identity and perception in a child-like parable. *A Bit Transcendental* (2001) continues his whimsical, winning studies of life's quirks.

If MSIA is to have a lasting legacy, it will be the result of the work of veteran animator Neil McInnes, one of the main forces in the establishment of the association. After years of making commercials and animated inserts for *Sesame Street*, watching the rise and fall of his own animation company, and devoting too much time to MSIA, McInnes released a film that lived up to his early promise and single-handedly validated MSIA. *Lovehound* (1996) is a collection of "dopey clichés" about a slickly pompadoured realtor and his opportunistic mistress. The story and wide range of jokes are secondary to the film's visual and aural effects, however. Against a rich, multi-layered soundtrack and backgrounds that present a polished, retro look, McInnes has orchestrated a playful series of squash-and-stretch routines in deep-focus settings, recalling the best of classic animation. *Lovehound* is what independent animation is all about.

Things to Come

With Brad Caslor's retirement and Cordell Barker's decision to concentrate on advertising, Manitoba animation has seemed to be in eclipse for the past ten years, even with the publicity garnered by Condie's CGI film *La Salla*. Barker's award-winning *Strange Invaders* promises to change all that. Indeed, a modest revival is on the horizon. Condie is currently exploring an Internet animation project, continuing his penchant for experimentation. Veteran animator Neil McInnes is hard at work on an as-yet untitled short film. And newcomers Derek Cummings and Anita Lebeau are taking NFB animation in entirely new directions, Lebeau with a colourful cel-animation portrait of her eccentric grandmother, *Louise*, and Cummings with *Mind Me Good Now*, a six-minute film adaptation of a children's story set in Guyana about a young boy and girl captured by a cocoya (sorceress) named Mama Zee.[7]

Still, it is clear that the value of influential institutions like the NFB, the WFG, and the CBC is diminishing. Far fewer *Sesame Street* inserts are being made in Winnipeg, limiting opportunities for local animators, whether veterans or beginners, to flex their muscles. The NFB has moved its production offices into smaller quarters, leaving MSIA, its workstations, and its animation stand without a home. More worrisome is the fact that under Jennifer Torrance, producer in charge of NFB animation and children's programming for the prairie region, animation no longer seems the priority it once was. Likewise, at the WFG, animation has lost status.

Computers, videos, and the Internet have created a new animation world. Fortunately, other institutions have responded. The University of Manitoba, Red River College, and several entrepreneurial technical and business colleges have offered training courses in animation for several years. Graduates from these programs, like Alain Delannoy, whose short film *Shuttle* (1997) was made entirely on video with the aid of computers, have already entered the animation marketplace and festival circuit. More promisingly, a new computer-animation business, Frantic Films, with a growing list of accomplishments, clients, and employees, has already captured international attention. Computer-generated visual effects for *Storm of the Century* (based on a Stephen King novel) and other Hollywood film and TV shows, plus local and national television commercials using Maya, a new 3-D animation program, mark the beginning forays in the creation of a new Manitoba animation era.

For twenty-five years, the Prairie Production Office of the NFB has provided substantial long-term contracts for local animation projects plus a national marketing and festivals branch second to none—which undoubtedly contributed to the international successes of its best films. The NFB also assisted independent animators with completion money, film stock, and in-house lab work, and supported both the WFG and MSIA. It is undoubtedly the engine that drives the local animation economy. Had the NFB not opened a regional production office in Winnipeg in the 1970s, there would be no *Getting Started, The Big Snit, Get a Job, The Cat Came Back*, or *Jours de Plaine*. There would be far fewer awards and four fewer Oscar nominations. Brad Caslor, Richard Condie, Cordell Barker, Neil McInnes, and Réal Bérard likely would not have become filmmakers, for they would never have moved to NFB Montréal headquarters to become animators; and even if they had, their films would not be the same. Working not only in their hometown but in their own homes, they were able to make animated films with a certain "shack-wacky" sensibility[8]—films featuring neurotic, isolated, usually housebound or recently loosed characters and made with an off-beat, slightly unhinged sense of humour. These quirky, distinctive films have added much to the animation tradition started by Norman McLaren. Regionalization of the NFB has been great for Manitoba, and good for the NFB too.

Notes

1   For an insider's analysis, see Ronald Dick, "Regionalization of a Federal Cultural Institution: The Experience of the National Film Board of Canada 1965–1979," in *Flashback: People and Institutions in Canadian Film History*, Gene Walz, ed. (Montréal: Mediatexte, 1986), 107–133.

2   See Jerry Beck, *The 50 Greatest Cartoons* (North Dighton, MA: World Publications, 1994), and also *The 50 Greatest Cartoons of All Time*, an eight-hour marathon program that ran on the Cartoon Network on American television in winter 1998.

3   Although a print remains, nothing else is known about *The Man Who Woke Up*, its distribution and exhibition, or the filmmakers who made it. Once it was finished, J.A. Norling went back to the US to make other industrial and documentary films. This film left no perceivable legacy.

4   The most fascinating figure from the family tree of Winnipeg animators is Charles G. Thorson, who worked for almost all of the American "animation factories" during the "golden age of American animation" and ended his career at PGA. For a complete account of his life and contributions to animation, see my book *Cartoon Charlie: The Life and Art of Animation Pioneer Charles Thorson* (Winnipeg: Great Plains Publications, 1998).

5   For a more complete account, see my article "The PGA Connection," *Animation World Magazine* 22 (May 1997).

6   For more information on the Winnipeg Film Group, see Gilles Hébert, ed., *Dislocations: Winnipeg Film Group* (Regina: Dunlop Art Gallery, 1995), especially the essays by Geoff Pevere and Patrick Lowe.

7   Karen Mazurkewich is less optimistic about animation's future in Winnipeg, but she overlooked some recent developments. See "Geeks from the Prairies" in her book *Cartoon Capers: The History of Canadian Animators* (Toronto: McArthur and Company, 1999), 155–68.

8   "Shack-wacky" is a local colloquialism for cabin fever. It is a layperson's description of a non-medical, non-pathological condition that results from confinement for several days or more due to excessive cold or blizzard.

Conjugating Three Moments in Black Canadian Cinema

Kass Banning

> Black filmmakers are not silkworms, they don't produce through their guts.
> —Stuart Hall

Shoutout to Viola

THE CONSIDERATION OF BLACK CANADIAN CINEMA summons a moment in our shamefully little-known civil-rights history, when the screen and blackness were inexorably linked. For me, joining black, Canada, and cinema recalls one woman's celebrated challenge to racial segregation in Nova Scotia. Predating Rosa Parks' Montgomery bus incident by nine years, in 1946 Viola Desmond stood her ground against the colour bar in a New Glasgow movie theatre.[1] While watching a Hollywood feature, she was forced from a seat designated for white patrons. When she objected to the Roseland's racially segregated seating policy, she was arrested, which led to the launch of a civil suit and eventual appeal to Nova Scotia's Supreme Court. Although Desmond lost on both counts, her efforts (as well as those of many others) stand as monumental test cases that exposed existing judicial prejudice and as precedents that helped to mobilize challenges to laws and racial attitudes, from community to national levels. While boldly demonstrating the costs of informal Canadian "raceless" laws, Desmond's case also underscored the paradox that while no mandates existed to enforce racial segregation, Jim Crow practices were alive and well.[2]

While the struggle of Canada's black filmmakers to produce images scarcely resembles Viola Desmond's choice to occupy a seat in a movie theatre, and the ensuing dramatic civil-rights struggle her action provoked, a correspondence nonetheless lingers. A mere decade separates this infamous incident—involving the right of a black woman to watch images in the public sphere—from William Greaves' film production with the National Film Board (NFB) in the 1950s. The movement from the struggle for black consumption of white images in spaces designated "public" to an analogous full-filmic citizenship has yet to be realized; a commensurate corpus of black-produced images by black filmmakers awaits achievement. My objective in what follows doesn't belabour these somewhat analogous inequities; I simply point to their symptomatic relation. The 1950s image of the lone William Greaves toiling in the NFB desert has nevertheless been eclipsed over the last decade by exponential black participation in the film and television industries and self-imaging in general. Compared to earlier eras, black production is at an all-time Canadian high. Fuller grasp of this seeming shift and apparent advancement, however, requires more of a conjunctural consideration of earlier patterns of black Canadian filmmaking.

Rather than tease out a unifying concept of black Canadian film or identify authentic characteristics that would distinguish black-authored film from its more dominant Canadian efforts, I observe black Canadian cinema as a process of becoming, as a practice that defies fixed categorization. As for the interstitial nature of "emerging" black Canadian film as constitutive, I will probe the critical interface black filmmakers negotiate between national institutions and diasporic, "outer-national" affiliations in three selected films. To various degrees, these strains, both intra and inter, inform both the subject matter and modes of address evinced in *Born Black* (Little-White, 1972), *The Road Taken* (Jacob, 1996), and *Rude* (Virgo, 1995). Neither list-motivated nor auteur-based, this chapter aspires neither to be comprehensive nor to exhaust analysis. Obviously, the range, repertoire, and achievements of black Canadian filmmakers cannot be fully considered here.[3]

Isolating three films for analysis does not signal their protean value nor legitimize their place in the history of black Canadian cinema. Rather, my selection serves to illustrate a diversity of formal and political responses to oft-recurring subject matter and concerns in black Canadian production. Although each film possesses distinct discursive, production, and reception contexts, each engages with black Canadian experience from a repertoire of histories and struggles that is both personal and public, further conjugating definitions of black Canadian film. Produced over roughly a quarter century, *Born Black*, *The Road Taken*, and *Rude*—while coming out of complex cultural circumstances endemic to black Canadian communities, both immigrant and settled—mark how black Canadian films are shaped equally by evolving local contexts and by global debates on black cultural practice and experience, both self- and other-defined, both lived and in the rarefied realm of critique. But relationships between black Canadian film and its audience (both black and multicultural) are mediated and transformed by the inherent governmentality of Canadian film[4]—its discursive strategies and organizational policies—and by recent forms of black popular culture and its cross-over global appeal. The films *Born Black*, *The Road Taken*, and *Rude*, mediated in different ways and to various degrees, indicate three moments in black Canadian film that are informed by odd mixes of, respectively, migrancy and social protest, governmentality and poetics, and translations of black youth culture housed within an art-film genre. At the same time, despite the cross-generic and formal range evident in the three texts' variously deployed accounts of a black Canadian public sphere, they share themes and preoccupations: the attention to and privileging of voice, in all its oral, political, and musical registers; explicit concern with black masculinity; and direct and indirect challenges to normative depictions of blackness and homegrown racism.

Roots and Routes

Black film production in the West, be it British, American, or Canadian, could be characterized as roughly following a similar trajectory over the past thirty years.[5] It is generally acknowledged that emerging black cinema from the 1960s through the 1980s was a response to the systematic exclusion and marginalization from film production, as well as misrepresentation and racist depiction in the mass media. While this phase of black imaging could be identified as corrective imaging, self-representation also served as a central conduit for agency and transformation.

Marked by a sense of urgency and pragmatism, the independent films of this period were made under remarkably limited financial constraints. In spite of the odds, this stage of redress produced histories that validated and "authenticated" black voices.[6] Black output, according to both American and British commentators on black cinema, was informed by "the realness dimension,"[7] that across genre, the factual presides.[8] Indeed, the pressing social issues of the day that largely comprised the prevailing subject matter of black films produced across continents conjoined to enforce the call for representational redress as necessary if not imminent. Sidestepping the pitfalls of periodization and its evolutionist connotations, it could be said that black Canadian work generally reproduces the content, shape, and address of these earlier practices. This direction, of course, was and remains overdetermined by governmental and institutional funding factors that dictate both the form and the subject of an individual film. At the same time, recent films by black Canadians share an archeological impetus with filmmakers of African descent globally. Fortunately for some documentary filmmakers, the project of excavating a "usable past" coalesces with the general pedagogic goals of the National Film Board (NFB).

Enter *Born Black*

Informed by a 1960s documentary aesthetic of economy and immediacy, *Born Black* offers a spirited mélange of conventional and not-so-conventional documentary forms and fictionalized re-enactments. Not surprisingly, the film shares thematic concerns and representational strategies with independent black documentary of the period. Informed by movements for social justice and inflected by the "self-help" mandate and activism of the black power movement and an emerging 1970s black cultural nationalism, *Born Black* squarely fits the designation "committed documentary."[9] Director Lennie Little-White,[10] then a student with Ryerson's Radio and Television Arts program, independently produced *Born Black*; according to its end credits, the film was "created from an idea of The Black People's Movement, York University."[11]

Pedagogical in intent and orientation, the film opens with the epistemological and ontological query: "Who are the blacks in Canada?" Its project is to sketch contemporary black Canadian specificity, to provide a counternarrative to the normative accounts of Canadian history and experience, and to bear witness to and assert black presence and achievement, past and present. Encyclopedic in scope, archaeological in impetus, serving as a template for later films on black themes, *Born Black* anticipates the more focussed efforts of black-authored film to follow.[12] Shot MOS throughout, with sound and image never synchronized, *Born Black* dizzyingly maps the broad fabric of black Canadian life. Exhibiting the virtues and weaknesses of the historical overview, the film predictably lacks depth, yet its resilient archiving renders it both curious and invaluable. It combines differing documentary modes of address that encompass what Bill Nichols has categorized as expository, observational, and interactive modes, resulting in a composite that relies heavily on the schizophrenic yet profoundly significant deployment of voice.[13] Through visuals culled from stunning original graphics, innovative adaptation of the cinema direct format, and dramatic punctuation, *Born Black* illustrates *présence africaine* from wildly opposing vocal registers. Despite the evident *frisson* in tone and address, the message is consistent. Black Canadians from the sixteenth century to the present have not lived, for the most part, an equitable existence. Although *Born Black* privileges black autonomy and self-reliance through its didactic delivery, strains of the larger society's liberal integrationist stance coincide; advocacy and activism share equal billing as the preferred route to equality.

Born Black divides roughly into three modes of address. The first mode, expository, uses a white male voice-of-god narration that offers direct commentary on the images. Part tour guide, part school-marmish historian, this authoritative voice grounds and conjoins with the "image-bite" graphics of Canadian blackness. Sightings include Mathieu de Coste, Canada's first recorded slave in 1608, slave communities from the deportation of Jamaican Maroons to Sierra Leone from Nova Scotia, Black Loyalist settlement, the "lived" and mythic significance of "the underground railway," the Ontario settlements of Buxton and Dresden, the life of Jeremiah Jenson (ostensibly the Uncle Tom of Harriet Beecher Stowe's *Uncle Tom's Cabin*), and black participation in the abolitionist movement. The use of graphics to illustrate the past could be rationalized by predictable tales of budgetary restraints, yet these rendered sketches emphasize the irretrievable nature of black history. Their sheer invention suggests and underscores the relative and inherent dearth of documentation of black life, from official records to enduring self-fashioned imagery.

The educating voice "explains" footage of railway porters, outlining the significance of the Brotherhood of Sleeping Car Porters for the politicization of black labour and communities across the country. Further observational illustrations of contemporary black existence follow, stressing the crucial role of self-sufficiency for self-determination. Informal and formal Toronto black organizations and meeting places—from barber shops and churches to lost institutions such as the Harriet Tubman Centre and the weekly publication *Contrast*, to the Third World Bookstore and Crafts that recently closed its doors—are conceived as contributing to a transformationalist politics, towards fostering a distinct black public sphere.[14]

While the white male voice of authority frames the hard facts of black existence (at times coming uncomfortably close to pathologizing its subjects), the basic movement of the film is towards self-consciousness and empowerment. To this end, *Born Black* gives voice to multiple testimonies of black Canadian experience. A rush of voices conjoins—in a sometimes staccato, sometimes lyrical manner—to give accounts that from time to time contradict one another. Although these cross-cut, sound-looped voices are non-synchronous and disembodied (except for the Bildungsroman-like "character," we are never offered the opportunity to match a voice directly to an image, yet there are often conceptual links), they work against the normalized effects of distance and objectivity suggested by the first expository voice of authority. Interspersed throughout, these clusters of various polyphonous "voices off" suggest an interiority that nevertheless supports the rhetoric of the central narrator. Over footage of instances of black Canadian life—from Toronto's Caribanna to black capitalism to interracial relationships—commentary runs from the conciliatory to the stridently oppositional. Through such multivocal means, playing off expositional opinion and interactive memory, black Canadian totality is suggested, but suggested through difference, through a stubborn refusal to synthesize black Canadianness into a totality. The strategic use of voice in *Born Black* accounts for differences of interpretation within a collective frame and incorporates a number of voices without fully assimilating them. Voices blend into a polyvalency, a collectivity framed in the discourse of social action, that at times speaks to Canadian blackness, at others, speaks for. The official tone of the initial expository mode is rendered weaker, and thus *Born Black*'s effect is both emphatic and multiple at once.

A dramatized quest of a young black everyman supplements the film's movement towards critical consciousness. The black Bildungsroman journeys down the road across Canada towards geopolitical and ontological enlightenment to answer the film's opening challenge. His presence obviously anchors the film's throughline, but the privileging of one social actor also grounds the success of the job-interview sequences. The contradicting voice-over justifications for rejection, either under- or over-qualification, register at a more visceral level than a more orthodox enumeration of prejudicial hiring practices. Sly Stone's lyrics to "You Can Make It If You Try" on the soundtrack ironically inflect the man's fruitless search for a job. Roadblocks notwithstanding, our stand-in retrieves the "history lessons" that have been suppressed due to the silencing effects of racism: self-determination and community determine spiritual and financial liberation. The lyrics of the reggae-inflected hymn that imbue the film's closing, "We are going, heaven knows where we are going, we know we can," parallel the narrative arc of *Born Black*: the road from struggle to fulfillment.

While the film's contemporary subjects occupy Canadian soil, their first-person narrated concerns were (and are) shared with populations throughout the west that stem from both migrancy and racism: employment and equity issues, unequal resources ranging from housing to education, fear of the consequences of assimilation, the value of black women, the integrity of the black family and related anxiety about interracial relationships, and insistence on equality and its activation through controlling community institutions to pursue self-determination. Fuelled by the language of national liberation movements and decolonization, civil rights, and the black nationalist phase of the struggle, *Born Black*, with its endearing black-is-beautiful uplift, zooms, and afro excesses, remains a landmark that attempts to recode the black Canadian image by stressing self-love, self-reliance, and autonomy. *Born Black* shares the goals of politically motivated filmmakers who covered black struggles elsewhere—to inform black viewers—yet it also attempts to reach a larger constituency through a shifting, if not schizophrenic, mode of address.[15]

Circumstances and delivery systems have indeed changed. Television has replaced the church basements and meeting halls of the 1970s, but alternative methods of archiving and approaching historiography continue to evolve nonetheless. In the context of a film like *Born Black*, the problem of reaching a black audience has paradoxically been alleviated by television. Yet the televisual, further exacerbated by the NFB and broadcasting guidelines across a broad spectrum, has unquestionably influenced the subject, address, and form of black film; cross-over requirements, supposedly dictated by the tolerance threshold of the dominant culture, have helped to shape seemingly less hard-hitting renditions of and positions on Canadian blackness.

Training the Nation/s
The Road Taken

Selwyn Jacob's *The Road Taken* focusses on one central aspect of black Canadian struggle fleetingly invoked twenty-four years prior in *Born Black*.[16] The film offers a lyrical and highly subjective account of Canada's sleeping car porters and their historical role in constituting a black public sphere. Yet it also, almost indirectly, explicates a historical black working class, providing a labour history of sorts of black battles for advancement and equality through trade unionism. Housed within a more liberal-inflected social-documentary format than its predecessor, *The Road Taken* privileges focus over scope, reciting the power to endure over dissent, and subjective psychology over activism.[17] Although dissimilar in style and tone, *Born Black* and *The Road Taken* share some defining characteristics, specifically their experimentation in voice and the maximizing of black musical traditions.

The Road Taken shares the realist orientation of black-authored NFB documentaries conventionalized in the 1980s,[18] yet it extends their somewhat predictable effects of pathos. Insisting that its subjects have ontologies, it centres on the individual men who served as Pullman porters. Yet the film does not exclude the social networks—local, national, and international—that framed their labour (and labour struggles). The outlines of the porters' lives are sketched with a mix of media representations. Archival photographs of porters, newspaper headlines, a range of promotional material produced over the century by the CPR and CNR of inviting train interiors and steely exteriors, footage of the multi-seasoned sublime Canadian landscape, and the grandeur of the trains themselves offer authorial, often touristic, sources.

The manner in which the porters' lives are recalled, however, gently pulls away from the veneer of these official discourses and traditional signifiers of "Canadianness." Relying primarily upon oral-history interviews with aged porters and commemorative reunions, the film's humanizing core remains indebted to the audio over the visual, specifically to subjective narration. Despite their age, the interviewed porters are articulate; although individuated to their own experience, they speak a sense of agency to and across generations. The porters share narratorial function with a central, overarching baritone voice and two men whose fathers served as porters. Voice here negotiates a double-edged function: part participants, part narrators, the two sons, both artists—one visual (Clifton Ruggles), the other a musician (jazz pianist and composer Joe Sealy, who recorded *Africville Suite* [1996] and also scores the film)—mediate between filmmaker and subject. While subsidizing the film's intersubjective grid, they also gain insight into their fathers and their relationships with them through memorializing.[19] Their reflections allow the ambivalent meaning and effects of this kind of labour to emerge more fully: that, although these men performed servile tasks uncomfortably recalling those of slavery,[20] these positions were highly regarded and sought after in black communities. But most significantly, their presence underscores how this moment has passed: that the formation and aspirations of a black Canadian middle-class sensibility were born of breaking through racialized labour segmentation.

Part vessels of oral history, part therapeutic agents, the film's voices do not constitute an authorial "I" in the usual sense. Conjoined with the reflective, at times versed, baseline of the film's central exposition and the two sons' accounts, the porters' testimonies offer subtle, almost soothing, counterpoint to the weight of "official" record of smiling and bending—read happily oppressed—sleeping car porters. *The Road Taken*, then, tells two stories: the simultaneous personal accommodation to racism and indignities, and the fight for full citizenship told by survivors of this era, coupled with the effect of this refusal of secondary status on families. Their struggles were neither in vain nor did they eventuate in tragedy. The insistence on generational affiliations at both structural and narrative levels registers a sense of both "getting over" and political accomplishment, of enduring not only for their families but also to participate in the dismantling of the glass ceiling that limited their own potential for job advancement, and, by extension, all black Canadians.[21]

The film's musical accompaniment plays a key part in communicating this theme of endurance. Composed by interviewee/narrator/musician Sealy, an instrumental blues score undergirds and strengthens the film's soulful rhetorical effectiveness. Working with the privileging of audio signifiers evinced throughout *The Road Taken*, music provides a typical affective resonance, but the subtext of this particular genre brings out an element of religiosity, inflected by nineteenth-century spirituals. The inherent musical cues of the blues establish mood, while their referents of faith, recognition of right, pride, and struggle cast the porters' narrative within a readily recognizable frame of reference that parallels and adds resonance to the conditions and the outcome of their struggle. At the same time, the generalized black struggle of slavery, evoked through African-American musical tradition, operates as an aesthetic supplement that works against the authorial denial cast by the "official" images. Affiliation through music, specifically the blues, thus aids identification with the film's subjects and the process of historical memory.

Those who served Canada's railway system also distributed goods and information to segregated and dispersed regions across railway lines,[22] assisting an informal web of black communication across North America. These parallel "clandestine" acts further underscore the film's central yet understated conceit: the porters are the supplement to Canada's romance with the rails. Given the real and mythic foundational role of the railway for Canada's nation building, the black porters, from the railway's inception, indicate blackness as constitutive of Canada itself. If the conditions that brought the Pullman car into Canada in the 1880s hinged on the labour of the black porter, we cannot imagine Canada without black presence. The transnational railway, then, initiates and evidences the nation, while enlisting black presence (mostly elided under slavery's residual effects) to serve both touristic and nation-building ends.[23] The railway, as Canada's founding myth, did not for black Canadians live up to its promise of progress. The participation of the porters, and their guaranteed deportment, on the other hand, assured a level of touristic comfort and perceived opulence to a burgeoning white middle class attenuating itself to modernity's codes of leisure.

From the early conjoined filmic efforts by Canada's railway interests and the state to promote a mythic vision of nationhood, through the various yet consistent attempts by the NFB, to the present ventures of the film festivals branch of Telefilm, film has helped to provide a centrist, statist function of "social cement," offering a homogeneous notion of what constitutes "Canadianness." Dominant forces have historically promulgated and administered specific infrastructures and institutions to effectively procure the cohesiveness of a national identity. "Technological nationalism,"[24] the pervasive thesis that the space-binding effects of technology—from the railway to the radio—birthed and sustain the nation, does not, nor cannot necessarily, acknowledge parallel black networks. Ironically, the black porter, while sustaining a broader national project through his labour, also covertly spread discursive black culture and politics. Within the bounds of national categories, blackness is simply complementary, Canada's structuring absence.

My insistence on the trope of the consummate quality of Canadian nationhood and blackness, suggested through the porters' tale, is conveyed most resolutely by indirection, if at all consciously. *The Road Taken* subtly implies this "confederation," at least for this viewer, but its obliqueness also discloses a rich object lesson. It points to how black relations with national institutions such as the NFB require constant negotiation; glass ceilings contain both ideological and innumerable subtle, informal other requirements.

After the Love Is Gone
Black Canada's *Rude*

Clement Virgo's *Rude* indicates a moment in black Canadian cinema when a series of social developments and a set of related discourses intersect. First, the simultaneous increased commodification of black expressive culture and its escalating status, visibility, and constitutive role in popular culture,[25] most notably youth culture; and the attendant degree to which the ubiquitous nature of popular culture itself has helped to forge and influence new forms of citizenship. Second, the emergence, relative success, and cross-over marketability of the 1990s black-authored "hood" films, an attainment partially secured by the historic identificatory role black males hold for white males.[26] Third, the specific relevance of technology to the circuits of production and distribution of black popular culture, and, in the context of *Rude* and to the role of its storyline, as both narrative motor and conduit to a more covertly defined black public sphere. Fourth, the solidification of the art film/first feature as the privileged genre and characteristic entry point for the (hypothetical) black Canadian auteur within the purview of both funding agencies and an image-consuming leisure-class populace. Fifth and most notably, new opportunities and infrastructures available to "emerging" filmmakers.[27] These generative conditions, coupled with *Rude*'s overarching theme of redemption deployed through the consistent reference to Christianity and rastafarianism, conveyed predominantly through reggae and other genres of black music, offer some traction to consider the centrality of voice in *Rude*, its extensive textual operations, and its far-reaching implications.

The popular press' "first-time/black-directed feature film" reception of *Rude* was typically devoid of critique. More importantly, reviewers displayed ignorance of black expressive culture, Canadian or otherwise. Generally celebratory, commentary emphasized the film's stunning stylistic virtuosity, its emergence as unique, its "Jamaican-Canadian" director as atypical, and its representation of "community" as notable. At the expense of exposing the film's layered referents and nuanced manoeuvres, both textual and expeditious,[28] the failure to effectively situate the film demonstrates just how far *Rude* lay beyond earlier critical frameworks for examining Canadian cinema.

Filmic challenges to critical assumptions based on national definition are never totally successful, as the conditions that ushered *Rude*'s possibility helped to realize a highly uneven and contradictory text.[29] What is of interest is how *Rude* negotiates the seemingly opposing discourses of the Canadian mainstream and local and diasporic black concerns. While *Rude* metaphorically operates within the broad outline of an imagined Canada, it signifies a number of spheres, imagined and real, public and private. Generalized Canadian preoccupations are suggested through thematic and stylistic means: a symbolic indigenous First Nations appearance, performed by a traditional "warrior" in the film's opening coda and also interspersed allusions to "the Mohawk"; repeated mention of the historical and social status of black Canadians that embellishes the themes of migrancy, belonging, and legitimacy, communicated by an illegal pirate radio broadcast;[30] the trope of traditional anti-American imperialist sentiment, embodied in the portrayal of the evil Yankee druglord, the film's only white central character; and the sense that technology (in this case, the camera) mediates experience.[31] While *Rude* commercializes and aestheticizes blackness, it conveys social reality, evinced in the ethnographic impulse of the dominant ghetto-centric narrative strand, perhaps a residue of a Grierson documentary heritage.

Rude speaks more directly to a black urban Toronto specificity through its saturated digitally reproduced skyline, its Regent Park exterior location (not used to realist effect to ground particularity), and its multi-accented use of voice and vocal references to the local from specific police divisions and racial profiling to significatory practices of a black urban working class. While embedded in the local, expressions of black identity are reconfigured and overlaid by sense of global centrelessness.[32]

Rude builds upon a range of diasporic cultural expression that is buoyed by the poetics of loss that define Tony Morrison's novel *Beloved*, the rastafarian inflections of Babylon, the ghetto-centric flourishes of the new jack film, the moral archetypes that lace African-American letters, and most significantly, its use of black music. Referencing and quotation, of course, are mainstays of artistic practice in general, but Paul Gilroy, among others, insist that a "cut 'n' mix" or synchretic dimension, most evident in black music, defines and sustains black expressive culture *in toto*. Henry Louis Gates would claim that this intertextual aspect supports his notion of signifying which entitles the idea of twoness: as both linguistic utterance and tropological referencing.[33] As the most privileged translation of black life and ideals,[34] integral to black social history, music lends authenticity and emotional power, especially to black representation. Employed to both diegetic and non-diegetic effect, the many subgenres of black music heard in *Rude* emphasize and comment on the various narrative strands, adding fluidity, poignancy, and even drama. The dissonant guitar chords of Jimi Hendrix, for example, underscore the inner discord of the coming-out character and the crisis brewing in the Yankee's lair. Inflected by spirituals and gospel music, the tunes "Brown Baby" and "Farther Along" editorialize the journeys of all the characters, with direct commentary annotating the window-dresser's experience. Reggae music is associated with the attendant black experiences of ghetto poverty and resistance. The popular and oft-employed "Many Rivers to Cross" that forms *Rude*'s theme song emphasizes resurrection and rebirth, but the tune also recalls the extra-diegetic plight (and voice) of Jimmy Cliff in the classic *The Harder They Come* (1973). My point, then, is not to disparage quotation but to stress how musical reference, regardless of subgenre, follows a progressive arc from struggle to fulfillment, indicating an elsewhere, be it simply "getting over," or Zion. Quotation facilitates narrative design, but it also dislodges the continuous preoccupations of identity and nationhood that obtain in Canada's dominant culture. To indicate an elsewhere forecloses the possibility of sameness, of endorsing a single and unified definition of Canadian identity.

Formally comprised of a triptych, three visually and generically distinct narratives mix with the soothing yet invective-laden voice-over of pirate radio DJ Rude over an Easter weekend. The central tale focusses on the conflict of two brothers, General and Reece. Deriving from the quintessential African-American trope of dashed hopes and from the plea "When are we going to be men?" (reminiscent of James Baldwin's *Sonny's Blues*), *Rude* nevertheless escapes formula by inversion, the most illustrative being the cop wife who saves her recently released man and family. The visual richness of General's Francis Bacon-inspired mural and the exhilarating pyrotechnics displayed throughout, coupled with experiments in sound, disrupt genre-proper requirements but also offer a fluidity that is difficult to pin down. At the same time, the ghetto aspect is played out in specific ways through conventional realism and the familiar conjuncture of prison, policing, and economics. Departing from films like *Boys 'n the Hood* that resolve in escape, *Rude* nevertheless closes with the circularity of death and redemption. Heavily inflected by the rastafarian themes conveyed in the music, this outer-national aural referencing works against what Paul Gilroy calls "the discourse of the hoods' implied localism [that] problematizes the potential for expansive diasporic identification and collective movement."[35] The insistence that the reconstitution of the black family is the normative route to redemption indicates both closer and more-distanced ground.

Conceptualized perhaps to represent the multiplicity of black experience, the three strands attempt to negotiate gender and sexual differences, but they are sacrificed to the privileged ghetto-centric story. The first narrative thread follows the young window-dresser Maxine through a weekend of spiritual crisis. Driven by art-cinema narration, this section expresses subjective strife at all registers: visual, aural, and narrative. Front-screen photography and video images foreground a sense of a haunting past. The second narrative offers a coming-out tale that is set in the hyperactive, hyper-male arena of boxing, to emphasized dramatic effect. Off-speed camera technique and repetition emphasize the turmoil endemic to contender Jordan's attempt to negotiate boxing and being gay. Both of these narrative strands offer critiques of a normalized black masculinity: one directed at its sexist manifestations, the other at its homophobic effects. Significantly, redemption is not afforded outside family limits, indicating perhaps how the growing interdependence of black filmmaking and the market has rendered multi-consciousness difficult to sustain.

Rude, a female pirate radio figure, is the film's centrepiece. She generates and sustains a narrative forcefield through the disposition of voice and its attendant gendered effects. Pirate radio has been used as trope and subject to register both strength of community and resistance to different effects in feature films that often privilege an aspect of youth culture. Pirate radio's transmissions of identity and alterity have been exploited in a number of films that range across continents, genres, and degrees of independent production evinced in *The Warriors* (1979), *Born in Flames* (1984), *Pump Up the Volume* (1990), *Do the Right Thing* (1989), and *Young Soul Rebels* (1991). The naming of the Rude character is also highly suggestive of a specifically Jamaican phenomenon. While rooted in earlier conceptions of rasta and its moralisms, the vernacular figure of Rude more accurately approximates the refashioned rudie-boy popularized in the 1960s that stylized political/cultural resistance.

Rude sets the film's real and narrative time; her sensually riffing lips articulate the goals of the film through insistent meta-commentary on the social and sexual conflicts of its characters, within its three narrative strands and the extended black public sphere of her listeners. The semantic registers of DJ Rude's voice intone the co-existing impulses of national language (Caribbean) and the more African-American-inflected black vernacular. These double acoustic markers operate across and inform the dialogic, call-and-response exchanges with her call-in interlocutors.[36] Her outlawed and self-named "disenfranchised diasporic voice" recalls Molly Bloom or Marylese Holder of *A Winter Tan*, or Mo's Mabley. Enacting the traditional trickster of black folklore, Rude talks dirty, sexualizing the "dozens."[37] While Rude remains somewhat of a cipher or ventriloquist, with her speech indebted to a masculinist discourse, she nevertheless takes on, overtly and reflexively; the forces that shape a black urban public sphere. In fact, the illicit and illegal suggestiveness of pirate radio signifies that black speech, and by implication "authentic" black expression, can only be conveyed through covert means. Obvious historical resonance aside, this trope extends generatively to the production and possibilities for black Canadian film, a commentary on the constitutive marginality of black expression within national definition.

The Push of the Local and the Pull of the Diasporic

Scenarios of domination have traditionally been held up to exemplify Canada's seemingly fragile, colonial relation to the United States (or Hollywood). Such ideas can be traced back to the generic meta-narrative concepts of identity propagated by Margaret Atwood, Northrop Frye, Harold Innis, and others. Setting up an antithetical relation with the US, and forged on negativity, these narratives stressed the debilitating effects of media imperialism and tended to present Canadian cultural production as homogeneous, adopting the hypodermic model of domination. Structural negativity propagated anti-American sentiment that smoothed over social divisions around audience. For our purposes, these models structurally prohibited an acknowledgement that the local is partially enabled by an "indigenization" of American or elsewhere-located diasporic products. These enduring models of Canadian cinema that were informed by an *a priori* Canadian identity, with its solidification in a 1970s cultural nationalism, are not, obviously, flexible enough to accommodate the constitutive transnational strain in black Canadian production (let alone the widely held view that all cultures are essentially hybrid).[38]

The continued presence and proliferation of black Canadian film in the past decade potentially disrupts and redefines staid definitions of Canadian film. Earlier paradigms that have provided the bedrock of thinking about Canadian film are not adequate to fully situate black Canadian film nor its emergence. The exhilarating global consumption of black film culture in the 1990s further suggests that the cultural-imperialism model has limited applicability when considering black Canadian films. (Indeed a paradox inheres in the fact that the commercial success of popular black US film has made black product much more palatable and indeed desirable to Canadian funding agencies.) *Born Black*, *The Road Taken*, and *Rude* eschew conventional, all-too-familiar themes of Canadian film as a national cinema—those that support historical nostalgia, invisibility, landscape imagery, "loser boy," or victim scenarios. Sharing strains of Canadian miserablism, these films could be classified as overdetermined by their national site of production.

Black Canadian film is a relational practice, in relationship to broader institutional and historical contexts of black filmmaking, local, national, and transnational. Three of the most important of these contextualizing sites are popular film, third cinema (recent black and otherwise), and Canadian filmmaking traditions, especially documentary. These cinematic histories directly and indirectly influence the political address and form of black Canadian film as much as they are reciprocally rewritten by locally black Canadian interventions. At the same time, however, the cultural capital that attends African-American production, both mainstream and alternative, has provided the enduring markers of achievement for young black Canadian filmmakers. In fact, the effects of this economy of desire, these connecting lines of influence, constituted within an American-dream imaginary, often eclipse the lived reality of producing films in Canada. And this tension, the desire for both commercial and artistic success, constantly rubs against the enduring aesthetic base line of mimicry and centrist governmentalization.

The productive space available to black expressive culture necessarily engenders tension. While participating in parallel channels as the dominant culture, films by Lennie Little-White, Selwyn Jacob, and Clement Virgo, and by extension all black Canadian cinema, work with and against the constraints of both community and state protectionist rhetoric. What is of interest is precisely how these interlinking forces are influenced by specific patterns of black diasporic film but, at the same time, are overdetermined by statist institutions. Yet the consistent traces of these films, registered pervasively through the ontological space of sound, speak "the experience that stands behind them," enabling what Stuart Hall eloquently describes as the surfacing "of elements of a discourse that is different—other forms of life, other traditions of representation."[39] Future criticism and study of this under-investigated genealogy of Canadian film can only materialize from a more considered assessment of these traces.

Notes

Material in this chapter was presented in earlier versions at various conferences over the last decade. Selected conference papers include "News From the North" (Questions of National Cinema, Ohio University, Athens, Ohio, November 12, 1993); "Race on Ice: Shading the Great White North" (Black Cinema: A Celebration of Pan-African Film, New York University, New York, March 29, 1994); "Situating Recent Black Canadian Cinema"

(SITES: African Canadian Video and Film Festival Saw Video Co-Op, Ottawa, September 30, 1995); "After the Love is Gone: Black Canada's Rude" (Society For Cinema Studies Conference, Ottawa, May 15–18, 1997). I am extremely grateful to the Canadian Studies program of the Department of Canadian Heritage for support in the writing of this chapter.

1   In 1955, Rosa Parks refused to move to the back of the bus. Her actions escalated to the momentous bus strike in Montgomery, Alabama, offering a much-canonized moment in American civil-rights history. In contrast to Viola Desmond, Parks has been revered in popular songs, films, and books, as well as in academic accounts.

2   The first statute to prohibit segregation on the basis of race followed one year after Viola Desmond's civil suit. See Constance Backhouse's thoughtful and detailed documentation of the Canadian civil-rights struggle: *Colour-Coded: A Legal History of Racism in Canada, 1900–1950* (Toronto: University of Toronto Press, 1999). Chapter Seven, "'Bitterly Disappointed at the Spread of Colour-Bar Tactics': Viola Desmond's Challenge to Racial Segregation," offers a thorough and illuminating account of this momentous case. Robin Winks' *The Blacks in Canada: A History* (Montréal and Kingston: McGill-Queen's University Press, 1997) remains the definitive historical overview on the Canadian context. Its original publishing date of 1971 betrays its methodological strains and, perhaps more significantly, indicates the tremendous need for new scholarship in this area.

3   See the National Film Board and Studio D's booklet *Black on Screen: Images of Black Canadians 1950's–1990's* (1992) for an annotated list of films. While useful, this account is by no means comprehensive. The omission of pioneer William Greaves' eight-year stint producing, directing, and editing more than eighty films at the NFB, and especially of his sole-authored film *Emergency Ward* (1958), a film that presages Frederick Wiseman's *Hospital* (1968), exhausts any claim as a definitive account. Moreover, Lennie Little-White's *Born Black* (1972) is also not included. While wishing to sidestep the implications of this not-so-hidden conjoining of agendas— to demonstrate both the NFB's early and continuous commitment to multiculturalism and to promote actively producing black Canadian filmmakers—I can only conjecture that the fact that both directors left Canada to return to their native countries (USA and Jamaica respectively) places them outside of the communities of interest. Perhaps Greaves' typical "race-neutral" NFB-circumscribed efforts disqualify them as black Canadian productions. Greaves' career trajectory suggests the boundless nature of black diasporic film and supports my contention that nation-bound frameworks alone are not sufficient for consideration of black Canadian film. In fact, his skills were transferred to New York's public broadcasting station WNET's renowned *Black Journal*, a black-operated television-journalism program directed to black audiences, which he headed as executive producer from 1968 to 1975. This program had a formative influence on a generation of black American documentary filmmakers. See Adam Knee and Charles Musser, "William Greaves, Documentary, and the African American Experience." *Black Journal* is still on the air, but is now known as *Tony Brown's Journal*. The NFB document's publication date of 1992 further excludes updating that would reflect the burgeoning and diverse directions black-authored film and video takes in the next decade.

4   I refer here both to tangible statist institutions such as the National Film Board of Canada, the Canadian Broadcasting Corporation, Telefilm, etc. and to the wider sense of term posed by Michel Foucault. Michael Dorland deftly applies the concept to the formation and inherent workings of Canadian cinema in *So Close to the State/s: The Emergence of Canadian Feature Film Policy* (Toronto: University of Toronto Press, 1998).

5   David James, "Chained to Devil Pictures: Cinema and Black Liberation in the Sixties," in Mike Davis et al., eds., *The Year Left Review* 1987: 125–38. For the implications of the use of realism in the black Canadian context, see my article "Rhetorical Remarks Towards the Politics of Otherness" and Cameron Bailey's "A Cinema of Duty: The Films of Jennifer Hodge de Silva" in *Gendering the Nation: Canadian Women's Cinema*, Armatage et al., eds., (Toronto: University of Toronto Press, 1999).

6   Redress, of course, did not begin in the 1960s. The jointly conceived Lincoln's Dream, released as *Birth of Race* (1919), for example, was, in Thomas Cripps' words, "a black cinematic rebuttal" to Griffith's *Birth of a Nation*. See Cripps, *Slow Fade to Black* (New York: Oxford University Press, 1993), 69. Successive reactions to distortion and heinous imagery across the decades perhaps indicate the tenacious sustainability of misrepresentation.

7   Clyde Taylor employs the term in his article "Decolonizing the Image: New U.S. Black Cinema" in *Jump Cut* 28 (1984). His conception of the realness dimension includes how dramatic time in black films is not separated from historic time. Valerie Smith also stresses the importance of the factual in "The Documentary Impulse in Contemporary U.S. African American Film," in *Black Popular Culture*, Gina Dent, ed. (Seattle: Bay Press, 1992).

8   It is precisely this "realness dimension," and by extension realism, that has contributed to the fact that most black films remain unchampioned, under-theorized, or at least under-analyzed by Canadian film scholars. In spite of protestations, realism remains unfashionable, which is indeed a stumbling block for the analysis of politically motivated, racialized texts.

9   Tom Waugh names the committed documentary's characteristics as a "declaration of solidarity with the goal of radical socio-political transformation," "activism, or intervention in the process of change itself," and "a subject-centred practice" which includes people involved in the issues depicted. See Thomas Waugh, "Introduction: Why Documentary Filmmakers Keep Trying to Change the World, or Why People Changing the World Keep Making Documentaries," in *'Show Us Life': Toward a History and Aesthetics of the Committed Documentary* (Metuchen: Scarecrow Press, 1984), xxii.

10 After his training in Toronto, Little-White returned to Jamaica, where he directed television and made two feature films, *Children of Babylon* (1980) and *Way Back When* (1985), noted for their social realism. See Mbye Cham, *Ex-Iles: Essays on Caribbean Cinema* (Trenton, NJ: Africa World Press, 1992).

11 This immediacy would seemingly contradict David James' claim that "independent black film developed out of the educational reforms produced by the black movement, rather than in relation to the movement itself" ("Chained to Devil Pictures," 262).

12 In fact, *Born Black* serves as a subject template for subsequent films that concentrate on aspects of black Canadian life. For example, the problems of migrant adjustment and the effects of policing in black communities are treated in Jennifer Hodge de Silva's *Home Feeling: Struggle for a Community* (1983). (The job-interview sequences in both films are markedly similar and used to ironic, sometimes comedic, effect.) Black settlement in Buxton is treated in Claire Prieto and Roger McTair's *Home to Buxton* (1987). Jacob's film *The Road Taken* explores the history of Canada's sleeping car porters in a more meditative fashion. Roger McTair's NFB-produced *Journey to Justice* (2001), released after the time of this writing, takes up the struggle of the Brotherhood of Sleeping Car Porters (as well as Viola Desmond's case) as one of Canada's definitive civil-rights moments.

13 I refer here to Bill Nichols' seminal categorizing of documentary narration and authority first published as "The Voice in Documentary," *Film Quarterly* 6, no. 3 (Spring 1983):17–30 and revised in *Representing Reality: Issues and Concepts in Documentary* (Bloomington: Indiana University Press, 1991). Nichols offers a typology of documentary modes which he defines as "basic ways of organizing texts in relation to certain features or conventions" (*Representing Reality*, 32).

14 While the initial historical bird's-eye view of *Born Black* offers a rather flat-footed whirlwind history of blacks in Canada, the expository narrator's accounts are often laced with irony. The eastern Ontario's white-owned and -operated tourist sites, for example, are countered with the suggestion of bogus claims to authenticity.

15 Many of the concerns and goals of *Born Black* reflect features of the ten-point Black Panther program: housing, education, and policing. David James claims the reciting of the ten-point plan became a generic convention of Panther films. California Newsreel's *Black Panther* (1972), for example, inserts the points while the camera tours ghetto streets. While *Born Black* includes footage of blacks in states of poverty (indeed, the moments when the film comes close to pathologizing), the use of interweaving voices corroborate the image, offering thematic coherency and texture. Through a similar interweaving voice strategy, Agnes Varda's *The Black Panthers: A Report* (1968), according to James, depicts the Panther spokesmen as speaking "with the voice of community, accurately representing their voices" ("Chained to Devil Pictures," 131).

16 *The Road Taken*, co-produced with Selwyn Enterprises and the NFB, also had TVO and Telefilm participation. Jacob successfully negotiated the NFB form in a film that deals with racism and identity, *Carol's Mirror* (1992). To date, Jacob's films exhibit a pedagogical and archaeological impulse to document black Canadian particularity. Earlier independently produced works include *We Remember Amber Valley* (1984), a sketch of

Alberta's first black settlement; *The Saint from North Battleford* (1989), a portrait of football star Rueben Mayes; and *Al Tasmin* (1995), on Canada's oldest mosque. Formerly based in Edmonton, Jacob now resides in Vancouver and works as a producer for the NFB as part of a Special Mandate Team for Cultural Diversity.

The films produced under the NFB's *Women at the Well* series, inaugurated by Studio D's New Initiatives in Film (NIF), could be said to anticipate several preoccupations and strategies evident in *The Road Taken*. These films chronicle the lives of black Canadian women through personal portraits: *Black Mother Black Daughter* (Hamilton and Prieto, 1989) assesses the historical contributions of black women in Nova Scotia; *Older Stronger Wiser* (Brand and Prieto, 1989) traces how the life experiences of older black women affect subsequent generations; and *Sisters in the Struggle* (Brand and Stikeman, 1991) builds on historical memory through individual accounts of racism and sexism, but moves past personal accounts to recognize the importance of the social, particularly black women's collectives, to resisting oppression. While *The Road Taken* shares their common intergenerational thread to connect the past and present, as well as a deft use of black music, evinced especially in *Sisters in the Struggle*, its effects seem more nuanced in both aesthetic and narrative registers. Perhaps this generates from the film's conditions of production.

17 My reading of *The Road Taken* is indebted to the many insights offered by a paper delivered by Warren Crichlow on a panel I chaired entitled "What is the Black and/or Canadian in Black Canadian Film?". Society for Cinema Studies, Ottawa, June 1, 1997.

18 Bailey stresses that the documentary realism of these films seeks "neither to shock nor seriously challenge the viewer, but reconfirm the norms of liberal conscience and national identity" ("A Cinema of Duty," 5).

19 Such familial fluidity also works against the commonplace of the aberrant black family, leaving little opportunity for the habitual pathologizing of black kinship.

20 Indeed, that is why they were hired in the first place. See Lynne Kirby's magnificent treatise on cinema, trains, and modernity *Parallel Tracks: The Railroad and Silent Cinema* (Durham: Duke University Press, 1997). She cites William H. Harris' remark in *Keeping the Faith* that "George Pullman's use of former slaves as porters for cheap labour would flatter whites' perceptions of their own status" (*Parallel Tracks*, 254). In spite of such planned effects, she argues, invoking Michel Foucault, that trains nevertheless offer heterotopic spaces that can potentially disrupt and reconfigure race and gender relations.

21 Ironically, their victory eroded a job base for blacks; it also came at a time of downsizing of the Canadian railway system and the porter job became attractive to white workers.

22 Porters dropped off the latest issues of the black press, Harlem's *Amsterdam Star News*, for instance. I am indebted to Mairuth Sarsfield, Jennifer Hodge de Silva's mother and author of the novel *No Crystal Stair*, for this information, related at a conference in Toronto on black theatre in June 1997. See Stanley G. Grizzle's *My Name's Not George: The Story of the Brotherhood of Sleeping Car Porters in Canada* (Toronto: Umbrella Press, 1998) for a highly personalized account of the struggles of the Canadian black porter. See Agnes Calliste's invaluable scholarship on the sleeping-car porters: "Blacks on Canadian Railways," *Canadian Ethnic Studies* 20, no. 2 (1988); "Car Porters in Canada: An Ethnically Submerged Labour Split Market," *Canadian Ethnic Studies* 19, no. 1 (1987); and "The Struggle for Equity by Blacks on American and Canadian Railroads," *Journal of Black Studies* 25, no. 3 (January 1995).

23 In fact, some of the "official" train and landscape footage is reminiscent of the late-nineteenth-century promotional scenics produced by the Canadian Pacific Railway to promote tourism and nationalism. See Peter Morris' *Embattled Shadows: A History of Canadian Cinema, 1895–1939* (Montréal: McGill-Queen's University Press, 1978).

24 See Maurice Charland's essay of the same title. He writes, "Note, however, that technological nationalism only defines Canadian ideals and opinion by virtue of their not being from foreign sources. This is significant because, in its reluctance or inability to articulate a positive content to the Canadian identity—and identity to be created—technological nationalism is a form of liberalism, privileging the process of communication over the substance of what is communicated" ("Technological Nationalism," 206).

25 See Stuart Hall's memorable essay "What is this 'Black' in Black Popular Culture?" in *Black Popular Culture*, 21–33. He qualifies, "American mainstream popular culture has always involved certain traditions that could only be attributed to black cultural vernacular traditions."

26 Eric Lott argues that black men have predominantly been gender role-models for white men since the 1840s. He claims the imitation of the styles of African-American masculinity is "so much a part of white men's equipment for living that they remain entirely unaware of their participation in it." See *Love and Theft: Blackface Minstrelsy and the American Working Class* (New York: Oxford University Press, 1993), 52. While Lott's point adds historical consistency to the mainstream appeal of this new genre, the fear and desire that necessarily undergirds the fetishization of the black male, and the subsequent social costs to him, should also be stressed.

27 *Rude* was produced with Toronto's Canadian Film Centre under the auspices of the Feature Film Project. While he was resident at the Centre, Virgo's script was chosen for development, a much-valued opportunity for first-time filmmakers. Here Virgo also completed his short film *Save My Lost Nigger Soul* (1993). The Cain and Abel narrative anticipates Virgo's third feature, *Love Come Down* (2000). His association with the Centre, however, was initiated by a summer institute for filmmakers of colour. To date, Virgo's features have won numerous prizes and accolades. *The Planet of Junior Brown* (1998) was listed as one of the best films of 1998 by the *Village Voice*.

28 One cannot find fault with journalists for their astonishment and subsequent overvaluation. My uneasiness lies in the precise nature of this engagement.

29 Stuart Hall explains: "[Popular culture] is rooted in popular experience and available for expropriation at one and the same time … By definition, black popular culture is a contradictory space. It is a sight of strategic contestation" ("What is this 'Black'," 26).

30 Again in itself a conceit, recalling how the porters' dissemination of the black press symbolically dismantled the coveted "technological nationalism" thesis.

31 See Arthur Kroker's *Technology and the Canadian Mind: Innis/McLuhan/Grant* (Montréal: New World Perspectives, 1984) for a definitive argument. The films of Atom Egoyan are also suggestive of the notion that technological experience discursively informs our cultural products. While both Egoyan and Virgo share the strategy of using video-imaging to point to the mediated nature of both representation and human interaction, its use does not signal decorative hipness. Video presence indicates trauma, historical memory, and its imminent erasure.

32 Albeit these references share a surface quality, and could be interpreted as shallow, what Rinaldo Walcott has named the "blackness of blackness." Among other shortcomings, Walcott critiques the film for its particular use of Africanisms and African-Americanisms, a practice that inhibits the full exploration of and grounding in the local. I believe Walcott's thoughts on *Rude* indirectly support my contention that blackness can only be articulated as a trace in popular film (or its attempted cross-over) because of the pervasive conditions I outlined in the beginning of this section. See "The Politics of Reading Third Cinema: Reading the Narrative of Clement Virgo's *Rude*" in *Pictures of a Generation on Hold: Selected Papers*, M. Pomerance and J. Sakeris, eds. (Toronto: Media Studies Working Group, 1996), 215–24. Reprinted in Walcott's collection *Black Like Who?* (Toronto: Insomniac Press, 1997).

33 See *The Signifying Monkey: A Theory of African-American Literary Criticism* (New York: Oxford University Press, 1988).

34 To name but a few scholarly efforts: Amira Baraka's *Blues People, Blued People: Negro Music in White America* (Westport, CT: Greenwood Press, 1963); Houston Baker's *Blues, Ideology and African American Literature: A Vernacular Theory* (Chicago: University of Chicago Press, 1984), and Paul Gilroy's *The Black Atlantic: Modernity and Double Consciousness* (Cambridge, MA: Harvard University Press, 1993) and *There Ain't No Black in the Union Jack* (London: Unwin Hyman, 1987).

35 Paul Gilroy, "It's a Family Affair," in *Black Popular Culture*, 308.

36 Like her fellow rudies, Rude stresses Jamaican patois through exaggeration and speed. To this end, voice and idiom are stretched, resulting in a purposeful wooden performance. Enlisting these speech acts points to the effects of transmission. See Edward K. Braithwaite, *History of the Voice: The Development of Nation Language in Anglophone Caribbean Poetry* (London: New Beacon Books, 1984) and Velma Pollard, *Dread Talk: The Language of Rastafari* (Jamaica: Canoe Press, University of the West Indies, 1994).

37 The dozens is a traditionally black urban game. In a form of verbal jousting, each person tries to come up with the most outrageous and original insult. See Geneva Smitherman's *Talkin and Testifyin: The Language of Black America* (Boston: Houghton Mifflin, 1977), and Gates, *The Signifying Monkey*.

38 Surprisingly, despite the current critical disfavour with nationalism, second-generation commentary on Canadian film, both popular and academic, continues to lament that "playing at being American" disrupts Canadian authenticity. In "In Our Own Eyes: The Canonizing of Canadian Film," Peter Morris adroitly traces this tautological tendency and argues that nationalist rhetoric or its residual traces continue to inform assessments of Canadian film. See *Canadian Journal of Film Studies* 3, no. 1: 27–44. Michael Dorland takes the argument further by claiming that cultural nationalism has historically been used for the purposes of self-interest. Although both accounts have made an invaluable contribution to scholarship on Canadian cinema, neither account extends consideration to how positions informed and propagated by nationalism exclude "emerging" filmmakers. As I have attempted to suggest, restriction is secured simply through structural relations.

39 Hall, "What is this 'Black'," 27.

Fishy

Geoff Pevere

IN THE YEAR 2000, FOUR CANADIAN MOVIES expressed a certain weirdness in the form of fish: *Maelstrom*, a story of romantic recovery told by a butchered but nevertheless loquacious fish; *waydowntown*, in which a fish makes a disconcerting appearance clamped to the knee of a man attempting a lunchtime quickie in an underground parking lot; *Violet*, in which a dead fish turns up at the birthday party of a woman convinced she is about to die; and *Two Thousand and None*, wherein a paleontologist with a rare and fatal swelling-brain disease discovers the world's oldest fossilized remains just before everything in his life starts to go baroque. It's a fish.

It's a coincidence, of course. At the risk of offending those whose livelihoods or backgrounds have ties with the harvesting of our waters, not since Pierre Perrault convinced the residents of l'Isle-aux-Coudres to revive their dormant beluga hunt—or since *Un zoo la nuit* imagined the salving of strained father–son relations in terms of a few lines cast out from the masculine sanctity of a shared boat—have Canadian filmmakers seemed to care so much about fish. Yet there they were, four of them. They showed up in the disparate works of four Canadian filmmakers of different regional pedigrees: one an Anglo Calgarian (*waydowntown*'s Gary Burns), one a Québec francophone (*Maelstrom*'s Denis Villeneuve), the third a Newfoundlander (*Violet*'s Rosemary House), and the fourth a Armenian central-Canadian (*Two Thousand and None*'s Arto Parmaganian).

Granted, four may not seem like much in the oceanic scheme of things, but four fish appearing in separate movies in a single year in a relatively small national cinema—which has hitherto demonstrated no conspicuous thematic interest in marine life—seems a coincidence too, well, fishy to be consigned to whim and happenstance. (If I haven't mentioned the fact that, in late 1999, the Toronto band Our Lady Peace released a CD titled *Happiness ... Is Not a Fish You Can Catch*—featuring a man in a bowler holding a fish on the cover—it's only because I am trying not to cloud the waters.) Moreover, there is the commanding fact that, in each movie, the fish serves a similar purpose to that which it did for certain surrealists and on the cover of avant-pop pioneer Captain Beefheart's ear-assaulting classic *Trout Mask Replica*: it is a signifier of weird, a signpost on the narrative freeway that announces we have officially passed the outer limits of normal.

In *Maelstrom*, the talking fish heeds us not to expect a story that honours the rules of conventional romantic storytelling, a fact that the creature's brutal filleting certainly stresses. In *waydowntown*, the fish on the knee—along with fleeting appearances of a caped superhero and the protagonist's occasional anti-gravitational tours of the office–mall complex in which the movie takes place—ripple the otherwise flat texture of corporate cubicle-ism which the movie sends up. The party-crashing killjoy fish in *Violet* sends our quasi-neurotic middle-aged matron-heroine into a state of bedridden self-seclusion: convinced the fish is a harbinger of a family curse that kills everyone at age fifty-five, she spends most of the days preceding her fifty-sixth birthday under the covers. In *Two Thousand and None*, the fossilized fish is an omen of the imminent disengagement from data-insulated normality. Shortly after he discovers it, the paleontologist learns not only that he is about to die from a swelling brain, but that he will lose his memory in the process, a bitter irony indeed for a digger of history and fisher of time itself. Even his dead parents start making appearances in his apartment.

In each of these movies, from the fish follows weirdness. But it is weirdness—and this is where it becomes compelling to students of the domestic cultural character—of a strangely ordered, almost official, variety. Both weird (in its announcement of logic's departure) and not weird (in the processed orderliness of the announcement). There seems, to me at least, something almost irresistibly Canadian in the fact that four moviemakers in a single year turn to the figure of the fish to find a metaphor for the flight from reason and convention.

Weirdness, understood here as the deliberate departure from realist convention for the sake of undermining convention itself, has long struggled to maintain a foothold on the stubbornly docudramatic surface of Canadian movies. Despite the fact that certain conditions of national experience would suggest a place where weirdness ought to flourish and thrive, in Canadian movies it has fought like weeds marching heroically against suburbia. In this country, weirdness is an underground movement as tenacious as it is outnumbered—and as systematically mown down.

To the extent that any traditions have managed to obtain within the slippery, tradition-dodging history of English-Canadian moviemaking, they have tended to favour those developments that incline in a direction almost precisely opposite that of the fantastical, the speculative, the whimsical and weird. It is instead a history of "documentary tradition," or of realist practices derived from "documentary tradition," particularly that galosh-on-the-ground hybrid of documentary technique and realist inclination sometimes called docudrama. In fact, docudrama long formed the centre of what passed for a Canadian canon: from the *verité* documentary innovations of the NFB's Unit B, through Pierre Perrault's non-fiction essays, the primary legacy of the first genuinely industrious period of Canadian-made moviemaking—from the late 1950s to early 1970s—was its apparent fidelity to practices rooted in documentary and post-documentary realism. This rootedness in turn led to the unavoidable if frankly peculiar implication that moviemaking in Canada—derived as it largely was from the commercially insulated practices of the NFB and public broadcasting networks—was more strongly associated with journalistic than artistic practices.

Indeed, the Canadian movies most likely to be cited as instrumental were those that demonstrated the strongest reflective tendencies: those that held the clearest mirror up to some form of national experience, that reported on some usually issue-based crisis in the social fabric: disconsolate adolescence (*Nobody Waved Goodbye*), Québec sovereignty (*Le Chat dans le sac*), regional economic and cultural disparity (*Goin' Down the Road*), marital crisis (*A Married Couple*), malevolent state power (*Les Ordres*), receding community tradition (*Pour la suite du monde*), or institutional abuse (*Warrendale*). If at all, Canadian moviemaking was valued as an extension of the realist, civically edifying practice of journalism—another vaunted domestic activity—and as such might have been good for civic awareness but considerably less so for the what-the-hell practice of art. And art, if you look at it with sufficient utilitarianism, is plain weird.

Yet it is precisely this pragmatic utilitarianism—often manifest as sheer hoser practicality—that has seemed to be the prevailing Canadian attitude to art. Its usefulness not as immediately apparent as say, a pair of skates, a snowplow, or a block heater, art squats suspiciously in the cultural character. There's something weird about it. Even in its arts, Canada has tended to favour weather-proof practicality. It is more comfortable with prose than poetry, representational painting (particularly of landscapes and animals) than abstract, Don Messer than Glenn Gould, Norman Jewison than David Cronenberg, David Cronenberg than Michael Snow, TV than movies, Wayne Gretzky than Toller Cranston, sport than art, and so on. Canada has kept art safely harnessed and leashed through systems of public subsidy, and ensured its marginalization by flooding the popular mainstream with unregulated pop-cultural imports. Even the more sanctioned forms of "classical" middlebrow arts, of the kind purring away in the confines of CBC radio broadcasting, are really not much valued, or they wouldn't be confined to the chopping block of CBC radio.

Certainly Canada is neither alone nor exceptional in this bull-necked philistinism: this is the way of the middle-class western world, or at least those parts of it where it is considered more newsworthy to score a goal than make a movie. But where it grows compelling in the Canadian context is the sheer effort such cheese-sandwich conformity requires, for Canada is actually a veritable hotbed of wanton, unwashed weirdness. Enforcing normality is work around here.

Consider the following conditions for the care and nurturing of the strange in this country. 1) Canada is a vast and uninhabitably forbidding country with a relatively minuscule population, where the populace wishes artists would go live somewhere else—and that's bound to warp any artist's sense of manifest destiny. 2) Canada is a largely English-speaking country stuck right next to the most powerful and pervasive English-speaking cultural juggernaut the world has ever known. Obviously this position plays havoc with any artist's sense of cultural sovereignty and identity. 3) Canada has no core national myth. Thus, while the disparate manifestations of the American experience are united by a subterranean myth of shared national destiny, Canada had to be pasted together with a railroad. (This is why so many otherwise absurd things—from railways and winter sports to radio hosts to news readers—are cast in the role of national glue, to be all that's holding this forever-falling-apart country together.) 4) Canada was not forged in the flame of revolution but through the interminable and orderly machinations of bureaucratic compromise; if anything explains the country's entrenched fondness for panel discussions, town hall debates, and waiting patiently in queues, this is it. And 5) Canada is a country suspended somewhere between the fading influence of British imperialism and the surging tides of American-issue corporate capitalism—or between high tea and high five. This place in-between certainly helps to create conditions of productively weird cultural schizophrenia.

But the salient point isn't the lack of pure, art-for-art's-sake weirdness in CanCult, but the fact of its marginality—the triumphant enforcement of that conservative, post-colonial, bureaucratic propriety. Given the preceding conditions, then, Canadian moviemaking has generated an inevitably rich tradition of paradigm-rattling, bird-flipping maverickism. From the perception-altering films of Michael Snow (and the generally robust tradition of Canadian avant-gardism) to the postmodern miasma of Winnipeg's Guy Maddin—whose first feature (*Tales from the Gimli Hospital*) incidentally contains a pioneering instance of fish—weird—the otherwise ice-smooth surface of Canadian movies has been regularly (and promisingly) scored and dented by interventions of sloppy strangeness: the Gaspé neo-Bergmanism of Paul Almond; the northern psychedelia of Gordon Sheppard; the cerebral bioshock of early Cronenberg; the arch symbolism of early Jack Darcus; the exuberantly earthy sensualism of Joyce Wieland; the deadpan, laser-precise pop-cult refraction of John Paizs. As this selective and illustrative list is meant to suggest, the point is not that Canada suffers any shortage of inveterate cine-weirdness; the point is the systematic suppression of that weirdness: in most of these cases, the weirder the work, the deeper its burial. With the blunt tenacity of that fishmonger bludgeoning our gilled narrator in *Maelstrom*, mainstream Canadian culture has beaten most of these names—and their work—right out of national memory.

You might wonder why. If weird intrudes so commonly and regularly on Canadian cultural practice as to seem almost natural, why must it struggle to find purchase anywhere but those pockets of specialty-boutique strangeness? Filmmakers like R. Bruce Elder, Mike Hoolboom, and Michael Snow continue to practise radically unorthodox filmmaking because that work politely observes the parameters of experimental practice: it makes no presumptions to anything other than marginality, and within those parameters it is duly celebrated and sanctified. It may question the epistemological paradigms of modern perception and discourse, but it is not uppity. No way it's going Hollywood.

And that's the crux of it, really. When one delves into the very notion of the thing called "Canadian cinema," one is sinking one's rubbers in something much more sensitive, complex, and problematic than just another national cinema. One may even be stepping into the very heart of the country's conflicted soul, the mine-strewn border where culture meets commerce, and where the impractical, poetic ideal of the country collides with the cold business of running it. There, weirdness and convention struggle not just for the sake of defining the territorial limits of normality, but for the global marketability of the country-as-business. And weird, in Canada's collective mind, is just not good for business. Movies, with all due respect to Alfred Hitchcock, are not only movies: they are one of the truly élite products of the global market. One of the defining economic units of post-Cold War globalization itself, cinema is the model for one market under Hollywood. Canadian movies, dependent as ever on state whim and priority for their existence—a necessary dependence when the commercial marketplace is largely off-limits—are therefore freighted with unreasonable expectation and prejudice. (The announcement, in mid 2000, that film-funding initiatives administered by the federal Heritage ministry would soon be determined according to box office performance is typical: like offering prizes for catching the most fish without going near the water.) Hollywood movies have come to set a production standard for feature filmmaking that skews all indigenous film-producing markets in its homogeneously entertaining and impossibly costly direction. Even more insidiously, Hollywood has set the standard of most people's notions of what proper movies are—including, as the box office-biased Heritage Ministry policy suggests, people who run the various departments and agencies that make Canadian movies possible.

In this context, homegrown cinematic weirdness is triply problematic. First, weird movies don't conform to mainstream standards. Next, weird movies lack obvious commercial potential—and movies, in global-think, are organs of commerce. And finally, weird movies represent the country poorly by emphasizing, in the most embarrassing fashion, how far below and beyond the Hollywood bar we fall. The last thing Canadians in the global economy want is to look weird. It's profoundly unbecoming.

Weirdness is thus viewed patronizingly, if not alarmingly, as a sign of arrested development or petulant killjoy nonconformity. This explains why weirdness has to be certified elsewhere before it warrants reluctant legitimization here (as the careers of Cronenberg, Atom Egoyan, and Guy Maddin testify). Even then, it is hardly a matter of straightforward recanting. Guy Maddin might be the most enthusiastically praised Canadian filmmaker everywhere but here since *Videodrome*-era Cronenberg, but it hasn't done much to lubricate the wheels of this inveterate square peg's career: he's produced four features in the same period that Egoyan has turned out six, a fact that probably has as much to do with the latter's more carefully modulated weirdness—particularly when compared to the former's full-bore neo-classical weirdness—as it does careful career management.

Fascinatingly then, those Canadian moviemakers who have managed to survive the process of cultural rendering have been those few—like Cronenberg, Snow, and to a certain extent Maddin—who have simply carried on, like one of those unstoppable apocalyptic viruses spreading madness and mutilation through Cronenberg's early movies, or maybe like one of the perpetual-motion cinematic devices once designed by Snow. And when they've managed, like these three have, to build a reputation despite the overwhelming and obvious official disinclination to their work (which was never more hostile than to early-career Cronenberg), isn't it somehow fitting that those reputations have so consistently been built outside of the country before gradually seeping back? You could read this as a sign that you have to go elsewhere to be a successfully weird Canadian (the Jim Carrey principle) or—more to the point, one should think—that weirdness in Canada is only accepted domestically if it has been certified elsewhere first. If, that is, the fish thrown overboard have been caught elsewhere. For it's there, somewhere offshore, that the frontier between plain weird and status weird would seem to preside.

If 2000 was the year of the fish in Canadian movies, the implications may not be entirely encouraging. While these numerous instances of simultaneous cinematic marine symbolism suggest that the tendency to strangeness in Canadian movies is as acute as ever, the fact that so much weirdness found itself processed into the same image can't help but give pause. When everybody comes up with the same weird idea, when weirdness itself verges on generic, well, how weird can it be?

Feature Filmmakers
and a Few Others

Directed by Phillip Borsos
Blaine Allan

"UNFULFILLED PROMISE" INEVITABLY PROVIDES THE CLICHÉ that neatly though inadequately characterizes the film career of Phillip Borsos. When he died in 1995 at the age of 41, he left an impressive, if modest, legacy. It includes six short films, a brace of television commercials, and five feature films, one that also exists in a longer format as a two-part television program. He did not live to see his fifth and final film released. Such a view of Borsos' promise largely bases itself on the early films of confidence and achievement: three short documentaries, notably, and his first feature. Through the last ten years of his life, he never regained the forthright praise he earned for *Cooperage* (1975), *Spartree* (1977), *Nails* (1979), and *The Grey Fox* (1982), all of which earned Canadian film awards. He followed those with a Hollywood thriller, *The Mean Season* (1984); a bleak but hopeful fantasy finally produced in collaboration with Disney, *One Magic Christmas* (1986); *Bethune: The Making of a Hero* (1990), an international epic, overreaching production, and logistical nightmare; and finally an adventure for young viewers, *Far From Home: The Adventures of Yellow Dog* (1995). While Borsos' filmmaking regularly overlapped with Hollywood, the conditions of Canadian cinema shaped his career. The circumstances of his life determined that his promise remained unfulfilled by the time of his death, but acknowledging promise also means recognizing the uncommon ambitions that his career encompassed and his films evidence.

For this discussion, I am concentrating on his best-known films, which circulated most widely, with occasional reference to two other documentaries, *Spartree/Making the Film* (1977) and *Racquetball* (1979), and two early shorts, *The Barking Dog* (1974) and *Cadillac* (1974). I am necessarily excluding a sponsored documentary, *Phase III (Regeneration)* (1977); two films that Borsos produced and Barry Healey directed, *Outtakes* (1977) and *The Morning After, The Night Before* (1979); and the commercials Borsos directed in Vancouver in the 1970s, which I have not yet seen. I am also bypassing the commercials he made in Toronto in the early 1990s. *Cooperage*, *Spartree*, and *Nails* share thematic and stylistic preoccupations with one another and with the features that followed; so do *Spartree/Making the Film* and *Racquetball*, but to tease them out in any depth would require more space than the rewards would warrant here. Immediately notable for their maturity, confidence, ambition, and skill, the suite of three award-winning shorts eclipses the other documentaries made in the same period and the student productions they followed. Professionally and textually, they lead directly into *The Grey Fox* and the feature films that dominated Borsos' career.

Information about production circumstances invariably conditioned response to Borsos' films after *The Grey Fox*. It too was a difficult case, but its award-winning achievement when few Canadian feature films drew praise overshadowed the problems in getting the picture in the can. To suggest their institutional character, it is possible to draw comparisons between Borsos' productions and well-known cases from the mavericks of US cinema, unusually (though, it turns out, appropriately enough) including John Cassavetes. Although ambitious, *The Grey Fox* originated with Borsos and was shaped by his and his close collaborators' hands, like Cassavetes' first film, *Shadows* (1959). Like Cassavetes, who followed that picture with studio projects, *Too Late Blues* (1962) and *A Child is Waiting* (1963), Borsos made a Hollywood venture, *The Mean Season*, his sophomore feature. *One Magic Christmas* drew on personal material but, like Cassavetes' *Husbands* (1970) or *Minnie and Moskowitz* (1971), also involved Hollywood partners. *Bethune* has no corresponding number in Cassavetes' career; he never took on such an overreaching logistical burden or period subject matter. For counterparts, we could look to the runaway epics Nicholas Ray or Anthony Mann directed in Europe for producer Samuel Bronston—*55 Days at Peking* (1963) and *The Fall of the Roman Empire* (1964), for example. Again like Cassavetes, who near the end of his career made the personal and intimate *Love Streams* (1984), shooting part of it in his own house as he had *Faces* (1968) years before, Borsos took to home ground with *Far From Home*, shot in his familiar territory, the lower British Columbia islands.

Borsos' documentaries demonstrate consistency of concept and execution, while his features display consistencies of different types, having more to do with Borsos' confidence in his approach to varying subjects and stories. *Cooperage*, *Spartree*, and *Nails* all concern traditional modes of work in a modern world. Barrel-building, tree-topping, and nail-making: each process has been done for years, and Borsos analytically depicts how such work is done in his time, whether that represents change or retention of traditional practice. These three films stand as a trilogy because of their shared concerns and styles, but it is not too big a step to include the lesser-known *Racquetball*, an exploration of the sport at a professional level, and *Spartree/Making the Film*, in which Borsos and his own crew are the professionals at work, exercising skills in a process, shooting a documentary that has its own history.

Of Borsos' five features, *The Grey Fox* and *Bethune* can be paired, as can *One Magic Christmas* and *Far From Home*. Although *The Mean Season* bears some correspondences to his other films, it also stands apart, as a fully fledged Hollywood production that Borsos undertook as a job for hire after the script was written; it is, moreover, the only film Borsos completed that was adapted from a work of previously published fiction. Historical in setting and based on verifiable events, *The Grey Fox* and *Bethune* concern protagonists who travel alone away from their homelands in moments of social change. One goes to Canada in the early years of the 1900s and the other leaves Canada for China during the Communist Revolution. They have outlaw status both in their home countries and in the lands where they relocate, but there they also attract the fascination, admiration, and even reverence of the people to whom they are foreigners. Contemporary stories *One Magic Christmas* and *Far From Home* depict families in crisis. In subgenres that typically imply young audiences or family viewing—Christmas fantasy and animal adventure—they incorporate the hard edges of trauma and the threat of family members' violent death that leaves the apparent survivors to cope with sudden loss. Each film also unfolds as a series of trials that the protagonist must endure.

The Hero

"A professional always specializes," says stagecoach robber Bill Miner to a callow jailbird trying to induce him to join in a bank heist. Borsos' male protagonists typically have skills and use them effectively. Miner explicitly draws our attention to this facet of himself, in that changing conditions require him to adapt his vocation from robbing stagecoaches to robbing trains. The documentaries all concern workers with productive and visually beguiling skills. Dr. Norman Bethune stands as a version of that staple character of medical drama, the brilliant clinician whose talents are valued but whose temperament makes him intolerable to the medical authorities. *The Mean Season*'s Malcolm Anderson is a reporter so good at his job that a serial killer, the object of his investigations, values him as a conduit of information to Miami's reading public. The Christmas angel Gideon has a job to do and does it with purportedly benign but actually ruthless efficiency. Perhaps the adolescent Angus, shipwrecked in *Far From Home*, offers an exception, although the film revolves around his learning the skills of survival in the wilds. He is an ordinary youth caught in exceptional circumstances that require him to adapt and learn to live long enough to be found. The film's protagonist arguably is not Angus, moreover, but the dog Yellow, whose keen survival skills are innate—or inscrutable to humans.

As Yellow and Angus might share the principal role in *Far From Home*, in its counterpart *One Magic Christmas*, the angel Gideon is not the protagonist who endures and changes. That role belongs to Ginnie Grainger, the working-class woman Gideon puts through a trial-by-ordeal in order to restore the childlike Christmas spirit that presumably survives dormant despite her material hardships and her reasonably embittered resolve. She is Borsos' only female character who can claim status as a protagonist. Her non-domestic work is a job—she is a supermarket cashier—and not a calling, profession, or skill. Her husband Jack has lost his own unidentified job, but aspires to use his talents to open a bicycle shop. His mechanical capabilities are more clearly identifiable than any Ginnie has that might plot her on the line of professionalism and skill that Borsos drew starting from the Sweeney Cooperage. In fact, part of the trauma of *One Magic Christmas* also stems from the apparent diminishment of any nurturing skills Ginnie might have had as a mother, now hardened in the face of both economic hardship and the consumerist demands of modern Christmas. Even there, the sentimental and more evidently caring Jack appears the more sufficient parent.

Where Angus and Yellow complement each other as they share the ordeal of *Far From Home*, Ginnie and Gideon are effectively antagonists, Gideon engineering the pain that Ginnie suffers. Gideon is charged to help one person who has lost the Christmas spirit to regain it, and he does so by effecting a series of incidents that strip Ginnie of her family. They culminate in a botched bank robbery, where bystander Jack is shot dead, then the thief gets away in Ginnie's car, with her two children in it, only to drive off a bridge into an icy river. While Gideon might cause Ginnie's grief, even in retrospect she does not seem aware of his machinations. The only encounter of the two is cloaked in mystery, not confrontation. Ginnie never has the opportunity to face down her supernatural tormentor, who is, in the film's moral scheme, acting for the greater good, in her interest, and in the interest of her family.

Apart from Ginnie, then, Borsos' heroes are males engaged in pursuits in which, in myth or history or both, men have predominated. Angel should be an equal-opportunity job, and at first it might seem that Gideon should be excused from this gender determination. The best-known films about benign angels or ghosts who meddle in mortals' lives, however, have typically involved male spirits. Of *It's a Wonderful Life* (1946), *Here Comes Mr. Jordan* (1941) and its remake

Heaven Can Wait (1978), *The Ghost and Mrs. Muir* (1947), *A Matter of Life and Death* (also known as *Stairway to Heaven,* 1946), *Ghost* (1990), and *Truly, Madly, Deeply* (1991), all but the first echo *One Magic Christmas,* in that a male, supernatural being influences an earthly woman, although in a romantic mode not present in Borsos' story. Even if he is an angel in the afterlife, moreover, in his mortal life as a cowhand Gideon had a conventionally masculine occupation, and he continues to wear the hat and duster of a Westerner, just like Bill Miner. For Borsos, Richard Farnsworth and Harry Dean Stanton evidently embodied Westerners. Although they were not completely interchangeable, he had first cast Stanton as Miner, and he had wanted Farnsworth to follow up his successful portrayal of Miner with a role in the Christmas film that Stanton ultimately assumed.

Not only are they men doing traditionally masculine jobs, but their dilemmas revolve around their work. Bill Miner is an outlaw of the American West, a fugitive pursued by the law, who also appears to be growing accustomed to a settled life in inland BC. Reporter Malcolm Anderson permits himself to be used by the serial killer Alan Delour in order to feed his own journalistic ambitions. Technically and socially, Norman Bethune is a surgical innovator, but as such is intolerable to the medical status quo and exiles himself first to Spain and then to China, where he finds himself more welcome than in Canada. Angus McCormick is still young, but he assists his father, a freight-boat operator, and their work puts them in the storm that shipwrecks the boy. Again, Gideon remains an exception, in part because his work causes him no discernible dilemma—he never appears to question his actions—but does for Ginnie. In part, Gideon's confidence derives from the film's demonstrable interest in how he does his work. If his job is to see that Ginnie regains her Christmas spirit, the film outlines the intricacies of the process, no matter that the process is more emotional than logical.

This concern for process forms a part of all Borsos' films, back to the documentaries. With a minimum of words, the trilogy of his best-known short films analytically describes physical tasks. The variously skilled workers who cut and shape staves, ends, and hoops, and assemble them into barrels constitute a collective hero of *Cooperage.* In a testament to the division of labour as it might have been practised in the nineteenth century and persisted at the Sweeney Barrel Company into the 1970s, Borsos finds the attractions and beauty in the ways the workers use tools and machine to manipulate wood and metal. With *Spartree,* he locates these qualities in a solitary man who scales a tall tree, chainsaws its top off, and sits atop the remaining trunk to smoke a cigarette. *Spartree* derives part of its visual force from the forest's natural beauty, but also from the step-by-step depiction of Hap Johnson's measured work at dizzying heights, unaccompanied by words after opening titles defining "spartree." Less deliberate, the companion work, *Spartree/Making the Film,* recalls *Cooperage* in its description of a process involving a team. The film concentrates particularly on the challenges met by the camera operators who had to mirror Johnson's work many metres up in order to shoot him at eye level and by the technicians who engineered the apparatus that enabled the elevated shooting in the forest. In his film about the making of his film, Borsos' presence remains significantly small, in deference to the craftspeople who provided the components for his documentary. *Nails* intercuts sequences depicting nail-making all in the present day, but representing manufacturing at different moments: a blacksmith fashioning nails one by one; an early, industrial model manufacturing them in quantity; and their modern mass-production. As in *Spartree,* Borsos avoids using words. Representing different periods, *Nails* has no single human centre or hero, although the film starts and ends with the smith and suggests endorsement of his craft.

With the features, Borsos has to situate his interest in the craft of his protagonists' work within more complex structures. While they may not be as dispassionately analytic as the documentaries in their depiction of the heroes' jobs, the features still ensure that their work forms an important part of the characters' definition. Bill Miner, for example, undertakes several jobs in the course of *The Grey Fox*, including oyster picker, mining engineer—his identity in Kamloops—and horse rustler, and Borsos depicts him doing all three at different points. His true profession, of course, was stagecoach robbery, now modified with the times to train robbery. The script is larded with references to techniques, such as "the Chapman method," where the passenger cars are separated from the engine and the mail car that holds the loot, that suggest both Miner's competency and the film's veracity. Miner's knowledge is such that he vests it in his accomplices—failing at first, resulting in a botched robbery in Oregon, and then more successfully with Shorty and the lucrative heist at Ducks Crossing.

Similarly, Norman Bethune's reputation is in part based on his technical innovations, which are woven, with appropriate explication, into *Bethune: The Making of a Hero*. Dramatizing a well-known episode in the Bethune myth, Bethune collapses one of his lungs as experimental therapy for his own tuberculosis and explains that disabling the lung permits the organ "to rest." During an operation, he becomes impatient with the conventional tools of thoracic surgery, and then finds inspiration in a cobbler's shears, with which he invents rib cutters with improved leverage. In Spain he devises mobile blood-transfusion units, and he brings to China methods of blood preservation, all the while explaining the processes and values of his own innovation. Not only in the straitened circumstances of the Spanish Civil War and Mao's war with Japan but also amid the medical establishment of Montréal, Bethune adopts a role as teacher. By his deeds and his words, he instructs in medical procedures and advocates for an equitable system of socialized medicine in Canada. In this, then, the film also adopts a didactic tone that mirrors Bethune the instructor.

Where Miner and Bethune are seasoned professionals who understand their respective crafts well enough to instruct, in *Far From Home* young Angus McCormick has himself to learn in order to survive. He has to innovate as a trapper and gatherer of food, he must devise shelter for himself and Yellow, and he has to consider his options and make decisions about moving or staying put for the best chance of being discovered in the thick forest where they are stranded. Angus has to improvise with what is available to him, and in that he resembles Gideon. If he has an overarching plan, he does not disclose it, and in any case has to gauge the responses of the Grainger family members in order for his plans to succeed. I have suggested elsewhere that the corresponding protagonists of *One Magic Christmas* and *Far From Home* might not be Gideon and Angus, but Gideon and Yellow, the dog.[1] Both other than human, they appear without logical cause and insinuate themselves into families. Without any special effects to convey magic, merely story and editing, Gideon simply turns up or disappears throughout *One Magic Christmas*. Similarly, Yellow shows up at the McCormick farm, where the family adopts him. After his apparently fatal fall when Angus is rescued, his reappearance, in the distance and with no depiction of his voyage back home, suggests the amazing. There are significant differences, of course, in that Gideon creates the traumatic situations endured by the Graingers, especially Ginnie, while Yellow suffers alongside Angus and his father when a vicious storm capsizes their boat and strands dog and boy on a remote shore. Inscrutably, both angel and dog, however, also protect their human confederates.

The Mean Season may stand apart from Borsos' other films in a number of ways, but like other Borsos heroes its protagonist practises his profession with skill. A reporter for the *Miami Journal*, he quickly becomes caught in a position reaching back to other news-and-crime stories, whether the social conscience of *Call Northside 777* (1948) or the farce of *The Front Page* (1931), wherein the reporter adopts the role of investigator.[2] Perhaps more so than other such films, apart from *All the President's Men* (1976), *The Mean Season* concerns itself with and implicates the processes of reporting news. Anderson picks up the story of the "Numbers Killer" only by chance. Like Hecht and Macarthur's Hildy Johnson, he is in the newsroom at that moment intending to quit the job—in Anderson's case to leave the torrid zone of south Florida for a more settled existence with his lover Christine, editing a small-town paper in Colorado. The initial call about a brutal murder enables him to do what his editor thinks he does best, however, and ultimately serial killer Alan Delour depends exactly on how well Anderson does his job as a reporter, at least for the killer's purposes. In fact, his failure to interrogate the information he is receiving in his direct link with the killer, which is to say his lapses in evaluating details in order to "get the story," constitutes one of Malcolm's key flaws.

Where there are heroes, there might be villains. Although Borsos' stories contain adversaries who throw the protagonists into relief, they remain remarkably clear of out-and-out villains. As a homicidal compulsive, *The Mean Season*'s Delour has the clearest qualifications, certainly to judge by the brutality of his crimes. Characteristic of a villain, he exercises power, both over his victims and over Malcolm and Christine, although with little motivational detail. (The source novel, John Katzenbach's *In the Heat of the Summer*, is set several years earlier than the film and situates Delour as a traumatized Vietnam veteran.[3]) As in many such films revolving around deluded killers, the perpetrator might appear as much the victim as his victims. Delour, however, capitalizes on Malcolm's ambition and his skills, leading him on with information and misinformation, thus suggesting fissures in his reporter's professionalism.

In cases such as *The Grey Fox* and *One Magic Christmas*, a protagonist himself might be seen to occupy the conventional position of villain, although the films work to obscure that. Miner is, of course, a thief, a fugitive, and a dissembler. The BC Provincial Police officer, Fernie, becomes his friend, however, even seeing that Miner will be warned when the Pinkerton agent, Seavey, is closing in. Seavey, wielding coercive power over Fernie, is the closest the film has to a villainous type. Neatly groomed and speaking with quiet confidence, he demonstrates the style of a figure in authority. Of course, the universe of the Western is rife with contradictions that cannot assure the moral or charismatic superiority of law and order over the outlaw. Gideon wreaks apparent havoc on the Grainger family. As some contemporary accounts worried, moreover, he looks more ominous than angelic—a view underlined at several points in his interaction with the film's child characters, for example, when Gideon surprises Abby on the street in the middle of the night. In a more potent instance, he appears in her bedroom in the night to draw her into his scheme, demonstrating his powers—both supernatural and emotional—by first destroying the treasured snowglobe her grandfather had given her and then magically restoring it.[4]

Norman Bethune encounters a number of professional and personal adversaries in the one and a half decades of his life dramatized by the film. In fact, his contentiousness predisposes practically all other characters to be antagonists or, perhaps more precisely, allies who turn into antagonists. This is endemic in his stormy marriage, and it pervades his relationship with his superiors in the Montréal hospitals. It characterizes his friendship with Chester Rice, the admiring writer (modelled on Bethune biographer Ted Allan) who becomes disillusioned with Bethune's drinking, womanizing, and self-disregard in Spain, which also cause the republicans to eject the surgeon from the country, leading Bethune to tar both the Spanish and Rice. Finally, in China where he tries to fulfill his mission to fight fascism, after excoriating, ostracizing, and humiliating a doctor, Fong, for incompetence, he realizes "the fascist in myself" and begs forgiveness, indicating the actual location of his antagonists and his wish to reform.

"I got ambitions in me that just won't quit," says Bill Miner to his sister, explaining why he has to give up the mundane and law-abiding work of harvesting oysters and leave the security of family. It sounds an unusual sentiment in *The Grey Fox*, since the elderly Miner, having been released from a long prison sentence, at that point might seem anything but ambitious. With the inspiration of viewing *The Great Train Robbery* in a nickelodeon, however, and having knocked would-be confederate in bank robbery Danny Young to the sawdust in a barroom fight, Miner's capabilities have momentarily risen into view, and he has acquired the tool of his trade, a Colt revolver. His skills and the required emotional capacity for violence are in place; only the opportunity to exercise those facets of his being awaits. The sentiment he expresses to his sister might easily be applied to Borsos' male protagonists in general. Miner, Anderson, and Bethune certainly harbour ambitiousness and the appeal of danger that both drives their characters and clashes with the lure of domesticity. Gideon's and Angus' ambitions may appear more moderated or qualified, perhaps because they are couched in jobs that need to be done—Gideon's as his assignment and Angus' in order to survive—but their resourceful drive to achieve their goals remains evident nonetheless.

Themes and Variations
The Grey Fox and *Bethune*

Borsos' heroes operate at points of change, and those changes are nowhere more evident in his work than in *The Grey Fox* and *Bethune: The Making of a Hero*. These two films stand at significantly different points in Borsos' career, and they represent different types of undertaking, although parallels exist even at the point of production. His first feature after the award-winning success of the documentaries, *The Grey Fox* and the story of train robber Bill Miner had been a project of abiding interest for Borsos for many years, although he had first imagined himself as producer and not director of the film. With the collaboration of Barry Healey, and having enlisted producer Peter O'Brian, Borsos assumed the director's job and set about making a distinguished Canadian version of a Western. Although the production was chronically underfinanced, what resources there were appeared on screen. *Bethune* had also been a commitment of long standing, although not for Borsos but for screenwriter Allan, who had known Norman Bethune and written, with Sydney Gordon, the first biography, *The Scalpel, The Sword*, published in 1952.[5] A film finally got underway when producers Nicolas Clermont and Pieter Kroonenburg took on Allan's project. They hired Borsos, by then the director of three feature films, to direct what turned out to be an arduous production and the most expensive Canadian film to that date.

The constructive myths of the Hollywood Western conventionally return to ideas of the frontier and settlement, and the imposition of European models of civilization on the developing territories of the United States. Borsos' film emphasizes the dimension of change over time rather than the conquest of space. The Canada of *The Grey Fox* is, as photographer Kate Flynn puts it, "a country in transition," although Borsos depicts a 1904 British Columbia already quite settled, with an occasional motor car, a fully industrialized lumber mill (the barrel factory of *Cooperage*), a Kamloops with handsome houses and church, board walkways, and a well-appointed hotel; and a railroad that ploughs through the mountains and along the rivers is perceived as profiteering exploiter that, in Miner confederate Shorty Dunn's words, " 'll shave you six ways to Sunday." Yet the film clearly situates Bill Miner as a personage in a story of personal and social change. Professionally, he has had to change himself, since his primary source of income, the stagecoach, has been supplanted by the railway. He gains inspiration to retrain when he watches a moving picture, a mechanical mode of communication that did not exist when he was last jailed. The film abounds in signs of industrialization, rapidly developing methods of communication and transportation, and resulting social change, articulated in Miner's conversations with Kate as they meet—first in a newspaper office and then as Miner hears her gramophone, another recent innovation—and then court. Perhaps the most striking is the murder–suicide of the Chinese family at the hands of the father, a crime scene to which Corporal Fernie calls Kate on Christmas Day to photograph. A stark sequence, it gains power from its spare dialogue and what it implies rather than says explicitly. Living, and dying, in undeveloped quarters, economically, socially, and physically the family exists on the outskirts of the town. Although unspoken, and almost twenty years after the fact, the image of exploited Asian immigrants recalls the construction of the Canadian Pacific Railway. The transcontinental railway "brings in ideas," in Kate's words, but not all beneficent ideas.

Miner adapts to such change, as I have already noted, most notably altering his job title from stagecoach robber to train robber. His story also revolves around settlement, community, and romantic love, however, and his adaptation to those lures. As a fugitive, of course, he has to conceal himself and remain separate from the social order, but Miner both engages and remains disengaged. He becomes part of the Kamloops community, building a cordial alliance with Fernie and a romance with Kate, but built on the lie of a false identity. Even his confederate Shorty, who knows him as a criminal, believes him to be George Edwards. Richard Farnsworth's characterization underlines Miner's reserve and distance. His placid demeanour breaks only once or twice in the film, when he cracks Danny Young across the face with a whiskey bottle and, later, when he slams Shorty against the hotel room wall for questioning Miner's relationship with Kate and, significantly, Miner's apparent satisfaction with a settled life apart from larceny.

By contrast, both the life and times of *Bethune* are more volatile. The revolution that Bill Miner encounters is industrial, but Norman Bethune puts himself into movements of international socialism, including the issue of socialized medicine in Canada, the republican response to fascism in Spain, and the burgeoning communist movement in China under Mao Zedong. Liberal and engaged in a practice with patients from Montréal's lower classes, Bethune propounds a fairer medical system for Canada but denies communist sympathies. Initially resistant, Bethune changes his commitment when he sees first-hand the medical system in Soviet Russia, although his sojourn there remains an off-screen experience that he relates in a filmstrip shown to his wife and friends. The on-screen wars in Spain and China form panoramic backdrops to Bethune's work. Donald Sutherland punctuates his mercurial Bethune with angry outbursts, for instance, when he arrives in China early in the film only to discover that a bomb destroyed the train and the gear on it, or when he discovers the ill-equipped hospital filled with gangrenous patients and castigates its director, Dr. Fong. Bethune's petulant anger, like much of his character's behaviour, appears to have as much to do with self—and the fascist he discovers therein—as it does with the conditions that provoke his reactions.

Miner and Bethune are distinctive for their respective roles as emigrants and strangers in the places they end up. Miner leaves the United States for Canada, then escapes jail and disappears in 1907, and purportedly travels to Europe the next year. Bethune leaves Canada behind for Spain and, ultimately, China, where he dies. Both depart their homelands for causes, Miner fleeing into BC on a stolen horse after the botched robbery and Bethune initially volunteering his practice in Spain after being asked to step down from his hospital post for mixing medicine and politics. His ejection from Spain then propels him to China. The people of the countries in which they are foreigners, moreover, make them objects of fascination and even adoration, gathering in great numbers to send them off. The entire town of Kamloops, it seems, assembles to see Miner and his gang board the train to prison, and hundreds of soldiers snake in procession through the hills, carrying Bethune's body to its resting place. Implicitly, then, both characters find a home somewhere not their home, but only as heroes and outsiders, as participants, but not fully belonging.

Both *The Grey Fox* and *Bethune* frame their biographies with signs of meta-historical authorship. Borsos situated *The Grey Fox* in relation to Miner's time and the Hollywood West with opening intertitles and black-and-white stock footage. These words and images introduce Miner, stagecoaches, and the West that he had inhabited before his incarceration, but also place his story in relation to the Western genre. As the end of the film approaches, with a final, underproductive robbery and flight, Borsos intercuts shots from *The Great Train Robbery*, recalling Miner's nickelodeon visit, and modified footage of Miner and his gang that resembles the early moving-picture images. In the final moments, titles fill in a conclusion to the story of Bill Miner after his conviction, implying a jailbreak and reunion with Kate. While these signs mark out a past and present at the beginning and end of *The Grey Fox*, Borsos constructs *Bethune* through alternation of Bethune's lifetime and reflection after his death, and builds a chronological mosaic, also alternating between China, where Bethune's life will end, and episodes of the previous fifteen years that lead him there. *Bethune* too has a frame, in that it opens and closes with Norman Bethune's funeral cortège in rural China. It unfolds, however, through extended flashbacks of Bethune's life linked by brief interviews and dialogues between the writer Rice and others who knew Bethune. It thus presents Bethune as a riddle, as something to be understood, his wife and friends as interrogators of his history. Implicitly it positions Rice, a character modelled on biographer and screenwriter Allan, as the writer of Bethune's history.

Outcasts both, Miner and Bethune assume positions as martyrs whose stories of expulsion, adoption, and sacrifice are related in retrospect. Told from a present or recent past, through the intertitles that introduce and conclude Miner's account or through Rice's interviews with Bethune's intimates, they lead from the fiction that forms the body of the two films beyond the films' conclusions and into a resonant future. Miner's story seems to end with his transfer to prison, but titles inform us that he escapes, and a set of enigmatic, concluding shots illustrate his flight in a rowboat into the mists over a body of water. Bethune's story ends at the film's beginning, with his funeral procession, reprised at the conclusion, but his reputational end extends with printed testimonials by Mao and the Chinese doctor, Fong, and finally an additional statement by Bethune himself, testifying to his commitment to social and medical justice. Both *The Grey Fox* and *Bethune* situate their protagonists as heroes and resolve biography and history as myth.

Variations

The Mean Season

As a professional, reporter Malcolm Anderson compares to other Borsos protagonists. More-over, like other Borsos films, *The Mean Season* situates him at a crossing point, like Bill Miner and Norman Bethune, between the thrills of his current work and the lure of domesticity. At the start of the film, as hurricane season—"the mean season," a radio voice informs us—begins, Anderson returns from a visit west to the *Miami Journal* newsroom, burned out by the work. Rummaging for a notebook, asked by another reporter what he has lost, he answers, "A little ambition ... drive ... time, mostly." He aims to leave ("again," his photographer colleague adds) and relocate to Colorado, which he likes, "especially ... the nature of their news." Contrasting the heat and storms of south Florida, which will play an important, sympathetic role in the film, implicitly with the idea of the Mountain West, the introductory sequence sets up alternatives based on job and location. Location means both physical conditions and what they connote, the West sug-gesting placidity and the South turbulence. It happens that a job running the *Greeley Tribune* also means moving to the hometown of his lover, Christine, and settling into domesticity, indicated in part by the jar of pickles he has brought her from her mother.

Before Malcolm returns to quit the *Journal*, in the credit sequence Borsos depicts the first of the murders, the shooting of a young woman on the beach, the assignment that keeps Malcolm from leaving the paper. His first inquiries, at the crime scene, an interview with the victim's mother, and writing and filing the story all unfold before he reunites with Christine, a school-teacher, at the end of her work day. The alternation between two concerns indicates Malcolm's choices, although the extended sequence depicting Malcolm's involvement with the case and the deferring of his reunion with Christine suggest the path that the narrative will take: Malcolm will be caught up in the lure of the story until its conclusion, and then he will make his choice.

It is perhaps tempting to see correspondences among Malcolm, Miner, and even Norman Bethune beyond their professionalism and in their relations to other characters. Malcolm, like Miner, has a confederate in a professional photographer. As with Kate Flynn, who is called on to record a crime scene (and who sees part of her work as documenting injustice), Andy Powell's job at the paper is to acquire evidence of crime and its circumstances; in both cases, photo-graphic evidence has a particular resonance. While Bethune has no such picture-taker in his life (although photographic evidence of conditions in Russia and Spain does play a significant role in Bethune's social conversion), he does have a chronicler-companion at least part of the time in Chester Rice. *Bethune* insists on its title character not only as a social activist and surgeon but also as a writer, like Malcolm, repeatedly depicted at a keyboard, writing the story at the centres of the respective films.

As a crime reporter, Malcolm stands outside the law, but like the fugitive Miner, he encoun-ters the law and enforcement officers. Miner's "good cop," BC Provincial Fernie, and "bad cop," the Pinkerton agent Seavey, are divided by nationality, their public and private status, and their demeanour, although they are collaborators—at least, so Seavey insists. Malcolm comparably negotiates the law through partners, the collaborative and younger Martinez and the antagonis-tic veteran Wilson.

Like Miner and Bethune, Malcolm is simultaneously the subject and object in his story, and both an agent of investigation and activity and someone who is investigated and acted on. Notably, he is caught in the contradictory position of the journalist who becomes a part of the story he is covering. As the person serial killer Delour contacts to respond to Malcolm's coverage, and then as the person to whom Delour drops leads, Malcolm also attracts press scrutiny himself. In part, however, this results from his collaboration with the police and his activities as a surrogate investigator. Both the Miami police and Delour the killer find themselves in the position of being able to use Malcolm, who in turn believes himself to be in the mediating position able to use both of them. Although Borsos establishes neither Bill Miner nor Norman Bethune in this type of intricate position, the situation Malcolm occupies also corresponds to their roles as outlaws who attempt to manipulate either side of law and disorder.

Theme and Variations
One Magic Christmas and *Far From Home*

Borsos used the names of family members when he imagined the two films that became *One Magic Christmas* and *Far From Home: The Adventures of Yellow Dog*. Early notes for the former, then titled *Father Christmas*, featured characters with his parents' and his siblings' names, and one version allegorized his parents' immigrant past.[6] In *Far From Home*, the two McCormick boys bear the names of Borsos' own children, Angus and Silas, and portions of the film were shot at the farm on a BC Gulf Island Borsos had bought not long before, his family's house the set for the McCormicks'. Stories of families under extreme stress, these two films are also distinctive for describing worlds where people have to endure onerous trials.

Both films revolve around comparably traditional nuclear families. The Graingers are Ginnie and Jack and their two small children, Cal and Abby, and the McCormicks are parents John and Katherine and their two sons. In both cases, Borsos tends to isolate one of the children as more important to the story, and has given each a non-human confederate or associate, the angel Gideon and the dog Yellow. The circumstances in each film demand that Angus and Abby act resourcefully and courageously in order to reach a satisfactory resolution. In order to achieve an end, both must also make an odyssey, Angus when he is stranded and seeking rescue, and Abby when she has to travel to the North Pole to retrieve her mother's letter to Santa Claus.

These odysseys follow traumatic events that rupture the families. After enlisting Abby's assistance in his mission to revive the spirit of Christmas in her mother, Gideon engineers events that result in Jack's death, followed by Abby and Cal's, leaving Ginnie distraught, with only her father. Gideon leads the children from the icy river in which they are presumed drowned, although they still have to be told that their father has died. Jack reappears, and although Ginnie is relieved and grateful for his return, the restoration of a true Christmas spirit remains incomplete, leading Gideon to usher Abby to the North Pole. There, in an industrialized operation of pulleys and belts that resembles the Sweeney cooperage, she meets Santa Claus, who pulls a letter from Ginnie Grainger, age seven, out of his files. This reminder, and confirmation of Santa's actuality, is the key step in Ginnie's complete rejuvenation.

In Angus McCormick's case, the film follows his odyssey after the wave that swamps his father's boat. John McCormick (called by his surname, usually) is recovered from the sea, but Angus and Yellow wash ashore. Where Gideon appears to tear the Graingers apart, nature removes one of the McCormicks, leaving the rest simply ineffectual. Although McCormick accompanies the air–sea rescue expedition looking for Angus, he can do little except identify where Angus has been. When a rescue officer tells the McCormicks that the search will continue as long as there is a "reasonable expectation" that Angus might be found, implicitly meaning found alive, Katherine responds, "I've got a reasonable expectation you're going to keep looking a long time." They are shown the obstacles, however, when she is taken aloft to see how nearly invisible the forest floor is from the air, and as the audience has already seen, how the surroundings where Angus and Yellow are lost keep them from being found. Where in *One Magic Christmas* the supernatural provides the impediment, in *Far From Home*, the natural rends the McCormick family.

As these précis suggest, both *One Magic Christmas* and *Far From Home* might be accused of structural flaws in their scripts. The apparent deaths of Jack, Cal, and Abby have no structural function except as means to wear down Ginnie by showing her how awful life can turn in a flash. Arguably, they also stand as punishments for her ill temper. It is only because Abby makes her trip and Ginnie sees the letter reminding her of the girl she once was that she also retrieves the Christmas spirit and Gideon's mission is accomplished. Similarly, Angus' capabilities are tested by his ordeal in the woods, but while he proves himself capable of survival in the wild, he returns to his family not directly resulting from his own resources but when the mechanical *deus ex machina* of a helicopter finally locates him and lifts him away. Moreover, although Yellow is lost in the rescue, he somehow saves himself and finds his way home, although the film does not indicate in any way how. These fissures in the script also underscore the importance of chance and, in the terms of each film, magic as components of their fictional worlds. In the case of *One Magic Christmas*, of course, Gideon does possess supernatural powers that enable him to change the course of events. Yellow, in *Far From Home*, may not explicitly be magical, but his appearances out of nowhere, in particular his reappearance after his apparent death, imbue him with mystery. When he first appears, Borsos situates him still and in the distance for Angus to discover, an image echoed in his reappearance at the end of the film. Borsos depicts Yellow in ways that tend to anthropomorphize the dog, cutting to him frequently as the family members talk about him, as if his actions might constitute reactions of understanding. He also exploits the inscrutability of an animal and the puzzles of its behaviour. When, for example, Katherine McCormick discovers that Yellow responds to commands, such as "sit" and "heel," she is actually finding that he is acting like an ordinary dog who has had training, but the sequence implies that Yellow comprehends and that he is something more than ordinary.

Both *One Magic Christmas* and *Far From Home* are resolutely modern in their settings, yet they pose themselves as less restrictively timely fables. Although the film had been on Borsos' plate for several years, the forces behind much of the tension surrounding the Graingers—the commercialism of Christmas, reductions in the workforce, and the recessionary strains on families that take their toll on mothers assumed to be a social adhesive—were evident in the mid 1980s, when the picture finally appeared. Although not nearly so oppressed by the fates of modern life, the McCormicks comparably incorporate into their otherwise apparently idyllic, rural lives the technologies and social forces that motivate adolescent boys such as Angus. In both cases, the resolutions they ultimately enjoy—the restoration of a Christmas spirit marked not only by Ginnie's transformation but also by Nicholas' actual appearance to her on Christmas Eve, and not only Angus' rescue but more importantly Yellow's reappearance from out of nowhere—occupy the realm of magic.

Form and Style

Whether train robber or surgeon, cooper or logger, angel or dog, Borsos constructs his heroes as larger or other than life and adopts commensurate imagery and style. Within a national cinema often associated with realism in variant forms as a hallmark, Borsos seeks to depict legend, fable, or myth, and his pictures reinforce such a view. That he constructs two of the feature films he initiated around the perceptions of children or adolescents—also suggested in Bill Miner's story by the boy to whom he gives an orange and who returns the favour on the bank robber's banishment to prison—is not incidental. Heroes of the type Borsos features depend on a willing suspension of moral regulation dependent on the assumption of evil, and require instead an investment in potential good, of a type associated with a child's-eye view. On the surface naïve, perhaps, this approach affirms belief in the capacity of people to interact for mutual benefit. Such a view determines Borsos' optic.

From the start, Borsos' documentaries attracted attention for him as a stylist, and he sustained that status through his career. The confidence that his documentary form conveyed might not have been anticipated in the earlier *The Barking Dog*, a parodic Western shoot-out, and *Cadillac*, a mock commercial for a 1950s-model luxury car. The combination of traditional and modern practices in *Cooperage*, *Spartree*, and *Nails* also brought a distinctive view of work, which Borsos caught and shaped with a restrained camera style, evocative sound design, and a minimum of words. Although the films suggest broader conditions of work—division of labour in *Cooperage*, logging practices in *Spartree*, and changes from artisanal work to mass-production in *Nails*—Borsos demonstrates a greater interest in what can be more immediately shown and heard, the ways things are made and done. The measured view, the sounds of machines, and overall taciturnity correspond to the professionalism of the subjects and the people who do the work. As Borsos presents them, most are men who go about their job with little bother and few words.

Logger Hap Johnson speaks not at all as he does his task. No one apart from the film crew is there to listen. Identification of film and subject is particularly notable in *Spartree*, since the cinematographers mirrored Johnson's actions as he scaled the tree he tops. As *Spartree/Making the Film* illustrates, they were rigged with ropes and pulleys that carried them up and down in order to capture the visual details of his work. While the labour involved in Johnson's job, and in making the film, is self-evident, Borsos conveys both the security of professional skill and spectacular exoticism. Although secured with safety equipment, Johnson is, after all, walking up a tall conifer. Chainsawing limbs as he goes, and finally lopping off the peak of the tree, he defies gravity while the falling timber clearly demonstrates what gravity can do and how far there is to fall. Similarly, while still the conventional documentary unit, invisible and silent, Borsos' crew captures views of Johnson's work at angles that unconventionally convey breathtaking heights. Yet while exploiting the spectacular, in the final moments as Johnson sits atop the swaying pillar and lights a cigarette, Borsos also indicates the familiar.

Complementing his films' interest in the craft of work, Borsos also imbues his films with the attraction of the old. Up to *Far From Home*, his films harked back to the past, frequently the earlier parts of the twentieth century, after the Industrial Revolution and the dissemination of steam and electrical power, but still an era driven by gears and cogs. His *mise-en-scène*, more than simply setting an verifiable backdrop for period stories, frequently includes props and design features that suggest the transition to the modern. The Sweeney barrel factory, the site of *Cooperage* that recurs as the lumber mill in *The Grey Fox*, is a signal location. Conceivably, it also served as a visual ancestor to Nicholas' North Pole workshop in *One Magic Christmas*, imagined as a Victorian industrial plant, with exposed drive belts and pulleys and furnished with wooden file drawers and brass fixtures. Bethune, whether in North America where he redesigns surgical tools or uses existing technology in new, unauthorized ways, or in Europe or China where he has to deal with remote locations and wanting facilities where he designs clinics to be portable for the war effort, brings the methods, implements, and machines of an inadequate past into the present day. Even *The Mean Season*, which might take place in the most resolutely modern of Borsos' settings, suggested technological transition in its time. Newspaper offices in movies and television had for many years rung, clattered, and zipped with the noise of teletypes and paper copy torn from typewriters. Although newspapers might have adopted computer technologies, that change was signalled only in the early 1980s, notably in the popular US television series *Lou Grant*, which during its run incorporated the change from typewriters to terminals at a large Los Angeles paper. By 1984, the *Miami Tribune* is so fully networked that not only does Malcolm Anderson compose his story on computers but his editor metaphorically looks over his reporter's shoulder as the story is drafted. In setting its hero adrift and lost in the woods, *Far From Home* exempts itself from such a transitional view. With the little he has salvaged, Angus has to make traps and snares, the devices that catch food. Borsos moreover juxtaposes the makeshift technologies, viewed up close as Angus hunts and gathers, with the wide view of the ultra-modern helicopters and airplanes of the search-and-rescue patrols looking for him.

Having shot his feature films in such diverse locations as BC and Washington, south Florida, southern Ontario, Montréal, Spain, and rural China, Borsos uses landscape expressively and impressively. If there is a characteristic Borsos angle on the land, it is the long view, frequently with human intervention only a minuscule feature in a broad field. The opening credits of *The Grey Fox* run over high angles of a forested valley, as a train snakes around the mountains, and similarly early in *Bethune*, the doctor's funeral procession, small enough in the frame to be barely visible at first, makes its way through the looming mountains of Yemen. These conventionally picturesque establishing shots suggest a relation of nature and human culture, but even the working-class housing of *One Magic Christmas* warrants such high and wide views, in the night-time shots of the Graingers' neighbourhood seen from Gideon's vantage point in a tree as the snow glows eerily in the streetlights, and in the view of Ginnie's family home, where her father lives, or of Nicholas' North Pole compound, structures surrounded by wintry vistas, deliberately comparable to the scene encased in Abby's snow globe. By *Far From Home*, the long view of a hinterland landscape adopts a threatening cast, all but swallowing the puny interventions of human culture. Where in *Spartree* Hap Johnson had been able to climb to the top of the woods and cut himself a place to be seen from the air, Angus and his dog Yellow all but vanish from view in the dense forests.

The evident appeal of landscape and setting to Borsos suggests the expressive properties of natural surroundings and conditions in his films. In *The Grey Fox*, he juxtaposes nature and culture, locating objects of the machine age amid the verdant BC interior—the railway itself, for example, the gramophone playing opera in the hills, or, set against the mountains, the bandstand where Miner and Kate waltz. Even the nondescript suburbs of *One Magic Christmas* receive a treatment of nature, covered in a December snow that first becomes the working-class neighbourhood but later appears a sloppy slush as Ginnie and Jack walk around the block on their way into the darkest of Gideon's trials. *The Mean Season* offers the one indisputable pathetic fallacy among Borsos' films. As the Numbers Killer's death toll rises and the tensions surround-

ing Malcolm multiply, hurricane season approaches south Florida. While Malcolm rushes to rescue Christine from Delour, in what appears to be their final encounter, black clouds roll across
the sky and the winds rise. Then the rain starts to fall. In such a structure, in fact, the weather
serves as a barometer for the truth of the drama, since it is only with the onset of rain and the
true realization of the storm that Delour appears for the last time, for his final confrontation with
Malcolm.

The lure of the heroic to Borsos determines the lure of the spectacular in his films. Sometimes cited for beguiling pictures at the expense of dramatic intensity, his work depends on the
capacity of the cinema to capture images and display them on a screen and a scale figured to be
larger than human life, but smaller than the bodies of the natural world.[7] *Bethune* provides one of
the most unfortunate ironies of Borsos' career, as an epic production conceived not only as a
two-hour theatrical feature, but also as a four-hour, two-part television broadcast. What the latter
gained in running time, it necessarily sacrificed in visual breadth. While the familiarity and smaller
scale of television might have served the history of Norman Bethune, they could not adequately
convey the spectacle within which Borsos set Bethune's passage from individual into myth.

⌇ ⌇ ⌇

In this examination of the films directed by Phillip Borsos, I have deliberately employed methods drawn from structural analysis. They offer ways to outline key thematic and formal features
invested in Borsos' feature films and documentaries. This discussion generally does not incorporate historical research or evidence beyond that provided in the films, whether directly concerning the films' production or broader circumstances of the cinema in Canada and elsewhere that
might have shaped the work. In addition, I have not drawn distinctions according to the participation of some collaborators who were important in Borsos' career, most notably writer and co-
producer Barry Healey, writer John Hunter, cinematographer Frank Tidy, and producer Peter
O'Brian. These are tasks for a much longer project. We are concerned for the moment with the
structure known as "Phillip Borsos," although even that figure is a historical being, moulded by a
matrix of forces and expressed through a network of signification.

Given his modest output over one and a half decades, the patterns that emerge on examination of his finished films, arranged in corresponding pairs with thematic consistencies, might appear both under-realized and too neat. A filmography that included his television commercials,
scripts, and unrealized projects would provide a more accurate picture of a restless professional
filmmaker. It might also suggest Borsos' capacity to grow and to grow diverse. His commitment
to film John Irving's novel *The Cider House Rules* and the eleventh-hour dashing of the project
have been well documented. He similarly committed himself to adapt Walter Miller's *A Canticle
for Leibowitz*, a devotion that persisted throughout his career. Along with another science-fiction
project about the boy adventurer Billy Buckles that Borsos announced at the time of *One Magic
Christmas* and the adaptation of Andreas Schroeder's novel *Dustship Glory*, the fantasist in Borsos
might have emerged more evidently. With *The Piece*, an original script that follows a handgun
from manufacture to disaster in a contemporary city, myth might have blended into bleak misfortune.[8]

Borsos lifted his eyes to the ambitions of his subjects, and he mirrored their progress. His visual style, consistent throughout his practice, conveys the esteem with which his people ought
to be held, no matter their circumstances. While they may live modest lives, they are held to

grander standards in greater schemes. The manual workers he observed in his documentaries practised work, as part of their daily lives, that was part of historical change and subject to forces of meaning that, while of the present, hark back to the past. Fleeing into settings new and unknown to them, profane heroes Bill Miner and Norman Bethune find their accomplishments magnified as they embody dreams of their adopted homelands, and they transform into myths in exile. Having been dared to venture into danger and having endured trials by ordeal, Ginnie Grainger, Malcolm Anderson, and Angus McCormick and Yellow all find their ways home, transformed. Although rooted in Canada, Borsos' films and his aspirations extended beyond the boundaries. While curtailed, his career traced a path that returned his practice as a filmmaker home, having endured the trials and earned benefits of his own.

Notes

1   See "*The Grey Fox* Afoot in a Modern World," in *Canada's Greatest Features*, Gordon Collier and Gene Walz, eds. (Amsterdam: Rodopi, forthcoming).

2   Or later versions, the best known *His Girl Friday* (1940) and *The Front Page* (1974).

3   John Katzenbach, *In the Heat of the Summer* (New York: Atheneum, 1982).

4   Jack Mathews, "Movie 'Angel' Could Spark Child Molesters, Critic Charges," *Vancouver Sun* (19 December 1985), F4.

5   Ted Allan and Sydney Gordon, *The Scalpel, the Sword: The Story of Dr. Norman Bethune* (Boston: Little, Brown, 1952).

6   Phillip Borsos, handwritten story outlines, 93-1928, c1983, Box 24, File 15, Phillip Borsos Accession, British Columbia Archives.

7   For example, Barbara Amiel, "*The Grey Fox* is Haute NFB," *Toronto Sun*, 10 April 1983, 12; or George Anthony, "Terribly Pretty, but Pretty Terrible," *Toronto Sun*, 11 April 1983, 32.

8   A filmography that includes some of Borsos' commercials accompanies my article "*The Grey Fox* Afoot in the Modern World." On *The Cider House Rules*, see John Irving, *My Movie Business: A Memoir* (Toronto: Knopf Canada, 1999), 50–56; "*Christmas* Open, Disney OKs Next Borsos Film *Billy Buckles*," *Variety*, 27 November 1985, 20. Phillip Borsos, untitled script, Box 34, File 7, Borsos Accession, 93-1928, BC Archives. Borsos, Notes, n.d., Box 24, File 22, Borsos Accession, 93-1928, BC Archives.

Janis Cole and Holly Dale's Cinema of Marginality

Kay Armatage

WHILE THE WORK OF JANIS COLE AND HOLLY DALE has received a fair amount of journalistic coverage in the Canadian press—especially Toronto-based media, and especially for their documentaries of the 1970s and 1980s—there has been no scholarly treatment of it. The recently published *Gendering the Nation: Canadian Women's Cinema* (1999), of which I was one of four editors, includes references to Cole and Dale, but there was no substantive article either in hand or in progress when the manuscript was prepared. This is somewhat surprising, as we now have a considerable Canadian feminist literature that attends to those women filmmakers whose work can be adequately assimilated into some sort of feminist rubric. As for the non-feminist critical discourse, we know all too well—even thirty years later—that women filmmakers haven't darkened that radar screen. So there remains a considerable gap in the critical and historical literature. The major figures, as canonized by the scholarly and journalistic establishment, remain almost exclusively men, and women filmmakers whose work eludes treatment by feminist critics are evacuated altogether from scholarly critical or theoretical discourse.

Journalistic treatment of Cole/Dale's work, on the other hand, has been steady from the start. As they have noted in interviews, they began to be treated as professionals in the press from their first student films, *Cream Soda* (1975) and *Minimum Charge, No Cover* (1976). Cole/Dale were renegades in the field of Canadian documentary, as it was dominated in the period by well-meaning bourgeois documentaries from the National Film Board (NFB) and the Canadian Broadcasting Corporation (CBC). They took on subjects that were deemed "deviant," even sensational: workers at body-rub parlours, hookers, transvestites, transsexuals, the criminally insane, and inmates of the notorious Kingston Prison for Women. As a result, their work gained a high degree of notoriety coupled with an excitement that bordered on prurience. They were interviewed by everyone from established poets to progressive lefties and respected film critics.[1]

Most interviewers wanted to know how Cole and Dale had gained access to their subjects. When the two brash, gorgeous young women responded that their subjects were their friends and neighbours, and laced their interviews with anecdotes of working in those same establishments (one article reported that Dale had been the manager of a body-rub parlour and helped to finance *Cream Soda* from money owing to her from the owner of the joint;[2] another article reported that Cole's father "ran a skid row hotel in Vancouver"[3]), the prurience quotient escalated accordingly. When newspaper articles included stills from the films—the norm in cinema journalism—they tended to be images of the "deviants" and transvestites from *Hookers on Davie* (1984). More often, however, the articles appended photos of the two luscious filmmakers, often wearing biker T-shirts or jean jackets, instead of film stills of their less photogenic subjects.

Such a journalistic embrace was remarkable not simply for its gender-driven excitement but for a new ingredient in the Canadian film scene. Here, for the first time in Canadian cinema, were not only working-class subjects but working-class filmmakers.[4] This was notable in a scene dominated not only by the patriarchs of the NFB but by the new generation of private-school alumni and university graduates who were recharging the Canadian film industry. Janis Cole and Holly Dale came out of Sheridan College (Toronto), renowned in the 1990s for its animators and computer wizards. But when they emerged from it, Sheridan College was tainted by the 1970s hierarchy that situated universities as bastions of the privileged middle class. After universities came the polytechnics and art schools, both of which tended to foster avant-garde filmmaking. Sheridan was a community college, known as a skills-training resource rather than a centre of higher learning. As an institutional source for filmmakers who would come to be noted for their documentary integrity, cinematic rigour, and concentration on social injustice, this was remarkable.

Throughout the 1970s and '80s, Cole and Dale managed to establish themselves among Canada's best-known independent documentary filmmakers, and in the 1990s they have transformed their careers into dramatic screenwriters and commercial directors (Cole and Dale respectively). As they are a respected team in Canadian filmmaking, their work deserves a close examination.

Work, Crime, and Class

One immediately observes that their films contribute forcefully to the discourse around class in Canadian cinema. Working-class subjects have been a staple of Canadian fiction classics from *Notes for a Film about Donna and Gale* (Owen, 1966) and *Goin' Down the Road* (Shebib, 1970) to the plethora of rural Québécois and Depression-era prairie narratives. Drifters, factory workers, farmers, and fishermen have struggled—often hopelessly—through indigenous narratives to the extent that a favoured characterization of the Canadian fictional hero was that of the loser, "clown," or "bully."[5] Groundbreaking documentaries such as *The Things I Cannot Change* (Ballantyne, 1967) and others in the NFB Challenge for Change series had also dealt significantly with both urban and regional poverty. Journalists despaired about our national identity, which seemed to produce no genuine heroic characters, either contemporary or historical. Nevertheless, Canadian cinema continued to produce a strategic discourse around work, poverty, and class, which—it may be argued in retrospect—contributed not only to the formation of an original indigenous cinema but may be seen to have affected the installation of Canada's social-safety programs massively inaugurated in the 1970s.

While Cole and Dale's work could be seen as simply carrying on this tradition, I would argue that from the beginning of their filmmaking careers they have significantly inflected the discourse on class with their emphasis on what George Bernard Shaw referred to in *Pygmalion* as "the undeserving poor." Their subjects are not the poor-but-honest folk helplessly caught in a cycle of social deprivation, but rather so-called deviants, white trash, abusive parents, and the most despicable of criminals. These subjects are consistently treated not only with empathy but with a social analysis that underlines their resistance to unjust social institutions, including not only the state and the law but the family itself. In films such as *Hookers on Davie* (1984), the lives and work of the protagonists—cross-dressers, rent boys, prostitutes, and drug addicts—are depicted with raucous exuberance and a stunning rejection of moral or social condemnation.

Such a depiction was consciously oppositional to the bourgeois norms of the NFB in general and of Studio D, the women's studio, in particular. Cole and Dale have said that when they sought assistance from Studio D for *Hookers on Davie*, they were counselled to centre the film around women ("housewives"[6]) who had been compelled by unfortunate circumstances into sex work—in other words, the deserving poor. At the time, Studio D had recently completed its own feature documentary on women sex-workers, the notorious *Not a Love Story* (Klein, 1981). That film, which aligned itself with the maternal feminism of Women Against Pornography, centred around a charismatic stripper (Linda Lee Tracey). *Not a Love Story* initially characterizes the protagonist as a deluded victim who is incapable of understanding her own exploitation, and proceeds to take her on a journey through the porn trade, eventuating a trajectory of consciousness-raising that finds her, at the end of the film, in abjection and repentance.[7] In contrast, *Hookers on Davie* leaves its protagonists as it finds them: ridiculing the johns who use their services and the social agents who seek to help them, comforting and helping each other when they get beaten up or strung out, battling out their extremely tough circumstances, and still managing to keep their street free from pimps. The film emphasizes their energetic cynicism and sharp-eyed awareness of the social institutions in which they operate their difficult lives.

Cole/Dale have delivered a prison theme in five films: *Thin Line* (1977), *P4W: Prison for Women* (1981), *Shaggie: Letters from Prison* (Cole, 1990), *Agnes Macphail* (1991), and *Dangerous Offender* (1996). They have taken sharp standpoints in all five films, but they are by no means consistently critical of the penal system.

Thin Line examines the Penetang Hospital for the Criminally Insane. The facility looks like a prison, complete with long corridors, blocks of locked cells, uniformed guards, and barred entrances separating one area from another. The inmates are the perpetrators of extremely violent crimes. One killed his mate because he had told her that if she woke him again, he would kill her. When she woke him again, he felt that he had to go through with it, and admitted that he felt nothing in doing it. One "slashed up a lot of people with a knife." Another admitted that while committing a robbery he had gone on to murder because in the prison system, murder is the most respected crime. Rapists and sex criminals form a significant portion of the population. While the facility has all the visible marks of a prison, it is in fact a hospital that treats the inmates as diseased and attempts to cure them. Both the speakers in the film and the film itself (through voice-over narration) praise the facility for its attempts at rehabilitation. Many forms of therapy are used, including alcohol and drug therapy; weeks or indefinite periods of time spent with another prisoner in "the Capsule," an eight-by-ten-foot cell with one-way mirrors allowing videotaping twenty-four hours a day; as well as more conventional forms of psychotherapy. The inmates—who are the only speakers in the film besides the narrator—are optimistic about the future of their rehabilitation process, and willingly undergo therapy. In later interviews, Cole/Dale assert that their position on the therapies was more complex than the film indicates:

> Dale: [*Thin Line* is] innovative—very much a *Clockwork Orange*, very supportive of brain-washing—all these subjects are sitting there saying, 'Being brain-washed is all right!'
> Cole: I think it opens your eyes to brain-washing rather than supports it. It throws a little shock into you to make you really think about it.

Dale: The intention of the film was to make you do that, look at it and say, 'My God! All these people are being brain-washed!' Some people who didn't look further thought we were supportive of brain-washing—but all we did was present the material.[8]

Cole/Dale seem to be taking each situation on its own terms. *Thin Line* was made in the period in which the filmmakers asserted their "humanism," which they defined as broader than feminism. Their empathy, equanimity, tolerance, even sympathy for the violent criminals of *Thin Line* are testament to the efficacy of this standpoint. Despite their disclaimers, however, and their adherence to an observational, non-judgemental direct cinema, *Thin Line* presents a marked retort to the systemic abuses of *P4W* and *Dangerous Offender*.

While *Thin Line* was being made, Cole/Dale were seeking permission to film in the Kingston Prison for Women, Canada's only maximum-security penitentiary for women criminals. It took six months to persuade the officials at Penetang to allow them access to the men-only hospital for the criminally insane, but the Kingston facility resisted their efforts for four years.

At first blush, *P4W* appears to be a progressive institution. The inmates wear their own clothes, decorate their cells as they please, receive visits from their children, and have considerable freedom of movement during the days when they gather in a lounge or move freely over the "range." They dye each other's hair, wear make-up and jewellery, listen to music, and play their own instruments. The filmmakers were permitted to interview the women in their own cells and to observe—in the rubric of *cinéma vérité*—activities in the coffee lounge, visitors' day, and so on.

The women inmates evidently welcome and trust the filmmakers. They invite them into their cells, display their photos and mementos, and casually caress their lovers. They speak openly about their crimes (murders of abusive husbands, drug busts, taking the rap for their boyfriends, theft) as well as about their families, love relations within the institution, addictions, and expectations for their futures on the outside. It seems at the outset that to some extent their lives are comfortable and safe within the prison.

The film is structured in several thematic sections, beginning with brief introductions of the featured characters. A longer segment follows, in which their crimes and sentences are revealed. Some of the most charismatic interviewees are serious criminals. One woman tells of repeated batterings from an abusive husband. Our initial horrified sympathy ("thirty-seven stitches in my face") gradually transmutes itself, however, as we eventually discover that she married and murdered more than one of them. One is "doing nine years for personal dope." Many are young, especially those on drug charges or bum boyfriend raps, and about twenty percent of the prison population is serving life sentences.

A long segment on relationships forms the second act of the documentary. The women tell stories of their families and children; one produces and sends a videotaped message to her child; a mother of an infant receives a visit from the baby; one tells of contacting her children only through official channels. A pair of lovers who met in the prison discuss their relationship in separate interviews, and are seen playing croquet outside, helping each other with make-up, and mourning their impending separation upon the release of one of the lovers.

The film presents a composite portrait of these women, through interviews, observation, and set performances (the young woman who plays the guitar and sings in the quiet of evening). As usual with Cole/Dale films, there is a visceral identification with the subjects, evidence of the filmmakers' empathy and of the socially charged import of the material. There is clearly a consciousness here that these women's voices are being heard for the first time and that the film has provided a platform for comprehension and sympathy for—primarily—the results of a gender-biased society which punishes women for fighting back, behaving aggressively, trying to get what they want, or being duped, silly, stupid, or greedy. While still adhering to the observational discretion of *cinéma vérité*, the film is stylishly constructed, punctuated by the clang of steel bars and hand-held tracking shots following the "screws" down the corridors.

In the final segment, a critique of the institution develops. In the initial scenes of this segment, a few women complain about the lack of skills training, efforts at rehabilitation, or dialogue between cons and matrons. They suggest various reforms—usually naïvely idealistic or wearily ironic. Quickly, however, the critique deepens in import and intensity. One inmate tells of the suicide of her friend who had been sent to "seg" (segregation) when she was depressed. The matrons had refused to respond to the interviewee's questions and eventually sent her to seg as well. No inmates were allowed at the inquest: only the matrons' version of the incident was reported. A woman says that within a twenty-month period, there had been three deaths. Another acts out a violent incident, and references to stabbings, beatings, and fights are frequent. This segment is interlaced with an interview with two young women whose arms are covered in homemade tattoos and scars from repeated slashings. They have taken their frustration and anger out on themselves.

Although the matrons smile at the filmmakers and seem comfortable with the process of filming, no guards or wardens are interviewed in this segment or in the film as a whole. The film gives voice to the women prisoners only. Their testimony then, coming from subjects previously confined to silence, is intensely urgent. The critique of the prison closes the film.

By no means coincidentally, the one-minute period drama that Cole wrote and Dale directed for the CBC Canadian Heritage Minutes series also hinges on penal reform. In the most compact of cinematic forms, *Agnes Macphail* (1991) tells the story—in sixty seconds—of Canada's first woman member of parliament. Macphail visited the Kingston Penitentiary for Men in 1932 and discovered the abominable abuses that were routinely practised there. Her raising the issue in parliament in a stunningly dramatic way—slamming a thick leather strap on the desk, as it is dramatized here—is credited historically with leading to the overhaul of the penal system.

While *P4W: Prison for Women* was an effective and startling film in its own right—Cole was barred from the prison after the officials viewed the film[9]—in retrospect, some of its significance in their body of work also resides in its introduction of Marlene Moore, the character who came to feature in their films well into the next decade. A minor character in *P4W*, Moore was released from prison and came to live with Cole/Dale

> for a while. She's one of the younger ones—the one with the slashed arms?—she was going to school and doing well until she got arrested again and is now sitting in the west-end detention centre. The arrest was the result of being influenced by seeing some ex-penners. She didn't really know how to cope with being with new friends.[10]

Moore's subsequent trials and death became the germ of the film that was to confirm the filmmakers' turn from a documentary team to screenwriter and director of feature films and television to dramatic feature filmmaking.

The feature drama *Dangerous Offender* (1996), based on a true story, depicts Marlene Moore's efforts to resist the penury of a life of incarceration—initially inaugurated by her own brutalized mother—from the time of her adolescence. Moore's resistance is literally inscribed on her own body, through the scars and welts that grotesquely thicken the skin on her arms as a result of re-peated slashings with razors, shards of glass or tin, and her own fingernails. She explains in the film that the slashings are her way of quelling the violent feelings of anger and loss that repeat-edly overcome her consciousness. Cole particularly was affected by Moore's death by suicide following the failure of the court attempts to incarcerate her for life as a "dangerous offender." Using optically treated excerpts from *P4W*, Cole made a short film, *Shaggie: Letters from Prison*. Shortly thereafter she began to write the feature drama based on Moore's life.

Comparison of *Dangerous Offender* with other films of the prison genre, such as *The Hurricane* (Jewison, 1999) and *The Birdman of Alcatraz* (Frankenheimer, 1962), throws scriptwriter Cole's approach to her subject into relief. The prison film is a subgenre of the crime film that centres on the difficult living conditions and volatile human interplay within the confines of a prison. Narra-tive conventions of the genre often include the difficulties encountered by ex-cons in adjusting to life "outside." In prison films, as in escape films, spectator identification is constructed around the inmates or a single prisoner who is either innocent or abused by the system. Many of the films push prison to the point of personal metaphor, signifying how one can become a captive of one's own flaws. These films are often about transformation, where prison becomes a sort of monastery, as in the middle section of *Malcolm X* (Lee, 1992) and in *Shawshank Redemption* (Darabont, 1994). The struggle of the usually male protagonist in confinement takes many forms, sometimes through out-and-out rebellion by the individual against the system (*Cool Hand Luke*, Rosenberg, 1967) and other times—*The Birdman of Alcatraz*—more inwardly. There are usually graphic portrayals of the violence that runs rampant in prisons, drawing ironic parallels to prison reform and supposed prisoner rehabilitation. Many of the films are based on real-life stories, in-cluding *Dangerous Offender*, *The Hurricane*, and *The Birdman of Alcatraz*.

Both of the films I have selected for comparison—*Hurricane* because it is the most recent ex-ample and *Birdman of Alcatraz* because it is generally considered a classic of the genre—depict the virtually lifelong imprisonment of the characters and their eventual release. All three films, including *Dangerous Offender*, dwell predominantly on the inside: the life in prison, the daily in-dignities and torments, and the suffering of the protagonists.

In *The Birdman of Alcatraz*, Burt Lancaster plays Robert Stroud, a withdrawn prison inmate who cures a sick bird that flies into his cell; he eventually becomes a world-renowned ornitholo-gist—while serving a life sentence. An overbearing warden (Karl Malden) eventually transfers Stroud to the notoriously brutal prison on the island of Alcatraz, but he is able to continue his research, abort a riot, start a romance, and eventually get his story out through a determined re-porter (Edmund O'Brien). The Stroud characterization is widely respected for the quiet dignity of Lancaster's performance. Wearing glasses and speaking quietly throughout, Lancaster por-trays the prisoner as an intellectual and a scholar; he is articulate, thoughtful, studious, and steadfastly determined. It is a portrait of intellectual resources and spiritual strength.

The Hurricane is based on the real-life story of Rubin "Hurricane" Carter, a New Jersey boxer who spent twenty years in prison for a triple homicide he didn't commit. A talented boxer and a defiant black nationalist who never hesitated to show his contempt for the white establishment, including the media, Carter is an exemplary subject for the combined genres of bio-pic and prison film. *Hurricane* works its way through all the usual prison-film conventions and addition-ally inflects the generic social issues (the injustice of the system, the brutalities of the institutions) with the element of race. Denzel Washington plays the Hurricane with "depth and concentration,"[11] but the dramatization constructs the character as a saint and a martyr unfairly treated by a racist justice system, rather than as a complex human being.[12]

As Amy Taubin writes in *The Village Voice*,

> It's a Hollywood adage that the political must be personalized and another that in order to attract a "crossover" audience, a film that features a black hero must provide white heroes as well. *The Hurricane* plays by those rules and as a result is far too tepid to either do right by Rubin Carter or expose the racism that exists unchanged in the 35 years since he was railroaded into prison.
>
> *The Hurricane*, [therefore], asks [Carter] to share equal time with a trio of white Canadian social activists (played by Deborah Kara Unger, Liev Schreiber, and John Hannah) and an African American boy (Vicellous Reon Shannon) whom they're fostering and who brings *The Sixteenth Round*, the autobiography that Carter wrote in prison, to their attention. In the film, this quartet then devotes itself full-time to Carter's appeals, eventually uncovering the evidence that wins him his release.
>
> As Lewis M. Steel, one of Carter's lawyers, writes in the January 3 issue of *The Nation*, the Canadians provided Carter with much needed psychological support but had almost nothing to do with the discovery of evidence or the legal processes. By concocting a fictional drama around their investigations, the film blurs the way an entire racist-tainted system of justice was rigged to reward and protect those who convicted Carter and to keep truth from being told. Similarly the film reduces institutionalized racism to the vindictiveness of one bad-apple cop (Dan Hedaya), who had it in for Carter from childhood. And most improbably, it provides a counterbalance for the bad cop in the form of a corrections officer who bends the rules to secure special privileges for Carter during his 20-year stay in the pen.[13]

Taubin's assessment of the film is convincing. Her review also points to the genre elements obviously in play—the simplistic constructions of the unjustly accused protagonist, the vindictive bad cop, and the sympathetic corrections guard who assists in ameliorating life in prison. Washington's performance also shows commonalities with others in the genre—like Lancaster, he wears glasses and speaks articulately, and his general demeanour is one of quiet dignity.

Dangerous Offender bears many of the marks of the genre: the daily indignities of life on "the range," the abuses from the "screws," the isolation of the inmates from each other and from themselves, the rigorous maintenance of the unjust social institution, the occasional good-heartedness of a sympathetic guard, and the difficulties of adjusting to life on the outside. In addition, in Cole/Dale's film, issues of gender and of cinematic construction of character inflect the comparison. *Dangerous Offender* is, first of all, one of the few films in the genre that features women protagonists. *Caged Heat* (Demme, 1974) is another film that features women protagonists, but the 1974 Roger Corman production belongs to quite another film group: the exploitation film (now often considered cult classics), of which women-in-prison was a subgenre. The marketing tagline for the release of *Caged Heat* was "Women's prison U.S.A.—Rape Riot and Revenge! White Hot Desires melting cold prison steel!" Leonard Maltin sums the plot like this: "Demme's first feature is tongue-in-cheek but otherwise typical women's prison flick, chiefly novel for being set in the U.S. instead of some banana republic, plus neat turn by [Barbara] Steele as wheelchair-bound warden. Has a sizeable cult following. Aka RENEGADE GIRLS."[14]

A more detailed summary says this: "A girl is caught in a drug bust and sent to the hoosegow. The iron-handed superintendent takes exception to a skit performed by the girls and takes punitive steps, aided by the sadistic doctor who is doing illegal electroshock experiments and raping drugged prisoners. After a while the prisoners put away their petty differences and plan the Big Prison Escape."[15]

In the same vein, we may recall *The Big Doll House* (Jack Hill, 1971): "Fast paced, tongue-in-cheek adventure shot in Philippines mixes sex, comedy, and violence in confrontation between sadistic warden and female prisoners. One of the earliest, most successful, and most influential of women-in-prison exploitation films. Followed by THE BIG BIRD CAGE. Aka WOMEN'S PENITENTIARY I."[16] And in case we thought this genre had died with the ascendance of the contemporary women's movement, there is *Cellblock Sisters: Banished Behind Bars* (Charr, 1995): "Sam Connor kidnaps his young daughters, April and May, sells them to strangers, and accidentally kills his wife when she attempts to intervene. Sixteen years later, April is an out of control outlaw who has come into a life of drugs and crime, while May has grown into a straight laced, refined woman. The plot thickens when April avenges her mother's death by killing her father, and May is sent to jail as the prime suspect. Fortunately, Detective Arman, instantly taken with May, fights for her innocence and tries to get her out before she is taken down by other hostile prisoners."[17]

While they are exploitation films, the plots of these movies give notice of the conventions of the genre: the innocent prisoner, the brutal prison environment, the bad warden and the sympathetic guard, episodes of sadism and violence not only between guards and prisoners but among the inmates, and finally the transcendent escape. These exploitation films are also laced with revealing costumes, large breasts, sexual activity of all kinds, and gratuitously explicit violence. Of these, only *Caged Heat* rises out of its exploitative genre, not merely as a result of Demme's direction but also because as the writer, Demme inscribes the text with his own subversive and feminism-aware politics, at least insofar as the sexy inmates rebel against exploitation and torture.[18]

Cole/Dale's *Dangerous Offender* by no means falls into the generic category of the women-in-prison movies described here. On the contrary, it situates itself as a serious social-issue film precisely in the vein of *The Birdman of Alcatraz* and *The Hurricane*. Cinematically as well as narratologically, the film takes pains to offer a raw and realistic portrait of Marlene Moore (played by Brooke Johnston), and it is precisely at this intersection that it diverges from *Birdman* and *Hurricane*. As opposed to the dignified, strong portrait of the martyred hero, *Dangerous Offender* offers a credible character study of a woman who has suffered deprivation of every kind—not only of her freedom, but also of emotional, physical, and intellectual stimulation. As for physical beauty, a staple of the women-in-prison genre, the male protagonists considered here win hands down. Hurricane is played by Denzel Washington, after all—no comment needed. And in *Birdman*, even portraying a reserved, middle-aged man, Lancaster has physical strength, perfect posture, and stately bearing. In contrast, the Moore character in *Dangerous Offender* is physically withdrawn: shoulders slumped, face and body lacking affect, hair lank and dirty, clothes unkempt, and the always-visible grotesquely scarred forearms.

In comparison to the male protagonists who heroically rise above their penury to nurture their own spiritual and intellectual pursuits, Moore suffers from massive discursive deprivation. Alternating between youthfully energetic, hopeful, and resilient behaviour and confused, inarticulate, and self-deprecating states, her only means of expression inside the prison is the inscription of her pain on her own body through the slashing of her arms. On one brief excursion to the "outside," she immediately pantomimes violent aggression, adopting as her own the false characterization imposed upon her by her family and the prison system. When the court fails to consign her to the dangerous offender category (mandating prison for life), she is flung into the contemporary urban world without any support and lacking any quotidian skills. She doesn't know how to feed herself, manage a social life, judge the safety of environments, or even buy a bus ticket. Terrified and ashamed of what she experiences as her own insufficiencies, she declines into abjection. The third act of the film charts this depressing spiral in episodic vignettes. Her death is the tragic end of the story.

The rigour of the portrait speaks once again to Cole/Dale's significant contribution to the Canadian cinematic discourse on class. Relentlessly refusing to glamourize, romanticize, or heroize, they nevertheless insist on the tragedy of lifelong deprivation, stemming from its roots in the brutality of a family of petty criminals and thugs parented by an overwhelmed mother who lacks comprehension of any kind. Moore's family heritage of poverty, brutality, and stupidity is then played out through the social, mirrored and magnified by the poverty, brutality, and stupidity of the penal justice system.[19] Rather than the Hollywood-style uplifting possibilities for transcendence represented through the individual heroics of the male protagonists of the prison genre, in *Dangerous Offender* we find the tragedy of the impossibility of freedom for a criminal who is a woman.

It may be useful to recall *Thin Line* here, for the optimism of the earlier documentary stands in marked contrast to the institutional analysis presented in *Dangerous Offender*. The male inmates of *Thin Line* seem to be convinced of the possibilities of their own "cure," and at the very least they acquire the clichés of self-help therapy as a means of personal understanding. Unlike the hospital setting of the documentary, the women's prison system offers no efforts at rehabilitation, no skills training, and no opportunities for the development of personal comprehension. The gender biases of the two penal systems are evident in the negligence of the women's prison, which seems to concur with a dominant ideology that treats even the most despicable male criminals as worthy of "saving," while consigning the women to darkness as cultural detritus.

These five films present a range of representations of working-class subjects. *Hookers on Davie* presents survivors who not only have skills of endurance but also a community of their like which is able to offer protection and comfort. *Thin Line* works within the confessional mode, using direct-to-camera interviews of the criminals, shot in extreme close-ups. The contrast between the intimacy of the interviews and the dulcet-toned formal voice-over narration provides an ironic complexity, resulting in something of a distance from the men who are its subjects. *P4W* returns to the confessional mode, giving its subjects voice and access to public discourse. The construction of the images is looser than that of *Thin Line*. The interviews are shot wider, giving the subjects room to breathe within the frame, and there is more panning and cutting away from the interviewees and jump-cuts within the interviews, all of which are considered devices that diminish intimacy. Nevertheless, the sense of urgency and authenticity of the women's testaments is palpable in *P4W*. *Dangerous Offender* may seem to contrast starkly with the earlier films in its portrait of a working-class woman. As a drama, it uses narrative and cinematic devices that produce heightened emotional effect and situates the plight of the protagonist at the level of tragedy, charting the inevitability of her isolation, deprivation, and abjection ending in death. What the films have in common, however, is the Cole/Dale commitment to realism coupled with empathy and an exacting refusal of liberal mythologizing.

Short Films

Both at the beginning and at the peak of their careers, Cole/Dale have turned out short films: *Cream Soda* (Dale's first student film, with Cole recording sound, 1975); *Minimum Charge, No Cover* (which Cole/Dale co-directed, 1976); *Dead Meat* (directed by Dale, story by Cole, 1989); *Shaggie: Letters from Prison* (Cole, 1990); and *Bowie: One in a Million* (Cole, 1999). All but *Dead Meat*, which Dale made as a dramatic exercise in her year in the Directors Program at the Canadian Film Centre, share a number of formal qualities that mark the short film as a cinematic mode in its own right. In particular, they are formal in structure and tend towards the non-narrative.

Cream Soda is set in a body-rub parlour, a type of business that was once legal in Toronto. Under the guise of massage, these businesses semi-covertly practised a form of sex-trade, offering erotic dance performances and other special services. The structure of *Cream Soda* is abstract, marked by repetitive actions: wide shots of men coming up the stairs to enter the establishment and women coming to the front desk to hand over money, close-ups of hands counting money, shots of the women sitting around waiting for the next customer, direct-cinema footage of two sex-workers changing clothes and kibitzing in the dressing-room, pans following workers escorting customers to the adjacent magazine shop or into the private rooms, tight shots of hands flipping through magazines featuring fetishistic photo spreads. A combination of wild and synchronized sound constructs an aural ambience of casual business-as-usual that is ironically undercut with the repeated playing of a recording of "Hey, Big Spender." The confinement of the diegesis within the establishment and the repetitions of the daily routines operate a closed and circular structure that ends with the women comfortably sitting together counting their earnings.

Minimum Charge, No Cover paints from a more varied palette. The opening shot of a hooker getting out of a car, backed by wild sound of a voice calling "twenty dollars—come on, twenty dollars," leads to the title and thence to an interior sequence. Three direct-sound episodes are intercut: an interview with a male-to-female transsexual sitting in a bathtub, her back slightly turned to the camera; domestic footage of a female sex-worker preparing a roast beef dinner for her child; a close-up interview with a young man who identifies himself as living a "faggot" (as opposed to "gay") lifestyle. All three types of footage begin *in medias res*, without introduction, identification, or contextualization. The jagged revelations of contrasting backgrounds, lifestyles, and aspirations are allowed to stand for themselves. In the second sequence, on the street, wide shots of pedestrian traffic on the sex strip, pans of neon bar signs advertising burlesque or topless dancers, a brief shot of a street tussle, and similar footage introduce three black transvestites in a street confrontation with the (unseen but heard) filmmakers.

The final passage takes place inside a bar where drag queens get dressed and made-up and perform a lip-sync and dance number. Disparate wild sound punctuates the audio track: the hooker at the beginning, a voice singing "God bless the child" later on, and the song of the drag performance at the end, which continues over the penultimate bracket syntagma of the performers taking off their wigs and eyelashes. Each passage is distinct, although unmarked. The structure doesn't recall the three subjects from the beginning or the street activity of the middle, but ends simply with the performance. *Minimum Charge, No Cover* presents a collage of thematically related footage in an open-ended and somewhat improvisational structure. There is no intervention through voice-over or visual verbal text, and the film ends with neither narrative nor cinematic resolution. Despite its brevity, it is a forceful piece, marked by a free-wheeling dynamism of subject matter and form.

The two short films made by Cole on her own take a somewhat more formalistic approach. Like *Cream Soda, Shaggie: Letters from Prison* (included in the NFB's *Five Feminist Minutes*, 1990) uses repetition forcefully in both the visual and auditory registers. The film returns to the character of Marlene Moore, first introduced in *P4W: Prison for Women*. *Shaggie* uses excerpts from the earlier documentary, but optically degrades the footage of Moore to a grainy, video-like texture. The images of Moore are intercut with several kinds of footage ranging from the highly stylized to documentary outtakes. There are sunlit home-movie-style images of a delightful child toddling towards the camera. Close-ups pan across Moore's handwritten letters on ruled paper. There are outtakes from *P4W*, including close-ups of a filthy toilet and rusted sink in a jail cell, tracking shots along corridors past rows of barred cells, and close-ups of graffiti on crumbling concrete prison walls. Other types of footage, including shots of Moore that are sometimes optically treated but at other times harshly raw (the close-ups of her tattooed and scarred forearms), are woven together freely.

The film is punctuated three times by highly stylized and gestural sequence shots. Twice the camera pans across a lineup of women looking directly into the camera, sullenly returning its gaze, and immediately reverses the pan across the same group, now behind bars. The third pan across the group of women reverses the sequence: the women are seen first behind bars, and then without bars, announcing a narrative moment of the possibility of parole. These three sequence shots not only break up the structure through their repetition and stark composition but also signal narrative shifts.

The narrative trajectory operates through the dominant visual motif of the film: stylized footage of a woman in silhouette with prison bars behind her. In discontinuous episodic syntagmas, the woman sits writing at a table, sweeps the floor, smokes a cigarette, paces back and forth, rocks autistically in a chair, bangs her head against the wall, takes a knife to her arm, and finally tears up a bedsheet and hangs herself from the prison bars. A coda formed by a collage of earlier footage, now including optically degraded images of the child, visually fills out a temporal structure that is primarily cut to the dictates of the audio track.

The soundtrack combines a variety of types of material, dominated by the vocal. A woman's voice reading the Twenty-Third Psalm ("The Lord is my shepherd, I shall not want") opens the film over footage of the smiling little girl on the street. That voice dissolves aurally just as the opening image dissolves visually; as the optically treated footage of Shaggie replaces that of the child, whispering voices on the soundtrack overlap the original voice and eventually cross-fade again into a single voice reading from Shaggie's letters.

Excerpts from the letters occupy the central and most extended passage of the film. Shaggie recounts her life in prison: she writes from "the digger" (segregation); tells of completing grade-nine English and going on to grade ten ("I'm surrounded by dictionaries"); looks forward to being trained as an embalmer and jokes that she will give half-price discounts to her friends; boasts that she has stopped slashing and later admits that she's in segregation again for cutting her arm ("fifty stitches, and thirty [days] inside"); and flatly notes that the acid burn that "happened" to her arm required seventeen days in hospital and repeated skin grafts. She goes through an emotional trajectory that includes intermittent states of frustration, renewed optimism, bravado, and finally despair. Each of the letters ends with a variation of "love and respect always" or "your friend always"—"love Shaggie."

As the stylized image of the woman in silhouette proceeds towards hanging herself, the single voice of the letter-reader abruptly ends, and whispering multiple voices repeat the

Twenty-Third Psalm. The words, though whispered, resonate with irony: "Yea, though I walk through the valley of the shadow of death, I will fear no evil. For Thou art with me. Thy rod and Thy staff, they comfort me ..." Over the visual coda, these whispering voices cross-fade into another multiple voice—louder, more urgently spoken—repeating a series of words that briefly occupied early moments of the film: "Frustration. Anger. Aggression. Hostility. Charged. Guilty. Punished. Steel bars. Concrete. Segregation. Boredom. Slashing. Pain ... Fear of people. Fear of self. Apathy. Surrender. Give up. Give in." With these words, the film ends abruptly on a cut to black.

Cole's most recent work, *Bowie: One in a Million*, is, like *Shaggie*, a *memento mori*. In the absence of arts council funding, Cole produced the film extremely cheaply, working with former students (non-professionals). The economics of production are mirrored in the economy of the visual register. The video image consists of still photographs and newspaper clippings, sometimes presented individually, but predominantly in collages of multiple images. Cole's own voice-over of her tightly written script drives the audio track.

Bowie tells of Cathy Bowie, a friend of Cole's older brother. She is introduced as a fun-loving, attractive, original, and unique individual—"one in a million." At the time, the originality of the singer David Bowie's performances and music matched their perceptions of their friend, who was then always referred to simply as "Bowie." As the film proceeds, Cole's narration tells of intermittent social encounters as the image presents snapshots of Bowie with Cole's brother, with Cole and Dale themselves, and in groups of friends. Bowie is dynamic in the photos, always smiling or laughing. After a time, she meets and marries a man, with whom she is happy for about two years. Just when Bowie is about to enact her decision to end the relationship, her husband shoots her with a rifle. In the trial, as Cole narrates, it is Bowie who is judged: for the way she dressed, her flirtatiousness, her love of partying. The murderer gets off with a light sentence—"a slap on the wrist," says Cole.

Here the narration shifts its purview to the wider social order. Cole relates that she began to notice news stories of women battered, raped, brutalized, and murdered by men. With a visual collage of newspaper headlines, the narration segues into a barrage of statistics: "Every year in Canada, hundreds of women are beaten or killed in their own homes. In North America, thousands. Worldwide, tens of thousands. Over the past few years, hundreds of thousands. In the past decade, over a million." The bitter personal narration comes to its double-edged, eponymous conclusion: "Bowie—she's one in a million." With this, the image shifts ironically to a close-up of Bowie, smiling charismatically into the camera's gaze.

This devastating short film speaks to the mature economy of Cole's recent writing, to her enduring commitment to women, and to the social injustices that must continue to be criticized and resisted. Together, these short films constitute a specific body of work, marked by cinematic economy, interest in unconventional subjects, and the filmmakers' continued willingness to take risks.

Calling the Shots

This morning, the day that I am in the midst of writing this paper, there was a stunning headline in the *Globe and Mail*: "Women filmmakers at the crossroads." The article was about the Sundance Film Festival (January 2000), at which 29 of the 113 features shown were made by women.[20] That's just over 25 percent. The second paragraph of the article starts thus: "Ten years ago, it would have been difficult to name more than three or four women (Lina Wertmuller,

Penny Marshall, Margarethe von Trotta, Jane Campion, Penelope Spheeris) directing feature films." The writer goes on to tout 2000 as a breakthrough year for women directors and concludes the piece with a quote from Barbara Kopple (*Harlan County USA*, 1976; *American Dream*, 1992; *Woodstock*, 2000): "In five years, they won't be writing articles about the increase of women filmmakers ... By then we'll be talking about children breaking into film with their digital cameras."[21] Kopple's statement, I take it, is meant to be optimistic about the future for women directors, rather than pessimistic about their imminent eclipse. Only Maggie Greenwald (*Ballad of Little Joe*, 1993; *Songcatcher*, 1999) strikes a realistic note in the piece as she says, "I've been around long enough that I can remember the last time it was called 'the year of the woman' [1993] ... but then there was that long period through most of the nineties when the only films you could get made were a certain kind of independent films" (the ones about guys with goatees, generally made by guys with goatees).[22]

I mention this ephemeral piece of journalism because it strikes a resonant note with Cole/Dale's 1988 documentary about women directors, *Calling the Shots*. In fact, contrary to the journalist's faulty memory, just over ten years ago women directors were making feature films in virtually every national film industry. After making the documentary film, Cole/Dale published some of the interviews in a book also titled *Calling the Shots*. The book profiles twenty women filmmakers, only a portion of the fifty interviewed for the film or of the ninety whose filmmaking work Cole/Dale researched.[23] Due to publishing economies, the book was limited to North Americans, thus eliminating some of the respected senior European filmmakers in the film, among them Jeanne Moreau, Mai Zetterling, Margarethe von Trotta, and Agnes Varda, as well as Asian director Ann Hui.[24] The book additionally includes interviews with four women filmmakers who became prominent in the five years between the making of the film and the publishing of the book.

I dwell on these numbers for a variety of reasons. In the Preface to *Calling the Shots*, Cole/Dale write,

> while there are many anthologies available that have presented the viewpoints of men who direct films, we have never found a similar collection that presents the personal accounts of women filmmakers. At best, one or two women have been included in a book that examines twenty or more men who work in the film industry. Upon discovering this, we felt a strong urge and necessity to fill that void in cinema literature. Second, while there are several books that examine feminist film theory, primarily through the analysis of women's on-screen image, or an analysis of alternative filmmakers working in avant-garde, documentary, counter cinema, or feminist film, we haven't seen any books that present a collection of contemporary viewpoints from a wide variety of women filmmakers, both mainstream and marginal.[25]

Their assessment of the literature is absolutely right, and remains right to the present day. While there have been several books on individual women filmmakers, as well as a couple of "companions" or encyclopedias,[26] there is still a lack of books that give a broad picture—either historical or contemporary—of women's creative production in film.

Perhaps this is as it must be. As Cole/Dale themselves write, "Some people would argue, why a book about women? After all women have now made it in the film industry."[27] While this is palpably false—to which the *Globe and Mail* article is telling testimony: since when does twenty-five percent representation mean women have made it, when we are more than fifty percent of the population?—other arguments may prevail. Isolating women filmmakers as a group may mask the differences among women by suggesting that women are a unitary category marked only by gender. Cultural traditions, sexual preferences, and racial identities are obviously equally compelling categories, and equally affect the examination of gender. There is also the ever-present fear of ghetto-ization—pigeon-holing women as concerned primarily with gender relations or feminist themes.

In addition to such arguments, since the early 1970s film theory has mounted a formidable challenge to an auteurist approach. Arguments against auteurism centre around the combination of the reification of the heroic Cartesian individual genius with the untheorized critical tools of pre-structuralist textual analysis. The search for "unities" of theme and style in the "body of work" produced a profile of an individual unalienated consciousness, flying in the face of the psychoanalytic emphasis on the workings of the unconscious (i.e., the split subject) and also obstructing the progressive social analysis offered by the methodologies of semiotics and structuralism. Auteurism also promoted the canonization of those filmmakers considered worthy of the "pantheon"[28] who, by definition, were those directors who had made a significant number of films over a long career (Hawks, Ford, Hitchcock, etc.). Even Peter Wollen's salutary reclaiming of auteurism for semiotics and structuralism chose Hawks and Ford for revisionary consideration.[29] Since few women directors had substantial bodies of work, they continued to languish outside the purview of auteurist methodologies.

The first feminist response to such a scholarly dilemma was the emphasis on gendered spectatorship in the critique of the canonical Hollywood text. As the decades advanced, attention to gendered spectatorship broadened to include the "gynetric" genres such as the women's film, melodrama, and television soap operas. Critical methodologies came to include the study of reception and address, arguing the empowering strategies of such genres for women spectators or the industrial implications of such gender-specific enunciation. These approaches amassed a significant theoretical toolkit packed with instruments capable of taking apart and rebuilding virtually any problematic construction as a productive retrofit for feminist readers. Nevertheless, these tools were not finely enough crafted to include more than a few films by women directors. The creative production of women filmmakers continued to be overlooked, resulting in considerable lacunae not only in historical knowledge but also in the instructional resources necessary to bridge that historical gap.

In *Streetwalking on a Ruined Map: Cultural Theory and the City Films of Elvira Notari*, Giuliana Bruno takes up the question of the female authorial voice.[30] Echoing Kaja Silverman's challenge to Roland Barthes' pronouncement of the death of the author, Bruno argues that Barthes actually wished to annihilate the paternal author rather than admit the possibility of female authorship. Bruno articulates a double authorial construction, for just as the death of the author announced the beginning of readership, feminist scholarship that centres on women figures constructs authorship not only for the woman director but for the woman writer as well:

As has been true for other female directors, the constitution of [Elvira] Notari's authorship has been a pure function of feminist criticism ... Overall, authorship is viewed as a
function of the modes of existence of discourse—its origin, circulation, and control—as
well as a function of the positions determined for, and shared by, possible subjects. In
this light, the historical scene is revealed as a set of historically changing experiences.[31]

Using Silverman's notion of constituting authorship through a process of identification, Bruno
retheorizes authorship as an intersubjective and interchangeable relation between mother/
daughter and author/reader: "Writing is mapped as a transitional site. Authorship becomes the
locus of interaction, a scene of libidinal exchange, where encounters as well as separations and
'little deaths' are staged ... The intersubjective predicament is another way to say, 'In a way, I *desire* the author: I need her figure (which is neither her representation nor her projection), as she
needs mine.'"[32] Bruno also argues the necessity for this relation on political grounds:

The constitution and analysis of Elvira Notari's authorial text are part of the general effort to rewrite history by empowering the female subject, texts, and readings. At this particular historical juncture, and as long as women such as Notari remain obscure(d), such
a cultural and political project is vital. Insofar as she was somewhat exceptional in her
early and productive engagement in the male-dominated field of filmmaking, giving
room to the authorial subject is a 'political' gesture for a feminist scholar. Because
Notari's authorship was suppressed, disregarded, and forgotten, not allowing for the authorial subject would only have continued the suppression.[33]

Finally, or perhaps first and foremost, there is simply the enormous scholarly challenge: other
than in a dictionary, companion, or encyclopedic form, how could one possibly assemble a book
that dealt adequately with the vast numbers of women filmmakers who have (admittedly inter-
mittently) worked in the international film industry throughout its history?

What *Calling the Shots* accomplishes is a time capsule. In both film and book, Cole/Dale have
selected a group of women filmmakers working in the period 1988–93. Some of them had just
"broken through" with box office successes; some of them were still struggling; some had received considerable long-term critical esteem. Neither the film nor the book pretends to be "representative"; at the same time, neither are the filmmakers exclusively white, straight, mainstream,
or young. All of them, however, are articulate and forthcoming.[34] They respond to the filmmakers' questions just as the subjects of Cole/Dale's film have always responded, with revealing anecdotes, personal reflection, thoughtful analyses, and—in some cases—wisdom.

Unlike the book, which is organized by filmmaker, the film is structured around specific thematic concerns, intercutting comments from the various interviewees along with illustrative clips
from their films. As in the book, however, "the subjects discussed are influences and inspirations,
breaking into the business, choosing and preparing the screenplay, a woman's point of view,
feminist cinema, sex and violence, censorship, women's on-screen image, working with actors
and crew, dealing with the money people, independent versus studio production, actress turned
director, and advice to aspiring filmmakers."[35]

The film begins with a gesture towards the historical roots of women's creative production in
film. Katherine Hepburn opens the film by recounting what it was like to work with Dorothy
Arzner, and is astonished to recall that at the time it seemed perfectly natural—rather than

"peculiar"—to work with a woman director. She recalls that Dorothy Arzner was simply accepted as a director in Hollywood, that she was "lots of fun and a damn good cutter." Her segment ends with Hepburn asserting—completely erroneously—that Arzner "was one of the first to prove that women are not completely foolish." While we are all fond of Hepburn in her dotage as well as in her youth, it is important to set the record straight here. One of the reasons that Arzner was so widely accepted as a director was that she was by no means the first woman in Hollywood who had held such a position. There had been many women directors during the silent era, among them Lois Weber, who in her heyday was the highest-paid director in Hollywood. It is not remarkable that Arzner was accepted at the time. What is mysterious is the fact that, as the studio system gathered power with the coming of sound, women directors not only became "peculiar," as Hepburn puts it, but vanished completely. From 1930, with Arzner's first movies, to the 1950s, with the emergence of Ida Lupino as feature-film director and powerful television producer, there were no other women working in positions of creative control until the 1970s.

Calling the Shots quickly moves to introduce the pioneers of contemporary women's filmmaking: Joyce Chopra, Martha Coolidge, Claudia Weill, Sandy Wilson, and Anne Wheeler. And with those introductions, the film moves into its first thematic block, the subjects' accounts of their first adventures in filmmaking: how they got started, what they thought it was all about, their first hair-raising moments on the set. All of them are cognizant of their positions as pioneers.

Joyce Chopra says that when she set out to make *Joyce at 34* (1973), about herself as a pregnant filmmaker, there were no other documentaries about ordinary people. There had been films about public events, race-car drivers, men on death row, she says, but no one had thought to make a film about an ordinary person. We now know that Chopra was one among many women who were making similar personal documentaries—about themselves, their next-door neighbours, their mothers and grandmothers—more or less autobiographical films that would come to be known as a virtual subgenre of feminist filmmaking. As Annette Kuhn writes, "If there is any structural principle governing the organization of feminist documentary film, it is that provided by autobiographical discourse ... Protagonists of these films are women who talk about their own lives."[36] Chopra also points, by implication, to the dearth of professional women film technicians at the time. She notes that when she approached Claudia Weill to shoot the film, the young cinematographer was still a senior in university.

Martha Coolidge is clear in her understanding that she was making an autobiographical film with her first film, *Not a Pretty Picture* (1972), but the final form of the film was somewhat slow to evolve. She didn't set out to make a documentary, she says, but rather a fictionalized account of the events that led to her own rape in high school. The necessity to set the fictionalized narrative in the context of a documentary about Coolidge's own experience of directing the film pressed itself on her during the process. As a result, *Not a Pretty Picture* was a sophisticated and innovative film that mixed drama with documentary in such a way that the emotional process that Coolidge was undergoing as she directed the narrative sequences became almost equally the subject of the film. Thus, the film asked telling questions about the construction of autobiographical narratives and the representation of traumatic events such as rape. *Calling the Shots* gives the filmmaker her due in this section, inserting substantial clips from *Not a Pretty Picture* and allowing Coolidge uncut breathing space in the frame and in the segment.

Jill Godmillow and Claudia Weill provide the transition to women directors' entry into feature filmmaking. In *Antonia: Portrait of a Woman* (1974), Godmillow had co-directed (with Judy

Collins) one of the first and most successful of the lost feminist heroines/positive role-model films, documenting the life and career of Antonia Brico, a once-famous orchestra conductor who had been forgotten by the public after she settled into teaching and conducting an amateur community orchestra in Denver, Colorado. Godmillow presents a telling critique of documentary method, arguing that by counting on the subjects of the film to provide the material, the documentary filmmaker shirks responsibility for what is said. Weill (*Girlfriends*, 1972) frankly admits that she got tired of waiting for documentary subjects to voice what she wanted them to say and spending months in the cutting room manipulating the footage to be sure they did so.

Amy Heckerling (*Fast Times at Ridgemont High*, 1982) strikes the first note of what becomes a dominant theme in the film: the intermittent nature of women's participation in the film industry. One of the new generation of women in Hollywood (like Martha Coolidge, working in teen genre films), Heckerling says that when she set out to become a director, only Elaine May was well known in the field. If she were in film school now, however, says Heckerling, she could point to Martha Coolidge, Donna Deitch, Claudia Weill, Joyce Chopra, and others.

Coolidge enters with her usual clear analysis. Yes, there was Elaine May, but she was followed by a gap. "Then there were the Joans—Joan [Micklin] Silver [*Hester Street*, 1975], Joan Tewksbury [writer of *Nashville*, 1975], and Joan Darling [*Two Worlds of Jennie Logan*, 1979]." And then there was another gap. Later in the film, Coolidge notes that, due to the financial success of *Fast Times at Ridgemont High*, Heckerling was one of the women directors who "opened the door." Throughout the documentary, others articulate the gap that Coolidge points to as one woman or a group of women filmmakers "opening the door." After each opening of the door, however, it seems to shut again. With its mis-remembering, the article in the *Globe and Mail* underlines this cycle continuing to the present day.

It would be misleading, however, to suggest that *Calling the Shots* approaches its subject with negativity. On the contrary: everything about the film is celebratory. For one thing, the production values of *Calling the Shots* far outstrip Cole/Dale's previous films. It is beautifully lit and shot, with each filmmaker in her own relaxed setting, and the editing is slick and professionally accomplished. Not only in its documentary surface is the film consistently upbeat, but the filmmakers—good-humoured, relaxed, articulate, and confident—strike consistently celebratory notes. This is not to suggest that they gloss over their struggles or their own mistakes. Sandy Wilson (*My American Cousin*, 1985) recalls that on her first day on the set she was most concerned about what to wear and, in ignorance, eschewed a script binder in favour of a little jewelled purse. Amy Heckerling tells of being stymied by the seemingly endless paradigmatic ways to shoot a car passing by. Martha Coolidge remembers being told to wear more make-up and never to say that she wanted to be a director, but to admit only that she aspired to "maybe, some day" become a production assistant. Karen Arthur tells of having to assert herself on her first day on the set by ordering the crew to tear down the set-up they had prepared without consulting her, only to allow them to reconstruct it later in the shoot. These anecdotes, while rueful and even self-deprecating, are told with the humour and confidence that arise from having overcome mistakes and adversaries. All are optimistic about their futures as directors.

Calling the Shots is an unapologetically talking-heads documentary. It consists entirely of direct-to-camera interviews with the directors, producers, and writers. The interviews are interspersed from time to time with film clips, still photos, or on-set *vérité* sequences. However, the dominant beat of the film is the voices, opinions, and images of the women filmmakers. The talk is incessant and it is fascinating. The filmmakers confirm, amplify, and contradict each other's views. Some are witty (Sandy Wilson recalls raising money by "dining for dollars"); some are bold (Lizzie Borden calls for women to make movies "that make us hot"); some are intensely personal (Penelope Spheeris reveals that she was beaten as a child, that she "was taught violence"); some are wise (Martha Coolidge is unfailingly intelligent). Jay Scott's review at the time divided the personae into types: Sandy Wilson is "the class clown," Penelope Spheeris "the tragic figure," Lizzie Borden "the erotic intellectual," Amy Heckerling and Martha Coolidge "the truthsayers," and Agnes Varda, Mai Zetterling, Jeanne Moreau, and Margarethe von Trotta "the European class acts ... They are virtually the only women who do not talk about financing." Scott caustically assigns Sherry Lansing, the first woman ever to head a major studio, the role of "the villain ... She characterizes Hollywood as a 'totally prejudice-free environment.'" He goes on to note that "it's enlightening to remember that Lansing produced *Fatal Attraction*."[37]

Despite their differences, however, what strikes one about the women as a group is their stylish, professional, and comfortably affluent self-presentations. Penelope Spheeris, whose facial gestures and manner of speech are rough and unpolished, is the only one who appears to come from a working-class background. All of them, including Spheeris, sport the fashion excesses of the 1980s: big hair, big shoulders, big earrings.[38] In this they provide a marked contrast to the subjects of Cole/Dale's previous documentaries.

One of the striking contrasts between the cinematic construction of the middle-class and wealthy subjects of *Calling the Shots* and the working-class subjects of the previous films is the rigorous isolation of the women filmmakers within the frame. They are constructed as ineluctably alone, as individual subjects, each occupying her own solitary cinematic space. Even when the subjects note the support and assistance of other women, they do so from within the individual close-up. Producer Barbara Boyle (*Desperately Seeking Susan*, 1985), for example, relates her involvement in Seidelman's first real commercial opportunity. Cinematically, the connection between the two women is constructed by intercutting the two interviews (in which Seidelman, by the way, neglects to mention Boyle's support). Joyce Chopra's account of working with Claudia Weill is similarly constructed. The women are associated through the editing, but not within the image. In the few sequences that feature group activity (Sandy Wilson and Martha Coolidge at work on set), the directors are the only women visible among the all-male crews.

In the other films, including *Minimum Charge, No Cover, Thin Line, Hookers on Davie*, and *P4W: Prison for Women*, there are some individual interviews, but the dominant notes in all the films are of relationships, community, partnerships, and social discourse. Even Marlene Moore, undoubtedly the most damaged and alienated of the documentary subjects, is interviewed (in *P4W*) sitting beside her slashing buddy. These earlier films construct what Thomas Waugh termed the "multiple subject," which he saw as characteristic of committed documentaries set in the Third World.[39] At its best, the multiple subject can challenge the western interpellation of the subject as enclosed and isolated within individual consciousness, thus obviating the alienating effects of the dominant cultural ideology.

The irony of *Calling the Shots*, articulated by Martha Coolidge, is that when women directors are successful, they are treated as individual exceptions (marked by "talent," as the villain Sherry Lansing says). When their films don't succeed financially, however, they are treated as a multiple category. As Martha Coolidge says, "The flops made by women directors are somehow held against all women directors."

To this day, *Calling the Shots* stands as a valid description of the position of women in the feature film industry. In fact, as Jay Scott writes, this "exhaustive, entertaining broadside against cinematic sexism" is "an examination not merely of women working in the movies, but of women toiling in any highly professional, male-dominated field."[40] The film has not been displaced by any more recent compendium. Perhaps someone will update the picture in 2000, the new year of the woman filmmaker.

The 1990s

Since *Calling the Shots* (1988), Cole and Dale have made no more documentaries together. Cole began to develop the script for *Dangerous Offender* (1996), wrote other screenplays (so far unproduced), and took up an appointment teaching screenwriting for the Ontario College of Art and Design. Dale was a resident in the Directors Program at the Canadian Film Centre in 1989, where she made the short film *Dead Meat* from Cole's story idea and developed the feature film *Blood & Donuts* (screenplay Andrew Rai Berzins, 1995).

Dead Meat is a jagged little pill, only ten minutes long, that sets a single sequence in motion to construct a narrative arc. A junkie couple, knowing the risk they are taking, sends the man off to the dealer to whom they owe money. The dealer punishes the junkie in a particularly cruel way. Stylishly shot and directed, the film is a narrative exercise that effectively demonstrates Dale's developing skills as a dramatic director.

Blood & Donuts is a delightful little vampire film that combines a trio of young characters: the vampire Boya, who comes back to life after being "in a bag" since 1967; Earl, an eccentric taxi driver who is in some kind of trouble with the mob; and Molly, the intellectual server at a donut shop in a derelict area of the city. The locations can be spotted immediately as consistent with Cole/Dale's earlier movies. The donut shop is populated by neighbourhood junkies, thugs, and bikers, and its set design is accurately threadbare. The fleabag hotel across the street, where Boya takes a room, is reminiscent of the setting of *Cream Soda*. A secondary character, Boya's lover from 1967, now aged by twenty-five years, works in a beauty salon in the same strip.

Blood & Donuts treats the vampire's taste for human blood as an unfortunate addiction. He's trying as hard as he can to resist, sustaining himself on the blood of rats and pigeons instead. The delightful taxi driver seems equally addicted to donuts and trouble. Although Boya's first transformation into a werewolf-like monster is surprising and horrifying for the gangsters, Earl and Molly seem to take his condition in stride, and the movie depicts them as a community of friends.

A hybrid, postmodern film that equally works from and mocks the generic conventions, *Blood & Donuts* combines comedy, romance, crime, and special effects in a snappy script. Dale's direction is adept and quirky, and Paul Sarossy's gorgeous cinematography lends the sleazy settings a moody, lustrous charm. Despite its economical budget, it is a creditable theatrical film and certainly succeeded as a calling card for Dale as a director. Since its release, followed almost immediately by *Dangerous Offender* (1996), Dale has been steadily employed as a director of commercials and episodic television.

Meanwhile, Cole has also been busy. With a number of screenplays waiting for production, she is currently writing a television drama based on the real-life story of Martin Kruze, a young man enticed into homosexual prostitution who eventually committed suicide.

ॐ ॐ ॐ

While Cole and Dale have recently described themselves as feminist, and while their work often deals with women, it by no means limits itself to gender issues, women's lives, or feminist themes. Casting a wide net predominantly outside the middle-class mainstream, their body of work is marked most urgently by its attention to marginalized registers of society and predominantly to resisters of social injustice. The subjects to which they attend are treated in the cinematic conventions appropriate to those registers: *cinéma vérité*, expressionistic short films, genre features, and social-issue dramas. Cole's and Dale's careers as independent women filmmakers must be noted not only for solidity but also remarkable longevity. At the same time, the present survey suggests that we must also recast the critical and scholarly assessment of their work as a consistent and forceful contribution to the discourse of marginality.

Notes

1 Victor Coleman, Alice Klein, George Csaba Koller, and John Harkness respectively.

2 Dale has denied this connection.

3 George Csaba Koller, "Street People," *Cinema Canada* 49/50: 58.

4 "We grew up in environments that were full of unusual characters that you don't meet in a nice middle-class, suburban type of living situation. We understood criminals, hoods, people who had sex hang-ups, street people." In Koller, "Street People," 59.

5 Robert Fothergill, "Coward, Bully or Clown: The Dream Life of a Younger Brother," *Take One* 4, no. 3 (September 1973). Reprinted in *Canadian Film Reader,* Seth Feldman and Joyce Nelson, eds. (Toronto: Peter Martin Associates, 1977).

6 John Harkness, "Nightworld: An Interview with Janis Cole and Holly Dale," *Cinema Canada* (June 1984): 12.

7 At the time, Holly Dale was quoted as saying that she would rather work as a waitress for a year than make a film like *Not a Love Story.* Cole added, "The problem with the Board is that they seem to believe that people want you to tell them what they should think. We'd like to believe that our audiences are a little more intelligent than that." John Harkness, "Canada's most successful ever indie documentary soon to open in the UK," *Screen International,* 21 April 1984, 10.

8 Victor Coleman, "Talking Pictures with Janis Cole and Holly Dale," *The Lictor,* 4 March 1982.

9 Cole joked in an interview with Victor Coleman, "I think it's because of my hair, but I'm not sure."

10 Coleman interview.

11 Amy Taubin, "Pulling Punches," *Village Voice,* 29 December 1999–4 January 2000.

12 Taubin, "Pulling Punches."

13 Taubin, "Pulling Punches."

14 Leonard Maltin's Movie & Video Guide, us.imdb.com/Maltin?0071266.

15 Ed Sutton, us.imdb.com/Plot?0071266.

16 See Maltin, us.imdb.com/Maltin?0066830.

17 See Maltin, us.imdb.com/Plot?0112649.

18 In his early films for Roger Corman, including *Caged Heat* and *The Hot Box* (Viola, 1972), which Demme scripted, he often inserted his own political perspective into the exploitation format. *The Hot Box* was sold as a women-in-prison movie, but its plot concerned four American army nurses captured by Cuban revolutionaries

(led by a thinly disguised Che Guevera). The African-American nurse becomes a dedicated guerrilla who returns to Los Angeles to fight the urban revolution with her own people.

19 Comparison of *Thin Line* and *Dangerous Offender* may note the place accorded to the mother. In *Thin Line*, a mother is interviewed as she crochets an afghan square sitting in an easy chair beside her pet bird. In its bare bones, the story she tells is similar to that of Marlene Moore's childhood. The mother admits that with an alcoholic husband and a family of eight children she was overwhelmed, and that as her son became unmanageable, she had to turn him over to the courts—at the age of five. In juvenile facility, the boy was abused repeatedly and sent from one institution to another until he ended up in a hospital for the criminally insane. Marlene Moore's mother, upon finding her daughter "unmanageable" at the age of twelve, likewise sent the child off to a juvenile corrections facility and thence into the prison system. We are set for apparently justified condemnations of the mother's negligence. In *Thin Line*, however, neither the inmate nor the film subjects the mother to such judgement. The mother is interviewed direct-to-camera in a medium shot, a standard documentary "legitimizing" or "authorizing" device, and she is allowed by the editing to say that she loves her son, just as he says that he understands her fears of and for him. Cole/Dale's amazing empathy is palpable here.

20 Doug Saunders, "Women filmmakers at the crossroads," *Globe and Mail*, 28 January 2000, R5. The article notes that the festival opened with a film by a woman: *What's Cooking?* (Chadha, 1999) and mentions also *The Virgin Suicides* (Coppola, 1999), *American Psycho* (Harron, 1999), *Girlfight* (Kusama, 1999), *Backroads* (Cheechoo, 1999), *Songcatcher* (Greenwald, 1999), *Love and Sex* (Breiman, 1999), *Committed* (Krueger, 1999), *Drop Back Ten* (Cochran, 1999), and *Soft Fruit* (Adreef, 1999).

21 Saunders, "Women filmmakers."

22 Saunders, "Women filmmakers."

23 Janis Cole and Holly Dale, *Calling the Shots: Profiles of Woman Filmmakers* (Kingston: Quarry Press, 1993), 12.

24 Lina Wertmuller, Liliana Cavani, Ulrike Ottinger, Monika Treut, and Jane Campion were, for a variety of reasons, not among the ranks of the documented.

25 Cole and Dale, *Calling the Shots*, 11.

26 The encyclopedias include G.A. Foster, *Women Film Directors: An International Bio-Critical Dictionary*, (Westport: Greenwood Press, 1995); Annette Kuhn and Susannah Radstone, eds., *The Women's Companion to International Film* (London: BFI, 1990); Barbara Koenig Quart, *Women Directors: The Emergence of a New Cinema* (New York: Praeger, 1988).

27 Cole and Dale, *Calling the Shots*, 11.

28 Andrew Sarris, *The American Cinema: Directors and Directions 1929–1968* (New York: Simon & Schuster, 1973).

29 Peter Wollen, "The Auteur Theory," in *Theories of Authorship: A Reader*, John Caughie, ed. (London: Routledge, 1991).

30 Giuliana Bruno, *Street-Walking on a Ruined Map: Cultural Theory and the City Films of Elvira Notari* (Princeton: Princeton University Press, 1993).

31 Bruno, *Street-Walking*, 234–35.

32 Bruno, *Street-Walking*, 24.

33 Bruno, *Street-Walking*, 235.

34 Chantal Akerman is barely present in the documentary, despite the critical esteem accorded to her films. From conversations with Cole/Dale during production of the film, I recall that she was largely edited out because she seemed unwilling or incapable of answering their questions in anything but monosyllables or shrugs.

35 Cole and Dale, *Calling the Shots*, 15.

36 Annette Kuhn, *Women's Pictures* (London: Routledge & Kegan Paul, 1982), 148.

37 Jay Scott, "True Confessions," *Globe and Mail*, 24 September 1988.

38 I remember showing the film to my class in the 1990s, and all we could see were the huge, dangling, jiggling earrings, which absolutely dominated the image. Jeanne Moreau wins hands down for longest, showiest earrings, biggest hair, and thinnest, longest cigarette.

39 Thomas Waugh, "Words of Command: Notes on Cultural and Political Inflections of Direct Cinema in Indian Independent Documentary," *CineAction* 23 (Winter 1990–91): 28–39.

40 Scott, "True Confessions."

Thirty-Two Paragraphs About David Cronenberg

William Beard

1. RIGHT FROM THE OUTSET, David Cronenberg has constituted a problem for English-Canadian cinema. He was a problem because he couldn't be fitted into any of the categories people were using to describe the phenomenon of distinctively Canadian feature film, or to prescriptively define the cultural and aesthetic strategies such a cinema ought to pursue. As time passed, Cronenberg's cinema evolved, and the models for Canadian cinema also evolved, but somehow the Cronenberg problem persisted—and persists still. For instance, consider the following statement: Cronenberg is the most substantial and important feature-filmmaker English Canada has produced, and if you subtract Atom Egoyan, second place isn't remotely close. This ought not to be a controversial statement, but it is, and most of the reasons that it is are themselves a reflection of the multiform crisis of nationalism, aesthetics, and economic and cultural status under the Hollywood thumb which has beset both the English-language film industry in this country and the critical discourse surrounding it for the past thirty years.

2. Beginning with the infamous *Shivers* scandal in 1975, wherein a fulminating Robert Fulford denounced the Canadian Film Development Corporation for putting public money into a cheap horror movie that featured slimy, crawling sex-parasites, Cronenberg became for several years a ritual enemy in the culture wars enveloping English-Canadian cinema.[1] Setting aside for a moment the essential Canadian versus American, serious-observation versus formula-junk aspect of this debate, Cronenberg also became a target at this stage of his career because his films were in such *poor taste*, so *low*. They did not share the accepted Canadian strategy of keeping their desperation bleak and muted in a depressively plain dramatic landscape. Instead they were loud and vulgar, and among other things their reception revealed the degree to which the desire for a Canadian cinema of which we could be proud was tied up with canons of respectability. The brand of cultural snobbery that denounced early Cronenberg decries not only the cheap and sensational but anything that too closely resembles the narrative formulas of popular movies. It is an attitude that in effect prohibits *any* kind of Canadian cinema not created by government subsidy for small festival and art-house audiences. In the context of the admirably drab, impeccably local human limitations depicted in *Nobody Waved Goodbye*, *Goin' Down the Road*, or *Wedding in White*, the revolting

excesses of *Shivers* and *Rabid* (1977)—and even *The Brood* (1979) and *Scanners* (1981)—made Cronenberg's films themselves seem to some like slimy sex-parasites in the clean and proper body of English Canada.

3. You can argue about the merits or weaknesses of Cronenberg's and Egoyan's cinemas, but these two are pretty much unique in the annals of English-Canadian theatrical feature film in one significant respect: the fact that they have remained productive and viable over a period of decades and have each built up a substantial body of work. The very real talents of other filmmakers (and one thinks immediately of figures like Don Shebib or Don Owen a quarter century ago, Phillip Borsos or Sandy Wilson more recently) so often faded or were cut off after a blaze of promise. Perhaps directors like Anne Wheeler, Bruce McDonald, and Patricia Rozema will yet be able to put together whole artistic careers in English Canada, banging out one considerable movie after another, but they're not quite there yet.[2] Cronenberg and Egoyan *are* there, and in any comparison by this criterion Cronenberg is senior. Quite simply, nobody else from his generation is still around, not to mention giving rise to cult-devotion, museum retrospectives, cultural prizes, international conferences, and book-length critical studies in four languages. He is the largest object in our cinematic landscape. In the context of a national cinema starving for some kind of sustained success, the question again arises of why Cronenberg couldn't just be seen as that much-longed-for beacon—of why this big, successful phenomenon has seemed to need to be worked around or painfully circumvented rather than just comfortably included in the conceptualizations of a desirable English-Canadian cinema.

4. The content of Egoyan's cinema is just as strange, twisted, obsessive, and repetitive as Cronenberg's, but because it is much quieter and more inward, because it always resembles something you would see at a film festival or alternative-cinema venue and is not tainted with low-genre sensationalism, it fits much more easily with an accepted model of "good Canadian cinema." Egoyan's films not only contain but are usually structured around (1) voyeurism and sick manipulation in the arena of sexuality; (2) fundamental delusions and "bad" substitutions in the arena of love; (3) narcissism and communicational dysfunction as personality traits; (4) severe pathologies within the family; and (5) a crisis of emptiness and over-mediation in the social realms of technology and representation. In its own way, this territory is as sensational as Cronenberg's, and thematically not so different from it. In particular, Egoyan's parade of characters who use mediating technologies and representations to distance themselves from the dangers of feeling is very reminiscent of Cronenberg's large collection of scientists and artists who use their professions in similar ways. But where Egoyan's proper multicultural foregrounding of racial/ethnic and gender difference and his proper demonization of white patriarchy have had the bizarre effect of rendering his neurotic excesses politically correct, Cronenberg has consistently created problems by dramatizing *his* neurotic excesses as noisy and explicit spectacles of transgression. So, notwithstanding their crucial similarities, the quick take has often been that Egoyan = Arsinée Khanjian staring moodily at a video screen and David Hemblen coldly humiliating somebody, while Cronenberg = Louis Del Grande's exploding head and Debbie Harry burning her breast with a cigarette.

5. Even those in Canada who disliked Cronenberg's films or disapproved of them as a model for the national cinema had to accept him as a figure of consequence once he began receiving respectful attention from critics abroad, and the process continued as he racked up

museum and gallery retrospectives and the award of the Chevalier dans l'ordre des arts et des lettres from the French government. As well, the films themselves started getting bigger budgets and more respectable casts, started moving fitfully away from creature effects and looking generally somewhat less weird and perverted, all of which helped to rehabilitate him from the charge of being a trash merchant. But Cronenberg's films, however comparatively gentrified they may have become, have always retained a deeply unpleasant quality somewhere. In *Dead Ringers*, *M. Butterfly*, and *Crash*, there are no creatures, special effects, or other overt evidence of an "immature" reliance upon sensational, low-culture, genre-narrative elements, but there are various forms of sexual pathology in profusion, a rottenness at the centre, and the pervasive odour of something disagreeable. Viewers who have always been repelled by Cronenberg are not going to be converted by this evolution—an evolution that has also, most clearly in *Crash*, brought the filmmaker closer to the realm of a pure art cinema. Cronenberg's ascent in his native country to the title of "respected film artist" has thus been accompanied by overtones of suspicion and unwillingness as well as confusion.

6. Cronenberg's early work did find admirers, both in Canada and elsewhere, who appreciated its scandalizing verve. It is highly ironic in this context that many of those admirers then began to cool towards the filmmaker's work because of exactly those qualities that rendered it somewhat more palatable to many of its first critics. This attitude seems to have particular currency among British *cinéastes*.[3] UK enthusiasts took up Cronenberg earlier than anybody (*Stereo* [1969] used to show constantly at the Notting Hill Gate cinema in London in the early 1970s), and the nasty and dishevelled aspects of his cheap horror flicks could overlap with, among other things, a punk-culture drive to outrage bourgeois norms (*Shivers* and *Rabid* remain cult favourites in the harder-edged club and rave scenes in Britain). You can find this viewpoint clearly on display in, for example, Iain Sinclair's little book on *Crash*, which continually repeats the refrain that Cronenberg's cinema was once cheap, messy, and genuine but now has become genteel, refined, and uninteresting.[4] And even Geoff Pevere's essay in the present volume refers several times, it seems to me slightly ominously, to "early Cronenberg" in such a way as to suggest that it is "authentically weird Cronenberg."

7. In the tale of the metamorphosis and decline of David Cronenberg, interesting filmmaker, it is often remarked that at a certain point he stopped writing original scripts: that since *Videodrome* (1983), every one of his films has been either scripted by someone else, co-scripted with someone else, or adapted from someone else's book or play. Cronenberg himself, who seems to follow the critical discourse about his work quite keenly, may even have responded to it with *eXistenZ*, widely described in the ancillary publicity as Cronenberg's "first original screenplay since *Videodrome*." A filmmaker who does not control his or her scripts in some ultimate way is in danger of being demoted from the status of *auteur* to that of *metteur-en-scène*, mere stager of somebody else's invention; and if there is one claim Cronenberg has wanted to maintain through thick and thin, it is that he is an original artist, not a formula hack. But the criticism that in depending on the original work of others for the kernels of his films from *The Dead Zone* (1983) to *Crash* (1996) he has abandoned an important creative autonomy seems to me ridiculous. The only Cronenberg film that does not scream "*Cronenberg!*" is *Fast Company* (1979), his drag-racing movie with John Saxon. All the rest, notwithstanding the presence of others' names at one point or another in the creative process, realize an artistic program that, far from being tainted by mixed authorship, is one

of the most consistent, self-contained, and even obsessively repetitive in world cinema over the past quarter century.

8. But there is a key here to the question of why Cronenberg has never quite occupied a comfortable place in the English-Canadian cinema environment he has from one standpoint dominated. While he was making cheap drive-in and fleapit fodder (those outlets still existed in the 1970s) with bad or unknown actors—or worse, importing porno-queen Marilyn Chambers for a momentary "straight" role in *Rabid*—he could be misidentified as a sellout to the lowest forms of Hollywood-aping commercial prostitution and a traitor to the idea of a serious, sober, and distinctive Canadian cinema. As he began to use big-name, but non-Canadian, performers like Oliver Reed and Samantha Eggar (*The Brood*), Patrick McGoohan (*Scanners*), and James Woods and Deborah Harry (*Videodrome*) in more and more central roles, he may have moved away from the shoddy-exploitation-movie stereotype, but he actually moved closer to the looks-too-much-like-Hollywood stereotype. And when he then arrived at offers of relatively big Hollywood production budgets and wide distribution, the resemblance was amplified to such an extent that many people had difficulty thinking of Cronenberg as a Canadian filmmaker at all. Now he was making *The Dead Zone*, adapted from a Stephen King bestseller by a third party, starring the likes of Christopher Walken, Brooke Adams, and Tom Skerritt, all for Dino De Laurentiis and Lorimar; followed by *The Fly* (1986), inspired by an old Hollywood B-horror-movie and produced by Mel Brooks for 20th Century Fox, with more American stars.

9. The argument here is that if it looks like a duck and talks like a duck, it is a duck. By contrast, the argument that Cronenberg's cinema—Jeff Goldblum, Dino De Laurentiis, and all—is essentially a *Canadian* cinema can seem too subtle and intricate to adherents of the opposite school. Mike Gasher provides an uncontroversial description of Canadian movies in the following terms:

> Canadian film, for the most part, does not subscribe to the same production values or the same thematic preoccupations as the dominant Hollywood commercial cinema. Canadian cinema is characterized by its difference from Hollywood, which owes a great deal to the context in which it is produced. Canadian films' small budgets, for example, speak to the Canadian industry's marginalization. Canadian cinema's lack of stars testifies to the lack of a media support system necessary to generate a public discourse around Canadian film ... Canadian films, for the most part, lack the aesthetic gloss of Hollywood cinema, explained partly by budget constraints, but also by filmmakers' concerns with unifying form and content.[5]

The Cronenberg exception is covered under "for the most part," but essentially what this argument observes is that Canadian cinema, in order to be recognizable as such, must have poor production values and marginalized production/distribution/exhibition, non-generic subjects, small budgets, no stars, and a relatively drab look. Cronenberg's post-*Videodrome* cinema, by contrast, has good production values, major distribution and exhibition, (often) some connection with generic narrative, larger budgets, stars, and a polished look.

10. From a thematic perspective, Cronenberg's work can be argued to be very close to the archetypal profiles of Canadian culture as advanced by Northrop Frye, Margaret Atwood, and Gaile McGregor (and I have argued just this in some detail elsewhere).[6] But one also must

remember some fundamental facts. Cronenberg, unlike, say, Norman Jewison or Ivan Reitman, has remained in Canada despite the opportunity to work elsewhere. He is not shy about depicting Montréal as Montréal in *Shivers* and *Rabid*, or Toronto as Toronto in *Dead Ringers*, and in other films has not called Toronto anything else except when the screenplay explicitly compelled it (*The Dead Zone*, *Naked Lunch*). Moreover, he always spoken about himself specifically as a Canadian artist. To my way of thinking, this is looking and talking like a Canadian duck, and a more elaborate argument for why Cronenberg should *not* automatically be thought of as just a Canadian filmmaker, no qualifications or disclaimers, is required than any that have been advanced so far. When Egoyan (*Felicia's Journey*), Phillip Borsos (*The Mean Season*), or Patricia Rozema (*Mansfield Park*) make films set or actually produced in other countries, it doesn't seem to affect their status as pillars of Canadian filmmaking, but Cronenberg continues to have trouble.

11. In his 1995 discussion of the problems created for a properly Canadian cinema by the presence of American genre models,[7] Jim Leach discusses Cronenberg's place in a nuanced way that recognizes the filmmaker's Canadian locus of production and self-description as Canadian, and summarizes some of the arguments for the Canadianness of his themes on the one hand and the international or <u>non-national nature of his entire project</u> on the other. He also recognizes that globalization, international co-production, and a host of other forces have made the Canadian-cinema-versus-genre-cinema opposition moot in many ways. But he too feels that Cronenberg de-Canadianizes himself by representing Toronto as simply a generic North American metropolis, and says that "the attempts to situate Cronenberg's films in a national rather than generic context often seem to obscure the ways in which the films are constructed and received."[8] One wants to reply to this by saying that Toronto *is* a generic North American metropolis, and that if the films are not received as Canadian, what this essentially means is that they are widely exhibited and advertised and people actually go to see them (it remains as difficult as it ever was to imagine a Canadian *popular* cinema that does not disqualify itself from Canadianness by its very popularity). As for the constantly cited problem of not identifying Canadian locations as Canadian, we might remember that English Canada is the only place in the world outside the United States itself where simply plunking the action down in a generic city and letting people talk would *not* immediately reveal its locale as "not the USA" through people's speech and the appearance of the setting: Canada does look like this, and we do talk this way. Anyway, at the end of Leach's discussion of Cronenberg, the impression remains once more of a large object that has to be manoeuvred around, taken account of, but not really absorbed.

12. Leach's primary opposition between Canadian cinema and genre cinema reflects the way many in this country have conceived the situation. A similar opposition between art cinema and genre cinema overlaps this territory to a substantial degree. In both comparisons, genre cinema is the undesirable choice. "The cinema we need"[9] is *not* a genre cinema; Hollywood North is basically a bad thing; and if Cronenberg's films are genre films, or even if they look too much like genre films, they are not the cinema we need. But the dualism of genre cinema versus national or art cinemas, however clearly it may mark itself in some areas, is intensely confused and problematical in others, and it can often obscure the situation rather than illuminating it.[10] In Cronenberg's case, the model is in any case only even notionally applicable in the films up to *The Fly*. *Dead Ringers* (1988), *Naked Lunch* (1991), *M. Butterfly* (1993), and *Crash* are not genre films by anyone's definition. (Of course they are also not place-centred,

realist little "stories of our own.") If we must choose a category, it would be "alternative" cinema—that broad catch-all where everything that is not mainstream can be thrown, a tank that includes national fish and art fish, but also lots of "alternative" genre fish. Sometimes these films open in a number of commercial theatres simultaneously, just like smaller mainstream movies, and sometimes they open only in specialized venues, independently run or set aside by the big exhibition chains for the odd art film or national film or off-the-beaten-track genre film. This is where Cronenberg sits at the moment.

13. In truth, Cronenberg's films have only ever fleetingly been a comfortable fit for the "genre" category. Even as cheap horror movies they always looked slightly alien—they were always "alternative" genre films. Only in Canada would anyone call him a genre filmmaker at any time after 1983. In many parts of the non-Hollywood world—in Europe, say—the whole convoluted debate about Cronenberg's place *vis-à-vis* genre cinema, national cinema, and art cinema would not have taken place at all. His cluster of characteristics, and in particular the difficulty in classifying him comfortably in any dimension, would simply be labelled "originality"—a still-prized quality in cultural production. As I said at the beginning, the arguments about him here are a mirror of our own cultural predicament. Cronenberg has difficulty pleasing the middle-of-the-roaders in the broad spectrum of popular movie-going, difficulty pleasing the sober-documentarist-localists who occupy one position in the debates about Canadian national cinema, difficulty pleasing the avant-gardists who occupy another, and difficulty pleasing the politically minded and the moralists who (in whatever context of Canadian public discourse) are always on the lookout for deplorable things to identify and denounce.

14. Cronenberg has come under a good deal of attack, much of it vitriolic, for his perceived sexual politics. This began with Robin Wood's essay in *The Shape of Rage*, which accused him of having a horror of sexuality, particularly of female sexuality;[11] continued with the angry denunciations of the scene of Deborah Harry's burnt breast in *Videodrome*; rose to an unsurpassable peak during the anguished aftermath of the Marc Lépine murders in 1989 when a woman on CBC Radio blamed the massacre on a climate of misogyny such as that perpetrated by the images in Cronenberg's films; and has continued in a scattering of feminist academic writing about Cronenberg during the late 1980s and 1990s.[12] Cronenberg's art depends on the operation and exploration of transgressive desire: he has talked about this many times, and it is plain to anyone looking at his films. The horror genre to which his work is often related has the transgressive quality built in (as Isabel Cristina Pinedo bluntly puts it, "it is the nature of fictional horror to transgress and violate all boundaries"[13]); and "transgressive desire" signifies the excitement and arousal that is stimulated through the entry into the forbidden. So if transgressive desire in Cronenberg's films *isn't* offensive, it's not doing its work. The problem arises because in the sub-Marxian political environment enveloping feminist and cultural-studies analysis (I speak as a wishy-washy social democrat here), it is essential to have an enemy who is not us, and to identify oppressive mechanisms that can be fought. In this context, transgressive art is not offensive at all but instead exhilarating and inspiring, because the transgression is against oppressive norms and systems that we of properly progressive political belief wish to repudiate. Robin Wood can politically validate the transgressiveness of some 1970s horror films (George Romero's or Larry Cohen's, for example) by invoking Gad Horowitz's notion of "surplus repression," wherein the process of socialization represses not only truly unacceptable wishes to kill others or do whatever we

want regardless of anything, but also perfectly acceptable ones such as those of sexual attraction towards members of our own sex; concomitantly, it is possible to unrepress selectively,
undoing "surplus" repression without disturbing the basic variety.[14] Progressive horror cinema is then truly horrifying only to adherents of the capitalist patriarchy; transgressive art is
offensive to somebody else.

15. But Cronenberg's films don't believe in surplus repression: specifically, they don't believe
you can unrepress only what it would be good to unrepress. Almost every one of his films[15]
offers the pattern of an unrepression that starts off as beneficial and ends up as dreadful because the process won't stop when it has accomplished what's good, but continues to cross
not only the boundaries that should be transgressed but also those that absolutely mustn't
be. Maybe the handiest example is *The Fly*, where what the hero needs is to get a girlfriend
and develop some confidence, but can't get that without also taking a transmutation into a
disgusting other species. Similarly, the hero of *Dead Ringers* wants to escape his emotional
encapsulation, the hero of *Naked Lunch* has to get in touch with his homosexuality, the hero
of *M. Butterfly* needs to be freed from bourgeois stultification, and the central married couple
in *Crash* must be released from their frozen alienation; and all of them get their wish to one
degree or another. Things turn out badly for all of them.

16. The idea of surplus repression and other similar beliefs is essentially optimistic in the realm
of the psychology, just as Marxism is essentially optimistic in the social realm. All human
problems are socially produced and perpetuated, and they are socially fixable. Cronenberg
belongs to another school—call it humanist, or proto-Freudian, or existentialist—which ap-
prehends the problems primarily as psychological rather than social. Human subjectivity is
undoubtedly socially constructed at some crucial level, as Cronenberg would doubtless be
the first to agree, but he is not very interested in analyzing exactly how its dysfunctionalities
are produced socially, still less in finding a socio-political project to ameliorate them. What
he *is* interested in is the spectacle of dysfunctional subjectivity and its ineffectual struggles to
live successfully in the world. He also feels that, for all practical purposes, psychological dysfunction is innate and inescapable (at least for his male protagonists) and that attempts to re-
engineer it will only inscribe its impossibility yet more deeply. In this he actually conforms
to one major stereotype of Canadianness: encapsulated, paralyzed by an over-awareness of
the other side of the argument or the harmful things that can follow any change of circumstances. It seems odd to describe Cronenberg as a cautious soul, but from a certain standpoint he is. In English Canada, we lack the temperament for revolution. Cronenberg is continually staging revolutionary transformations, but they all end badly. He sees the need for
revolution clearly enough; it's just that he sees the other side of the question with equal clarity. He is a pessimist.[16]

17. Cronenberg's early features—*Shivers, Rabid, The Brood,* and *Scanners*—are the closest to being
real genre films, particularly in the old pre-auteurist dismissive connotation of "downmarket
formula pictures." The first two particularly sit recognizably in a pile of low-budget 1970s
renaissance-of-horror movies, of which the most interesting would include Romero's *Night
of the Living Dead* and *Dawn of the Dead*, Tobe Hooper's *The Texas Chainsaw Massacre* and
Eaten Alive, Wes Craven's *The Last House on the Left* and *The Hills Have Eyes*, and Brian De
Palma's *Sisters*.[17] In addition to having a more accomplished visual aesthetic than any but the
last of these, Cronenberg's films are distinguishable from the others by their set of highly
idiosyncratic tropes. The most prominent are a constant interest in medical science and

forms of transgressive, often sexualized, "radical" research and experimentation, and a consuming obsession with the body as a thing apart from the rational self and a site of raging epidemics of sexual desire and disease—hence descriptions of Cronenberg's cinema as "body horror" and "venereal horror." So powerful and uniquely focussed are these repetitions that Cronenberg was recognized as an auteur very early on. (This didn't really help him, though, in the national-cinema debate, where the pro- versus anti-Cronenberg exchange was likely to go "But he's an auteur!" "So what, he's a Hollywood auteur!")

18. Like a number of their genre fellows, *Shivers* and *Rabid* stage the systematic affronting of social norms and propriety. In *Shivers*, highrise-apartment dwellers seeking comfortable vacuity and anonymity are transformed into voracious sex-predators by a mad doctor who implants them with squirming eight-inch parasites. The messy, sensational spectacle that results is indeed an outrage, not only to bourgeois propriety but to good taste, respect, refinement, discrimination, and even intelligence. When a parasite crawls up Barbara Steele's vagina while she's taking a bath, viewers of all persuasions are shocked and appalled, but then bifurcate instantly into the amused and the angry. A question here is the extent to which the film's rampage through standards of restraint too closely resembles a kind of adolescent glee in mere nose-thumbing. It's a difficult task, assaulting the citadel of responsibility responsibly. But the film isn't just anarchically gleeful; it's also horrifying and disturbing. Cronenberg's ultimate aim is to be serious, and that is apparent even in *Shivers*, where the forces of compulsion and revulsion at work are bigger and more lasting than the irony and satire.

19. Another question, here and in *Rabid*—and then later in *Videodrome, Dead Ringers, Naked Lunch,* and *Crash*—is prompted by images of sadomasochistic sexual violence. In *Shivers,* these include the opening strangulation and corpse-slashing, the bathtub parasite, and the later scenes featuring one of the female characters with a bloody bandage over her mouth. This transgressive sexuality is partly disavowed in the early films and partly just folded into the general presentation of transgression going on all over the place. Musing on the story in William Burroughs' *Naked Lunch* of "the man who taught his asshole to talk" and then couldn't get it to shut up, Cronenberg says,

> The talking asshole, and I mean *no* disrespect here, is Burroughs himself, in the sense that it's the part of you that you don't want to listen to, that's saying things that are unspeakable, that are too basic, too true, too primordial, and too uncivilized and too tasteless, to be listened to, but are there nonetheless.[18]

This can stand as Cronenberg's credo with respect to all the transgression of his work. If the artist, ransacking his unconscious like he's supposed to, comes up with images of sadistic sexual desire, well, that's what's there. In the early films, the moral and ethical horror of transgressive desire is not "placed" with much certainty. Later, though, beginning with *Videodrome*, this desire is presented insistently as not only harmful to others but also horribly destructive to the subject who entertains it.

20. As horror movies in general calcified during the 1980s, Cronenberg's films just kept getting more personal. *The Brood* is a fine little movie: dark, compressed, strikingly original, less marred by substandard acting than *Shivers* or *Rabid* (or the subsequent *Scanners*, for that matter). In its no-exit anguish and family-trauma introversion, it is more "Canadian" in theme and disposition than his earlier films, but it was barred still from recognition by its

"genre" elements. "Psychoplasmics," this film's mad-science, is a "radical" psychotherapeutic method designed to manifest the patient's problems as bodily growths—very Cronenberg. The therapy's most sensational outcome is Samantha Eggar's ability to conceive and give birth to child-creatures of her rage, carried in an external abdominal sac, a spectacle that, when it is finally revealed, causes both her husband and the film's viewers to gag with revulsion. This drew the fire of feminist critics for whom it was another example of Cronenberg's monstrosification of the female body, and it is exactly the kind of thing that seemed to require the film's classification as genre cinema. Without distractions such as these, *The Brood*'s truly bleak and hopeless narrative, with its insistence on the pathologies of family life that are doomed to be repeated generation after generation, its desolating spectacle of the suffering of children and other innocent parties, and its muted, sombre mood and equally damped-down palette, would no doubt have been quickly recognized as acceptably if not in fact stereotypically "Canadian."

21. *Scanners* is not Cronenberg's strongest film, having unignorable plot holes and other evidence of hurried and impecunious production. In the thematic progression of his work, it is notable as by far his most optimistic film, the only example in which the outcome of a "radical" experiment (again in medical science), a revolutionary incursion of the body into the realm of the mind, does not end disastrously. The "scanners" of the title are telepaths who don't read minds but interact with the nervous systems of others, at times violently, as in the notorious example of the exploding head; but the protagonist scanner, instead of coming to some dreadful end as a result of the ensuing imbalance, actually masters his gift and finally melds psychically with his evil sibling, emerging for a flash as a kind of successful fusion of opposites before the suspiciously hurried ending of the film. In spite of its countless unique Cronenberg fingerprints, *Scanners* is arguably more of a real Hollywood genre movie than anything he has ever done except *Fast Company*. It is crammed with action-plot elements to such an extent, and so effectively, that the inconsistencies and loose ends of the narrative are scarcely troublesome, and it has the (more or less) happy ending Hollywood movies are supposed to have. Opening in an off-peak month, this inexpensive and flawed but dashing and imaginative little film actually managed to be the top box office earner in the US for a week and to spawn a cult following and three sequels (none of them involving Cronenberg). This commercial success had far-reaching consequences for Cronenberg, moving him permanently from low-budget to medium-budget productions and ensuring his subsequent films a wide distribution. It also—ironically, in view of the Hollywoodness of the whole process—forced the Canadian cultural establishment, high and low, to pay some serious attention to him. The sickeningly familiar principle that you'll never get respect in this country until you get it in some other country was demonstrated one more time. There was a short delay while the concept of an internationally successful Cronenberg was assimilated, and then the Academy of Canadian Cinema published a book about him[19] and gave him a Best Direction Genie for his next film, *Videodrome*.[20]

22. *Videodrome* is the film that marks the dividing point between nasty, messy, early Cronenberg and more mainstream middle Cronenberg. It is the last film really embraced by devotees of the earlier manner; it won the filmmaker his first Genie award and thus his first official recognition in Canada; and it was the Cronenberg film chosen for the forthcoming anthology entitled *Canada's Best Features*.[21] It is a pivotal work in so many ways. Formally, it moves further away from generic horror and SF than anything since *Crimes of the Future* (1970). An

independent TV producer, looking for transgressive new material to broadcast, encounters a program featuring what appears to be "real torture and murder," which, however, causes severe hallucinations that both stimulate his sadomasochistic sexual desires and allow him to be controlled and manipulated by the devisors of the program. After murdering several people, he shoots himself in a decaying ship's hulk. This story still contains "genre" components—special effects depicting bodily mutations and other impossible events—and also elements of a thriller plot. But the omnipresence of first-person hallucinations presented in the same register as everything else means that the "real" events of the story are so scrambled as to be unknowable. Viewers struggle hard to construct a conventional narrative as they watch the film, but they are doomed to failure. In this respect, *Videodrome* is as anti-narrative (and of course anti-genre) as *L'Année dernière à Marienbad*. Is this bad story management or avant-garde daring? *Videodrome*'s sensational genre-movie signifiers on the one hand, and *Marienbad*'s puritanical art-movie signifiers on the other, are what make this question possible, rather than any formal differences between the films. Like so many of Cronenberg's films, *Videodrome* is impossible to classify: burningly intense, chaotic, indelibly surreal, absolutely like nothing else.

23. *Videodrome* also contains a crucial breakthrough in the areas of theme and character. Finally Cronenberg has arrived at a protagonist who can truly incarnate (in the somatic as well as the metaphorical sense) the compulsive desires and anxieties found in all his work; finally both the exercise of transgressive imagination and the ground of transgressive disaster are united in a single personage who can now begin to enact the monstrous and pathetic drama of the dysfunctional male subject. It is a drama that comes to seem an entirely logical and necessary resting-point of the shifting, out-of-focus tableaux of the earlier films, and James Woods in *Videodrome* becomes the first in a line of suicidally impossible males that will be continued with pulverizing reiteration through each of Cronenberg's next five films. Now, instead of the hysterically mutated females of *Rabid* and *The Brood*, it is the male whose body is inscribed with horrific aberrations, and it is the male who has, in effect, created this monstrosity in himself through the operation of his own transgressive desire rather than its being visited on innocent bystanders by some megalomaniacal "research" project practised by a distant mad-scientist patriarch. *Videodrome* still has mad scientists and transgressive females—and indeed also disease-creating video technology and predatory corporations—but its most insistent activity is to delve inward, into the subject, into desire and its humanity-destroying dangers.

24. *The Dead Zone* and *The Fly* mark Cronenberg's closest relationship with the Hollywood-industry machines of production and marketing, the former a movie opening everywhere, with the names of Stephen King, Dino De Laurentiis, and Christopher Walken more likely to strike the eye than that of David Cronenberg, the latter an upmarket 1980s "remake" (like *Invasion of the Body Snatchers* or *The Thing*) of a cheap 1950s SF movie starring the hot married couple of Jeff Goldblum and Geena Davis. Both films were extremely un-Hollywood, however, in ending in the suicide of the sympathetic central character, and both were full of Cronenberg touches—utterly unmistakeable in *The Fly*. Moreover, to viewers keeping a close eye on the progression of Cronenberg's work, these films didn't look like moves into more mainstream commercial production, but instead like absorbing follow-ups of thematic innovations begun in *Videodrome*. Both films have heroes whose "monstrosity" is an indirect consequence of their sexual relationships with women—actually, the films are a mirrored pair in

this respect, as Walken suffers for saying no to coitus with his girlfriend, while Goldblum suffers for saying yes to his—and both dwell in agonizing detail on the disintegration of an encapsulated male whose ego-subjectivity is simply unable to tolerate the incursion of desire and the body. In both films, the genre elements and the commercial elements alike are finally overwhelmed by a quality foreign to both of those types—a penetrating sense of sadness and loss.

25. *Dead Ringers* showed even more clearly how forcefully Cronenberg could deviate from the commercial stereotype while operating, so to speak, with Caesar's coin. A film admired widely enough to provoke lamentations in the US that it didn't get an Oscar nomination,[22] its story of twin gynecologists who swap women without their knowledge, become terminal drug addicts, and finally commit suicide was virtually a prescription for not-a-Hollywood-movie—strange and unpleasant and devastated. In any event, it is Cronenberg's masterpiece to date. Above all, more than any of its predecessors, it is a deeply, overwhelmingly *sad* film, insisting unmissably on a quality of pathos and loss that is present in so much of his best work, but from which we may be distracted by the transgression and revulsion intermingled with it. *Dead Ringers* comes right in the middle of the whole series of films (beginning, again, with *Videodrome*) in which the hero turns into a pathetic monster. Here the hero is a monster from the beginning: he's a twin. This twinness signifies the impossibility of his subjectivity (all this reads beautifully through a Lacanian lens, or a Kristevan one), whose awkwardness and encapsulation are once again tied to the traumatizing othernesses of sexuality and the instinct to keep them at arm's length with some kind of instrumentalizing "science"—here, literally enough, gynecology. Avoiding now any overt "genre elements," Cronenberg makes a film that is simultaneously as kinky and alienating as anything of his and yet one which somehow finds a route to some of the deepest constituents of male subjectivity. It's also visually his most aggressively clean and high-modernist yet, having, much of the time, the real look of an art movie.

26. *Naked Lunch* represented a culmination of a number of things in Cronenberg's career. William Burroughs had been an object of his admiration and even imitation ever since his undergraduate days, and now he was finally making a cinematic translation of this admiration (rather than "adapting" the book as he had long thought about doing). Burroughs' hallucinatory literary outpourings possess not only a beautiful directness of style but also a superabundance of tortured ugliness, anguished paranoia, and hysterical loathing that makes them more truly horrifying than anything Cronenberg has ever done. It is ironic, then, that Cronenberg's *Naked Lunch*, adapted from an established literary classic with the author's blessing and following closely upon the award of the French Order of Arts and Letters, should have cemented his new status as *artist* with such firmness—simultaneously winning him Best Direction and Best Screenplay Genies and baffling its relatively few mainstream viewers so thoroughly that its resemblance to art cinema became unmistakable.

27. Moreover, in neglecting the book's skimpy and fragmentary narrative elements and deciding instead to offer a kind of psycho-biographical fantasy on the life of Burroughs as he was writing it, Cronenberg's film becomes not simply an art film but a kind of manifesto on the nature and construction of the transgressive artist—a category which certainly contains Burroughs, and to which Cronenberg aspires as well. The film presents scenes from the life of the Burroughs character transformed so completely by phantasmagorical drug hallucinations that the status of the events is as ontologically unreadable as those of *Videodrome* (to

which *Naked Lunch* is a pure sibling). Insect-typewriters that talk through dorsal assholes, seven-foot alien monsters called Mugwumps, drugs made out of insecticide or giant black centipedes: these are only a few of the delirious features of the film's world—features that paradoxically land this art movie back in the land of "genre-element" creatures and special effects. Sex is there, too, an uncomfortable amalgam of half-disavowed homosexuality (Burroughs') and half-smuggled-in heterosexuality (Cronenberg's). Pushing past all that to the film's basic allegory of artistic creation, though, what one discovers is this: artistic creation begins in the desire to commit a crime and then its actual commission (the hero's "accidental" shooting of his wife on the instructions of a hallucinated insect representing his own homosexual misogyny); and it realizes itself in the final penetration and dispersal of the mists of self-deception in an ultimate recognition by the artist of his condition—which is not simply transgressive but actually humanly destructive and morally horrifying. This man, this artist, is left as a figure suffused in dreadful self-knowing melancholy, a clear fellow to all of Cronenberg's surrounding suicidal heroes.

28. *M. Butterfly* is almost everybody's least favourite latter-day Cronenberg film. Of all his literary adaptations (of which only *The Dead Zone*, *M. Butterfly*, and *Crash* are really adaptations), this is the one in which the film seems to be fighting the original (Henry David Hwang's Tony-winning play, based on the true story of a French diplomat in China who lived in a sexual relationship with a Chinese opera performer for twenty years while thinking he was a she). Cronenberg takes Hwang's Brechtian agit-prop play and transforms it into a solidly realist pocket-David-Lean production, seeking to invest the *prima facie* absurdities of the hero's predicament with the gravity necessary for him to become another exemplary Cronenberg subject destroyed by his own liberating project. The protagonist is once again emancipated and then monstrosified by a sexual breakthrough—this time in embarking upon a grand romantic union in which he will dare to play the masterful imperialist European male to the colonized Asian woman whose secret desire is to be dominated—only to discover that the entire inflated mythic undertaking is based on a comically elementary error. The result is perhaps the most deflating of all Cronenberg's deconstructions of male subjectivity, indeed something of a thesis film in its presentation of a man who meticulously assembles his own calamity and who is torpedoed explicitly not by the sexual other but by the sexual-other-in-his-head. *M. Butterfly* seems weighed down not only by its (relatively) lavish costumes and settings but by the specificities of Hwang's sexual and postcolonial politics, and even by its exhausted attempt to restage the inspired collaboration with Jeremy Irons from *Dead Ringers*. It was the sixth straight Cronenberg film to unfold a tragedy of male psychology, and judging by his two projects since then, even Cronenberg may have thought he had gone to the well once too often.

29. After dressing up Toronto as Tangier and New York in *Naked Lunch*, and (at least for some of the interiors) as Beijing and Paris in *M. Butterfly*, Cronenberg removed the action of J.G. Ballard's novel *Crash* from West London to Toronto. In a striking and, to Canadian eyes, blackly comic reversal, he came under attack from British "psychogeographer" and poet Iain Sinclair for betraying the singular localness of 1970s-London grot in the book by recasting it as the smooth high-tech anonymity of contemporary Toronto.[23] But I would say that the movie is more or less flawless: you may not like it, but it is what it is perfectly. Its very beautiful, ultra-controlled, antiseptic cinematography and découpage are superimposed on subject matter that is incendiary in its provocation, and the result is both a real art movie and a

curiously exact counterpart to Ballard's surgical prose coldly relaying demented and porno-graphic material. Car-accident victims performing kinky couplings in strange automobilic contexts in ways that equate sex with violent bodily injury and death, everything encased in a cinematic apparatus of obsessive, puritanical preciseness: that's *Crash*. When the Cannes jury awarded the film a special prize for "daring, originality, and audaciousness" over loud protests recalling the good old days of mixed receptions for Antonioni and Godard, Cronenberg must have glowed with satisfaction, a certified transgressive artist. Many view-ers attracted by the sensational publicity were disgusted not by the pathology of the charac-ters and the action, but by the fact that instead of hot sex they got frozen high-modernism. Lost in the controversy, at least to some degree, was the fact that *Crash* signalled a major departure for Cronenberg: away from anguished stories of impossible personal subjectivity and (back) toward a more detached vision of a community of people afflicted with a bizarre condition.

30. After the commercial disappointments of *Naked Lunch* and *M. Butterfly*, after what we might call an "alternative art movie" in *Crash*, after all the stuff about so many adaptations from the work of others, Cronenberg's latest film, *eXistenZ*, returns again to "genre cinema." It was grouped conveniently by reviewers with a handful of Hollywood virtual-reality/SF movies—*Dark City*, *The Matrix,* and *The Thirteenth Floor*—that came out around the same time (1998–99) in one of those odd little concentrations that happen repeatedly in commercial filmmak-ing. All of these movies are strange and offbeat, but *eXistenZ* is by a healthy margin the strangest of them all. The plot is baroquely convoluted and finally disappears up its own tail, so that the film has no closure at all; and the characters, the dialogue, the virtual-reality gizmos, and above all the design and feel of everything have an outlandish idiosyncrasy that is smaller, more grotesque, and more willfully messy and off-turning than anything in their Hollywood counterparts. Like some other Cronenberg films (*Videodrome*, *Naked Lunch*), it did disappointing initial business but began almost immediately to develop a cult following. If almost everything in *Crash* is excessively clean, then almost everything in *eXistenZ* is exces-sively dirty—and not only dirty, but yucky. Both the "real" world and the virtual worlds of the movie are incredibly, insistently drab and down-at-heels, almost a caricature of the con-dition of dereliction that always surrounds Cronenberg's doomed protagonists as they start to go under. And as the film proceeds, the revolting-viscerality quotient keeps rising and ris-ing, until, in sequences like the ones in the Chinese restaurant or the slaughterhouse-factory, it is inescapably clear that the disgustingness of all this is funny—moreover, a joke at Cronenberg's own expense. Cronenberg is almost always classified as a postmodernist—in disregard of his tragic outlook and strongly modernist/existentialist set—but to my way of thinking, *eXistenZ*, with its self-parodic humour and its weightless recursive reality-loops, is his first genuinely postmodern film.

31. Caution and melancholy are essential characteristics of Cronenberg's films; but these de-scriptors seem counter-intuitive when applied to a cinema whose glaring, almost hysterical, insistence on the alarming and unprocessable otherness of the body is so horrifying. In the end, though, it is the combination of these very different qualities that perhaps best defines his cinema. On the one hand, there are the sharp stabs of revulsive fascination and instinc-tive anxiety rising to panic, the unfailing sense for what is alien and alarming, the spectacle of flagrant bodies overrun with mutation and disease. On the other, there is the impossible subject encapsulated and exiled from wholeness and functionality, with his sad destructive

strategies for coping with this condition through the instrumentalizing mechanisms of "radical" science or (later) "radical" art, and the even sadder and now suicidally terminal failure of these strategies. This is the oscillation or dualism of Cronenberg—especially in that crucial cluster of his best work between *Videodrome* and *Naked Lunch*. As a *cinéaste* and artist he has special attributes as well: a clean and focussed camera-eye, a superb sense for the subtle powers of décor and setting, and a genuine native surrealism that can achieve images of penetrating and unnerving suggestive power. Altogether, there is nobody quite like him.

32. If the old model of Canadian cinema—the realist and anti-genre cinema, serious and local, recognizably true and ours—has had difficulty absorbing Cronenberg, a more recent model struggling to be born in the past twenty (and especially the past ten) years may not just have assimilated him but actually imitated him. In *Mondo Canuck*, Geoff Pevere and Greig Dymond point insightfully to a whole cluster of films and filmmakers that seem to constitute a "school of Cronenberg"—a list that includes Egoyan, Mike Hoolboom, Bruce McDonald, Guy Maddin, and Patricia Rozema.[24] You might want to dispute this or that specific inclusion, but now that another half decade has passed you'd also want to add a few names, for example Don McKellar and Lynn Stopkewich. How did this happen? Generally speaking, Canada has been moving in this period towards multiculturalism, and its old crisis-of-no-essential-identity has been to a degree subsumed into postmodernism's jamboree-of-no-essential-identity and had some of its ache soothed in the process. The old "deference to authority" model has been crumbling,[25] and now to be Canadian is, as a Molson's commercial a couple of years ago had it, *both* to disapprove of an American corporate boss on our old staunchly traditionalist lines for wanting to use a Fox-type "zoom-trail" puck in hockey telecasts *and* to heave him physically out the door with our new-found liberating "I'm not putting up with this shit" arrogance (this latter in effect saying, "I'm more American than you are!").[26] In the midst of this transformation, the sickness and perversity of Cronenberg films can be seen as positive values, objects for emulation, and even emblems of identity. It's a kind of cinema that still makes a lot of people in this country unhappy. But the kicker is that Cronenberg's essential bleakness and defeatedness—and also that of Egoyan, McKellar, and others—are more traditionally Canadian than anything else in the brave new world of multiformity, re-conceptualization, and celebration of difference.

Notes

1 Robert Fulford [as Marshall Delaney], "You Should Know How Bad This Movie Is—You Paid For It," *Saturday Night*, September 1975.

2 Actually, Wheeler's résumé is now pretty impressive in this respect, and perhaps it is unjust to exclude her from this tiny group. But a good deal of her work has been for television, and this part of her output is, I would say, as important as her theatrical films. Only Cronenberg and Egoyan have succeeded so consistently in the brutally difficult world of making theatrical projects—very personal ones at that—in a Canadian context. The picture would also look very different if we were taking francophone Québec film into account.

3 There are, of course, exceptions to this pattern (Chris Rodley is one Brit who has stuck with Cronenberg throughout this phase), just as there are those who from the beginning accepted Cronenberg as a properly and admirably Canadian filmmaker, insisted upon his importance and centrality, and have not wavered in this view. Prominent in this group are Piers Handling, Peter Morris, Geoff Pevere, and Maurice Yacowar.

4 Iain Sinclair, *Crash* (London: British Film Institute, 1999). As well as conducting his own critique along these lines, visible in several places, Sinclair quotes the similar opinion of independent filmmaker and critic Chris Petit, who describes Cronenberg as starting "with lowbrow pretensions" but becoming "this vaguely middle-

brow to highbrow director" (36). Sinclair also characterizes Cronenberg as now being "the asset-stripper of the modernist cult canon" (12).

5 Mike Gasher, "Decolonizing the Imagination: Cultural Expression as a Vehicle of Self-Discovery," *Canadian Journal of Film Studies* 2, no. 2–3 (1993): 98. A footnote to this passage goes on to quote Atom Egoyan to the effect that glossiness is a quality Americans, but not Canadians, can believe in: "'We're certainly able to create the glossiness, the slickness; unable to make it believable unless you really believe it'" (Gasher, 104 n.9).

6 See my "The Canadianness of David Cronenberg," *Mosaic* 27, no. 2 (June 1994): 113-33. See also Piers Handling, "A Canadian Cronenberg" in *The Shape of Rage: The Films of David Cronenberg* (Toronto: General Publishing, 1984); and Gaile McGregor, "David Cronenberg and the Ethnospecificity of Horror," *Canadian Journal of Film Studies* 2, no. 1 (1993): 43–62.

7 Jim Leach, "North of Pittsburgh: Genre and National Cinema from a Canadian Perspective," in *Film Genre Reader II,* Barry K. Grant, ed. (Austin: University of Texas Press, 1995), 474–93.

8 Leach, "North of Pittsburgh," 482.

9 In his original conception of the phrase ("The Cinema We Need," *Canadian Forum*, February 1985), Bruce Elder thought of this cinema not only as non-generic, but as non-narrative, in fact avant-garde. But the essay gave rise to a long debate (reprinted in Douglas Fetherling, ed., *Documents in Canadian Film* [Peterborough: Broadview Press, 1986]) in which different models of "the cinema we need" were presented and discussed.

10 Leach also recognizes this, but it doesn't seem to interfere with his primary argument.

11 "Cronenberg: A Dissenting View," in *The Shape of Rage,* 115-35. Wood's argument here was a further articulation of points he had made more briefly in his seminal essays on the recent horror film in *Film Comment* and with collaborators in *The American Nightmare* in the late 1970s. Some of this material is reprinted in Wood's *Hollywood from Vietnam to Reagan* (New York: Columbia University Press, 1986).

12 See especially Florence Jacobowitz and Richard Lippe, "*Dead Ringers*: The Joke's on Us," *CineAction!,* Spring 1989: 64–68; and the many references in Barbara Creed's book *The Monstrous Feminine: Film, Feminism, Psychoanalysis* (London: Routledge, 1993). In her most recent article on Cronenberg ("The naked crunch: Cronenberg's homoerotic bodies," in *The Modern Fantastic: The Films of David Cronenberg,* Michael Grant, ed. [Westport CT: Greenwood, 2000]), Creed describes herself as a "Cronenberg fan" (85); but it would be impossible, I think, to guess this from reading the remainder of her critical work.

13 Isabel Cristina Pinedo, *Recreational Terror: Women and the Pleasure of Horror Viewing* (Albany: SUNY Press, 1997), 5.

14 See Wood, "An Introduction to the American Horror Film," in *The American Nightmare: Essays on the Horror Film,* Andrew Britton et al. (Toronto: Festival of Festivals, 1979), 7–11.

15 *Scanners* is an exception, and the early art films *Stereo* and *Crimes of the Future*, while not exactly deviating from the basic mindset, are so different in narrative form that it doesn't make much sense to talk about them in this way.

16 Caution and conservativeness are among the qualities Wood attributes to Cronenberg. I can agree with Wood about this up to a point, but to suggest as he does that this means the politics of Cronenberg's work are regressive and repressive is going too far. Cronenberg does not believe in the perfectibility of man (maybe woman, but not man), but this doesn't *ipso facto* render him regressive.

17 This list comprises much of the canon of Britton et al.'s beautiful little book *The American Nightmare*. Other enthusiasms of that volume include Romero's *The Crazies* and *Martin*, De Palma's *Carrie*, and the collected works of Larry Cohen, especially *It's Alive!, God Told Me To*, and *It Lives Again*. Cronenberg fits in pretty effortlessly here, except that his films are excluded from the pageant of resistive/progressive allegory most of the others are constituted as, and are condemned as politically regressive by Wood, as mentioned above. During the 1980s, the horror genre moved upmarket following the commercial success of some of these films (notably *Halloween* and *Carrie*), and we came into the era of the multiple *Halloween* and *Nightmare on Elm*

Street movies from which we have yet to emerge. But the cheap horror movie continued to exist in the 1980s and after, and generated its own "classics" in this period, including the canonical rape-revenge duo of *Ms. 45* and *I Spit on Your Grave*. Carol Clover's splendid *Men, Women, and Chainsaws* (Princeton: Princeton University Press, 1993) covers much of this material. One might also note that "Hollywood North" was a contributor to this process (via films like *Death Weekend* and *Black Christmas* in the 1970s and *Prom Night* and *Terror Train* in the 1980s), and that it was Cronenberg's resemblance to *this* group that nationalists especially didn't like about him. Doubtless they were confirmed in their views when he made what looked something like his own 1980s upmarket horror movie, *The Fly*.

18 Interview in the London Weekend Television *South Bank Show*, "The Making of *Naked Lunch*," 1992.

19 This was *The Shape of Rage*, to which I contributed a lengthy survey of Cronenberg's films to that date. This study had received initial backing from the Canada Council and was eventually expanded into a more ambitious project with the addition of several other essays under the editorship of Piers Handling and published by the Academy in association with General Publishing.

20 The Best Picture award went to *The Terry Fox Story*, a fact that speaks volumes. Cronenberg subsequently won Best Direction Genies for *Dead Ringers*, *Naked Lunch*, and *Crash*, but *Dead Ringers* is the only film to have won Best Picture.

21 *Canada's Best Features*, Gordon Collier and Gene Walz, eds. (Amsterdam and Atlanta: Rodopi Press, forthcoming), contains a chapter on *Videodrome* by Suzie Sau-Fong Young.

22 Jeremy Irons' performance as both the twins was highly esteemed as well, and it was generally felt that his Best Actor Oscar two years later for *Reversal of Fortune* was in compensation for his not getting it, as he should have done, for *Dead Ringers*.

23 See, for example, Sinclair's *Crash*, 75–76, 87–88, 90–94.

24 Geoff Pevere and Greig Dymond, *Mondo Canuck: A Canadian Pop Culture Odyssey* (Scarborough: Prentice Hall Canada, 1996), 40–41.

25 Cf. Edgar Friedenberg's book on Canadian culture, *Deference to Authority: The Case of Canada* (White Plains, NY: M.E. Sharpe, 1980); and Peter C. Newman's updated model as described in *The Canadian Revolution, 1985–1995: From Deference to Defiance* (Toronto: Viking, 1995).

26 The ironies of this advertisement are endless. Among them is the fact that the actor playing the American boss is a Canadian (Dan Lett), putting on a none-too-convincing Yankee drawl for all the world like another Toronto with fake licence plates dressed up as New York.

The Cronenberg Effect
Wayne Rothschild

THE CRONENBERG EFFECT IS ONE OF THE GREAT PLEASURES left to us in cinema: Cronenberg is our Kafka. His cinema is also a crucial site for thinking the body in relation to politics—or if one prefers, the body in relation to itself (there is no difference). By situating itself where the body cannot adhere to itself, Cronenberg's work reopens the disfigurative aesthetic of the surrealist and modernist traditions against the pastel (read pallid) background of contemporary ("modern") culture. Politics transforms the power of bodies into the field of social relations. Political power is body power; it must move and transform our physical reality into the field of social relations.

The Cronenbergian intersection of the body with the external other (representation and technology) articulates the difficult cross-wired connection between society and sexuality. We are all wired into the body through the social field; this is not an accidental process. Society incorporates us through our sexuality. This process is necessarily uncomfortable and unsatisfactory; the body does not hold.

The ties that bind the body to society: that is what I am trying to get at through the work of Cronenberg. Cronenberg gives aesthetic form to the ties that bind us to society. The other is always already inside the subject. This inside other represents the trans-individual character of subjectivity;[1] Cronenberg literalizes always-dysfunctional subjectivity as the screwed-up tie between mind and body. It typically takes the form of technology and media. This is the Cronenberg effect: that unhappy union of the body and technology. In that sense, all Cronenberg's work is an aesthetic/political commentary on the destructive fusion of body and machine. *Shivers, Rabid, The Fly,* and *Videodrome* all are about technology gone sour and fusing with the body. The "instruments for operating on mutant women" in *Dead Ringers* powerfully figure the violent fusion of technology, the body, and desire. The twins' world is a microcosm of a dysfunctional society. Tied to the other in their identity and their sexuality, they are alienated in an absolute sense. The twins' world goes from the cold of Italian (Antonioni) modernism to the chaos of "action" (Pollock or Albert Ayler) abstract expressionism. It is a social world that is locked in a binary field of arid rationality or total decay.

The space between subjects and between the subject and itself is where the trans-individual character of subjectivity is carried out. Individualist theories of the subject (as self-enclosed individual and consciousness) rely on the invention of a transcendental subject or ego to make the arrangement work. The world of Cronenberg is a world without transcendence, where structure and subject collide in an immanent field. Immanence in Cronenberg occurs in a fractured/fracturing field. In *Shivers, Rabid,* and *Videodrome,* the immanent field of trans-individual subjectivity is one of technological or scientific mutation; in *The Dead Zone,* it is the empathetic ability for time travel. The identical character of *Dead Ringers'* twins gives the problem of the trans-individual character of subjectivity a peculiar poignancy.

The individual in Cronenberg is an illusion and an impossibility. In his films, consciousness is never the cause of itself. And indeed consciousness may itself be the problem, a dis-ease of the body. The narrative arc of Cronenberg's film is that white, male, individual consciousness is a dead end with suicide as the only solution. In *Dead Ringers,* for example, the twins are already both a split and doubled subject, just as we are each the double of the other: no one exists without the other inside of them. The twins are society, triangulating their (male) desire through women; heterosexual desire fails because their only real relation is with each other. The homosocial thematic runs through to its dead-end conclusion.

The radical character of the political/aesthetic operation in Cronenberg's films is that it is always carried out in a violently doubled dialectic. Cronenberg, in his cinema, presents a rationalism against reason, a masculinism against itself, and a body that cannot hold in a society that does not work. His male subjects are dominating obsessives gone hysteric, gone schizophrenic. His characters cannot deal with either difference or sameness. The split and doubled Cronenberg subject is better with his brains blown out than on the street or a couch. This is not escapist cinema, because there is no escape.

I am trying to capture the dynamic ambiguity of Cronenberg's work by posing the divisive questions that constitute its problematic. Arguably, the best way to distinguish art from ideology (and I still think it is essential to distinguish art and knowledge from ideology) is to see the way in which a work opens and develops its own contradictions. Cronenberg's work is about making us uncomfortable in our day-to-day dysfunctionality. He takes up some bad positions in his films, but he mobilizes them against themselves and typically against himself. If Cronenberg is about the individual, then it is the individual against "himself": divided, at a dead end and with the other always-already inside. If Cronenberg is interested, as I am arguing, in the problem of collectivity, then it is a collectivity that is divided, uncomfortable yet unavoidable. If Cronenberg's films focus on the masculine—if they are guy films—then, like Hitchcock's, they are guy films from hell: part of their aesthetic power is to issue a withering critique of themselves.

The problem of the body in Cronenberg must be handled in dual and opposing directions. On the one hand, the social is not a body, but the body is social: in this body critique of the social, we have the now-traditional critique of the negative effect of society on the body. Cronenberg's work is pervaded by a critique of the invasive character of power and technology. On the other hand, the body is the metonymy of society: in this social critique of the body, the body may stand for society itself. In that case, the disfigured body, so familiar in Cronenberg, stands in for disfigured society. Society is not whole and neither is the body. The divisions of society and split subject may not be identical, but they are interlocked. The anti-ontology of

Cronenberg's world undoes any sense that we are at one with ourselves. Cronenberg's world gives aesthetic life to a kind of negative pantheism, to mis-paraphrase Spinoza: neither god nor nature. Mind and body are intimate but neither in synch nor separable.

The disfigured body in Cronenberg should be subject to a dual reading. More obviously, the films are about the resistance of the body to the social; disfiguration is Cronenberg's body-critique of society. In this reading, although the social is not a body, the body is itself social. The divisions of society are played out in the violation of the body. But also: the mind–body split is a figure for class division, the division between mental and manual labour (and the mind is on the side of the boss). When subjectivity is working, the subject is the state writ small. Cronenberg's body-critique confronts the way in which technology and media deform the body. If the mind in Cronenberg takes the position of the controllers, then the body typically figures the working classes. At times, this figure is inert or commanded by the mind, at least when it does what it is told. At other times, the body is figured as the site of irrational desire that has lost its mind. Like all modernism, the Cronenberg effect works through the stylization of alienation because there is no other choice. A more pleasant art would only efface reality. But Cronenberg's work also contains a social critique of the body. In this reading, the body is the metonymy of society. Cronenberg's deformed bodies stand for a society that is sick in itself, a society that is not whole because it is so deeply divided and yet can imagine itself as whole and functional, democratic and collective. When body and mind come together, then, it is the possibility of a different kind of political power: socialism.

This socialism may be feared or rejected, or even completely unrecognized, in Cronenberg's cinema, but it is possible and necessary: consider the alternatives. Cronenberg's individual is disfigured in advance, always part of a collective field of power that has mutated out of control. There is always the possibility of repressive right-wing control—as seen, for example, in the state's actions in *Rabid* or the predatory corporations in *Scanners* or *Videodrome*—but that is even worse. Does it matter whether *Videodrome* or the disfigured body causes the right-wing/corporate conspiracy or the conspiracy generated the disfigured body? In either case, it is sick.

This methodological communism treats liberty and equality as questions immanent to any social field; in other words, any form of collective life must account for any inequality in that field. It is inevitable that someone, sometimes almost everyone, will question any form of power: without justice, there will be no peace. Communism reconfigured as absolute democracy can then be used as a way of posing questions to culture and society. This unconscious communism is exactly what Cronenberg, in film after film, is after; whether or not he likes it is another question (I doubt that he does). The choice in Cronenberg is stark: socialism or suicide.

This unconscious communism is also a communism of the unconscious. The unconscious in Cronenberg is a powerful trans-individual force, directly in *Shivers*, *Rabid*, and *Videodrome*; desire and collectivity are interchangeable in a kind Freudo–Marxist sexual communism. In *Shivers*, a "mad scientist" creates a formula that unleashes a sexual revolution that violently overthrows the subject, consciousness, and individuality. It is clear in the film that, however liberating, this is not a desirable conclusion; but it is also clear that this subject is itself the result of a bland, repressive conformism. The sterile society is in many ways the cause of this unclean and workable response. The "revolution" of the 1960s may not be endorsed but, in the vision of this film, the 1960s' critique of contemporary society as alienating and unlivable is palpable and compelling.

Rabid, I believe, must be re-read in the light of Québec nationalism as "rabid nationalism." Set in the Montréal of the 1970s, this film is again about a mutation: of science, as usual, out of control. Sex and violence fuse in a terrifying de-subjectifying process. In the end, the only control is violent, military suppression of the disease and its human carriers. This cold, calculated cure is worse than the disease. Although the disease is not coded as Francophone, I think nationalist radicalization, especially the October Crisis, is the object of the film. The portrayal of the military response would then present the film's critique and rejection of the War Measures Act.

The infamous "new flesh" of *Videodrome* is exactly the kind of post-individual sexual communism that Cronenberg figures in his early films. The ambiguity, and therefore the power of the film's ending, lies in the viewer's not knowing whether this is a suicide or a future. The film may not be a poem to the positive form of collective power, but it does not ignore it either. In typical fashion, the film's ending is both ambiguous and ambivalent; it is unclear what happens or even what it wants.

In *Dead Ringers,* society seems to have disappeared completely into the double problem of the identical twin brothers—a literalization of the split subject. But this is in many ways the most acutely political of Cronenberg's films. The subject doubled and split carries forward the problem of the society-other inside of us: the twins are (male) society. The Mantle twins provide an almost mechanical mapping of the failure of the "regime of the brother." As figure for the split subject, they are split by the stereotypical "difficulty of difference," but it is the difficulty of sameness that drives the narrative. The twins are the dysfunction of the homophobic character of the normative narrative. They sleep with women to sleep with each other—without, of course, sleeping with each other. Elliot is insensitive to women because he is actually only ever sleeping with Beverly and therefore himself. Beverly may be "the sensitive one," but it is his homophobia mixed by his fear of the violation of the incest taboo that leads to the tragedy of the film's end.

In the normative narrative, men exchange women among themselves to bind themselves to each other through a field that is simultaneously both desire and aggression. For example, in *Casablanca*, Rick binds himself to the society of men and collective action by giving up Ilsa and going off to kill other men (Germans) with Renault, who has, not coincidentally, been flirting with Rick throughout the film. In Bergman's *Persona*, the field is reversed, as women exchange men in an inversion of the typical (sexist) pattern. *Persona*, the cinematic double of *Dead Ringers*, completely inverts the pattern in working through the relations of power and desire between women exchanging men. White racism in America is typically organized around sexual exclusion and miscegenation (*Birth of a Nation* is the obvious example). Social position and sexuality are intimately intertwined in all narrative.

The tragedy of *Dead Ringers* lies in the homophobic character of the socialization process, because Bev cannot sleep with Elliot, and Elliot is only ever sleeping with Bev (however indirectly). The crisis may begin with Bev's heterosexual attachment to Claire, but the plot thickens. Elliot seems to be "the shit" because he only sleeps with women to sleep with Bev. Interestingly, Bev thinks Claire is cheating on him because he misinterprets the fact that Claire's gay assistant answers his telephone call. In the end, this is a love story in which Elliot sacrifices himself for Bev. To put it another way, Elliot accedes to his disembowelment and death because that is the only way he can be penetrated by Bev. This is the typical homophobic solution: violence substitutes for sex. It is an unsatisfactory solution—a kind of suicide and a prelude to suicide. In effect, the brothers die together.

Bev uses the "instruments for operating on mutant women" in order to find the absolute in-side the woman, but it is of course not to be found in the body. This absolute voyeurism simply carries to its conclusion the logic of the twins' sexual obsession with knowledge. The general im-plication is that knowledge is about an intellectual mis-recognition of sex and sexual difference. Consider the girl who tells the young twins that she knows for a fact that they do not know what "fuck" is: again, presumably they never find out.

The narrative arc of *Dead Ringers*, and it is typical of Cronenberg, is individual and collective suicide. In *Shivers*, sexual desire runs towards complete dis-individualization, the death of the subject. In *Rabid*, *Videodrome*, and *The Fly*, the path is much the same. The mind undoes the body or the body undoes the mind; they are inseparable and at loggerheads. Both technology (as a certain kind of discipline of the mind on the body and nature) and the body or nature are ulti-mately destructive.

Mirror to mirror, the twins in *Dead Ringers* incarnate the powerful anti-ontology implied in the theoretical agenda of the great structuralist and post-structuralist thinkers. The film literal-izes both the problematic of the split subject and the subject as the double of society in the fic-tive field. Lacan's insight that the subject mis-recognizes itself in the other and the other in itself has no more poignant realization than this film. The divisive, dissonant, and uncomfortable power of this body without ontology is indigestible to contemporary theory; this modernism without "post" is a powerful antidote for much of what ails both contemporary theory and con-temporary culture. Specifically, just as any politics without the body is a dead end, any politics of the body which is not also a politics of society (collective action) is on an intellectual and politi-cal road to nowhere. The Cronenberg body—doubled, split, and disfigured—is social all the way through.

This is what I call the Cronenberg effect: the uncanny feeling of the power of the outside that is already inside. Located where the body does not adhere to itself, this discomforting aesthetic thinks beneath the skin. The Cronenberg effect is a way of giving form to the immanent relation of the body to politics. It is possible to read in this disfigured body a powerful trope for the total dis-function of contemporary societies. The mind–body split, so crucial in Cronenberg, is, in part, a function of the social division of labour. Cronenberg's work forces us to experience our society's dead end as our own: there is no way out. Bonded to our society through our sexuality, we should always be able to read about our socialization through our sexualization. Politics in the era of mass radicalization is a passionate politics, typically figured in terms of the excess of desire. Contemporary politics and culture are framed by the disappearance of the politics of desire, or the disappearance of mass politics into desire. Cronenberg's work directly figures the disappearance of a mass political desire into a desire without politics. Further, our inability to deal with sexual sameness, or with sexual difference, marks the subjective impasse of contempo-rary societies. There is something in Cronenberg that points beyond that, to a positive theory of collective power (I am thinking especially of the conclusion of *Videodrome*, but it is furtive and problematic). In *Dead Ringers*, the social bond is intolerable and unavoidable, a dead end, unless ...

Notes

1   My methodological approach is shaped by the Althusserian project as it developed in relation to Spinoza. See particularly Etienne Balibar, *Masses, Classes, Ideas: Studies on Politics and Philosophy Before and After Marx*, James Swenson, trans. (New York: Routledge, 1994); Pierre Macherey, *The Object of Literature*, David Macey, trans. (Cambridge: Cambridge University Press, 1995); Warren Montag and Ted Stolze, eds., *The New Spinoza* (Minneapolis: University of Minnesota Press, 1997). From a Marxist, but not Althusserian, perspective see Antonio Negri, *The Savage Anomaly: The Power of Spinoza's Metaphysics and Politics*, Michael Hardt, trans. (Minneapolis: University of Minnesota Press, 1991).

Repetition, Compulsion, and Representation in Atom Egoyan's Films

Monique Tschofen

A recursive structure results when you perform the same operation over and over again, each time operating on the product of a previous operation.
—Brian McHale

Repetition changes nothing in the object repeated, but does change something in the mind which contemplates it.
—Gilles Deleuze

SCARCELY FORTY YEARS OLD, Toronto-based filmmaker Atom Egoyan has proven himself to be astonishingly prolific. He has managed to complete eight short films, three operas, several installations, extensive work for television (including episodes for *Alfred Hitchcock Presents*, *Friday the 13th*, and the made-for-TV movie *Gross Misconduct*), and eight feature-length films in which he has more often than not taken responsibility for the writing and producing as well as the directing. Since 1984, when *Next of Kin* was nominated for a Genie Award for Best Director, his features have earned him innumerable awards and accolades in Canada and abroad. Much of his early fame in the international scene came as a result of Wim Wenders' gesture at the 1987 Festival of New Cinema and Video in Montréal when Wenders offered the prize money for Best Film he had been awarded for *Wings of Desire* to Egoyan, the young director of *Family Viewing*. *The Adjuster*, from 1991, won Best Canadian Feature at the Toronto Festival of Festivals as well as the Special Jury Prize at the Moscow Film Festival. *Exotica* was the first Canadian film in more than a decade to be invited to compete at the 1994 Cannes Film Festival, where it won the International Critics Prize. *The Sweet Hereafter* also had its premiere at the 1997 Cannes Film Festival, where it won the Grand Jury, International Critics, and Ecumenical Jury prizes before going on to win eight Canadian Genie awards, including Best Picture and Best Direction. Egoyan also received Academy Award nominations for his direction and screenplay adaptation of this film, unprecedented recognition for a Canadian director of a Canadian movie. For his successes, he has been offered five honourary doctorates from Canadian universities, inducted into the Order of Canada, elected a member of the Royal Canadian Academy of the Arts, and even knighted with a Chevalier dans l'ordre des arts et des lettres by the French government in 1996.

As the filmmaker who, perhaps more than any other working today, has produced a corpus that systematically and coherently reveals the work of postmodern culture and attendant processes of globalization, Egoyan has made sure that his films are always unsettling and never easy. He reveals the pressures brought to bear on the conception, practice, and representation of communication in an age of spectacle and simulation by exploring past the point of obsession some of the principle (cinemato)graphomanias of our times—that is, our fetishistic relationship with recording technologies which include audiotape players, answering machines, photo booths, home video, surveillance video, television sitcoms, family photographs, and film. From his earliest shorts to his features, Egoyan reveals the way ever-proliferating technologies of reproduction mediate and ultimately transform our sexual, familial, professional, social, and economic lives. His is an aesthetic of distancing and displacement in the Freudian and the geographic senses of both words. Against the instabilities brought about by the mobility of persons, culture, and commodities, Egoyan fixates on haunting conceptual slippages that disrupt some of the few remaining touchstones: home, place, self, family, sex, and money. Still, under their cool surfaces and conflicted textures, Egoyan's films all argue for a kind of existential accountability in the way we live and represent our own narratives. *Egoyan tends to the unbordered.*

Full Circle

It is perhaps inevitable that Egoyan would be hailed as one of Canada's great auteurs because his work is so internally consistent. With the release to the festival circuit of his most recent film, Samuel Beckett's *Krapp's Last Tape* for the Dublin-based Beckett Film Project, Egoyan's corpus has come full circle with a truly fearful symmetry, returning him directly to his roots in the theatre. When Egoyan was a student in international relations at the University of Toronto and later with Toronto's Tarragon theatre, he wrote a series of absurdist plays. By 1979, he had more or less abandoned the stage, turning instead to film as his chief medium of expression. He explains:

> I felt that in a lot of the drama I was writing I was just treading over material that other people had done. I was so influenced by Pinter or Beckett that I never really found my own voice in the drama I was doing. It was easier for me to feel confident about my direction and scripting when I was making films. I was able to absorb influences, let them pass through me and grow outside of them more easily than I could with theatre.[1]

His first short film, produced in 1979 with the financial assistance of the Hart House Film Board at the University of Toronto, offered an unabashed homage to Beckett. *Howard in Particular* deals with an old man's retirement from his assembly-line work at a company that makes fruit cocktail (a detail that allows Egoyan to slip in the requisite absurdist banana). At his "party," Howard finds he is the only attendee. Left entirely alone in a claustrophobic room, he sits mute while his boss, who claims to take a special interest in him as an individual—in "Howard, in particular"—addresses him demeaningly from an audio recording. The audiotape tells essentially the story of Howard's work for the company, but rather than praise him, the voice on the tape recalls every one of Howard's failings at the company and weaves these episodes in with gossipy testimony from colleagues. After making Howard pose for a photo for the company's records hopping like a "sad bunny," the voice on the recorder asks Howard to send the next retiree in. The taped process, now personalized to address "David, in particular," begins again, in assembly-line fashion. The slippage between Howard's celebration and humiliation is amplified by the particular absurdity of the juxtaposition of medium and message: a highly personalized rhetoric of abuse is conveyed through a highly depersonalized recording device.

An audio recorder also figures prominently in Beckett's play *Krapp's Last Tape*. Krapp celebrates his birthday by listening to diary-like audiotapes he made thirty years earlier and recording a new entry for the archive. For Beckett, the technique of juxtaposing two "versions" of one man's voice—one live, one recorded and replayed—sheds light on the workings of memory. The past bypasses the workings of memory to speak directly into the present (although to further confound the tense of representation, Beckett's stage directions specify "a late evening in the future"), but its voice is filtered, re-presented, and thus detached from the body and self that articulated it then as well as from the one that listens to it now. And yet, the play argues that even though detached, documented, and meticulously organized, the past can never be controlled; the repressed returns in unpredictable ways to disrupt and disturb. With his fingers at the controls of the tape player, Krapp rewinds and fast-forwards through the parts of his narrative that might offer personal catharsis and philosophical revelation, but in so doing, returns inadvertently to the narration of a failed intimate encounter which finally underlines the loneliness of his self-reflexive interactions with a machine.

Egoyan explains his long-standing interest in *Krapp's Last Tape*: "It seems to me to be the ultimate statement about how technology can both soothe and torment you at the same time and how memory is affected by these recordings that Krapp has made."[2] Beyond this shared interest in the double valence of technology as prosthesis and as irritant, Egoyan's driving obsessions with the impossibility of true dialogue, with missed and misread attempts at intimacy, with the way identity is refracted by ever-proliferating forms of mechanical reproduction, with the workings of memory against forgetting, and with structures built recursively around the fragment, all can be seen to replicate Beckett's. Here lies one of the keys to Egoyan's work: in order to come to terms with his oeuvre, one must embrace the aesthetics of the hybrid text wherein two or more media work against each other to carry the narrative. More importantly, one must also embrace the cultural logic of the fast-forward and the rewind, as well as its core symptom: repetition.[3] From his early work in short films like *Howard in Particular* and *Peep Show* (1981) through *Felicia's Journey* (1999) and *Krapp's Last Tape*, Egoyan paces over the same territory. On a structural level, his films build up fugal patterns to their inevitable crescendo while they parody and pastiche a range of genres, character types, and images. On a diegetic level, his characters suffer from reminiscences and forgetting, return compulsively to the primal scene, as they act out fundamentally narcissistic behaviours.

Baroque Structures
Repetition within the films

Structurally, Egoyan's films tend to be complex and convoluted. They typically work to establish layer upon layer of parallelism as they move between concurrent plots and subplots, and they demand that the viewer take an active role in piecing the fragments of narrative back together to reconstitute lost time. In his first feature, *Next of Kin* (1985), Egoyan works to correlate the theme of doubleness with a number of structural strategies of doubling. Peter, who is in family therapy because he spends "a lot of time pretending," discovers the satisfaction of giving "direction" to people's lives. After watching the videotaped therapy sessions of an Armenian family whose problems stem from giving up their infant boy to foster care, Peter decides to insert himself into their narrative. By playing the role of their missing son, he experiments with different modalities of artifice, control, and direction. The conceit of an audio-recorded diary (perhaps also in homage to Krapp's diary) allows Egoyan to repeat events. Peter acts out scenes and then reports on them in his audio-journal entries, which are offered to us in voice-over sometimes two or three times. These repetitions serve to underline Peter's particular psychopathology, the same psychopathology that guarantees the cinema's ability to carry our collective and personal narratives and deliver "happy endings": Peter is able to mediate just as he is able to re-present. In other words, his "successes" in bringing all the members of his new family together occur because he is able to set the stage by translating the raw, painful, and chaotic material of life into legible representation. Peter's Armenian father also demonstrates his mastery of this skill when he feigns a heart attack that prompts his wife and daughter to respond, predictably, with love and concern. As the film works self-consciously through the familiar clichés about family to produce a happily-ever-after ending, *Next of Kin* suggests that we respond more powerfully to repetition than to originality, to the familiar than to family, to acting than to being, and to narrative than to life.

While *Next of Kin* exploits the narrative possibilities of audio-recording, in subsequent, more formalist films, Egoyan often constructs plots that function as analogues to other mechanical devices treated in the plots themselves. *Family Viewing* (1989), for instance, offers a meditation on the idea of "remote control." Scenes shot with the competing textures of film, video, and television are deftly interwoven to invoke two related functions of the same technology: channel flipping and rewinding or fast-forwarding.[4] The story is of an Oedipal struggle as a son wrestles with his father for control of his family's past and future narratives. The father, Stan, who works for a company that distributes video recorders, has been erasing the home movies he had long ago made of his family—his mother, his wife, and their son—by recording over them with home pornography he makes of himself with his new lover. (These sex scenes are doubly mediated: for the video camera, Stan makes his partner Sandra act out a script narrated over the telephone by a sex worker.) His son, Van, is naturally anxious about this erasure of the images that concretize his own family history, give shape and presence to his memories of his missing mother, and grant meaning to his functionally absent, catatonic grandmother. Van struggles to restore the integrity of his family's story by rearranging things in the "real" world, clumsily and sometimes inadvertently working to bring all of the women in his father's life under his own influence.

At the turning point in the film is a charming *mise-en-abyme*: plot mimics structure which itself mimics the technology of representation perhaps most closely associated with postmodern culture.[5] Van is staring at a television screen over his grandmother's hospital bed as a show is ending, when he notices that the woman in the bed next to his grandmother's has just died. He turns his gaze to the room, and proceeds to switch the body of this dead woman with the body of his mute grandmother. In doing so, he effectively scripts a new ending to his own family's narrative as well as for that of the telephone sex worker. Believing that his own mother has died, Van's father is no longer able to control her future or erase her present. The sex worker, who in reality has lost her mother, is perversely entitled to prolong her relationship with a mother figure when she is enlisted to look after Van's grandmother. Egoyan explains that Van "doesn't really understand the full implications of what he is doing, that mentality of things just being switched and 'plot points' being added to one's life is something that is obviously derived from his television watching."[6] The paradox that Van never does come to realize is that, in his attempts to do things differently than his father, Van replicates his father's errors. Both men strive to direct the lives of those around them, and for both men, bodies are interchangeable insofar as they can be used to act out clichéd narratives scripted in advance. Building an increasingly frenetic pace as the film flips from texture to texture and subplot to subplot, *Family Viewing* explores the impossibility of feeling "connected" when one's history and memories are in large part determined by the artificially constructed imagery of unstable media, when one's relationships are forged out of linkages as casual and arbitrary as those between television channels, and when control is always mediated through grossly simplistic narrative archetypes.

Television remains the connecting link and controlling metaphor in *Speaking Parts* (1989), but here the director explores parallels between three additional professions involved in the "creation of illusions" through standardization and repetition: hotels, the cinema, and the sex industry. Nothing is as it appears in this film, and yet everything is monotonously the same. Stressing repetition over difference, Egoyan casts characters from the same mould and constructs them uniformly in two dimensions. They experience loss and desire, but their drives are refracted through an infinity of mutually reflective surfaces, and so can never assume any depth or substance.

Although the core narrative has to do with a series of triangular relationships, a more complex geometry of mirroring governs the way the four major characters are positioned in relation to one another. Lisa, a housekeeper in a hotel, is drawn to Lance, an awkward bit-part actor working in the housekeeping department with her. In her fanatic pursuit of his image, she forges a relationship with the video-store clerk who nightly rents her the handful of movies Lance has appeared in. The video clerk, like Lance, lives a double life: when not acting or doing laundry, Lance works part-time as a gigolo in the hotel, while the video clerk spends his evenings freelancing as a videographer of weddings and orgies. Lisa does not relate romantically to the video clerk, but she does use him as a substitute for Lance. He listens to the explicit and implicit questions about love, images, and story that she cannot address to Lance directly, and challenges some of her assumptions by showing her how the images she fetishizes are constructed and controlled. Meanwhile, another symmetrical subplot centres around Clara, a screenwriter staying in the hotel, who somewhat physically resembles Lisa. Like Lisa, Clara is fetishistically drawn to video images of an absent male—in this case, of her own dead brother. When she sees that Lance resembles her brother, Clara tries to enlist him to fill the role of the absent object of her desires by procuring his sexual services and trying to get him cast as the lead in the film that will be made of the script she has written. As the central focus of two women's iconophilia, Lance appears to be motivated only by the narcissistic desire to disseminate his image through whatever means necessary. (Egoyan surreptitiously literalizes a pun on dissemination and insemination here: the gigolo and the actor both are involved in a kind of sterile reproduction.)

Clara's brother is dead and Lance will not speak to Lisa. Each woman's complex game of substituting persons for one another functions to compensate for the fact that the object of her desire does not speak. The title of the film is thus highly paradoxical, because throughout *Speaking Parts*, speaking is the antidote for the fantasy world of surfaces and images; but at the same time, speaking is entirely subordinated to and informed by image making. Lisa quips that "there is nothing special about words." Clara does not choose silence, but her script remains confusedly mimetic because it is born out of a world of surfaces, screens, and mirrors. She is driven to ensure that her own life story be reproduced on screen as faithfully as possible to the original, but the producer sees clearly that her story is an unoriginal, rather smarmy tale of a brother's love and self-sacrifice. When the producer makes these parts speak on screen, in the context of a highly melodramatic talk show, he makes explicit all of the latent clichés and stereotypes that give structure and shape to desire in the age of mechanical reproduction: speaking is only a part of a larger economy of mediated communication, and there is no talk that is not scripted in advance.

Commenting on how so many of his films are structured around "channel-hopping," Egoyan also points out his indebtedness to an earlier artistic tradition built around repetition—the fugue.[7] Indeed, in his remarks on his film about Bach's Cello Suite #4, *Sarabande*, a film that connects several different storylines, Egoyan explains:

> As a filmmaker, I've been profoundly influenced by the Baroque technique of counterpoint. Bach makes extensive use in the Cello Suites of this idea of multiple musical lines stating, reinventing, and echoing melodies. I wanted to find a dramatic equivalent to counterpoint in the writing of the film. Thus, ideas and even snippets of dialogue are repeated or restated throughout the scenes. More obviously, I have made extensive use of dialogue and sound overlaps from one scene onto another.[8]

His comments about *Sarabande* apply equally to his structural strategies in all his other polyphonic films. From his very first short films through made-for-TV productions like *Gross Misconduct* to his latest features, Egoyan's narratives imitate the fugal structures of exposition and development through subjects, counter subjects, answers, and inversions.[9]

In *Exotica* (1994), as in *Speaking Parts*, three storylines are brought together. Here, however, Egoyan allows mechanical devices and specific technologies of representation to remain in the background while he foregrounds the things that happen to the bodies of the people who live among them. The structuring metaphor is again visual, but Egoyan refers us to practices with much longer histories than film or television when he builds the film around dance in the form of the low-cultural practice of striptease and its high-cultural counterpart, ballet. Both striptease and ballet are intimately related to music, both rely on costuming to conceal and reveal,[10] and both offer erotically and emotionally charged spectacles of "perfect" bodies moving rhythmically to produce palettes of colour and texture. *Exotica* explores the paradox at the heart of such activities: spectacular uncoverings and discoverings betray the ultimate disappearance of bodies— of the body—offering up images of presence to conceal the fact that something is lost.

The film's central themes of loss and longing are announced in a dream-like flashback sequence in which a young couple falls in love while they are searching for a corpse.[11] A younger Eric explains to Christina: "It seems to me that every time I am about to get a hold of something or someone, it's bound to slip away." She answers, "Maybe you want it to slip away, the thing you think you're about to have." The three interrelated storylines about desire, loss, and exchange develop around these statements, and even more than in *Speaking Parts* or *Family Viewing*, Egoyan allows the different strands to echo off each other. Francis, who works for Revenue

Canada, has lost his daughter and his wife. He works through his grief by hiring his niece to "babysit" his empty house while he goes to the strip club Exotica to watch Christina's school-girl strip act. (We discover in the film that this activity repeats an earlier pattern: when Christina really was a schoolgirl, she would come to his house to babysit his daughter.) Christina's act condenses and displaces a number of his anxieties. Dressed as a schoolgirl, brimming with "special innocence" in the same kind of uniform his daughter once wore, but also the very woman who once babysat his schoolgirl daughter, Christina evokes for him the times before his trauma and loss and allows him to forget his pain. However, as she lifts her skirt and opens her shirt, Christina dramatizes innocence lost—her own, because the film suggests that she might have suffered from incest as a child, but also Francis' murdered daughter's—and thus forces him to re-member and repeat his loss.

If Francis returns compulsively to a metaphorized and glamourized scene of the crime when he visits Exotica, Eric resembles a broken record. What is it about a schoolgirl? he asks the audience and Christina every time she walks on stage. He has lost Christina, the person who connects him most to his younger, more idealistic self; as with Francis, his loss is connected with a child and a betrayal. We discover that Eric had been contracted to impregnate Zoe, the night-club owner who employs him as a DJ and Christina as a stripper; upon learning of the transaction, Christina leaves him. In a third storyline, Thomas, who runs an exotic pet store that Francis is auditing, negotiates still another kind of loss. After lovingly smuggling birds' eggs into the country, taped to his stomach, he takes himself repeatedly to the ballet to act on his desires for intimacy. One of the male lovers he picks up at the ballet (who happens to be the customs agent who watched him enter the country) robs him of the eggs and betrays their intimacy. Dance, be it striptease or ballet, thus evokes the way characters relate to each other, striving for closeness through performance rather than touching, at the same time as it evokes the way the storylines echo and answer each other and are rhythmically punctuated.

By identifying and exploiting the similarities between strategies of fragmentation and repetition in forms such as the fugue and dance, as well as in forms such as the TV talk show and home porn, Egoyan is able to draw out important nuances in the way we make and use culture. His is never the unethical or affectless postmodernism many accuse him of reproducing. In *Sarabande*, for instance, the differences between performance as artifice and performance as truth are shown to be as blatant as the differences between disease and healing. Egoyan's work clearly calls for healing and truth over symptom and artifice.

Compulsion and Control
Repetition between the films

If Egoyan's plots weave convoluted structures according to a logic of echo and reply, fast-forward and rewind, or channel-flipping, he seems to build these plots out of similar elements. Most obvious is his deliberate attempt to cast actors who look alike. The presence of his wife, actor Arsinée Khanjian, in all of his feature films ensures a stunning continuity throughout his work. (One French book on Egoyan's work puns on her name, suggesting that Arsinée is really "l'art-ciné."[12]) But Egoyan also tends to hire actors who look like her. In *Speaking Parts*, Lisa, Lance, Clara, and her dead brother all resemble each other to the point of absurdity—it is often difficult to tell exactly who is speaking. Egoyan exploits their resemblance to one another to dramatize the way in which specular technologies cause identity to become unstable and relationships to become hauntingly narcissistic/incestuous. Says the director,

> what the film is about, ultimately, [is] the fact that people resemble each other and have the ability to play certain roles based on their ability to remind someone of someone else. It's always a matter of finding a form or texture which reflects the underlying psychology of what the film is about. In *Speaking Parts*, it was about substitution, projection, and people living with other people as images and being able to trade and barter those images.[13]

Egoyan's comments about "substitution, projection, and people living with other people as images" also apply to *Exotica*. Christine and Zoe are doubles; they have the same long, curly hair and appear to have been lovers. His comments could apply equally well to *Calendar* (1993), a film premised on a man's attempt over the course of a year to come to terms with the loss of his wife. The protagonist—a photographer, whose job is to deal with images of things rather than the things themselves—hires a dozen escorts, who more or less resemble Arsinée in their dark hair and accents, to come for dinner at his house and, following his cue, perform the same scene, turning their backs to him and speaking lovingly in another tongue to someone else.

Just as bodies repeat throughout Egoyan's films, so do character types. In *Howard in Particular*, Egoyan introduces an ambiguous figure who remains a constant in his oeuvre. The boss, voiced by Egoyan himself, is an authority figure whose powers mime those of the director as he barks out whimsical orders designed to make others act in unnatural ways. Characters in subsequent films reveal similar compulsions for constructing scenes, directing parts, playing roles, and otherwise re-presenting: Peter (Patrick Tierney) in *Next of Kin*; the Producer in *Speaking Parts* and Stan in *Family Viewing* (both played with an icy monomania by David Hemblem); Noah Render in *The Adjuster* and Eric in *Exotica* (both played by Elias Koteas); Egoyan himself as the photographer in *Calendar*; the lawyer Mitchell Stephens (Ian Holm) in *The Sweet Hereafter* (1997); and the caterer/serial killer Hilditch (Bob Hoskins) in *Felicia's Journey*.[14] Their authority is grounded in their access to technologies of reproduction—they are associated with audio and video recording devices as well as pens and ledgers—and is wielded indiscriminately in relation to other characters' life stories.

Indeed, the consistency with which Egoyan's films return to a figure obsessed with narrative control and mastery permits a reading of his more recent films—specifically *The Adjuster*, *Exotica*, *The Sweet Hereafter*, and *Felicia's Journey*, which otherwise seem to be moving away from Egoyan's signature cinematographomanias in their increasing devotion to constructing well-rounded characters—as logical and necessary continuations of his earlier work. Peter in *Next of Kin*, Stan in *Family Viewing*, the Producer in *Speaking Parts*, and the photographer in *Calendar* are all obviously involved in cinematic activities: attached to recording devices, they offer clear and self-reflexive analogues to the role of the director. But in his later films, Egoyan extends the metaphor into other realms to offer a tension between the figures involved in re-presentation and those they would seek to control. The insurance adjuster Noah Render in *The Adjuster* documents everything about his customers' lives before their tragedy so that he can replicate it, but he does not restrict himself to such essentially passive mirroring. Rather, Noah repeatedly issues blatant imperatives, telling his customers what they should be feeling even if they have no feelings. Eric in *Exotica* narrates and ultimately dictates men's experiences in the nightclub as he frames and interprets the scenes the strippers choreograph. In *The Sweet Hereafter*, Egoyan relies on a clever pun that connects the practice of law to the practice of authoring, producing, or directing, when he has the lawyer Mitchell Stephens urge his clients repeatedly to let him "represent their anger." Stephens must document the crash and wanders through the town site with video recorder or notebook in hand. He elicits and then sorts out the competing versions of stories from the townsfolk; but of course, like Eric in *Exotica*, Stephens subtly attempts to force the narrative away from some directions and towards others. Finally, Hilditch in *Felicia's Journey* picks up lost young women, gains their trust, videotapes their confessional conversations, and stores them in an archive alongside videos of his mother's 1950s television shows; but his authorial functions do not stop there. Initially offering to help his latest victim find the happy ending to her love story, Hilditch acts concerned, makes up stories, invents characters, orders costumes and props, and manages in part to impose a darker ending when he convinces Felicia to abort her child and attempts to murder her as he has the other women.[15]

Egoyan has remarked on the cultural and social powers granted to those who have the means to produce images and stories: "our society is divided into people who make images and people who watch images. Authority is granted to people when they have the ability to turn themselves into producers."[16] But Egoyan's films insist on what is at stake when such authority is applied without responsibility; artist/author/director figures in Egoyan's oeuvre are always radically separated from themselves, and to varying degrees, like Howard's boss, disembodied and untouchable. Moreover, like the "very near-sighted (but despectacled)" Krapp in Beckett's play, they cannot see.[17] In *Calendar*, for instance, the narrative is predominantly conveyed in the first person: what we see is either explicitly filtered through the perspective of the photographer who speaks from behind the camera in the sequences shot in video, or is implicitly slanted to represent his perspective in the sequences shot in film. As critic François Jost confirms, the photographer is in all respects a "narrator": his gaze is central and controlling.[18] Nevertheless, the narrative clearly conveys that the photographer/narrator does not see what is going on. Although his gaze determines the composition and framing of the camera image, he cannot see beyond the frame. He records the growing chasm between himself and his wife, and the growing intimacy between his wife and their driver; but even when he replays these images after the fact, he cannot make sense of his own document. Authorial and directorial control, Egoyan seems to argue, comes at the price of other kinds of vision and insight.

All of his controlling characters, for instance, exhibit compulsive behaviours very much in keeping with Freud's return of the repressed. After suffering a trauma, his characters seem "obliged to repeat the repressed material as a contemporary experience instead of ... remembering it as something belonging to the past."[19] In *Exotica*, Egoyan explains, "there's this man who goes to this sex club every night. There's something quite habitual about that and he doesn't quite understand the damaging effect of this type of behaviour merely because he's allowed himself unquestioned access to repetition."[20] Likewise, Christina's strip act allows her to re-enact more safely the trauma of possibly incestuous relations she had as a youth. In *The Adjuster*, Noah Render inserts himself into the intimate lives of the families whose lives have been devastated by fire with the same incantatory phrase: "you don't feel it now, but you're in a state of shock." He often choreographs his "adjusting" so as to repeat scenarios that were typical for the families before their trauma. For instance, after examining intimate photos of a gay couple, Noah is shown naked and in bed with one of the men, assuming intimate poses that mirror the photos he studied. Says Egoyan: "I think that *The Adjuster* went about as far as you could go in render-ing characters almost completely absurd because of their inability to define themselves. There was something quite humorous at some level about the repetitive patterns of behaviour that the people were forced to re-enact over and over again."[21]

Intriguingly, these characters' compulsion to return to and repeat scenes is shown to be the particular consequence of loving and losing in an age dominated by the image. In the age of mechanical reproduction, precisely because communication is always mediated, intimacy is difficult and relations tend towards narcissism. Egoyan asks,

> Can people live through imagistic representations of life? If they can, do they then need to gain control of how those representations are made? And if these questions can be answered 'yes' and 'yes,' at what point do people fall in love with the representation of the loved one? Maybe they are really falling in love with their own ability to conjure up that image. Does the love then become narcissistic?[22]

An early short film that announces the major themes of *Exotica*, *Peep Show* is set in a location devoted to the production of spectacles, something between a pornographic pleasure dome and a shopping mall. A voice intones "Welcome to Stardust, where under our magical dome the crude vulgarities of the outside world disappear as we add colour to your most subtle desires ..." but reminds customers of the one rule: "you are not to touch." A man enters a photo booth alone with the intention of responding to a personal ad that seeks "an ordinary man for mutually fulfill-ing relationship." The photos that come out reveal him in increasingly intimate poses with a na-ked woman. His frustrations are two-fold. On one hand, the photos will not provide the kind of image that would prove he is an "ordinary man" capable of a "fulfilling relationship." On the other hand, the salacious photos remind him of the lack in his life, of the emptiness he would fill. His frustrations increase until he kicks the photo booth and police officers escort him away. What is at stake in the film is the way representation both dictates and frustrates our most subtle desires, setting out, for example, narratives about the body and intimacy that work only to lead us away from the body and direct contact. Imagistic representations of life, the film argues, can lead to a double bind.

This particular double bind is beautifully dramatized in the opening sequence of *Exotica*. Thomas stands across from the customs officer who will later become his lover for a night, sepa-rated by a one-way mirror. Thomas does not see the future lover staring into his eyes. He simply examines his own reflection, without knowing that the technology of the mirror screens the fact that his gaze is intertwined with a much more complex series of gazes. On the other side, the officers look beyond faded reflections of their own faces, trying to "read" and analyze whatever is hidden, which they have to find. Voyeurism, narcissism, and suspicion are bound together in the way images reflect and deflect.

For Egoyan, narcissism does not just dictate relationships with others; the self is also problematized through its reliance on ephemera. In *Family Viewing*, Van feels horror as the recorded images of his childhood are erased. Hilditch in *Felicia's Journey* lovingly pockets a min-iature of himself as though to preserve a connection with a former, smaller self. Egoyan in fact sees these two characters as similar. Van, says Egoyan, was "of that first generation of kids who might have had their childhood videotaped. In this same sense, Hilditch is of that first generation of kids who had their childhood mediated, through this very bizarre participation on his mother's cooking show."[23] Neither character can adequately separate self from representation, and this explains their radical alienation.

If these characters suffer trauma because of an inability to define themselves, Egoyan offers a counterpoint. Against those who would control and direct narrative are those who would be responsible to it, who attempt to work against "cultural and personal erasure."[24] Their strategies are what Michel de Certeau calls "tactics,"[25] and they poach both techniques and meanings from those who would use the power of image-making technologies and the power of narrative to control. In *The Adjuster*, against Noah, whose language relies on the imperative, Hera uses an interrogative strategy. She asks him, "Do I make you feel stupid?" "What do you mean?" he responds. "When I say something which deserves consideration, and you respond without thinking, how do you feel?" she asks again. Although he answers "I feel fine," she get the last word with her retort: "I thought you might feel stupid." Against Mitchell Stephens' work, grounded in anger, of (legal) re-presentation, and against her father's betrayal of the "beautiful rock star" fantasy he constructed, Nicole in *The Sweet Hereafter* steals the tactic of lying. She deliberately misrepresents her recollection of the accident because she realizes that in so doing, she will put an end to the lies that led her astray. Through these and other similarly rebellious characters, Egoyan argues that control fails without responsibility.

As with Mediation, So with Migration

Responsibility—to people and to their stories—is essential in the Egoyan universe because his is at all times a geography "characterized by global networks and an international space of information flows; by an increasing crisis of the national sphere; and by new forms of regional and local activity."[26] One of the most important tensions that informs Egoyan's corpus, and the element that ultimately directs his work beyond the concerns announced by Samuel Beckett, is the result of migration. Atom was three years old when his parents, Armenian refugees living in Egypt, chose to move to Victoria, British Columbia. Egoyan often describes the peculiar trauma of having to learn a new language and forgetting the old one. Silence is thus not only a marker of the primacy of the visual in the society of the spectacle, but also of the absurdities that surround translation and consequently communication in the global village. When in *Speaking Parts*, Lisa mutters in her foreign accent to the man in the video shop that "there is nothing special about words," her comment resonates with an ironic ambiguity.

Arjun Appadurai confirms what Egoyan's films have long dramatized: that there is an intimate connection between the forces of globalization that prompt migrations and the practices of postmodernism through media that fragment and atomize. Appadurai explains: "The story of mass migrations (voluntary and forced) is hardly a new feature of human history. But when it is juxtaposed with the rapid flow of mass-mediated images, scripts, and sensations, we have a new order of instability in the production of modern subjectivities."[27] Both migration and mediation are strategies of distancing, and both are the consequences of the "restructuring of information and image spaces."[28] Moreover, migration has a destabilizing effect akin to that of the specular and image-making technologies Egoyan's films critique. Egoyan himself suggests that the experience of immigration forces you [to] realize that personality is something that you construct. The moment that you become self-conscious about that construct, that induces a sense of alienation and disenfranchisement. That's what I'm more interested in—that notion of what it is that people have to do in order to feel at place, and the degrees of self delusion that they suffer in order to convince themselves that they have found their place amidst the havoc.[29]

Whether explicitly or implicitly addressing immigration, Egoyan's films explore the fragility of both the family and the concept of home, while his characters seem to be startlingly placeless. In *Open House* (1982), one of his earliest films, Egoyan shows the intimate relationship between architecture, our memories, and future-oriented desires. A man posing as a real-estate agent brings a young couple into an old house emptied of nearly all its contents; it has just been painted a blank white. In the front rooms, the owner pitches the house to the prospective buyers as she tells stories about better times; in a darkened room in the back, a man projects slides onto drop cloths that resemble screens. The pretend real-estate agent's goal is to prompt the owners of the house, his own catatonic father and depressed mother, to remember the good parts of their past. The young couple tours the house in anticipation of their future; as they navigate the spaces of the older couple's memories, however, the young couple betray the fact that they are about to build their lives on a shaky foundation of posturing and lies. The encounter of these two families in the space of a house that has been stripped of all signs of its occupants' individuality offers an uncanny portrait of before and after: family and home both are problematic terms because they rely on manufactured selves. An order of instability is built into the family romance from the outset because in contemporary times, the space of memory is without ground, subject to erasure, while geographic space is placeless. As Gertrude Stein once said, "there is no there there."

In *The Adjuster*, Noah's is a mobile and consequently selfless/selfish body.[30] He perpetually floats through the virtual spaces left blank after the devastation of fire as well as the most placeless spaces of modern life—the motel and the suburb—landing only when he forces himself to replicate scenes of intimacy with other people's families. The final scene of *The Adjuster* shows that Noah is not even the patriarch of his own family, the one he lives with in the prop-filled, isolated showhome. His wife, child, and sister-in-law were also once his clients, a fragment of a family that offers merely another locus in which to perform his ritualized and ultimately empty caretaking. In *The Sweet Hereafter*, Mitchell Stephen's body, like his drug-addicted daughter's, is also highly mobile. Both move restlessly in cars through a foreign landscape, but as the opening scene in the car wash reveals, cars are not safe places. Both attempt to forge connections through the technology of the telephone, but the phone usually offers only bad connections. The lawyer's hotel room, like the hotel rooms in *Speaking Parts* and *Family Viewing*, offers only a simulacrum of a home. That connection and, more importantly, touching are impossible for him in this setting is hardly a surprise.

Calendar is Egoyan's most explicit film about journeying, exile, and home. The reason the protagonist has lost his wife has to do with a trip the couple took to their homeland in Armenia to photograph churches for a calendar. For the woman, the journey is a homecoming. She penetrates the history, the landscape, and the monuments, and allows herself to be carried away by the language and song. Meanwhile, the man maintains at all times an unbridgeable distance between himself and his homeland, refusing even at the prompting of his wife to engage, touch, or feel. His body parts seem to be melded to technologies of reproduction: camera, telephone, answering machine, television, video player, remote control, pen and paper. These props mediate all of his relationships, and disrupt the rhythms of conversation and the patterns of intimacy.

In a melancholic scene, the photographer refuses to step away from the camera he is setting up to go for a walk, despite his wife's coaxing. "It's not a question of wanting to go or not," he confesses. "It's much stranger than that. What I really feel like doing is standing here and watching. Watching while the two of you leave me and disappear into a landscape that I'm about to photograph." *Calendar* thus offers a clear formulation of two kinds of distancing, one the result of media and mediation, the other the result of motion. The spaces of the film, metropolitan Toronto and the countryside of Armenia, themselves stress both distance and distancing. North America's tight, geometric, claustrophobic interiors are contrasted with the fluid, organic lines of the Armenian landscape. The bland, repetitive conversations in the metropolitan environment contrast with the long-chronicled histories associated with the churches integrated into the Armenian hills. The dehumanization that results from the daily rhythms imposed by technologies of mechanical reproduction (such as answering machine and television) in placeless Toronto contrasts with the sensual richness of lives punctuated by vigorous and passionate performances of song and speech in Europe. The New World of the photographer himself is frenzied, panicked, and profane while the Old World, represented by the photographer's wife and their tour guide, seems pastoral, serene, and sacred. These oppositions establish an elegiac tone and provide the basis for Egoyan's critique of the forces of a globalizing postmodern culture.

At the end of *Calendar*, in a message left on his answering machine, Arsinée, the Echo to the photographer's Narcissus, speaks about his hands:

> It's strange, but the strongest memory I had is not of any of the churches, but of the time we drove into that huge flock of sheep. You took your camera out, and as you were taping, he placed his hand on mine. I remember as I gripped his hand, watching you grip your camera so tightly, like you knew what was happening behind you. Did you know? Were you there? Are you there?

Her verbal description of this scene is perfectly cinematic, although it is never filmed because it is never seen by the photographer's superficial gaze. Her recorded voice fading into a far-away echo, she describes a parallel montage of close-ups of hands gripping. His hands are attached to his camera; hers make contact with her lover's hands. A potent metaphor for the themes of touch that run through the film, the scene recapitulates the two kinds of coupling that run throughout Egoyan's work—body and machine versus body and body—and thus establishes mediation and intimacy as binary oppositions. Arsinée's questions, "Did you know? Were you there? Are you there?", which fade into a far-away echo, explicitly address the problem of his knowledge and his vision. His narcissistic gaze precludes knowing. Preoccupied with framing, lighting, and composition, he neglects gestures and meaning; involved with surfaces and appearances, he neglects depths. His practices of image-making detach him from the corporeal world and thrust him into a universe of machines, screens, reflections, and copies. But the solution to his quandary is shown to be remarkably simple. After twelve months in which he compulsively repeats a scene of betrayal and abandonment with women who resemble his wife, he is able to break the pattern when he abandons his script, puts away his recording technologies, and responds sincerely to the escort.

Egoyan's films are informed by the trauma of his own immigration and consequent forgetting of his homeland as much as by the traumas particular to life in the age of mechanical reproduction, but they are amplified by another order of historical forgetting: our collective amnesia about the Armenian genocide, which has been reproduced through silence and has erased many from home and homeland. Egoyan often talks about how the genocide can be read into all of his films that touch on Armenia, particularly *Next of Kin, Calendar,* and his for-TV film *Looking for Nothing.* He has also stressed that the genocide and its forgetting implicitly inform all of his other narratives:

> The Armenian genocide hasn't just been repressed. It's this very curious type of denial where, in the face of so much openness about the nature of holocaust, the Armenians are in a curious position where the perpetrators have never really admitted it. There's a vagueness about the whole event. And as it recedes more and more into our history, as the century has found other events to deal with, the necessity of finding out what happened in Armenia at the turn of the century seems to be diminished. Yet, as an Armenian, its emotional consequences are still overwhelming.[31]

The death and destruction that run through such films as *Exotica* and *The Sweet Hereafter* force the kinds of questions Egoyan believes must be posed of Armenian history. What happens to families and communities faced with such large-scale loss? How can the remembering of trauma not succumb to repetition, compulsion? What can bridge the distance between people enough to allow healing to take place? In *Felicia's Journey,* Egoyan explores the problem of mass killing but offers here a more explicit statement about the dialectic of remembering and forgetting. Egoyan says of Felicia,

> What I ultimately found so powerful about her passage is that she comes from a place where oral tradition is very important, where stories are told, where a great-grandmother speaks in an ancient tongue, letters are hand delivered and everything is done by direct contact and transmission. She then enters into this universe where she's lost, but through contact with evil and ultimately through the recitation that Hilditch gives of the names of the women that he's taken away, she uses this oral tradition to reconstruct her own dilemma. That history actually reflects her own experience and she almost has a sacred duty now to commemorate those names. That is very much based on her tradition. Irish culture is all about remembering the names, but the names that her father has given her don't have meaning for her anymore, whereas the names that she's just heard from the mouth of this killer do.[32]

Another "tactic" to be used against erasure and forgetting, commemoration does not involve the technology of rewind, fast-forward, or channel-flipping, as explored (à la Beckett) in *Next of Kin* and *Family Viewing,* nor does it involve the kinds of voyeuristic and fetishistic displacements of desire explored in *Speaking Parts* and *Exotica.* Rather than merely repeating, commemoration connects people to each other and to their past.[33]

ᕁ ᕁ ᕁ

Jean Baudrillard writes that "to exit from the crisis of representation, you have to lock the real up in pure repetition."[34] Indeed, this crisis of representation is precisely the crisis that Egoyan's films have negotiated and is also the strategy his films have adopted. Throughout his corpus, Egoyan has built his hybrid texts out of the conflicting and contrasting textures of media such as television, home video, and film. Consistent with his dedication to fugal patterns, his work has been built around point and counterpoint: moving or static image, high or low resolution, full-colour spectrum or subdued tones, play or replay, amnesia or remembering, voyeurism or seeing. Hamid Naficy has remarked that Egoyan reveals an "accented style" typical of exilic filmmakers, marked by

> paradoxical and contradictory themes and structures of absence and presence, loss and longing, abandonment and displacement, obsession and seduction, veiling and unveiling, voyeurism and control, surveillance and exhibitionism, descent relations and consent relations, identity and performance of identity, gender and genre, writing and erasure, the dense intertextuality of film and video, and the technological mediation of all reality.[35]

The logic of the paradox is everywhere in his work. Egoyan's feature films, shorts, and television shows begin with a fundamental irony that is as serious as it is playful: the director levels an incisive critique against the very media he employs to convey this critique, while taking to the point of absurdity the very compulsive behaviours that characterize his labours as a film director: voyeurism, control, and mediation. Against paralysis, fear, and silence, he produces his dizzyingly challenging films; against loss and trauma, he reproduces laughter.

His devotion to the logic of the paradox is best captured in the short film addressed to his son, *A Portrait of Arshile*. Structured as an epistolary film narrated and translated almost simultaneously by Egoyan in English and Arsinée Khanjian in Armenian, *Portrait* explains the origins of their son's name. "You are named after a man who painted a portrait of himself," they begin, but then offer a qualification. The portrait was based on a photograph taken in Armenia. "His mother," they explain, was "a devoutly religious woman ... named Shushanyk. Her son, the person you are named after, was called Bostanyk. Your name is Arshille." The reason this artist who painted portraits based on photographs changed his name has everything to do with Armenian history: the mother dies of starvation in the painter's arms. Later, looking at the portrait, the painter was afraid of disappointing her, of bringing shame to his name, so he changed his name to Arshille Gorky: "you are named after a man who changed his name because of what he felt of his mother's face. His mother's face, which now stares from the gallery wall into a land she never dreamed of." Contained in these dense four minutes of film based on a painting based on a photograph are countless contradictions: a "portrait" that depicts two people, and an act of naming that refers to an act of renaming. The telling is also intriguing. Narration and translation do not work against each other as they do in films such as *Calendar*; both blend with Arshille Gorky's work to remember and commemorate the traumas of genocide and exile. Against the void of a *mise-en-abyme* worthy of any great postmodernist and from the depths of a history wrought with sorrow emerge two interwoven tales of parental tenderness and filial love. The world may well be absurd, and the mobility of persons, culture, and commodities may well disrupt home, place, self, and family, but Atom Egoyan works through these dialectics with remarkable wisdom and grace.

Notes

1 Marc Glassman, "Emotional Logic," in *Speaking Parts,* Atom Egoyan (Toronto: Coach House Press, 1993), 51.

2 Bruce Kirkland, "Egoyan's 'dream project.' Director thrilled to make Beckett film with John Hurt." *Toronto Sun,* 24 August 2000.

3 Repetition may well be one of the touchstones of modernity; more recently Arjun Appadurai, Fredric Jameson, and Jean Baudrillard have linked their analyses of the commodity culture of consumer capitalism to the broader theories of repetition of Sigmund Freud, Søren Kierkegaard, Gilles Deleuze and Felix Guattari, and others.

4 Many of Egoyan's films develop this theme. For instance, in a highly voyeuristic scene in *Calendar,* shot so that a clear view of the action is obstructed, it is impossible to tell whether Egoyan plays with a remote control or himself while he sits watching tapes of his wife and foster child; the remote control is a phallic object, and its use is masturbatory.

5 Quoting Ulmer, Robert Ray quips in an encyclopedia entry on postmodernism that "[t]he best way to understand postmodernism is to think about a pun: in French, poste means 'television set' ... Postmodernism is really postemodernism, what happened when modernism met TV." See Robert Ray, "Postmodernism" in *Encyclopedia of Literature and Criticism,* Martin Coyle, Peter Garside, Malcolm Kelsall, and John Peck, eds. (London: Routledge, 1990), 137.

6 Ron Burnett, "Atom Egoyan: An Interview," *CineAction!* 16 (Spring 1989).

7 Glassman, "Emotional Logic," 48.

8 Egoyan, "Director's Statement," *Sarabande Suite #4: Yo-Yo Ma—The Films,* www.sonyclassical.com/releases/ 63203/films/direct_4.html; accessed 30 January 2002.

9 Peter Harcourt points out another way to think of "Egoyan's desire to achieve a contrapuntal structure for his films" that applies to *Exotica* as to *Felicia's Journey:* "Skilled in music and theatre, he thinks out his film's structures in deliberately musical ways, like three-part inventions as we know them from Bach. Furthermore, the absurdist repetition of situations and scraps of dialogue bestows upon his narrative a serial dimension" ("Imaginary Images: An Examination of Atom Egoyan's Films," *Film Quarterly* 48, no. 3 [Spring 1995]: 5). Serial killing and serial culture, Mark Seltzer argues ("Serial Killers," *Differences* 5, no. 1 [1993]) correlate, and Egoyan is certainly not unaware of this relationship.

10 This notion of costuming, disguising, and concealing, pandemic in the Egoyan corpus, finds an analogy in the *trompe l'oeil* of the house in *The Adjuster.* The library, for instance, contains only the shells of books.

11 Egoyan explains: "I find the cinema is a great medium to explore ideas of loss, because of the nature of how an image affects us and how we relate to our own memory and especially how memory has changed with the advent of motion pictures with their ability to record experience ... And people in our society have the instruments available to document and archive their own history. In my earlier films, I was exploring this in a quite literal way" (Richard Porton, "Family Romances," *Cineaste* 23, no. 2 [1997]).

12 Danielle Hibon, *Atom Egoyan* (Paris: Galerie Nationale du Jeu de Paume, 1993), 16.

13 Porton, "Family Romances."

14 Egoyan comments on how his controlling characters are analogues of himself: "When I noticed that character [Mitchell Stephens], I became very inspired by him. As a director, I'm always drawn to the characters who are close to conducting themselves in the way that I do. There's an aspect of my job that involves manipulating people, that involves trying to seduce people and gather people and follow me into a project. In a way, I, like any filmmaker, am a pied piper" (Porton, "Family Romances").

15 Egoyan comments on the way Hilditch's occupation evokes serial culture (television and film) as well as serial structures: "It's almost become a job. The representation of serial killing in contemporary film culture makes it an occupation, like lawyering, which I explored in *The Sweet Hereafter*. That's the only way I can understand the preponderance of this particular abnormality. We're fascinated by it because it represents the most extreme moral transgression, but it's done repeatedly. The seriality of the action becomes interesting to us structurally, because it alludes to fate and inevitability and our ability to stop it" (Cynthia Fuchs, "Interview with Atom Egoyan" in *Pop Matters*, 24 November 2000).

16 Porton, "Family Romances."

17 Samuel Beckett, *Krapp's Last Tape and Other Dramatic Pieces* (New York: Grove Press, 1957), 9.

18 François Jost, "Proposition pour une typologie des documents audiovisuels," *Semiotica* 112 (1996): 134.

19 Sigmund Freud, *The Standard Edition of the Complete Psychological Works of Sigmund Freud*, vol. 18 (London: The Hogarth Press, 1957), 18.

20 Porton, "Family Romances."

21 Porton, "Family Romances."

22 Glassman, "Emotional Logic," 47. Tracing the etymology of Narcissus to the Greek word "narcosis," Marshall McLuhan offers the following short summary of the myth of Narcissus, which does much to explain the neuroses about touching throughout the Egoyan corpus:

> The youth Narcissus mistook his own reflection in the water for another person. This extension of himself by mirror numbed his perceptions until he became the servomechanism of his own extended or repeated image. The nymph Echo tried to win his love with fragments of his own speech, but in vain. He was numb. He had adapted to his extension of himself and had become a closed system. (*Understanding Media* [Cambridge: MIT Press, 1995], 41.)

23 Donato Totaro and Simon Galiero, "Egoyan's Journey: An Interview with Atom Egoyan," *Hors Champ*, www.horschamp.qc.ca/new_offscreen/egoyan.html; accessed 28 November 2000.

24 Porton, "Family Romances."

25 Michel de Certeau, *The Practice of Everyday Life*, Steven F. Rendall, trans. (Berkeley: University of California Press, 1984), xix.

26 David Morley and Kevin Robins, *Spaces of Identity: Global Media, Electronic Landscapes and Cultural Boundaries* (London: Routledge, 1995), 1.

27 Arjun Appadurai, *Modernity at Large: Cultural Dimensions of Globalization* (Minneapolis: Public Worlds, 1996), 4.

28 Morley and Robins, *Spaces of Identity*, 1.

29 Kevin Lewis, "The Journeys of Atom Egoyan," *MovieMaker* 36, www.moviemaker.com/issues/36/egoyan/36_egoyan.html; accessed 24 November 2000.

30 This thematics of mobility might explain Van's name in *Family Viewing*.

31 Porton, "Family Romances."

32 Richard Porton, "The Politics of Denial: An Interview with Atom Egoyan," *Cineaste* 25, no. 1 (Winter 1999).

33 At the moment of this writing, Egoyan is rumoured to be planning to produce a film that specifically deals with the Armenian genocide, thus completing another circle in his work.

34 Jean Baudrillard, *Simulations*, Paul Foss, Paul Patton, and Philip Beitchman, trans. (New York: Semiotext(e), 1981), 142.

35 Hamid Naficy, "The Accented Style of the Independent Transnational Cinema: A Conversation with Atom Egoyan," in *Cultural Producers in Perilous States: Editing Events, Documenting Change,* George E. Marcus, ed. (Chicago: University of Chicago Press, 1997), 184–85.

The Tuxedoed Fallacy
Intratextual Audiences in Two Films by François Girard
Brian McIlroy

FILM STUDIES HAS BEEN SEIZED by many theoretical and methodological trends over its history. One of the major theoretical approaches of recent years has been concerned with understanding and configuring audiences, a pursuit that has direct precursors in the 1930s and 1940s, notably in Britain with the Mass Observation project.[1] In this essay, I want to chart briefly some of these audience studies, considering their theoretical manoeuvres as a backdrop to François Girard's two award-winning films of the 1990s. If the last decade has brought the audience back into the film-studies radar with its intrinsic claims that the text and author/director are effectively dead or meaningless, then Girard's work is a parallel discourse that inserts what I call here the intratextual audience into our imaginings. I choose the term *intratextual* because the words *diegetic* and *non-diegetic* as used by Carol Clover in her article "Judging Audiences" refer best to internal audiences in classical Hollywood cinema. Girard's works do not easily fit this paradigm.

Unlike Hollywood films (save a segment of the musical genre, trial movies, and sequels), Girard's films recognize the importance of audiences, their absence or presence, their homogeneity or heterogeneity; the films do so intratextually, displacing inherent meaning from traditional narrative and traditional authors in a fashion influenced by postmodernism and poststructuralist theory. Yet it might be more accurate to say that *Thirty-Two Short Films about Glenn Gould* (1992) and *The Red Violin* (1998) are an *internal* working through of Tony Bennett's concept of viewing formations, and in this way Girard ironically allows the text and writer/director to reclaim some primacy that audience studies has threatened to assume for itself outside the text and its creators.

The Shapes of Audience Study

The major outlines of audience studies reveal that their authors and practitioners believe that meaning, however difficult to ascertain, lies outside the text and writer or director. Meaning may lie in genre, but it is more likely to reside in the critical consensus of academics, journalistic reviews, film-industry press kits and marketing campaigns, star study, and interviews with actual audience members. Barbara Klinger, for example, analyzes the various ways in which the films and persona of Douglas Sirk went through a series of reformulations from the 1930s onwards. These changes in viewing formations thus have a historical component and can be tracked successfully if the film is noteworthy or popular, emanates from a major Hollywood studio, and contains stars. Klinger's study makes the obvious connection to Rock Hudson's makeover in the critical field once his HIV/AIDS condition became public. Hudson was once the great heterosexual male pin-up, but his films were later reinvestigated for gay and queer readings, given the then-strong correlation between the disease and homosexuality.

For her methodology, Klinger relies on Tony Bennett's work on viewing formations that underscores his 1987 book on the Bond films and places importance on establishing the premise that a film, or a literary text for that matter, has its meaning produced for it at a particular moment in time. A text does not mean the same thing to audiences in different periods or to audiences from different cultures. Furthermore, audience divisions by gender, race, and class must also be taken into account. The scholarly task, therefore, is to find out what these meanings were and suggest why they came to be. Another factor to bear in mind is that our readings of a text today most likely carry with them an awareness of how the work has already been viewed. To use an architectural analogy, we often move along a continuum from the romanesque through the gothic and baroque to rococo in our appreciation.

Problems exist here, of course, as with any methodology. Klinger, for example, omits any empirical analysis of actual audiences for Sirk's films, regarding them as too prone to subjective variations. By contrast, in their 1998 book, Martin Barker and Kate Brooks focus specifically on 136 cinema-goers who agreed to be interviewed on attending the Sylvester Stallone film *Judge Dredd* (Cannon, 1995) and employ discourse theory to make meaning of the offhand comments viewers are likely to make before and after seeing a film. Jackie Stacey's 1994 book *Star Gazing* draws on 300 female interviewees in their sixties and seventies who recalled their affection for female stars of the 1940s and 1950s. Stacey is correct to point out that feminist psychoanalytical criticism too often posits an ideal spectator which the text is assumed to seek, while an overemphasis on empirical studies reliant on memory can skew the conclusions of what kind of cultural work the films (or stars) actually accomplished at a specific historical period.

Clearly, a balanced approach to viewing formations would combine the historical research of Klinger and the more spontaneous research of Barker and Brooks, allied to a strong theoretical conception of the spectator. But equally, critics must recognize that there are those filmmakers who problematize the audience *within* their productions. We do not have a satisfying theoretical vocabulary for these works. We might label them postmodern, poststructuralist-influenced, art film or—the last redoubt of desperation—experimental or avant-garde. They invite a flexible audience response, a far cry from the mainstream Hollywood product, which continues to attract the focus of academics.[2] In addition to the inadequate theorizing of non-Hollywood production, we do not have a sufficient vocabulary to discuss the audience response to documentaries or to different definitions of text. As to the latter, the fragmented figure of Glenn Gould in *Thirty-Two Short Films* and, more playfully, the violin in *The Red Violin* are destabilized texts in constant formation and reformation. The notion of destabilized texts fits neatly with much of art-film practice, as outlined programmatically in David Bordwell's thoughts on the art film (1979), and in Janet Staiger's thoughts on niche art-house audiences (1992).[3] Unquestionably, Girard's first feature-length English language film seeks and finds a highbrow audience. To a degree, this audience is predetermined by Girard's clear intellectual bent, his serious attitude to interviews in newspapers and magazines, and his post-screening discussions at festivals. To another degree, it is reflective of the production team that allows him to "authorize" his works.

François Girard and Rhombus Media

Alongside these theoretical concerns, it is still possible to place Girard in the auteur category within English-Canadian cinema on the basis of his two English films. Both productions were made under the aegis of Rhombus Media, produced by Niv Fichman, noted originator of films on composers Manuel de Falla and Kurt Weill. Both were co-written with Don McKellar and photographed by Alain Dostie. Both films deal with musical topics of a cerebral nature, locking the works into high modernism. It comes as no surprise to learn that Girard's past and recent documentaries have relied heavily on a musical theme, including *The Secret World of Peter Gabriel* (1994), a concert film; and a contribution to the 1997 TV series *Yo-Yo Ma, Inspired by Bach*. A striking aspect of Girard's first French-language feature, *Cargo* (1990), is its musical score, which makes up somewhat for its rather convoluted narrative structure. The interest in musical arrangement can be traced back to Girard's rendition of Carbone 14's staged performance *Le Dortoir* (1990). As André Loiselle remarks, the latter film bears "witness to his formalist predilections and mastery of devising cinematic correspondences for the primarily perceptual structures of choreography and musical composition."[4] To this astute comment, one could add Girard's later interest in temporality and history in *The Red Violin*, which set cinematic challenges of their own.

More generally, Girard has undoubtedly crossed a barrier: he has moved artistically from his Québec roots and culture to English Canada through his study of Glenn Gould, to the international scene with *The Red Violin*, which fittingly won an Oscar for Best Music, Original Score (John Corigliani). Any extratextual viewing-formation study would deeply consider this boundary crossing from French Canada to English Canada. Politically, one is not surprised at Central Canada's embrace of Girard's work (four Genies in 1993 for *Thirty-Two Short Films*, eight Genies in 1999 for *The Red Violin*) when you consider such awards "prove" that Québec filmmakers can work successfully with Ontarians on Canadian and international projects. Further, it would have to consider the culture of Rhombus Media, a Toronto company formed in 1979 by Barbara Willis Sweete, Niv Fichman, and Larry Weinstein that focusses successfully on the performing arts. Rhombus has also been involved with feature films apart from Girard's work, such as Don McKellar's *Last Night* (1998), so it is a company with its own niche, an aura that affects all its projects. But in this essay, I want to show how Girard's films incorporate the viewing formation concept intratextually. I suspect this quality in his work makes his films attractive to intellectuals concerned with the constant conversation between the academy and the visual arts.

Thirty-Two Short Films about Glenn Gould

In the introduction to the published screenplay, Denys Arcand mentions that he saw Glenn Gould perform. His response is eminently quotable: "Now at that point in my life I had never heard *The Goldberg Variations*. Listening to them for the first time played live by Glenn Gould is a little bit like losing your virginity with Marilyn Monroe: you never entirely recuperate from it."[5] Here Arcand alludes to the central problematic of many a biographical film on a reputed genius or celebrity: how can one capture the essence of that greatness while also fairly addressing other aspects of his or her life? Gould and his music are the text that can only come alive by interaction with an audience, real and created. As Girard explains, "It was clear that there was no way to make only one film and say what it was to think and know about Glenn Gould."[6] No grand narrative was possible for writers Girard and McKellar, since that assumes a confidence in knowledge about their subject (which, given Gould's reclusive habits, would have been impossible) and an equal confidence in the audience for such a film. Gould's life does not have the shape that dramatic feature films such as *Shine* (Hicks, 1996) and *Hilary and Jackie* (Tucker, 1998), to take two recent examples, clearly have. (This does not stop researchers from creating one: Peter Ostwald's recent biography suggests that Gould suffered from Asperger's syndrome, which might allow a future filmmaker to attempt the "brilliant musician with disability" genre with the Canadian musician as the subject-hero.) A complex and contradictory man, Gould was interested in contrapuntal musical forms, which explains his attraction to Bach and the structures he created for his famous radio play, *The Idea of North*. In choosing thirty-two short films to represent the idea of Gould, Girard and McKellar lean on the divisions of Bach's *The Goldberg Variations*, ensuring that their film resembles a musical work in itself. In addition, they actively seek out a polyphony of voices "about" Glenn Gould without privileging any specific one. If it is true that Gould could hold many thoughts simultaneously and found expression for this in his music, then the form of Girard's film is fitting. These voices produce and suggest various kinds of viewing formations of Gould the man mostly melded with Gould the musician.

One kind of viewing formation is raised as a concept to be interrogated by Glenn Gould himself in an article he published in *High Fidelity* magazine in February 1974, playfully entitled "Glenn Gould Interviews Glenn Gould About Glenn Gould," and which Girard realizes as "Gould meets Gould." To Denys Arcand and the others who saw Gould perform that evening, a particular viewing formation of the brilliant, eccentric performer was created, an *event* that Arcand some forty years later can still recall. But Gould, frustrated by this type of audience and the wide range of acoustics and pianos, gave up concert performance in 1964 at the age of thirty-two. The need for an embodied artist to give a live visual representation is dismissed by Gould as the tuxedoed fallacy:

> To me, the ideal audience-to-artist relationship is a one-to-zero relationship. First, I'm not at all happy with words like 'public' and 'artist'; I'm not happy with the hierarchical implications of that kind of terminology. The artist should be granted anonymity. He should be permitted to operate in secret, as it were, unconcerned with—or better still, unaware of—the presumed demands of the marketplace, which demands, given sufficient indifference on the part of a sufficient number of artists, will simply disappear. And given their disappearance, the artist will then abandon his false sense of 'public' responsibility, and his 'public' will relinquish its role of servile dependency.[7]

Behind this statement we hear echoes of D.H. Lawrence and James Joyce's Stephen Daedalus on the artist, but most of all Gould wished his audience to hear, not to see. In his turn to technology via recording, Gould could achieve a certain perfectionism which live performance, with all its variables, could not. Glassman and Loiselle rightly point to the influence of Innis and McLuhan on Gould's decision to seek the technological route. Yehudi Menuhin voices the counter argument:

Of course, from a purist's stance, he had a point. In a concert hall, some people can hear or see better than others. Sometimes, in large churches people are seated behind pillars and can't see. The acoustics may be exaggerated—something may be too loud or not loud enough. The volume is too loud, or the reverberation hurts your ears. He was right, it's not always ideal. But that's part of life. For me, that exists as a living element.[8]

Gould's interview with himself is both a parody of the search for the Holy Grail—the one piece of biography that will reveal the genius of the pianist—and a serious contemplation on the public consensus about an artist that journalists and academics strive to sculpt and present as fact. The voices of the film are many: the musical collaborator Bruno Monsaingeon, the violinist friend Yehudi Menuhin, the people he used to phone for company, the interviewers for famous magazines, and the flurry of questions from different interviewers in the section "Questions with No Answers." The main point of having this series of interviews (throughout which the voice of Girard is omitted) is for the audience to construct their Gould, the musician or the man.

The film is a mixed genre in itself, neither fully documentary nor fully fictional. It tends to borrow techniques popularized in such experimental documentaries as Errol Morris' *The Thin Blue Line* (1988), which relies on recreation of a wrongful murder conviction to convey aspects to which we could not have access in the real world. Girard keeps true to Gould by using his own words as much as possible and working around them visually. Morris, for example, is notable for setting his interviewees down in a chair at a specific distance from the camera and lets only their words emerge on the film. Girard follows this practice throughout, suggesting Gould's own belief that the artist should be invisible as far as possible. Girard also draws on some of the best-known shots to speak to the *cinéaste*. The shot of Gould in "The Last Concert" dipping his hands and forearms in the sink with a container of tablets in the foreground and a door in the background is framed in an eerily similar fashion to the famous deep focus shot of Susan Alexander's suicide attempt in *Citizen Kane* (Welles, 1941). While this may seem disrespectful to Gould by comparing his undoubted talents with an untalented fictional singer, there is an intellectual link between the two, since it reaffirms Gould's dismissal of the embodied spectacle of musical performance.

That audience of one that Gould valorized is given form in the "Hamburg" section. Here Gould is seen dictating a telegram from the phone in his hotel room as a chambermaid makes up his room. Room service arrives with a record. Gould motions for the chambermaid to wait while he puts it on the turntable. At first reluctant, the maid gradually listens and enjoys the piece, finally realizing as she picks up the record cover that Gould is the performer. She thanks him. It is an austere sequence of shots, and yet it encapsulates Gould's passionate obsession, the power of music to elevate the everyday world, and Gould's happiness that an ordinary person can hear what others will pay large sums to hear him play—less well—in the flesh.

Letting people speak naturally is at the core of Gould's tapestry in his radio play *The Idea of North*, but contrapuntalism is best rendered by Girard in the previous section, "Truck Stop." The filmmaker reveals Gould slumming at a roadside diner. He has been listening on his car radio to the popular songs of Petula Clark, for whom he had an odd obsession. It seems he comes here not for the food but to listen to the symphony of conversations that move in and out of audibility, imagining himself as some sort of conductor. Girard suggests that the simultaneity of several voices is harnessed by Gould and reformulated into his radio documentary as the main technique.

A documentary filmmaker usually creates a specific viewing formation for an audience who may or may not accept it, just as many books are written on the same subject but, rightly or wrongly, only a few are deemed worthy or definitive. Girard deconstructs the process of traditional documentary by being playful, by inviting contradiction, by answering few questions. A conventional audience study of Girard's film would no doubt reveal a popularity contest among the short films' aesthetic merits. In its collage-like quality, any empirical analysis of scenes of Girard's film would probably find that Gould's true essence was unknowable and that he was multifaceted. Yet Girard still places Gould as a genius who took radical decisions in giving up concert performance and retreating to the studio. Gould knew that his records were selling well worldwide, and perhaps the greatest compliment to his music is in the section "Voyageur," where we learn that a piece that he recorded was sent into the heavens in search of an alien listener.

The Red Violin

If *Thirty-Two Short Films* entertains the notion that a text (Gould as subject) can help create (or limit) its own audiences and reception, then *The Red Violin* moves in the other direction, showing how an apparently inanimate object (the red violin) means different things in different cultures and different times. Bennett's viewing-formations concept could not be better articulated, even if the violin appears to be passive, unencumbered by its past lives. The film navigates five periods in diverse locations: seventeenth-century Cremona, Italy, where the violin is created amidst a tragic story of death in childbirth; eighteenth-century Vienna, where a child prodigy is trained to impress possible patrons; nineteenth-century Oxford, where virtuoso Frederick Pope plays passionately with the instrument, making women swoon; twentieth-century Shanghai during the Cultural Revolution, where the instrument must be hidden from view; and present-day Montréal, where an appraiser must establish authenticity and an auctioneer must establish a price for the instrument. Throughout the film, Girard and McKellar make interesting use of a tarot card reading in the Italian section to introduce the other segments. We also return to the auction scene in Montréal at various points, always from a different perspective of the previous one. The film is thus both linear and non-linear; or, musically speaking, it comprises five verses with recurring and variable choruses.

The Italian section begins in a cavernous studio with the suggestion of the Renaissance in full flight, revealing master craftsman Niccolo Bussotti attending to his apprentices. Bussotti checks out the labours of his employees, destroying one violin-in-process that he deems of poor quality. His studio obviously makes instruments for "true artists" to play and for cultured audiences to appreciate; he is a man concerned with perfection and beauty. The writers' conceit is that it takes DNA sampling in the late twentieth century to discover the great romantic moment of Niccolo Bussotti. He takes his most valued instrument, intended for his future son, and varnishes it with the blood of his wife, who has died giving birth; the brush he uses is created from the dead woman's hair. The two great loves of his life are therefore encased in one instrument, reputed to be his last violin. The viewing formation here is that of the quality art object of artisan culture which is linked, but not exclusively so, to a commercial value.

One of Bussotti's criticisms of poor-quality violins is that they become instruments for monks and courtesans to "pluck," by which he means their owners have no aesthetic sense. Ironically, the red violin's fate is to be traded to a monk's orphanage in Austria where it is employed to give young boys a sense of self-worth. Here we see the role of music as healer of emotions. The boys also play for the beauty of God as a group, downplaying the possibility of individualism. Nevertheless, even the monks see a gift from God when they hear it. In the form of Kaspar Weiss, a child prodigy, violin teacher Poussin sees his passport to financial success and fame. In the process of seeking preferment for Weiss, Poussin illustrates the need in this society for musicians to have patrons in order to survive and prosper. Poussin gets his chance to succeed only because a baron on his way to Prussia needs a young musician as part of his entourage. There are no profitable free-standing performances here, so the well-played violin becomes an attribute of this hierarchical, elitist, and almost feudal society. The death of Kaspar Weiss due to his refusal or inability to play in front of such monsters and in such circumstances gives the violin a living value-laden presence. Clearly, as Bussotti would doubtless have believed, not all audiences are worth playing for.

Ripped from the coffin of Kaspar Weiss, the violin then passes along from gypsy to gypsy. This section is full of lust, life, and travel; it is a form of sexual awakening, culminating in the section profiling the affair between Frederick Pope and Victoria Byrd. This short narrative has come under withering criticism, since it is viewed as exhibiting either bad acting or embarrassingly poor direction. Certainly, it is highly melodramatic, but for a reason. The violin has moved from the womb-like cavern of the studio, to the gentle tutelage of the monk's orphanage, to the rarefied air of the Vienna social scene, and now to the energetic, sexually active, histrionic adolescence in the hands of the gypsies and Frederick Pope. In this latter viewing formation, the violin is played to provoke strong emotions and is foreplay to sexual satisfaction. This point explains why Victoria, having discovered Pope and a gypsy girl in the throes of sexual intercourse, shoots the violin, calling it a "sluttish muse," rather than punishing either of the lovers. The sensuous atmosphere created in this section conjures up the writers of English Romantic period—a Byronic philanderer crossed with a Coleridgean opium-smoker in Frederick Pope, and a passionate Mary Shelley-figure in Victoria Byrd.

Undoubtedly, the strongest episode in detailing how the violin's treatment reflects a culture is the Chinese section, which might be seen as the violin's age of maturity. Traded by Frederick Pope's Chinese servant in Shanghai, the violin is eventually bought for a little girl, Xiang Pei. She grows up to be the head of a cultural unit among the socialist realism of the Cultural Revolution. It is a delicate task since she clearly does not believe in the new orthodoxy; she must hide these feelings along with her past love of Western music. Girard and McKellar write in a most compelling scene. After a performance by the cultural unit, the visiting political commissar uses the occasion to lambaste Western music, calling it all "empty formalism."

An instructor of music is dragged in to be humiliated for teaching Western music and instruments. He is about to be purged when Xiang Pei comes to his rescue by softening his punishment. The burning of the violin the teacher is carrying impels Xiang Pei to find her own hidden red violin. In the process, she is discovered by her son Ming, who, while apparently agreeing to keep the existence of the violin secret, in the tenor of the times of betrayal reveals all to his father, who reports his wife's activities. While Xiang Pei's future is unknown, she enables the violin to survive by convincing the disgraced music teacher to hide it. In this society, the violin is representative of a Western capitalist bourgeois threat; it speaks to the past and tradition, and this is naturally a problem for the communists seeking to break the stranglehold of former ideologies. But what the short narrative valorizes is the inexorable pull of art and family gifts, which has a close resemblance to the opening Italian section.

The final section in Montréal might be termed the era of collectibles. Throughout the film, we have visited the auction room in preparation for the final sale of the red violin. We have also been introduced briefly to the representatives of those who seek to claim the violin as their own: Mr. Ruselsky, the practising violinist and collector; Ming, as an old man, perhaps wishing to capture something of his mother's precious past and, at the same time, redeem himself; the buyer for the Frederick Pope Foundation; the modern-day wealthy monks of the orphanage where Kaspar Weiss was first noticed. Finally, Charles Moritz, the American instrument appraiser who has been seeking the red violin most of his professional life, substitutes a copy for the real violin in order to please himself and to present a gift to his child in the way that Niccolo Bussotti had intended. While the auctioneer is concerned only with the prestige of selling the famed red violin and the price it will attract, the Pope Foundation and the orphanage appear to be attracted to it to create a museum piece—a wry comment on the institutionalization and popular marketing of our cultural heritage. It is perhaps fitting that the violin, after trips through Europe and China, should end up in the "New World" to begin its travels again.

↪↪↪

Many years ago, Seth Feldman wrote an influential essay on the silent subject in which he argued that, in both style and character, English-Canadian cinema is distinctive in its passiveness. To a degree, this characterization is also true of Glenn Gould in *Thirty-Two Short Films* and, most clearly, the violin in *The Red Violin*. But by choosing the topic of art, and musical performance in particular, in both films Girard intratextually raises the constructed nature of audiences and their viewing formations. It is a nice irony that whereas Gould tried to control his reception by relying on studio recording, Girard's apparently scattered approach to portraiture deconstructs and destabilizes any hope of a single viewing (and auditory) formation. While more condensed, controlled, and fictional than the Gould film, *The Red Violin* creates specific intratextual audiences, with historically contingent viewing formations. In the end, Girard's films are poststructuralist-influenced works that essentially aspire to make extratextual academic audience study redundant.

Notes

I'd like to thank André Loiselle for lending me copies of *Cargo* and *Le Dortoir* as well as his article cited below in preparation for this essay.

1   See Jeffrey Richards and Dorothy Sheridan, *Mass-Observation at the Movies* (London and New York: Routledge and Kegan Paul, 1987).

2   See Melvyn Stokes and Richard Maltby, *Identifying Hollywood Audiences: Cultural Identity and the Movies* (London: British Film Institute, 1999).

3   "The Art Film as Mode of Film Practice," and *Interpreting Films: Studies in the Historical Reception of American Cinema*, respectively.

4   André Loiselle, "François Girard's Glenn Gould and The Idea of North," *Reverse Shot* 1, no. 3 (Fall 1994): 13.

5   François Girard and Don McKellar, *Thirty-Two Short Films about Glenn Gould* (Toronto: Coach House Press, 1995), 7.

6   Quoted in Mark Glassman, "In Search of Glenn Gould," *Take One: Film In Canada* (Winter 1994), 17.

7   Girard and McKellar, *Thirty-Two Short Films*, 34.

8   Girard and McKellar, *Thirty-Two Short Films*, 66.

Greyson, Grierson, Godard, God
Reflections on the Cinema of John Greyson
Christine Ramsay

"THE BOURGEOISIE IS NOT MY AUDIENCE," John Greyson has always insisted. As Douglas Bell suggests apropos of Greyson's most recent film, *Uncut* (1997), with his "experimentation and loose exuberance," the director is "always after something else," and the "reasonable expectations of a general audience" simply aren't it.[1]

Emerging from the Toronto gay community in the late 1970s into the Toronto arts community's radical video movement in the 1980s, what Greyson *is* after has always been political intervention for alternative communities and audiences. Listed in *Take One*'s "100 Great and Glorious Years of Canadian Cinema—The Sequel," Greyson is celebrated in Canadian film and video circles for the "unique combination of wit and didacticism" he brings to the issues of queer culture, making him "a force for the mainstream to reckon with." Well-known in North America in the 1980s as a producer, distributor, promoter, writer, documentarist, video artist, teacher, and activist (he has taught video at the California Institute for the Arts in Los Angeles, studied at the Centre for Advanced Film Studies in Toronto, and is always in demand as a speaker at universities and festivals), Greyson has gone on to develop an international reputation in the 1990s: *Urinal* (1989), *The Making of 'Monsters'* (1991), and *Zero Patience* (1993) did extremely well at the Berlin Film Festival, while *Lilies* (1996), his third feature, won a Genie Award for Best Picture.[2]

Greyson's work as a cultural *agent provocateur*, he tells Peter Steven, began at home, where he was always encouraged to "paint, write, and do plays."[3] His education in a technical high school rather than university, he intimates, may be partly responsible for his irreverent grass-roots, tinker-with-the-form attitude to his art and to the cultures he engages with (whether gay rights groups, AIDS Action Now, or the Canadian media and the CBC). Bringing art and politics together through humour to challenge and subvert conventional ways of seeing and "expand how we look at the world" has always been his forte. Even in his earliest work, Steven observes, his iconoclastic bent is evident:

The Visitation (1980) is a pseudo-documentary combined with performance sequences on gay life in Toronto, as narrated by a fictional gay radio station. *Manzana por Manzana* (1982) and *To Pick Is Not to Choose* (1983) function as much more conventional documentaries, on Nicaraguan and Ontario farmworkers respectively. Both tapes were created in close collaboration with the local farmworkers' organizations. Yet even with these tapes Greyson inserts striking, often humorous interventions into the talking-head testimonies—singing intervals by a young Nicaraguan and by 1960s TV-style corny farmers.[4]

Moreover, the political left to which he himself subscribes—the left, whether straight or gay, for whom "humorous art, especially of the camp and tacky variety, never seems quite proper"—is itself subject to his high spirited barbs. "In the late seventies," Greyson says, "there was an incredibly well established gay community, so the humour in the tapes and performance pieces was partly a way of taking that on, and to a certain extent laughing at some of the arrogant aspects of gay culture. You always reject your elders, I suppose."[5]

With his overtly didactic commitment to "producing new content" as a community documentarist who lampoons "institutions and conventions," one might expect Greyson's work to be heavy-handed and decidedly monologic, but that is not the case.[6] Rather than outright "rejecting" his elders or the cultural institutions and conventions he wishes to challenge, Greyson achieves a profound dialogic engagement with them. The conceptual heterogeneity and formal heteroglossia[7] of his tapes and films inflect the didacticism of their queer politics, lending them their unique and highly original flavour as complex socio-cultural documents of his lived culture.

According to Peter Steven, as a gay activist influenced by traditions in social documentary and video art who also places great store in the power of popular forms not only to entertain but to enlighten, Greyson must be understood as a powerful force at the centre of "new documentary" in Canada. By "shaking up conventional documentary forms," "challenging us to look more carefully at the social, cultural and political patterns and habits we have set for ourselves in Canada," and "creating new types of working relationships with the people or groups documented," these new documentaries work as hybrids to "fuse forms, contents and contexts" in new ways.[8] In such work, Steven argues, meaning resides in what Nick Browne calls the "supertext," the complex set of relationships between texts, audiences, and cultural formations. "The full meaning of a tape or film," he writes, "includes everything displayed on the screen and heard on the sound track *as well as* all the references leading into it and away from it in the eyes, ears, and minds of the audience"[9]—and, I would emphasize, the *author*. For what Steven is describing as the key impulse of Greyson's particular articulation of new documentary is in fact what Mikhail Bakhtin celebrates as the dialogic imagination, where mind, creativity, and embodied subjectivity are understood as elements in relation to others, to lived culture, and to history in the endless dialogue that constitutes human reality. As Michael Holquist suggests, the master assumption of the dialogic imagination is that "there is no figure without a ground," no text without context, no single voice without the languages and events of culture, no authorial word without the words of others that go before and come after.[10] To *author* is to *answer* to "the text of our social and physical universe" and to participate in "shaping the world," producing new content by entering with one's own voice into the multitude of voices that "jostle each other within the combat zone of the word."[11]

John Greyson has always seen himself as a guerrilla film- and videomaker, throwing himself as a marginalized voice from the queer Canadian cultural scene into the "combat zone" to challenge the words of his elders in the interests of an alternative, politically aware audience formation open to expressions of socio-sexual dissent.[12] "A progressive culture," Greyson says, is a dialogic culture: "by definition contested, contradictory, and combative. Oh, and hopefully fun."[13] Unapologetically intellectual on the one hand and unabashedly ironic and playful on the other, his work is a provocative hybrid of popular film genres, video art, ideological critique, and subcultural in-jokes in which, in true guerrilla style, he "supplies the pieces but expects the audience to put them together."[14] Speaking from and to several discursive worlds at once, Greyson draws together an eclectic audience of queers, Canadian cultural aficionados, and college types steeped in critical thinking to participate in the making of new meanings. For Greyson, as for Bakhtin, authoring is always a question of "engaging and negotiating with your subjects, since you share their subjectivity."[15] An artist is not a romantic genius hived off from others and the dialogue, but is profoundly imbued with and answerable to their cultural context.[16] Hence, for Greyson, making his art involves *inter*subjectivity, "a social contract of responsibilities, of respect for differences within a group. Imposing a particular political or artistic vision is inevitable, and can't be erased, but it can also become selfish. To me anyone who 'stays true to their vision' at the expense of their subjects is a pig and ends up walking all over people!"[17]

Centring primarily on gay and lesbian experience of the last two decades with issues such as the formation of a queer nation and the struggle for queer identity (*Kipling Meets the Cowboys*, 1985; *Moscow Does Not Believe in Queers*, 1986), the AIDS epidemic (*The Ads Epidemic*, 1987; *The World Is Sick [Sic]*, 1989; *Zero Patience*, 1993), washroom sex (*Urinal*, 1989), and the surveillance and regulation of desire by religion and the state (*Lilies*, 1996; *Uncut*, 1997), Greyson audaciously dialogizes, politicizes, contextualizes, and localizes them for a Canadian festival and gallery audience interested in queer current events and the media propaganda surrounding them. For example, *Moscow Does Not Believe in Queers* documents Greyson's own trip to film the gay contingent at a Soviet youth conference, but borrows from Rock Hudson submarine movies to satirize Soviet socialism and sexual politics. *Kipling Meets the Cowboys* foregrounds the importance of American cowboy fantasies to gay male identity formation through musical numbers that play with the historical figure of Rudyard Kipling while tracing the post-World War Two transition from British to American forms of cultural imperialism. His work on AIDS is similarly sweeping and heteroglossic, with both *The World Is Sick (Sic)* and *Zero Patience* critiquing media representations of the disease. *The World Is Sick (Sic)* documents the reality of drug-company profiteering at the Fifth International Conference on AIDS held in Montréal in 1989 with the help of actual members of Toronto's AIDS Action Now group and a drag send-up of CBC newscasters. *Zero Patience* adapts the story of Gaetan Dugas, the Canadian flight attendant made a scapegoat in the media for bringing AIDS to North America, into a witty musical fantasia in which Dugas returns as a ghost and has an affair with Victorian sexologist Sir Richard Burton. Historical figures are constantly paraded in order to juxtapose contemporary values with those of the past, as well as to parody journalists and the media in Greyson's form of new documentary. In *Urinal*, bisexual personalities from gay and lesbian history (Frida Kahlo, Sergei Eisenstein, Langston Hughes, Oscar Wilde) come to 1980s Ontario to analyze the media frenzy over OPP surveillance of gay washroom sex, while in *Uncut*, former Canadian Prime Minister Pierre Trudeau's rumoured bisexuality becomes a central thread in a narrative about circumcision, three gay men named

Peter, and issues of copyright and ownership of the image in our media-saturated world. Thus, as Steven suggests, a consistent formal strategy emerges across Greyson's work: his tactics "swing wildly between direct cinema documentary and the highly articulated and layered conventions of art video" in order to subvert "the dominance of cinema by stirring the conventions of video art into cinematic fiction and documentary."[18]

As a Canadian interested in documenting his society and effecting social change, Greyson stands in the long shadow of John Grierson and the history and traditions of the NFB. Asked by Steven whether there are particular conventions in mainstream documentaries that really bother him, Greyson replied, "Voice-of-God narration is pretty high up on my bad list. At the same time I can think of good reasons to use it as a way to shape content and capture information, etc."[19] Undeniably, there is a decidedly Griersonian didacticism and stridency running throughout Greyson's work as he follows, in principle if not in style, the father's tenets: that "documentary, above all, must have a social purpose" and that "documentary ... not be separated from the community ... served."[20] Taking these dictates seriously, what Greyson strives to do above all in interpreting Canada to (queer) Canadians is to "dialogue" with the various groups he represents[21]—whether Ontario farmworkers, urban activist-intellectual art circles, or people living with AIDS. But rather than perpetuating the division between filmmaker and subjects that the voice-of-god style inevitably depends on to deliver "the authoritative truth," the "trick" for Greyson is to "try and erase that divide" by introducing to the social documentary self-reflexive narrative strategies that suggest internal criticism, multiple perspectives, and conflicting truths. [22] As Kass Banning argues, Greyson's new form of documenting our world by queering it involves questioning not only accepted truths but ways of knowing in Canada and, in fact, "questioning the certainty of 'knowing' in the first place."[23]

This leads us to another cinematic elder whose influence Greyson also integrates while slyly interrogating: Jean-Luc Godard. While Greyson is interested in social content, in documenting social realities, and in speaking to and for communities and their issues, he is also committed to philosophical, political, and formal questions about art and knowledge, such as "how representations are constructed and who constructs them."[24] In Greyson, the populist didacticism of Grierson meets the stylized cinécriture of Godard, re-inventing the essay-film and its collage structure for a more complex, late-twentieth-century videated reality. As many critics have observed, underlying every one of Greyson's films is a highly constructed polemical argument after the fashion of early Godard, counter-cinema, and the critique of the system from within. For Banning, Laura Marks, and Robert Cagle, for example, Greyson's is a true "cinema of ideas," awash in anti-narrative devices and Brechtian distancing techniques—the "analytical tools of cultural criticism" by which he questions the myths, received wisdom, and homophobia of his lived culture.[25] Writes Cagle, "Greyson always locates himself firmly inside the culture that he examines and in which he lives and works. He adopts/adapts academic methodologies to develop challenging and yet always entertaining works that reflect his desire both to voice a critique against the system and to effect radical change in the face of an 'epidemic of signification.'"[26] Greyson's work, like Godard's, is rife with sharp analysis that undermines our belief in the singular truths of the status quo while borrowing the forms and conventions of popular culture and Hollywood (in Greyson's case, most typically, the musical) to deconstruct normative forms of signification and their meanings, and to amuse.[27] Unlike Godard, however, Greyson's project is to clutter not only the text and its structure and content with the signifying traces of his authorial voice, but to dialogize the media of signification as well, stirring, as Steven suggests, the conventions of high-art cinema into those of independent video art and social documentary for his own, queer purposes. In a media-saturated world, where "[t]his year's bourgeois conventions are sometimes last year's cutting edge," Greyson knows only too well that all forms and conventions have "historical perspective" and a definite shelf life.[28] But as a guerrilla who wants to reach his audience by any means necessary, everything goes. Hollywood and high art, past and present, the popular and the political converge and are scrambled to achieve a truly overdetermined essay effect. Greyson comments,

> I'm most interested in taking conventions and playing with them—not rejecting them. I think that's more useful ... I've never liked the arrogance of the straight white avant-garde film tradition. For me ... [a]rtists have an immense responsibility to communicate and respond to their audiences.[29]

For Greyson's dialogic imagination, high art, the fictional forms of popular culture, and documentary exist together in a heteroglossic world; as a gay activist documentarist, he sees it as his responsibility to speak as many of the languages he shares with his culture as he possibly can, "taking chances" with both form and content to continually open the dialogue to new audiences.[30] "My work has never attempted to convert an uninformed or hostile public and bring them over to the wonderful world of gay liberation. The tapes wouldn't really recruit anyone. My work tries to invite people in. I want to engage with feminists, start a dialogue, such as, 'Here's what gay men are up to, what do you think?' "[31]

Hence his foray, with playwright Michel Marc Bouchard's *Lilies*, into "straight" (melo)dramatic feature filmmaking,[32] a departure of sorts from the ironic play with the musical that characterizes most of his other work. It is a departure that has received relatively little critical attention or analysis, a situation that I would like to redress here, given the festival attention and accolades the film has enjoyed, as well as its clear political and thematic resonances with the rest of Greyson's oeuvre.

Using the forms and conventions of the "women's picture" to stage a gay love story that questions patriarchal authority by exposing the sexual hypocrisies of the Catholic church in 1950s Québec while simultaneously exploding current homophobic norms of acceptable gender behaviour, Greyson certainly succeeded with *Lilies* in engaging and impressing a feminist audience.[33] Noreen Golfman writes, "In its high calibre look, its almost intimidating sensuality and its fearless challenge to the masks of institutional authority, *Lilies* is a little masterpiece, probably the most exciting Canadian feature of the year."[34] And for Laura Marks, Greyson's works have always been highly relevant to feminism in their attempt "to subvert the masculine project"—a project that establishes a distance from the male body in order to abstract men and enable them to stand in, as if transparently, for a general social and political authority. "Anonymity," she writes, "is a condition of male power. When the male body is revealed in its particularity it loses that abstraction that bestows upon men the illusion of authority."[35] How do Greyson's films and videos subvert this masculine project? In challenging white masculine authority and its imposed categories of gender behaviour and compulsory heterosexuality by bringing the queer male body—whether naked or in drag, cut or uncut—singing and dancing decidedly into view. From the ribald shots of "jolly group sex" that accompany the country-and-western singalongs by multi-racial cowboys in *Kipling Meets the Cowboys*, through the "soft-core hockey/dance routine" to the *Hockey Night in Canada* theme music that unearths the "sexual ritual behind the rigid rules of sport"[36] in *The Making of 'Monsters,'* to the found footage of the "peter meter," which measures "the angle of an erection to determine whether or not an image of the penis is 'obscene'" in *Uncut*, the gay male body has undeniably been a key locus of subversive signification for Greyson.[37] But what is particularly interesting about *Lilies* is that, with the move into the forms and conventions of melodrama and so into a deeper development of character, the director comes to focus less exclusively on the *body* as the central site for questioning the masculine project and turns to the equally important site of *affect*. In the past decade, many popular feature films have begun to thematize the crucial problem of affect for masculinities, and *Lilies* suggests the extent to which Greyson the social documentarist continues to keep his finger on the pulse of contemporary culture and its concerns.[38] Abandoning the critical yet emotionally distanced and distancing tools of his "prickly, ironic video-art roots"[39] in this "men's women's picture" with a seditious drag twist, *Lilies* emerges as a moving story of gay love that challenges the masculine project's equally problematic distance from male *emotion* and exposes the complex levels of homosocial desire that the masculine masks of institutional authority struggle to suppress.

This is not to suggest, however, that none of the earlier work informs *Lilies*. On the contrary: the question of male emotion is clearly grafted onto the layered essayistic-intellectual structure Greyson has always favoured, and his cheeky treatment of his forefathers, and queer current events, remains visible. In this case, the subject matter shifts away from documenting queer nation, AIDS, washroom sex, and the regulation of gay desire by the state to a less didactic, more poetic treatise on the deep forms of homosocial bonding existing in but repressed by the Catholic church; thus the elder being challenged shifts from Grierson and Godard to God himself!

Lilies begins in 1952 Québec, in the thick of the Duplessis regime, as Bishop Jean Bilodeau (Marcel Sabourin) visits a Québec penitentiary to hear the confession of murder convict, Simon Doucet (Aubert Pallascio). The bishop expects to give absolution, but the tables are turned and Bilodeau is forced to revisit his own sins of forty years earlier, acted out for him and Simon by other inmates and guards in the prison chapel. As the play unfolds, it is revealed that in 1912 Bilodeau (Matthew Ferguson) and Simon (Jason Cadieux) were classmates with Count Vallier de Tilly (Danny Gilmore) at a Catholic boys' school in Roberval. They acted in the Italian poet Gabriele D'Annunzio's highly eroticized play about the torture of St. Sebastian, *The Martyrdom of St. Sebastian*, and Vallier and Bilodeau vied for the love of the beautiful Simon. In a fit of jealousy and rage at his friends' eventual romantic coupling, and suffering denial of his own sexual orientation, Bilodeau causes the death of Vallier and casts the blame on Simon, who is given a life sentence. The film is densely layered, self-reflexive, and Brechtian in structure, alternating between the prison and Roberval, and using the same actors to embody different characters in both settings in this play-within-a-play-within-a-play-within-a-film about socio-sexual dissent. Thus, as Golfman observes, Greyson situates 1952, the work's present, in "the stark male prison world" of Duplessis Québec, "thereby forcing an uncomfortable analogy between then and now ... a frighteningly judgmental and intolerant time in which religious fundamentalism marries right-wing individualism in the service of homophobia."[40]

What is particularly striking about *Lilies* as a dramatic feature is the way Greyson—ever self-reflexive in his use of form and content, and ever self-conscious in foregrounding the intellectual and emotional dialogue he seeks with his audiences—plays with gender stereotypes through the subversive potential of melodrama and melodramatic tableaux.[41] Those stereotypes involve, on the one hand, what Richard Dyer has called "the homosexual as sad young man," and, on the other hand, "the woman scorned" by men in patriarchal culture. For Dyer, the affective image of the homosexual as a sad young man (melancholy, emotionally overwrought, and inevitably feminized) is ubiquitous in our culture, and he traces its lineage from Christianity and the Romantic poets through Freud. As a Christian symbol, the sad young man is embodied in the spectacle of "a naked, suffering young man, either Jesus or one of the martyrs, notably St Sebastian," and is part of the latent homosexual structure of Christianity. At the same time, he is also distinctly Romantic and subject to Freudian discourses of inversion: "feminized" in his "long-haired, ultra-pale looks," "hyper-emotional" personality, and excessive closeness to his mother, he thus articulates patriarchal "correlations between physical appearance, emotional capacity and gender identity"[42] based on what Chris Faulkner has called a "philosophy of difference which defines being antithetically" in terms of harmful gender dichotomies.[43] "Both physically and narratively the sad young man is a stereotype of impermanence and transience," Dyer suggests, often inhabiting a "half-world" between the straight one that wants to mould his desire to suit the norms of emotionally repressed straight white masculinity, and the queer one he yearns to inhabit.[44]

St. Sebastian as sad young man is at the centre of *Lilies'* subversive gay politics. In Vallier, Simon, Bilodeau, and the tableau of their relationships (mounted for us by Greyson in their first scene together as they rehearse the St. Sebastian play in Roberval), we have the director's self-aware personification of the roles of the "half-world" in men's experience. The scene is staged and performed to foreground them as distinct types along the male homosocial continuum. Vallier, of course, is more or less out. Comfortable in his sexuality, he loves Simon openly and without shame. "Tell me you love me," he demands, pressing his body ardently against Simon's. Simon's position is more ambiguous. He *is* the exceptionally beautiful St. Sebastian, the icon of the stoically suffering, self-sacrificing, emotionally reticent white male subject in patriarchal culture, as well as that icon queered and sexualized, as he relishes the thought of being tied up by Vallier as the Archer Sanaé and penetrated by his arrows.[45] Yet living in the "half-world" between gay and straight, his love for Vallier is something he can't immediately bring himself to face.[46] Indeed, his father beats him savagely for it, and a marriage to the mysterious French aristocrat Lydie-Anne de Rozier (Alexander Chapman) is quickly arranged to keep Simon from Vallier and their attic trysts.[47] Then there is Bilodeau, the closeted homosexual who also loves Simon but, sexually rejected by him, ruins Simon's life and his love for Vallier. Here Greyson is clear in his layered symbolic use of Bilodeau both to queer the Catholic church and to expose the prison of masculinity in our culture. Throughout the play, Bishop Bilodeau is literally and figuratively trapped in the closet of the confessional booth and shot through its bars, the character resonating for Canadians with the scandals of the past decade involving the sexual abuse of young boys (from the residential schools to Mt. Cashel orphanage) by Catholic priests. It is the prison of masculinity, Greyson suggests, that has caused such suffering, as male religious authorities hide behind their institutional masks and gilded cloaks, and homosocial desire is pathologized. In *Lilies*, however, Greyson turns this prison of repressed masculinity into a melodramatic stage for the liberation of gay men. The prisoners in the film "act up," so to speak, using camp and drag and the kind of over-the-top theatricality Greyson loves to tell the moving and very beautiful love story of Vallier and Simon, and to expose the sad hypocrisy of the closeted Bilodeau, the Bishop who spends his life avoiding "something tremendous" that once happened in the attic and cannot be spoken: that he is homosexual and a murderer. As Dyer suggests, what out homosexuals have succeeded in facing about the sad-young-man image is that "one could not go on being him" and live an authentic and fulfilling life at the same time.[48] Like the best of the early gay liberationist films, *Lilies* takes the form of "the sexual political education of a sad young man who comes to realize that if he is unhappy it is not because of himself but because of social oppression."[49] Accordingly, Simon defies his father and the compulsory heterosexuality Roberval society tries to enforce by abandoning Lydie-Anne and attempting to run away with his true love, Vallier. However, trapped in the attic by Bilodeau on the morning they are to escape, Simon and Vallier are left to die with their love. It is only because Bilodeau cannot bring himself to let *his* true love die that Simon lives. Leaving his rival Vallier behind, Bilodeau rescues Simon but returns himself to the closet by testifying at trial that it was Simon who murdered Vallier after an argument about the need to terminate their "sick" relationship. The tragedy Bilodeau is eventually forced to face through Simon's belated revenge is that his own life as a man of God, in the closet of the confessional, has been a complete sham.

But so, Greyson suggests, have been the lives of the women in the story as they become disillusioned in their roles as haute bourgeois ladies, pampered and adored by their "gentlemen." If *Lilies* is a scathing indictment of the oppressiveness of the Catholic church and compulsory heterosexuality for gay men, it is also an overt political comment on the oppressiveness of the heterosexual contract for women in patriarchal culture. Finally facing the fact that Simon will never love her because he really loves Vallier, Lydie-Anne de Rozier takes Vallier's mother, the Countess Marie-Laure de Tilly (Brent Carver), down with her, revealing to the latter that her longed-for husband, the Count de Tilly, is never returning to Roberval but has in fact established himself in Europe with a new wife and child and completely forgotten that Marie-Laure exists. The suggestion, of course, is that Lydie-Anne knows this because she herself has had an affair with the Count. Together, Lydie-Anne and the Countess are Greyson's double indictment of the stereotype of "the woman scorned" in androcentric culture: the Countess as the aging wife cast aside for a younger model; Lydie-Anne as the exoticized black woman, exciting for a time but soon used and discarded, first by the Count (or someone like him) and then by Simon. However, where women scorned are often the butt of jokes about feminine cloyingness and hysteria, and are themselves turned into the problem in mainstream representations of the type, under Greyson's direction we empathize with rather than mock their vulnerability, humiliation, and emotional pain.[50]

Using the tools of the women's picture—tableau, masquerade, and melodramatic excess—to tell the story of women's suffering under oppressive patriarchal forms of socio-sexual relations, Greyson further thickens the symbolic weight of the *mise en scène* by having the parts of Lydie-Anne and the Countess played by men. However, where in his previous work Greyson has tended to use "bad drag" for comedic effect, in *Lilies* he uses "straight drag" for dramatic effect, bringing the emotional experience of women and gay men under patriarchy together in solidarity.[51] Kept women betrayed, wives, or closeted men: we all play parts in the service of the smooth running of patriarchal culture and the privilege of straight white men, *Lilies* clearly suggests. Moreover, we lie to ourselves in the name of the Father. Simon does, by placating his father's demands that he stop playing with boys and marry Lydie-Anne; Bilodeau does, by accepting social and church pressure to deny his sexual orientation; and Marie-Laure does, by creating a European fantasy life in Roberval and letting her cruel, duplicitous husband off the hook by killing herself. It is Lydie-Anne, in the moving scene between them in the drawing room, who forces the Countess to face the truth that she herself knows so well: that "all men are liars" and that all of Roberval is laughing at both her own and Marie-Laure's humiliation. As Lydie-Anne whispers the awful truth of their masquerade and self-deceit in Marie-Laure's ear, Greyson frames them in tableau, as mirror images, their Edwardian rectitude no longer masking their pain.

The dénouement comes directly after, as Greyson cuts to the Countess and Vallier at night, in the rowboat, on their way to their ultimate disillusion in the forest. The Countess knows she must give up her son—the only person who ever loved her—in order for him to live an authentic adult love with Simon. It is, symbolically, the night of Vallier's birthday, and the Countess becomes witness to Simon's birth as a gay man as well as he (finally, openly) acknowledges and declares his love for her son. She leaves them to pack her things for her ostensible trip back to Paris, and Greyson intercuts her preparations with their lovemaking, suggesting that Vallier's new life now requires her disappearance. Vallier and Simon follow her to her forest grave. "The hour has come for me to return to Paris," she says as she lies down in the dirt. "Your every move must be merciless. Steady and precise. Don't cry. We have to take leave of each other some day. It's the law of nature. Don't cry. Will you ever get rid of this habit? Don't spoil my legacy. Play the part. Play the part." Realizing he himself must give up his mother and her madness for the sake of his own life, Vallier reluctantly and painfully agrees to play his part in *her* legacy as a bourgeois mother, enabling her swan song in the sacrificial structure of the maternal melodrama. Crying "Look what your beloved Simon is giving up for you," she determines to give up her life for him as well. Reluctantly, Vallier strangles his mother with her scarf, lays a stem of white lilies on her breast, and, crying hysterically, falls into Simon's arms.[52]

As Patricia Hlachy suggests, "It is astonishing that Carver, despite his achingly human evocation of the Countess, was shut out of the Genie nominations," and equally so that Danny Gilmore and Alexander Chapman, nominated for best performance by an actor in a leading role as Vallier and best performance by an actor in a supporting role as Lydie-Anne, respectively, did not win.[53] In any case, the emotional register does not "belong" to women, Greyson's casting and directing, and these men's performances, seem to be suggesting, any more than it is anathema to men. As Hlachy observes, "there is nothing camp about these queens of hearts."[54] Clearly, for Greyson the affective identities of the male characters in *Lilies*, whether played straight or in drag, allow for what Christopher Faulkner has called "the production of a difference which *exceeds* the difference 'permitted' by the dominant order."[55] In Greyson's hands, the trope of the homosexual as sad young man in love with other men becomes an excessive and empowering image of a different kind of masculinity: a queer masculinity involving men openly displaying emotion, "holy sensitivity," and "stunning good looks" in the service of "overwhelming erotic experience and escape from the dreariness of real manliness."[56] *Lilies* grafts the power of a gay camp sensibility's use of drag to foreground the role-playing and masquerading that goes on in men's and women's lives across our culture onto the power of the popular form of melodrama both to put us in touch with our feelings as human beings and to critique the society in which we live. It is a film that deftly dialogizes forms, contents, audiences, institutions, and politics to create new meanings and, potentially, new identities—what Faulkner would surely applaud as *affective* identities that might help us imagine socio-sexual relations, and people, differently.

By way of conclusion, I will suggest that in John Greyson, the Canadian cultural landscape has produced an important queer voice: a dialogic imagination that works with the language, events, and forefathers of our shared discursive reality to speak the concerns of alternative communities and audiences, and in effect, to test what Faulkner has called the very limits of social possibility.[57] Whether he works in film or in video, with feature-length or short format, through the unbridled energy of the musical or the emotive potential of the melodrama, Greyson consistently seeks to challenge the masculine masks of institutional authority that have historically attempted to regulate and control desire, subjectivity, and sexual identity in their own interests. Using Canadian current events as a context for outing historical figures (from Brecht and Weill to the fictional composite Bishop Bilodeau) and as a vehicle for challenging aspects of heteronormative masculinity as a masquerade (from cowboys and hockey players to prime ministers and priests), his oeuvre documents, deconstructs, and de-deifies in the name of Grierson, Godard, God ... and Greyson's own socio-sexual dissent. There is every reason to expect that his next film, *The Law of Enclosure*, will carry on this admirable legacy.

Notes

Thanks to Chris Faulkner for pointing me toward Cavell's work and the connection between the attic in melodrama and the closet in Roberval.

1   Douglas Bell, "Greyson's exuberantly eccentric film defies description: *Uncut,*" *Globe and Mail*, 3 July 1998, C9.

2   Other awards include Audience Award at the 1997 Austin Gay and Lesbian International Film Festival for *Lilies*; Grand Jury Award for Outstanding Narrative Feature at the 1997 L.A. Outfest for *Lilies*; Audience Award at the 1997 San Francisco International Lesbian and Gay Film Festival for *Lilies*; Best Canadian Feature at the 1996 Montréal World Film Festival for *Lilies*; Best Canadian Feature Film Special Jury Citation at the 1993 Toronto Festival of Festivals for *Zero Patience*; Best Canadian Short Film at the 1991 Toronto Festival of Festivals for *The Making of 'Monsters.'* The latter film is out of circulation until 2001, due to a controversy over Greyson's use of Kurt Weill's music and image (Greyson cast a queer goldfish in one scene to represent Weill, and his estate has withdrawn all music rights). Distributors are anticipating a re-release of the film in 2001 when Weill's music passes into the public domain. See R. Bruce Brasell, "Queer Nationalism and the Musical Fag Bashing of John Greyson's *The Making of 'Monsters,'* " *Wide Angle* 16, no. 3 (1995): 33.

3   Peter Steven, *Brink of Reality: New Canadian Documentary and Video* (Toronto: Between the Lines, 1993), 148.

4   Steven, *Brink of Reality*, 147–48.

5   Steven, *Brink of Reality*, 148–49.

6   Steven, *Brink of Reality*, 151, 152.

7   Mikhail Bakhtin uses the term "heteroglossia" to describe the simultaneity of dialogues—speakers' perspectives and ways of speaking, or utterances—that characterize the social world as a polyphony of discursive forces. "Heteroglossia is a way of conceiving the world as made up of a roiling mass of languages ... All utterances are heteroglot in that they are shaped by forces whose particularity and variety are practically beyond systematization. The idea of heteroglossia comes as close as possible to conceptualizing a locus where the great

centripetal and centrifugal forces that shape discourse can meaningfully come together" (Michael Holquist, *Dialogism: Bakhtin and His World* [London and New York: Routledge, 1990], 69–70). Greyson's films and tapes, as his unique authorial utterances, emerge self-consciously out of this polyphony of discourses, playing with the centralizing or official forces of discourse to open them up, dialoguing with the utterances that come before, borrowing the forms and conventions of the past to fashion new meanings for the future.

8   Steven, *Brink of Reality*, 8.

9   Steven, *Brink of Reality*, 82.

10 Holquist, *Dialogism*, 22.

11 Holquist, "Answering as Authoring," *Bakhtin: Essays and Dialogues on His Work*, Gary Saul Morson, ed. (Chicago and London: University of Chicago Press, 1981), 70, 59.

12 Steven, *Brink of Reality*, 149, 239.

13 *Canadian Dimension* 31, no. 3 (May–June 1997): 11.

14 Graham, "*Uncut* is going to drive some people nuts," *San Francisco Chronicle*, 8 January 1999, C3.

15 Steven, *Brink of Reality*, 150.

16 See M.M. Bakhtin, *Art and Answerability: Early Philosophical Essays by M.M. Bakhtin*, Michael Holquist and Vadim Liapunov, eds.; Vadim Liapunov, trans. (Austin: University of Texas Press, 1990). See also Giovanni Palmieri, "'The Author' According to Bakhtin ... and Bakhtin the Author," in *The Contexts of Bakhtin*, David Shepherd, ed. (Australia: Harwood, 1998), who suggests that the author can only be understood "against a complex, polyphonic series of relationships" involving the author's own world, the narrative world, and the reader's world (55).

17 Steven, *Brink of Reality*, 151.

18 Steven, *Brink of Reality*, 147.

19 Steven, *Brink of Reality*, 149.

20 Peter Morris, "After Grierson: The National Film Board 1945–1953," in *Take Two: A Tribute to Film In Canada*, Seth Feldman, ed. (Toronto: Irwin/Festival of Festivals, 1984), 184.

21 Steven, *Brink of Reality*, 149.

22 Steven, *Brink of Reality*, 149.

23 Kass Banning, "Queerying John Greyson's *Zero Patience*," *Take One* 3 (Fall 1993), 20.

24 Steven, *Brink of Reality*, 150.

25 Respectively, Kass Banning, "Queerying John Greyson's *Zero Patience*," 21; Robert Cagle, "Tell the Story of My Life ... The Making of Meaning, 'Monsters,' and Music in John Greyson's *Zero Patience*," *The Velvet Light Trap* 35 (Spring 1995): 70; and Laura U. Marks, "Nice Gun You Got There: John Greyson's Critique of Masculinity," *Parachute* 66 (1992): 28.

26 Cagle, "Tell the Story of My Life," 70.

27 Where social-change documentaries have been terrified of humour because it seemed like mocking the oppressed, Greyson insists on breaking the taboo by making documents for social change that also entertain. For Greyson, humour has always been an important and empowering mechanism in allowing oppressed groups not only to fight back but also to loosen up and laugh at themselves as well as the conventions, institutions, entrenched ways of seeing that control them (Steven, *Brink of Reality*, 152). For this reason, he has always admired the surrealists, and Magritte in particular: "He was both incredibly philosophical and playful. He knew that his audiences weren't going to follow too far with scientific theories of perception, etc. so he made his paintings engaging and popular" (Steven, *Brink of Reality*, 152).

28 Steven, *Brink of Reality*, 149.

29 Steven, *Brink of Reality*, 149, 152.

30 Steven, *Brink of Reality*, 149.

31 Steven, *Brink of Reality*, 154.

32 Greyson's film is a more-or-less faithful adaptation of Bouchard's critically acclaimed hit play *Les feluettes ou la répétition d'un drame romantique* (1987). It has been translated by Linda Gaboriau as *Lilies or the Revival of a Romantic Drama* (Toronto: Coach House, 1990). Greyson, working on the script with Bouchard and Gaboriau, rewrites the play's ending somewhat, having Bilodeau trap Simon and Vallier in the attic rather than have Simon lock Bilodeau out, and himself and Vallier in, in order to carry out a kind of lovers' combination marriage vows/suicide pact. In any case, both versions end with Bilodeau rescuing Simon and leaving Vallier to die. See also an account of the adaptation and production process by Barbara Mainguy, "*Lilies*: The Adaptation of Michel Marc Bouchard's Award-winning Play," *Point of View* 30 (Fall 1996): 35–39.

33 Not to mention the general Canadian film culture as well. Nominated for fourteen Genies, *Lilies* took away four, including Best Art Direction, Costume Design, and Overall Sound, as well as Best Picture, thus beating out the favourites (Canada's premiere auteur, David Cronenberg and his film *Crash*, as well as Bruce McDonald's *Hard Core Logo)*.

34 Noreen Golfman, "Flowers for Greyson's Queer Cinema," *Canadian Forum* 75 (November 1996): 27.

35 Marks, "Nice Gun You Got There," 27, 29.

36 Marks, "Nice Gun You Got There," 30, 29.

37 Tony Rayns, "Uncut," *Sight and Sound* 8, no. 10 (October 1998): 60.

38 See, for example, *Prince of Tides* (Streisand, 1991), *Dead Man Walking* (Robbins, 1995), *Affliction* (Schrader, 1997), *Good Will Hunting* (Van Sant, 1997), and *Magnolia* (Anderson, 1999).

39 Liam Lacey, "John Greyson, an uncut above," *Globe and Mail*, 30 May 1997, C3.

40 Golfman, "Flowers for Greyson's Queer Cinema," 27–28.

41 Recent work on melodrama is particularly interested, as Pam Cook suggests, in tracing in its representations of the bourgeois family "the convergence of capitalist and patriarchal structures" in order to expose the relationships between power and gender. See Cook's *The Cinema Book* (London: British Film Institute, 1994), 73. As a theatrical genre involving the passions, melodrama has a long history. Thomas Elsaesser has argued that "in the hands of gifted directors and at the right historical moment it can be used to critique the society it represents" (Cook, *The Cinema Book*, 75). Pathos and irony can be used to externalize suppressed feelings onto the decor, gestures, and events of the *mise en scène*, creating, in effect, an excessive display—or melodramatic tableau—of the oppressive forces at work on women and men in bourgeois culture.

42 Richard Dyer, "Coming out as going in: The image of the homosexual as a sad young man," in *The Matter of Images* (London and New York: Routledge, 1993), 77–79.

43 The logic of which dichotomous thinking goes "If he's half naked, vulnerable, and emotional, he must be a woman." Christopher Faulkner, "Affective Identities: French National Cinema and the 1930s," *Canadian Journal of Film Studies* 3, no. 2 (Fall 1994).

44 Dyer, "Coming out as going in," 88, 86.

45 As Dyer suggests, the story of St. Sebastian has a decided appeal to gay men, with its erotic subtext involving the love of Sanaé, the Archer, for Sebastian. According to legend, Sebastian was a soldier in the Roman army (ca. 283) who made numerous converts to Christianity by curing afflictions and freeing slaves. When it was discovered that Sebastian was Christian, Emperor Diocletian and Caesar ordered him executed. He was tied

to a tree, shot with arrows, and left for dead, but then nursed back to health by an empathetic woman. Denouncing Diocletian for his cruelty to Christians, Sebastian was finally beaten to death. He is celebrated as the patron saint of archers, athletes, and soldiers, and is appealed to for protection against plagues (see "St. Sebastian" in *Catholic Online Saints*, www.saints.catholic.org/saints/stsindex; accessed 3 May 2001). The parallels between Sebastian's plight and the persecution of gay men are obvious; the status of Sebastian as protector against plagues has clear resonance for gay men in the age of AIDS; and there is a certain masochism in Sebastian's yearning to die in order to "escape eternal darkness" and be reborn that appeals to the homosexual-as-sad-young-man stereotype. Thus, St. Sebastian has become an important figure for gay culture. Under Greyson's direction, however, irony, humour, and sexual innuendo bubble under the surface and over the top of the staid Christian version of the story, as Simon's interest in being tied up offers a gentle nod to contemporary gay S/M sexual practices, and Vallier and Simon simply carry on kissing when Father Saint-Michel, the priest directing the Roberval production who asks for as much fervour as the boys can muster, leaves the stage to find Bilodeau.

46 A confusion perhaps best symbolized in his pyromania, which, significantly, is displaced onto Bilodeau and becomes the latter's *modus operandi* toward the end of the film, as he sets Lydie-Anne de Rozier's balloon alight to prevent her from taking Simon away and then the attic to prevent Vallier from doing so.

47 The attic "half-world" of Roberval's Saint Sebastian's School for Boys is the place where Simon and Vallier retreat with their hidden love and, by extension, the metaphorical stand-in for the closet as well as the site of what is clearly Bilodeau's "homosexual panic." For an elaboration of the concept of homosexual panic, which she sees as endemic to heterosexual males since broad developments in Western social formations beginning in the nineteenth century, see Eve Kosofsky Sedgwick's *The Epistemology of the Closet* (Berkeley: University of California Press, 1990). The attic in the melodramatic tradition, of course, is a highly overdetermined image: the psycho-sexual site of dirty secrets, of the forbidden, of the unspeakable, and, often, of madness. See Stanley Cavell's *Contesting Tears: The Hollywood Melodrama of the Unknown Woman* (Chicago and London: University of Chicago Press, 1996) for a detailed examination of the philosophical meaning of closets, "private chambers," outside of which "something tremendous cannot be spoken" (153). Bilodeau forms a central figure in Greyson's tableau as his homosexual panic crescendos near the end of the film, when he finally begins to speak his fascination with the boys in the attic and offers to help them escape to a "Garden of Eden" where "no one will ever find us." "I'm so glad to be your friend again," he says to Simon. "We're gonna pray so hard. We're gonna tell each other all our bad thoughts. I'm not going to the seminary any more. It's more important to dedicate my life to a saint. Give me a kiss. A little saint's kiss." When Simon rejects Bilodeau's religiously couched sexual advances, the latter panics. "Then you two can rot in hell," he screams, setting the room ablaze and abandoning his "sick" companions to each other.

48 Dyer, "Coming out as going in," 90.

49 Dyer, "Coming out as going in," 89.

50 See, for example, *Fatal Attraction* (Lyne, 1987) or *Play Misty for Me* (Eastwood, 1971).

51 For Greyson, "a man in drag is always an overdetermined image," and drag history has a number of "different streams" and permutations (Steven, *Brink of Reality,* 153). With the "bad drag" involving the CBC reporter in *The World Is Sick (Sic)*, Greyson suggests, there is "no mistaking the reporter for a real woman"; in fact, she looks more like "Harpo Marx," which cues the audience to take her and the institution she symbolizes less than seriously (Steven, *Brink of Reality*, 88, 153). With the "straight drag" in *Lilies*, however, the subtlety of the drag performances cues a more profound contemplation of masquerade, gender values, and the fluidity of gender identity in our culture.

52 The funereal lilies of the title thus manifest overtly in Greyson's melodramatic *mise en scène* as a double political symbol for feminists and gay men: on the one hand, of Marie-Laure's death as the self-abnegation patriarchal family structures and values require of women and mothers; and on the other hand, of Vallier's coming of age as the awakening of an out homosexual who leaves behind the crippling "excessive closeness to his mother" of the sad-young-man stereotype.

53 Patricia Hlachy, "Lilies," *Maclean's,* 11 November 1996, 76.

54 Hlachy, "Lilies," 76.

55 Faulkner, "Affective Identities," 16.

56 Dyer, "Coming out as going in," 90.

57 Faulkner, "Affective Identities," 10.

Srinivas Krishna
and the New Canadian Cinema
Lysandra Woods

WITH TWO FEATURE FILMS TO DATE, Srinivas Krishna is in the process of redefining both what it means to be Canadian and what it means to be a Canadian film. Alongside a mainstream discourse that would have the young, white Joe represent, on behalf of Molson's, the righteousness of Canadians against a befuddled American audience who think we all say "ah-boot," Krishna evinces no interest in either Joe's beer-guzzling agenda or the overdetermined insecurity that has governed Canada's on-screen relations with its gigantesque neighbour down south. The fact that Krishna ignores Joe's plight only sets into relief how much of English-Canadian cinema still takes Joe (or a Joe-like conundrum) as a given. Neither are Krishna's films, *Masala* (1991) and *Lulu* (1996), exemplary of what has heretofore been the popular, accepted means of representing alterity within Canada. Cameron Bailey calls this paradigm "the cinema of duty" and describes it as

> Social-issue oriented in content, documentary realist in style, firmly responsible in inten-
> tion—[it] positions its subjects in direct relation to social crisis, and attempts to articulate
> problems and solutions to problems within a framework of centre and margin, white and
> non-white communities.[1]

Suffice to say that Krishna's works do not fall neatly into this schema: he champions heterogeneity rather than homogeneity, relishes problems rather than solutions, and prefers the confrontation rather than the liberal platitude.

Perhaps due to this position, Krishna is hardly a consistent voice. The task of discussing his two films as working along an auteurist vein (shared themes, interests, styles, and tones) is at best a dodgy prospect: his films can be put into dialogue with one another, but they disagree as often as they concur. Tracking his films, one runs the inverted course from postmodernism to modernism: the breezy headiness of *Masala* has all but vanished by the time we reach the sombre *Lulu*, a transition that suggests the two modes are more firmly intertwined than is often admitted, working off instead of supplanting one another. Indeed, the fascination of examining

Krishna's still-nascent body of work is the manner in which gender, race, pop, and identity inflect both the postmodernism/modernism debate and the two forms themselves.

Coming from the perspective of marginalized voices, *Masala* and *Lulu* produce a space for dissonance, one that has long been open in Canada's National Film Board documentary practice but seldom seeped into English-Canadian features. However, if Krishna exhibits a radical documentary spirit, his films eschew any aesthetic of the *cinéma-vérité*/direct-cinema brand, opting instead for a studied artifice. *Masala* especially throws reality and realism to the wind, offering up a concoction of postmodern pastiche—high camp, musical numbers, otherworldly communications, historical incidents, and caricature—that calls to mind John Greyson's *Zero Patience* (1993).

The comparison is apt. *Masala* and *Zero Patience* offer fractured, critical portraits of life on the straight, white, and narrow road of Canadiana. These films do not rest on defining themselves within Bailey's framework of centre and margin, white and non-white (or straight and queer); rather, both send forth a dialectical version of what it means to be Canadian, to be East Indian, or to be queer. This dialectic, by its insistence on hybridity, questions the putative stability of any "normative" centre. Both films also offer much unabashed fun, and this itself is something of an anomaly on the English-Canadian cinematic landscape.

In a sense, *Masala* and *Zero Patience* argue that the postmodern moment is nowhere more clearly articulated than within minority communities, existing under the double aegis of "us" and "them," fragmented between a local sense of self and a conflicting, overarching national narrative. In an interview with Roy Grundmann, Krishna reflects on these tensions, tensions that in some sense rely on postmodernism for an articulation, if not a tenable solution:

> *Masala* is a mixture. All these different spices come together in Indian cooking, forming a flavour that wasn't there before; neither is it there in any one of the particular spices—one of the things is greater than the sum of its parts. But it's a very tenuous unity. Mixture to me is about purity and impurity, authenticity and inauthenticity ...[2]

The masala movie is a Bollywood genre, full of high emotion and usually revolving around the antics of a three-generation household upset by the arrival of a Westernized daughter-in-law. Maintaining a few Bollywood-style musical sequences, *Masala* goes on to toy with the formula: moving the setting from Bombay to Toronto, switching the Westernized daughter-in-law for the Westernized ex-con Krishna, and bringing in the god Krishna and a subplot concerning a valuable postage stamp. *Masala*, then, opens up a forum in which various incarnations of popular culture mingle with the sacred and sacredly Canadian. Refusing to play the popular off the authentic, the film upsets distinctions between the two, charting the difficulty of situating them as wholly disparate entities: the masala movie is "authentically" Indian; it is also "authentically" pop. "Krishna" is a god; he is also an ex-con.

Caught between competing directives of home, tradition, modernity, and the present, and wary of favouring one ingredient over the other, *Masala* serves up a mishmash. This strategy is borne out in the film's hodgepodge of cultural imagery: the blue-skinned god Krishna adorned in a Toronto Maple Leafs jersey, Lallu Bhai's kitchen table covered in an array of Indian dishes and an air popper churning out a seemingly never-ending bowl of popcorn. Indeed, if Godard called his characters the children of Marx and Coca-Cola, Krishna's could well be the children of curry and popcorn: the former being history, tradition, and home, and the latter being the movies.

Movies, television, all things pop weave themselves into *Masala*'s tapestry, and perhaps the friendly greeting they receive marks the greatest distance between *Lulu* and *Masala*. Withholding judgement one way or another, the mediated image in *Masala* is a fact of the contemporary landscape, although accepting this fact can be a mitigated enterprise. Tellingly, for the female character, Rita, enjoying the mediation involves a rewrite. That is, while her Uncle Lallu Bhai and her cousin Anil construct a dream life very much along the grain of patriarchy, the sort of material one finds in every beer commercial or mainstream film, Rita must read against it. She, like the film itself, understands that pop culture (at times) must be tinkered with and repositioned to gain satisfying purchase. Lallu Bhai, Anil, and Rita all experience exotic fantasy sequences, but whereas the former pair revel in an imagined space that would allow them mastery over a domain of adoring, nubile women—Lallu Bhai on stage at his fashion show surrounded by half-clothed models and Anil in bed with his hoped-for fiancée—Rita's fantasy, incorporating the same mélange of English, Hindi, Bollywood, and music video as her uncle's, resituates the gender codes in her favour. Casting herself as the daring adventurer, Rita flies off into the wild blue yonder while her ex-boyfriend Anil is left behind, stretching his arms outwards in the typically feminine position of yearning. The imaginings of Anil never amount to more than fodder for masturbatory sessions, whereas Rita, and even Grandma Tikoo, arranges elements of the popular to feed her reality. Bollywood-inspired landscapes or television become the avenue through which conflicting desires can be melded: Rita can be an independent woman, the sexy star of a Bollywood film, and insist that she will not go to medical school but take flying lessons; Grandma Tikoo can live in a Toronto suburb and commune with the god Krishna via her VCR.

In contradistinction to *Masala*'s benign positioning of both popular culture and the technology that is its livelihood, *Lulu* regards the two as forces of oppression for its eponymous protagonist. Lulu "meets" her future husband, Lucky (a total loser), through a cheesy East–West Connection mail-order-bride video, which has each woman walk onto the stage and smile while a game-show-like voice-over lists her various attributes—a representation that elides the dire circumstances that have put the women on stage in the first place. In the department store where Lulu works, a stack of monitors play a rap video containing intercut footage of the Vietnam War to match its funky street beat. The screen in *Lulu* is pernicious, chewing up histories and individuals, spewing forth a barrage of meaningless imagery. Even a kindly intentioned Chilean documentarian who is making a film to give voice to Canadian refugees fails to record Lulu's story on tape (although he does capture Lulu's husband at his stubbornly aggressive worst). Lulu never finds a space to narrate herself or place her story within a broader context; indeed, the film argues that no such space exists, that the other's story remains beyond the threshold of a dominant Canadian narrative: Lulu is left marooned, and popular culture further obfuscates her situation.

The postmodernity of *Masala* and the modernity of *Lulu* stand as a testament that the chasm between the two movements is as much about attitude and tone as it is about content. In *Masala*, the popular is an obstacle course, but one that can be navigated; in *Lulu*, the popular is a monstrosity that thwarts Lulu's voice rather than providing her with the material for, at the least, an imaginative self-expression. This demonization of the mass media calls up a prominent split in the postmodernism/modernism entanglement—a split that has everything to do with gender. In her essay "The Terror of Pleasure: The Contemporary Horror Film and Postmodern Theory," Tania Modleski notes that, for many critics, the postmodern and the modern boil down to how the two map themselves in relation to pleasure or popular art. Modleski observes that proponents of both modernism and postmodernism exhibit a tendency "to make mass culture into the 'other' of whatever, at any given moment, they happen to be championing—and, moreover, to denigrate that other primarily because it allegedly provides pleasure to the consumer."[3] However, this targeting of pleasure (or, as Lionel Trilling named it, the "specious good") may, for women, be cause for concern. Modleski maintains that

> [this] point needs to be stressed, since feminism has occasionally made common cause with the adversarial critics on the grounds that we too have been oppressed by the specious good. But this is to overlook the fact that in some profound sense we have also been historically and psychically identified with it.[4]

Thus, through a series of conflations—the popular with pleasure and pleasure with woman—the woman ironically stands in for a force she also has a stake in challenging. The way out of this double bind could well be postmodernism, if, as Modleski argues, postmodernism is not viewed as simply carrying forth modernism's "subversive" agenda but in fact revamping its very terms, specifically in regards to pleasure.

Modleski's paradigm keenly asserts itself in the gap between *Masala* and *Lulu*. Neither film grants mastery to its male characters or, for that matter, to anyone in the text, yet *Masala* views this situation with a certain amount of humour, even liberation, evincing no nostalgia for the days of an unquestioned male voice of authority. *Lulu* is prone to brooding—a tone that Lulu herself partakes in, but one that also plays out against her. In this sense, the film adheres to Modleski's thesis, in that

> the mastery [modernism] no longer permits through effecting closure or eliciting narcissistic identification is often reasserted through projecting the experience of submission and defencelessness onto the female body. In this way the texts enable the male spectator to distance himself somewhat from the terror. And, as usual it is the female spectator who is truly deprived of "solace and pleasure."[5]

The film is sympathetic towards Lulu, yet at the same time one could argue that the film as much participates in as critiques Lulu's predicament.

Lulu is kept cryptic, frustratingly enigmatic; lacking a voice, she is simply a body of exchange between the various men in her life, a body on which they can write out both their frustrations and desires: her father insistently arm wrestles with her; her husband and his friend, Clive, situate Lulu in a sexual triangle that has more to do with their personal rivalry than it does with her. Sex in *Lulu* is simply a commodity market, whereas in *Masala*, Rita and Krishna can experience a mutually salutary fling that offers Krishna one of the few personal ties he respects. Consuming bodies, bodies consumed, objects of exchange saturate *Lulu*: Clive works for a nebulous corporation that purchases human corpses for parts; a joke nudie pen and an engagement ring travel from character to character (suggesting that it is the material world, not the emotional, that binds); Lulu herself functions much like an object, a physical presence rather than an individual. To represent this state of affairs is obviously not to condone it, but it is, after all is said and done, what the film offers: a text that on the one hand rejects consumption and pleasure, but on the other provides Lulu for male solace. She pays for the male crisis through both her body and her silence.

The point is not that postmodernism is female-friendly while modernism is not, but that the series of conflations Modleski pinpoints do work as structuring elements in *Lulu*, leaving its heroine nowhere. By opening itself up to the charges of courting pleasure (both diegetically and extradiegetically), *Masala* renders a site for both female voice and fantasy. Moreover, if male mastery is mourned in *Lulu*, the mourner is most obviously Lulu's white husband, Lucky. The film's modernist bent is to some degree the result of Lucky's perspective, a projection of his quiet hysteria as his marriage slowly unravels. Perhaps the transgressive aspect of *Masala*'s own brand of postmodern adversity is that it chooses not to mourn the loss of mastery but to revel in its possibilities.

Masala intuits that to be a visible-minority male in Canada is already to be at one remove from the site of power, but this position is not covertly assuaged by launching an attack against the female body. The film has other targets in sight, most notably the structures, strictures, and myths of a putatively harmonious multicultural nation. On this front, *Masala* channels its pop landscape to decidedly critical ends. Modleski notes that Fredric Jameson laments "the fact that art is no longer 'explosive and subversive,' no longer 'critical, negative, contestatory ... opposi-tional' and the like," but has demeaned itself by "incorporating images and stereotypes from our pop cultural past."[6] But what shall art contest? Capitalism, of course—but does only one site of contention exist? If the effects of capitalism do not affect equally, Jameson himself is dangerously near a position of universality and seems to be championing a monolithic course of opposition.

By asking who is the "our" in "our pop cultural past" and what is the popular, *Masala* contests the very model that Jameson supposes we all know exists—not an entirely innocent presump-tion. The popular in *Masala* is unsubtitled Hindi, Bollywood movies, American music videos, television, and the campy god Krishna, all of which make Modleski's case compelling when she argues that "perhaps the contemporary artist continues to be subversive by being nonadversarial in the modernist sense."[7] By appropriating pop rather than repudiating it, while pointing up that this embrace of popular culture is not akin to welcoming the conditions of production from which it springs, *Masala*'s critical work is very much about pulling off the blind from "us" and "them" relations, deconstructing the ideals on which the modern state fashions itself.

Set within the South Asian community of Toronto, *Masala* interrogates community itself, for the absence in the film is precisely any cohesion or connection. Initially, this lack is set off by the arrival of the young, hoodlum-like Krishna in the lives of his upper-class relatives, a milieu that cannot contain this familial black sheep. However, Krishna's arrival only serves to expose the al-ready-existing fissures, and once the surface starts cracking, all the fault lines give way: subcul-tures within subcultures, race, gender, class, and generations all fragment beyond easy reconcili-ation. *Masala* avoids any trite solutions and concerns itself with posing difficult questions. What does it mean to be a community? How can community function within an intricate matrix of conflicting demands that set members at cross purposes? The characters in *Masala* are too diverse to fall under any one unifying aegis: what does it mean that multiculturalism denies this, opting instead to slot Other communities into the liminal space marked beforehand to contain difference itself as a homogenous grouping? At issue, then, is the dominant narrative of pleasing cultural diversity that is multicultural Canada. *Masala* undoes this version and sends up the multicultural agenda as a specious gesture, ensnaring Other communities safely away in the margins—a peculiarly Canadian version of ghetto-ization.

Multiculturalism is a modern-day version of bread and circuses. It encourages a lot of commotion through an ongoing series of cultural events, temple openings, and parades, but the noise tends to drown out dissonance and distract from access to real power. The rituals of participation come to replace rather than reinforce community: Krishna is killed in the street while the rest of his family is absorbed in various facets of a Krishna parade. Throughout *Masala*, a culturally diverse Canada is overseen by the slick minister of multiculturalism, a man who divides the members of the South Asian contingent between those who play by his rules and benefit, and those who do not—potential "revolutionaries" unable to, in his words, "compromise."

However, the compromise on which multiculturalism thrives works against minority cultures. Through the divine workings of the god Krishna, Harry Tikoo comes to take possession of a valuable Canadian stamp, and for the first time ever Harry finds himself with a stake in the national thing: "I have the stamp and people notice me." The stamp itself is a fairly tongue-in-cheek version of Canadianness, the first stamp to depict an animal—Canada's national beaver—rather than a *Homo sapiens*. Harry's reluctance to part with the stamp is condemned by both the Canadian government and his family: the former considers Harry an incendiary element while the latter is angry that Harry will not sell a stamp that could erase the family debt. Working in collusion with Harry's daughter, the minister offers Harry an out, which he accepts. He donates the stamp to a newly created museum of philately where he will act as guest curator. Multiculturalism, *Masala* argues, is an attempt to ensure difference never lays any claim to power or economic gain, and Harry fumbles his one chance to bargain. The "revolutionary" is quieted, accepting a comfortable, albeit peripheral, haven.

The museum is, of course, opened in an officious manner, replete with ribbon-cutting and speeches. No doubt it will be spin-doctored as another instance of a multicultural success—the food at the event is a mixture of both Western and Eastern goodies. What gets lost in the official translation is that instead of challenging white supremacy, multiculturalism duplicates its workings. In accordance with critic Slavoj Zizek, *Masala*'s perspective is that

> Multiculturalism is a disavowed, inverted, self-referential form of racism, a "racism with a distance"—it represents the Other's identity conceiving the Other as a self-enclosed "authentic" community towards which he, the multiculturalist, maintains a distance rendered possible by his privileged position. Multiculturalism is a racism that renders its own position devoid of all positive content (the multiculturalist is not a direct racist, he doesn't oppose to the Other the particular values of his culture), but nonetheless retains this position as the privileged empty point of universality from which one is able to appreciate (and depreciate) properly other particular cultures—the multiculturalist respect for the Other's specificity is the very form of asserting one's own superiority.[8]

The gap between the patronizing rhetoric of the minister and the young hoods who terrorize Bibi (and later kill Krishna) is minute indeed, for both positions come from a belief in the right to make a judgement call: appreciate or depreciate. *Masala* proposes that multiculturalism fails not in reifying theory into practice, but in its very tenets: offering not a break with but a reformulation of systemic racism.

Masala's critique of multiculturalism carries over into its representational strategy, foregoing either positive roles or nuanced characterization in favour of broadly drawn stereotypes. This gambit has garnered much negative response, but the move encompasses ground that positive or individual portraits would fail to cover. In an interview with Cameron Bailey, Krishna has defended his choice, stating,

> These are stock characters in the way you would find stock characters in Restoration comedies. But every stock character here has some kind of slippage. What I'm trying to do is say that things aren't what they appear to be, people aren't the stereotypes they appear to be ...[9]

So, for instance, Grandma Tikoo, initially the stalwart upholder of tradition and homeland, also covets the food processor of her nephew's wife, claiming the mortar and pestle an inferior appliance. The Sikh terrorist everyone assumes is heading an arms-smuggling operation is, in fact, delivering the written history of the Sikh people on his revolutionary toilet paper: "Everyone has time to read on the loo." Uncle Tikoo, the epitome of obsequiousness—he apologizes for his clumsiness when he is knocked over by a garbage can Krishna kicks at him—turns momentarily intractable when the stamp falls into his possession. Anil's arranged bride, churned out to him in a sari and veil, proves resolutely "modern" when she rejects him as a wimp (as she has rejected 250 other men). The stereotype goes only so far before it breaks down; nonetheless, despite the breakage, characterization functions for the most part within recognizable types. But this ploy pays dividends of its own.

Within the general anti-realist framework of the film, stereotypes pointedly draw attention to the currency in which Other communities trade within dominant discourse (a parody of the "authentic" community), while attempting to own these types for divergent ends. As Richard Dyer has observed in his book *Gays in Film*, the drawback of normative representation is

> [t]hat these norms themselves, by their focus on uniqueness and inner growth, tend to prevent people from seeing themselves in terms of class, sex group or race. The very density, richness, refinement and 'roundness' of these characterizations ... make it very difficult to think of there being solidarity ... collective identity.[10]

As much as collective identity is lacking in the film, it wants the plurality of community to take precedence over any one viewpoint, a de-centring that undoes a representational norm that would idealize the individual and all the baggage the individual entails: namely, the foregrounding of "experience" over ideological effect or social policy.

Stereotypes reinforce the sense that the characters are stuck, defined by meagre parts that prove stifling. Krishna tries on a posture of rebel-without-a-cause alienation to voice his disgruntlement, yet the role that allows him to voice his anger also keeps him in a position of economic impoverishment and isolated angst, leaving him increasingly vulnerable. With bitter irony, his death comes at the hand of a surly white youth who has obviously bought into the same tough-guy stance of disaffection.

Characterization in *Masala* carries a dual register: on the one hand, forcing the conflict to play out at the level of the communal; and on the other, invoking stereotypes as the literal translation of Canada's official multiculturalism, which, the film suggests, is founded on situating

Other communities in reductive and stagnant roles of hyphenated Canadians. The final stand-off, between an armed group of Canadian Mounties and the Sikh "terrorists," insists on the recognition that otherness is always already operating within a circumscribed space, calling up the fervour over correct Mountie headgear—a moment when popular opinion deemed the other had crossed the line. *Masala* parlays multiculturalism as a plan that both rests on and perpetuates stereotyping, an elaborate double bluff that offers the other the opportunity to remain other as long as that role will not impinge on the "rights" of dominant culture.

This being the case, *Masala*'s representational strategy further worries the divide between authenticity/inauthenticity within the arena of self-identity. Stereotypes send up identity as performative rather than essential (an aspect further underlined by the use of actor Saeed Jaffrey, who plays three roles); the disjuncture within the stereotypes offers identity as a series of provisional alliances and continual modifications rather than a foretold entity. Within the postmodern state, Cindy Patton argues that

> identity operates performatively in a practical and temporary space, a situation ... Competing rhetorics of identity interpellate individuals to moral positions that carry with them requirements for action. Identity is an issue of deontology, not ontology; it is a matter of duties and ethics, not of being.[11]

Masala views this incarnation of identity politics as a viable mode; troubling, though, are the limitations and paucity of the "proper" action.

Roles, performance, stereotypes, and identity also preoccupy *Lulu*, the paradox of Lulu's move to Canada being that she finds her new environs offer no chance for her to partake in the putative freedoms of the modern state. Instead, the move entrenches Lulu as a stereotype: a submissive, diffident Asian beauty. Stuck in front of her vanity table every morning, Lulu goes through an elaborate face-painting ritual, a voiceless geisha aware that she is trading on her looks and equally aware that, finally, they give her purchase on nothing. She arranges her life so that she sees as little of Lucky as possible, dividing her time among work at a cosmetics counter in a glaringly impersonal department store, writing letters to a former lover (possibly husband) whom she left behind, and visiting her ailing mother and irascible father. The locations Lulu traverses are treated almost theatrically, with little sense of theme. Instead, each is a set piece, introducing an arena in which Lulu plays out her disparate roles of worker, wife, refugee, and loving daughter—roles that do not reward her with a forum in which she can tell her own story. Her job is mind-numbingly dull, keeping her trapped behind a counter as her boss screens her on a video-surveillance monitor. Her marriage is a sham: Lucky claims to love her but is unwilling (or unable) to call her by her name, Quyen, referring to her as Lulu, a nickname that, as his friend Clive comments, belongs to a pet. Imagining her created anew for his needs, with no past outside her appearance on an East–West Connection video, Lucky provides no opportunity for Lulu to give voice to her life. His attitude is mirrored by that of her father, who greets her visits with an onslaught of complaints and reprimands, never considering (or caring) that his daughter may have frustrations of her own.

Between her morning ritual, the dislocation of space, even her "stage name," Quyen is performing in a limited play, one in which she never has the choice lines and one in which her function is reduced to image. Her husband could not resist her on video viewing, and Clive claims to love her "from when I first saw you." But the trade into which Lulu is able to enter gives her little currency: she merely keeps herself in circulation like the objects around her. Simultaneously, while her image betrays her, it also protects her: the mask she paints on every morning is her buffer zone. Her choice seems to be either specious interaction or complete isolation, with the former being a bit part in another's fantasy, and the latter leaving her alone with her guilt over abandoning a loved one and uprooting her parents to a country that her father loathes.

Lulu, though, is finally offered a way out, and interestingly, this option comes from her mother—it takes a woman to shatter the film's modernist melancholy. After the sudden death of her father, Quyen discovers that her mother has sold his body. Shocked by the news, she berates her mother's decision, only to be greeted with a matter-of-fact question: "How much is the cheque?" (the first line her mother speaks). Acutely aware of her father's wish to return home, Lulu murmurs, "Dad would be so angry with us." But the mother's response to this is unexpected for both Lulu and the viewer: "As if we could ever please him. Don't blame me. Your father blamed me so much. He couldn't see me. He could only see his regrets. Save your pity for the living." By speaking to her daughter in this fashion—adhering to a convention of sorts—Lulu's mother offers her comfort by sharing a kind of oral history. But this spoken account prefers forgetting to remembering. The final shot of the film has Lulu sitting once more in front of the vanity table, though now she is not making up her face but tearing up her stack of unanswered letters. Lulu practices a tentative smile (a smile that looks like it hurts). On this ambiguous note, the film ends.

The words of Lulu's mother clearly signal a departure from *Lulu*'s moodiness; less clear is whether or not this will prove liberating. As far as the diegetic text goes, the mother provides a bracingly pragmatic elixir to the various men in the film, all of whom want to romanticize notions of love, honour, and loyalty despite the fact that they cannot live up to the imperatives this code would demand. Lucky may rail against Clive for selling her mother's body, but when Clive is not looking he wrestles the wedding ring off her finger. Lulu's mother ties the film to *Masala*, ephemerally recovering a buoyant attitude in which all bets are off and no expectations will be met according to tired formula.

Either figuratively or literally, both films stipulate that going home is not an option. This is a view Krishna has discussed with Grundmann in reference to a real-life incident that shows up repeatedly in *Masala*:

> There was a plane that blew up over the Atlantic, going back from Toronto and Montréal to Bombay—they suspected Sikh terrorists. I knew people on that flight from the University of Toronto. Almost four years after that, I started thinking about the incident in terms of the question, "Can one really go home?" Home, it seems, is not the place one has left. The problem is the search for authenticity and origin. Upon returning to where one has come from one won't find these things because one is already destabilized.[12]

This is the very destabilization that *Masala* takes glee in exploiting: by questioning the longing for authenticity, the film sends up authenticity itself. In *Lulu*, the longing fuels a modernist quest, but in the end Quyen's mother suggests that to crave the authentic, to crave your home rather than your surroundings, is to pave the way for misery and regret. In terms of Canadian cinema, the contribution of Krishna's work is the manner in which his films smash open what it means to take Canada for a home.

In closing, then, I will return to the beginning: to the Molson's beer campaign, a series of ads that insist on recognition for both the ferocity with which they declare their Canadian-Canadianness and for the import they inadvertently shed onto the riskiness of any discursive identity. As Kieran Keohone notes of the Molson's campaign, as much as it patrols the boundaries of national identity, it also unwittingly advertises

> the hollowness, the original Lack (of meaning) which underpins the identity Canadian ... One could imagine other articulations of "what Canada is all about": a portrayal of the enjoyment of Afrofest, or the enjoyment of various Others not represented in the dominant articulation: a representation of life (existence/enjoyment [?] on a Native reserve; a wife being beaten up by a drunken husband: isn't that equally "what beer [read "what being Canadian"] is all about"?).[13]

Aren't curry, Krishna, Bollywood, and Vietnamese mail-order brides equally Canadian, especially if we are, in fact, a multicultural nation? Portrayals of otherness, of course, abound in Canadian cinema. The distinctiveness of Srinivas Krishna's contribution is that *Masala*'s modernity, and even the manner in which *Lulu* finally throws over its modernist journey, celebrates the arbitrary nature of the discourse, rather than attempting to create an inviolable mould for future reference.

Notes

1   Cameron Bailey, "What the Story Is: An Interview with Srinivas Krishna," *CineAction!* 28 (Spring 1992): 38.

2   Roy Grundmann, "Where Is This Place Called Home?" *Cinemaya* 23 (Spring 1994): 19.

3   Tania Modleski, "The Search for Tomorrow in Today's Soap Opera: Notes on a Feminine Narrative Form," *Film Quarterly* 33, no. 1 (Fall 1979): 693.

4   Modleski, "The Terror of Pleasure," 699.

5   Modleski, "The Terror of Pleasure," 699.

6   Modleski, "The Terror of Pleasure," 700.

7   Modleski, "The Terror of Pleasure," 700.

8   Slavoj Zizek, "Multiculturalism, Or, the Cultural Logic of Multinational Capitalism," *New Left Review* 255 (1997): 44.

9   Bailey, "What The Story Is," 43.

10   Richard Dyer, "Stereotyping," in *Gays In Film*, Richard Dyer, ed. (New York: Zoetrope, 1984), 36.

11   Cindy Patton, "Tremble Hetero Swine!" in *Fear of a Queer Planet: Queer Politics and Social Theory*, Michael Warner, ed. (Minneapolis: University of Minnesota Press, 1983), 148.

12   Grundmann, "Where Is This Place," 24.

13   Kieran Keohone, "Symptoms of Canada: National Identity and the Theft of National Enjoyment," *CineAction!* 28 (Spring 1992): 21.

Fire and Ice
The Films of Guy Maddin
Steven Shaviro

1. "To ME, THE PRIMARY COLOURS OF MY LIFE are yearning and humiliation, in a melodrama ... [W]ith unrequited love, it's not over until you've totally humiliated yourself."

2. This is Guy Maddin, describing his 1997 film *Twilight of the Ice Nymphs*. But the remark could apply just as well to his three previous feature films: *Tales from the Gimli Hospital* (1988), *Archangel* (1990), and *Careful* (1992). Maddin's movies are all delirious poems of romantic misery. They all play with the form of melodrama to tell stories of unrequited love. They all wallow in feelings of yearning and humiliation. And one more thing: they are all extremely funny.

3. Maddin's films are driven by a tension between romantic excess on the one hand and absurdist humour on the other. This could also be called a contradiction between gorgeous-ness and camp, or between the beautiful (rather than the sublime) and the ridiculous.

4. In the first place, Maddin's films are visually ravishing. They are beautiful, frame by frame, in a way that has almost nothing to do with meaning or plot. The backlighting, the shadows, the frontal close-ups, the figures in silhouette, the arbitrary jump-cuts: these all seem to exist for their own sakes. Maddin's images are entirely non-functional. They do nothing to advance the story. They are also not means of thematic expression, because they have nothing beyond themselves to express; they arrest the gaze, rather than moving it onward. Maddin's images belong to a cinema of spectacle, or a "cinema of attractions" (in Tom Gunning's well-known phrase), rather than to any sort of narrative impulse.

5. At the same time, Maddin's films are chock full of narrative, even to excess. They tell stories, full of exaggerated twists and turns, with extreme emotional responses, in the tradition of stage and silent-film melodrama. Melodrama has always been a paradoxical genre, having both a conformist and a critical edge. On the one hand, it is shamelessly populist and kitschy. This is why it has so often been scorned by high-minded critics. It invites the viewer to indulge in vicarious identification with its characters. It plays on this identification in order to wring out cheap emotions. On the other hand, as Thomas Elsaesser and other scholars have pointed out, melodrama is often extremely self-conscious. In the films of Sirk

and Fassbinder, among others, melodrama presents the gap between aspiration and achievement, or between the characters' dreams and their reality. In this way, it promotes critical reflection about the emptiness of ordinary bourgeois life.

6. Maddin's films insist on being "melodramatic" in the most pejorative sense of the term. Both their plot twists and their emotional displays are arbitrary, unmotivated, and excessively histrionic. Maddin's films indulge the feelings of yearning and humiliation in such an over-the-top way that these feelings come to seem like unreal poses. The situations that provoke them are too ridiculous for the audience to enter into them or identify with them. When we watch Maddin's films, we are always laughing at the characters, rather than crying along with them. In this way, the critical and conformist edges of the genre exchange places. The gap between aspiration and achievement is no longer a social condition on which we are invited to reflect: it becomes, instead, a metaphysical absolute. Emotional excess no longer provides the occasion for over-identification. Rather, it becomes the source of a new kind of alienation effect. We do not "naturalize" the story in our minds, but revel in our distance from the spectacle.

7. There is a word for the situation I am describing. In Maddin's films, melodrama is transformed into camp.

8. Maddin himself rejects this characterization. He says in an interview that he has no desire for cult-film status and no particular "allegiance" to the idea of camp. He would "rather be considered 'decadent' than 'kitschy' or 'tacky.'" He wants people to say about his work: "'Wow, is this ever rich and strange.' That's what I'd rather have, not 'Wow, is this ever hokey.'"

9. In short, Maddin wants us to take the emotional predicaments of his characters seriously, even though he makes it impossible for us to do so. He wants us to find his *mise en scène* dreamy and poetic, even though he makes it ludicrous with incongruous details. But this may well be less of a contradiction than it appears to be. In Maddin's movies, it would be wrong to say that emotion is emptied out and turned into camp. The logic is rather the reverse: camp is the enabling condition for a particular kind of emotional expression. Ludicrousness is the mask under whose cover the cultivation of extreme feelings becomes possible. We cannot help looking ridiculous when we are overcome with passion, or driven by desires that have no hope of success and no rational grounding. It is only by opening oneself to such ridicule, and acknowledging it internally in the form of shame, that one can transform oneself into a work of art, in the way that Oscar Wilde recommended. Camp, for Maddin, is a shortcut to radical aestheticism.

10. Maddin's sense of absurdity is at one with his sense of beauty. When I watch Maddin's films, I am absorbed by beauty, pulled into a state of ravishment. At the same time, I am distanced by the films' flagrant display of phoniness, their stagy sets and highly mannered acting. But the gorgeousness and the absurdity have at least one thing in common: they are both equally gratuitous and ungrounded. They are non-utilitarian and non-functional; there is nothing that justifies them, nothing which they are *for*. This is what makes Maddin's movies so decadent, rich, and strange.

11. Consider a scene from *Twilight of the Ice Nymphs*. As Peter (actor uncredited) and Zephyr (Alice Krige) make love, the tide rises and waves wash over their bed. Later, when their passion has been spent and the tide has gone out again, Peter casually picks up a lobster from

among the sheets and tosses it back into the water. What are we to make of such an image? Its absurdity is matched only by the insouciance with which the film offers it to us. For this incongruous lobster is not a symbol. It is not a metaphorical visitor from the depths of the unconscious. It is just there, a gratuitous gift of the sea. It is a decadent detail, precisely because it has no ulterior use, and it does not come up again elsewhere in the film.

12. Maddin's love of gratuitous detail can be linked to an even more important trait: his self-conscious archaism. Maddin crafts all his films to look like old-time movies. This willed anachronism is most evident in *Tales from the Gimli Hospital* and *Archangel*, both of which are shot in black and white to emulate the look of silent film. These films have extensive musical soundtracks, but their dialogue is sparse. They use title cards, exaggerated gestures and facial expressions, heavy-handedly ominous close-ups, and stylized make-up reminiscent of the 1920s. The result, though, is not so much to imitate films from the 1920s as it is to replicate the stereotypical ideas we have about such films now. Pantomime was never so exaggerated in actual silent films as it is in Maddin's parodies. Nor were D.W. Griffith's own melodramas ever quite so "melodramatic" as Maddin's simulations of them are. Maddin does not try to reinvent silent film as a new medium, in the way, for instance, that Aki Kaurismäki does in his recent film *Juha*. Rather, Maddin resurrects silent film precisely in its oldness, its decrepitude, its inadequacy, its failure to keep up with historical and stylistic change.

13. Maddin's point is not to return to an earlier time but to dramatize the impossibility of such a return. His films do not bring us back to the era of silent film. Rather, they demonstrate how long ago that era was, and how far away from it we are now. In his two black-and-white films, Maddin deliberately reproduces effects that have to do with the aging of movie prints, rather than with the way such prints would have looked when they were first released. His lighting, for instance, is often streaky or washed out. His special effects, like the repeated sequence of a World War One aeroplane flight in *Archangel*, are made to seem rudimentary and obviously unreal. For this is the way old special-effects techniques tend to look, in the wake of technological improvements that have surpassed them.

14. *Careful* is Maddin's first work in colour, but it adopts poses that are just as archaic as the previous pseudo-silent films. For one thing, *Careful* lacks a full-fledged colour scheme. Rather, everything is bathed in an oversaturated yellow glow. This simulates the effect of tinting the individual frames, as was often done before the advent of reliable colour film stock. *Careful* also parodies a mostly forgotten early film genre: the German "mountain film" (*Bergfilm*) of the late 1920s and early 1930s. Eric Ames describes the genre as follows: "The films used melodramatic plots, typically involving accidents and last-minute rescues, and usually featuring male heroes. On another level, they represented 'elemental' nature and pantheistic ideas while flaunting the power of technology, the camera's ability to exhibit alpine views (shot on location)." The ideology of mountain films was quite appealing to the Nazis; it is noteworthy that Leni Riefenstahl got her start in mountain films, starring in a number of them and directing one.

15. *Careful* is set in a high alpine valley, where everyone must speak quietly for fear of starting an avalanche. Nature is a burden and a source of guilt rather than something to be celebrated or struggled against courageously. Nature is also ostentatiously artificial in Maddin's film: it is evident that everything has been shot on a sound stage. In place of heroism and vitalism, *Careful* centres around ideals of servitude and repression, together with incestuous fantasies and Oedipal guilt. As Maddin summarizes the plot, "Whenever anyone unburdens her- or

himself of their true feelings, they're punished in an Old Testament fashion with a maiming or an instantaneous death."

16. In all these ways, Maddin gleefully inverts the original connotations of the mountain film. The result is to distance the genre yet further from us, to drain it of whatever vitality it may have had. Indeed, this is precisely why Maddin chooses as his target a genre that few people have even heard of, much less seen or even remotely cared about. Postmodern films often strive to revitalize old genres, either by upscaling them with big budgets and high-tech special effects (as in the *Star Wars* series), or more interestingly by updating and cross-fertilizing them (as when *Blade Runner* combines *film noir* with science fiction), or else by appropriating them through tongue-in-cheek *homage* (as Quentin Tarantino does with blaxploitation films). In contrast to all these examples, *Careful* only makes its chosen genre seem mustier, less vital, and less relevant than ever.

17. We generally think of movies as unfolding in the present tense, even if they are set in the past and even if their narrative structure involves flashbacks. The vividness and immediacy of the film-going experience trumps everything else. The fact that images seem to move—and their overwhelming presence on a large, illuminated screen while we are seated anonymously in the dark—gives film an overwhelming sense of the *now*. This was already the case in the silent era. The impression of immediacy is even greater today, thanks to powerful speakers and multi-channel sound. Gilles Deleuze insists, nonetheless, that "it is a mistake to think of the cinematographic image as being by nature in the present." Other temporal relations are possible. It is difficult, but not impossible, for film to evade the present. In *Cinema 2: The Time-Image*, Deleuze traces the different ways that modernist filmmakers (starting with Orson Welles and the Italian Neorealists) have worked to detach film from the present tense and open it up to other tenses and different forms of temporality. The only thing these various approaches have in common is that they all disrupt our usual habits of perception.

18. Maddin's (mis)appropriation of past genres is his way of making films that do not unfold in the present tense. *Careful* evokes the mountain film, and *Tales from the Gimli Hospital* and *Archangel* evoke silent-film melodrama, in order to produce the sense that everything in them is already past, already out of date, already lost. Another way to put it is that these films are not about remembering or bringing the past back to life in the present. Rather, they are about forgetting: watching the present slip away into the past, consigning that past to oblivion, and yet remaining enthralled by such oblivion.

19. The main characters in *Archangel* suffer from amnesia and cannot remember whom they are in love with. In a parody of Freudian repression, they repeat the past while remaining unable to grasp it. And in *Tales from the Gimli Hospital*, Einar (Kyle McCullough) recalls violating a female corpse, who turns out to have been the fiancée of his hospital mate Gunnar (Michael Gottli). The two men come to blows over something that is irreparable. They proceed to wrestle in the shadows, in a ridiculous extended sequence that is the closest the film comes to a climax. The characters in both films are trapped, less in the past than in their distance from the past, from which they can neither recover nor free themselves.

20. *Twilight of the Ice Nymphs* is similarly oriented toward an irrecoverable past, even though it does not replicate any particular genre or style from the 1920s or 1930s. With its garish colours, static camera, and exaggerated acting, *Twilight of the Ice Nymphs* seems like an archaic experiment in colour cinematography gone awry. We cannot help feeling that it *should* have come from the era of early film. *Twilight of the Ice Nymphs* has a built-in sense of

obsolescence. Everything in it seems hopelessly passé and outdated. The film is stilted and airless, like a kitschy souvenir preserved under glass. Its images come to us like delirious, half-forgotten dreams.

21. An exquisite radiance suffuses nearly every frame of *Twilight of the Ice Nymphs*. The film takes place in the mythic land of Mandragora, where the sun never sets. Each scene is backlit in gorgeous tones of gold, silver, or pink. The diffuse light streams horizontally through the forest and along the shore. It glistens over the long necks and tiny heads of the ostriches on the ostrich farm. It makes even the most common objects glow with an unearthly sheen. It burnishes the actresses' pale skin and illuminates the pastels of their costumes.

22. Such a light is not found in nature. It is something extra, something we add to what we see. It glimmers only in our nostalgia and yearning, or in the artifice of a movie studio. It connotes idealized retrospection and therefore pastness, rather than present-day actuality. Maddin creates an unreal world of wistful dreams and tacky glamour. *Twilight of the Ice Nymphs* is ironically nostalgic. It makes the motions of returning us to the past, but the past it brings us back to is one that never was. Or more precisely, the events of the film are always-already faded into the past. There has never been a time when they would have been present. Disappointed love is always looking back to a moment of erotic plenitude that never actually was, but that is constituted after the fact. We only encounter the gleam of the midnight sun in retrospect. That is why these heart-rendingly lovely tints are the colours of yearning and humiliation.

23. The temporality of *Twilight of the Ice Nymphs* is perfectly exemplified by what Juliana (Pascale Bussières) tells Peter as she abandons him: "This might have been the day we first knew we loved each other, and my kissing you now would not have meant goodbye." The speech is a past conditional, compounded with negation. It expresses a potential state of affairs that is nonetheless both contrary to fact and no longer present. The speech also loses in conviction, and thereby perhaps gains in poignancy, by virtue of the fact that it is spoken three times in the course of the film. What seems at first a spontaneous utterance (at least to the admittedly limited extent that anything in the film can seem spontaneous) is transformed into a speech repeated by rote. The second time Juliana speaks these lines, she seems to be under the hypnotic control of the sinister mesmerist, Doctor Solti (R.H. Thomson). The third time, she is evidently quoting herself and referring Peter to the previous occasions. In this way, the consummation of erotic bliss, the focus of Peter's desires, continually recedes further and further into the past, without actually ever having taken place. We cannot ever pinpoint the moment at which anticipation turned into nostalgia and vague yearning gave way to lost memory.

24. *Twilight of the Ice Nymphs* continually evades the finality of the present moment. This is also to say that every character in the film is driven mad by the pangs of unrequited love. Peter allures Zephyr only to spurn her, in the same way that Juliana first allures and then spurns him. For her part, Juliana is disturbingly entranced by Doctor Solti, who seems to value her less the more he is sure of controlling her. The Doctor also toys sadistically with the affections of Peter's gawky sister Amelia (Shelly Duvall). And Amelia, in turn, suffers the ambiguous advances and persecutions of her handyman at the ostrich farm, the aged eunuch Cain Ball (Frank Gorshin).

25. Beyond these entanglements, all of the characters in the film seem subject to the whims of Venus, whose enormous statue looms over the shore. Even the Doctor is vulnerable to the flawless beauty and unrelenting coldness of the goddess of love. He embraces the statue, seemingly willing it to come to life. But Venus' only response to the characters' ardent prayers is to topple down upon them. The statue has already mangled the Doctor's leg, making him a cripple, before the film begins. It falls again, crushing Zephyr to death, at the climax.

26. Despite its delicate beauty, the light of the midnight sun is cruel and implacable. It uncovers all secrets. It forbids repose. It tracks the characters relentlessly, leaving them no place to hide. These people all seem lost in an insomniac stupor. Sometimes they wander aimlessly through the woods. Other times, they hold a single posture, as if frozen. They break down in paroxysms of futile passion. They gesture emphatically, to no avail. They don't engage in conversation, so much as they declaim vehement speeches to one another. Indeed, Maddin post-dubbed the dialogue, and had all the actors speak in different accents, in order to get this sense of disconnection.

27. *Twilight of the Ice Nymphs* dramatizes its characters' various hopeless infatuations in a series of ludicrous *tableaux vivants*. The film lurches from one lurid, embarrassing incident to the next. Each scene reaches new, operatic depths of despair and entombs yet another blasted emotion. All the while, overwrought romantic music plays on the soundtrack. Eventually, Amelia loses her mind and murders Cain Ball; meanwhile, Juliana and the Doctor drive Peter to the utmost depths of despair and humiliation.

28. When Peter cannot stand it any longer, he cries out to the trees in the forest, whom he thinks of as his only remaining friends. In a lovely absurdist touch, he calls upon each species of tree by name. Peter begs the trees to crash down and obliterate them all. It is a wonderful melodramatic moment, full of rhetorical sound and fury: if I must perish, then let the whole world perish along with me. For an instant, the wind rages as if responding to this plea. But in the end, of course, nothing happens. The world remains unmoved by Peter's ridiculous gesture. For why should things be tailored to the measure of his desperation and longing? Ultimately, frustration is every bit as fleeting, and as disappointing, as desire. Even Peter's overwhelming sense of desolation finally succumbs to disillusionment.

29. Each character in the film struggles with the dead weight of the past, which is also the fatality of his or her desire. Each event in the film is shadowed by the ghost of all the things that did not happen. That is why the film cannot take place in the fullness of a living present. Things are always in process of fading away, and saying their farewells.

35-mm Non-Fiction
An Interview with Ron Mann
Jerry White

AMONG CANADIAN DOCUMENTARIANS, RON MANN is something of an anomaly. He has never had more than an arm's-length relationship with the National Film Board (NFB), operating more along an "independent filmmaker" model that is much more common in the United States than in Canada. He has made films about subjects that don't at first seem as earnest or engagé as a lot of Canadian documentary, such as comic books (*Comic Book Confidential*, 1988), 1950s dance crazes like the Twist (*Twist*, 1992), or a history of pot (*Grass*, 1999). And unusually for any documentary filmmaker, Canadian or not, his films regularly get some form of theatrical release and are often shot in the expensive medium of 35 mm, as opposed to the grainier but less costly 16 mm (which often prohibits a theatrical release, since so few venues outside the non-profit sector still have 16-mm projectors).

In the interview that follows, Mann talks about how he thinks of himself as an "independent filmmaker," a term that notoriously means all things to all people. In Canada, though, it is especially rare to find a documentary filmmaker with any real claim to that title, given how totally central the NFB is in the production of non-fiction film. While some of Mann's films have received limited NFB funding, almost all of his work has been made through his independent production company. He says this is because he can't make films by committee and deals badly with big bureaucracies like the NFB. I think, though, that this is only part of the reason he is uninterested in state-sponsored filmmaking. Throughout his career, Mann has tried to build a genuinely alternative structure for filmmaking in Canada—not least through his own films. For them, he employs (and, he proudly points out, decently pays) a very small army of researchers and editors, most of whom also get some share in the profits. Being paid for work is too often unheard of in independent feature films, and the notion of profit-sharing would be anathema to the culture of the NFB. Mann is closer to an American model of non-governmental, semi-commercial filmmaking than to the usual mode of production for Canadian documentary, but he also takes his responsibility to the people who work with him, and for him, much more seriously than the average American indie. He seems to understand that, for most people, this is a job, and they cannot be expected to mortgage their own futures for the sake of his non-commercial artistic vision. Indeed, Mann has also acted as a producer and mentor for a younger generation of Canadian filmmakers, positioning himself at the centre of the Ontario New Wave of the 1980s.

Another reason for his reluctance to work with the NFB is no doubt because of the topics that Mann has taken on. It is not impossible to imagine an NFB documentary about Toronto's Rochdale College (like Mann's 1994 *Dream Tower*) or famed CanLit publisher Coach House Press (like Mann's 1983 *Echoes Without Saying*), or even on American avant-garde jazz (like his 1981 classic *Imagine the Sound*). But it's much harder to imagine the NFB having much interest in films like *Comic Book Confidential*, *Twist*, or *Grass*, all of which are extremely well-researched investigations into less-than-respectable areas of contemporary culture—and what's more, contemporary *American* culture. There is certainly a palatable streak of Amer-o-philia running through Mann's work, although not of the Ken Burns variety. Indeed, as I mention in the interview, Mann has become a kind of anti-Ken Burns. Where Burns projects a comfortable, liberal-patriotic Americanism, Mann's films project the view of an outsider Canadian, curiously and critically investigating the ways in which the culture has been subverted. Where Burns makes copious use of archival materials to give his films a sense of historical weight and unimpeachable truth, Mann uses those same kinds of images to show how the truth has been manipulated and distorted by the powerful. Burns is the architect of a revisionist version of twentieth-century America. Mann wants to revise that history too: he's much less a builder than he is a termite (to borrow a particularly vivid image from one of the United States' best film critics, Manny Farber).

His peers in documentary filmmaking, though, are indeed Americans. Mann frequently mentions Emile de Antonio's influence on him, but his films are close to the work of satirical archive-raiders like Kevin Rafferty and Pierce Loader (*The Atomic Café*, *Heavy Petting*) or Terry Zwigoff (*Louie Bluie*, *Crumb*). Rafferty/Loader and Zwigoff also get modest theatrical exhibition and have, in their quirky way, encouraged people to re-evaluate some of the more contradictory aspects of American cultural history of the twentieth century. That kind of re-evaluation is, in the right hands, a politically radical act.

JW: Maybe you could tell me a little about how you started making films.

RM: I was a projectionist at my parents' house for home movies. My father used to have an 8-mm camera, he used to take a lot of home movies, and the real inspiration to make movies ... You know, as a kid—I have three kids now, and kids are fascinated with things that rotate—I was always fascinated by the way the take-up reel worked, staring at it, and we used to have these get-togethers where my father used to show these home movies, and I used to like performing for him. Next door to our house was a Cinerama movie theatre, and we used to go, I would say once or twice a week. And the Cinerama movie theatre was a real movie palace. It was where I saw *This Is Cinerama*. The first movie I saw was a documentary [*chuckles*]. That was the movie that started off with a roller coaster ride—it was mind blowing, I remember some kid in front of me threw up. I thought that you go to the movies just to throw up. And then my father was a TV repairman, so I was always stuck in front of the television, absorbing *Twilight Zone* ...

JW: So your cinematic formation came from extreme spectacle and television?

RM: Well, I'm definitely a child of television. It's not so much television, actually, it's more the spectacle of cinema, of Cinerama. I mean, they had beach party movies ... I remember standing in line for *Hard Day's Night*, which really is still my favourite film. It really changed my life. It was like a rock-and-roll concert. I think one of the reasons I became a filmmaker is because I wasn't good enough as a rock musician. I had a band, and I thought that movies were like a second to a career in rock and roll. But *Hard Day's Night*, it was a real event; I don't think that night you could hear any of the dialogue, people were screaming so loudly. And it was kind of a documentary too ... And a lot of the touchstone works that inspired me, *Shadows, On the Road, Pull My Daisy*, all seemed like they were spontaneous, but they really were carefully scripted.

JW: Is that what you're trying to integrate into your work, a sense of spontaneity?

RM: Yeah, authenticity ... because we kind of grew out of that, that 1960s reaction of trying to find authenticity in your work and trying to be true ... It's like what Ginsberg promoted, first thought, best thought. So I started to make films because my aunt gave me a Super 8 camera when I was twelve years old. Actually, I'm sort of concerned, because the Cinémathèque Québecoise is giving me a retrospective that includes some of those Super 8 films, I dunno, some of those should stay in the archive. My archive, actually, is at the Art Gallery of Ontario, and some of those Super 8 films are there. But those films are about it being a hobby ... some of the films were inspired by this NFB director who made this film called *Very Nice, Very Nice*—I've forgotten his name ...

JW: Arthur Lipsett.

RM: Yeah, yeah. Because my first film was just five frame shots of my impressions of downtown Toronto. And you always sort of begin with documentary, because you can't afford actors, you can't afford art directors, so a lot of the work was just what I could do with a roll of film and this camera, and slowly I started to get more complicated. I started to do animation. When I was sixteen, I worked at Sam the Record Man, and I worked there for about three years, and I saved a lot of money and made the move to professional filmmaking, which was 16 mm, and made my first 16-mm film when I was sixteen called *Flack* (1975), which was about friends of mine who lived beside gypsum factory, and how we kind of devolved from a political society to an apolitical one, and all we could do was just talk about a problem. And I wrote and shot it and edited it, and it looks it, it's pretty crude. It was influenced by a film called *Ice* (Robert Kramer, 1975) and Cassavetes' *Shadows* and Antonioni's *The Red Desert*, which was about the emotion of boredom. And Norman Mailer's *Maidstone*. A lot of my ideas at the time corresponded to the films I was seeing at the Roxy in Toronto ... At the time this is where you'd be introduced to films like *Millhouse* by Emile de Antonio, playing on a double bill with *Repo Man* [*laughs*]. Just so you know, I have always been a great fan of Hollywood films, it's not oil and water to me. I like *Truck Stop Women*, I like *Tout va bien*; I really was a cinephile in that way. In 1976, I started going to the Cannes Film Festival. I was seventeen years old and sleeping on the beach, just to watch movies ... And I started to see movies that you'd never see here, and started to know about other filmmakers, you know I ran into Werner Herzog, and it was there that I got advice from Elia Kazan. I was trying to make a decision about whether to go to film school, and he said study everything but film, and go make films.

JW: So did you go to university?

RM: I went to Bennington College, in Vermont. They didn't have a film program. You couldn't really get an education from Bennington because of its library, which was very small at the time, so I went to the University of Toronto, and graduated from the U of T. It was there that I met Joe Medjuck, who was an advisor and a good friend; Joe hired me in 1984, with a film called *Listen to the City*. Ivan Reitman was the executive producer at that point; I had a three-picture contract with Ivan Reitman Productions.

JW: That was after you had done what?

RM: Well, in university I studied everything but film, except for a few classes, and Joe was an advisor on a screenplay I had written. So after unsuccessfully trying to mount a film about a rock concert in Toronto called Heat Wave, with people like Talking Heads, The Clash—it was about New Wave bands—I began a career of making documentary films. In 1978, David Fine and I decided to do a series of films together. Those included *Depot*, which was inspired by the Tom Waits song "Depot, Depot," and a number of animated films, including *The Only Game in Town*, which won ... the Genie? ... well, some award from the Academy of Canadian Cinema, which blew the film up to 35 mm, and it played in theatres across Canada. It played in front of Cheech and Chong's *Things Are Tough All Over*, a sign of things to come! So we did a series of films together, and through those, we met a distributor named Murray Swaydon at International Telefilm. Murray was your classic old-school distributor, and he talked to me about making a feature film. And so one day I was up at his office, and the headline was about a riot that had happened at Ontario Place with a band called Teenage Head. And he said, this is what we want! We want you to make a film that will cause a riot. And so that's how this Heat Wave concert film started, because he knew, somehow, the accountants involved with that. So I met with the accountants, and they looked at my film, *The Only Game in Town*. And they said, look, you're really talented, but we think you need an experienced producer. And they said that they had the money, and all I had to do was get an experienced producer. So I thought, who am I gonna get who was an experienced producer, you know, I was twenty years old, and I didn't know. Except I had my friend from Bennington, David Siegel, who did documentary work with the political filmmaker Emile de Antonio. I had seen his films at the Roxy, and so I called up De [de Antonio's nickname], and I flew to New York with my film, *The Only Game in Town*. That film was about poker, and De was a great poker player. So I told him about this concert film I wanted to make, and how I needed an executive producer. And he really got off on young people, he was really inspired by them, I think I inspired him and he inspired me. And he loved the game, he loved to be involved, he loved the wackiness of these kids, and these bands he'd never heard of. I remember playing him the Talking Heads for the first time ... [*laughs*]. So we were on the phone daily, because he was my executive producer. And five days before we were about to film, the accountants revealed that they didn't have the money, and I had lost five, maybe six thousand dollars. For me, twenty years old, that was bigger than my student loans! So I went back to Murray and said, OK, we have to do this film, but I've got this other idea, and it was gonna be bigger than Teenage Head. I had been a jazz fan for years, and I really wanted to make a film about avant-garde jazz. At the time this was the tax-shelter years in Canada, and I was able to go to doctors and dentists, to finance this film about avant-garde jazz. And people went along with it. I had co-producer Bill Smith, from *Coda* Magazine, and we created what was the first feature documentary about—and had the privilege of filmmaking with—Cecil Taylor, Archie Shepp, Bob Lain, and Phil Dixon, who by the way co-taught black filmmaking at Bennington. I was turned off by the music of the early '70s, from '73 on I was pretty much a jazz person. I was playing jazz music, I was listening to it all the time, I was going to Charlie Mingus, Roland Kirk. The inspiration for *Imagine the Sound* came when I was at Bennington. I took LSD with Jay Knapp and we went down to the University of Massachusetts, he had just had a stroke, so he was playing with just one side of his body—six instruments, all at the same time, which is what Roland Kirk did. Then Roland Kirk died a few months later and, um ...

JW: So that was the germ of the idea, you wanted to do a film about Roland Kirk?

RM: Yeah, absolutely. He passed away and I remember Eric Dolphy once saying at the end of a record, "music's in the air and then it's gone." And that profoundly influenced me, because I understood ... there needs to be a recording, there needs to be an imprint, there needs to be a record of alternative culture, because otherwise it's in the air and it's gone.

JW: So is that what you feel your calling is, then, to provide a record of this stuff?

RM: I wanted to give recognition to visionary artists who were heroes and who I grew up with. That's really been my project, from the very beginning. In making films about artists like William Burroughs or Alan Ginsberg or Robert Crumb, you know these were people of whom there needed to be some historical record. Because there wasn't any. Remember in the early '80s, which is when I began making these films, there was this kind of ... seeing the '60s as some failure, that everything was just reduced to some kind of experiment that failed. And I felt a responsibility to set the record straight. So a lot of what I originally wanted to do ... what De was doing in his films. Remember de Antonio was really the influence, he was like my mentor. In fact, I almost didn't want to do documentaries because I would just never be as good as him, I just felt ... I should do something else. But De's films were so inspiring. And when you look at all of his films, it's like a history of the Cold War. But it's an alternative history. And it's a history of a patriot. He was a radical filmmaker, but he really loved his country.

JW: So that's the kind of history you wanted to write.

RM: Yeah, I wanted to do culturally what he was doing politically. But I had a different aesthetic. His was more ... he called it brute or rough, and mine was more elegant. It was a kind of Hollywood-ization of the documentary. I managed to give a start to a lot of filmmakers, like Bruce McDonald, I helped Atom Egoyan or was inspiring to Atom, Peter Mettler, people like that. I was part of a group of people in Toronto, where I was doing this fairly young. *Imagine the Sound* was the first film that had a little bit of history, and later on my films became more historical. *Comic Book Confidential*, I'd say that it's a profile of twenty-three comic-book artists in the context of history. The dynamic of that narrative is going from the beginning of comic books to the present. And the other thing that I think I do besides recognizing these visionary artists is uncovering secrets, and that is because the official history is presented to us but we want to capture alternative history.

JW: I'm interested in this idea of Hollywood-izing the documentary. I think that is a lot of what you're doing.

RM: Well, I have this very arrogant approach ... A lot of it has to do with elevating the form of documentary. I look at documentaries dramatically, to tell a story. Because my films are theatrical. I saw these films in the movie theatres, and that is my audience. I am not a TV journalist. The other thing is, I think television's a giant trash heap. Everything is reduced to the form of a TV documentary, and those pieces are just in-between soap commercials. The films that I made, the documentaries that fall under the tradition of theatrical documentary ... as the technology changed, Dolby became more common, etc., and also as the independent film movement started in the '80s, you began to realize that you really needed to entertain an audience. I love the form of documentary, you can do so much with it. But to look at the film as a narrative, because we start with the script. You know, de Antonio's films were very much a Shakespearean drama. A drama about McCarthy, *Point of Order*—it's structured like Shakespearean tragedy. What documentaries had ... the underpinning was dramatic. The other thing I use is comedy, which not a lot of other filmmakers do, but that's influenced by de Antonio's films too, which is the irony to get across points. Nobody had ever really done comedy before in documentaries, before de Antonio. But some of my films got rid of the omnipotent voice, so condescending was the traditional voice-over.

JW: So how about the Woody Harrelson voice-over in *Grass*?

RM: He's the conscience, I think ... It needed a way to condense one hundred years of history, and I couldn't do it with the narration. Woody is factual, except at the very end. He's really the voice of the film, and we needed a voice, a point of view. The one thing about de Antonio that always made him crazy was this idea of *cinéma vérité*, or objectivity. The idea of elevating the form of documentary was from the very beginning something that I wanted to do. But I thought that if you could do this with high art ... You know a lot of these movies, whether it was *Romeo and Juliet* or the Royal Shakespeare Company on film, there was always this lavishly reproduced play, and I thought you could do this with the avant garde. Because traditionally they haven't been treated with that kind of respect. I was also trying to control the artist's work, putting them in a neutral environment, in a studio, where I had more control. In a way what I wanted to do was have the movie be a performance. I didn't film the audience, which is something that Martin Scorsese did in *The Last Waltz*. So that the film itself becomes a performance, so the event itself is live, and it worked. Because there was cheering in the theatre after a performance; they clapped. In the same way that *Hard Day's Night* brought the same kind of reaction, in the same way that in *Twist* people started to dance in the aisles. That's really what I was after. You know, kids today are used to ... a lot of film is software for your home theatre. I look at that and say, you know, I have a home theatre, I'd love to see and hear my films in digital at home. I was the first person to do letterbox, the first documentary on CBC to use letterbox.

JW: Which was what?

RM: *Dream Tower*. There was a huge argument about it. And I was involved with Bob Stein at the Voyager Company, who also letterboxed. The real legacy of the Criterion Collection is letterbox; no one had done that before. Because I thought of myself as a *cinéaste*, that's the form I worked with, that's the ratio I worked with.

JW: I want to get back to this *vérité* thing. I think that your stuff is a major departure from most traditions of Canadian documentary. It's almost a reaction against that. It's less a product of a history of the NFB than it is a product of Toronto in the '80s. Are you put off by a lot of Canadian documentary?

RM: No, no. I mean, two weeks ago I was at my first documentary festival, in Sheffield. I've always been ... I helped start the Toronto New Wave. These were friends of mine, all pretty much the same age, who were working on each other's films, were interested in these other films. There was this kind of synergy, with all these people ... Holly [Dale] and Janis [Cole] and Barry [Weinstein] were just starting out, those were the only people who were really friends in the documentary world. And they had a different tradition of making films. My influences were really de Antonio's work, and international cinema. I don't remember ever going to the NFB crowd.

JW: Why is that, do you think? I mean, you really are almost the only successful documentary filmmaker in Canada to have no relationship with the NFB at all.

RM: My influences were really academic. I never even thought of myself as a filmmaker, I thought of myself as a cultural historian. What I would do is make films, projects that I really ... I just never really followed the "film" path. I was an entrepreneur. I didn't take government money. I guess that's what it was, I thought that was kind of crooked. I thought that if you were gonna make a movie, you should be responsible and make money back for the investors.

JW: Do you think this had a major influence on your films, this economic imperative?

RM: But also, I can't work for anybody. I couldn't work in a bureaucratic way. Everything I did was so idiosyncratic. A lot of it was because I couldn't explain it to anyone. And a lot of people didn't want to get involved with me. I mean, making films about jazz, about poetry? Talk about uncommercial. And especially Beat poets? And a lot of my experience is the push for the Canadian experience. I grew up with this notion, like what Henry Miller said, there should be no borders. And I do agree with that. For me it was a human experience. It was how the alternative culture affected me. I've always been outside of the mainstream. Even when I was a kid, all my friends were listening to the Archies, and I was listening to the Fuggs or Bob Dylan, or to John Coltrane.

JW: But both of you were listening to American culture.

RM: But a lot of it was North American culture. For me, I don't think you can divide Canada and the United States. For me, the divide is straight culture and alternative culture. I was always in an alternative culture, from the very beginning, from when I was reading. My brother gave me Bob Dylan records. I was somehow on the flip side of what everybody else was listening to and doing. And the NFB was to me another way of looking at ... at least at the beginning, because now I'm working with the NFB, *Dream Tower* was somehow ... But later on I realized, Canadian culture needs to be ... we need to somehow have some kind of reflection, we need to have these stories, need subsidization, because otherwise they won't have any kind of ... I mean, I enjoy the "I Am Canadian" commercials, I get a real charge out of them, because I deep down think, yeah, we are being barraged by American culture, but that's straight culture we're being barraged with. The reason I did *Dream Tower* is that it's about alternative culture in Canada. That doesn't preclude that my work was exclusively about American culture, because everybody was reading that stuff, or everybody was listening to that stuff. Everyone I knew who was hip, anyway.

JW: So was American culture a signifier of hipness or subversion to you?

RM: Well, no. I mean, when I read *Howl* and *On the Road*, it really spoke to me about what was going on in my life. I was a kid in the suburbs that really wanted to experience the world, so I stuck out my thumb and started hitchhiking, inspired by *On the Road*. I didn't realize at the time that he was French-Canadian! For me, a lot of it was about looking at the world and seeing how fucked up things were, which by the way is great for comedy. And a lot of it was this idea of being influenced by Paul Goodman, an educator and social thinker. I remember Paul Goodman, and I read a book called *Growing Up Absurd*, and I just completely identified with his utopian way of looking at things. Utopian didn't mean that it wasn't popular to change things, things were kind of fucked up. So I was involved from the very beginning with the many movements that expanded my mind and rejected this kind of nationalist idea. For me, this is gonna sound corny, but I am a child of the Woodstock nation. I identified with hippie culture, in the US and Canada, it didn't make a difference to kids. It was all about the music I was listening to. It signifies that subculture. What I was reading and what movies I saw was just part of this nonconformist attitude I had. I also realized that it was very hard to find this stuff. I think there are a lot of factors that influence me as a Canadian filmmaker. A lot of it has to do with having the ability to criticize the US. And that comedy, I think Canadians somehow can look at the US and say, hey, I recognize. You might not recognize that this is your heritage, but we do, and so do Europeans. I mean, *Dream Tower* is specifically Canadian, but people around the world do identify with it, with alternative education And this, by the way, in the '80s, when everyone said you gotta go back to the basics, and everything that happened in the '60s in education were failures. So I don't think you can't move forward, I don't think you can just stamp it out, and say it's not valuable, or reduce it to sex, drugs, and rock and roll. There's a way that the right rewrites history.

JW: I think of your stuff as an anti-Ken Burns.

RM: Oh yeah, he's very nationalist, very flag-waving. And that scares me about his *Jazz* [2000], what he's doing. Even though he licensed some of the Cecil Taylor performances from *Imagine the Sound*. I'm glad he paid.

JW: Not only ideologically, but formally too.

RM: That's right, yeah, I have a voice that's my own, that's not bought and paid for by some corporation.

JW: That style of documentary became more and more the standard, after *The Civil War*. Do you feel pressure to conform to that by broadcasters or funders?

RM: Um, no. I cannot work by committee, my work is just so individual, and in a way I pay for it. I paid for the freedom and the luxury of time, to work things out on my own. I've always seen a model for myself where de Antonio was, in his basement, working out new ideas for movies. I really loved that his entire wall was filled with … it was just simple, he was just a filmmaker. And his influences, by the way, were painters. He saw film, especially documentary, as an art form. It's not about corporate sponsors, putting the content in a form that is watered down. I drive to put out my own versions. What's satisfying to me is when … I'm making films for those artists. If I can satisfy those artists, I've done my job. Because I'm representing their history. I'm not a jazz musician, I'm not a poet, I certainly can't draw, I definitely don't dance. So I have to be careful, to be so true to their work. And to be sort of true as an independent filmmaker.

JW: So does that need to represent conflict with the idea of documentary as an art that was so important to de Antonio?

RM: No, no, they go hand in hand. He was a painter, and he was friends with those people, so they would open up. He saw film as being an art, but his art … He used collage, in the same way that Robert Rauschenberg would use collage, or John Cage would use collage. He saw collage as a twentieth-century art form, in the way that I do, I kind of sample like a DJ. These artifacts are testimonials, and they show us attitudes and the consensus of our times. You know, you manipulate these historical records, to get across your point of view.

Ultimately, though, what De was doing was a form of propaganda, a form of agit-prop filmmaking. And from the very beginning, I wanted to turn people on to jazz musicians, recognize that comic books were a great literary form. So you're using this work, and it's a collage form, but it's propaganda, to get across your message, an alternative viewpoint. The compilation form is the hardest form to work in. A lot of it has to do with the licensing of the materials. And that is certainly an economic censorship that happens ...

JW: Have you had good luck with archives? Have you had trouble?

RM: Oh yeah, they've become my best friends. People like Rick Prelinger, he's a collector, a social historian, he owns 75,000 cans. Mostly social dinosaurs, called Mental Hygiene films, real ephemeral. Anti-drug films, you know. He and I have collaborated on a number of projects. And Fred MacDonald, another private collector, and UCLA, they've been really helpful. I rely on them. I mean, you have to be really careful, because a lot of this stuff has been sold to big corporations. Those corporations own our history. You can't access Fox Movietone News. And that's dangerous. They're in the hands of people who won't allow them to be accessed. And also, there's a difficulty if you're making political films, if they disagree with your agenda, then they deny you access. So I think *Grass*, among all my films, is the most blatantly political, and I'm very proud of it. One thing I'm proud of is that I look back on my films and I say, you know, they make a difference. They're a record somehow, they kind of set the record straight. So I'm proud to work in that documentary form, because they do ultimately make a difference. But the archival work is so difficult, because to tell a story you do rely on the historical material and you may not have access as an independent filmmaker. But that form is so dangerous, your best friend is the person who gives you EO insurance. I also have a socialist way of making films. The people who work on my films, some of whom have worked on my films for years, own the film, so some of the profits go back to them. The principal creative people can get something. I mean, not someone who got me an egg-salad sandwich ... In a way, it's just the spirit of this collaborative work, making films which are outside of the film mainstream. I work somehow in isolation. There's only fifteen documentary filmmakers who get theatrical releases. I'm not part of that whole television ... I don't know how to pitch a documentary to a commissioning editor.

JW: So your films have no life on broadcast?

RM: They do. There's a TV station in Toronto run by Jay Switzer, City TV, and they've been supporting my films from the beginning. I would not be making films if it were not for Jay Switzer. What City TV was trying to do was provide a real alternative. They really do support independent film, work that television could bring was intelligent programming. But they've had more success outside of Canada.

JW: So there's a major difference in how your films are received in the US or Europe? Why is that, do you think?

RM: Well, I think that I have an international reputation, in the same way that Atom does. I mean, Atom is a superstar; I'm not a superstar. But somehow, my films are being recognized, in the same way that those artists are being recognized. People catching up, saying oh yeah, Robert Crumb. I think Terry [Zwigoff's 1995 film *Crumb*] had a lot to do with that, but *Comic Book Confidential* was kind of a breakthrough movie. It somehow got people more interested in the alternatives.

JW: So why would your film open at the South by SouthWest Film Festival [in Austin, Texas], but not at Vancouver? Do you have a sense of what in the Canadian cinematic landscape is less friendly than the American or European landscape?

RM: Well, I have been supported by the Toronto Film Festival. I mean *Twist* was the closing gala. Piers Handling and Wayne Clarkson have been hugely supportive of my work. But my films have a theatrical market, and there really is more, outside of Canada, more opportunity. There's more than four or five cities where it can play theatrically in the United States. There's more of a distribution system that allows them to go to colleges and universities, so I can do tours. And the truth is that a lot of the artists in my films are American, so the histories are American histories. And there's this real need to see these kinds of films.

JW: So you said earlier that you had a three-picture deal with Ivan Reitman?

RM: Yeah, I was writing a Bill Murray comedy called *Hoods in the Woods*. And I used to have these big fights with de Antonio about it. A lot of people talk about Hollywood, and they don't know what they're talking about, and I wanted to have that experience. And I had a great time. And I was shooting a behind-the-scenes documentary on *Legal Eagles*, and I got introduced to Jules Feiffer and Will Eisner, and started filming *Comic Book Confidential*. Now a lot of what I do costs money, and there's a lot of people today who say that you make documentary films because they're cheaper, with DV. I mean, a lot of it is an excuse to exploit people: "I made a film for thirty thousand dollars." What does that really mean? It means that your sound editor didn't get paid, and your DP deferred. You've gotta be careful with this new generation of DV people. And the broadcasters, who will say, oh yeah, we'll pay you three thousand dollars for this thing you worked on for three years.

JW: So tell me a little bit about what you've done as a producer.

RM: Well, I produced Peter Wintonick's *New Cinema Tapes* in 1983. It's about the Montréal Festival of New Cinema, so it has people like Michael Snow, Chantal Akerman, de Antonio. That was at the beginning of the independent film movement. And then I executive-produced a film, Robert Kennedy's film *The Special of the Day*. And I did *Brakhage*, that Jim Shedden directed. And next year I'm gonna be producing a film that Gerald Peary is going to direct, that's going to be a history of film criticism. In the '80s, a lot of young filmmakers came to me, and I helped them. And a lot of that comes from De, who used to say that if we don't help each other, we'll never move ahead.

A Canadian
(Inter)National Cinema
William MacGillivray's *Life Classes*
Robin Wood

This essay is reprinted from Robin Wood's book *Sexual Politics and Narrative Film* (Columbia University Press, 1998) and had appeared earlier in a slightly different form in *CineAction!*. In both instances, it follows a similarly detailed consideration of Anne Wheeler's *Loyalties*.

THAT I AM DEVOTING TWO CHAPTERS of a book mainly concerned with rereadings of generally recognized "classics" to studies of two Canadian films, both obscure and one (*Life Classes,* 1988) virtually unknown outside Canada and barely known within it, will appear to some merely quixotic, to others perhaps no more than a token gesture of gratitude to the country that has been my home for the past twenty years. Nothing could be further from the truth. Within Canadian film culture I have made myself thoroughly unpopular for my alleged lack of interest in Canadian cinema, and, worse, for my openly expressed dislike of certain films that have received far greater national acclaim and international recognition than the two I have singled out. To yet others, it may appear both pointless and frustrating to write at length on films they may never have a chance of seeing—but if nobody draws attention to them, what hope have they of *ever* gaining recognition? So let me make this clear: I write about *Loyalties* and *Life Classes* because I love them; I went so far as to include the latter in my list for the last *Sight and Sound* international critics poll to choose the ten best films ever made. With *Life Classes* especially, I am aware of no incongruity in giving it place beside the works of Ozu, Renoir, Ophuls, etc.

The titles *Loyalties* and *Life Classes* (both wonderfully apt and precise in relation to the films) are not exactly "box office." Would the films have received more distribution if they had been called, respectively (and plausibly), *Psycho Rapist* and *Take Off Your Clothes?* But then, the patrons of *Life Classes,* especially, would have been as audibly disappointed as those who attended screenings of Godard's 1964 *A Married Woman* (*Une femme mariée*) when it played briefly at a soft-core porn theatre in London advertised as "Twenty-four hours in the Life of an Adulteress!!!"

The phrase "conceptual underpinnings" occurs twice in *Life Classes*. The first time, it is used by the pretentious woman who interviews Mary Cameron (Jacinta Cormier) for employment shortly after she arrives in Halifax from the remote seaboard of Nova Scotia, to express her superiority to a young woman who enjoys "painting by numbers." The second time, it is used by the art historian whose lecture Mary attends, with reference to De Kooning, Kandinsky, etc., to describe the concerns of various modern artists: that it is not the outward appearance but the inner energies and tensions that structure an art work. The theme, if not the phrase, is further developed in the instructions of the teacher of the life classes for which Mary becomes a model, a woman presented as intelligent and sympathetic and who influences Mary's development. I deduce from this *(a)* that director William MacGillivray would like to point our attention to the "conceptual underpinnings" of his film, beyond the "realist" level of character, action, and behaviour, but *(b)* that he has a dread of appearing pretentious. Diffidence seems to me an important component of the authorial personality that gives *Life Classes* its particular distinctness and distinction (it is the least arrogant, rhetorical, or ostentatious of films); intelligence is another. Taking the hint, I shall concentrate on the film's thematic level, examining five concerns which continuously interpenetrate: feminism; the relation of present and future to the past; the country/city opposition; the different artistic modes available in contemporary culture; attitudes to the media and technology. If "diffident," the film is certainly not unambitious.

Mary Cameron never becomes fully aware that she is part of an international political movement (though her friend and workmate Gloria is, asking during a seminar about "the politics of being a woman artist in Germany today"), and the word *feminist* does occur in the film. Yet the most obvious and dominant level of its discourse—the "evolution of a woman's consciousness"—is unmistakably feminist, every lesson that Mary learns being both personal and more-than-personal. I might justly have described the film as being about "the evolution of a *feminist* consciousness." It is (for better or for worse—I don't mean this as a value judgement) *more* explicit about this than the earlier film with which it most invites comparison, Bertrand Tavernier's *A Week's Vacation* (*Une semaine de vacances,* 1980). It is a comparison to which *Life Classes* stands up remarkably well (no small tribute, as *Une semaine...* remains among the best work of one of the contemporary cinema's most distinguished figures), considering Tavernier's enormous advantages—long experience of feature filmmaking, working within a long-established and vital artistic (and critical) tradition, with incomparably superior financial resources and technical facilities. In fact, I am never aware, in watching *Life Classes,* of any technical shortcomings: MacGillivray has the true artist's ability to find the means fully to realize his concerns within the available resources, and there is never any sense of a discrepancy between ambition and technique. I have heard the term *minimalist* applied to the film, presumably as a means of describing the strict economy of MacGillivray's style: it is a film entirely devoid of frills and flourishes, there is no attempt to woo the audience with a seductive charm (which is one of the things about it I find so captivating), and, aside from the use of slow motion in the credit sequences, there is a total rejection of cinematic rhetoric (the 360-degree tracking shots, which I shall discuss later, are strictly functional, not decorative or "show-off").

Against the complete confidence and authority of the Tavernier film, one must acknowledge a certain hesitancy and reticence, the "diffidence" I spoke of earlier: it is what gives the film its engaging freshness, with its suggestion that this filmmaker from Nova Scotia and Newfoundland, lacking the long cinematic tradition that nurtures a Tavernier, was having to reinvent cinema all over again for himself. These are qualities that have been theorized by Canadian critics, preoccupied with defining an indigenous national culture, where none exists, as peculiarly Canadian. *A Week's Vacation* is every bit as "French" as *Life Classes* is "Canadian" (or "provincial Nova

Scotian"), but no one as far as I know has found it necessary to apply that term to pigeonhole it and, in doing so, by implication drastically circumscribe its significance. MacGillivray's film belongs to the world (or at least deserves to). The hesitancy and reticence can be equally attributed to the supposition that MacGillivray is a profoundly honest person tackling issues of immense international cultural significance gently and unpretentiously, feeling his way rather than making assertive statements.

If I had been shown *Loyalties* and *Life Classes* unprepared, and asked to guess which was made by a woman, I would unhesitatingly have chosen *Life Classes*. This is partly because *Loyalties* adopts unquestioningly the mode and norms of the dominant (hence patriarchal) tradition—in my opinion a perfectly defensible strategy, but one to which many feminist writers on film have expressed strenuous opposition. The style and enunciation of *Life Classes,* on the other hand, consistently suggest a search for an alternative mode of expression subtly deviating from the norms by a process of selection and emphasis (we are not talking *Riddles of the Sphinx* here). Further, the enunciation is characterized by qualities our culture tends to regard as feminine (sensitive and reticent, as against the forceful and direct "masculine" address of *Loyalties*). Even the treatment of David Sutton in Anne Wheeler's film might be read as a not uncommon form of male masochism and guilt, as against the feminist firmness with which Earl (Leon Dubinsky) is treated in *Life Classes.*

More important, however, is the extraordinary intimacy and inwardness of MacGillivray's relationship to his central figure, both actress and character. This impression is by no means contradicted—rather the contrary—by the fact that we feel we "know" Mary Cameron rather less completely than we "know" the women of *Loyalties*. The latter have the life of fully realized fictional characters, fully known by their authors who created them. The "life" of Mary Cameron is something more than that: she is allowed to retain something of her mystery, the not-quite-knowability of a human being. In other words, the relationship of filmmaker/actress/character is rather more complex here. Though I shall postpone discussion of the opening and ending credit sequences—the framing prologue and epilogue—one aspect is relevant here. In a shopping mall, we are led to watch a supposed television interview with Jacinta Cormier, supposedly attending the premiere of *Life Classes* in Halifax and questioned about the character she plays. Her genuine response expresses a complex combination of empathy and uncertainty, with "I guess" a key phrase: "She's a product of the culture ... and a victim, I guess ... and the changes that it's going through." She is both like and unlike Mary: "I grew up in a small town too, and like her ... I was [pause] *forced* [sounds uncertain of the word's appropriateness], I guess, to leave home ... Mary eventually becomes more ..." (sentence left incomplete). Was the role difficult for her? "Yes ... No, not really. I came to know her. Not that it was easy. She's a very complex character. I'm still not sure I fully understand her or her motives." Mary Cameron is, of course, a fictional character who does not exist outside the film. But Jacinta Cormier does, and she both is and is not Mary Cameron. There is then the relationship of MacGillivray to Cameron/Cormier, which seems at once symbiotic and distanced, and which determines the viewer's relationship: we both identify with Cameron/Cormier and study her.

Mary's development, while in some ways dependent upon the family and environmental background, which she never entirely abandons, is accelerated by the move from Cape Breton to Halifax. The small town/country community is never sentimentalized, either past or present. The film's view is that, if there ever was once a form of "organic culture" there of any character or distinction, it is now irretrievably lost, and nostalgic laments for its passing would be a waste of time; if it ever existed, its traces have been thoroughly obliterated by the irresistible flood of consumer capitalism, technology, and the media. The predicament of Mary's grandmother, drifting into senility in almost total isolation ("No one has any time for old ladies") eloquently sums up the sense of cultural deprivation which the film shares with the Alberta of *Loyalties:* on the one hand she clings to otherwise long-abandoned straws from the past (memories, snatches of Gaelic), on the other her days are passed propped in front of a TV screen watching the "stories" (as she calls indiscriminately whatever drifts before her consciousness—soaps, sitcoms, newsreels, commercials...). Neither is the city in any way glamourized; but it is presented as offering Mary opportunities for self-realization, for reaching an awareness (of herself, her potential, her social position) that she could never have reached in the country.

Central to this process of self-realization is Mary's discovery of herself as an artist, the various stages of which coincide with MacGillivray's inquiry into the modes of contemporary art and his defence of a qualified representationalism, leading to an implied congruity between Mary's paintings and his film (hence further confirming his identification with his leading character). Before I examine those stages (which are essential to the film's structure, both narrative and conceptual), I must confront one possible objection, the question of plausibility. Mary's somewhat abrupt discovery of authentic creative gifts (it is not clear exactly how much time passes between her first attempts at "personal" expression and her solo exhibition, but it appears to be a matter of months rather than years) imposes some strain on credulity.

The point I want to make is that, while arguably *improbable,* it is not *impossible.* Many of the attacks on Realism have centred on the assumption that it can only endlessly reproduce what is already there (external appearances, social structures) and is powerless to change it. But why should Realism be tied to probability? Why not a Realism of the *possible,* allowing for greater freedom, the potential for leaps of the imagination (both the filmmakers' and the characters')? Mary's progress (essentially a "leap of the imagination") is validated by the spirit and progress of the film itself, its commitment to change, to the *making possible,* to increased awareness, experimentation, audacity. The stages of Mary's self-discovery are sufficiently complex and suggestive to provide a basis for this leap into the possible.

Painting by numbers

It is greatly to MacGillivray's credit that he never invites the viewer to feel superior to, or find ridiculous, Mary's painting-by-numbers, the first of her attempts to find an outlet for her creativity. Within the context of an impoverished rural culture—the obliteration of its past compensated for by nothing more fulfilling than supermarkets and television—Mary's loving care is felt as bringing a certain validity to an essentially non-creative medium, and is respected as such. We are aware from the outset of Mary's native intelligence, her capacity for reflection, criticism, discrimination, autonomous judgement; at this stage her creativity lacks any awakening in the form of a model or an external stimulus, any sense that more ambitious work is possible.

The interview

At the employment agency in Halifax, Mary's attention is drawn to an abstract, minimalist painting on the wall. The woman interviewer asks what she thinks of it, referring pretentiously to her own interest in "conceptual underpinnings." We register Mary's response ("Mine are better") as funny, certainly, but not stupid: its naïveté is set against the other woman's condescension and assumption of superiority, and Mary's confidence in the value of her own work—a confidence that does not strike us as arrogant—is an important pointer to the speed with which she develops her talent.

The lecture on modernism

Mary accompanies her friend Gloria (her fellow-assistant in the department store where she gets a job, and part-time art student) to an art history lecture (the scene in which the term "conceptual underpinnings" recurs). Back in Gloria's room she expresses bafflement and hostility ("pictures you can't even make sense of"). We need not take this as MacGillivray's attitude to all abstract art (to identify with someone does not involve necessarily sharing all his/her opinions, and the film in no way satirizes the lecture); both Mary's exposure to modern art and her (initial) rejection of it mark an important stage in her critical evolution—her artist's sense of what interests *her*, rather than the critic's sense of what is of value. It is at the end of this scene that Gloria suggests that Mary supplement her income by "sitting" for $12 an hour.

The life classes

Mary's exposure of herself as nude model, itself an important step in her evolution as a person, is accompanied by her exposure *to* certain concepts of figure drawing that are crucial to her artistic development: both aspects of the experience teach her the lesson of freedom, the casting off of constraints imposed by her earlier environment. The teacher (a woman this time) instructs the students to make quick sketches ("gesture drawings") catching the body's action as Mary adopts different poses. The sketches are "not supposed to look like anything," the positive response to Mary's negative "pictures you can't even make sense of"; the aim is to capture the "inner core," not to produce outlines. At home afterwards with her child Marie, Mary attempts her first autonomous sketches, trying to capture the "inner core" of the small girl's body.

If I remember correctly, Julia Lesage once remarked at a conference that men should be banned from photographing women for at least ten years. I hope she would allow an exception in the case of MacGillivray. The way in which Jacinta Cormier is shot in the nude scenes (it might be taken as exemplifying the distinctions made in John Berger's thesis on the nude in the seminal *Ways of Seeing*, a work I have found much more helpful than Laura Mulvey's celebrated "Visual Pleasure" article) implies a distinction between two terms that are frequently confused— being looked at and being objectified. We are invited to *look at* Mary, as at once a beautiful woman and a person, the two being inseparable (nowhere in the film is she treated as merely *physically* beautiful). At no point is she objectified; we are always in intimate contact with her feelings; she is consistently a person rather than a body. The first scene in which she appears nude is eloquent on this point: we share her embarrassment and intense unease as she poses within a circle of students for the first time, even as the camera compels us to watch her, as if our presence were adding to her discomfiture. This is the least pornographic of films: the human body is progressively demystified, its anatomical detail no longer a dirty secret, source of sniggers, and titillation, but mature, matter-of-fact reality. Hence nudity in the film, instead of being an act of oppression, becomes a liberating experience for both Mary and the movie's audience. It is important that Mary's nudity is balanced later by full-frontal male nudity: the young men participating in the avant-garde television "happening," and more especially Earl (the father of her child), the scene in which Mary persuades him to pose naked for her answering the three "life classes" sequences, the demystification of the body capped by the demystification of the phallus.

Crucial to the presentation of nudity and the nonobjectifying look at the female body is the set of three life-classes sequences, which constitute a formal progression in which similarity and difference are marked by the *mise en scène*. Each consists mainly (though not exclusively) of a 360-degree tracking shot around the studio, as Mary poses naked for the students, yet each offers a different perspective, the three taken together adding up to a three-dimensional description of the experience of the life class. In the first, Mary is the centre of attention and empathy (shrinking, embarrassed, wondering if she should feel humiliated), the students kept in the background, anonymous and undifferentiated. The second focusses on the students, absorbed in the work, the teacher moving around to inspect their efforts, Mary entering the frame only later in the shot, the camera stopping when she is central to the image. The third shot concentrates on the students' drawings, the various (and markedly diverse) representations of Mary's body (or its "inner core"): while Mary is kept frame centre throughout, her body is repeatedly concealed by the sketches as the camera circles.

The German artist

Gloria takes Mary to a special seminar celebrating the visit of a German sculptress, illustrated by slides of her recent work—a series of smooth bone- or horn-shaped abstract objects. The lecture, read in translation by another woman as the artist presides in silence, is verbose and obscure, an outpouring of pretentious jargon delivered reverentially. Question time follows, but the audience has by now been intimidated into total silence. At last Mary raises a series of simple practical questions ("What are these things made of? ... How big are they? ... How does she carve them so perfectly?") which are then relayed in translation to the artist, her answers paraphrased by the translator: "She has carpenters do it ... She doesn't paint them herself, she has someone else do it..." "How come they don't tip over?" Mary asks. "She has a computer design them." Mary is driven to the ultimate question: "What does *she* do?" (The artist is becoming increasingly defensive/aggressive.) "She just *thinks* of these things." The sequence takes up again the notion of "conceptual underpinnings," carrying it to its parodic extreme: the totally alienated art of a "sculptress" who has no physical contact whatever with her materials. (At the same time, it is important that the objects are beautiful rather than grotesque or merely absurd, and Mary's questions—"How does she carve them so perfectly?"—implicitly acknowledge this. Nothing in this film is simple except its enunciation.) Although Mary is too diffident to be aggressive, the scene reminds me strongly of the Ursula/Loerke confrontation toward the end of Lawrence's *Women in Love:* the naïveté, which can easily be made to look like stupidity when faced by arrogant pretentiousness, comes across as a healthy and fundamentally intelligent response. In relation to MacGillivray, the scene is a reminder that, if our attention is being drawn to "conceptual underpinnings," this is not to negate our sense of the filmmaker's art as a fully human engagement, nor to invite us to neglect the film's flesh and muscle in favour of its skeleton.

Children's drawings

Exploring the country home she has inherited from her grandmother, Mary finds some of her own childhood drawings, from before she learned to "paint by numbers." The film does not explicitly connect this to her artistic development, yet it links Mary's adult art to another of the crucial issues, the sense of the past and its relation to the future: a so-far unproduced screenplay of MacGillivray's which I have been privileged to read contains the line "If we lose the past, we lose the future." We may also recall the importance of child art in the work of certain key modern artists (Klee, Miró).

The television "event"

This sequence draws together so many of the conceptual/thematic threads that I shall have to return to it. The film's ambivalent attitude to the event itself (a semi-organized "happening" in which the participants, male and female, naked, encased in cylindrical plastic curtains, perform songs associated with some important period of their lives in order to release memories and emotions in a stream-of-consciousness monologue) is epitomized in the presentation of the organizer, intelligent and efficient but bossy and inconsiderate (she also refers to women as "girls"). If the event is *almost* ridiculous, it is saved by its aim and function (realized especially through Mary herself, singled out by the television camera for the unconstraint with which she gives herself): the cathartic significance of self-discovery and self-revelation, the exposure without shame of the whole human being, of which the physical nudity is but the outward sign. Mary uses an avant-garde "happening" for the expression of, simultaneously, her commitment to the past and her sense of the need for change. The predominantly positive nature of the scene should effectively counter any suspicion that MacGillivray is hostile to modernism or to experimental art. His film is itself modernist in its audacities.

Drawing Earl

The film's presentation of Earl in many ways parallels that of Eddy in *Loyalties*. Both are working-class men of limited education who develop a sensitivity and a kind of rough grace through their ability to love, and more importantly learn to respect, a woman. It is their ability to learn and to adapt that makes possible the generosity with which the films treat them. Earl consistently recognizes Mary's superiority—not in class or education, but in intelligence, awareness, and sensibility: her superiority both to him and to their small-town environment, the superiority that leads Mary's peers to see her, quite unjustly, as a "snob." Mary is quite clear on the subject of Earl's limitations, refusing to tie herself to him in marriage, her affection for him having its source in sexual pleasure. Early in the film, when, confronted with the fact of Mary's pregnancy, Earl asks her what she's going to do (adding "I wouldn't make much of a ..."), she promptly responds with "I know what I'm *not* going to do. I'm *not* marrying *you* ... We both know what you do best, Earl. That's why we're where we are." Yet, while still at the end of the film refusing marriage (which he now wants), she never rejects Earl either, developing a certain respect for him because of his capacity to learn. There are three crucial steps in the progress of the relationship: *(a)* Earl, by chance, and thanks to his satellite dish, watches Mary's television appearance; in the course of the monologue she refers—with irony and affection—to his "great family jewels," linking this to her mother's and her own pursuit of the "family jewels," the women's quest for potency. It is this that provokes Earl's departure for Halifax in a spirit that combines pique with admiration; *(b)* Mary persuades Earl to pose for her in the nude. The film's theme of the liberating effect of nakedness is thus extended to the male, Earl gradually overcoming his extreme uneasiness at having "the family jewels" exposed to objective female scrutiny; *(c)* Earl attends Mary's art exhibition, discovering—with initial horror but swift acceptance—her revelation of his nudity to the public gaze. In the film's overall schema, *b* corresponds to Mary's first engagement at the life classes as a nude model, and *c* to her naked television appearance.

The art exhibition

Clearly, Mary's art exhibition, consisting exclusively of nude studies of Earl and delightfully billed as a "One Man Show," is the culmination of the process I have traced, the film's trajectory. We are not asked to view Mary as a great artist, and the show is not a particular success; the emphasis is on her own personal development, her realization of her talent combined with a feminist deployment of it, the returning of the gaze onto the naked male body. The sketches ("gesture drawings," as in the life classes) are at once representational and distinctively modern (like MacGillivray's film).

One of the film's major concerns (which also happens to be one of mine) is the tension between the need to acknowledge and respect the past and the need to distance oneself from it, the need for a sense of tradition and the need for radical change. One may begin a discussion of MacGillivray's characteristically intelligent exploration of this tension with the song that runs through the film as *leitmotiv*, and its precise function:

> My child is my mother returning,
> My mother, my daughter, the same.
> She carries us all in her yearning,
> Our sorrow, our peace, and our pain.

In itself, the song can be read as a succinct summation of the response of women to oppression throughout the history of patriarchy. Its function in the film is somewhat more complex. Mary and her mother Mary and her daughter, both are and are not "the same": the same as the victims of oppression, quite distinct in their responses to it, the responses that their changing cultural situations make possible—the song's essentialism and resignation are powerfully countered by the film's progression. Mary's sense of the importance of preserving a continuity with the past is at all points accompanied by her need to break with it; it is not a paradox that her commitment to the past gives her the strength to take control and determine her own future. The commitment is of course highly selective: Mary identifies (through the song learned from her grandmother, which she sings interchangeably in English and Gaelic, the "second language" she claims in her employment interview) with the women's line, both the transgressive mother who left and the nontransgressive grandmother who stayed (but who tells Mary, in one of her moments of perfect lucidity, "you should have left long ago"). The father, unable to forget the affront to his male ego ("She made a fool of me, Mary, in front of everyone") has tried to obliterate the mother altogether, burning her letters and all photographs of her. Despite his efforts, the generations all come together in the scene after the grandmother's death when Mary and Earl explore the house she has bequeathed: Mary finds photographs of her mother and grandmother, and Marie, though left behind in Halifax, is "present" on the T-shirt Mary gives to Earl ("You can wear it in the tavern and brag to the boys"). It is important that she chooses, for the print, a photograph in which Marie appears to be crying: Earl will not be allowed the comforting illusion that everything's just fine.

This commitment to the women's line, the identification with oppressed women through the centuries, is accompanied (logically enough) by a firm rejection of the patriarchal nuclear family and the institution of marriage that is its foundation and sanction (if *Loyalties* is equivocal on this issue, *Life Classes* is not). Mary implicitly endorses her mother's abdication (despite the fact that the mother abandoned her as well as her husband) and reconfirms her independence by rejecting marriage to her child's biological father (as delivered by Jacinta Cormier, the last line of the film, the two simple words, "No, Earl," becomes one of the film's great lines, caustic, affectionate, and rock-firm all at the same time). It is characteristic of the film's (and Mary's) generosity that this rejection of patriarchal authority does not necessitate a rejection of *people*: Earl and the father are both present and acknowledged in the final scene.

The treatment of technology and the media, like every other aspect of the film, is highly intelligent. It is also consistent with the city/country opposition and the film's firm rejection of "Canadian pastoral" and all that goes with it: Mary, to retain her links with everything in the past that matters to her, will return to her grandmother's house every summer, but her future is in the city. The film opens (after the credits) with the installation of Earl's satellite dish, and it is partly through this that the attitude is defined. The dish accrues strong positive connotations: it is Earl's means to self-respect and dignity (his "phallus," if you will, despite its inappropriate shape, but a strictly non-oppressive one) in an environment that clearly does not encourage a sense of self-worth. It becomes the community's access to a wider world—picking up the program in which Mary participates and broadcasting it to both Earl and her father, forcing the latter to confront at last the negativity and self-insulation of his own attitude ("He said my mother was a whore," broadcast to the world in Mary's monologue) while initiating an entire new development in the former. More important, it becomes the individual's means of serving the community of which he is a member, in defiance of capitalist interests and authority: Earl is facing prosecution for using his dish to service more than one house. His friend has built a de-scrambler, but the American channels "went crazy," changing their code every few seconds. In case we mistake this for simple nationalist anti-American diatribe, Earl is made to add that "the worst is the RCMP": it's the system and its minions that constitute the enemy. While it is never spelled out, the film's commitment to a form of socialism seems as clear as its commitment to feminism.

On the one hand, the dominance of the media, the capitalist function of television to fill up leisure and inhibit thought, is presented firmly: the grandmother sitting passively in front of "the stories," Earl and his friends boozing it up while watching sports programs. On the other, the film never shows the least inclination to indulge in nostalgic wish-fulfillments of a return to the simple life in a technology-free "natural" environment. MacGillivray's point is clear: it is not technology that is the enemy but the people who control it; more precisely, the socioeconomic system which it is made to serve and sustain.

I want, in conclusion, to return briefly (at the risk of some repetition) to the pivotal sequence of this perfectly constructed film, the avant-garde television performance. It is one of those marvellous sequences that guarantee the authenticity of works of art—the place where "it all comes together," where all the disparate themes, as in a piece of complex contrapuntal music, are suddenly caught up, revealed as the interlocking parts of a whole. The concept of the sequence is extremely audacious, the action arguably implausible and potentially risible: another triumph, in fact, of a "realism of the possible."

All the themes I have explored are simultaneously present, their essential unity made manifest so that a summation of the sequence can stand also as a summation of this chapter. Mary, naked, sings her song (both in Gaelic and English); her monologue definitively "places" the men in her life (father, lover) and defines her relationship to them; it also establishes her commitment to her errant mother, the other links in the female line (daughter, grandmother) being "present" in the song itself. The celebration of continuity is contained within a celebration of innovation (the avant-garde "happening," which also defines artistic creation in terms of the human and the personal, in terms of "nudity" and the refusal of shame, in terms of rootedness in lived experience). The show itself is independent, broadcast via satellite, using advanced technology but outside the control of the dominant ideology or corporate capitalism. Finally, it is important that the woman artist who conceived and organizes it is *from* New York, and the transmission is intended primarily *for* New York. The film takes in its stride this extreme instance of "cultural im-perialism": if "the enemy" is not technology, it is also not simply the United States, but the sys-tem that controls both (and Canada).

After eight years, *Life Classes* remains the finest Canadian film I have seen, but it doesn't require the qualification. In terms of the richness and density of meaning, it can stand beside any of the films discussed in this book, and deserves to be widely known and generally accessible.

Outlaw Insider
The Films of Bruce McDonald
Steve Gravestock

> If you want to drive, you gotta kill.
> —*Roadkill*

BRUCE MCDONALD OCCUPIES A UNIQUE, somewhat paradoxical position within the Toronto film scene. From the outset of his career, he has been seen in opposition to the other filmmakers who emerged alongside him in the mid 1980s and early 1990s. His four feature films—*Roadkill, Highway 61, Dance Me Outside,* and *Hard Core Logo*—boast a decidedly accessible, pop-culture feel, a mood that separates him from contemporaries like Atom Egoyan, Peter Mettler, and Jeremy Podeswa. McDonald's work seems to belong only tangentially to the art-film genre, and his films are not overtly influenced by the great European directors in the same way that, for example, Egoyan's films are. *Hard Core Logo* screenwriter Noel S. Baker probably put the finest point on this division in his book *Hard Core Road Show: A Screenwriter's Diary,* where he claims, "With one or two exceptions, Bruce is the only English-Canadian director I can think of who makes 'fun' movies."[1]

McDonald's outlaw image also sets him apart from his contemporaries. Journalists typically paint him as a rebel, more at home on a Harley than in a limousine.[2] His first big public success came in 1989 when *Roadkill* won the Toronto City award at the Toronto International Film Festival. In his acceptance speech, McDonald announced that he was going to spend the prize money ($25,000) on a big chunk of hash. The statement offended some, delighted others, and is repeated in almost every article written about him over the course of his career (including this one). A few years later, he again raised the industry's collective hackles when he invited a biker gang to a party at the same festival.[3]

Yet, as Baker notes, the image is, well, an image. According to Baker, McDonald "calls the rock 'n' roll persona he maintains 'a dog and pony show.' ... He usually wears jeans, army boots and untucked shirts ... but maybe twice a month he has this other look: beige chinos, a truly conservative shirt ... the unaffected, studious film nerd. I suspect that this is who Bruce really is when the dogs and ponies have gone home."[4]

McDonald is intimately connected with these filmmakers—in fact, he has played a key role in the development of the highbrow art cinema Toronto has been known for since the mid 1980s. He attended Ryerson Polytechnic Institute at the same time as Peter Mettler, did sound on Mettler's *Scissere* and edited the follow-up *The Top of His Head*, and went on to edit Atom Egoyan's *Family Viewing* and *Speaking Parts*, and Ron Mann's *Comic Book Confidential*. In 1980, he helped found LIFT (Liaison of Independent Filmmakers of Toronto), a filmmakers' co-op that has become one of the city's crucial institutions; and in 1988, he edited a key issue of *Cinema Canada* that championed Egoyan, Mettler, et al. It was, of course, entitled the *Outlaw Issue*. Revealingly, the politics of the issue are cultural rather than radical, a trait common to this group, as Cameron Bailey points out.[5]

The style, form, and surface details of McDonald's films have fuelled much of the confusion. True, all of his films are linked to the road movie, arguably the pop genre with the tawdriest, hippest roots (from *The Wild Angels* to *Easy Rider* to *Wild at Heart*). But some of cinema's most subtle masters (Kaurismäki) have also used the format.[6] And one couldn't easily claim the genre's history was free from pretension: Hopper's *Easy Rider* and *The Last Movie* are the two most obvious examples. We could also include the first movie that made a real impact on McDonald, *2001: A Space Odyssey*.[7]

Granted, none of McDonald's films claim the broad territory of *Easy Rider* or even *Two-Lane Blacktop*. His films are far too specific and too modest to evoke the "mood of a generation."[8] The typical McDonald protagonists are arrested adolescents, overage teenagers who, as Lester Bangs once put it, "couldn't make themselves a peanut butter sandwich." Which doesn't mean that McDonald's variations on the genre are mere fluff. In fact, McDonald has used it to explore a variety of significant themes. *Highway 61*, for example, uses the journey motif to comment on Canada's bizarre envy of the United States, while *Hard Core Logo* is a hellish tour of a band's collective psyche. McDonald's road films are unique in part because of their specificity and modesty. (It's what separates him from probably his most obvious American contemporary counterpart, Jim Jarmusch—whose work I find far less intriguing and vastly more pretentious.[9]) One could say the same about his sense of humour, which often lulls the viewer into a false sense of security.

His work is strewn with references to rock and roll—from legendary figures like Bob Dylan to obscurities like The Poppy Family to mainstream bands like Bachman-Turner Overdrive. Where his contemporaries quote from Jean-Luc Godard, McDonald is as likely to use guitar solos as reference points.[10] Three of his films take place within the lower echelons of the music business. *Roadkill*, in fact, functions as a virtual who's who of Toronto rock circa 1987.[11] In interviews, McDonald uses rock imagery to describe his development as a filmmaker.[12] But music is as much a milieu as it is a subject for McDonald. McDonald's work is populated by artists and pseudo-artists, and music is almost always their chosen field. As McDonald himself matures as an artist, his figures get closer and closer to becoming true creators. In each film, though, there is a critique of the notion that artistic creation somehow relieves artists of responsibility. In his first three films, the characters' development is linked, in part, to the development of their art or their relationship with it. In *Hard Core Logo*, the band's refusal of responsibility and maturity signals their artistic, moral stagnation.

Canadian documentary filmmaker Ron Mann (*Imagine the Sound, Comic Book Confidential, Twist*) is closest to McDonald in spirit. Like Mann, McDonald is obsessed with alternative histories and mythologies, ranging from local legends like Toronto band A Neon Rome (the source for *Roadkill*) to myths about the blues to a desire to exoticize Canadian locations.[13] And McDonald shares a similar abiding interest in pop-culture marginalia. (His dream project, one he has been working on since *Roadkill*, is an adaptation of the cult comic book *Yummy Fur*.)

More than any of the other Toronto filmmakers mentioned, McDonald is a moralist. Each of his films arrives at a moral destination. And with each new film, the stakes are raised. *Roadkill's* Ramona achieves independence on her own terms. In *Highway 61*, Jackie accepts responsibility for her action while Pokey seasons his naïveté with experience. Silas and his friends, who have a much harder road than McDonald's other protagonists, forfeit innocence for maturity in *Dance Me Outside*. McDonald's darkest and best film, *Hard Core Logo*, illustrates what happens when the characters refuse to grow.

♂ ♂ ♂

Born in Toronto in 1954, McDonald made his first short film, *Let Me See (...)*, in 1982 and followed that with *Knock! Knock!* in 1985. A mock documentary, *Knock! Knock!* follows a filmmaker as he invades people's bedrooms to find out about their sex lives, prefiguring Tom Green's favourite set-up by more than a decade and establishing one of McDonald's own tropes: the overeager filmmaker as recorder, meddler, and incompetent. This figure appears again, reconfigured, in McDonald's first feature, *Roadkill* (1989); McDonald revives the character in *Hard Core Logo*.

Roadkill

Shot in black and white, and co-written with frequent collaborator Don McKellar, *Roadkill* is based on a semi-infamous Toronto rock legend. In the early 1980s, a punk-psychedelic band called A Neon Rome featured lead singer Neil Arbic, a disciple of Zen Buddhism who one day took a vow of silence.[14] For months, he refused to speak, communicating only by singing or writing notes. McDonald's initial plan was to make a documentary about the band, which was garnering rave reviews everywhere but in Canada. Unfortunately, the group broke up before the film was started, but this "legend" is incorporated into the film, which is constructed as a partial parody of Francis Ford Coppola's stoner classic *Apocalypse Now*. Ramona (Valerie Buhagiar)—an intern for an apparently coked-out Toronto rock promoter—is sent to northern Ontario to retrieve the Children of Paradise, a band that's gone AWOL. Her orders: "Terminate the tour with extreme prejudice."

The first of McDonald's arrested adolescent heroes, the shy, almost invisible Ramona is uniquely ill-equipped for the assignment. She's so mild-mannered her parents don't even acknowledge her departure. Her isolation is underlined in her first scene. She walks her bicycle around Toronto's Little Italy neighbourhood during the Easter Parade (featuring a spectacularly brutalized Christ—other participants flog him as he walks), separated from it all by her Walkman. Moreover, Ramona can't drive—an activity that serves as a key signpost throughout the film. For her, driving becomes a means to assert herself and her independence. It's initially presented as a comic mystery. Ramona grills Buddy (Larry Hudson)—a permanently stoned cab driver who bullies Ramona into letting him drive her several hundred miles to northern Ontario—about whether it's difficult to drive. (He answers, "No, you just need a good tape deck and some pot.") As Glassman notes, the film is also part feminist parable.[15]

During the lengthy drive north, Buddy regales Ramona with apparently tall tales about the famous musicians he knows, all of which she tunes out by slapping on her Walkman. Her action suggests that her isolation is, to a significant degree, self-imposed. When Ramona spots the Children of Paradise's van, she leaps out, kicks an apparent vagrant out of the van, then charges into a nearby diner to find out who left the van there. Two members of the band are inside trying to order food. They tell her she's mistakenly kicked their drummer out of the van and that their lead singer has abandoned them to finish a spiritual quest. Ramona calls her boss, but while she argues with him, the band and Buddy desert her, leaving her alone and Walkman-less to contemplate her next move. This sets up a recurring motif in the film, with Ramona being adopted by guides, including a silent hotdog vendor and a would-be serial killer, who hide their true natures or identities.

Ramona is soon picked up by a roving camera crew headed by an overeager director, Mr. Shack (McDonald himself). Like Ramona, they're supposed to hook up with the band, but since they can't find them, they're using this opportunity to shoot a poorly conceived documentary. The director begins teaching her to drive, but the lessons are cut short when Ramona runs over a hedgehog. They leap out and photograph it, and the director consoles the distraught Ramona by saying, "It's part of driving. If you want to drive, you gotta kill."

This scene sets up one of the crucial conflicts in the film. Independence and maturity are invariably yoked to insensitivity, and even slaughter. McDonald and McKellar pack the first section of the film with images of small animals being killed or eaten. The film opens with a parody of the *Hinterland Who's Who* films, featuring a rabbit menaced by Shack's RV (which bears the motto "Move or die").[16] A later guide, Russell Skelly (screenwriter McKellar), casually runs over a rabbit and roasts it on his car's engine, then declares he wants to be a serial killer. (Ramona's own decision to assert her independence is established comically through similar imagery: after she decides to take the assignment, she bites the head off a chocolate Easter bunny.) In each case, Ramona is offered entrance into this world, and in each case, she refuses. (She's visibly upset by the dead hedgehog, and refuses to eat the rabbit Russell cooks.) Tellingly, she is ultimately taught how to drive by a teenager, and when she finally winds up behind the wheel by herself, she diligently swerves away from wayward animals.

Violence and its equation with maturity are satirized through apparently innocuous Russell, one of the most awkward characters in the film. He also provides a means to mock the Canadian inferiority complex. "It's usually seen as an American thing, but it doesn't have to be," says Russell of serial killing; one could easily say the same thing about filmmaking.

Another index of Ramona's developing independence is her ability to suss out true and false guides. She dismisses Buddy, the cabdriver, as a fraud, although it turns out that his stories, or at least some of them, are true. Shack is a confused amateur; the seemingly benign Russell is a serial killer. The silent hotdog vendor who rescues Ramona is actually Matthew, the missing lead singer. (The theme of false identity is underscored in the penultimate scene, when Matthew talks about the false identity he's created for himself.) Ramona's final guide is the best: a teenager who not only teaches her how to drive but also offers her his car. Their relationship is markedly different from Ramona's relationships with the other men in the film. She initiates him as much as he teaches her.

The film reaches its climax with a surreal bloodbath. Determined to help everyone, a suddenly independent Ramona organizes a concert. It will allow her boss to recoup his money, give the movie crew to get some great footage, provide the tormented Matthew with a way out of a life he finds increasingly pointless, and, bizarrely, let Russell establish himself in his chosen career. Unfortunately, her boss arrives early and slaughters almost everyone present, except Ramona. The scene ends with Ramona taking the mike and welcoming everyone to the club, assuming Matthew's role as the artist propelling the narrative (it is his disappearance that sparks her mission in the first place) and taking control.

It's an ending that's more than somewhat problematic. Is it a fantasy, or a reminder that real evil exists? (Everyone Ramona has encountered has been relatively benign, at least to humans.) One assumes that Ramona's initial plan was to fake Russell's murder of Matthew, but there's nothing specific to support that contention. More significantly, the conclusion is jarring and basically throws us out of the movie. It feels as if McDonald and company are reaching for a big ending, regardless of how it fits with the material. However, as mentioned earlier, the scene underlines one of the basic misconceptions about McDonald. He's far less a realist than he first seems, and his comic touch doesn't mean that his characters operate in a benign world.

Despite the baffling ending, *Roadkill* is a truly admirable first feature, boasting wit, style, and a considerable amount of skill. As I watched the film for the first time in almost ten years for this article, it seemed better, more trenchant than I remembered it.

Highway 61

Highway 61 (1992), written by McKellar, represents a quantum leap forward in every way imaginable. The tone seems far more certain and McDonald's skill with actors has improved considerably; in particular, Valerie Buhagiar's performance is far stronger. The film won the Best Director Award at the San Sebastian Film Festival.

The film begins with a similar axis to *Roadkill*, but this time the arrested adolescent figure is split in two. One the one hand, there's Pokey Jones (McKellar), a barber and would-be trumpet player from Pickerel Falls, Ontario. Every night, Pokey gets in his Mercury Galaxie, the only thing his parents left him, and tries to leave. Each time he fails to muster enough nerve. On the other hand, there's Jackie Bangs (Buhagiar), a self-described "fugitive from a heavy-metal road crew." If Pokey has no experience, Jackie has nothing but experience. She first appears in a heated battle with her boss during a concert, then steals a sizable stash of drugs. Hopping on the first available bus, she winds up at the absolute end of the line: Pickerel Falls, Ontario. When Pokey becomes a local celebrity after finding the frozen corpse of a kid in his backyard, Jackie sees a way to smuggle the dope across the border: in the corpse. Claiming to be the kid's sister, she cons Pokey into driving her to New Orleans via rock music's legendary Highway 61. It doesn't take much to convince Pokey. It's the same trip he's been planning for years. (The scene as they hit the road yields one of McDonald's most indelible images: Jackie trying to hitchhike while sitting on the kid's coffin.)

In hot pursuit is Mr. Skin (Earl Pastko), a self-proclaimed Satan, who traded the kid a pair of concert tickets for his soul. Skin plans to collect no matter what. He seems in large part a variation on the old blues legend about Robert Johnson selling his soul to the devil.[17] This time, instead of frauds, the protagonists must deal with self-delusion, a much nastier foe. Pokey presents himself as a musician, but he's reluctant to play in front of anyone (a trait first noticed, of course, by Mr. Skin). When he and Jackie split up and he's forced to busk for money, Pokey pulls out his trumpet, strangles a few notes, then switches to something he's more comfortable with: barbering. The blow-up between Jackie and Pokey climaxes with Jackie telling Pokey, "You're no fuckin' musician; you're a barber, a small-town barber, a Canadian."

Pokey's self-delusion is compounded by his intense, juvenile adulation of the US. "They have a different way of doing things here," he writes his buddy Claude, immediately after he and Jackie cross the border. "Hard to believe, but everything you've heard about America is true. I've already seen some incredible landmarks that would blow you away." McDonald then cuts to an obviously awed Pokey. The cause? A pedestrian middle-American driveway leading to the childhood home of Bob Dylan. (McDonald is tweaking his own, well-documented obsession with Dylan; like Pokey and Jackie, he took the trip too.) McDonald undercuts Pokey's astonishment even further through a montage focussing on the Minnesota landscape, consisting primarily of desolate fields with the odd road crew and impromptu scrap yard (read garbage dump) popping up every now and then. Pokey's arrested adolescence, of course, is linked not only to his innocence, but to Canada's own unique inferiority complex about its neighbour.

Conversely, Jackie is wised-up and cynical. She casually boosts things from a variety store, steals from rural clotheslines, and robs the sad-sack Watson Family (a low-rent, state-fair pop group consisting of three spectacularly untalented pre-teen girls, led by their clearly insane father) of what appears to be their life savings—all without any second thoughts. It's when she visits her old friends, faded rock goddess Margo (veteran Toronto stage actress Tracey Wright) and her paramour, Otto (Vancouver rocker Art Bergman), that things hit home. A nightmare version of retired rock sirens from Patti Smith back, Margo is a near-vegetable, interested only in watching her own videos over and over again. Otto can barely take care of himself, let alone Margo. He decides to entertain Pokey and Jackie by letting chickens loose and demanding that they kill their own supper. (Both Pokey and Jackie refuse to kill any of the fowl—a decision that echoes Ramona's refusal in *Roadkill* and prefigures Silas' indecision in *Dance Me Outside*.) During their split, Pokey's insults cut as close as hers: "You'll end up dying in slow motion," he warns.

At the same time, Pokey and Jackie are on a very different plane, spiritually speaking, from the people they meet. Pokey's pop dreams look quite sane compared to those of the demented stage father Mr. Watson (played with exemplary verve by a rather wearied-looking Peter Breck, perhaps the best use of an aging American TV actor prior to Guy Maddin's casting of Frank Gorshin in *Twilight of the Ice Nymphs*). Jackie's hedonism and self-centredness appear quite mild when contrasted with Mr. Skin's demented actions or the spaced-out antics of Margo and Otto.

McDonald and McKellar paint a bleak portrait of America. A charity bingo in a small town turns out to be for a truly worthy cause: a new satellite dish for the clubhouse. Everyone Mr. Skin propositions gladly signs over their soul, usually with a thrilled expression and the stock response, "Are you serious?" Skin's customers include Claude (for a fifth of bourbon), a hobo (for twenty dollars cash), an Elvis Presley impersonator (for memorabilia), and one of the Watson sisters (for beauty and fame). Although much of the spiritual desolation happens south of the border, the film pointedly underlines the fact that Canadians are not exempt, tweaking our own prejudices about American greed.

One of the biggest pleasures we get from watching *Highway 61* is McDonald's improved sense of detail. More significantly, the moral landscape of *Highway 61* is much richer and more completely fleshed out than that of *Roadkill*. Instead of concluding with a disruptive bloodbath, McDonald and McKellar immediately place us in their Manichean world, a world where psychology, morality, and maturity are inextricably linked. The more demented characters operate as nightmare versions of Jackie and Pokey's destinies. At the same time, McDonald questions his own counter-culture beliefs and prejudices. As Marc Glassman notes, the film exposes the "lie of counter-culture capitalism, the selling of hard drugs."[18]

Pokey and Jackie also represent a further elaboration on a theme set up in *Roadkill*. Instead of serving art, they claim to create or embody it. They don't do it very well, and their acceptance of their flaws represents both a moral and artistic victory. By the end of the film, Jackie accepts that her actions have connotations and repercussions (that her life isn't a work of art); she decides not to sell the drugs. Pokey accepts that he isn't an artist, an admission that allows him to do something useful and poignant (he plays as the coffin, with the drugs still inside, floats out to sea).

Dance Me Outside

Dance Me Outside (1994) is McDonald's most adult film, although it is the only one to deal specifically with teenagers. Much of this maturity can be attributed to the fact that the film transpires within a close-knit community and that the principals make much more serious decisions. Unlike the arrested adolescents of *Roadkill* and *Highway 61*, they embrace and confront adulthood instead of being conned, coaxed, or forced into it.

McDonald was effectively hired to make the film by one of the patron saints of Canadian cinema, Hollywood veteran Norman Jewison, who purchased the rights to the W.P. Kinsella stories several years before. (McDonald had met Jewison while trying to raise money for *Knock! Knock!*, then chauffeured Jewison while he was working on *Agnes of God*.) Yet *Dance Me Outside* seems as much a McDonald film as its predecessors. Co-written by McDonald, McKellar, and new collaborator John Frizzell, and set on a reserve outside of Parry Sound, the film focusses on Silas Crow (Ryan Black), his best friend Frank Fencepost (Adam Beach), and their attempts to deal with women, maturity, racism, violence, and justice.

Silas and Frank suggest a native version of Jack Kerouac and Neil Cassady. The more thoughtful, reserved Silas is a nascent writer. (Both Silas and Frank plan on being mechanics, but they must write stories about their lives as part of the entrance exam, a device that basically drives the narrative, partially propelled by Silas' voice-over.) Silas is energized and amused by the antics of Frank, a born performer.

Once again, the film illustrates a quantum leap forward in technique, evident from the opening scene in which McDonald introduces us to a wide variety of characters. Following a brief, ominous prologue in which Silas offers a crow his last cigarette, only to be bitten by it, *Dance Me*

Outside opens with a flurry of returns and introductions. The first to arrive is Gooch (Michael Greyeyes), a local legend just released from prison. Gooch is admired by Silas and Frank, and the girls in their gang, in particular Little Margaret (Tamara Podemski), are equally excited by his return. Only the perspicacious Sadie (Jennifer Podemski), Silas' girlfriend, has doubts, lecturing them on the perils of looking up to someone who's served time.

Silas welcomes Gooch at the local bar, the Blue Quills, in a scene that parodies the steely-eyed stand-offs of Sergio Leone's spaghetti westerns. Gooch seems chastened by his prison term, but embittered by the news that Illianna (Lisa LaCroix), his old girlfriend and Silas' sister, is married. Coincidentally, Illianna is bringing her husband, Robert (Kevin Hicks), a white liberal lawyer, to meet the family that weekend.

Everyone gathers that evening to attend a dance at the Blue Quills, all expecting fireworks between Illianna, Robert, and Gooch. In the end, the excitement comes from an unexpected source: local white thug, Clarence Gaskill (Hugh Dillon). Proving his newfound maturity, Gooch refuses to make a scene and simply ignores the attempt of one of Gaskill's gang members to provoke him. Silas and Frank foolishly respond instead, sparking a melee that in turn provokes the break-up between a puzzled Silas and an infuriated and frustrated Sadie. Meanwhile, Gaskill lures Little Margaret outside, rapes, and murders her. He's immediately apprehended but given a ridiculously light sentence. The desire for justice drives much of the remaining action.

Throughout the film, most of the major action happens off-screen—from Little Margaret's murder to the subsequent killing of Gaskill. This strategy mirrors Frank and Silas' moral and intellectual immaturity: they also miss the point, and the key actions always happen when they aren't around. Within the community, it's the women who act and make decisions. "The stories we drew from ... were about the way the women in the community really run the show," said McDonald in a 1994 interview.[19] In contrast, the men play games. Frank and Silas take Robert out to indoctrinate him into the family, while Illianna, who's desperate to have a child but cannot because Robert is not up to it, sleeps with Gooch. The indoctrination ceremony is played for comedy, satirizing white liberal stereotypes about Native culture. At the same time, it signals Robert's acceptance into the family, as his frenzied, crazed actions endear him to Frank, Silas, and their friends.

Similarly, when Sadie organizes a legal protest against Gaskill's sentence, Silas and Frank mistakenly trash the car of the activist she brings in to motivate them. When Gaskill is released, Frank, Silas, and Coyote form an ill-conceived plot to kill him. The women prove more ingenious than the men in this instance as well, exacting vengeance with startling precision. This motif is underlined by Frank's repeated, unanswered question: "Are women thinking something?" Using stereotypes to their advantage, Sadie and her group escape prosecution because of prevailing prejudices (i.e., women are incapable of such an act, and even if they were, probably couldn't pull it off).

In place of the counter-culture mythologies that drive its predecessors, *Dance Me Outside* critiques prejudices, presenting Native teenagers in untraditional, contemporary terms. "We saw it as a teenage movie in the spirit of *River's Edge* and *Boyz 'n the Hood* ... I want teenage kids to see this movie. The way white teenage kids would see *Boyz* and say it's cool to come from East L.A.

The only ghetto we have in Canada is an Indian reservation," said McDonald in a 1994 interview.[20] Moreover, Silas is a more genuine artist than Pokey. His artistry is inspired by real, objective concerns, actual moral dilemmas.

Hard Core Logo

Hard Core Logo (1996), McDonald's undisputed masterpiece and last feature film to date, is the most elaborate, layered exploration of his favourite themes. Although touted as his most commercial and accessible work, it is also his darkest and most forceful. Based on Vancouver writer Michael Turner's novel of the same name, the film was scripted by a new collaborator, Noel S. Baker.[21]

A fusillade of techniques and formats much like the novel it is based on, the film is beautifully conceived, offering McDonald an ideal opportunity to demonstrate his ample skills. The film is presented as a mock-umentary, and mixes colour, black and white "documentary" footage, fake found Super 8, wish-fulfillment slow-motion set pieces, interviews, voice-overs, monologues, bizarre near-surreal imagery (a toy car stands in for the band's van), a ritual slaughter à la *Apocalypse Now*, and journal entries. McDonald plays a director (named "Bruce") who has been hired to record Hard Core Logo's last tour.

At the instigation of lead singer Joe Dick (Hugh Dillon), legendary Vancouver punk band Hard Core Logo reunites to play a concert in honour of their mentor, Bucky Haight (Julian Richings), who has lost the use of his legs after being attacked by a crazed fan. The proceeds go to No Guns, a local political group. (McDonald's witty, apolitical stripe is evident here; despite the fact that many of the Vancouver punk bands, unlike their Toronto counterparts, were fiercely political, no one pays any attention to the group's spokesperson.) Joe then convinces the band to reunite for one last tour, in part as a tribute to Bucky. They are to follow a crazed, elliptical route through western Canada to Winnipeg and back again.

The band is an odd assortment of borderline personalities: drummer Pipefitter (Bernie Coulson), described as a force of nature, pure appetite; reflective bassist John Oxenberger (John Pyper-Ferguson), who has in fact already had a severe nervous breakdown; callow, egotistical, star guitarist Billy Tallent (Callum Keith Rennie); and Joe Dick, a sleazy, desperate manipulator and egomaniac—and, of course, the band's spirit, spokesperson, and conscience. Joe is the kind of arrested adolescent who can't help but drag things down to a schoolyard level in the name of truth. That said, the band is a vital and genuine punk unit, committed to, and trapped by, its anarchic, fuck-you sensibility. And Joe's rants are as bracing (and on some level true) as those of punk icons Johnny Rotten or Joe Strummer. He effectively sealed the band's anonymity when, at a big New York showcase, he pissed in a record company executive's gin and tonic and hollered, "Sell that, you corporate weasel!"

As one would expect from McDonald, the band's songs—with lyrics written by Turner and music by veteran Toronto band Swamp Baby—are carefully done and sound authentic. The film is packed with priceless riffs on rock mythology, from Billy's speech about how aggressive music is a dead end (which apes Eric Clapton's defense of the pap he's produced over the last two decades) to the ironic repetition of The Poppy Family's sappy ballad "Which Way You Goin', Billy?".

Like *Highway 61* and *Dance Me Outside*, the film focusses on two characters, Joe and Billy. Since the band split up, Joe has been doing nothing (writing songs and "playing acoustic gigs," he tells the documentary crew, obviously embarrassed). In fact, Joe has never played with another guitarist, an index of his abrasiveness and his connection with his former bandmate. Billy, on the other hand, has been playing with big-time Seattle group Jennifur (a subplot that echoes *Highway 61*'s exploration of US envy), and he's about to sign with them permanently. When the group is interviewed by journalists (mostly of the college variety), this issue comes up repeatedly, which drives Joe up the wall. Joe describes the group as being like a gang, but it's more like a marriage between him and Billy. McDonald and company illustrate just how far they've got under one another's skin when Billy calls Joe a bitch: he immediately looks sheepishly around as if he is going to get caught.

It is an intense love–hate relationship, with a private language (such as the scene where Joe and Billy play the "I'm invisible" game or the road game where they come up with fake Canadian band names, like MacArthur Parka and Sled Dog Afterbirth). The tempestuous nature of their union suggests countless real ones, including Jagger and Richards, Strummer and Jones, or just about any band you care to name. Joe describes the differences between himself and Billy self-servingly but accurately: "Billy wants the models and limousines; I'm happy with the taxicabs and hookers." The comment sets up an axis of ethics versus greed, committed visionary versus talented hired gun. This dichotomy collapses as we learn more about Joe, whose notion of ethics invariably puts himself first.

As the tour proceeds, Joe effectively woos Billy, trying to get him back into the fold—although we're unsure whether Joe wants to reform the group or just wants Billy back in his life. In some ways, the film plays like a twisted version a screwball comedy: *The Awful Truth* with mohawks. Of course, Joe's pursuit of Billy is in part ideological, a preference for hookers instead of models. But Joe's ideology is a convoluted mixture of punk philosophy, self-interest, and suppressed desire, each aspect exposing the limitations of the other.

As with any rock band, the rhythm section has little or no actual power, except by siding with Joe against Billy or vice versa, or through observation. Indeed, Oxenberger's journal entries offer a fascinating commentary on the band. Oxenberger raises the favoured McDonald motif of fake identity. Both Billy and Joe, well into their thirties, go by the punk names they made up more than a decade ago. Oxenberger wonders if they can even remember their true names. (He's sure Pipefitter can't.) The commentary gets richer and more erratic as the tour proceeds, things begin to fall apart, and Oxenberger loses his medication. He even suggests that Billy and Joe slept together, although it's hard to determine the credibility of the statement, given how far gone he is. Of course no one notices that he's lost his meds except the mercenary filmmakers, who do nothing.

There's no audience at one of the shows; a gig gets cancelled; Joe is picked up by two prostitutes who promptly steal the band's money (like *Roadkill*'s Children of Paradise, Hard Core Logo aren't as tough as they claim). Billy loses the Jennifur gig because he doesn't return to Los Angeles quickly enough. (Significantly, he doesn't tell the rest of the band members, an act which, when exposed, sparks another row and one of the funniest lines in the script, when Pipefitter tells Billy, "Fuck you, Mr. Rock-Star-No-More.")

General nastiness abounds, as do cruel practical jokes, pervasive insensitivity (Pipefitter reads Oxenberger's journal aloud), lies, and a variety of behind-the-back slagging. Billy confesses to the film crew that he always thought Haight was a bore and that Joe's emulation of him was ridiculous. (But Billy plays Bucky's guitar as if he was holding something sacred.) Each of them is forced to confront consequences and realities they rather wouldn't. A former groupie shows up with a daughter Billy is convinced is his. Joe realizes he's never going to be able to keep the band together.

When a gig is cancelled, Billy suggests they go visit Bucky Haight to see how he's doing, a suggestion Joe resists vehemently, at least initially. When they arrive, they find out the entire premise of the reunion is built on a lie: Bucky is worse for wear but still physically intact. They get drunk and drop acid, slaughtering a goat. When they leave, an incensed Bucky—who's raised self-pity and self-abuse to an all-consuming art form—effectively cuts Joe off. This act rings both true and false. Given the moralizing that surrounds punk, I don't doubt that Bucky would have reacted this way. However, it might have been more amusing, more true to the punk ethos if Bucky had responded positively to Joe's chutzpah. Given punk's own background in fraud and outrage, it is possible an old punk would have loved such an over-the-top con.

They head back to Vancouver, knowing that news of Joe's lies about Bucky's condition is probably already out. Perversely, this has somehow endeared Joe to Billy. He defends Joe when someone accuses him of lying, claiming he touched Bucky's stumps himself. And he begins discussing recording together, minus the rest of the group. (We might feel more distressed if Pipefitter hadn't tried the same thing with Billy earlier, pathetically hitting him up for a gig with Jennifur.) That falls apart when Billy gets a fax from his manager, telling him Jennifur's guitarist is back in rehab and the job is Billy's again. Gutlessly, he hides it from Joe, but the film crew shoots Billy surreptitiously and show the footage to Joe. (Perversely, they're somehow more pissed at Billy than Joe, despite the fact that Joe has conned and abused them.) The gig climaxes in a brawl between Joe and Billy. Afterwards, Joe kills himself in a drunken stupor, an act that is honest to his punk credo and suggests an ideologically purer version of Sid Vicious' infamous flameout. As Oxenberger notes, Joe looks like he's carrying a cross. At the same time, the filmmakers underline the limitations of Joe's credo: it's one that can't accept growth or stability. (Prior to the Sex Pistols' tour of the United States, Greil Marcus observed—prophetically—that the band would either take America by storm or it would kill them.) McDonald and his cohorts admire Joe's notion of integrity, but they're smart enough to reject its extreme adolescent romanticism. (Interestingly enough, the original script ended with everyone going their separate ways. As the shooting proceeded, though, it became clearer that someone's death was inevitable.)

The dark side of machismo and arrested adolescence, *Hard Core Logo* is the only McDonald film without a substantial female character. The women in the film are abused or ignored by the band, which becomes a self-containing, almost hermetically sealed unit, one that prohibits growth on any level. Joe is the only character who grows even slightly. His odd acquiescence when they decide to visit Bucky Haight suggests that even he is tired of his bullshit. But faced with living outside of the only (mal)functioning family unit he's ever known—and unable to accept his own complicity in his fate and his faults—he refuses to move on.

The film is also McDonald's most powerful statement on art and the responsibility of artists. Embroiled in an ethos that prohibits any sort of compromise or sense of responsibility, the band and its members necessarily self-destruct. *Hard Core Logo* also illustrates the inevitable end of the apolitical punk ethos, where outrage and self-interest are the key principles—although this notion of destructive art is certainly not limited to the punks in the film. The other principal figure is the filmmaker, who is as much vengeful instigator as observer.

ༀ ༀ ༀ

Much of McDonald's work seems committed to elaborating on one of the key themes of his favourite rock critic, Lester Bangs. Bangs succinctly argued against the romantic notion that artists were somehow a separate race of human beings, who didn't need to abide by the same basic rules as others or were exempt from similar concerns. Like Bangs, McDonald is, in part, an apolitical moralist. The closest McDonald gets to politics is an intense cultural nationalism, linked to a notion of do-it-yourself self-sufficiency. At the same time, his films are acutely aware of economics. Nearly all of his characters wind up penniless at some point. To some degree, the apolitical nature of his films is a function of the arrested adolescent state of his characters. Unable to deal with basic issues or see beyond immediate concerns, politics is a luxury they're not about to pursue.

To some degree, McDonald is the victim of the success of the art-film movement in Canada. The pop surface of his films sometimes make them seem far slighter than they actually are—and in many ways his aesthetic is foreign to the Canadian film industry, which leaves popular art to the United States, a dangerous and possibly disastrous course. Then again, McDonald's work is interesting because it injects pop with a hint of the underground—in part because he shows us what popular culture can (and can't) actually mean, a project that is as unpopular and artistic as they come. *Hard Core Logo* functioned as McDonald's swan song to adolescent myths. Perversely, it was his least successful film commercially. Not surprisingly, given the finality of the film, he did not make a feature film for several years afterward. He has devoted himself primarily to television work, including the series *The Rez* (based on characters from *Dance Me Outside*), *Twitch City* (which suggests what the lives of his early characters might have been like if they hadn't hit the road; the show is written by McKellar), and *Platinum*, a series about the recording industry; two TV movies, *American Whiskey Bar*, an adaptation of another Michael Turner book, and *Scandalous Me: The Jacqueline Susann Story*. In 1998, he made a stellar short film, *Elimination Dance*, based on a work by Michael Ondaatje. And in January 2001, he produced a documentary on musician Robbie Robertson for CBC's *Life & Times* series.

Happily, he has recently finished work on another feature film, *Picture Claire*. Advance word is that it is more commercial and accessible than his other work—but then, people have said that before.

Notes

1 Noel S. Baker, *Hard Core Road Show: A Screenwriter's Diary* (Toronto: House of Anansi Press, 1997), 7.

2 "And despite what he describes as 'his people's' attempts to downplay his image, McDonald, 32, is determined to remain true to his nature: that of the uncompromisingly pure street artist." Angela Baldassarre, "Where do you want this killing done? Out on Highway 61," *Eye Weekly*, 13 February 1992, 27.

3   McDonald has a flair for promotion, a trait welcome in an industry that often seems too polite, reserved, and insular. His films have always arrived with cross-promotional items, including comic books in the case of *Highway 61*; an illustrated screenplay for *Dance Me Outside*; and, believe it or not, a tribute album to a band that never existed to accompany *Hard Core Logo*.

4   Baker, *Hard Core Road Show*, 36.

5   For a key article about this group of filmmakers, see Cameron Bailey's "Standing in the Kitchen All Night: A Secret History of the Toronto New Wave," *Take One* 28 (Summer 2000): 6–11. It outlines significant similarities between McDonald, Mettler, Egoyan, Don McKellar, Ron Mann, Patricia Rozema, and John Greyson.

6   Says McDonald: "People have this thing about road movies. They think you roll up the spliffs and just head on down the road hollering OOEEE!, making it up as you go along. In fact there's an incredible amount of pre-production." Steve Gravestock, "On the Road with Bruce and Don," *Innis Herald* 27, no. 1 (January 1993): 12.

7   Paul Eichhorn, "Bruce McDonald Gets Off the Road" *The Late Harvest Journal of Creative Culture* (Winter 1994–95).

8   McDonald's view of his forays into the genre, and the genre itself, are characteristically modest and unpretentious. "I didn't grow up thinking that road movies were this great art form that I absolutely loved. True, there were films like *Paris, Texas*; *Two-Lane Blacktop*; *Vanishing Point*; but to me they were just great movies. These first two movies were like work-out films for me, the first two I've formally directed. I really like them. At the same time, I try to keep them in perspective ... You have to learn your craft. Working this way really keeps you or your toes because you're out there where you don't have any safety net. It's a great trial by fire" (Gravestock, "On the Road with Bruce and Don," 12).

9   Even the most perspicacious Canadian critics have done flip-flops when trying to place McDonald within this tradition. "*Highway 61* combines the freewheeling rock-on sixties of *Easy Rider,* minus the romanticism about drugs, with the deadpan eighties wit of road movie specialists Wim Wenders (*Paris, Texas*) and Jim Jarmusch (*Down by Law*), minus Wenders' self-conscious philosophizing and Jarmusch's self-conscious aestheticizing." Jay Scott, *Globe and Mail*, 14 February 1992. In other words, key elements.

10   See, for example, the comic echo of the guitar solo from BTO's "Let It Roll" in *Highway 61*.

11   These include Leslie Spit Tree-O, A Neon Rome, Nash the Slash, Handsome Ned, and The Sidewinders, to name just a few.

12   "I'm still learning how it all fits together in the same way a band goes out on the road to get its chops together before it plays Lee's Palace or whatever" (Gravestock, "On the Road with Bruce and Don," 12).

13   "We have to come up with things that are unique ... which somehow set us apart from the regular Hollywood production. This is what people are responding to overseas, in American and in Canada ... When you pretend that Canada is someplace else you end up with bland faceless places ... You make it in Toronto or Sault St. Marie that's gonna add to it, not subtract. Look at the way music mythologizes a place, like when Grand Funk sang about Little Rock. That place takes on a mythical grandeur because it's in a song. But Little Rock isn't much different from Kapuskasing" (Gravestock, "On the Road with Bruce and Don," 12–13).

14   A Neon Rome was fodder for many bizarre stories. Arbic would supposedly call people on the phone during the period when he vowed not to speak and would hum or tap on the receiver until people realized it was him. Another rumour was that Arbic and the band were asked to appear in the film, but their agent asked for too much money.

15   Marc Glassman, "Rockin' On the Road, The Films of Bruce McDonald," *Take One* (Summer 1995) is a fine overview of McDonald's career up to and including *Dance Me Outside*.

16   Mainstays on Canadian television throughout the 1960s and 1970s, the brief *Hinterland Who's Who* films offered tidbits about Canada's wildlife, all featuring the same sonorous, helpful narrator. They've also been parodied, notably, by SCTV.

17 Walter Hill's *Crossroads*, Greil Marcus' *Mystery Train*, and even the Coen brothers' *O Brother, Where Art Thou?* invoke the same myth.

18 Glassman, "Rockin' On the Road," 19.

19 Steve Gravestock, "The Outsiders," *Venue* (Fall 1994).

20 "Adam Beach had done a couple of features, but this is the first contemporary thing he's done. He's usually cast as the silent Indian, so he was thrilled to be able to wear a Metallica T-shirt and rock out and stuff," says McDonald. "And the cast could sort of claim the here and now as theirs, and not just go through the motions. It was an attitude they had. It was irreverent and not a holy, polemic attitude. They felt freed just by that. It was like 'Oh yeah, this is like today. We can do what we usually do.' It wasn't like 'I want you to be really quiet and hunt the deer, talk to grandfather.' I think that made them all tremendously excited" (Gravestock, "The Outsiders").

21 The novel is based on Turner's own band and invokes Vancouver punk legends D.O.A.

The Radically Moderate Canadian
Don McKellar's Cinematic Persona
André Loiselle

ALTHOUGH DON MCKELLAR (B. 1963) HAS ONLY ONE feature-length film to his directorial credit, *Last Night* (1998), he has developed a reputation within Canada's film culture that places him at the centre of a group of English-speaking auteurs who emerged from Toronto in the mid to late 1980s and have now achieved international recognition, including Atom Egoyan, Patricia Rozema, Peter Mettler, John Greyson, and Bruce McDonald. As a matter of fact, Cameron Bailey argues, McKellar is the one who "knits this group together," who is "the most important to this group *as* a group."[1] This position as the cornerstone of the new Canadian cinema is no doubt due in great part to McKellar's collaborative involvement in multiple film and television projects as writer, actor, and director. However, McKellar's rise to the stratosphere of popular film culture in this country (which may or may not prove to be a flash in the pan) also rests on the persona he has constructed through the roles he has performed in his and other filmmakers' works, as well as through the content and structure of the screenplays he has written and the feature he has directed. This article proposes that Don McKellar's success results from his cinematic incarnation of an *idea* of popular English-Canadian culture that appeals to a certain segment of the population, for they recognize in it the embodiment of the radically moderate, ironic, multicultural Canadian. McKellar does not merely express his own Canadian identity in his work: he makes the very idea of Canadianness—its association with self-deprecating humour and perverse civility as well as its self-perception as a cultural mosaic—an object of mild-mannered derision.

Initially active on Toronto's alternative theatre scene, whence his inclination for collective work,[2] McKellar first contributed to Canadian cinema in 1989, when he wrote and appeared in Bruce McDonald's first feature, *Roadkill*, something of a northern Ontario version of *Heart of Darkness*. McKellar teamed up with McDonald again in 1992 for *Highway 61*, which he also wrote and starred in; in 1994 for *Dance Me Outside* (1994), which he co-wrote; and in 1998 for McDonald's short *Elimination Dance* and the much-written-about TV series *Twitch City*. McKellar also collaborated closely with Québec *cinéaste* François Girard on the screenplays for *Thirty-Two Short Films about Glenn Gould* (1993) and *The Red Violin* (1998). Although McDonald's and Girard's films are analyzed in detail elsewhere in this volume, McKellar's role in these films warrants consideration here, for it sheds light on the structure and meaning of *Last Night*.

The Embodiment of Canadian Irony

Very much unlike its American "equivalent," Francis Ford Coppola's *Apocalypse Now* (1979), *Roadkill* does not deal with significant events or powerful characters. Rather, it focusses on a timid woman, Ramona (Valerie Buhagiar), who embarks on a mundane search for an irrelevant renegade rock band. In the dreariness of its northern Ontario location, the platitude of its subject matter, and the marginality of its heroine, McKellar's screenplay foregrounds its Canadianness to the degree that it becomes a running joke; but a running joke that is only moderately funny, of course. Shot in black and white, with a generic deadpan acting style and numerous references to the tradition of boring documentaries that many English-Canadian children grew up watching on TV (including its opening sequence which clearly parodies any number of NFB wildlife films), *Roadkill* makes fun of English-Canadian culture in a radically English-Canadian way: by delivering an emphatically understated commentary on the absence of anything emphatic. The only event of importance is the mass murder at the end of the film. Ironically, but not surprisingly, even this climactic moment is rendered banal by the pedestrian line spoken by the killer, Ramona's boss: "Ramona. Tomorrow morning at the office, nine o'clock. Don't be late." Even the shooting of a dozen people in a bar seems dull when it takes place in northern Ontario. To McKellar and McDonald's credit, the film manages to avoid the trap of becoming insipid by depicting insipidity through a keen self-awareness of its function as an inside joke. It is a purposefully Canadian version of an American road movie, and as such, the film succeeds in getting a few laughs by stressing its wilful failure to live up to Hollywood standards. The victims of Ramona's "killing spree" on the road are not cops and other authority figures, but the small animals who live and die on the margins of the highway.

The radically moderate Canadianness of the film is perhaps most obviously expressed in the character McKellar wrote for himself, Russell, whose career ambition is to become a serial killer. Russell's matter-of-fact attitude towards his "line of work" is meant to be recognized as "typically Canadian" in the passionless civility he expresses when discussing this shocking topic with Ramona. As such, Russell is reminiscent of David Cronenberg's character in McKellar's first short film, *Blue* (1992). Here Cronenberg parodies a respectable carpet-factory executive who is addicted to pornography. Cronenberg's affected detachment in his portrayal of the character's casual inclusion of hardcore porn in his trivial, carpet-related daily routine foregrounds the shielding of immorality behind the mask of propriety. What must be stressed is that McKellar is not only depicting the factory boss as an incarnation of a sort of Toronto-the-Good decorous depravity; he also presents it as an already highly recognizable cliché that suggests a typically English-Canadian critique of English-Canadian morality. McKellar expressed this ironic self-reflexivity when he said that "the impulse for making *Blue* was sitting by the pool, looking at the mansion [at Windfields estate], thinking, 'Gee, this would be a great place to make a porno film'."[3] That McKellar so flippantly reveals the inspiration for his putative critique of debauchery behind the veneer of respectability was, in fact, his own interest in making a dirty movie within the posh decor of the Canadian Film Centre mansion does not merely imply that he is aware of the decadence hidden behind classy façades, but rather that he is fully aware of this awareness. In other words, it could be argued that McKellar made *Blue* not so much to denounce civilized perversion as to underscore that this attitude is readily recognizable by "progressive" Canadians as a characteristic of the conservative constituent of Canadian culture.

The commentary on self-critical conservative depravation in the Canadian context is as evident in Russell's dialogues as it is in *Blue*. For instance, one of Russell's main ambition is to demonstrate that it is possible for a Canadian to be successful in this most American of activities. As he says,

> I am a serial killer ... It's more of an American thing traditionally. But it doesn't have to be. It's like everything else. There's this colonial attitude about it, that if you want to make it you have to go down to California or something. But I am going to change all that ... There's not a lot of opportunities up here for social mobility. You can either become a hockey player or take up a life of crime. And I had weak ankles so there you go.

There are several layers of irony deployed in Russell's comments, including his highly colonized or "Cyclopean" response to colonization, which demonstrates that the dominated culture can be as competent as the colonizer in the latter's field of expertise.[4] He also establishes an implicit link between hockey and criminal behaviour as practices that *seem* totally opposite but are in fact two sides of the same coin. The film reaches an even higher degree of derision when Russell, after having shot only one person, sees his success ruined by Ramona's boss, who shoots him along with a dozen other characters.

More ironic still is another scene in which the would-be serial killer walks out of a bar absolutely furious because he dislikes the shocking performance of the band playing on stage. The would-be killer's self-righteous critique of the band's violent act comes across as an effective parody of the Canadian tendency to reproach others for engaging in conduct that Canadians themselves may adopt.[5] McKellar's self-righteous serial killer very much mirrors this attitude typical of the "imaginary Canadian," who projects onto others what s/he refuses to see in her/himself.[6]

But where McKellar proves most skillful in his construction of the radically moderate Canadian attitude is in the use of irony *itself* as a device that is recognizable as typically Canadian. Indeed, Russell is not merely an ironic character. He actually *stands* for Canadian irony, just as the carpet-factory executive in *Blue* stands for the progressive Canadian's idea of the perverse conservative Canadian. Over the last several years, irony has been heralded by writers and essayists, ranging from Vancouver's one-hit-wonder playwright John Gray to the University of Toronto's godmother of CanLit Linda Hutcheon, as a most typical mode of discourse among Canadians. Hutcheon not only suggests that "irony is a wonderfully covert way for repressed Canadians to express either aggression or enthusiasm," but also argues that the essential doubleness of Canadian culture makes it a particularly fertile ground for irony: "There certainly seems little in Canada that is not (or has not been) inherently doubled and therefore at least structurally ripe for ironising."[7] Irony, for Hutcheon, is thus the natural literary outgrowth of Canadian history and culture. Along the same lines, according to Jamie Dopp, Margaret Atwood's *Survival* (1972) interprets all of literature in this country in terms of "an essential irony thought to be at the heart of the Canadian."[8] And Gaile McGregor, in her voluminous *Wacousta Syndrome* (1985), notes that "the single adjective most often applied to Canadian literature by critics is probably 'ironic.'"[9] So many critics of Canadian literature and art share this Hutcheonian fascination with the idea that "speaking Canadian" means speaking with "the forked tongue of irony," that irony itself has now become less a description of actual cultural practices than a canonized discourse framing Canadian culture as a whole.[10] The earnestly light-hearted and obtusely clever chapter titles of Geoff Pevere and Greig Dymond's *Mondo Canuck* (1996) bear witness to this exaltation of irony as Canada's national idiom.

McKellar seems fully aware of this institutionalized use of irony, for he characterizes Russell not so much as an ironic embodiment of the Canadian ethos as an embodiment of Canadian irony, where the very enactment of irony is gladly perceived as representative of the radically moderate Canadian. Pokey, McKellar's character in *Highway 61*, functions in the same way and actually comes across as a more straightforward, ironically less ironic, embodiment of Canadian irony.

Another radically Canadian version of the American road movie, *Highway 61* follows Pokey and Jackie (Valerie Buhagiar) as they drive down Highway 61 from Thunder Bay to New Orleans to deliver the body of Jackie's "brother" which, unbeknown to Pokey, contains drugs. Pokey's lifelong dream has been to follow this road that encompasses the history of popular music, and Jackie's request that he drive her and her dead "brother" to Louisiana allows him to fulfil this dream. Early in their trip, Pokey explains to Jackie his relationship to Highway 61 and, implicitly, to American culture in general:

> Pokey: When you travel south on 61 from Thunder Bay to New Orleans, what you're really doing is tracing the history of popular music back to its roots. I lived all my life on the northern tip of the highway and I studied and I read. I never left home, but I know every inch of this highway. I know it inside out. Ask me a question if you like. Ask me anything.
> Jackie: Do you want to have sex with me?
> Pokey: No, I am fine. Thank you.

This exchange, not unlike dialogues between Russell and Ramona in *Roadkill*, contains a fair amount of "Canadian irony." Obviously, Pokey's "polite innocence" (in Brian Johnson's words from 1992) in declining Jackie's offer comes across as the typical Canadian response to a sexual advance. More importantly, however, Pokey's devotion to American popular music, his in-depth knowledge of a highway he has never travelled, foregrounds the ironic condition of a section of Canadian culture that is entrenched in Americana.

As they drive "deeper into the American psyche" ("High-octane"), Pokey realizes that the United States is not quite the land of dreams he was expecting. Guns, violence, and madness are rampant, with a would-be devil, Mr. Skin (Earl Pastko), stealing the body of Jackie's "brother" and burning Pokey's beloved old car. The low point in Pokey's exploration of the deep American south comes when, shortly after Mr. Skin has burnt his transportation, Pokey decides to leave Jackie to her own devices and must resort to his trade as a barber to make enough money for a bus ticket. The leader of a biker gang, riding into the small Mississippi town in which the protagonist is stranded, threatens to shoot Pokey if he cuts him while shaving him. Pokey not only gives him a great shave but also charms the biker. The biker says, "You must have a hell of a lot of nerve; why did you agree to that?" and Pokey timidly replies, "Well, I am pretty used to guns by now. And anyway I knew I could always slit your throat before you could shoot me." There follows a moment that represents the fulfillment of a great Canadian dream, namely, the taming of a gang of savage American bikers by the radically gentler, kinder, moderate Canadian. Pokey's "gently sardonic edge," the "bumbling gallantry of a northern Ontario Buster Keaton" that characterizes his persona, according to Martin Knelman, are the qualities that allow him to win the day, become a typical Canadian hero, and even get the girl in the end. Without having to resort to violence (i.e., the American way), he still manages to reach his goal.

Certain reviewers have praised *Highway 61* for its genuine commentary on Canada–US relations. Mike Beggs, for instance, wrote that the film "serves as an update on Yank–Canuck relations. It really hits home when [Jackie and Pokey] part briefly in the South, and she screams at him, 'You're not a f'in [sic] musician, you're a small-town barber. A Canadian.' Such dialogue rings true throughout."[11] Beggs fails to see that the metalepsis that joins the barber to the Canadian in this "truthful" dialogue is so farfetched that it does not function as an actual comedic insult but rather as yet another instance of a *parody* of Canadian self-deprecating irony. McDonald and McKellar are again fully aware that their film is not an *actual* criticism of non-ironic America and a promotion of ironic Canadian culture, but rather a replica of the Canadian's sense of self-irony *vis-à-vis* the US. McDonald sees the film as "a weird look at America. It replicates the classic Canadian attitude towards the States: a combination of repulsion and attraction."[12] Clearly McDonald and McKellar are not looking at the US through a candid Canadian eye but rather are commenting on the "classic Canadian attitude" towards America by replicating it. Not that *Highway 61* does not also make fun of American culture. But as Shlomo Schwartzberg points out, McDonald and McKellar are "having a grand old time puncturing American notions about themselves and those of their fellow Canadians as well."[13]

Much of McKellar's success in his collaborations with McDonald rests in his ability to construct personas and narratives that are aware of their own place in Canadian culture and do not simply reflect the Canadian imagination but make Canadianness the very core of their ironic commentary. Similarly, much of the appeal of *Twitch City* results from McKellar's self-consciously playful merger of the theories of English-Canada's two most revered intellectuals: Northrop Frye and Marshall McLuhan. As McKellar's character, Curtis, remains ensconced in his "garrison" while his body is extended towards the imaginary "global village" through TV, it becomes almost impossible for the spectator not to respond to *Twitch City* as an inside joke on the part of a student from the University of Toronto who had to write a paper on Canadian Literature but decided to make a sit-com instead. Even when McKellar works in his "serious" mode, especially in his collaboration with Girard, he continues to make films that consciously embody Canadianness rather then simply observing aspects of Canadian culture.

Mosaic Narratives

Very few Canadian fiction feature films offer biographies of our cultural icons. *Thirty-Two Short Films about Glenn Gould* stands as one of the more successful instances of this marginal practice. One of the reason for this success might be that, rather than documenting the life of Gould through a traditional bio-pic not unlike Borsos' *Bethune* (1990), Girard and McKellar decided to make a film that *incarnates* the pianist, a film that manages to be "littéralement à *l'image* de Glenn Gould," as Michel Sineux puts it.[14] As I have argued elsewhere, Girard and McKellar made a film "in accordance with Gould's own perception of himself. Taking as [their] point of departure Gould's statement that the best biography would be a fiction [... they venture] to approximate the character's self-representation as a bundle of eclectic fabrics no less intricate than the score of a Bach symphony."[15] At one level, then, McKellar and Girard's screenplay for *Thirty-Two Short Films* is comparable to *Roadkill* and *Highway 61* insofar as there is an attempt not merely to show their Canadian subject *through* the transparent cinematic medium, but to integrate it within the manifest structure of the film. Not unlike the way Russell and Pokey embody Canadian irony, *Thirty-Two Short Films* embodies Glenn Gould.

This embodiment of Glenn Gould can be construed at another level as an embodiment of Canadian culture itself. As a British reviewer wrote, this cinematic portrait of Gould "is elegiac, austere and amused: Canadian, you might almost say, in its cool, intelligent, elegant non-conformity."[16] The opening shot of the film, with Colm Feore's Gould walking alone in the middle of "the freezing expanses of Canada," as a film critic from *The New Yorker* observes,[17] recalls at once famous figure-and-ground paintings (such as those of Jean-Paul Lemieux) and *The Idea of North*, which defined much of Gould's self-image. As such, the opening scene is significant to this argument because it clearly suggests Canada to its spectators. This inscription of the *idea of Canada* on screen, rather than the simple display of a Canadian idea, is achieved through a threefold mode of connotation: first by introducing Canada's best-known classical musician, in all of his polite eccentricity, as one of his landmark recordings, *The Goldberg Variations*, is heard on the soundtrack; second by signifying the Canadian landscape as it has been constructed in the visual arts; and third by implying Gould's radio program *The Idea of North*. This radio program is a montage of voices relating, in an often incomprehensible but always highly musical sound amalgam, five people's experience of solitude in the Canadian North.

That *The Idea of North* is suggested in the very first shot of the film and explicitly referred to in the central vignette of the film, episode sixteen, dedicated to the radio program itself, is of particular interest to us because it links Glenn Gould to Canada as well as to the structure of the film as a whole. Talking about his radio program, Gould once said that "this contrapuntal radio documentary [is] about as close to an autobiographical statement as I am likely to make at this stage of my life."[18] Gould's contributor on the project, James Lotz, also said that the program should have been called "The Idea of Glenn Gould," because the five monologues harmonize Gould's own polymorphous psyche.[19] The idea of Glenn Gould, the idea of North, the idea of Canada, the idea of music, and the idea of McKellar and Girard's film all share the common traits of non-linearity, multiplicity, juxtaposition, parallelism, and contradictions within harmony. Truisms about Canada, such as its mosaic complexion,[20] its diffused, shifting northern geography[21] comprising a multitude of separate but unified regions and sub-regions,[22] and the lack of closure of its cultural narrative,[23] all emphasize the harmonious juxtaposition of different histories, spaces, identities, constitutions, lineage. *Thirty-Two Short Films about Glenn Gould* is similarly structured as a mosaic, to use a favourite Canadian cliché, with its thirty-two disparate but attuned vignettes that seek to parallel Bach's intricate, multi-layered, and constantly shifting musical composition, at the same time as it personifies Gould's own convoluted character. As Sineux remarks, the film "propose en trente-deux instantanés ... autant de facettes qui, comme un puzzle ou une *mosaïque*, tentent de cerner ... la personnalité prétendument insaisissable de l'artiste."[24] While, unlike *Roadkill* and *Highway 61*, the purpose of Girard and McKellar's film is not to parody Canadian irony, the crux of *Thirty-Two Short Films about Glenn Gould* remains very much the manifestation of Canadianness through a mosaic narrative that bespeaks of highly recognizable Canadian subjects.

The mosaic narrative of Girard and McKellar's *The Red Violin* is equally, if not even more, "Canadian" than that of *Thirty-Two Short Films about Glenn Gould*. Not only does it unfold as a partition of eclectic narrative lines that remain distinct yet unified through the central device of a violin passed from generation to generation, but the blatantly multiculturalist character of the plot, transpiring in North America, Europe, and Asia, renders it a cinematic materialization of the stereotypical ideal of Canada's ethno-cultural diversity. Even a most cursory reading of the film reveals its entrenchment in the official ideology of this country. As Marc Glassman notes in passing, "*The Red Violin*, as a cultural production, risks its financial survival on a point that can only be perceived as good old-fashioned Canadian linguistic politics, [showing] characters in Cremona speaking Italian and those in Shanghai speaking Chinese."[25]

Of course, mosaic narrations are not exclusively Canadian. It could be said, for instance, that such narrative structures, which encourage multiple identifications, are typically feminine in their form.[26] Even then, however, they would retain a degree of Canadian specificity, for certain critics, such as Coral Ann Howells, have suggested that much of what distinguishes feminine writing "might be said to characterize Canada's national image at home and abroad."[27] This feminization of Canada has been seen as either the result of the Canadian's feminine recoil before the harsh, masculine landscape,[28] or the outcome of Canada's counter-revolutionary (feminine) tradition as opposed to the revolutionary (masculine, Oedipal) history of the US.[29] Either way, an argument could be made to support the idea that even if the feminine, mosaic narrative might not be *uniquely* Canadian, it is quite typically, if not stereotypically, Canadian.

Furthermore, the very production context of the film makes it the perfect example of what someone like Pierre Elliot Trudeau might have envisioned as the ideal Canadian movie. A French-speaking Montréaler working with a devout Torontonian, both born in 1963, the year L.B. Pearson's newly elected Liberal government established the Royal Commission on Bilingualism and Biculturalism that would lead directly to the proclamation of Trudeau's policy on multiculturalism in 1971, and admitting that they share "la même culture,"[30] while remaining opened to "global" influences: one could hardly wish for a more heartwarming emblem of this great Dominion. Interestingly, when accused of having made too much of an "internationalist" film, Girard insisted that *The Red Violin*, produced by Niv Fichman's Toronto-based Rhombus Media, "est vraiment un film de Montréal."[31] Indeed, instances of multicultural Canadianness in *The Red Violin* abound. But in spite of the foregrounded Canadianness of both *Thirty-Two Short Films* and *The Red Violin*, these productions were not seen by critics as being Canadian to the point of annoyance. The same cannot be said of McKellar's only feature-length film to date, *Last Night*.

Canadian to the Bitter End

While *Last Night* was rather well received both in America and Europe, it is intriguing to note that the issue of its Canadianness often emerges as an irritant in reviews from foreign critics. One of the most negative commentaries came from British reviewer Richard Kelly, who wrote in *Sight and Sound*, "Few millennarian dramas have been so muted and mild-mannered as [McKellar's] directorial debut. One would like to forswear cultural stereotypes, but as a vision of terminal chaos and decadence, *Last Night* is deeply bourgeois-Canadian ... [McKellar's] prickly, nebbish persona can't give the movie a spine."[32] In the US, many reviews were much more positive than Kelly's. But some critics remained annoyed by the lack of action in the film and identified this narrative lethargy with Canadian culture. Bob Ivry of the New Jersey newspaper *The Record* exclaims,

> Naive me! I always thought there was so little difference between Canadians and Americans that having that border between the two countries was a mere formality. I was

wrong. Canadians are different from you and me, in ways that pop up in surprising places. In *Last Night*, the differences in sense of humor and in artistic sensibility are stark ... The pace of *Last Night* is taxingly slow ... I actually found myself rooting for the end of the world to come sooner. There: The ugly American has spoken.[33]

Even those who clearly liked the film still saw *Last Night* as a work whose Canadian origins are central to its meaning. Steve Murray of the *Atlanta Journal*, who actually preferred the Canadian version of the apocalypse to its American counterpart in *Armageddon* (1998) and *Deep Impact* (1998), writes:

> The end of the world has inspired Hollywood filmmakers to send casts of thousands screaming through the streets and to flatten New York and Paris with special effects. For our neighbors to the north—or at least Canadian writer-director-actor Don McKellar—the final apocalypse is treated with a dry wit and a sense of decorum that consciously tweaks that nation's reputation for civility.[34]

Stephen Holden of the *New York Times* also notes the typical quiet desperation of Canadians on doomsday: "As it methodically links together a group of quirky Canadians living in Toronto during the final hours before an unidentified cataclysm, *Last Night* offers itself as a smart, stiff-upper-lip alternative to a movie like *Armageddon* ... Everyone in the film, even those who are rampaging in the streets, seems resigned."[35]

Not only foreign reviewers noted *Last Night*'s definite Canadianness. Peter Howell of the *Toronto Star* also perceived the film as radically Canuck:

> *Last Night* might just be the Canadian movie to end all Canadian movies ... It's populated by more Canuck faces than you'd see at a sugaring off party, including Sandra Oh, Sarah Polley, David Cronenberg, Geneviève Bujold, Callum Keith Rennie and Randy Bachman. Had McKellar thought to add cameos by Gordon Pinsent, Maury Chaykin and Don Cherry, plus an intro by Elwy Yost, *Last Night* would be ready for burying in a time capsule below the Peace Tower ... McKellar knows this country well enough to suppose that, faced with impending oblivion, we'd all keep on being just as selfish, petty and bureaucratic as always. As typically Canadian as always, in other words ... *Last Night* might just be too damn Canuck for its own good ... It would have been nice if McKellar had managed one decent riot ... [E]ven God's Frozen People would have to thaw a bit when faced with this reality. But for the most part, he has us dead to rights. This is the way the world ends, not with a bang, but with everyone wearing clean underwear.[36]

While McKellar might not have thought about asking Gordon Pinsent to appear in the film, he is certainly fully aware that *Last Night* is a parody of typical Canadiana, including his own well-known persona. As he told Geneviève Royer in an interview for the Québec film magazine *Séquences*, "Le personnage que j'incarne dans *Last Night* utilise cette image un peu *nerd* et ironique qu'on me connaît ... Le personnage que [Cronenberg] incare se veut une parodie de certains Torontois, ceux qui se rendraient au bureau la toute dernière journée de l'humanité—responsables, jusqu'à la fin du monde!"[37] Incidentally, he has admitted to the same degree of self-parody in *Twitch City*: "My character in *Twitch City* ... is a kind of caricature of a perception some people might have of me."[38] It does not come as a surprise, therefore, that the film's Canadianness would be pointed out by so many critics, for *Last Night* is indeed quite radical in its depiction of the moderate Canadian.

Here, McKellar merges his tendency to ironize on Canadian irony and his inclination for mosaic narrations—telling the parallel stories of several characters spending the last six hours of their lives praying, preparing their suicide, having sex with as many people as possible, trying to isolate themselves from the world, or simply doing their job—with pretty much every other criterion necessary to make a "good Canadian film." In an article on canon formation in Canadian cinema, Peter Morris identifies a few characteristics that films *must* display in order to be accepted in the family of valued Canadian films, along with works ranging from *Goin' Down the Road* (1970), *Mon Oncle Antoine* (1971) and *The Apprenticeship of Duddy Kravitz* (1974), to *I've Heard the Mermaids Singing* (1987), *Un zoo la nuit* (1987), and *Jésus de Montréal* (1989). One of the criteria Morris foregrounds as having been instrumental in the development of a canon of Canadian films starting in the 1960s is the acknowledgement of Canada's fundamental biculturalism.[39] Every canonized film listed here includes characters from Canada's other linguistic group. Other canonized English-Canadian films that do not necessarily include French-speaking characters, such as *The Grey Fox* (1982), might still imply French Canada by mentioning Montréal, for instance. Québécois films that do not have any dialogue in English, such as *Les Ordres* (1974), can nonetheless comment on relations between Québec and English Canada. Working self-consciously within this tradition, McKellar created Mrs. Carlton (Geneviève Bujold), Patrick (McKellar) and Craig's (Callum Keith Rennie) former French teacher, with whom Craig has sex and to whom Patrick speaks with the attitude of a shy schoolboy. Arguably, the main reason that Mrs. Carlton would have to be a French teacher, rather than an English or math teacher, is that McKellar wants to parody (or expose) this mandatory reference to the Francophone other in Canadian cinema. Patrick's pathetic attempt to speak French might also be a gentle satire of all the well-meaning Torontonians who try to speak French but fail miserably. Either way, it attests to McKellar's awareness of the bicultural cliché.

Another criterion for canonization appears in Morris' article under the rubric "The Winds of Realism." Morris explains, "Perhaps the most widely accepted critical premise of the period was that Canadian narrative films were conditioned by a realist tendency."[40] Again, although much is made of the fact that McKellar and his contemporaries were "Canada's first generation of feature filmmakers to make virtually no contact with the documentary tradition. Not one of them ever worked in or for the National Film Board,"[41] McKellar conspicuously positions himself within this tradition of Canadian cinema. While, unlike *Roadkill*, it does not explicitly reproduce the codes of documentary, *Last Night* undoubtedly follows the axioms of realism. Shot on location in Toronto with a marked absence of fantastical special effects and an identifiably realistic (read understated and psychologically based) acting style, the film even has a musical soundtrack that is not strictly speaking diegetic but that finds a fully realistic justification in a radio program dedicated to playing the top 500 songs of all time.

Morris' final criterion is "that Canadian cinema is a negative cinema focused on victims and losers."[42] Beside the fact that McKellar has admitted to always identifying with victims in disaster movies,[43] the characters who move in his film are, if not unadulterated losers, certainly not heroes, and from the start accept that there is nothing they can do to escape their fate as victims of whatever it is that will destroy the world at midnight. The only moment that *could* have been heroic isn't: David Cronenberg's character, Duncan, confronted by a bully with a shotgun, remains cool and says: "I am not afraid of you ... You are the one who's afraid ..." But this heroic moment is discredited by the fact that Duncan's brains still end up splattered all over the kitchen floor.

In this scene, as in many others, one of the central characters of *Last Night* encounters nameless members of the mob roaming the streets of Toronto. Almost invariably, these marginal male characters are portrayed not as savagely brutal killers, as one might expect to see in an American film, but rather as petty bullies. McKellar's buddies McDonald and Girard, for instance, appear in the anonymous roles of insignificant hoodlums armed with comparatively inoffensive baseball bats rather than machine guns. As though just before writing his screenplay he had read Robert Fothergill's influential essay on 1960s and early '70s Canadian cinema, "Coward, Bully, or Clown" to which Morris refers, McKellar peppers his narrative with irrelevant bullies and constructs his two main male protagonists, Patrick and Craig, as variations of the Coward and the Clown figures. While both Patrick and Craig share traits from both the Coward and the Clown, Patrick is almost a perfect embodiment of the former type: "The essential characteristic of the Coward," says Fothergill, "can be summed up in that splendid word, 'pusillanimity'. He can be quite appealing at times—sensitive, mild—and a woman can find herself drawn to him; but with these qualities comes a deep down gutlessness that renders him incapable of reciprocating her commitment."[44] Patrick, not unlike Pokey, is indeed an endearing man, and his profound melancholy ensuing from the death of his girlfriend a few months earlier accentuates his sensitiveness. But he chronically resists, out of fear it seems, the attraction he feels for the female lead, Sandra (Sandra Oh). Both *Highway 61* and *Last Night* close with McKellar's character kissing his female counterpart, but as is customary in Canadian cinema, the male protagonist "wins the girl almost by accident."[45] In *Last Night*, Patrick agrees reluctantly to partake in Sandra's double-suicide plan, which she can no longer fulfil with her husband, Duncan. At the last moment, however, incapable of pulling the trigger that would kill Sandra, Patrick kisses her as the image fades to white. As for Craig, with his boyish charm, polite depravity, and sexual goofiness, he is very much the classic incarnation of Canadian cinema's archetypal Clown.[46]

Interestingly, McKellar also follows Fothergill's prescriptions on female characters. "A central quality in women, to which these films pay tribute, is their greater authenticity," Fothergill notes. "They are in touch with their feelings, and they express them ... To women is attributed a different and more integrated consciousness which does not always calculate before it speaks, which is more open to the world."[47] Sandra is a more "authentic" and more "open" character than Craig and Patrick, and many critics have viewed her performance as the key quality of the film.[48] "What sets [*Last Night*] apart and makes it an exceptional viewing experience," remarks Marc Glassman, "is the performance of Sandra Oh as a woman desperately trying to get home to her husband. 'She carries the emotional weight of the film,' acknowledges McKellar."[49] The fact that the female character carries the emotional weight of the film is so emblematic of Fothergill's reading of Canadian cinema that one is inclined to perceive Sandra as a parody, albeit a serious one, of the quintessential Canadian female role.

While not itemized by Morris, there are other deeply entrenched traits of Canadianness that critics have recognized and that McKellar seems to go out of his way to incorporate in his film. The sense of alienation and identity crisis, ascertained by Geoff Pevere as a "defining characteristic of Canadian films in general," evidently comes across in Patrick's behaviour.[50] He is at once alienated from his family, who ask him in vain to spend the last minutes of their lives together, and suffers from an identity crisis following the recent death of his lover, Karen. Along the same lines, Maurice Yacowar's argument that Canadians see themselves as outsiders in their own country and that the "very marginality [of film characters] makes them the representative Canadian"[51] is echoed in McKellar's focus on a handful of characters who *do not* join the party to end all parties, but prefer to stay in the margins, praying, having sex, trying to commit suicide, mourning their lovers, or sitting at work in front of a computer. As such, McKellar's characters clearly attest to Christine Ramsay's suggestion that "the Canadian imagination is simply more culturally predisposed to contemplate life from the margins."[52] Even more esoteric theories on the Canadian cinema apply to *Last Night*, such as Deborah Knight's notion of "Exquisite Nostalgia" characteristic of Canadian films "which seem to be marked by the recognition of incompleteness" and "also profoundly by their inscription of deferral by delay of pleasure, a pleasure which can only be experienced insofar as it is drawn out in time."[53] McKellar's film functions entirely around the notion of delay, operating primarily through the countdown of the remaining six hours before the end of the world. This delay is rendered even more flagrant in the final moments of the film, as Patrick and Sandra's double suicide is endlessly deferred into the continuous circularity of the camera movement, before the proverbial colourlessness of the Canadian protagonists is overexposed into oblivion.

ꝏ ꝏ ꝏ

Last Night lends itself to every standard, and not so standard, reading of Canadian cinema. It is a film that demands to be viewed not as an interpretation of certain aspects of Canadian culture but rather as a parody or critical replication of the themes and characters that have been established as representative of Canadian culture. The endearing qualities of moderation and irony that Patrick, Pokey, and even serial-killer Russell display, like the mosaic narrative structures common to most of McKellar's screenplays and the presence of several other acknowledged standards of traditional Canadian films, are all aspects of his cinema that appeal to some Canadian spectators. Such viewers recognize in these contributions to our national identity not so much popular Canadian culture itself but the idea of popular Canadian culture as it has been formulated in commentaries on film, television, and other arts, at least since the 1960s. McKellar has thus established himself as a central figure of contemporary cinema in this country less because he is necessarily the most talented filmmaker working in Toronto today than because he, more than anybody else, has brought the *idea* of Canada to the foreground of Canadian cinema. Through his radically moderate disclosure of Canadian clichés, his subtly relentless ironizing about Canadian irony, there is an emphatic understatement about Canada's civilized perversions or perverse civility; and in his timidly categorical negation that there is anything "cool" about Canada, McKellar has actually succeeded in making Canadianness cool. And that is no small achievement.

Notes

1 Cameron Bailey, "Standing in the Kitchen All Night," *Take One* 28 (Summer 2000): 10.

2 For information on his theatre career, see Craig MacInnis, "Bruce and Don on the Highway to Hell," *Toronto Star*, 6 October 1991. For information on his collective impulses, see Mark Glassman, "*Last Night*: In the Year of the Don," *Take One* (Fall 1998): 14.

3 Brian Johnson, "School for celluloid: the Canadian Film Centre is a leading place to learn 'the literature of our generation'," *Maclean's*, 23 November 1998, 125.

4 Clyde Taylor, "The Ironies of Majority–Minority Discourses" in *The Mask of Art: Breaking the Aesthetic Contract—Film and Literature* (Bloomington and Indianapolis: Indiana University Press, 1998), 165.

5 A sad but revealing example of this typically Canadian attitude is found in Kathleen Kenna's vehement criticism of American gun culture in the *Toronto Star* immediately following the Columbine High School shooting in Littleton, Colorado on 20 April 1999. (See Kathleen Kenna, "Land of 220 million guns," *Toronto Star*, 24 April 1999.) Kenna's self-righteous tirade against violence in America was made as bitterly ironic as Russell's criticism of the violent punk band a few days after the publication of her article when, on 28 April, a similar shooting occurred in Taber, Alberta. The shooting in Alberta did not deny the fact that American culture is drenched in violence, but certainly undermined the Canadian "holier than thou" stance. Herman Goodden of the *London Free Press* added another ironic twist to this sequence of tragic events when he threw back responsibility for the Taber shooting onto American media, writing "Everyone knows that the Taber, Alta. high school shootings last April ... were inspired by the obsessive, ubiquitous Columbine coverage." (See Herman Goodden, "Reckless Coverage Spawns Copycats: News Directors Should Rein in Reporting of Tragedies," *London Free Press*, 26 April 2000.)

6 See Bruce Elder, *Image and Identity: Reflections on Canadian Film and Culture* (Waterloo: Wilfrid Laurier University Press, 1989), especially pages 10–12; and Anthony Wilden, *The Imaginary Canadian* (Vancouver: Pulp Press, 1978).

7 Linda Hutcheon, *Splitting Images: Contemporary Canadian Ironies* (Toronto: Oxford University Press, 1991), 12, 15.

8 Jamie Dopp, "Who Says That Canadian Culture is Ironic," in *Double-Talking: Essays on Verbal and Visual Ironies in Canadian Contemporary Art and Literature,* Linda Hutcheon, ed. (Toronto: ECW Press, 1992), 43.

9 Gaile McGregor, *The Wacousta Syndrome: Explorations in Canadian Landscape* (Toronto: University of Toronto Press, 1986), 419.

10 Linda Hutcheon, Introduction, *Double-Talking*, 29.

11 Mike Beggs, "McDonald road film subversive epic," *Taxi News*, May 1992.

12 Schlomo Schwartzberg, "*Highway 61*," *Performing Arts in Canada*, 1 April 1992.

13 Schwartzberg, "*Highway 61*."

14 Michel Sineux, "*32 Short Films about Glenn Gould*: Glenn Gould revisité," *Positif,* January 1995, 36.

15 André Loiselle, "François Girard's *Glenn Gould* and The Idea of North," *Reverse Shot* 1, no. 3 (Fall 1994): 9.

16 Mark Sinker, "*Thirty-Two Short Films about Glenn Gould*," *Sight and Sound,* 4, no. 5 (July 1994): 55.

17 Anthony Lane, "The Gould variations," *The New Yorker*, 18 April 1994, 105.

18 From Otto Friedrich, *Glenn Gould: A Life and Variations,* quoted in Loiselle, "François Girard's *Glenn Gould*," 9.

19 Loiselle, "François Girard's *Glenn Gould*," 10.

20 Tamara Palmer Seiler, "Melting Pot and Mosaic: Images and Reality," in *Canada and the United States: Differences That Count,* David Thomas, ed. (Peterborough: Broadview Press, 1993), 303.

21 Margaret Atwood, *Strange Things: The Malevolent North in Canadian Literature* (Oxford: Clarendon Press, 1995), 8.

22 William Westfall, "On the Concept of Region in Canadian History and Literature," in *A Passion for Identity: Introduction to Canadian Studies,* Eli Mandel and David Taras, eds. (Toronto: Methuen, 1987), 228–29.

23 Laura Mulvey, "Magnificent Obsession," *Parachute* 42 (1986): 11.

24 Sineux, "*32 Short Films about Glenn Gould,*" 36

25 Marc Glassman, "The Epic Sound of Melodrama: *The Red Violin* reaches the screen," *Take One* (Winter 1999): 10.

26 See Tania Modleski, "The Search for Tomorrow in Today's Soap Opera: Notes on a Feminine Narrative form," *Film Quarterly* 33, no.1 (Fall 1979).

27 Coral Ann Howells, *Private and Fictional Words: Canadian Women Novelists of the 1970s and 1980s* (London and New York: Methuen, 1987), 3.

28 McGregor, *The Wacousta Syndrome*, 171.

29 Seymour Martin Lipset, *Continental Divide: The Values and Institutions of the United States and Canada* (New York: Routledge, 1990), 59–63.

30 Geneviève Royer, "François Girard: Jeux sans frontières," *Séquences* 200 (January–February 1998): 37.

31 Royer, "François Girard," 37.

32 Richard Kelly, "*Last Night,*" *Sight and Sound* 9, no. 7 (July 1999): 44.

33 Bob Ivry, "Out with a Whimper—Doomsday Should Have a Little Pop," *The Record*, 5 November 1999, 8.

34 Steve Murray, "Movies: A wacky, eloquent apocalypse unfolds," *Atlanta Journal and Constitution*, 10 December 1999.

35 Stephen Holden, "*Last Night*: Stranded in the City, On Doomsday to Boot," *New York Times*, 5 November 1999.

36 Peter Howell, "End of the world, Canuck style," *Toronto Star*, 23 October 1998.

37 Geneviève Royer, "Entretien: Don McKellar," *Séquences* 200 (January–February 1998): 19–20.

38 Glassman, "In the Year of the Don," 12.

39 Peter Morris, "In Our Own Eyes: The Canonizing of Canadian Film," *Canadian Journal of Film Studies* 3, no. 1 (Spring 1994): 32.

40 Morris, "In Our Own Eyes," 35.

41 Bailey, "Standing in the Kitchen All Night," 7.

42 Morris, "In Our Own Eyes," 36–37.

43 Royer, "Entretien: Don McKellar," 21.

44 Robert Fothergill, "Coward, Bully, or Clown: The Dream-Life of a Young Brother," *Take One* 4, no. 3 (September 1973), reprinted in *Canadian Film Reader*, Seth Feldman and Joyce Nelson, eds. (Toronto: Peter Martin Associates, 1977), 236–37.

45 Fothergill, "Coward, Bully, or Clown," 238.

46 Fothergill, "Coward, Bully, or Clown," 238.

47 Fothergill, "Coward, Bully, or Clown," 239.

48 See Gilles Marsolais, "*Last Night*: Don McKellar" *24 Images* 93–94 (1998); and Bob Ross, "A *Night* to reconsider," *Tampa Tribune*, 19 November 1999.

49 Glassman, "In the Year of the Don," 15.

50 Geoff Pevere, "Middle of Nowhere: Ontario Movies After 1980," *Post Script* 15, no. 1 (Fall 1995): 13; originally published in *Les Cinémas du Canada*, Sylvain Garel and André Paquet, eds. (Paris: Editions du Centre Pompidou, 1992).

51 Maurice Yacowar, "The Canadian as Ethnic Minority," *Film Quarterly* (Winter 1986–87): 19.

52 Christine Ramsay, "Canadian Narrative Cinema from the Margins: 'The Nation' and Masculinity in *Goin' Down the Road*," *Canadian Journal of Film Studies* 2, no. 2 (1993): 39.

53 Deborah Knight, "Exquisite Nostalgia: Aesthetic Sensibility in the English-Canadian and Québec Cinemas," *CineAction!* 11 (Winter 1987–88): 32.

Deepa Mehta as Transnational Filmmaker, or You Can't Go Home Again

Jacqueline Levitin

"STRANGELY ENOUGH," DEEPA MEHTA STATED to an audience in Vancouver in March 1999, "more than any time, I feel really Indian—more than I ever have."[1] Born in India in 1950, Mehta immigrated to Canada in 1973, and the question of her nationality frequently surfaces in interviews. Asked to clarify what she intended by her statement of Indianness, Mehta declared, with some exasperation, that the whole question of nationality no longer interested her. The real issue, she said, was where could she make the films that impassion her?

Since that day, Deepa Mehta has had cause to rethink the issue of identity and location because India, the place where she decided to shoot her films, has become temporarily inaccessible to her. In the early months of 2000, while beginning to shoot *Water*, the third in her trilogy of films that began with *Fire* (1996) (*Earth* [1998] is the second), she again met opposition from the Hindu Right. Mehta's difficulties with conservative forces began with the distribution of *Fire*, the first film she shot in India.[2] *Fire* tells the story of a lesbian relationship that develops between emotionally neglected sisters-in-law in a middle-class, joint household. Opposition mobilized in November–December 1998 when the film was launched in India. For two weeks, Mehta's opponents ransacked theatres and terrorized audiences in Mumbai (Bombay), Delhi, and Pune until the government stepped in to restore order; it also required that *Fire* be sent back to the Censor Board.[3] With *Water*, Mehta's opponents initiated their campaign even before production commenced. After only a few days of shooting, Hindu fundamentalists mounted demonstrations, destroyed sets, burned Mehta and her actors in effigy, and staged a protest mock suicide to force the production to shut down. They claimed the script was disrespectful of Hinduism and its holiest city, Varanasi (Benares), the film's location. (Rumours of its anti-Hindu contents proved impossible for the production company to contradict.) Mehta, they said, was purposefully controversial; her interests were solely commercial, to make money from portraying India negatively to the world.[4] Even some liberal voices agreed that Mehta could be seen as a "symbol of insensitive foreigners trampling on sacred soil."[5] Mehta's company later explained that the opposition to the production might have been set off by their dismissive response to a minor government official who wanted distribution rights to the film.[6] Was Mehta's film company then naïve to the ways power works in India, assuming standards of artistic freedom that belong not to

India but to the West? Although the production had obtained all required approvals,[7] local authorities sided with the protestors, declared the presence of the film production a provocation to public order, and required the company to cease shooting. Successful in driving Mehta out of Varanasi, her opponents further vowed that her company would be driven from wherever in India they attempted to shoot.[8] Mehta's supporters, in turn, initiated a letter-writing campaign calling attention to a situation of censorship by violence and intimidation. The Indian government, they claimed, failed to take timely action.[9]

Why such opposition in a city that, although indeed holy, is host to production companies shooting action films and love stories almost daily?[10] The assault on Mehta's films exceeds prior attacks and censorship involving local artists and filmmakers.[11] The filmmaker has become embroiled in the decades-old polarization between left and right, secular and theocratic in India, a battle that extends beyond India's borders via the non-resident players of the South Asian diaspora. For detractors and defenders, Mehta may be simply a pawn in the current chapter of this civil conflict. But through her filmmaking, and in the international responses she has rallied to her defence, she has also taken a role, both national and international, in this conflict.

In this essay I will discuss Deepa Mehta's career and filmmaking, but I see these aspects as inseparable from the contexts of production and consumption of her films, the socio-cultural politics of Canada and India, and the effects of the globalization of media generally. Her record is similarly inseparable from an understanding of the particular challenges she faces as an independent, transnational filmmaker. Transnational filmmaking is a category that has gained notable prominence lately. One can think of those filmmakers now making films all over the world who left China in the aftermath of Tiananmen Square in 1989, and others in self-exile from Hong Kong since the return of the island to Chinese control in 1997, and global influences upon media within China, particularly recently.[12] In India, filmmakers effect a transnational-like trajectory when they cross the North–South linguistic border. (The split is between Sanskrit-derived languages such as Hindi and those speaking unrelated Dravidian languages.) In popular Indian film, one finds a new internationalism of plots as attention shifts to the potential profits to be made by reaching a diasporic audience.[13] All this is accompanied by a hybridization of styles and frequently a lack of attention to place, turning precise locales into generic cities. It is something I witness daily as my own city, Vancouver, becomes Phoenix or the Bronx for international production companies in search of cheaper locations. These are the effects of an increasingly globalized film and television market. In India, they are particularly noticeable since the launching of cable and satellite television in 1991.

Without entering the debates concerning the definition and theory of transnational filmmaking, it is worth associating the term with a discussion of Mehta's films. While transnational filmmaking is not a homogeneous category,[14] filmmakers traversing political and cultural borders, literally and figuratively, generally face a similar set of obstacles. The focus here, then, will be on Deepa Mehta as a filmmaker manoeuvring her way through the challenges characteristic of transnational filmmaking. In turn, an investigation of the particularities of Mehta's career, both in North America and in India, will contribute to our understanding of transnational filmmaking generally, and demonstrate the practical impact of media's globalization on filmmakers. As this study will illustrate, transnational filmmaking does not exist in a vacuum; rather, it exists in symbiosis with the dominant and alternative cinemas and in constant negotiation between the global and the local at the moments of encoding of meanings and moments of decoding and re-coding. Viewing Mehta as a transnational filmmaking allows her films to be read and re-read not only as individual texts produced by authorial vision and generic conventions, but also as sites for intertextual, cross-cultural, and transnational struggles over meaning and identities.[15]

The Hyphenated Filmmaker
Transnational by default

In North America, the tendency is to recognize the duality of the immigrant's identity by label-ling individuals with a hyphen. In Europe, the practice appears variously to be the wholehearted adoption of the individual (e.g. the Rumanian-born artist is considered French) or—and here the desirability of the immigrant is an issue—to cite only the country of origin, though it may be a generation later. India, which has highly specialized categories of identity, does not easily adopt the foreigner and is suspicious of its own emigrants.

Two quotations will be useful to understanding the implications of these different mindsets and their effects on the transnational filmmaker. The first comes from an exchange with S. Gurumurthy, one of Mehta's opponents in the *Water* controversy.[16] But first, some details about *Water* are necessary as background. *Water*'s story takes place in the 1930s in a house for widows in the holy city of Varanasi on the Ganges. In the past, a widow of certain caste standing was considered to die in part with the death of her husband. Although she might be no more than ten years old (and there is a child widow in Mehta's scenario), Hindu tradition forbade her from remarrying or returning to her family, and required her to refrain from all pleasures. Conse-quently, widows went to places such as the house in Varanasi in Mehta's film to live out their days in abstinence. Another widow in *Water*'s script—Mehta's historical research demonstrated that there were many like her[17]—has been forced to prostitute herself but is now in love with a follower of Gandhi.

The interviewer asks Gurumurthy,

> Q: Several movies are made about people working in various professions. Films are made about widows also. Is it the fact that this lady is trying to sell an aspect of India to the western world that makes you angry?
> A: Yes, first of all, she is from abroad. She is not a resident of India; she is a Canadian citizen. If an outsider makes such films, there will always be suspicion that he/she is doing it with an ulterior motive.

After a moment, the interviewer returns to the issue:

> Q: Do you feel an Indian would never have viewed the problems of the widows the way Deepa Mehta has done?
> A: An Indian will never look at the issue the way Mehta has. If he does, there is some-thing wrong with his Indian-ness.

The arrogant tone of Gurumurthy's response, his simple distinction between Indians and outsid-ers, and automatic distrust of the latter, and his certainty about what constitutes an essential "Indianness" reveal much about nationalism and religion in India today.

In a discussion of Mehta's film *Fire*, Ratna Kapur proposes that the controversy over *Fire* ex-emplifies a struggle over the definition of culture currently taking place in India. The targeting of sex and sexuality, she says, "betrays an underlying fear that sex is something that is threatening to Indian cultural values, to the Indian way of life, to the very existence of the Indian nation."[18] Kapur's argument is that all sides in the debate over *Fire*—feminists and lesbian groups, as well as Hindu rightists—displayed an uncomplicated understanding of culture as static and unchanging.

In arguing in defence of Mehta's film that homosexuality has always been a part of Indian culture, lesbian rights advocates mistakenly assumed that the definition of Indianness is immutable, and that validation and legitimacy could only be established by appeals to history. They did not, asserts Kapur, challenge the essentialist story about culture. The film itself, says Kapur, was more progressive than its defenders in its recognition of the fluidity of culture.[19] She invokes Stuart Hall to argue for a cultural identity that is not based on a sense of unity, but includes points of difference in addition to points of similarity. The danger in not following Hall's model, she says, is setting up Indian culture in opposition to the "modern," the outsider, or the "West"—where feminism has continually been cast. She concludes, "*Fire*'s significance lies not so much in representing sexual pleasure between women, as it does in representing this relationship in the context of a joint Hindu family household at this very moment when the Right is in power"[20]—and largely determining the outcome of cultural controversies.[21] I will return to the debate over ownership of the definition of Indianness later.

The second quotation, from the *Village Voice*, talks about *Such a Long Journey* (1999), a film by another (sometimes) transnational filmmaker living in Canada, Sturla Gunnarsson, born in Iceland. The film is based on the 1991 novel of the same name by Indo-Canadian writer Rohinton Mistry and takes place in 1971 in Bombay. The reviewer introduces the film this way: "Acted by Indians in English, produced with British and Canadian money, and directed by an Icelander with American TV to his credit, *Journey* has an acultural lostness about it, meant for all races but expressive of none. It's a sensation bound to grow more common as globalism trods on." He then tempers his negative criticism: "Gunnarsson's movie rises above this vague dispossession, particularly in its respect for the textures of Bombay."[22]

Other than the reviewer's notably inadequate vocabulary to describe the audience of transnational filmmaking ("meant for all races [*sic*] but expressive of none") and his mistaken identification of Gunnarsson as an Icelander, his comments raise at least two further questions. The first relates back to the reviewer himself: what qualifies this reviewer to pronounce judgement on a film set in India while he, himself, sits in New York? If he finds that Gunnarsson's film manages to "rise above this vague dispossession, particularly in its respect for the textures of Bombay," is it because he has knowledge of the textures of Bombay and of the precise period of Gunnarsson's film? Is such knowledge necessary for the critic to respond adequately to a transnational film such as Gunnarsson's, or those of Mehta's trilogy? Who is the ideal critic or spectator of transnational films? These questions, of course, can be asked in relation to all films, but they are more pressing for the transnational filmmaker because *authenticity* is a criterion front and centre in critics' minds.

The second question raised by the *Village Voice* article relates to the reviewer's comment that the film has an "acultural lostness about it." Assuming that the reviewer is correct, that the film is "unsituated," how can the transnational filmmaker avoid this pitfall? How can she situate herself in a particular culture while simultaneously aiming the film at an international market? And how does the goal of making a film that is both situated and international determine the approach taken by the transnational filmmaker?

Humanism or Globalism?

> I wanted [*Fire*'s] emotional content to be universal. The struggle between tradition and
> individual expression is one that takes place in every culture. *Fire* deals with this specifically
> in the context of Indian society. What appealed to me was that the story had a resonance
> that transcended geographic and cultural boundaries.[23]

For Deepa Mehta, the problem of reaching a transnational audience can be resolved by finding universal situations and emotions. As Mehta pursues her transnational film career, she appears increasingly to be turning to humanism as a model. Humanism assumes a basic emotional and experiential stratum on which all human beings can communicate. And although ideological criticism has demonstrated the hegemonic underpinnings of what humanists assume to be "universal," humanism nevertheless has reappeared as an ideal for communication across and within borders. Mehta frequently mentions Indian filmmaker Satyajit Ray, describing him as a humanist and a strong influence on her work.[24] Ray, as the director mostly of minority Bengali-language art films, was better known outside his country than within, and within India only to an educated elite. His *Pather Panchali* (1955), the first in his Apu trilogy, was among a vanguard of foreign films able to cross into the Western market.[25]

What did Western audiences see in this work? The Apu trilogy *is* situated in a precise Indian locale, but the simple life of rural poverty that Ray renders in beautiful black and white was not his own experience. Does his film then exemplify successful translating across national borders based on a situatedness, or rather the internationality of a particular class' sensibilities—that of those who control the marketplace? Similarly, Mehta mentions that she was pleased that so many women in India responded to her film *Fire*—women who were simple housewives.[26] What then of the younger (but not middle-aged) men that Mehta says also appreciated her film?[27] Are the positive responses to her film an argument for universalism or evidence of the role ideology plays in audience response?

The debate over culture within India, as noted earlier, is mirrored by a process of acculturation taking place in the South Asian diaspora by means of popular Hindi films. Rachel Dwyer notes a tendency in recent Indian film to place characters in a variety of geographic locations.[28] By including foreign locations or even tourist destinations within India as both real and imagined spaces, these films acknowledge India's new mobile middle class, as well as the important market of the South Asian diaspora. These films propose, Dwyer asserts, that the Indian can feel at ease anywhere, "because what really matters is a sense of home, somewhere to belong, a *watan* or *desh* ('homeland'), sanitized and acceptable, with no trace of it being in any way inferior to or more 'backward' than the west."[29] Increasingly, she says, even for young audiences, "home" is defined by Indian values. Indian values are negotiable, but the films of the exceedingly popular Yash Chopra demonstrate that even (or especially) for younger audiences, "being Indian has to do with a survival of values."[30] Younger generations may "prefer Hollywood films for action, but they much prefer their romantic films to come from Bombay."[31] The romantic films appeal to a South Asian diaspora, Dwyer states, but are not watched by "Euro-Americans," because the Indian values they display "are not those of the modern or postmodern world, but those of a world that is almost feudal: family (*khaandaan*), honour (*izzat*), modesty (*laaj*), and increasingly, religion, as opposed to work, companionate marriage, self-knowledge, or the pursuit of happiness."[32] Is Hindi cinema, she asks, "one of the world's most globalizing cultural forms which is not American and is not in English?"[33] Her article argues that it is.

Interestingly, Mehta's interviews never mention a feeling of alienation from India, although she left more than twenty-five years ago. In one interview, she mentions reading Luis Buñuel's autobiography, *My Last Sigh*.[34] "Buñuel," she tells the interviewer, "talks about the importance of characters being rooted to a place. He says that any character that is honest and rooted to a place immediately becomes universal because human emotions are universal. I think this is true." Authenticity of place must have been on Mehta's mind as she considered where else she could possibly continue shooting *Water*, whose meaning is enmeshed in its Varanasi locale. But place, as this quotation from Mehta interprets it, is potentially as mobile as the notion of home described by Dwyer because Mehta links it to a notion of "honesty." Mehta believes she can be universal (humanist) by presenting characters who are born honestly from the world of her experience, i.e., her personal (but competing) set of Indian values. Beginning with *Fire*, she has written all her own scripts. "For a long time I was confused about my identity," Mehta told an interviewer in 1998 in India:

> I've never felt Canadian. I used to be upset about being called a 'visible minority,' that's what they called coloured people there. I used to come to India and was called an NRI here [Non-Resident Indian]. The problem was not about belonging anywhere, it was a dislike for labels ... Now I feel very happy being who I am, Deepa Mehta.[35]

The happiness, it seems, comes from a trust in her own (mobile) authenticity and memory, and her decision to draw upon it.

Dwyer and Mehta's comments return us to the question raised in relation to Sturla Gunnarsson's film: what can be considered authentically national in the globalized world of filmmaking? A consideration of Mehta's career in terms of three aspects will illuminate her further negotiation of the problem: money, style, and theme.

It Pays To Be a National

In interviews, Mehta frequently complains that she has not had luck financing her films in Canada. She claims it is because they are not considered to be sufficiently "Canadian." What she refers to, but of which the readers of her interviews are likely not aware (and Mehta typically makes no attempt at clarification), is not an essential Canadian identity to which her films fail to conform but rather the criteria employed at both the federal and provincial levels to determine assistance to film production and distribution in Canada.[36] In the case of the federal culture institution, Telefilm Canada, these policies were put in place to ensure that Canadian taxpayers' money was used to support Canadian talent—essentially to protect the Canadian film industry from being overwhelmed by foreign, predominantly American, production, as had historically been the case. By setting criteria that institutions could use to assist film production, or offering incentives to production in Canada through tax credits, regulators hoped to build a strong indigenous industry.[37] Mehta's first feature, *Sam & Me* (1991), which was shot in Canada and tells the story of a friendship that develops between a newly arrived young Indian immigrant and his charge, an old and dotty Jew, the father of his uncle's employer. Mehta complains that *Sam & Me* was not deemed "Canadian enough" to receive government financing.

Mehta hired Indian writer Ranjit Chowdhry, himself a recent arrival to Canada, to write and act in *Sam & Me*.[38] Neither Canadian citizens nor permanent residents, Chowdhry and then-little-known Indian actor Om Puri, who plays the young Indian's sycophant uncle, did not count as Canadians under the institutions' point system, which considers the citizenship of a film's key personnel. It is unlikely that Mehta would have found experienced local talent to play the roles, and in this the point system is prejudiced against the scripts of ethnic filmmakers, but Mehta additionally complains that the evaluators at Telefilm Canada were simply not interested in her version of multiculturalism. Desperate to complete her financing, Mehta appealed to Britain's Channel Four and ITC Distribution. Both agreed to invest. Mehta could feel justified in not compromising her story or her choice of cast to meet institutional criteria when *Sam & Me* won an honourable mention in the Caméra d'or (first features) category at the Cannes Film Festival in 1991.[39] The success of *Sam & Me* catapulted Mehta into a bigger league.

While showing *Sam & Me* at the London film festival, Mehta was surprised with an offer from George Lucas to direct an episode of his television series *Young Indiana Jones Chronicles* (the episode entitled *Benares*, 1992). This was followed by an offer to direct *Camilla* (1993) and, in 1994, another offer from Lucas to direct the final segment of *Young Indiana Jones Chronicles*, a movie of the week entitled *Travels with Father*. Mehta speaks highly of her experience with George Lucas, whom she found both respectful and supportive.[40] Her experience with *Camilla* turned out to be less happy.[41] Produced with Canadian and British financing, *Camilla*, like *Sam & Me*, was about a relationship across generations, here between two women. The script appealed to Mehta, and the film's budget of $11 million was the largest ever given to a woman filmmaker in Canada.[42] Mehta was able to work with top actors: Jessica Tandy as the old woman who seeks to travel from Georgia to Toronto to recapture her past, and Brigitte Fonda as the young woman who unwittingly helps her escape her controlling but well-intentioned son, and gains self-confidence in the process. Mehta later claimed that she did not recognize her film once the producers got through re-editing it, although she was blamed for its failure.[43] As a consequence, Mehta found herself with no new offers to direct.

The effect of this "failure" on Mehta was a promise to herself to make only those films for which she had passion and over which she could maintain artistic control.[44] With these criteria in mind, she turned again to finding production financing.

Fire, *Earth*, and *Water* are all executive-produced by Mehta's companion David Hamilton, which means that, although there are collaborating producers involved and the budgets have been smaller ($1.6 million for *Fire*, and $3.2 million for *Earth*), financing and control now stay in family hands. As well, $3.2 million goes much further in India than it does in Canada—a practical reason to "feel Indian" and shoot in India.

Style and (Trans)Nationality

> I see the evolution of a hybrid filmmaking. There is film being made that is not 'Bombay' and not 'Western' ... In terms of talent, production design, how the director deals with actors and characters [which] have a sensibility that is no longer one that comes out of Indian cinema.[45]

Mehta consistently works with the same creative team and, when possible, the same actors. Her crew is a United Nations of film. Her director of photography is usually Giles Nuttgens, who is British. His first assistant is French, and his third assistant, Italian; Mehta's first assistant director is Hungarian. Nuttgens has worked on every one of Mehta's films except *Camilla* since they met on the *Young Indiana Jones Chronicles*; so has producer/line producer Anne Masson and production designer Aradhana Seth. Editor Barry Farrell worked with Mehta on both *Camilla* and *Fire*. Ranjit Chowdhry has a role in *Camilla* and plays the family servant, Mundu, in *Fire*. Mehta claims she would have used him in *Earth* had his Hindi been better. Nandita Das, whose debut in film was as the younger sister-in-law in *Fire*, was given starring roles in both *Earth* and *Water*, while the widely admired Shabana Azmi, who plays the elder sister-in-law, was to appear again in *Water*.[46] A good understanding of her intentions as director is paramount to Mehta: she consults with key personnel as soon as she has a script. Her attempts to build a close-knit crew have been rewarded by their fierce loyalty.[47]

Clearly communicated intentions are perceptible across Mehta's films. Similarities of style and point of view mark them all, aspects of which can be attributed to her Indian origins. Like her later films, *Sam & Me* contains a surprising number of characters and perspectives, something not typical of North American filmmaking. It is, however, reminiscent of the multiple plots of popular Indian films, or even of Mehta's experience growing up in a large joint Indian household where one was aware of others' perspectives.[48] Mehta was raised on a diet of popular Hindi-language films ("Bollywood" cinema, for Bombay, the film capital of India—the number of films it produces exceeds Hollywood), which she would view in the cinemas owned by her film-distributor father in her home town of Amritsar, near the border with Pakistan.[49] These films are predominantly melodramas. Categorized as "masalas," these typically include at least one love story and, despite extraordinary adversity, ensure that moral order and social stability are restored by film's end.[50] Songs and dances are dispersed liberally throughout. The screenplays of popular films are also frequently published, which is why suspicions must have increased when Mehta refused to release the screenplay of *Water* for her critics' perusal: when Bollywood's films are simple variations on plot, being secretive about one's screenplay is not an issue.

Even in the huge canvas of the partition story in *Earth*, history, in typical Mehta fashion, is told by way of a story of individuals. Individuals are accorded a dignity in their varying perspectives. Even the British, whose decision to divide India along patterns of Muslim and Hindu settlement is widely held to be at least partly responsible for the bloodshed that followed, are treated with sympathy as individuals. A statement by the British commander, "India is the only home I've known," is presented with the same respect accorded Sikh Sher Singh's lament, "Lahore is my home." (As in the configuration noted by Dwyer, the word "home" is always given particular resonance in Mehta's films.[51]) It is likely the film's focus on characters who are identified by religious group (personality here takes a secondary place) that causes many spectators to remember *Earth* as more sympathetic to the Hindu Indian perspective on partition than to the Muslim point of view. Although the film's most appalling images of bloodshed (the train stacked with hacked-up bodies) depict the killing of Muslims, we remember better the image of Shanta, the Hindu ayah, whose hiding place is discovered through the cunning of the vengeful Muslim Ice Candy Man, as she is dragged away at the film's end to what we suppose is a terrible death. (Masseur, also a victim of Ice Candy Man, is depicted as less obviously a Muslim than his murderer; for Shanta, he is willing to become a Hindu.)

The disappearance of Shanta, the beautiful nanny of Lenny, the young Parsi girl through whose eyes the story is told,[52] affects us more because Mehta's stylistics here involve us with the individual characters. As in Bollywood film, Mehta works on a heightened emotional register and, Hollywood-style, through a relay of looks to "suture" us into the film's world.[53] Cutting back and forth between the terrified Shanta, her tormentor Ice Candy Man, and Lenny, who has been tricked into revealing her ayah's hiding place, we watch Shanta disappear into the mob. Shifting between Lenny's helplessly guilty gaze, Shanta's terror, and Ice Candy Man's frozen determination, the scene is given a more intense emotional presentation than it receives in Bapsi Sidhwa's understated autobiographical novel *Cracking India*,[54] upon which Mehta based her scenario.

Mehta employs emotion and the child's literal perspective to grab her audiences—here, in order to lead them to experience what for both her and Sidwa was the incomprehensible splintering of a peaceful community. The breakdown of relationships in Shanta's multicultural circle of admiring friends, in particular the destruction of the tense but balanced triangle of the ayah and her two suitors, Masseur and Ice Candy Man, is an allegory in miniature of the explosion along communal lines that occurred on the national scale. (Some, however, argue that this accepted—

ideologically humanist?—version of events ignores the parallel divisions that occurred along religious *and* economic lines.) Mehta's focus on multiple perspectives is intended to help us understand how former friends could become capable of killing each other. Ice Candy Man's murderous rage follows his discovery of his anxiously awaited loved ones among the hacked-up dead. (How else could one fathom every individual slaughter if not by someone, himself, emotionally deranged?) We share Ice Candy Man's point of view as he opens the door of the train to the lifeless but still blood-dripping victims of a Hindu massacre while music swells in the background.

This last image of partition violence may be rejected as unsubtle and emotionally exploitative, but it is the unfolding of the love story, told like a Bollywood melodrama, that most cheapens Mehta's historical portrait. In *Earth*'s narrative, unrequited love becomes the dramatic cause of a partition mob's violence. Mehta's film does not end happily in the manner of Bollywood models. The fate of *Earth*'s characters, in part, was already determined by history. But the vision of the ayah being dragged away is not where Bapsi Sidhwa ends her novel. There, we find the ayah many months later, a captive, but still alive. If, as Mehta says, all those later pages were anti-climactic and unnecessary to the story, the scene in the film of ayah's disappearance also permits *Earth* to end like all of Mehta's films: with the pain born of experience.[55] In Mehta's film world, happiness is typically poignant and ephemeral.

Mehta's films are highly production designed, and she writes all the details into her scripts.[56] Even when we are not consciously aware of it, their colour schemes affect us—the saffron orange, white, and green of *Fire* (the colours of the Indian flag), or the buff tones of *Earth*. Although Mehta was not able to film *Earth* in Lahore, and Delhi substitutes, her use of an earth-tone palette makes Lahore a palpable place, and we share the physical agony of having to leave it. She is also sensuous in her use of fabric. One remembers the hanging folds of netting that enclose the lovemaking of the sisters-in-law in *Fire* like a breathing cocoon, or the billowing sari—orange, she says, the colour of passion—as the two women gather their laundry on the rooftop in a scene that marks their growing attraction to each other. The production design of her films—remarkably intricate, especially in scenes that depict South Asians, even the South Asians in the made-in-Canada *Sam & Me*—is suggestive of the detail of traditional Indian painting and sculpture or fabric art.[57] The rich textures and colours of the house that Nik joins in *Sam & Me* contrast—like the lively multicultural mix of people who live there—with the unwelcoming anonymity of colour and texture that characterize the house of his employer. Even the old man, Sam, feels happier in Nik's home. But still more indicative of Mehta's negotiation of her Indian and Canadian identities in her role as transnational filmmaker is her use of language, music, and symbol.

Sam & Me is in English. Mehta uses Indian music, but only diegetically, quoting from an Indian film and a religious tape; for background music, she uses jazz and reggae. Style transformations towards Indianness begin with *Fire* and *Earth*. *Fire* was shot in English. Mehta wrote the screenplay in English and explains that she did not have the money to have it translated into Hindi before shooting, although her claim about the script's untranslatability is disputed by at least one of her critics.[58] A Hindi version came only with the film's Indian release. With *Earth*, she was able to have her script translated before production, and English plays only a minor role in that film; all characters speak their appropriate languages. Considerations of language are extremely important in India. Hindi is the language of north India, although Hindi speakers are the country's largest single language group. Speakers of Urdu (primarily Muslims) understand oral Hindi without difficulty but not written Hindi, and Hindi is resented as culturally imperialist by those in the south. While English is spoken by most of India's educated elite, many view it as the language of colonization. As well, language is of paramount importance in the distribution of a film. Although European markets find subtitles acceptable, American audiences will stay away from a film that does not speak their language. That Mehta made a film such as *Earth* in the languages of India's communities is a commitment both cultural and financial.

With *Fire*, Mehta began her association with lyricist Javed Akhtar and composer A.R. Rahman. In Hindi popular film, a musical film tradition, the music director and lyricist are as significant as the stars. Akhtar, who worked with Mehta on *Fire* and *Earth* and was engaged to write the songs for *Water*, has been described as the "most popular lyricist [in India] today."[59] Rahman, whose early work was exclusively for south Indian directors, became well known across India when films such as Mani Ratnam's *Roja* were dubbed into Hindi in the early 1990s and became runaway hits.[60] He has since composed for Hindi-language films, and his work on *Fire* was his first venture into an English-language production. Although still young, he has already become a star composer, known for his fusion of Indian and Western instrumentation.[61] His music for *Fire* and *Earth* is considered outstanding. With *Earth*, closer to the Bollywood tradition, Mehta dares bring the music forward (the ayah even sings, Bollywood playback style, at young Papoo's wedding), but she still reserves it as background support for the drama as in Western film models. Indian critics have lamented its minor role.[62]

As for stars, another mainstream Indian film tradition, Mehta's choices have generally been determined by actor quality, not stardom. With *Earth*, Mehta has gone for quality *and* star power. For the difficult role of Dil Navaz, Ice Candy Man, who must transform himself from charmer into murderer, she chose Aamir Khan, the most popular performer of Bollywood according to a poll by the *Times of India*.[63] For Masseur, the second suitor of *Earth*'s Shanta, Mehta chose Rahul Khanna, an unknown in cinema circles, but famous with his fans as an MTV VJ. Both are fair-skinned and handsome in the Indian popular film way. Gesture and situations in the film (for example, kite flying as a sexual stand-in as Ice Candy Man's arms entwine Shanta) would be familiar to Bollywood audiences. And, like Bollywood's female stars, Nandita Das, if not presented as a Hollywood-style sex object, is still presented as much the object of visual desire for the film audience as for her admirers in the world of the film.

For style, Mehta's increasing tendency not to explain things for a foreign audience should also be mentioned. Popular Hindi film typically includes mythic references. The characters of Indian epics populate daily life; both revered and familiar, their stories are widely known. In *Fire*, Mehta refers to epic stories in the names she gives the two sisters-in-law, Sita and Radha, goddesses "whose attributes of virtue, self-sacrifice and devotion to their respective husbands have come to represent the hallmarks of Indian womanhood as it is imagined."[64] (Anticipating the stir that a film with a character named Sita who engages in a same-sex relationship would cause in India, Mehta agreed to change Sita to Nita for the film's Indian release.[65]) She includes, as well, the story of Sita's trial by fire (the *agnipariksha*) as it is traditionally told in the Ramayana: although Ram perhaps believed his wife to be faithful to him, to prove her innocence and purity before others, he required Sita to pass through fire and emerge unscathed. Mehta explains that she employed the story three times in the film to make its significance clear.[66] However, in the one scene that depicts the story on a purely allegorical level (prior scenes have been re-enactments in drama or as video within the film), it is Radha, not Sita, who emerges alive from the fire in which her husband, angry because abandoned, leaves her to die.[67] In this altering of the traditional mythic tale, Ratna Kapur sees Mehta's radicalness: "Culture is invoked to counter the dominant cultural tale"; in choosing to abandon her husband for Sita, Radha is found guiltless.[68]

In contrast to *Fire*'s explanatory presentation, much in *Earth* can be missed if one is not attuned to the religious and political signifiers of clothing, architecture, accents, and language. Mehta does not go out of her way to make sure her audience follows her use of symbols and icons. For example, she makes no particular effort to assure they recognize that Muslim mosques and Hindu temples are silhouetted together against the sky, that the name Singh identifies a character as a Sikh, or that the servant's choice to become a Christian both puts him out of reach of Muslim vengeance and releases him from the stigma of Hindu caste. Such a lack of explanation is surprising in a film that seems more likely destined for a non-South Asian audience than for one already familiar with the partition story.

Although still making hybrid films, it seems Mehta is becoming "more Indian" in her aesthetic choices. Or is she simply demonstrating good business sense? Today, as things Indian become chic, is explaining less desirable?[69] Do stories of another country's problematic issues, wrapped in almost-Bollywood tales of sex and death, sell?[70] Are negative stereotypes of India commercially exploitable—as Mehta's Hindu fundamentalist critics contend, as even Madhu Kishwar, the editor of the Indian feminist journal *Manushi,* asserts[71]—placing *Fire* in a self-serving tradition of India-disparaging that began with the British?[72] To judge from the box office success of Hollywood's xenophobic plots and characterization, perhaps so. As the daughter of a film distributor and exhibitor, Mehta early on developed good instincts for what helps a film's success. However, Mehta sees her films as countering, not perpetuating, stereotypical depictions of India. In *Fire*, for example, she explains she is dealing with the experiences of an Indian urban middle class that numbers more than the population of the United States, but is ignored in Indian cinema's evocations of the British Raj or in Satyajit Ray's images of rural life embraced by the West. The closeness of the women's relationship in *Fire*, Mehta says, was inspired by her mother's closeness with her own sisters-in-law; an understanding of Radha's hesitancy to leave her husband developed during her own struggle to leave her marriage;[74] *Earth* was born from the stories told to her as a child living in Amritsar; and the real oppressions of widows told in *Water* are well documented in the work of scholars she has read. These justifications, however, are not sufficient to convince vehement critics such as Kishwar or Rima Banerji (who lives in Canada and also writes for *Manushi*) of the innocence of Mehta's motivations.

Reception
The struggle over interpretation

According to Banerji, *Fire* "recycles a number of stereotypes popularly consumed as monolithic truths about South Asian life. [These are] reinforced in the West, but also within elite sectors of Indian society ... This first myth—that the already subjugated Hindu woman's identity is forever at the crossroads of dharma [the Hindu/Buddhist moral code of behaviour] and kama [the god of love]—is a familiar feature of discourse centring on Indian women."[75] Following a line of criticism developed by Kishwar in an earlier issue of *Manushi*,[76] Banerji further contends, "Even if we accept for the moment that Mehta's notion of Radha and Sita is the primary and legitimate one—that they are objects of male exploitation (and in many versions of folklore, they are not!)—we cannot take these two figures as uniform representatives of how Indian female identity is imagined ... Even if we just limit ourselves to Hindu religious narratives, the prominence of Durga, Kali, and Chandi literally point to another story."[77] Banerji says that neither the image of woman-as-oppressed nor woman as modelled on the fearful spirit of shakti[78] can explain the everyday lives of India's females. Women "use and are used by the two extreme sets of symbols in complicated ways."[79]

As a resident of Lajpat Nagar, the community in the outskirts of New Delhi that Mehta claims to be the location of *Fire*, Kishwar critiques the film for inaccuracy in its depiction of isolated family life and the public working roles of the women.[80] Her argumentation—as if fictional films were documentaries—is suspect, as is her motive for singling out Mehta for a lengthy four-part critique while not according the same extended treatment to examples of the very sexist and clearly unrealistic Bollywood cinema. But Kishwar claims Mehta has brought Kishwar's wrath on herself:

> If Ms Mehta had described [*Fire*] as one more domestic melodrama dealing with marital incompatibility due to the insensitivity of some husbands, I would have confined this review to assessing how well the film deals with this well-worn theme ... It is only because she labours hard to call the marriages of Radha and Sita "Hindu marriages" and attributes their failures and crudities to the Hindu worldview that one begins to view Deepa as one more among a growing tribe of Indian women who have understood that there is a lot of money to be made by portraying the real and imagined miseries of much-pitied Indian women in the western market.[81]

Kishwar also resents all the publicity Mehta was able to generate around her film. (The Shiv Sainiks "took her bait and expressed outrage at her self-confessed attack on Hindu culture.") Kishwar titles her critique "Naive Outpourings of a Self-Hating Indian." For her, Mehta is insensitive to the legacy of insecurity brought by colonization: "She [Mehta] admits to thinking in English," Kishwar even offers as proof.[82] If Mehta were more Indian, she would be more sensitive to the already-wounded pride of her countrymen.[83] The vehemence of Kishwar's attack makes the reader suspicious, but the gist of her argument cannot be mistaken: Mehta's vision is inauthentic and foreign, and Kishwar is in a position to know it.

For her part, Mehta states, "Moving away from India [to Canada] provided me with perspective and made me fearless."[84] The abiding effect of inculcated tradition on Indian women became more apparent to her as she struggled in Canada between a nascent feminism ("I had read Virginia Woolf's *A Room of One's Own*") and what she realized was the self-censorship of deeply inculcated prohibitions against divorce.[85] As a filmmaker living in Canada, she found the courage to say things that an Indian woman typically could not dare say. She describes *Fire* as a film about lesbians, but first of all as a film about choices: tradition must evolve to be alive, and women should have the right to choose a different path from what tradition expects of them; becoming lesbian is just one such choice.[86]

For Ratna Kapur, whether or not Mehta's portrayal is accurate is unimportant. In summary to her discussion of *Fire* and the debate in India over ownership of the definition of culture, she states, "*Fire* attempts to situate the love story between Radha and Sita in a specific cultural context and a familial location ... Whether fantastical or real seems irrelevant. This is the context as it exists in the imagination of a first generation Indian immigrant to Canada."[87] This comment shocks me. For Kapur, although Mehta's challenge to rigid tradition is more effective than the position of local lesbians, *Fire* is simply the results of the imaginings of a "first generation Indian immigrant to Canada." Does she not see Mehta as at least a transnational, and a legitimate player in this debate? I doubt that Kapur is restating here the essentialist position that she herself discredits. Rather, her generous postmodern accepting of difference simply deflates all position-taking. In contrast, what is clear in looking at the films themselves is that living abroad has sharpened Mehta's sense of moral indignation and outrage. In film after film—those made in Canada and those made in India—she attacks prejudice and injustice, defending the "other" and allowing no one off the hook.[88]

Born into a family relocated because of partition, Mehta was already a transnational by birth. Following her new husband Paul Saltzman to Canada in 1973 was a second dislocation. She had begun documentary filmmaking after completing her master's degree in philosophy at Delhi University (by accident, she recalls, while considering whether to continue on to a PhD[89]). In Toronto, Mehta, together with Saltzman and her brother, Dilip Mehta, formed a production company, Sunrise Films.[90] Mehta worked as an editor, directed for episodic television (the company specialized in children's series[91]), and made television dramas before attempting *Sam & Me*. Mehta claims she "would have died" if she had been unable to make *Sam & Me*.[92] Although she did not write the screenplay, the idea was hers and she collaborated closely with the writer, Ranjit Chowdhry. It is clear that she put her heart into the film.[93] More than a tale of a young Indian abroad, the film is an indictment of a country that is multicultural in name only. Coming from a comfortable family background, Mehta had been shocked in Canada to find herself viewed as a brown-skinned "other."[94] Perhaps her Canadian experiences forced her into feeling Indian.

Mehta's is not a Manichean universe. Typically, her characters are not only right or wrong, or good or bad. Sam, the old man in *Sam & Me*, is at first full of prejudice against South Asians. Although, as Jews, Sam and his family are justified in feeling paranoid about anti-Semitic prejudice, being victims themselves does not let them off the hook. Mehta champions the victims of intolerance, but she examines their own personal record for bias—usually with the humour of irony. Nik's cab-driver friend, for example, wanting to educate Nik about the cultural insensitivity of hegemonic Canadians, prepares him to hear the standard litany of his ignorant white fares, but the demonstration fare fails to perform. At other times, Mehta's method is more indirect. An example is the repeated image of the black neighbour watching from his window, ignored by South Asians, Jews, and Chinese alike, who comes magically to the rescue when Sam collapses during a joyous game of cricket to which he has not been invited.[95]

Mehta may not be subtle in her characterizations (Kishwar points out all the blunt instances of male sexual deviance in *Fire*[96]), but she is discriminating in her choice of actors and how she directs them in their roles. Ashok (Kulbhushan Kharbanda), Radha's husband in *Fire*, for example, has begun a program of abstinence from sexual relations because Radha is unable to conceive a child. Devoted to his guru (whose "testicles have become too big for his loin cloth"—a description mocked by Kishwar), he believes sex for pleasure only is wrong for a spiritual man. Occasionally Ashok asks Radha to lie down beside him—but only as a test of his will power. A dutiful Indian wife, Radha lives with this arrangement. Ashok is unconcerned that Radha herself might have desires and, spurned, tries to leave Radha to burn to death at the end of the film; but until this act Ashok displays a face that is more likely to inspire our sympathy than our ill will.[97] Indeed, Indian viewers have cited Ashok's generosity in choosing not to divorce Radha for being barren.

What I, from my perspective in Canada, have termed Mehta's sympathy for differing perspectives and "moral indignation" against all instances of intolerance has been described differently by Kishwar. Interestingly, we both note the same scene for particular examination. This is not surprising, because the restaurant scene from *Fire* "jars." Not beautiful, as are so many of

Mehta's scenes, and not about the growing intimacy between Sita and Radha, it follows instead Jatin (Jaaved Jaaferi), Sita's husband by arranged marriage, who is spending the afternoon with his Chinese girlfriend, Julie (Alice Poon). Julie is the woman Jatin would have married if he had been allowed a choice (men are also oppressed by tradition, Mehta indicates)—and if the independent and ambitious Julie would have accepted to live in a joint Indian household; instead they continue their relationship as lovers. The restaurant scene directly follows a scene with the sisters-in-law in the family house. It is the festival of Karvachauth and, while Jatin dines with his lover, Radha and Sita are spending the day fasting and refraining from any liquids to assure the long life of their husbands. (Sita's line "I'm so sick of all this devotion" marks the change of scene.) The restaurant scene also includes Julie's father (Avijit Dutt), and someone we presume to be Julie's brother. The scene "bothers" because, other than for the useful juxtaposition noted above, it is not clearly motivated in terms of plot. We do not know Julie's family—we have never seen her father or brother before and never will again for the rest of the film. This scene seems to be written for us, the audience, alone.

According to my interpretation, the scene is unusually complex and also unusually imprecise. It gives a confusing history of Julie's father—fleeing the Cultural Revolution (i.e., from mainland China) but reminiscing about Hong Kong—as he declares his preference for "shitting comfortably" reading the *Kowloon News* rather than on a hole in the ground like "stupid, bloody Indians." Are Julie and her father and brother there simply to signify "generic Chinese" (the actor who plays the father actually appears to be of mixed race), to tell us that prejudice against Chinese (only Chinese?) exists in India and that the Chinese are consequently bitter? The boy recounts that he has been called "Chinky." I do not doubt that such an event could happen, but I wonder at the level of insults the father heaps in revenge. Perhaps the scene is staged to show Julie, who was earlier depicted as rebellious, acting now like a traditional daughter and doting wife—like Radha and Sita in fact—in the presence of her own father. (In a classic-style Chinese dress, she feeds Jatin choice tidbits.) But why does Mehta go to the trouble of telling us Julie has learned to speak English with an American accent? Is it to say Julie recognizes that hegemonic power lies with American, not Indian, English? Or was the actress just incapable of any other accent? Mehta's presentation of Julie is so caricatured that we do not know if we are to admire or disparage her ambitions. Most likely, the scene's purpose lies in its depiction of a hierarchy of power and otherness. The depiction of Julie's father's confrontation with Jatin seems calculated to bring Jatin down a peg or two. Jatin may lord it over Sita at home, but he must accept revenge-inspired racial insults from a man to whom, for Julie's sake, he cannot show disrespect. (Race here seems to substitute for gender in the equalling of scores.) Jatin's response to the father's barrage is measured: "You are right, sir. We Indians are a very complex people." Complex, yes, because there are certain parts of Indian culture that Jatin himself would rather leave behind. The tangled motivation for the scene is reminiscent of a scene in *Sam & Me:* the sudden appearance of the black neighbour and his saviour role serving to prove the ill-founded logic of the South Asians' counter-racism.

This same scene is interpreted quite differently, however, and with none of my ambivalence, by Mehta's critic in India, Kishwar, who sees in it a further attack on the traditional joint family. Kishwar begins by commenting on the film's depiction of Radha and Sita's demanding mother-in-law:

> The Indian family system is also condemned as stifling human happiness because we are
> still foolish enough to believe that our old parents should be taken care of by their own
> children rather than consigned to old age homes or left to fend for themselves. Jatin's

Chinese girlfriend, who wants to live in Hong Kong, refuses to marry him because she would feel suffocated in a "joint-family" ... The Chinese girlfriend's father seems to give vent to deep hatred for Indians which sounds more like Ms Mehta's own disdain for fellow Indians.[98]

Kishwar concludes, "True enough, Ms Mehta. Some of us even enjoy pouring shit on the heads of our fellow Indians because it has become a lucrative proposition in the western market."[99]

Kishwar continues her attack on the scene in another installment, where she describes Jatin's response not as "measured," as I assess it to be, but as "sheepish" and thus totally unrealistic:

If Deepa knew the basics of Indian family life, she would know that Indian men grow up expecting to be pampered and honoured like little gods by their prospective in-laws. Their inverted racism may manifest itself in accepting insults from a western woman but they certainly don't take such shit from an ethnic Chinese woman or father-in-law. Mehta's lack of understanding and mean-spirited caricature of middle class family life among urban Hindus is amazing considering Deepa Mehta claims to belong to such a family.[100]

A Chinese person couldn't possibly act superior to us, Kishwar seems to say, especially a Chinese woman. Why, we are superior to them! I find Kishwar's explanation of the "realistic" response Jatin should have displayed to be proof that Mehta was right in her assessment of Indian racism: there is a hierarchy of difference in India.

By Way of Conclusion
Globalization again

You cannot isolate India anymore. Global telecommunications have made it an impossibility.[101]

Could Mehta have gone on to make films with the controversial and complex perspectives of *Fire* and *Earth* in Canada? One of the differences between Mehta and her compatriot Sturla Gunnarsson is that Gunnarsson is a blond Icelandic-Canadian and Mehta part of a visible minority. In Canada, as a relatively unknown filmmaker with brown skin, Mehta was expected to make only films that relate the minority's experience, and in predefined terms. *Sam & Me* did not stay within those terms and presumably this is why it was not of interest to Telefilm. Canadian film critic Kass Banning terms it "being pegged by 'race'." "Ethnicity," she says, "brings an attendant particularism that annuls the possibility of making allegorical statements."[102] "Pegged by race," and not a lesbian herself (although being a lesbian is an additional liability), Mehta likely would not have been funded by Canada to make *Fire* as a film about lesbians and, allegorically, about the hold of tradition and a call for choice. Certainly, it would not have been accepted if it were construed to possibly critique (please, no controversy) rather than celebrate ethnic communities. Nor would she necessarily have been understood if she presented *Earth* as concerned with the *reinstatement* of difference in a formerly accepting multicultural community, because Canada officially knows nothing of real multiculturalism: "If people can see minorities as real human beings, complexities, flaws and all," Mehta has remarked, "then maybe we'll all be able to talk to each other."[103] Interestingly, despite Mehta's claims that she is no longer interested in making immigrant stories like *Sam & Me*, she has continued to make films about multi-culturalism and identity, although no longer in Canada. In the mode of *Sam & Me*, in *Fire* and *Earth*, and one presumes also in *Water*, Mehta continues to allow difference to be controversial (i.e., real difference as opposed to quaint and insignificant ethnic displays). She has persisted in attacking the non-acceptance of difference and the resulting hierarchy of relationships whether difference is based on race, gender, sexuality, age, religion, ethnicity, or class.

Coming back to the initial discussion, which involved globalization, the film *Water*, and democratic institutions, Mehta's filmmaking reminds us that globalization can be seen in a positive light. The experience of the anti-WTO demonstrators in Seattle in November 1999 showed that globalization is not just an opportunity for market forces to operate internationally but also for citizens and citizens' groups to meet across borders and join forces. There was a palpable excitement in Seattle as trade unions, women's groups, ecology groups—individuals and organizations from all over the world—recognized their common interests across difference and felt the power to make their voices heard. If I state that the constant theme of Deepa Mehta's films is the need to accept difference and intolerance for narrow-mindedness (and she has been successful in rallying international response to the notion that in India her different opinions are being attacked), it is to suggest that her films and her film practice speak against the imposition of monocultures of power and identity. Mehta brings the question down to the individual level. She makes our role in the global political and social economy a personal, moral decision. The struggles of Mehta's characters remind us finally of Deleuze and Guattari's description of human beings as "desiring machines."[104] Although entrenched bigotry, the weight of tradition or powerful political figures may try to tie these "desiring machines" down, to contain and use their energy, the desiring machine cannot be encircled forever. Despite the troubled moments that typically mark the finales of Mehta's films, one has faith that all is not lost and that desire will eventually break out again in a wild and uncontrolled flow.

But does Mehta also participate in globalization as a monoculture of style? One recognizes in her films the pull of the market, vacillations in style that correspond to the attraction of successful formulas. Returning to the accusations against *Water*, and Kishwar's critique of *Fire*, it is necessary to finalize the discussion of whether Mehta's films are purposefully controversial and exploitatively commercial in their depictions of female oppression and the stranglehold of tradition. As for the issue of controversy, I would answer that becoming a thorn in the side is one of the few ways that an independent transnational filmmaker with a minimal publicity budget can get her work noticed. In a global world where advertising budgets for commercially destined films are typically equal to the cost of production, I see her choice to make *Fire*, *Earth*, and *Water* as a trilogy as a simple but brilliant marketing strategy. (She says her inspiration comes from Ray's Apu trilogy). I also understand why she might entice journalists to pay attention to her with talk of the provocative content of her films. However, if Mehta's accounting of profits of the controversial film *Fire* is correct, exciting controversy doesn't pay because *Fire* hasn't earned her a penny despite its prizes and public success: being forced to withdraw a film does not help profits.[105] But this might be a lesson learned in hindsight.

Without agreeing to calls for censorship, we need to acknowledge some legitimacy in the claims of Mehta's critics. In India, it is difficult to separate moral rigidity and dogmatic anti-modernism from the still-painful legacy of colonization. Remarkable in all the interviews with Mehta's detractors is the subtext of a wounded pride. In this Kishwar is right. Whether or not *Water*'s opponents were professional protestors and people manipulated into marching, as Mehta asserts, the fact that nationalism can still be an effective tool for mobilization speaks to

India as a society that remains troubled. These are messages from those who are not like Mehta (wealthy enough to receive an English education and able to be coddled by her family in India or to retreat to Canada when the going gets rough)—that is, from those who may not have shared in the fruits of England's colonial presence. International privilege is the one power differential that Mehta herself has not addressed.

It is possible that Mehta may no longer be as attuned to Indian culture as she might have had she never left, but I doubt she exploits the miserable image of women. It is possible that rather than rallying Indian women to their rights with *Fire*, as Kishwar accuses, she was instead making them self-conscious and fearful of censorship for expressing the physical closeness typical of women in joint families, and the lesbian outcome arguably was not necessary in a film about the choice to leave a bad marriage. I think Mehta honestly wanted to do good, but the brush of the transnational filmmaker may be too broad to suit both India and Western audiences. For even feminist critics like Kishwar, the choices of a transnational filmmaker may make Mehta seem to be the unsubtle and presumptuousness outsider. However, Mehta risks the wrath of local critics to a greater extent than most transnational filmmakers because her films take on controversial subject matter.

Deepa Mehta's films fit comfortably within transnational filmmaking. Their narrative source is memory filtered through nostalgia, but also through critical distance. They are concerned with but unbothered by the transformation of identity, with culture as mutable and subject to pressure. They evidence a filmmaker in a constant dance with her home and host cultures, and with differing models of cinema-making, from Hollywood to Bollywood and from Canadian to regional Indian cinemas; and Mehta is savvy to global trends. Transnational films place heavy demands on their readers to recognize sources of style and inspiration; in many ways Bollywood looks like Hollywood. A critic of transnational films should ideally be more than in step with the filmmaker's experiences and cultures to assess her films' authenticity and influences. Reading interviews with Mehta only in Canada or only in India can leave the critic confused, or mistakenly certain about where Mehta stands on issues. She is known to contradict herself depending on whom she is talking to and where she is giving the interview; but this can likely be attributed to the transnational filmmaker survivor game. It is as transnational and not as woman filmmaker that I have examined Mehta's career here; I have not even questioned the gender politics that may be involved. Looking at her career, one is aware of a strong auteur presence and also of a strong public personality, the latter perhaps the result of necessity. The demands of transnational filmmaking, more intricate even than other types of filmmaking, call for a strong public persona, especially in the case of the female filmmaker. Nevertheless, Mehta is indeed simply who she is. She is neither and both Indian and Canadian. By this time, she has herself become transnational: too buffeted by the trials of immigration and the complications of international filmmaking, too world wise to call any one place home.

Post-script

It is now August 2001 and Deepa Mehta has returned to Canada. She says she has left but not abandoned the project *Water*; she is waiting for the political climate in India to change. In the meantime, she is working on two projects. The first is a comedy produced by David Hamilton, interestingly titled *Bollywood Hollywood*, which she will soon shoot in Toronto and for which Telefilm Canada, this time, has been very supportive. (How could they now ignore her international reputation?) The second is an adaptation of Alice Walker's *By the Light of My Father's Smile* for Columbia-Tri Star, with Sarah Green producing. This production is slated to shoot in spring 2002, and Mehta seems optimistic about it despite, once again, finding herself without economic and thus artistic control. Mehta seems enthusiastic about working with Sarah Green, who is known for producing for other independents such as David Mamet and John Sayles. And Alice Walker specifically suggested Mehta for the director role. [106]

Notes

1 Kass Banning of York University, Toronto, conducted a public interview with Deepa Mehta on 27 March 1999 for the Women Filmmakers: Refocussing conference (held 19–21 and 26–28 March 1999 and organized by Jacqueline Levitin, Judith Plessis, and Valerie Raoul). The interview is excerpted in Jacqueline Levitin, "Deepa Mehta: Making Films in Canada and India" (in *Women Filmmakers: Refocussing,* forthcoming). I am grateful to the work of Kass Banning, and to Valerie Raoul, Thomas Waugh, and Narendra Pachkhede who generously offered me their comments at various stages of this essay. I also thank Moninder Bubber for her excellent assistance in my research.

2 Initial opposition came from Mahila Agadhi, the women's wing of Shiv Sena (warriors of the god Shiva), militant Hindu nationalists and anti-Muslims, and the governing party of the western state of Maharashtra, whose capital is Mumbai. Mahila Agadhi is widely quoted as making this interesting comment: "If women's physical needs are fulfilled through lesbian acts, the institution of marriage will collapse" ("Ban *Fire*, says Sena Mahila Aghadi," *Express News Service* [4 December 1998]). Hindu nationalists have also denounced *Earth* and demanded that the government ban the film.

3 It originally passed without a single cut. Mehta filed a court petition naming Balasaheb Thackeray, Shiv Sena chief in Bombay, as the central figure behind the attacks against *Fire*.

4 For the accusation of commercialism, see, for example, the interview with S. Gurumurthy by Shobha Warrier in the online Indian journal *Rediff,* "If a widow remains a pure widow, she is respected," www.rediff.com/ news/2000/mar/31inter.htm.

5 "'Mehta showed a lack of sensitivity to local culture. As an artist you have to be concerned about boundaries,' counters writer Pankaj Mishra, author of a new novel set in Benares, or Varanasi as the city is also known. 'She came with an international crew. They spread a lot of money around. In a poor country like India, that can cause resentment'" (Robert Marquand, "Film Stirs Hindu Radical Rage," *Christian Science Monitor* 92, no. 57 [14 February 2000]: 1).

6 "Everything appeared to be just great until one of the state government people, someone who doesn't have an official title but is like a lackey to the UP Minister for Tourism, came to Varanasi and told us that we could shoot the film if we used his friends to cast the film. I told him that the film was already cast. He said OK, but could we use his friend's wife to star in the film and also use this friend to find all the extras. The final straw was when he demanded I give him distribution rights to the film. So I basically told him to buzz off. We'd been working for about four weeks doing pre-production at that stage. Two days after I'd told him to take a hike, murmurs began in the city that I was making a film that was anti-Hindu, and which denigrated the widows, the ancient Indian culture and the people of Varanasi. And within days it catapulted into something massive. We were amazed how organized and well-oiled the machinery was" (see Richard Phillips, "Deepa Mehta speaks out," World Socialist Web Site, www.wsws.org/articles/2000/feb2000/meht-f15.shtml). Mehta later denied this comment in a reply to the *Hindustan Times* on 19 May 2000. The *Hindustan Times* had published an article on 3 May 2000 attacking both her and the World Socialist Web Site's campaign to defend her (see "Filmmaker Deepa Mehta replies to an attack in the *Hindustan Times,*" World Socialist Web Site, www.wsws.org/articles/2000/may2000/dm1-m19.shtml). Walsh rewrites Mehta's statement to indicate that the individual was a "film commission guy" (see David Walsh, "The Case of Deepa Mehta and the Defense of Artistic Freedom," *Cinema Scope* 4 [summer 2000]). In later statements, Mehta praised the *Hindustan Times* for its judicious covering of events. Two articles on the *Rediff* website (Suparn Verma, "I won't deal with thugs, says Deepa" [www.rediff.com/news/2000/feb/07deepa.htm], and Onkar Singh, "*Water* will not flow back to Varanasi," [www.rediff.com/news/2000/feb/09water1.htm]) make reference to the question of requests for roles or distribution rights. Singh's article names the individual as "Manjul Rakesh." Says Mehta, "What embarrasses me so much is that they are focussing their attention on all this while Kashmiri Pandits are being slaughtered. I mean we are just making a film" (see Verma, "I won't deal with thugs"). Distracting the public might be the real issue.

7 Foreign-funded films must pass through a lengthy process to obtain permits. This became a requirement following the embarrassment caused by French filmmaker Louis Malle's seven-part television series *Phantom India* (1969). The American film *City of Joy* (1992) caused a similar stir. Traditionally, Indian film censorship is sensitive to slurs against any religion or community so as not to spark communal violence.

8 An interview with Shyamdeo Ramchaudhary shows the Bharatiya Janatha Party (BJP) legislator's casual attitude to the violence against the production: "When there is a mass movement people cannot control their sentiments" (see Suparn Verma, "If your intentions are honourable make the script public," *Rediff*, www.rediff.com/news/2000/feb/02inter3.htm). The BJP, the political arm of the Hindu Right, heads the coalition government that gave authorization to Mehta's production. The party is currently in power at the federal level.

9 The controversies around *Fire* and *Water* are covered in many publications. On *Water*, see the excellent early summary by Robert Marquand, "Film Stirs Hindu Radical Rage." See also the interviews conducted in *Rediff* (www.rediff.com/index.html) and articles posted on the World Socialist Web Site (www.wsws.org). Mehta has this to say about the Vishwa Hindu Parishad (World Hindu Forum): "The VHP, in particular, has been rabid. VHP leader Ashok Singhal has been saying the film will only proceed over his dead body ... We were told by the UP [Uttar Pradesh state] Chief Minister that they didn't want someone of this stature killing himself, that it would produce rioting and therefore the film should be stopped" (see Phillips, "Deepa Mehta speaks out"). The Rastriya Swayangsevak Sangh (RSS), the principal Hindu organization in India and the organization involved in the 1948 murder of Mahatma Gandhi, similarly opposed the film.

10 Pamela Constable, "Roiling Sacred Waters," *Washington Post*, 23 February 2000.

11 Protests and attacks on individuals and property have also been mounted against local filmmakers and artists. Muslim actor Dilip Kumar, who has been under police protection since 1991, saw that protection increased when fundamentalists demonstrated outside his house following his public support of Mehta in December 1998. Following the attacks on the theatres, Mehta, Kumar, and four others filed a petition with the Supreme Court of India seeking intervention for the peaceful screening of the film (cf. Note 3). As a result, Mehta and the other petitioners were also placed under protection. See T. Padmanabha Rao, "S.C. directive to state in 'Fire' case," *The Hindu*, 16 December 1998, 10; and Walsh "The Case of Deepa Mehta." (Walsh's article and interview with Mehta is also posted on the *World Socialist Web Site*.) On censorship, see also the *Rediff* interview with Govind Nihalani, one of the first Indian filmmakers to encounter protests ("If a film or a book can tarnish our culture, which is more than 5000 years old, then what kind of culture is this?" www.rediff.com/news/2000/feb/16inter.htm). Saleem Kidwai reports that attacks have increasingly been directed against Muslim and Christian targets. See Saleem Kidwai, *Interpress Service* (10 December 1998).

12 Examples include Ien Ang, Clara Law, John Woo, Evans Chan, Wong Kar-wai, and, of course, Jackie Chan. Hong Kong filmmakers who make genre films may have an easier time translating them across borders, but sensibilities and references remain particular to a locale. Several Chinese directors have managed to make only one film outside China and then have gone back. Chinese director Zhang Yimou, who never left China to film but has received foreign backing, has nevertheless been criticized for being insufficiently Chinese. Very few transnational filmmakers are female.

13 For the north–south movement of films, see Uma Magal, "Indian Cinema Fifty Years After Independence: A Cinema of Ferment," *Asian Cinema* 10, no. 1 (Fall 1998). However, Narendra Pachkhede has pointed out to me that, as early as 1928, filmmakers such as the Hindi-speaking Mani Lal Tandon were making box office hits in Tamil without knowing the language. For attention to the diaspora audience, see Rachel Dwyer, "'Indian Values' and the Diaspora: Yash Chopra's Films of the 1990s," *West Coast Line* 32 (Fall 2000).

14 A filmmaker from Hong Kong working in Hollywood, for example, experiences aesthetic pressures unknown to the independent filmmaker whose concerns may be overwhelmingly monetary, while a filmmaker from South East Asia who makes a film in the Middle East will likely experience a set of pressures different from those experienced by both the industrial or independent filmmaker working in Europe or North America, pressures which are likely monetary, political, or religious.

15 The term "transnational" is used variously. Mehta's films, in part, might be seen in terms of the "exilic" film. Canada, as the crossroads of various cinematic models and rich in the variety of its cultural make-up, is particularly suited to transnational filmmaking. Hamid Naficy has added a new term to the vocabulary: "accented film." Among the growing proliferation of literature on the subject, see Naficy's *An Accented Cinema: Exilic and Diasporic Filmmaking* (Princeton: Princeton University Press, 2001); and Sheldon Hsiao-peng Lu, ed. *Transnational Chinese Cinemas: Identity, Nationhood, Gender* (Honolulu: University of Hawai'i Press, 1997). My definition of the auteur in transnational filmmaking in part borrows the words of Narendra Pachkhede, an accurate description of my findings. In my discussion of Mehta's trajectory, I have profited from Stuart Hall's "Encoding/decoding" in *Culture, Media, Language* (London: Hutchinson & Co., Ltd., 1980), 128–38.

16 Gurumurthy is the convenor of the group Swadeshi Jagran Manch that announced its members planned protests throughout the country if Mehta continued to attempt to shoot (See Warrier, "If a widow remains a pure widow"). See also S. Ramchaudhary's comment, "The Ganges is the most revered place for us, to call it *Water* is so insulting! Calling it plain Water!" (In Verma, "If your intentions are honourable").

17 See Sutapa Mukerjee, "Widows defend film-maker's vision of their lives," *Vancouver Sun,* 12 February 2000, E21. Amitabh Bhattacharya, a Sanskrit scholar and a Brahman, is quoted by Marquand: "In the early part of the century, about half the widows here [Benares] ended up as prostitutes, about a quarter were concubines for wealthy Brahmans, and a quarter remained pure for God" (Marquand, "Film Stirs Hindu Radical Rage").

18 Ratna Kapur, "Too Hot to Handle: The Cultural Politics of *Fire,*" *Feminist Review* 64 (Spring 2000): 53.

19 Mehta and others insist that Hinduism traditionally accepted interpretations and variations of its epic stories and that it is, in its essence, open to change. For example, there are many versions of the Ramayana story.

20 Kapur, "Too Hot to Handle," 61. Citing a number of feminist cultural theorists, Kapur notes the significance of the film's challenge is precisely because of its location in the home: "In the late nineteenth century, the Hindu revivalists reconstituted the home—along with sex and sexuality—as a 'pure' space of Indian culture, uncontaminated by the colonial encounter" (54–55).

21 The split in India between Left and Right noted by Kapur, with the Right represented by religious nationalists, goes back to the period preceding the founding of the independent Indian state. Gandhi had opposed the pressures of religious nationalists to divide colonial India along religious lines. However, he seemed to accept without difficulty the proposition that a multicultural independent India would use Hindi written language for all legislative activity.

22 Michael Atkinson, "Entangling Alliances," *Village Voice* 45, no. 12 (28 March 2000): 120.

23 Jayne Margetts, "Deepa's Doctrine," *Celluloid Interview*, www.thei.aust.com/film97/cellindeepah.html.

24 "He is the greatest humanist filmmaker that I have ever known." Masterclass with Deepa Mehta, 27 March 1999, at the Women Filmmakers: Refocussing conference. Sharon McGowan was the facilitator.

25 The film was shown at the 1956 Cannes Film Festival.

26 Says Mehta: "The housewives really had put down their vegetables and their cooking and everything aside and were saying, 'How dare somebody tell us that this film is not meant for us!'" (Levitin, "Making Films in Canada and India").

27 Bapsi Sidhwa, "Playing with *Fire,*" *Ms.,* November/December 1997, 78.

28 See Dwyer, "'Indian Values' and the Diaspora," 19–24.

29 Dwyer, "'Indian Values' and the Diaspora," 21.

30 Dwyer, "'Indian Values' and the Diaspora," 23.

31 Dwyer, "'Indian Values' and the Diaspora," 23.

32 Dwyer, "'Indian Values' and the Diaspora," 22.

33 Dwyer, "'Indian Values' and the Diaspora," 23.

34 Richard Phillips, "If people want to separate they should understand what it would really mean," World Socialist Web Site, www.wsws.org/sections/category/arts/intviews.shtml. Buñuel was himself a transnational filmmaker, moving between his native Spain, France, and Mexico.

35 Vinita Ramchandani, "Passionate Plots: Deepa Mehta explains the emotion that connects her films *Fire*, *Earth* and *Water*," *The Week Magazine*, www.the-week.com/98dec06/enter.htm.

36 CAVCO (the Canadian Audio-Visual Certification Office) administers the Canadian Film Tax Incentive Program, with certification also from the CRTC (the Canadian Radio-television and Telecommunications Commission). Its policies are adopted by the provinces to suit their varying goals in encouraging local film production. Telefilm Canada operates as the national agency for film and television financing, while most provinces have film offices to handle financing at the provincial level.

37 Canada negotiated an exemption for culture under the 1989 trade agreement with the United States. The North American Free Trade Agreement (NAFTA), which expanded this agreement to include Canada, the United States, and Mexico, calls for the gradual removal of tariffs and other trade barriers on most goods produced and sold in North America effective 1 January 1994. Many in the cultural community in Canada, however, have expressed doubts about the effectiveness of these agreements to adequately protect the independence of Canadian culture.

38 Janis Cole and Holly Dale, *Calling the Shots: Profiles of Women Filmmakers* (Kingston: Quarry Press, 1993), 137.

39 Masterclass with Deepa Mehta.

40 Levitin, "Making Films in Canada and India."

41 Martin Knelman, "Sleepless in Toronto," *Toronto Life*, 28, no. 1 (January 1994).

42 Cole and Dale, *Calling the Shots*, 135.

43 Kathleen Wilkinson, "Filmmaker Deepa Mehta is on *Fire*," *Lesbian News* 23, no. 2 (September 1997): 38.

44 "After *Camilla*, I felt that in the future, if I ever made another film, I wanted to have control of the process. I wanted to make films that I believed in. Films that reflected something I was going through in my life." In Walsh, "The Case of Deepa Mehta," 25.

45 Renan Ansari, "Interviews with Deepa Mehta and Naseeruddin Shah," *Himal* 11/12 (December 1998).

46 Azmi, apart for being a respected actor, is also active in social causes and has been appointed a member of the Rajya Sabha, the upper house of the Indian Parliament.

47 Mehta's actors and crew stood by her during the *Water* controversy, gave interviews, and issued communications of support. George Lucas placed a full-page statement in *Variety* and was among the many international members of the film and arts community who were public in their support.

48 "It's not that I can't do it with two people, it's just that I seem to gravitate to stories that bounce off many people because I like different perspectives." Masterclass with Deepa Mehta.

49 Knelman, "Sleepless in Toronto," 36; and Cole and Dale, *Calling the Shots*, 136. Mehta's father's Hindu family was among those forced to abandon neighbouring Lahore at the time of partition in 1947. Millions of Muslims moved to the newly created Pakistan and millions of Hindus over new borders into India in a bloody exchange of populations that is still vivid in people's memories. Mehta recalls this period in her film *Earth*, or *1947*, as it was titled for its Indian release.

50 Uma Magal notes that there has been a fusion occurring lately between masala and "parallel" cinema, with its concentration on social/political content. Magal, "Indian Cinema Fifty Years After Independence."

51 *Fire*'s challenge to tradition's authority literally takes place in the home, and the two sisters-in-law are forced out of the home at the end. The old Jewish man in *Sam & Me* wants to "go home" to Israel before he dies.

52 The Parsi community was considered neutral in the partition conflict.

53 See Kaja Silverman, *The Subject of Semiotics* (New York: Oxford University Press, 1983), especially 194–236. The exact mechanism of involvement (the idea comes from Christian Metz's psychoanalytic study of the cinema) is highly disputed in film circles, especially when it is applied across national and time boundaries. Nevertheless, a relay of looks is assumed to be at the basis of a certain spectator involvement.

54 The original title was *Ice Candy Man*.

55 In her letter to the *Hindustan Times* in defence of Mehta during the *Water* controversy, Bapsi Sidhwa writes, "I have been misquoted as saying that I was unhappy with the film. This is untrue. Sure, the film ends differently from the book. But the film had to end the way it did: the impact would have been weakened otherwise. The screen exerts its own dramatic demands. I understood this even while the film was being made, and Deepa did not do anything without consulting me." The letter is reprinted as "They are punishing Deepa for deflating their egos," World Socialist Web Site, www.wsws.org/articles/2000/may2000/dm2-m19.shtml. See also Sidhwa's earlier *New York Times* article "Watching My Novel Become Her Film," *New York Times*, 5 September 1999.

56 Masterclass with Deepa Mehta.

57 Another Indo-Canadian, Srinivas Krishna, is similarly elaborate in the production design of his debut feature, *Masala* (1991).

58 Madhu Kishwar is disparaging about Mehta's excuses for not translating the film before production: "She cites two sentences as examples of the profundities in the script that were untranslatable—'The concept of duty is over rated,' and 'The Swamiji's testicles have grown too big for his loin cloth.' See "Naive Outpourings of a Self-Hating Indian: [Part 2 of 4]," *Manushi* 109 (November 1998).

59 Magal, "Indian Cinema Fifty Years After Independence." Akhtar is also the husband of actress Shabana Azmi.

60 The state of Tamil Nadu is also a major source of popular-style Indian film.

61 A.R. Rahman was born in 1966.

62 See, for example, Sunder Kumar's review of the album of *Earth*'s music.

63 The poll was cited on the official site for the film *Earth*, 1947earth.com/home.html, now taken down.

64 Kapur, "Too Hot to Handle," 55. Interestingly, the mother-in-law, who would normally play the role of ideal woman and who, according to Mehta, represents tradition, here is mute and paralyzed.

65 It is not clear from accounts if she was pressured into making this change, which occurred in both the English and Hindi versions. Rumours about the change generated much media discussion in India.

66 "To make sure we do not miss the point, there is the repeated visual replay of mythical Sita's agnipanisha scene from Ramanand Sagar's TV serial *Ramayan*, as well as repeated enactments of Deepa Mehta's scripted pseudo-folk Ramlila spiced with lots of cheap melodrama. To quote her: '[the agnipariksha] happens three times in the film, to make sure that ... it wasn't just me indulging in the agnipariksha for Radha and Sita, but that [the film is set] in the whole context of tradition, and the stereotyping of Indian women, that we, I, the actors understood where they were coming from.' (*Trikone*, October 1997)" (Kishwar, "Naive Outpourings [Part 2 of 4]").

67 This is perhaps also an allusion to bride burning by "accidental kitchen fires" for insufficient dowry. Such practices, at the time of the making of *Fire* and still today, are denounced by women's groups in India and abroad.

68 Kapur, "Too Hot to Handle," 57. Geeta Patel also reminds us of the religious narratives' stories of Radha "as the sexually transgressive woman/*gopi*/wife who leaves at night to meet her lover Krishna, the dark lord" ("Trial by *Fire*: A Local/Global View. Talking with Geeta Patel," *Gay Community News* 24, no. 2: 10–17). Patel offers an interesting discussion of the film's reference to the Ramayana, noting that it is the text associated with Gandhi and the notion of the perfect kingdom where good men live by ethical action.

69 See Dwyer, "'Indian Values' and the Diaspora"; and Pratibha Parmar's documentary *The Colour of Britain* (1994), about South Asian artists, resident in the United Kingdom, who have been redefining the British national self-image.

70 The sex scene between Shanta and Masseur is given prominence in *Earth* as *witnessed* by both the girl and Ice Candy Man. It is not in the novel.

71 *Manushi: A Journal about Women and Society* is described in its masthead: "*Manushi*, founded in 1978, is a serious journal which aims to bridge the gap between academic/scholarly writing and popular literature. The magazine analyses political, economic and social issues from a people-oriented perspective ... *Manushi* sees itself as playing a catalytic role towards making our society more just and humane."

72 "This device of professing sympathy for the 'oppressed' Indian women in order to condemn the traditions and culture of all Indians has a more than two century-long history. After the establishment of pax-Britannica in India, and the emergence of a new class of natives who began to challenge the legitimacy of the British Raj, oppressed Indian women became a favourite prop of our colonial rulers and missionaries" (Kishwar, "Naive Outpourings [Part 4 of 4]").

73 "My father used to say to me when I was growing up: 'Deepa, you must remember two things in life. One, you never know when you're going to die, and two, you never know how a film is going to do'" (in Sidhwa, "Playing with *Fire*," 78).

74 Sidhwa, "Playing with *Fire*," 76–77. In interviews, Mehta frequently points to these aspects as sources of her inspiration. Note that her calculation of the size of India's middle class is likely incorrect, and Ray more often depicted the middle class in his films than the rural poor, although these films are less well known abroad than the famous Apu trilogy.

75 Rima Banerji, "Still on *Fire*," *Manushi* 113 (July 1999).

76 "Is it true that Sita's unfair banishment and agnipariksha is the most dominant aspect of Indian gender traditions? Are not Shiv and Parvati in Indian tradition the most popular archetypes of happy, blissful conjugality, including euphoric joy in sexual union, the most celebrated couple of Indian mythology? After all, the supposedly traditional Indian woman keep fasts on Monday to pray to be blessed with a Shiv-like husband—not for an incarnation of Ram ... In one part of Indian tradition, there is a parallel tradition of spiritual quest via sexual union at a level of sophistication rare in most other cultures ... What about Indian women and goddesses who appear as Durga, Chandi, Kali and in a host of other fierce and benevolent forms? ... Such women and goddesses are not only an integral part of village lore but a living role model for women of all ages throughout India ...What sells in the international media market is the unidimensional stereotype of India as solely a land of beggars and oppressors, a country where brides are commonly burnt to death for money and consumer goods" (Kishwar, "Naive Outpourings [Part 2 of 4]").

77 Banerji, "Still on *Fire*."

78 See Lalitha Gopalan, "Avenging Women in Indian Cinema [Part 1 of 3]," *Nivedini—A Sri Lankan Feminist Journal* 5, no. 1 (June 1997).

79 Banerji, "Still on *Fire*."

80 "I can say with confidence that such a family as this is not likely to exist among the community she portrays. One of the key hallmarks of Indian family life, especially in a Punjabi neighbourhood like Lajpat Nagar, is that there is constant interaction with neighbours and relatives. But Deepa Mehta has cooked up a new variety of Indian family to conform to her schematic picture of all round oppression ... I have heard of artistic license, but this is a curious case of sociological license! The West has not only the onerous task of teaching us how to be liberated from our culture, but also how to learn to talk and chat with our own families" (Kishwar, "Naive Outpourings [Part 3 of 4]").

81 Kishwar, "Naive Outpourings [Part 4 of 4]."

82 Kishwar quotes from *Trikone*, October 1997, "Naive Outpourings [Part 4 of 4]."

83 Kishwar, "Naive Outpourings [Part 4 of 4]."

84 "I can be uninhibited about the subject ... I do not have to think about repercussions—as I would in India" (Ansari, *Interpress Service*).

85 Kishwar questions the truth of this claim to being tradition-bound since Mehta's was a love marriage and not an arranged marriage. Kishwar, "Naive Outpourings [Part 4 of 4]."

86 Levitin, "Making Films in Canada and India."

87 Kapur, "Too Hot to Handle," 60–61

88 As Kapur points out, the women's refuge at the end of *Fire* is the Nizam-ud-din tomb, a Sufi shrine, "the space of another 'other'" within India society. Kapur, "Too Hot to Handle," 54.

89 Masterclass with Deepa Mehta.

90 Dilip Mehta, a photojournalist, is the subject of Mehta's television special *Travelling Light: The Photojournalism of Dilip Mehta*.

91 Programs such as *Danger Bay* and *My Secret Identity*. Knelman, "Sleepless in Toronto," 37.

92 Levitin, "Making Films in Canada and India." Mehta expressed the same burning need to make *Fire*: "I just knew that if I didn't make that film, I'd die" (Sidhwa, "Playing with *Fire*," 78).

93 "It was a labour of love. Passion. Pain. Some people call their films a labour of love, I call this one a labour of anger" (Cole and Dale, *Calling the Shots*, 137).

94 "Mehtamorphosis," *Chatelaine*, November 1993.

95 See Kass Banning's discussion of this scene in "Playing in the Light: Canadianising Race and Nation" in *Gendering the Nation: Canadian Women's Cinema*, Kay Armatage, Kass Banning, Brenda Longfellow, and Janine Marchessault, eds. (Toronto: University of Toronto Press, 1999), 296–97.

96 Kishwar, "Naive Outpourings [Part 3 of 4].

97 Kulbhushan Kharbanda is another in Mehta's repertory of actors. He plays Boldev, Nik's taxi-driver friend, in *Sam & Me*. The character's experiments with abstinence from sexual pleasure has been interpreted by Mehta's critics as a disparaging reference to Gandhi, who is known for his own experiments with abstinence.

98 Kishwar, "Naive Outpourings [Part 2 of 4]."

99 Kishwar, "Naive Outpourings [Part 2 of 4]."

100 Kishwar, "Naive Outpourings [Part 3 of 4]."

101 Ajay Singh, "Burned by Home *Fire*s," *Asiaweek* 25, no. 2 (January 1999): 48–49.

102 Banning, "Playing in the Light," 290.

103 Cole and Dale, *Calling the Shots*, 135.

104 Gilles Deleuze and Felix Guattari, *Anti-Oedipus: Capitalism and Schizophrenia*, Robert Hurley, Mark Seem and Helen R. Lane, trans. (Minneapolis: University of Minnesota Press, 1983).

105 "Onkar Singh: 'There are others who allege that you deliberately create a controversy with a view to selling your film.' Mehta: 'How can I sell a film [*Water*] that is never going to be made! *Fire* was released [in India] one year after it was released elsewhere. It had been running for three weeks before Shiv Sainiks attacked theatres in Delhi. Till date I have not made even a single penny from that film'" (Onkar Singh, "The Film Has to be Shot in Varanasi," *Rediff*, www.rediff.com/news/2000/feb/01inter2.htm).

106 Telephone interview with Deepa Mehta, 17 August 2001.

Political Alignments and the Lure of 'More Existential Questions' in the Films of Patricia Rozema

Lee Parpart

PATRICIA ROZEMA'S FILMS ARE FILLED WITH IMAGES OF FLIGHT. If her characters aren't hang-gliding in pairs or fantasizing about flying solo through the skies of Toronto, her camera is floating along a line of blown glass windows or soaring over an abandoned British estate made to look like Jane Austen's Mansfield Park. Rozema readily admits that much of her work is driven by a search for transcendence, and she speculates that her affinity for all forms of flight—literal, figurative, symbolic—is probably a holdover from her upbringing in a strict Dutch Calvinist household. "I am attracted to a kind of utopian vision," she told one critic. "In *I've Heard the Mermaids Singing* you have the reality, and then what *could* be—and that's probably just me doing another version of heaven."[1]

But the liquid sensation and skyward thrust invoked by her movies involve more than a set of motifs and aesthetic interests. Given that Rozema describes herself as "lapsed now, for sure"— having turned away from Calvinism during college, at about the same time she realized she was attracted to women—it is, not surprisingly, often an overtly questioning and eroticized version of utopia that seems to circulate in her films. "I'm hungry for a kind of euphoria," she said in connection with her third feature, the lesbian romance *When Night Is Falling* (1995). "I haven't done it yet, but I want to make a film where people sit down and their hearts are in their mouths the entire time and they can hardly breathe, you know. Then they get a rush of release at the end."[2]

Audiences and mainstream reviewers have willingly soared along with the Toronto film-maker and let themselves be seduced at various times during her fifteen-year career, which spans five features, three short films (*Passion: A Letter in 16 mm* [1985], *Desperanto* [1992], and *This Might Be Good* [2000], a five-minute festival anniversary film), and an experimental documentary about J.S. Bach titled *Six Gestures* (1997). As has been reported many times, her astonishingly successful 1987 feature debut, *I've Heard the Mermaids Singing*, earned Rozema and producer Alexandra Raffé a famous six-minute standing ovation at Cannes, won that festival's Prix de la Jeunesse award for best first film by a young director, and secured Rozema's position at or near the crest of what would later be described as Ontario's New Wave.[3] Audiences were charmed by Sheila McCarthy's performance as Polly Vandersma, an "organizationally impaired" temp worker and amateur photographer who goes to work for a chic art gallery and has her ideas about art, sexuality, and standards of aesthetic judgement tested in a confrontation with her suave, bisexual boss. Brian D. Johnson calls it "one of the most astounding first impressions in the history of Canadian cinema," and various sources have suggested that the film helped to re-shape the agenda of Canada's publicly funded film industry, directing more attention to artist-driven films and driving down film budgets for a time.[4] From an initial budget of $350,000, *Mermaids* went on to earn roughly $6 million, playing in some 50 US cities and topping #17 on the *Variety* billboard.[5] Canadian film funding bodies responded by funnelling more resources into artist-driven films, hoping for another hit, while *Mermaids'* unusually high profits gave arts bureaucrats an excuse to drive budgets down on other projects. If Rozema and Raffé could produce an international hit for less than half a million dollars, they argued, other Canadian auteurs-in-waiting should be able to do the same.

In comparison with *Mermaids*, Rozema's follow-up effort *White Room* was nothing short of a critical disaster. Audiences expecting more the same gentle whimsy they found in Rozema's debut were faced instead with a serious, at times painful, meditation on voyeurism, deception, and the high costs of fame: a darker and more demanding approach to some of the same themes Rozema had explored in *Mermaids*.[6] All but a few critics loathed the film, calling it muddled, ridiculous, unoriginal in light of her debut, and lacking in subtlety. One male reviewer reportedly told Rozema he felt "emasculated" by the film's lead character, Norman Gentle (Maurice Godin), a blocked would-be writer from the suburbs who turns to peeping through windows in an attempt to learn more about the world.

What most critics failed to appreciate, however, are the intricacies of *White Room's* experiments with narrative structure. Although the plot revolves around Norman's affair with a reclusive artist named Jane (Kate Nelligan) who is the voice behind a murdered pop singer named Madeleine X, *White Room's* deeper subject matter has to do with the epistemological status of fiction. As Deborah Knight has suggested, the film's anti-realist aesthetic and overt play with fairy-tale conventions—including opaque references to a simplified, "once upon a time" framework and an inventive splitting of the standard "happily ever after" ending into idealized and macabre forms—situate *White Room* as "a film concerned with story-telling as *fabulation*, story-telling as the construction through time of a fictional world in which the principal conventions of realist narrative practices do not (and need not) apply."[7] Like most of Rozema's other films, from *Mermaids* to *Mansfield Park*, *White Room* is also directly concerned with "the nature of artistic creation and expression, the various aspects of human experience that threaten either to transcend or to escape capture in representational systems (language, music, film, etc.) and the sometimes translucent boundary between fantasy and reality."[8] But *White Room's* attention to storytelling as fabulation or artistic expression *per se* is only one part of its agenda. Through the character of Norman, Rozema also seems to be offering a trenchant critique of the potentially destructive force of androcentric storytelling structures. Norman is not just that stereotypical Canadian figure of the paralyzed male artist; he is also that potentially dangerous creature, a seemingly innocent and well-intentioned young man whose unexamined investments in traditional narrative and inability to break free of the type of story that demands sadism spell fatal trouble for not one but two women. In the first instance, Norman stands idly by while Madeleine X is raped and killed, unable to act or take his eyes off the spectacle before him, while in the second case it is his own (still clichéd) attempt at storytelling that indirectly leads Jane to take her own life.

Rozema has predicted that *White Room* may someday earn a larger and more appreciative audience.[9] But aside from Knight's article and a few attempts to mine the film's themes in relation
to Canadian motifs of voicelessness, it has elicited little interest, except as an example of the
"second-film trap" awaiting Canadian auteurs who are unleashed onto bigger-budget projects
with little support or experience from their debuts.[10] Since *White Room*, however, Rozema has
gradually honed her craft, reined in the darker aspects of her vision—perhaps at a loss of some
seriousness in her oeuvre—and won her way back into the affections of many viewers and critics.
Her lyrical lesbian romance *When Night Is Falling* (1995) was warmly received in many quarters
for its lavish visuals (shot by *Mermaids'* cinematographer Doug Koch) and its unorthodox,
slightly tongue-in-cheek use of a traditional narrative structure to explore the theme of lesbian
love. The film stars Rachel Crawford as Petra, a counter-cultural circus performer who meets a
theology professor named Camille (Pascale Bussières) and gradually coaxes her latent lesbian
desire to the surface, seducing her away from her boyfriend of three years, Martin (Henry
Czerny), and the promise of a prestigious position at a Calvinist college. Functioning partially as
a lesbian retelling of the Cupid and Psyche myth, *Night* was also intended as a cross-over film
that would appeal to lesbian viewers while also gently coaxing heterosexual audiences into accepting its lead characters by unfolding their story within a safe and familiar generic framework:
the classic romance. Some critics found the effort strained and the plot oversimplified. In an otherwise favourable article, for example, Brian D. Johnson commented that the film's "feather-
weight plot unfolds with the mock-naïveté of a Harlequin romance."[11] Most reviews, however,
were generally favourable—more than a few male critics purred in print over the film's semi-
explicit lovemaking scene between Bussières and Crawford (a scene that led *Night* into trouble
with American censors and caused the film to be released unrated in the US)—and *Night* went
on to win several audience favourite awards at international film festivals.

But it is Rozema's fourth feature, a deliberately "unfaithful" yet historically informed adaptation of Jane Austen's *Mansfield Park* (1999), that has helped establish her as a seasoned film artist
capable of producing commercially and artistically successful work from within a range of different voices and traditions. Austen specialist Claudia L. Johnson greeted the film as the culmination of all her hopes for a smart and politically engaged adaptation of Austen's writing: "Finally a
director has taken real risks and reaped real rewards with her work, treating her novels not as a
museum piece or as a sacred text but as a living presence whose power inspires flight."[12] Rozema
has since made a quick fifth feature, adapting Samuel Beckett's *Happy Days* for the Irish series
Beckett on Film, and has signed on to make two more films with Miramax, the American production and distribution company owned by Harvey Weinstein, who handled *Mermaids'* US distribution and financed *Mansfield Park*.

In spite of her intermittent success with audiences and critics, Rozema's work seems to
present many scholars with a paradox. Her status as a lesbian filmmaker (or a bisexual one, according to some profiles—Rozema seems to want to preserve an essential ambiguity on this
point) has led some academics to expect that she might choose to engage with issues of central
concern to feminist and queer film theory.[13] Rozema, however, has resisted becoming closely
identified with any group other than her fellow directors in the Ontario New Wave, and has defined her film practice as neutrally as possible, while still dealing provocatively with the issue of
lesbianism in three of her five features. Declaring herself a feminist but clearly distancing herself
from the term "feminist filmmaker," she has avoided many of the representational strategies
associated with feminist counter-cinema and has forged her own idiosyncratic version of a
seductive, narrative-based film art that foregrounds visual pleasure while frequently subsuming

politics within "more existential questions."[14] And while it is true that her films have brought a questioning attitude to narrative that has earned some of them the label of "metafictions," Rozema's experiments with form and storytelling structure have not always shielded her from accusations of liberalism, naïveté, and even (paradoxically, given her own sexual orientation) homophobia.

Feminist film theorists in particular have written scathing attacks on her work for its tendency to reflect "the sparest of feminist principles," and have criticized Rozema's self-described habit of sweetening difficult or controversial subject matter by putting "beautiful, beautiful sugar on the pill."[15] More than anything, there is a sense that Rozema has a rare opportunity to match her often-marginal subject matter with a rigorous approach to ideology and representation, but that she has consistently chosen a safer route—one strewn with sexless thirty-one-year-old waifs (Polly in *I've Heard the Mermaids Singing*) and eye-catching lesbians traipsing through the most traditional of romantic plots (Camille and Petra in *When Night Is Falling*).

One of the clearest expressions of disappointment with Rozema's work from a high-placed source appears in Teresa de Lauretis 1990 *Screen* article "Guerrilla in the Midst: Women's Cinema in the 80s." In an argument geared to distinguishing between real and illusory alternatives to patriarchal cinema, de Lauretis charges Rozema's debut with wearing the mantle of a feminist film while in reality undermining the movement in significant ways. According to de Lauretis, *Mermaids* belongs to a subset of films (including *Bagdad Café*, *The Color Purple*, and *Desperately Seeking Susan*) that seem to take up feminist objectives but ultimately fail to "engage the current problems, the real issues, the things actually at stake in feminist communities on a local scale." Such films, she adds, "ostensibly legitimate women's ability to succeed in the world as it is, and even to live independently of 'men,' " yet "in their more or less overt homophobia, [they] all but delegitimate the feminist argument for an autonomous definition of female sexuality and the far more radical independence from the heterosexual social contract—the social institution and the symbolic categories of heterosexuality."[16]

De Lauretis focusses her critique on the film's fairy-tale structure, its portrayal of Polly as a naïve "modern-day Cinderella with a camera and aspirations to art," and what she considers its exploitative use of a lesbian subplot. She particularly objects to the fact that *Mermaids'* semi-closeted lesbian couple, the biblically named curator Gabrielle St. Peres (Paule Baillargeon) and her lover, artist Mary Joseph (Ann Marie Macdonald), turn out to be the perpetrators of an art-world fraud and are punished for their transgressions, while Polly remains asexual to the end, misreading her own attraction to Gabrielle as a harmless version of mother-love. In a plot geared to emphasizing the gulf between Polly as the "pure" artist and Gabrielle (the curator) as a pretentious poseur, it is the discovery that Gabrielle has been passing her publicity-shy lover's luminous paintings off as her own that finally shatters Polly's overwhelming admiration for the curator and leads Polly to regain trust in her own instincts as a photographer. De Lauretis objects to the way this plot twist tends to construct Gabrielle as "a female man and a bad phallic mother" whose crime and secret lack must be exposed by Polly and captured in the form of a video confession. And she argues that it is "difficult to see what lesbianism has to do with the story," except perhaps as a sensationalist device "to take the place of 'the kind of action or violence or sex that get automatic attention and commercial success'—the kind, that is, which Rozema decries (and which would have cost more than a few shoestrings)."[17]

De Lauretis quotes Rozema at length in order to illustrate that her film and her account is built on "the sparest, most tenuous of feminist principles," and cuts her interpretation short with a comment that the film is not worth the time it would take to analyze it more fully: "I do not care to speculate further on the less conscious or unexpressed fantasies behind *I've Heard the Mermaids Singing* (the reference to T.S. Eliot is no less a naïf than the rest of the film), though its reception as an exemplary film of women's cinema is ground for serious self-questioning by those of us who still want to claim the term for a feminist political project."[18]

Part of what seems to fuel this critique—along with genuine distaste for *Mermaids'* themes, characters, and representational strategies—is a palpable sense of disappointment, of hopes raised and then dashed on the beach. Evidence of this can be found in the emphasis given to Rozema's film compared to more obviously androcentric texts. De Lauretis dispatches films such as *Fatal Attraction* and *The Jagged Edge* in one long paragraph, calling them "obviously antagonistic, anti-feminist attempts to devalue the gains that a very few women may have made in social equality and, at a deeper level, to delegitimate the feminist demand for women's self-definition and sexual independence from familial—or male-centred social relations."[19] She saves her real rancour for the film that should have been a friend. A work like *Mermaids* is particularly odious, de Lauretis implies, because one can point to "conscious strategies, on the part of the director, by which both feminism and lesbianism are on the one hand appropriated and legitimated, and on the other pre-empted of their sociological and subjective power, reduced to a new angle to sell 'more existential questions.'"[20]

To be sure, Rozema's relationship to feminism and lesbian identity politics has never been easy or, for that matter, easy to assess. Like many filmmakers who choose to work in or near the mainstream, she has been suspicious of labels that might lock her into serving or speaking to one group at the expense of others. She speaks about not wanting to be reduced to the status of a lesbian auteur, explaining that she can't "problematize" sexual orientation enough to make it her primary subject matter:

> If I had said 'OK, this is what I am, I'm a lesbian filmmaker who makes lesbian films,' it wouldn't be a broad enough palette for me. Because it's not my only ... I don't want to be a professional homo. It's not enough. It's not interesting enough.[21]

Rozema has also issued flatly contradictory statements about her interest or lack of interest in gender as a category and feminism as a political project, statements that have left her open to charges of inconsistency and opportunism.[22] Ultimately, many of Rozema's comments seem to reflect her belief in the theoretically discredited but still widespread notion that all art can and should be kept separate from politics, or what she terms "polemics": "I can be political outside of my work, and there can be things that seep into my work; but in my fiction, for me to consciously promote a course of action in terms of gender politics would weaken it." Echoing a (pre-structuralist) belief in the self-present author as the punctual source of meaning within artistic discourse, Rozema has boldly claimed that she is "trying to present a Patricia Rozema perspective on things, a completely individual perspective rather than a 'feminist' one"—she acknowledges that when she follows her own artistic impulses, "women tend to respond," but she says advancing the goals of feminism is not one of her conscious strategies.[23]

Rozema has occasionally been faulted for just this sort of talk, and her work has been read as stemming from a naïve view of gender and "the sparest, most tenuous presumption of feminist principles."[24] But I do not think it is too far-fetched to argue that her well-known resistance to the labelling practices of a strict, 1980s-style identity politics now seems increasingly in alignment with queer theory's suspicion of fixed identities and insistence on the fluidity of all subject positions. As Carol-Anne Tyler notes, queer theory has gained its critical edge by calling into question norms and assumptions about the stability of identities: "Ultimately, queers must question any identity, even a queer identity, since the very fact that it is fixed enough to be recognizable implies an idealized norm and an imperative to identify with it."[25] To call oneself a lesbian, then, is to invoke a fluid and highly mediated set of associations:

> 'The lesbian,' like any other identity, is an effect of representation, a negotiation between language users who (re)create themselves through their linguistic performances, their encoding and decoding or writing and reading of signs. And no matter what we bring to these negotiations, something will always be missing which is finally more ourselves than everything else we are: what we had to negate to represent a self in the first place.[26]

Queer theory, Tyler argues, "describes a relation with alterity, in which calculation comes undone and the name or identity fails."[27]

It seems possible, even likely, that Rozema's resistance to identity politics may have more to do with a pragmatic desire to keep her artistic options open and "have it all," as she recently put it, than with a rigorous deconstruction of social labelling practices.[28] But it is worth noting that a number of the perspectives from which her work has been attacked for its lack of political effectivity have themselves begun to seem too narrowly defined. Marion Harrison, for example, was clearly working within some prescriptive and essentialist version of an "images of women" approach to feminist cinema when she wrote a 1989 *CineAction!* piece attacking *Mermaids* on some of the same grounds that appear a year later in de Lauretis' essay.[29] *Mermaids*, according to Harrison, "only fools us into thinking it is a feminist film," whereas "attention to the filming technique, the narrative construction, the characterization and the treatment of voyeurism and sexuality all reveal that the so-called *positive images of women in this film are undermined*."[30]

Both Harrison and de Lauretis object to the film's depiction of Polly as a pathetic, cloying, degraded specimen of womanhood, and point to what they see as *Mermaids'* (and Rozema's) indifference to the "real" conditions of women and thinly veiled hostility to the actual concerns of feminism. Harrison's article is framed as a response to a *Cinema Canada* piece by George Godwin, who praises the film (within the terms of a fairly straightforward feminist psychoanalytic reading) for short-circuiting the oppressive system of looks in traditional cinema by using formal and narrative means to interrupt the spectator's anonymity.[31] From the moment Polly steps into frame and reveals herself as both the creator and the subject of the flickering video images that open the film, Godwin writes, the "[voyeur's] pleasure of illicit looking" is called into question and made strange: "The distance between the cinematic object and the spectator is collapsed and in the immediate awareness of our act of looking caused by Polly's looking at us, we must readjust our accustomed approach to film; we must justify our looking or look away." Given Rozema's frequent return to the image of Polly addressing the spectator in the video portions of *Mermaids,* he writes, "Our only viable choice, if we are not to reject the film outright, is to re-establish our pleasure in looking by aligning our gaze with Polly's own (as we traditionally align our gaze with the active male subject's gaze)."[32]

Harrison acknowledges that Godwin's interpretation may be "quite justified in its own right," but suggests that a more practical reading of the film is needed because the "average viewer" is likely to leave the theatre with "a more obvious analysis" that has little to do with psychoanalytic processes. Her main objections relate to the film's characterization of Polly and its depiction of the lesbian relationship between Gabrielle and Mary. Polly, she points out, is "the name given to a parrot"; her life as a thirty-one-year-old, sexless, female bachelor seems "blinkered and unfulfilled," and her use of a video camera to convey the film's narrative amounts to a case of internalized oppression: "Polly, as video-maker, places *herself* in a position where the audience looks down on her ... along with distancing Polly from the audience (via the two cameras), [the video device] creates a sense of Polly's distant awareness of herself, and of life in general."[33] Harrison finds the other characters and their relationships equally problematic, and once again her reasoning seems based in a frustrated desire for more affirmative images of women:

> Feeble efforts at dialogue between Polly and Gabrielle, Polly and Mary, and Mary and Gabrielle create little sympathy for these women. Gabrielle is set up in the film as a role model for Polly, yet there is little for us or Polly to admire about her; in fact, she seems to be a symbol of male intellect and power, running a business and interacting with men on their own terms, using their language.[34]

Harrison's critique also reflects her desire for a more subtle and politically engaged approach to lesbian sexuality. *Mermaids'* handling of this subject is "glossed over" and gratuitous, she argues, "providing the *look* of lesbian life but glossing over how that life feels and what it means to lesbians." But it is not only Mary and Gabrielle's relationship that strikes her as shallow and underdeveloped; more worrisome, she implies, is the fact that *Mermaids* sets Polly up to grow and develop as a result of her encounter with the curator, then never allows her to move beyond the "timid, adolescent sexuality" that characterizes her at the start of the film: "There is no evidence that Polly, a once-fragmented individual, is now unified and secure in her knowledge of herself or even has discovered a path to those ends."[35]

Aside from simply asking too much of this or any film, the demand implied here for a steady progression in the moral, sexual, and mental health of *Mermaids'* female characters is symptomatic of a prescriptive strain that defined much of the work in the "images of women" school of feminist film theory in the 1970s and into the '80s. As Agata Smoluch points out, such a reading fails to recognize that meaning within texts "cannot be isolated at any one of [its] various levels or in any one of the character representations, but only exists within the totality of discourses that make up the text." By arguing that Polly's image is "trite and offensive to women" simply because her character falls short of an ideal representation of female strength and self-possession, Harrison takes the narrative too literally, assuming a straightforward authorial endorsement of Polly's character, and creates the problematic impression that "the only recourse for resistance is through constructing utopian representations of women and lesbians."[36]

De Lauretis' essay is equally problematic in its appeal to a placeless, ahistorical definition of feminism as the standard against which *Mermaids* is said to fail. It is striking, for example, that although her larger framework for thinking about the difference between alternative and feminist cinema rests on an appeal to "real issues" and "things actually at stake in feminist communities on a local scale," her reading of *Mermaids* fails to consider the film in relation to its national context. While other critics may have gone too far to situate Rozema's oeuvre alongside a set of characteristics that have been assumed (or asserted) to be uniquely Canadian—characteristics ranging from timidity and difficulty with expression to a "metafictional" concern with margins, boundaries, and unorthodox approaches to narrative—de Lauretis errs at the other extreme, ignoring some fairly obvious references to nationally inflected forms of female fantasy (Polly flinging off her maple-leaf toque while fantasizing about flying over Toronto, for example) and generally neglecting her own call for a contingent definition of feminist and women's cinema that might be alive to local conditions. While paying attention to such conditions may not have fundamentally changed de Lauretis' views on the film's implied homophobia, a more case-sensitive, localized reading of the film can bring to light certain internal and culturally specific dynamics shaping *Mermaids'* approach to gender, sexual orientation, and linguistic competence.

To take just one example, it seems important to read Polly's attraction to "the curator," Gabrielle St. Peres, in light of a larger pattern of attention to the strained and desire-soaked relations between Anglophone and Francophone characters in Rozema's work. One of Rozema's recurring themes, appearing in both *Mermaids* and her 1992 short film *Desperanto,* has to do with the awkwardness and anxiety surrounding English Canada's seemingly repressed desire to be liked by—and to be *like*—French Canadians, who are simultaneously envied and, by some accounts, discriminated against and colonized from within. Rozema's Francophone characters tend to be so much more culturally sophisticated and linguistically competent that her less polished Anglophones can only struggle vainly to keep up.[37] *Desperanto*'s klutzy Toronto housewife, Anne Stewart (Sheila McCarthy), epitomizes this type of figure. After saving up for years, Stewart heads to Montréal for a wild weekend away from her normal routine. When it looks as if she may end up stuck in her hotel room watching Denys Arcand's *Decline of the American Empire* on TV, she forces herself to venture out in her best outfit (a wasp-waist white dress that is "so five years ago") and blunders her way into a chic house party. Armed only with her phrase-book French and a head full of clichés about the exotic French-Canadian other, the naïve lady Anglo (a return of sorts to McCarthy's role as Polly in *Mermaids*) proceeds to break every rule of decorum and misread every cultural sign in her midst. Craig MacInnis called *Desperanto* "one of the great caricatures of English-Canadian anxiety and awkwardness," and quoted Rozema explaining that the film is meant to say to Québec, "I know why you find us geeky. And you're *right*!"[38]

A similar pattern forms part of the subtext of *Mermaids*. While Paule Baillargeon's character, the curator, comes from old money earned in a Swiss chocolate-manufacturing business, the English–French divide as an overdetermined site of awe, envy, and desire is still very much a factor. After learning that the curator wants her to come and work at the Church Gallery, Polly rides her bike through Toronto practising the greeting "bonjour," which still comes out as "bon jure." And she tells the viewer, through one of her videotaped confessions, that one of the things she always admired about the curator was her delicate way of speaking: "The thing that I will always remember about her is her voice. She had a French accent on everything she said. She would say 'Type this Polly,' only she would say 'Type *this*, Poll-é.'" Knowing about this pattern of representation in Rozema's work and its deep roots in a century of Anglophone and Francophone relations within Canada tends to complicate any direct reading of Gabrielle's character in *Mermaids* as simply phallocentric, fraudulent, or due for punishment. She is all of the above, but she is also a source of genuine envy (as well as real admiration) in a context that on some level seems to privilege her character's access to that distinctly Canadian form of social manna: Francophone sophistication.

One of the more suggestive issues raised by Harrison and de Lauretis has to do with Rozema's tendency to craft her narratives as though feminist and lesbian utopias have already been achieved. This strategy, with its debatable appeal to a form of agency based on sheer optimism, is evident not only in *Mermaids* but also in Rozema's third feature, the rhapsodic lesbian romance *When Night Is Falling*. Both films tend to present lesbianism as a relatively unproblematic choice, paying scant attention to the personal, political, and economic costs of living "outside the safe house" of heterosexuality, and generally depicting lesbianism as a problem for the church but not the rest of society.[39] In *Mermaids*, for example, Gabrielle St. Pere's only stated objection to a relationship with Mary stems from the fact that in her line of work at the Church Gallery, she comes into contact with "a lot of ministers." This obstacle is quickly set aside, and for the remainder of the film Mary and Gabrielle enjoy a relatively problem-free existence as live-in lovers, insulated, perhaps, by their involvement in the art world. In *When Night Is Falling*, which elevates the issue of organized religion and homosexuality to a fully developed subplot, the church once again emerges as the primary obstacle to the fulfillment of lesbian desire.[40] The film's lead character, Camille (Pascale Bussières), works as a mythology instructor at a Christian college and resorts to lying to the college's rector (David Fox) in order to hide her growing attraction to Petra (Rachel Crawford), a beautiful lesbian performer with the counter-cultural Sirkus of Sorts. Later, Camille risks her position at the college by openly contradicting the church's position on homosexuality, arguing that the God she serves would not be so cruel as to condemn gays and lesbians to eternal damnation. The film's only overt suggestion of pressure on lesbians in the secular world occurs briefly near the end, when Camille reacts angrily to some of Petra's circus performers who have playfully taunted the couple for showing affection at a party. Petra reminds her that these are "some of the kindest people on earth" and asks Camille what she plans to do when "the really mean fuckers in the world start laughing at you, because they will."

The blissful assumption of a safe house for lesbianism is one of the things that most bothers Harrison about *Mermaids*. She argues that the film "fails to comment on or even hint at the social pressures that act on lesbians" and that "the contradictions and pleasures inherent in lesbian life are entirely absent." Clearly puzzled (or just put off) by the lack of fit between her reality in 1989 and the film's optimistic view, Harrison asks, "Is this a utopian vision of some future acceptance of lesbian sexuality?"[41] Something similar is implied by de Lauretis' comment that it is "difficult to see what lesbianism has to do with [*Mermaids*'] story," since even to raise the issue of relevance in relation to a lesbian subplot is to assume that lesbianism must be specifically motivated within narrative rather than simply forming part of its backdrop or world of assumptions, as heterosexual relationships have done since the first days of cinema. The fact remains, however, that the "relevance question" was probably a fair one to pose of *Mermaids* in 1989 and 1990, before the rise of "lesbian chic" made it fashionable (if not entirely acceptable) to depict women's desire for women in films and television shows ranging from *Go Fish* and *The Incredibly True Adventures of Two Girls in Love* to the Ellen DeGeneres show and, more recently, both *E.R.* and *Buffy the Vampire Slayer*. The degree to which this climate of surface acceptability was *not* a part of *Mermaids'* reception in 1989 is clearly illustrated by Harrison's now-startling remark that "As lesbians, Gabrielle and Mary traditionally will be seen by the audience as whores, reinforcing the stereotype of the evil lesbian or, at least, of the bad girl." She also writes of an "ever-present expectation, from the viewer's standpoint, that the lesbian theme will either blossom or explode, providing the film with traditional sexual conflict."[42] While this may have been true of some audiences when *Mermaids* was initially released, I would speculate that contemporary viewers are probably far less likely to assume that a lesbian theme must "blossom or explode" in order to deserve a place in a narrative.

The fact that the question of lesbian relevance fades from view for the most part in the criti-cal response to *When Night Is Falling* offers a useful illustration of how much has changed theo-retically and in terms of public attitudes in the eight years between Rozema's first and third fea-tures. Although Smoluch raises the possibility that *Night* may be open to charges of "sexual in-difference" stemming from its depiction of Petra and Camille's lesbian relationship within the terms of a heterosexual dynamic of Cupid and Psyche, or hunter and prey, other critics who have written about the film's approach to lesbianism have not raised the issue or have indirectly praised the film for its very tendency to assume the validity of lesbian desire.[43] This, for example, seems to be part of what Shameem Kabir suggests when she points out that lesbian desire in *Night* is allowed to circulate in refreshingly unspectacular (or, as she puts it, "fluid" rather than "phallocentric") ways:

> These women are not obsessed with their partners but enamoured, not fixated but in love. Their desire seems not to entail permanent possession, control, domination or sub-ordination, but respect and reciprocity. They support lesbian desire through a plurality of positionalities.[44]

Kabir does, however, point to the potentially troubling presence of a different utopia in *When Night Is Falling*: a possible racial utopia implied by Petra's status as "another black character who is not seen to be articulating her blackness."[45] Lisa Kennedy briefly hovers over the same ques-tion in an otherwise glowing *Village Voice* review when she asks "why isn't more made of Petra's race?"[46] Smoluch, meanwhile, argues that while *Night* has helped to create lesbian visibility in the mainstream sector, the film may also be open to charges of reducing lesbian desire to a state of narcissistic doubling or identification, while relying on racial difference (however weakly defined it may be within the film) to produce a distinction between the lead characters.[47] The latter point is in keeping with Adrienne Rich's observation that "race occupies the place vacated by gender" in some lesbian relationships, where race serves as a "marker of difference" in the lack of gender differences.[48]

I find it difficult to decide between these seemingly opposed views. It seems possible that both narrative directions alluded to here—the tendency to minimize Petra's blackness and the tendency to draw on race to manufacture a sense of difference between the lovers—are being pursued simultaneously, with racial difference being mined only as much as "required" (within the confines of an otherwise highly traditional romance plot) to heighten the sexual tension be-tween Petra and Camille. As Kabir's comment implies, the film does tend to flatten out any cul-tural specificity that might be associated with Petra's race. A light-skinned black woman, Petra travels with an avant-garde circus that is run by a white couple and largely staffed with white performers, sleeps with white women, and does not appear to have any black friends other than a few non-white co-workers in the Sirkus of Sorts, none of whom have speaking parts. The film makes no mention of her race, focussing instead on other obstacles to Petra's relationship with Camille, such as the church and Camille's boyfriend and career. For Kabir, however, the move to downplay (or perhaps just ignore) Petra's blackness is ultimately unimportant, since *When Night Is Falling* does a great deal to humanize Petra and little, if anything, to pathologize or infantilize her: "Petra is not attempting to pass physically as white, because her blackness is a given. She seems integrated with the white culture without having to become white-minded as a result of this contact."[49] Describing herself as "a black subject who has been hungry for healthy imaginings of us" (and, furthermore, as a lesbian whose own relationships have often been with white women), Kabir attests to feeling "glad to see the imaginings of [Petra] as strong, though vulnerable, as capable and confident, desirous and desirable."[50]

Petra is not attempting to pass physically as white, because her blackness is given. The assumption here seems to be that one effective (or at least passable) way of constructing racial difference within narratives is to posit blackness as "given" rather than making it the subject of the film or writing characters in such a way that they are clearly seen to be "articulating" their blackness. Although Kabir also implies that Petra's unarticulated blackness is something that she had to overcome in her response to *Night*, one could, perhaps, read her as ultimately suggesting that where blackness is truly "given" within narrative (rather than simplistically and oppressively taken to be "the same" as whiteness), questions of racial difference can give way to a healthy *assumption* of equality that then allows the film to stray far and wide from a strict focus on identity politics. The same argument could, perhaps, be used to justify Rozema's habit of depicting lesbianism as a relatively unproblematic choice with few attendant social pressures. The fact that Rozema was denied this justification in two important feminist critiques of her work in the late 1980s but that her continued interest in lesbian and racial utopias provoked little direct criticism in the mid 1990s stands as a further indication of how much has changed with regard to lesbian representation between Rozema's first and third features.

Questions having to do with race, sexual orientation, and utopian longing surface rather forcefully in connection with Rozema's fourth feature, *Mansfield Park*, with results that suggest a certain continuity and also some notable differences from her earlier work. Rozema's reinterpretation of Austen's third novel can, in many ways, be considered her most overtly political work to date. Rather than simply trying to reproduce the novel on film, Rozema has self-consciously and audaciously reshaped it, not only drawing on Austen's early stories and letters but also turning to contemporary critical re-readings of the novel's race politics and approach to gender for inspiration. Rozema's departures from the text, which appear sensational on the surface, are intended to, and in many ways do, honour the spirit of the novel by reviving key features of the social and political context in which *Mansfield Park* was written and originally received. Downplaying the pomp and furnishings that have become a staple of Austen adaptations in recent years, Rozema instead delivers a trenchant reading of the seamier side of life at Mansfield, asking and answering a question that many traditional approaches to the novel (including a faithful but dull two-part 1985 BBC miniseries directed by David Giles) have ignored, but which is arguably one of the book's major subjects: who was paying for the privileges enjoyed by the British landed gentry during the Regency period? Or as Rozema likes to put it, "Who was paying for the party?"

The party, as described in the novel, is going on at a large country estate in Huntingdon, owned and presided over by parliamentarian and slave trader Sir Thomas Bertram and his vacuous wife, Lady Bertram. The couple share Mansfield Park with their four children, daughters Maria and Julia and sons Edmund and Tom, while tolerating the presence of Lady Bertram's meddling sister, Aunt Norris, who spends much of the novel living at the family's parsonage. When Aunt Norris thinks to help their much poorer sister by adopting one of her many children, Fanny Price is plucked out of her squalid home in the busy naval town of Portsmouth and brought to Mansfield Park to live indefinitely. The plot from then on tells the story of a kind of blood infusion into the corrupted British aristocracy from the healthier lower classes. In Edward Said's nice description, "the poor niece, the orphaned child from the outlying city of

Portsmouth, the neglected, demure, and upright wallflower," Fanny joins the country estate, faces many obstacles and some meanness of spirit from the inhabitants, but "gradually acquires a status commensurate with, even superior to, that of most of her more fortunate relatives."[51] The novel suggests that she accomplishes this through pure force of will and moral goodness, qualities that distinguish her from Sir Thomas' spoiled daughters and dissolute older son, but that align her with her cousin Edmund, whom Fanny adores from the start and eventually marries. Along the way, Fanny comes under intense pressure from the family to agree to a marriage proposal from Henry Crawford, the rich but unreliable rake who comes to know the family well during long visits to Mansfield Park with his equally slippery sister, Mary Crawford. The strongest pressure to agree to this unwanted marriage comes from Sir Thomas, who appears to believe he owns Fanny and works to convince her it is her duty to accept a proposal that would benefit her family financially. The campaign is called off only after Henry loses patience and reveals his true colours in an extramarital "fracas" with Sir Thomas' older daughter Maria, wife of the pompous and dim-witted Mr. Rushworth. The novel ends with an external authorial narrator swooping in to "restore every body, not greatly in fault themselves, to tolerable comfort, and to have done with all the rest."

Rozema launches her adaptation on an audacious note by taking Austen's heroine, the intensely shy, passive, and morally unimpeachable Fanny, and transforming her into a witty, irreverent, and active protagonist with a gift for writing and storytelling borrowed directly from Austen. Rozema's Fanny is still quiet, self-deprecating and, as Mary Crawford notes, "as fearful of notice as other women are of neglect," but she comes equipped with a wild imagination and a quick wit, complex views on women's role as chattel, and firm opinions about the evils of slavery. Taking over as the film's clear-sighted narrator, Rozema's Fanny Price gets all the film's best lines, most of them borrowed from stories that Austen wrote as a girl, including "Henry and Eliza," "Love and Friendship," and her mock "History of England," with other references gleaned from Austen's correspondence and her first novel, *Northanger Abbey*. As Claudia L. Johnson has pointed out, this unapologetic innovation ironically serves to bring the film closer to the overall tone of the original by foregrounding "what many of us love about Austen in the first place, what other movies never deliver: Austen's presence as a narrator."[52] From the point of view of authorship, *Mansfield Park* also stands as the culmination of a working method that Agata Smoluch, following Mikhail Bakhtin, describes as dialogical and intertextual—a tendency, that is, to combine genres, quote specific films, and import various cultural texts such as poetry, classical mythology, fairy tales, and the Bible directly into her films.[53] By contributing some of her own writing to the mix, supplementing paraphrased passages from *Mansfield Park* with her own attempts at Austenian dialogue, and weaving all of the elements into a narrative that resembles Austen's original text but also departs from the novel in narratively and politically significant ways, Rozema sets herself up as "one of the speakers" contributing to a polyvalent transformation of the novel into audio-visual form.[54]

Having substantially remade Austen's heroine, Rozema then goes on to expand the novel's muted, half-dozen references to the Bertram family's slave-run West Indies sugar plantations into a full-fledged abolitionist subplot. In practical terms, this means tripling the number of references to slavery and the West Indies while putting abolitionist sentiments directly into the mouths of her characters, including references to the anti-slavery writings of one of Austen's favourite writers, Thomas Clarkson, and a critical look back at Thomas Long's racist *History of Jamaica*.[55] One wholly invented scene even has Fanny stumbling upon an artist's book that includes William Blake's abolitionist sketch "Man on a Meat Hook" and other artist's renderings of slaves being raped and brutalized by white plantation owners, including the novel's patriarch, Sir Thomas Bertram.[56]

Rozema has said she amplified the slavery subplot in order to help contemporary viewers grasp the subtle critique that would have resonated in the minds of Austen's readers at a time when abolitionist debates were very much in the air—discussions that are too much a part of the past to resonate with audiences in the same way today. By airing those debates and importing historical details such as Blake's artwork and references to Clarkson's abolitionist writings into her script, Rozema says, she has simply taken what was implicit in the novel at a certain point and made it *explicit* for a new set of readers.[57] Her approach has won some influential fans, including Johnson, who has championed it as a historically informed, adventurous, and appropriately dark version of a novel that has too often been read as a straightforward rags-to-riches romance. Describing a longstanding disagreement between those Austen fans who prefer to think of her as "serene, domestic, and placid writer" and those who prize her "for very different qualities—for the energy, the irreverence, and the wicked sharpness of her wit, for the keenness of her social commentary on a world where morals and manners are often at odds," Johnson concludes that "Rozema's [adaptation] best captures why my half of the world loves Austen."[58] With *Mansfield Park*, in other words, Rozema begins to receive credit for possessing a clear political vision and a firm feminist agenda—the very things that have been most in question in earlier discussions of the rest of her oeuvre.

Another noteworthy gesture that has helped create this impression has to do with Rozema's introduction of a lesbian subplot—one that may or may not receive subtle support from within the novel. Whereas Austen emphasizes a vaguely defined mutual "fascination" that takes hold between Fanny Price and Mary Crawford, especially during Edmund's absences from Mansfield Park, Rozema transforms this ambiguous connection between the characters into an unmistakable *frisson* of sexual attraction, initiated by Mary and received with faint curiosity by Fanny. This well-publicized but ultimately minor subplot is contained within two main scenes. The first follows Mary as she visits Fanny in her room and ropes her into a sexually suggestive rehearsal designed to convince Edmund to take on the role of Anhalt in the lascivious German play *Lover's Vows*, which the Bertram children almost get around to staging as a "home theatrical." (The scene calls for Mary to wrap her arms around Fanny's neck while explaining that "None but a woman can teach the science of her own sex"—a heated moment that serves to convince Edmund he should take the part.) The other scene unfolds on a rainy day when Fanny is soaked to the skin while gathering fruit near the parsonage. In a version of the scene that is only slightly more suggestive than that in the novel, Mary leaps to Fanny's aid, helps her out of some of her wet clothing, and takes the opportunity to inspect Fanny's "fine form."

Although both scenes could perhaps be viewed as Rozema's gift to her lesbian fans, the mode of address employed in these encounters is far from unambiguous. As I read it, the desire expressed in both scenes carries a strong whiff of triangulated desire (one of Rozema's favourite motifs, familiar from both *Mermaids* and *When Night Is Falling*) and is complicated by the fact that Mary and Fanny are, during most of the film, in direct competition with each other for the same man. While neither character has admitted as much by the time these lesbian-tinged flirtations take place, Mary's dawning awareness of the situation seems implied by her behaviour at a "coming out" ball held in Fanny's honour. After watching Edmund and Fanny from a distance of several feet, Mary waits for Fanny to leave and then approaches Edmund with the sudden, half-joking demand that he should "admit [he is] in love with Fanny Price." Edmund manages to reply "Of course I love Fanny. But there are as many types of love as there are moments in time." One could easily follow the lead set by de Lauretis in her discussion of *Mermaids* and ask what lesbianism has to do with *Mansfield Park*'s narrative, except as a means of adding a hint of homoerotic cachet to what is ultimately the expression of a heterosexual aim by both women (i.e., Edmund's undivided attention). Lesbian viewers might wonder what they are expected to take from these scenes, given the degree to which they are presented as "perks" within a plot driven for the most part by straight desire. But as Johnson has indicated, passion in both the film and the novel tends to be "mobile and bewildering,"[59] and these scenes are no exception. If Rozema's other films are able to assume the presence of lesbian utopias, *Mansfield Park* responds to its source material and pursues a more ambiguous agenda: that of subtly coaxing lesbian desire to the surface while leaving it tantalizingly unclear whether there is anything more at stake between these two young women than a platonic fascination born of distrust. If there is any kind of shared impulse underlying these otherwise distinct representational strategies, it may have to do with the fact that Rozema is continuing to assert her right to define lesbianism in any way that pleases or makes sense to her, regardless of what might seem politic or popular. Fortunately for her, these are more permissive times than when she began her career. In a theoretical climate geared, as Carol-Anne Tyler suggests, to questioning all forms of fixed identity, a touch of triangulated, amorphous desire may be just the ticket.

Notes

1 Robert Cagle, "Canadian Filmmaking in the Face of Cultural Imperialism," *Reverse Shot* 1, no. 2 (Summer 1994): 9.

2 Cameron Bailey, "Intense Auteur Unleashes Risky Lesbian Romance," *Now*, 4–10 May 1995, 30.

3 Geoff Pevere, "Middle of Nowhere: Ontario Movies After 1980," *Post Script* 15, no. 1 (Fall 1995): 9–22. Originally published in *Les Cinémas du Canada*, Sylvain Garel and Andre Paquet, eds. (Paris: Éditions du Centre Pompidou, 1992). Pevere describes Ontario's New Wave as "one of the most vital and productive booms in the history of the country's cinema"—a major "semantic reversal" that saw the artistic heart of Canadian filmmaking shift from Québec to Ontario during the 1980s. Rozema was a key player, along with Atom Egoyan and Bruce McDonald, while David Cronenberg solidified his reputation and earned international auteur status during the 1980s.

4 Brian Johnson, "Sex and the sacred girl," *Maclean's*, 8 May 1995, 93.

5 The $6-million figure was current as of 1995, as reported in Johnson, "Sex and the sacred girl," 93. The information about *Variety* and *Mermaids'* US theatrical run appears in Michael Posner, *Canadian Dreams: The Making and Marketing of Independent Films* (Vancouver/Toronto: Douglas & McIntyre, 1993), 19.

6 Both films feature subplots that emphasize the splitting of the artist into public and private selves: one self to produce the creative work, another to perform in public or deal with the critics. In *Mermaids*, this arrangement is exposed as a fraud, whereas in *White Room* it takes on more of a sympathetic hue. Within that film's analysis of fame, Jane's decision to retreat from the world of public performances and media attention is made to seem rational.

7 Deborah Knight, "Metafiction, Pararealism and the 'Canon' of Canadian Cinema," *Cinémas* 3, no. 1 (Fall 1992): 138.

8 Knight, "Metafiction, Pararealism and the 'Canon'," 138.

9 MacInnis quotes Rozema as saying *White Room* is a picture "that still hasn't received its due. But it will. It will." Craig MacInnis, "Patricia Rozema ... unbound," *Toronto Star*, 17 February 1995, D1.

10 Other second films in this category include *Beefcake* (Fitzgerald, 1999), *Touched* (Ransen, 1999), and *Drive, She Said* (Shum, 1997).

11 Johnson, "Sex and the sacred girl," 93.

12 Claudia L. Johnson's introduction to Patricia Rozema, *Jane Austen's Mansfield Park: A Screenplay* (New York: Talk Miramax Books, 2000), 10. This essay originally appeared in the *Times Literary Supplement* and was not, to my knowledge, commissioned by Rozema.

13 On the matter of whether she is lesbian or bisexual, Rozema had this to say in 1995: "I'm still uneasy about discussing [my sexual orientation] publicly. I guess I would have called myself bi six or seven years ago. I don't know. There are a lot of delightful men in the world. But I'm gradually coming to the conclusion that I'm primarily lesbian" (Johnson, "Sex and the sacred girl," 94). More recently, Agata Smoluch has written of Rozema as a "bisexual filmmaker" who has "resisted [the lesbian community's attempts to claim her] and prefers not to be categorized as a lesbian." Agata Smoluch, "(Con)texts of Hybrid Authorship: Canadian Cinema, Feminism, Sexual Difference and the Dialogic Films of Patricia Rozema," unpublished master's thesis, York University, 1999, 79. The reference to "more existential questions" is found in Chris Bearchell, "A Canadian Fairytale: Chris Bearchell Talks to Patricia Rozema about Taking Her First Feature to Cannes," *Epicene*, October 1987, 25. Rozema is quoted as saying that gender "seems like a category of such minuscule significance to me ... I'm interested in more existential questions."

14 On her resistance to labelling and identity politics, Rozema told critic Cameron Bailey, "As soon as I'm identified as belonging to any group, the brat in me tries to show how I don't belong. So to make a lesbian love story, and to be in the position of being called a lesbian filmmaker, frightens me because I see it as one category among many" (Bailey, "Intense Auteur," 32).

15 Bailey, "Intense Auteur," 32.

16 Teresa de Lauretis, "Guerrilla in the midst: women's cinema in the 80s," *Screen* 31, no. 1 (Spring 1990): 17, 19.

17 de Lauretis, "Guerrilla in the midst," 19. It is not clear from de Lauretis' discussion why lesbianism needs a special motivation to appear within narrative, although from her positive discussion of *She Must Be Seeing Things* it appears she favours lesbian narratives that work to situate lesbianism critically within an explicit analysis of representation. There is little room in this theory for assuming the "right" of lesbian characters to exist in any narrative, regardless of the film's commitment to an explicit critique of lesbian identity and representation.

18 de Lauretis, "Guerrilla in the midst," 20.

19 de Lauretis, "Guerrilla in the midst," 18.

20 de Lauretis, "Guerrilla in the midst," 20.

21 de Lauretis, "Guerrilla in the midst."

22 See, for example, Smoluch, "(Con)texts of Hybrid Authorship," 33. In a 1993 interview, Rozema was quoted as saying, "I'm distinctly feminist. My films assume feminism. That's the best way I can say it. They assume feminism, it's in their foundation." In 1997 she was quoted as saying, "There's a strain of feminism that seems to suggest that you can create only heroic female characters ... I could never write a film where people would say, 'My films *assume* feminist principles.'" Smoluch, who was working as Rozema's personal assistant at the time of this writing, cites these statements side by side. The first appeared in Janis Cole and Holly Dale, *Calling the Shots: Profiles of Woman Filmmakers* (Kingston: Quarry Press, 1993), 183. The second appeared in Judith M. Redding and Victoria A. Brownworth, *Film Fatales: Independent Women Directors* (Seattle: Seal Press, 1997), 210–11. Taken together, these statements do seem contradictory. However, Rozema's work may assume feminism without her necessarily wanting audiences to be able to detect that assumption, since (in her view) that would mean she has failed as an artist. This is a common attitude among artists who may embrace the goals of a particular political movement but who still believe in the goal of using art to express "universal" themes. The assumptions underlying a defence of art as universal are vulnerable to a number of well-known criticisms. Much feminist work in aesthetics and epistemology, for example, has been geared to demonstrating that all knowledge, including artistic expression, is best viewed as "situated," or as carrying within it a wide

range of meanings and assumptions relating to the identity, desires, and socioeconomic standing of the speaker and the culture of which she is a part. See for example, Carolyn Korsmeyer, "Pleasure: Reflections on Aesthetics and Feminism," *Journal of Aesthetics and Art Criticism* 51, no. 2 (Spring 1993), and selected articles in Peggy Zeglin Brand and Carolyn Korsmeyer, eds., *Feminism and Tradition in Aesthetics* (Pennsylvania: Pennsylvania State University Press, 1995).

23 Peter Brunette, "'Shut up and just do it!' *Sight and Sound* 60, no. 1 (Winter 1990–91): 57.

24 de Lauretis, "Guerrilla in the midst," 19.

25 Carol-Anne Tyler, "Desiring Machines: Queer Re-Visions of Feminist Film Theory," in *Coming Out of Feminism?* Mandy Merck, Naomi Segal, and Elizabeth Wright, eds. (Oxford and Malden, MA: Blackwell Publishers, 1998), 155.

26 Tyler, "Desiring Machines," 157.

27 Tyler, "Desiring Machines," 172.

28 When asked about her much-publicized resistance to labels, Rozema said "I'll take any embrace I can get. But I don't want to be limited by that embrace. But that's just always the trade-off. You are welcomed, you feel warmth and affection when you belong to a group, but when you belong to a group you are monitored more closely, and you can be castigated for not doing or saying the right things ... Basically, we just want it all. We want freedom but we want stability and love too, we want all of the advantages of being single, but we want domestic bliss as well. We want it all and we'll never get it." Interview with the author, 28 December 2000.

29 Marion Harrison, "*Mermaids*: Singing Off Key?" *CineAction!* (Spring 1989): 25–30.

30 Harrison, "Mermaids: Singing Off Key?", 25.

31 George Godwin, "Reclaiming the subject: A feminist reading of *I've Heard the Mermaids Singing*," *Cinema Canada* 152 (May 1988).

32 Godwin, "Reclaiming the subject," 23.

33 Harrison, "Mermaids: Singing Off Key?", 26.

34 Harrison, "Mermaids: Singing Off Key?", 27.

35 Harrison, "Mermaids: Singing Off Key?", 28–29.

36 Smoluch, "(Con)texts of Hybrid Authorship," 61, 64.

37 The one noteworthy exception to this pattern occurs in *When Night Is Falling;* here the Francophone character is a conservative theology professor who must be dragged into an acceptance of her own lesbian desire by the Anglo circus performer, Petra. This raises the issue of race, since it seems possible that Petra's greater spontaneity is being subtly or subconsciously "explained" within the narrative by her blackness. For a largely positive (and unabashedly personal) reading of lesbian identity and racial difference in *When Night Is Falling,* see Shameem Kabir, *Daughters of Desire: Lesbian Representation in Film* (London and Washington: Cassell, 1998), 101–10.

38 Craig MacInnis, "Rozema hits nerve in unity wrangling," n.d. Located in "Rozema" file in Cinematheque Ontario's Film Reference Library, Toronto.

39 Yvonne Rainer writes that to "call [herself]" a lesbian is "not only a statement of sexual preference, it is a way of pointing to where I—and others like me, for the same, also different, reasons—live: outside the safe house, on the edge, in the social margin." Rainer, "Working round the L-word," in *Queer Looks: Perspectives on Lesbian and Gay Film and Video*, Martha Gever, John Greyson, and Pratibha Parmar, eds. (New York and London: Routledge, 1993), 13; as cited in Tamsin Wilton, *Immortal Invisible: Lesbians and the Moving Image* (New York and London: Routledge, 1995), 5.

40 For a slightly different view, see Smoluch, "(Con)texts of Hybrid Authorship," 91. Although she acknowledges that lesbianism is presented as a relatively unproblematic social choice in *Night*, Smoluch argues that the use

of formal and intertextual strategies to "offer the lesbian lovers up as being *the same* as any of the star-crossed lovers of their heterosexual counterparts" actually amounts to a "defensive portrayal of lesbian sexuality that knowingly treats lesbianism as a threat." She sees the move to present lesbianism as "natural" (i.e., hetero-sexual) as problematic because it "denies the potential differences involved in lesbian relationships."

41 Harrison, "Mermaids: Singing Off Key?", 29.

42 Harrison, "Mermaids: Singing Off Key?", 29.

43 Smoluch, "(Con)texts of Hybrid Authorship," chapter 4, especially pages 83–85. She points to contradictions stemming from Rozema's strategy of placing a taboo and potentially alienating subject matter within dominant codes of representation: "Specifically, the contradiction between the desire to represent a form of sexuality that is not heterosexual by embedding it within a typical 'heterosexual' narrative romance, is what de Lauretis would term 'sexual indifference.'" Smoluch cites Teresa de Lauretis, "Sexual Indifference and Lesbian Representation," passim.

44 Kabir, *Daughters of Desire*, 106.

45 Kabir, *Daughters of Desire*, 103.

46 Lisa Kennedy, "States of Grace," *Village Voice*, 21 November 1996, 38.

47 Smoluch, "(Con)texts of Hybrid Authorship," 84, 93–95, 104.

48 B. Ruby Rich, "When Difference Is (More Than) Skin Deep," *Queer Looks*, 321.

49 Kabir, *Daughters of Desire*, 103.

50 Kabir, *Daughters of Desire*, 103.

51 Edward Said, "Jane Austen and Empire," in *Mansfield Park and Persuasion*, Judy Simons, ed. (New York: St. Martin's Press, 1997), 108.

52 Johnson, "Introduction to *Mansfield Park*," 5–6.

53 Smoluch, "(Con)texts of Hybrid Authorship," 32 and 46–47.

54 This brief quote from Silverman comes from her discussion of the limits of auteur theory and her attempt to reconcile the feminist political need for a theory of female authorship with the poststructuralist assault on authorship as a category of expression. Silverman argues for a distinction between the author "inside" and "outside" the text, and suggests that "the director may in certain situations constitute *one* of the speakers of his or her own films, and that there may at times be pressing political reasons for maximizing what might be said to derive from this authorial voice." Kaja Silverman, *The Acoustic Voice: The Female Voice in Psychoanalysis and Cinema* (Bloomington: Indiana University Press, 1988), 202.

55 I count a total of sixteen brief and more extended mentions of slavery in Rozema's shooting script. These range from passing references to elements of *mise en scène* (such as a lithograph from Antigua that appears several times) to fully developed scenes complete with invented dialogue.

56 The images, as identified in the screenplay, include details of severely chafed wrists, titled "Oronooko's Wrists"; a group of young white boys raping a black girl, titled "Our Neighbours"; a building out alone in a field, titled "Slave Prison"; a close-up of an enraged Sir Thomas with a whip in his hand; and another image of Sir Thomas about to be fellated by a slave woman. Patricia Rozema, "Jane Austen's *Mansfield Park*," 128.

57 Interview with the author, 28 December 2000. This assertion is likely to be controversial, given debates into the feasibility of recovering the historical conditions underlying literary texts. Antony Easthope, for example, has argued that "texts cannot be adequately analysed in relation to a definition of a particular social and historical context," because they "exceed that context not only diachronically, always temporally going beyond a given reading, but also synchronically, always available to another reading at the same time, even in the supposedly 'original' moment when they were first produced." Rozema, according to this view, could never hope to restore *Mansfield Park* to the social totality of which it was a part because such a totality is always unavailable, radically un-readable, and in a sense never existed. Anthony Easthope, *Literary Into*

Cultural Studies (London: Routledge, 1991), 113; as cited in Barbara Klinger, "Film history terminable and interminable: recovering the past in reception studies," *Screen* 38, no. 2 (Summer 1997): 107.

58 Johnson, "Introduction to *Mansfield Park*," 10.

59 Johnson, "Introduction to *Mansfield Park*," 8.

States of Emergency in the Films of Anne Wheeler

Susan Lord

ANNE WHEELER IS A PROLIFIC CANADIAN FILMMAKER. Born in Alberta, she has lived for the last decade in British Columbia. Her ties to region are clear in her oeuvre: her prairie and Alberta films inhabit their locations and have, not unlike the landscape (at the risk of bad cliché), moved laterally across a range of themes and have insisted on plumbing the depths of historical memory for the visible evidence of the violence of that repressed and contained past. Her West Coast projects clearly draw from Vancouver's iconic neighbourhoods ("the Drive") and workplaces (the docks), as well as from BC's particular experience of World War Two in the internment of Japanese Canadians. Wheeler herself has explored some of the "Hollywood North" terrain as a director.

Although she has never made an experimental film, her work has also spanned genres and modes of representation, beginning with salvage documentaries such as *Great Grandmother* (1975) and *Augusta* (1976), the interactive "consciousness-raising" documentary *Happily Unmarried* (1977), and a mixed-mode documentary, *A War Story: Based on the Diaries of Dr. Ben Wheeler* (1981), which is structured around very moving and beautifully shot re-enactment footage. Her work in the mid 1980s begins with short dramas, *One's a Heifer* (made for the CBC-TV series "Program X") and *To Set Our House in Order*, and takes us to her best-known and most accomplished films, *Loyalties* and *Bye Bye Blues*. Later, Wheeler undertook made-for-TV movies and miniseries, such as *The War Between Us* (1995) and *The Sleep Room* (1998). In the early days, she worked on the staff of CBC *For the Record* series, the series for which *A Change of Heart* was made, and she has the credit of writer and producer for the made-for-TV film *Diane Kilmury: Teamster*. She has also recently directed a number of episodes of television shows, including *Ray Bradbury Theatre, Cold Squad,* and *da Vinci's Inquest*.

Over the course of her career, she has run the gamut of production contexts from independent productions with the company Film West, formed in the early 1970s, to work for the CBC and National Film Board (NFB), to co-productions with what was Atlantis, and Allarcom and Barna Alper, to co-ventures with cable stations such as Lifetime. Odeon, NBC, and, of course, Alliance/Atlantis are among her most recent credits. These production contexts tell the story of dramatic and incremental changes in Canadian film funding and cultural policy, from Trudeau-era Local Initiatives Programme (LIP) grants to co-ventures to multiculturalism to NAFTA. While

Wheeler has written and directed a number of her films, her production history is rich with co-writers, scripts written by others or based on novels and short stories. Most notably, however, Wheeler's filmography, more than that of any other director of her generation, betrays a long-term commitment to representing gender alongside racial and ethnic difference.

Curiously and disappointingly, though, there is almost no critical literature on this filmmaker whose eighteen film-direction credits alone (at least twenty-six together with TV credits) certainly outrank many other "Canadian" filmmakers for whom much critical discourse has been generated. The fortunate exceptions to the dearth of writing on Wheeler are the tremendously insightful discussions of *Loyalties* in Brenda Longfellow's essay on gender, landscape, and colonial allegories, and in Robin Wood's essay on *Loyalties* and *Life Classes*. Tom Waugh's "queering the canon" project includes a discussion of *One's a Heifer*, based on a story by prairie writer Sinclair Ross, and *Cowboys Don't Cry*. Otherwise, most of the source material used here comes from the pages of industry reviews, such as *Variety* and *Alberta Report*, and cultural history and policy analyses.[1] This essay, then, represents the first attempt at a comprehensive study of Anne Wheeler's films. As such, it is meant to function both as a survey of key themes and issues laced across some eighteen films made over twenty-five years and as a provisional analysis of the effects on a body of work of late-1980s changes in cultural policy and Canadian politics. As I hope here to provide historical and discursive contexts for viewing the work, and examples of how one may find these contexts illuminating the films' forms and styles, a different occasion will better serve close textual readings. Although I am unable to resist some textual work on the early films in particular, this effort at an authorship study locates the "author" through a number of different, and sometimes incompatible, methods—institutional, filmic, cultural, historical, economic—making this more a work of cultural history than film theory.

Major Themes and Issues

Overall, Wheeler's work evinces a set of intersecting themes: colonialism and violence intersect with prairie patriarchy. This form of patriarchal governance of land and family is inextricable from Canadian mythologies of wilderness; together they generate an anti-modern sociality, an ethos against which female friendships and affective male relationships are established across often quite radical differences, differences that are themselves prescribed through institutionalized violence that services nationalism. There is also an ongoing interest in World War Two and the immediate postwar period in Canada, largely informed or inspired by the biographies of her parents. *War Story* is based on her doctor-father's diaries written while in a Japanese prisoner-of-war camp in Formosa (Taiwan); he was imprisoned for most of the war, during which time he ministered to countless sick and dying men. *Bye Bye Blues*, a feature fiction film, is based on the mother's experiences as a "grass widow" during this same time, playing piano in a dance band to secure food and running shoes for her children.

As persistent as these themes are, we find that in the late 1980s they begin to be treated quite differently than they had been in the previous decade. My analysis is in part motivated by an interest in how and why Wheeler articulates different approaches to representing gender and cultural difference, with the shift in perspective most clearly marked with the last of the "prairie" films, *Bye Bye Blues*, in 1989. This film itself is pivotal in a number of ways, particularly because it registers the extrusion of gothic elements, leaving us with a very accomplished, if less difficult, woman's film. The generic use of melodrama then structures most of the films made in the 1990s.

But it is *Loyalties*, made in 1986, that represents the culmination of a project begun in 1975, a project that sought to bring to representation the private suffering of public violence. In so doing, the films disclose the primacy of the role of what Marx called "sentience" as that which is intrinsic to the *work* of creating intersubjective relationships from which the making of a single self is indissociable. In other words, the self does not exist prior to, and apart from, its relations with others, and those relations, a co-working of all involved, produce the selves of all involved in them. From those relations, sentience, a capacity for empathy and the insights only empathy can provide, is no mere addendum to the formation of social relationships with others but is entwined through them at every moment. As the films disclose, the gender ideologies that prescribe masculinity as isolated self-making and femininity as privatized selflessness are interlaced with race ideologies that prescribe whiteness as specific and raceless, and colour as undifferentiated. These ideologies are symptoms of the colonization of the life-world by power.[2] Wheeler's early films strive to articulate the sentient subject as one who is born from the link between action and suffering (i.e., the doer is always and at the same time a sufferer). And action is, as Hannah Arendt put it, "never possible in isolation; to be isolated is to be deprived of the capacity to act ... Action, moreover, no matter what its specific content, always establishes relationships and therefore has an inherent tendency to force open all limitations and cut across all boundaries."[3] The disclosure made by and in the films is also then an act of destruction insofar as it rejects with critical force the normative gender and race narratives formed and managed through the language of "tolerance." The films not only represent intersubjectivity as the prior ground of subjectivity; they also propose community as that which can be based on bonds of empathy and affection. Such a community is subcultural, utopian in its imagination of a space beyond power. In this way, Wheeler is participating in—to a more or less radical degree—a social imaginary dramatized in the Canadian docudrama tradition. Seth Feldman's insightful essay on the Canadian docudrama analyzes how in many of the films made for *For the Record* "protagonists work their way from a rejection by one group toward their acceptance by another sub-cultural entity."[4] It is my analysis that Wheeler's later films tend to normalize and stabilize power, merely adjusting who sits where; and the issues addressed by the films are privatized, either through legal discourses or domestic relations.

What happened in the late 1980s to motivate this change in ethical, political, and aesthetic attitudes? As critical as I am of what I perceive to be a loss in the 1990s work of an incisive interrogation of these themes, I wish also to consider the entire oeuvre in terms of one question: does the use of melodrama for the content of the violence of colonialism and its aftermath merely affirm liberal multiculturalism (and its variant liberal feminism) or does it create sublimated, excessive, emotional experiences that effectively do not permit the text of colonial patriarchy to close after the last commercial?[5] And, given the Canadian tradition of a "cinema of outsiders," do Wheeler's 1990s mainstream productions push the outsider to the inside?[6] In other words, in congruence with official multiculturalism, is the imaginary circulating in this body of work one that "de-marginalizes" gendered, sexual, racial, ethnic, and class "others"? And to what effect? How does this rhyme with other changes in the discourse of national identity in the same period? And, finally, how are those discourses tied to money? In an effort to answer these questions, I will outline the work done in the two periods, sketching the production contexts in which Wheeler worked and analyzing the cultural politics of the mid to late 1980s. I will weave my analyses of the films throughout, tracking themes and textual strategies.

The Periods

My division of Wheeler's oeuvre into two parts is based in the first instance on a change in the films' signifying density. I would not say that Wheeler's films have ever been intensely "writerly": she has never participated in avant-garde or experimental textual practices and has stayed faithful to naturalist dramatic conventions and the tradition of realist documentaries of the Studio D variety. However, in the films of the 1970s and 1980s, those conventions are deployed in a manner that registers an as-yet inexpressible depth subtending the fears, grief, and tensions manifested in the archival documents, and dramatic narratives and their characters. I see a link between this auteurist textuality and the development of a project through the decade 1975–86, from *Great Grandmother* to *Loyalties*, that is motivated by a complicated and urgent set of political and ethical questions. Foremost among them are those provided by feminism, undoubtedly of a liberal sort but which is informed—more than is the case for most white women working in this period—by a race politics of a particularly prairie form: cowboys and Indians. Along with feminism, issues of colonialism (with its poverty and violence) as opposed to multiculturalism, and thus regionalism as opposed to nationalism, inform and motivate the stories that are told and the form in which they are presented.

Loyalties and *Change of Heart* (1984) are both feminist melodramas centred in the domestic sphere, and both understand that sphere to be the repository of public and political values, systems, and processes.[7] Even while the screen time prioritizes the physical spaces of "hearth and home," that space is a net of signs that permits us and the female characters to analyze the public sphere and its institutions. A similar, if less critical, deployment of melodrama structures *The War Between Us* and *The Sleep Room* as they engage with the realms of law, medicine, and government.

Change of Heart, written by Sharon Riis (Wheeler's co-writer on *Loyalties*), stages the encounter of tradition and modernity very differently than we are used to seeing it. Technological modernity usually represents the colonizing processes—and in Canadian cultural studies and philosophy from Grant and Innis to Peter Harcourt, technological modernity is a particularly national sign. But according to Wheeler, a "prairie" type of patriarchy offers a different version of this binary. The father is tradition: land worked with minimal technology, family run with as little modernization as possible. It is this masculinity—embodied, literally, as force and strength—that secured the grid against Natives and cultivated a nation. Having raised four children (one of whom died as a boy) on a farm run by her nasty husband Bob, Edna chooses, with the help of a woman friend, to leave and live on her own. Bob, the aging patriarch, refuses to sign over the farm to his eldest son, which would allow the purchase of a tractor, because this technology stands as a sign of his absence—a sign of the end of a particular form of governance of land and family.[8]

However, modernity and modernization are, for Edna, preconditions for autonomy. Leaving the farm to go to work (because of hard financial times) introduces her to comradeship, respect as a person, economic independence, and community. She works at an adult-education centre in the city and spends her days with a heterogeneous group of people: other women, Native people, and immigrants who are learning English. It is in this context of difference that she flourishes. She leaves behind not just a failed marriage and a disrespectful husband; she is also freed by the excavation of a terrible secret that has bound the household in fear and grief. Edna had silently borne the unspeakable grief and guilt over the loss of her son, until it is disclosed that he was killed in a farming accident because his father "bullied" him to be a "man." Once on her own, Edna says, "I'm ashamed of myself for being treated as less than human all those years. I may be unhappy but at least I'm alive." The possibilities for new and previously unimaginable ways of living emerge from intersubjective and modern forms of sociality.

Narratives such as Edna's participate in the discourses and fantasies of women's popular culture such as those found in the 1950s woman's film, with their hopes for a different form of society on the horizon. The early Wheeler films offer the critic a rich "gothic" archive for an "auteurist" study: the dramatic tensions in *To Set Our House in Order, One's a Heifer, Change of Heart,* and of course *Loyalties* are articulated by troping on gothic themes of female paranoia, obscured vision, attributions of life to inanimate objects, the domestic space as terrifyingly unsafe, the undead, and the secret. As Longfellow has written about *Loyalties,*

> It appropriates melodramatic, generic conventions to feminist critique but its textual predecessors are less likely to be found among romantic melodramas than among the darker gothic romances of *Jane Eyre* or *Rebecca*. Founded on the suspicion that the thin veneer of civility in bourgeois marriage masks a deeply malevolent brutality against women, the gothic is preoccupied with the struggle to name the source of domestic horror. Structured by an enduring tension between the said and the unsaid, between the appearance of domestic harmony and its dark foreboding underside, the gothic textually embodies the terror women experience as targets in a patriarchal society.[9]

While women's relationships and subjectivity form the main content of these films, gothic devices destabilize normative gender roles and hetero-normative relations in *One's a Heifer* by presenting an encounter between a fatherless pubescent boy and an older, psychologically distressed man. The malevolence that seems to haunt the man and his house, complete with howling wind, stuffed owls, and intimations of a dead woman buried somewhere on the farm, never completely vanishes; but neither does it yield anything dangerous. In fact, the old bachelor cares for the boy; and the momentary and fragile affection between them gives representation to a non-normative homosociality.[10] The gothic trope is at work in *To Set Our House in Order,* but the agent of oppression is the grandmother of our young heroine. The house is unbearably clean, lifeless, and tense with secrecy. As in the best eighteenth-century novels of the "popular sublime," the house speaks: the stairwells seem shared by ghosts, and life and death live side by side. Again, the film ends with the secret being revealed and order restored. But the young girl will be forever changed by the revelation and the events leading up to it. As these two examples also show, surrogates for colonial patriarchy are not exclusively male, nor are redemptive relations the sole property of women.

Wheeler's documentary projects are also textually rich. For instance, although her first two films *Great Grandmother* (an early Studio D film) and *Augusta* are both clearly located in the feminist project of the 1970s, which sought to recover the previously invisible lives of women past and present, Wheeler's use of dramatic devices produces a pervasive suspense—a suspension of certainty—and thus a form of identification with the experience of feeling the presence of danger. The use of archival footage and interviews in combination with harrowing re-enactments of childbirth and death in *Great Grandmother* and the strategic use of specific techniques at key moments of Augusta Evans' narration of her life as a Native woman facilitate simultaneously the ethical relation Vivian Sobchack and others have theorized for our encounter with archival images, and the empathetic and affective spectatorship common to the viewing of fiction film. A similar double register for very different content is at work in *A War Story*.

Relative to the early films, the work of the later period suffers from a kind of textual inertia. These generic, movie-of-the-week melodramas—most of which provide some CBC-of-the-90s style of pedagogy—are all about important topics and stories. However, it appears that when run through the industry standards of the 1990s, the textual complexity, the affective intensity, and thus the critical potentiality are diminished. The stylistic signs now facilitate televisual spectatorship: that is, a foil upon which viewers can cast their own emotions and fantasies. The generic text imagines a generic spectator, however diverse and contradictory the spectator's uses and gratifications may be.[11] In this period, the locations and address shift from a regional to national point of view; historical exposés of the national past provide the material for two large television projects: *The War Between Us* (1995), written by Sharon Gibbon, about the internment of Japanese Canadians during World War Two, and *The Sleep Room* (1998), written by Anne Collins, about the CIA-related drug and behavioural testing on psychiatric patients in Montréal from 1955 to 1964. With these, the work clearly continues to participate in the social-conscience drama that historically distinguishes CBC productions from the movie-of-the-week fodder made south of the border. Wheeler also made *The Diviners* (1993), based on Margaret Laurence's novel, and *Better Than Chocolate* (1999), a "romantic comedy" about sexual minoritization, filled with hyperbolic and generally uninteresting characters (the exception is the male-to-female transgender whose role is discussed later). What persists, then, from the early period into the later is the revelation of repressed knowledge hidden under myths about how nice a place Canada is. But there is a change of textuality and attitude that signals a much larger contextual shift: from a political and ethical critique of racism, of patriarchal governance, and of nationalism to something more akin to a moral argument against intolerance. Put another way, the shift is from decolonization to multiculturalism, from collective to individualist consciousness.

There are biographical reasons for the changes in style and production values notable in Wheeler's oeuvre: at the end of the 1980s, she moved from her home in Edmonton to the West Coast (the hub of "Hollywood North"); for a director whose work is so carefully tied to region and location, this move is significant to the work. But more crucially, there were major changes taking place in the Canadian film industry and policy. Although the Department of Communications' 1990 annual report states its goal to be "nation building" ("helping Canadians share their ideas, information and dreams"), the actual conditions for making films in Canada in the 1990s were driven ever more intensively by the post-national movement of "global capital" facilitated by the Free Trade Agreement, signed in 1989, and NAFTA, signed in 1994.[12] The resultant shift toward the development of US audiences through co-ventures, as opposed to the projection of the imaginary Canadian in the nation-building cultural-funding imperatives of the 1970s and early 1980s, was registered in many creators' film practices. As Longfellow and Dorland are careful to point out, though, the tie between nationalist cultural policy, public money, and the private film industry dates back to the late 1950s; and the "tax shelter films of the 1970s and the innumerable other examples that followed were also committed to mimicking foreign (read 'Hollywood') textual, marketing and industrial practices as means of achieving market undifferentiation."[13] Nonetheless, the politics of regional and cultural specificity, tied as they are to imaginaries about land, work, and community, clearly informed and were inscribed in many films of the 1970s through mid 1980s. This is especially true for the films produced in the *For the Record* series, as well as those produced or co-produced by Atlantis before the late 1980s.

Atlantis, a co-producer of *One's a Heifer*, *To Set Our House in Order*, and *Cowboys Don't Cry* (as well as four of the feature films in the 1990s) underwent a major change of direction and personnel in the late 1980s. Janice Platt, co-founder with Michael MacMillan and Seaton McLean, left the company in 1989. She had been Wheeler's producer on two dramatic shorts and was committed to making Canadian stories. MacMillan's interest turned southward, redirecting the company's mandate and monies, making Atlantis one of Canada's leading TV producers and distributors, and the largest "client" of the co-venture policy, beginning with *The Ray Bradbury Theatre* in 1985. By 1987, close to 80 percent of Atlantis' revenues came from outside Canada, 55 percent from the US and 25 percent from Europe.[14] Wheeler's feature *Cowboys Don't Cry* (1987) was the only co-produced Canadian feature film Atlantis made in 1986–87, and from the feature came the TV series which had all but erased the traces of regionalism.

Because Wheeler came out of *Loyalties* broke, she happily took the Atlantis offer to write and direct this film about a cowboy and his son—especially attractive was the fact that the money was in place.[15] Wheeler's script is based on a novel that she "wasn't in love with," so while writing the script, she changed the leading male characters into women. Once she was satisfied with her female rodeo characters, she changed their names back to those of men. This fascinating process is just one of many forms of authorial inscription unavailable to the subsequent writers and directors of the *Cowboys Don't Cry* television series.

Cultural Politics

Of equal, if less direct, import, the late 1980s and early '90s was a period of intense contestation in the spheres of Native, feminist, and cultural politics, with much public debate about artistic appropriation and systemic racism in the funding bodies, Japanese redress, feminist backlash, and redemptive masculinity. Bill C-93, the Canadian Multiculturalism Act, was passed in 1988. In the period 1989–92, the Canada Council, the Ontario Arts Council, and the Toronto Arts Council undertook studies of racism and cultural bias in their organizations and their allocation of funds. The NFB's Studio D launched New Initiatives in Film, and the legal struggle for Native self-government was clearly part of the land-claims discourse. The critical literature on official multiculturalism is plentiful and instructive; particularly relevant to my purposes here are the studies by Eva Mackey and Smaro Kamboureli.

Eva Mackey's *The House of Difference* considers the complex relationship between multiculturalist and nationalist discourses in Canadian policy and media in terms of the idealizations and ever-renewable forms of containment and control the state exercises over cultural difference and Native identity:

> The New Multiculturalism Act, despite the shift to a concern with "race relations," and the transformation of dominant society, is still primarily a form of state intervention into the cultural politics of diversity. The intervention not only appropriates and institutionalizes diversity for the project of nation building in the manner of earlier multicultural policy, it now proposes that multiculturalism is a national resource in the context of global capitalism. It still limits multicultural diversity to symbolic rather than political forms, because in the political arena, members of ethnic groups are *individual* members of their groups or the larger society ... Although 'multiculturalism' could be seen as vastly different from the more overtly racist and assimilationist policies of earlier governments, the

institutionalization of difference and 'tolerance' drew on previously existing patterns ... the degree and form of *tolerable* differences are defined by the ever-changing needs of the project of nation-building.[16]

I quote Mackey at length because her comments reflect the analysis provided by many others. She also highlights the link between the bill and globalization (earlier she cites a 1987 policy document that clearly asserts links between "multicultural resources," free trade, and economic progress), and brings to the forefront a major point in Kamboureli's article. Bill C-93, the Canadian Multiculturalism Act, legislates ethnicity and as such addresses its constituents as individuals before the law. But Kamboureli goes further, noting that in the language of the Act, ethnicity is mobilized as a nation-narrative:

> Although a condition of difference that becomes an instrument of marginalization in Canada, ethnicity is rendered by official multiculturalism as something residual to it ... Ethnicity loses its differential marker and becomes instead a condition of commonality: what all Canadians have in common is ethnic difference.[17]

The address to everyone and no one is common parlance in the operations of global capital. Longfellow writes about this in terms of new "international" co-productions of films such as *The Red Violin*:

> Within the film itself, the proliferation of difference acts as a way of eliding any overarching parochial sense of national belonging. The enunciating location of the film is, precisely, nowhere, at least nowhere within the groundless and all enveloping textual folds of international style.[18]

These comments may seem remote from our discussion of Wheeler's work, but I wish to consider how they form both the background and some figures (or their absence) in the foreground of the films.

In response to a question about "appropriation" in a 1990 interview, Wheeler said,

> I won't make another native film. I decided that when I was making *Loyalties* four years ago. It was not a comfortable position. No matter how you try to get into someone else's skin, you can't ... I think that native people should have their own government and make their own films. I have been offered, especially since *Loyalties*, numerous films ... Many of these films have come to me because the people know that to some degree I have the native support ... But I have said no. I don't want to do another one. I make fairly big films now, and I make a pretty good living, which I don't want to make on the backs of the native people.[19]

However much these comments indicate a form of political solidarity and an ethical standard for work, I am drawn to one question: what cultural and social conditions make such a statement utterable? It is curious that she did not reflect on, for example, a collaborative writer/director/producer project with a Native writer or director, given how notoriously difficult it was to secure film funding in this period and how regularly she does collaborative projects. And, in fact, she has since made a film with Native representation, this time through the mediation of CanLit: *The Diviners*. Rather than working through the difficult, fragile politics of the issue, her quote suggests she removed herself from its reach. And the filmic record bears this out. I am not judging what Wheeler should have done or what kinds of films she should have made. Rather, I wish to point out how her statement underscores the complex yet definite operations of governmentality as it functions to organize identity and difference in the realms of cultural production. As individuals under the law, we have the right not to act; as individuals under the law of multiculturalism, it is our right and our duty to differentiate. As Dot Tuer points out,

> From the vantage point of ethnic communities, visible minorities and aboriginal peoples, national unity constructed from subsidized culture pays lip service to difference while funding uniformity, invokes democratization while preserving the structures of elitism. As it turns out, cultural subsidies are not only engaged in benign neglect, but in active deceptions: constructing what Tony Wilden so eloquently describes as an Imaginary Nation ... the discourse of the multicultural mosaic has functioned as a ideological shield to protect the actual funding bodies from scrutiny while they, simultaneously, must defend their very existence against continuous attack from various proponents of the right. Or, such was the case until recently.[20]

The "until recently" referred to is the point when the Canada Council, the Ontario Arts Council, and the Toronto Arts Council responded to the charges of systemic racism and other forms of cultural inequity by sponsoring studies into their operations. The controversy that erupted in response to these reports pivot on two related points: appropriation and autonomy. Cameron Bailey states that "in a country where a working artist is almost by definition a government-funded artist, [the systemic racism of the arts councils] amounted to state-sanctioned cultural apartheid."[21] As a result of people of colour, ethnic minorities, and "majorities" actively forming coalitions and destabilizing the official discourse, the councils developed processes and funding formulas consistent with the aims of anti-racism. No similar, internal review of funding was undertaken by Telefilm or the CBC; and with the Multicultural Act came specific monies for groups contained under the designation "heritage." These external, contextual realities bear upon the content of Wheeler's films in subtle but important ways.

Locations and Communities

In *Cowboys Don't Cry* (1988) and *Bye Bye Blues* (1989), the two films made after *Loyalties*, we cross a lot of prairie: from one rodeo to another, one town's dancehall to another. *Cowboys Don't Cry* takes place in contemporary times; *Bye Bye Blues* is set in the during World War Two. There is not a single Indian in either film. This would be disappointing but unremarkable had the films been made by almost any other white Anglo filmmaker. But Wheeler made *Augusta*, her second film, and *Loyalties* was one of the most courageous dramas produced in Canada in the 1980s.

There are some socio-historical explanations, which also go some way toward explaining the specific cultural politics of the prairie. In the case of *Bye Bye Blues*, the historical reality of the apartheid "pass law" was still in effect during the period represented in the film. From the end of the 1885 North-West Rebellion until 1956, the majority of Native people on the prairie were not permitted to leave reserves without a "pass" provided to them by a local Indian Department official. In July 1885, Assistant Indian Commissioner Hayter Reed recommended fifteen measures for the "future management of Indians"—and not just those implicated in the rebellion.[22] These measures were adopted by John A. MacDonald; they included hanging specific individuals, abolishing the existing tribal system and ousting "rebel" chiefs and councillors, dealing with all who could be charged with crimes "in as severe a manner as the law will allow," and suspending annuity payments to rebel groups, with any further monies understood as a gift and not a right. The pass law had the effect of severely constricting the movement—and thus communication—of most Natives on the prairie. Even if the pass law was not in effect for a particular tribe, the Indian Act of 1876 had already provided the means by which to restrict movement and communication, and erase visibility and cultural presence by, for instance, stating that Indians could not participate "in any show, exhibition, performance, stampede or pageant in aboriginal costume without the consent of the Superintendent General or his authorized agent."[23] The period 1876–1951, overlapping with the period of the pass law, is referred to by Gerald McMaster as "the Reservation Period," "with implications of imprisonment and the extinguishment of religious and cultural freedom."[24] This "backstory" is relevant to *Bye Bye Blues* because the film registers this historical reality—whether intentionally or not—and thus brings us a story of cultural isolation alongside one of subjective flourishing.

Containment is part of the colonial imaginary, and how Wheeler treats it, as well as the landscape upon which that imaginary projects itself, can be seen through an analysis of her 1976 film *Augusta*. This NFB documentary is about a Native woman who, in her eighty-eighth year, remembers "the gold rush, the cattle ranchers, Indian trails, river steamers, stage coaches ..." The voice-over that opens the film belongs to the announcer for Radio Caribou, which broadcasts messages to people in the 100 Mile House and Williams Lake area: "To Augusta Evans at Deep Creek, I'll meet you at the bus stop tomorrow morning and we can go into town and do some shopping, and that's from Edna Blankenship." As the image-track shows us Augusta preparing to leave her small house for the bus, the film's narrator, who turns out to be Edna Blankenship, a Native woman who has known Augusta for many years, tells us that Augusta lives at Deep Creek, fifteen miles north of Williams Lake, alone in a little cabin without electricity or running water; she lost her status as a Shuswap Indian in 1903 when she married George Evans, a taxpayer.

As the film proceeds, Augusta becomes the main narrator of her own story, which is filled with remarkable acts of courage and generosity. When she was very young, she ordered a medical book from the Eaton's catalogue, read it, and became a midwife. Augusta tells us, "Midwives in those days charged; I didn't believe in that ... not among the Indians; we were taught to help one another. I didn't care about no money; I saw a woman die and decided that wouldn't happen again." This autonomy was also practised within her own home: she was feeding cattle while suffering with labour pains, making it back to the house to give birth to a daughter all alone. She was in bed for three days and when her husband came home drunk, "I was so angry I started whipping him in bed."

The film carefully negotiates the ethical terrain of ethnographic filmmaking, with the image-track attentive to Augusta's physical movements and space, responding to her gestures and words by changing the shot range. And, still radical for an NFB documentary at that time, an eighty-eight-year-old Indian woman provides her own voice-over. But there is one especially remarkable piece of footage: Augusta has gone to the Soda Creek Reserve for Sunday mass. We learn that she was born there and her grandfather was the chief. When she was four, she was taken to St. Joseph's Mission School where she was forced to live for nine years without her family, culture, or language. Augusta then begins singing a hymn. The image-track shows an extremely long shot of largely uninhabited landscape; the contemporary view dissolves into an archival photograph of the mission school. With this simple technique, Wheeler twists the conventions of landscape imagery—showing an inhabited past and an empty present. This seemingly simple convergence of two different times in the visual space before us calls on an ethical spectatorship perhaps more urgently than does Augusta herself: the right to amnesia is the right of the victor of history. In this simple dissolve, the landscape is remembered by the film as a space of loss.

Wheeler's films disclose a deep commitment to their locations. It is that interest that works either to reveal an almost structuring absence, as with *Bye Bye Blues*, or to play upon the colonial tropes, as in *Loyalties*. The settler imaginary, which structures the wilderness against civilization, evident in so much "Canadian" visual culture, is not the dominant trope in prairie visual culture. The paintings and drawings from the nineteenth and early twentieth century show the prairie to be peopled—or, more accurately, worked. There are plenty of "wide-open spaces," but the images often contain bales of hay, tilled fields, or cows.[25] In both *Bye Bye Blues* and *Loyalties*, the relationship between the symbolic value of the landscape and the point of view accorded the camera is extremely important. In both films, the white female character "arrives" from elsewhere (India in the former and England in the latter), and it is her point of view through a window that shapes our introduction to the location and its unfolding narrative. *Loyalties'* Lily Sutton arrives in Lac La Biche by air, giving us a location of unpeopled wilderness. This view of landscape, formed as it is by the "dreamwork of imperialism,"[26] becomes one term in a dialectical interracial relationship between Lily and Roseanne, the Native woman whose daughter is raped by David Sutton, Lily's husband. The colonial stereotypes of Natives of and in nature is critiqued through a subtle series of reversals that structure the film—and include recognitions of class difference—as well as through pointed statements, such as the one made by Roseanne's mother, Beatrice. Referring to a beautiful, pristine lakeshore, Beatrice tells David that her people lived there "until white people wanted to live here and they called us squatters." In the process of relaying the point of view for the film between Lily and Roseanne, where Roseanne becomes the *primary* source of identification[27]—the "implicit feminist spectator, the film's moral and political centre"[28]—the primary location for their relationship shifts from the Sutton house to Beatrice's home on the reserve. The specificity of the relationship between land and identity is thus founded not on the transcendental sublime or pastoral imaginary but on the history of politics, power, and loss.

Bye Bye Blues introduces us to the landscape in much the same fashion *Loyalties* does; however, this time, the transformation of perception occurs due to Daisy's subjective flourishing rather than due to a complex intersubjectivity. The spectatorial address thus begins and ends with an individual (woman) rather than shifting and destabilizing identity's formation. *Blues* opens in India, where Daisy's husband Teddy is stationed. The numerous shots of a crowded, colourful market seem merely to function in contrast with the subsequent images of wide open prairie. Teddy is transferred to Singapore, and Daisy and her two young children move back to her home in Alberta. From a farewell party in India (hosted by Susan Woolrich, the actress who played Lily in *Loyalties*), Teddy's loving gaze at Daisy dissolves into Daisy's rueful gaze through the window of her train car. The landscape is cold, scrubby, and empty. Yet the cut to her young son's point of view gives us an image of a few children playing and skating on a pond. "Not too many people," he says. "Canada is a new country," says Daisy; "and India is an old country," says the boy. This differential of home and away is never destabilized through an introduction of counter-information about the old and the new within Canada. However, many of the long prairie views provided as establishing shots for scenes throughout the remainder of the film—almost all with farm houses, barns, or tractors in the frame—are remarkably like the prairie realist landscape paintings mentioned earlier. This settler view of the location gently reminds us that we are, after all, seeing the region from a point of view located in the particular and embodied story of a "grass widow" during the war. As Daisy reacquaints herself with the place she knows as home, the prairie comes to be shot by Wheeler as a place of great beauty, with a natural diversity of land forms and colours. The conceit that ties the land's transformations to Daisy's subjective flourishing demonstrates a shift in the symbolic value of landscape: from a contested space that can disclose the traces of stories of action and suffering, to a private enclosure reflecting individual dreams.

Girl Talk, Boy-to-Men, Male-to-Female

As is true of Edna in *Change of Heart*, Lily in *Loyalties*, Joyce in the documentary *Happily Unmarried*, both women in the TV miniseries *The War Between Us*, and all the women in *Better Than Chocolate*, Daisy's subjective flourishing is inspired by affective solidarity with other women, as well as the financial autonomy afforded by work and the rejection of patriarchal governance. Unlike previous films, Daisy's flourishing is also fed by an erotic relationship with a man. However, it is the scene in the bathtub with Daisy's sister-in-law Frances, where they get drunk and talk about sex, that stands as the pivotal moment between the syntagma of father's home and her own. Throughout Wheeler's films, the relationships between women (as I have shown) and relationships between men (in *One's a Heifer*, *Cowboys Don't Cry*, and *A War Story*) displace the normative heterosexual compact that drives most narrative, and certainly most melodramatic, film. As Thomas Waugh has urged,

> let us then now take a second tour through imagery of masculinity in Canadian film history as a means of wondering what it might look like to see queerness not on the margins, but as a troubling centre and structuring absence, provoking a final reflection that will not provide answers but perhaps point to several areas where we can roll up our sleeves.[29]

ᔆ ᔆ ᔆ

I have called this essay "States of Emergency" because this condition—in its double meaning—is the affective and narrative centre of the (narrative) films and the object of analysis in the documentaries. Many of the films stage an encounter with the other which is rife with enacted, remembered, or potential violence. From the early documentaries to *Better Than Chocolate*, Wheeler makes films about the violence of the state as it is embodied by its patriarchal surrogates and enacted upon the bodies of the racialized and sexual others. In the earlier works, unlike the later generic melodramas and romantic comedies, Wheeler's project, while certainly feminist, was also decolonizing, for it is that first, foundational violence of colonization that permits the other violations to circulate. However, this is not decolonizing cinema as we have come to know it through third-cinema strategies and their counterparts of political modernism. There is nothing formally disruptive, nothing in the form to indicate that there is a problem of meaning, of signification. There is not, in other words, a noticeable politics of form. As mentioned earlier, there is instead a repeated reliance on melodramatic conventions to deal with a range of issues, many of them not traditional melodramatic material. I wonder, then, if the disruption, while not found in the deployment of third-cinema strategies, exists through the use of melodrama to produce a particularly Canadian variant of that genre.

Anchoring her critique of colonial patriarchy in relationships between women and relationships between men, Wheeler is able to employ, with justifiable ease, melodrama's major tropes. While the private sphere is certainly investigated in Wheeler's melodramas, she does not obey the genre's historically defined limits of hearth and home. As many theorists have insisted, this genre has a social critique at its centre. Wheeler opens the genre to race relations, homosexual and homoerotic narratives, feminist narratives of solidarity and flourishing; and in so doing, she devises a radically liberal vernacular for the Canadian imaginary.

Notes

1   This material includes Richard Collins, *Culture, Communication & National Identity: The Case of Canadian Television* (Toronto: University of Toronto Press, 1990); Victor Dwyer, "Company of Women: A Largely Female Crew Shoots a Canadian Classic *The Diviners*," *Maclean's*, 15 June 1992), 51–52; Gary Evans, *In the National Interest: A Chronicle of the National Film Board of Canada 1949–1989* (Toronto: University of Toronto Press, 1991); "A Frightening Time: A Film Revisits Canada's Internment Camps," *Maclean's*, 7 November 1994, 66; Larry Hannant, "The Sleep Room," *Canadian Historical Review* 80, no. 4 (December 1999): 698–705; Gail Henley, "On the Record: *For the Record*'s Ten Dramatic Years," *Cinema Canada* 117 (April 1985): 18–21; Katherine Koller, "Anne Wheeler: The Woman Behind the Camera," *NeWest Review* 12, no. 8 (April 1987): 18; Jeff Laffel, "*Bye Bye Blues*," *Films in Review* 41 (November/December 1990): 558–59; Mary Jane Miller, *Turn Up the Contrast: CBC Television Drama Since 1952* (Vancouver: University of British Columbia/CBC Enterprises, 1987); Paula Simons, "Bye Bye Blues, Hello World: Anne Wheeler and Allarcom Go For the Big Time," *Western Report* 22 August 1988, 32–33; Diane Turbide, "The Sleep Room," *Maclean's*, 12 January 1998, 66; Alison Vermee, "Anne Wheeler and the Drama of Everyday Life," *Take One* 4, no. 9 (1995): 38–41. Thanks to Marlena Little for helping me with the research; and thanks to Paul Kelley, Janine Marchessault, and Brenda Longfellow for their invaluable and informative conversations about this paper.

2   The concept of the "colonization of the lifeworld" was deployed by critical theorist Jurgen Habermas in his study *The Philosophical Discourse of Modernity: Twelve Lectures* (Frederick Lawrence, trans. [Cambridge: MIT Press, 1987]), in an effort to articulate the extent to which the economic, bureaucratic, and administrative functioning of industry and the state has come to structure those relations previously thought to be outside those spheres (i.e., the space of everyday life, intimate relationships, cultural practices, etc.).

3   Hannah Arendt, *The Human Condition* (Chicago: University of Chicago Press, 1958), 188, 190.

4   Seth Feldman, "The Electric Fable: Aspects of the Docudrama in Canada," *Canadian Drama* 9, no. 1 (1983): 44.

5   The literature on the woman's film as a critical variant of the melodrama is vast. Of particular interest here is Catherine Russell's reading of the film *The Company of Strangers* in *Gendering the Nation: Canadian Women's Cinema* (Toronto: University of Toronto Press, 1999), for its deployment of the genre and mode of address. Also useful is the work by theorists such as Christine Geraghty, Ana Lopez, Juliana Burton, and Marcia Landy, who have considered the ways in which Hollywood melodrama is appropriated for the articulation, and critique, of gender and national identity (British, Mexican, Italian).

6 My consideration of this question is greatly informed by Christine Ramsay's article "Canadian Narrative Cinema from the Margins: 'The Nation' and Masculinity in *Goin' Down the Road*," *Canadian Journal of Film Studies* 2, no. 2 (1993): 27–50.

7 Although I will be referring to *Loyalties* throughout this article, I have elected to give attention to films that as yet have not been analyzed, and for detailed analysis refer the reader to Brenda Longfellow's article "Gender, Landscape and Colonial Allegories in *The Far Shore, Loyalties,* and *Mouvements du désir*" in *Gendering the Nation: Canadian Women's Cinema*; and Wood's article "Towards a Canadian (Inter)national Cinema: Part 2: *Loyalties* and *Life Classes*," *CineAction!* 17 (September 1989): 23–35.

8 As events of recent years have shown, this also spelled the beginning of the end of the family farm, with agribusiness buying farms from the banks that gave tractor loans. The economic reality of farm life is well beyond the scope of this paper, but we need to recognize the conditions in order to maintain a critical view of the modernity in which Edna finds liberation.

9 Longfellow, "Gender, Landscape and Colonial Allegories," 172–73.

10 Thomas Waugh, "Queering the Canon," conference paper given at the Annual Meeting of the Film Studies Association of Canada, University of Alberta, May 2000.

11 For more on this, see Ien Ang, *Watching Dallas: Soap Opera and the Melodramatic Imagination* (London: Methuen, 1982).

12 See Brenda Longfellow, "*The Red Violin*, Commodity Fetishism, and Globalization," paper given at the 1999 Annual Meeting of the Film Studies Association of Canada, Université de Sherbrooke (a version is forthcoming in *Canadian Journal of Film Studies*); Ted Magder, *Canada's Hollywood: The Canadian State and Feature Films* (Toronto: University of Toronto Press, 1993); and David McIntosh, "Memes, Genes, and Monoculture," in *Money, Value, Art* (Toronto: YYZ Books, 2001).

13 Longfellow, "*Red Violin*" and, as discussed in Longfellow, Michael Dorland, *So Close to the State/s: The Emergence of Canadian Feature Film Policy* (Toronto: University of Toronto Press, 1998), 67.

14 Magder, *Canada's Hollywood*, 211.

15 Jane Evans, "Filmmakers Don't Cry? An Interview with Anne Wheeler," *NeWest Review* 15, no. 3 (February/March 1990): 17.

16 Eva Mackey, *The House of Difference* (London: Routledge, 1999), 69–70.

17 Smaro Kamboureli, "The Technology of Ethnicity: Canadian Multiculturalism and the Language of Law," in *Multicultural States: Rethinking Difference and Identity*, David Bennett, ed. (New York: Routledge, 1989), 215.

18 Longfellow, "*Red Violin*."

19 Evans, "Filmmakers Don't Cry," 18.

20 Dot Tuer, "The Art of Nation Building: Constructing a 'National Identity' for Post-War Canada," *Parellélogramme* 17, no. 4 (1992): 28.

21 Cameron Bailey, "Fright the Power: Arts Councils and the Spectre of Racial Equity," *Fuse* 15, no. 6 (Summer 1992): 20. A number of issues of *Fuse* and the artist-run centre periodical *Parallélogramme* published between 1987 and 1993 contain essays related to the issues addressed by Bailey.

22 Blair Stonechild and Bill Waiser, *Loyal Until Death: Indians and the North-West Rebellion* (Calgary: Fifth House Publishing, 1997), 215. As is well known, and well documented in Stonechild and Waiser, the number of tribes and chiefs involved in the rebellion was hugely exaggerated by the state.

23 Quoted in Gerald McMaster, "Tenuous Lines of Descent: Indian Arts and Crafts of the Reservation Period," *Canadian Journal of Native Studies* 9, no. 2 (1989): 213.

24 McMaster, "Tenuous Lines of Descent," 206.

25 For a fascinating visual history of the prairies, see Rosemary Donegan, *Work, Weather, and the Grid: Agriculture in Saskatchewan* (Regina: Dunlop Art Gallery, 1991).

26 W.J.T. Mitchell, ed., *Landscape and Power* (Chicago: University of Chicago Press, 1994), 10.

27 Wood, "Towards a Canadian (Inter)national Cinema," 23–35.

28 Longfellow, "Gender, Landscape and Colonial Allegories," 175.

29 Tom Waugh, "Cinemas, Nations, Masculinities: The Martin Walsh Memorial Lecture (1998)," *Canadian Journal of Film Studies* 8, no. 1 (Spring 1999): 22–23. As my focus has been on women and race relations, I direct the reader to Waugh, for he includes *Cowboys Don't Cry* and *One's a Heifer* in his "canon queered" project.

3

Aboriginal Voices

Studio One
Of Storytellers and Stories
Maria de Rosa

> But do you see that when you take the word history and separate it in half, it tells you that
> it's "his story." And we want ... to tell our story also. The true story of our people.
> —Michael Mitchell

GRAYDON McCREA, EXECUTIVE PRODUCER of the National Film Board's documentary productions in western Canada, recently noted that "one of the most remarkable and appropriate transformations within the Canadian film and television industry during the last ten years or so has been the place occupied by aboriginal filmmakers." He reflected that

> ten years ago, only a handful of First Nations filmmakers had ever directed a film at the
> NFB—a number which has, over the span of a single decade, soared to dozens—forever
> altering the opportunities for aboriginal filmmakers throughout the industry in Canada.
> Decades from now, it will be seen as one of the most important developments in the his-
> tory of the Canadian film and television industry.

Integral to this development has been the National Film Board of Canada (NFB). The NFB has had a long history of making films about Canada's Indian, Métis, and Inuit peoples, a history that dates back to the early 1940s. Because of this history, it was not surprising that in 1991, the NFB announced an initiative that would forever transform the landscape of aboriginal film and television expression by creating a film studio for aboriginal peoples: Studio One, for "First Peoples." [1] The creation of the Studio was seen by some aboriginal filmmakers as

> an extension of ... social activism within the Native community ... [in order] to [have] a
> space that would enable Native stories to be told, by the Native community ... In fact,
> Studio One was intended as part of the tradition of storytelling: of how Native Nations
> speak to one another about what it means to be part of a nation, a territory, a cultural
> belief system. [2]

Film and video are seen by the aboriginal filmmaking community as being "ideal carriers of stories, conduits for histories, conveyors of dreams."[3]

The establishment of Studio One has also been described "as a first stage of a long but exciting journey to close the circle."[4] The journey has not been without its challenges, but Studio One has changed the culture of the NFB and, more importantly, the environmental landscape of aboriginal cultural expression. Without a doubt, Studio One, which has now developed into the Aboriginal Filmmaking Program at the NFB, has been a catalyst for a renaissance that is taking place in the aboriginal film and television community—a renaissance of storytelling. By many accounts, this renaissance is authentic, in that stories are finally being told by aboriginal peoples, for aboriginal peoples, *in their own voices.*

The NFB as Scribe of Aboriginal Stories

> Films are a bridge so Native people can be reached directly through their own voices.
> —Alanis Obomsawin

That the NFB would be the agency to launch an aboriginal film production studio in 1991 was unsurprising. For fifty years prior, the NFB had been an important "scribe" of the stories of aboriginal peoples, having produced more than a hundred films, mostly documentary, about aboriginal peoples.[5] These films spoke to cultural resistance and survival, aboriginal rights, land claims and self-government, spirituality, traditions, the struggles of Native women, racism and poverty, and myths and legends. The audiences for these films range from children to the elderly, from medical professionals, social services workers, and teachers to parents, self-help groups, community organizations, and individuals.

As some have observed, the reasons for the NFB's role as scribe include

> the fact that until recently, there were few organizations producing such films ... the fact that aboriginal peoples represent a significant population, occupy extensive territory and maintain values (for example, respect for the land and appreciation of the natural world) that are shared widely in Canada and respected and admired elsewhere ... [and the fact] that some non-aboriginal filmmakers have been approached [to make films] by members of aboriginal communities either because of their skills or because of their commitment.[6]

The NFB's affinity for aboriginal stories dates back to the 1940s when the Board produced such films as *Land of the Long Day, People of the Caribou, NorthWest Frontier,* and *Totems.* In the 1960s, the first-ever Indian film crew came into being at the NFB as part of an initiative called Challenge for Change. This project involved the production of a series of films about social issues sponsored by several federal government departments. Set against the backdrop of "the political milieu of the American Indian Movement (AIM) in the U.S. and related land claims and self-government struggles in Canada," the goal of Challenge for Change was to use film as a catalyst for social change and political empowerment.[7] The NFB believed that the needs and aspirations of aboriginal people could best be expressed and documented by an all-aboriginal crew. The results of this initiative came in 1968 with the release of *The Ballad of Crowfoot,* the first-ever documentary directed by an aboriginal director, Willie Dunn. This film is now considered a classic with its haunting account of the opening of the West. A number of other films were made by aboriginal people as part of this series, including Buckley Petawabano, Michael Mitchell, Duke Redbird, and others. These films are seen as "historical documents of Indian and Inuit ways of life and outlets for aboriginal points of view."[8]

Few from this generation of filmmakers pursued careers in film; most went on to pursue careers as chiefs, teachers, politicians, and journalists in their respective communities. In describing his experiences, Michael Mitchell, a member of the first Indian film crew, foreshadowed the importance of the creation of Studio One and the building of an aboriginal film community:

> when we left the National Film Board, the Indian film crew all went back to their home reserves ... As a result of our training and the problems for our people in this country ... I went around Ontario talking to different leaders about education for young people ... Our greatest concern is in audio-visual ... We are trying to get down what our elders have to tell us, and we have to do it quickly ... We need to know what it is about our people that we should keep...
>
> ...
>
> [T]he hardest thing has been to change that [stereotype] and ... the historical perspective being taught [in schools]...[9]

Filmmaking as a continuum of storytelling

Increasingly, the aboriginal community saw a need to produce a written record for future generations and to pass on accurate content. These priorities were at the core of a "movement" in the aboriginal community in the 1970s and 1980s as "the need to reclaim traditional culture and transmit it to the young" took on urgency.[10] There was also "an outcry against cultural appropriation regarding some films where cultural misrepresentations [had] occurred or cultural liberties [had] been taken."[11] In many ways, the issue about content was really about who was creating the content.

Both aboriginal people and non-aboriginal observers recognized that the content of aboriginal media, including film, should be shaped by aboriginal people. In fact, studies as early as 1972 had already documented the negative impact that a lack of Native-produced television programming was having on aboriginal communities. As Gail Valaskakis, professor at Concordia University (and Dean of Arts in the early 1990s) and member of the Advisory Committee for Studio One, pointed out, First Nations peoples, particularly those living in northern communities, were feeling "culturally dislocated."[12] Several studies had found that Native-produced film and video were especially effective in strengthening First Nations culture, languages, and communities.[13] As Valaskakis writes,

> aboriginal producers and audiences clearly use access to visual media to express and share the cultural reality of their lives: to document, experience, share knowledge, express identity, speak to each other across generations and build community, in short, to tell their own stories.[14]

Over time, as aboriginal peoples discovered that storytelling had an affinity with filmmaking, a greater number of aboriginal people wanted to tell their stories. Carol Geddes, a Tlingit filmmaker from the Yukon and Studio One's first producer, noted, "the affinity between filmmaking and storytelling is most important ... visual media such as film and video are uniquely appropriate to cultures which have traditionally relied on the spoken word, music and drawings to communicate."[15] There was also an increasing concern for a "more balanced cinematic view of historical events" being expressed by aboriginal peoples.[16] This concern was tied to the issue of cultural ownership: some people felt that "the majority of financial benefits generated by the interest in native stories [was] being enjoyed by non-native producers, writers, directors and technicians."[17]

With a few exceptions (Alanis Obomaswin and Gil Cardinal), all films made by the NFB before Studio One were made by non-aboriginal people. Graydon McCrea, Executive Producer of the North West Centre in Edmonton, where Studio One was housed, recalled that the films that explored the cultures of Canada's first peoples were not by Native directors and producers.[18] That the NFB understood the importance of integrity of voice in making films was demonstrated in its establishment of Studio D in 1974, the world's first production unit dedicated to women. The NFB created Studio D to empower women with the tools and skills necessary to tell their own stories. Films needed to be made by women, for women, and about women. The NFB hoped to play a similar role in "mobilizing the creative energies" of aboriginal filmmakers and enabling aboriginal voices to be heard.

The Board's role as scribe of aboriginal stories was, in many ways, integral to the NFB's "process of familiarizing Indian, Métis and Inuit peoples with the tools of the visual media."[19] This process would soon culminate in Studio One—a defining initiative for aboriginal stories waiting to be told.

Studio One
1990–96

They [aboriginal peoples] must have the resources to reach the screens of their communities and of this country with their perspectives and values woven implicitly into the fabric of the cinematic stories they themselves choose to tell.
—Graydon McCrea

While it is difficult to determine the exact moment of Studio One's birth, the path leads to Wil Campbell, a Saskatchewan-based Native filmmaker, and Roger Trottier, professor of Native Studies at the University of Saskatchewan, who, in 1990, approached Graydon McCrea about organizing a meeting to discuss the participation of aboriginal peoples in the Canadian film and television industry. With the NFB's assistance, the first Aboriginal Film and Video Symposium was held in Edmonton in April 1991, bringing together some fifty aboriginal people involved in film and television production in Canada to discuss the barriers they faced in telling their stories on film and video, including,

- ᧘ the view that Native stories were seen to be "non-commercial" and of "narrow-market interest" to traditional production financiers and agencies;
- ᧘ traditional production financiers did not generally accept the experience level of aboriginal producers for investment purposes;

    ☞ the difficulty for aboriginal producers to access pre-sales or licences for broadcast-
    ers, thus making it impossible to fulfill the strict criteria of funding agencies such
    as Telefilm Canada and provincial funding agencies.[20]

In the report that emerged from the symposium, one area requiring immediate action was the
establishment of a facility within the NFB devoted exclusively to the training, experience, and
technical support of aboriginal filmmakers. The other areas, according to MacPherson and
Campbell, included the creation of an aboriginal-film development fund, a national aboriginal
broadcasting service, and the establishment of an organization that could represent the interests
of aboriginal filmmakers nationally. These initiatives were critical if aboriginal filmmakers were
to tell their stories, and the Aboriginal Film and Video Art Alliance (AFVAA) was formed to
implement them.

The birth of Studio One

Against the larger backdrop of the AFVAA working to create a viable aboriginal filmmaking sector, on 9 June 1991 the NFB announced its intention to create an aboriginal studio, to be called
Studio One, that would "contribute to providing aboriginal filmmakers with a greater opportunity to tell their stories and document their lives on film."[21] While the Studio would be based in
Edmonton at the NFB's North West Centre under the supervision of Graydon McCrea (producer
of award-winning films on native issues), an aboriginal producer would be named to head the
Studio. The overall goals of Studio One were as follows:

    ☞ to give aboriginal filmmakers the resources to tell their own stories and to
    address the communication needs of their own people;
    ☞ to enhance the film and video production skills of aboriginal peoples;
    ☞ to provide effective distribution outlets for these productions so that their
    intended audiences may be reached.[22]

Beginning in the fall of 1991 with an initial annual budget of $250,000, the Studio would develop
over two years in three phases:

    ☞ *Phase 1: Apprenticeship and Training*: Studio One will co-ordinate with NFB studios
    across Canada, the placement of approximately ten native filmmakers and crafts-
    people on a variety of productions for the purpose of professional development.
    ☞ *Phase 2: Vignette Production*: A commitment of $10,000 will be made to each of ten
    selected candidates for the production of a short vignette on film and video.
    Projects chosen for this phase will be those which can be undertaken without can-
    didates having to leave their communities. This will maximize the opportunity for
    native filmmakers to gain experience with production technology, and will ulti-
    mately expand the community of aboriginal production personnel.
    ☞ *Phase 3: Documentary Film Production*: Established native producers and directors
    will find the studio an important resource for their projects.[23]

The two-year plan was based on acquiring financial and creative collaboration in the amount
of $1.4 million in year one and $1.3 million thereafter from private- and public-sector organiza-

tions.[24] Funds for the Studio were to be sought from government departments, corporations, and private foundations. That Studio One had much to accomplish is underlined in the words of Carol Geddes, who was appointed the Studio's first producer shortly thereafter:

> As First Nations people move into an era of greater self-determination, one of the important aspects of that self-determination is to interpret our own realities in media ... and we must take the means of production of our images into our own hands as a way of taking our place as distinct cultures in Canada.[25]

Wil Campbell, named associate producer of the Studio during its start-up phase, noted that one of the challenges for the Studio would be to ensure that its programming reached native communities and, in turn, fed back into the Studio's programming process.[26]

A Time of Triumph and Challenge

Studio One's first year has been described as one of triumph and challenge: triumph because an avenue of opportunity had finally opened up for the aboriginal film community; challenge because the Studio was developing and "reflecting on [its] identity."[27]

Aboriginal people saw a significant role for the Studio. In creating their own images, aboriginal filmmakers would counter misrepresentation of aboriginal peoples in mainstream media and provide cultural education to young people. Studio One's specific objectives were identified by Carol Geddes as follows:

- ☞ Counter non-representation and misrepresentation of aboriginal peoples in mainstream media.
- ☞ Address the lack of meaningful cultural education for aboriginal peoples and the issue of appropriation of cultural images by non-aboriginal producers.
- ☞ Provide and assist with the professional development of aboriginal peoples in the film and video industry.
- ☞ Provide an environment compatible with the unique cultural aspirations of Canada's aboriginal people. To do this, the Studio is committed to provide an atmosphere sympathetic to special cultural ways in which to work, that is, use of elders for consultations, consensus models for decision making, etc.
- ☞ Provide for equal access for each group of Canada's aboriginal peoples.
- ☞ Provide opportunities for the expression of contemporary themes in film and video production.[28]

In its first year, the Studio focussed on developing initiatives. For example, in response to an urgent need to develop specific skills within the aboriginal filmmaking community, Studio One introduced First Nations/First Video, a ten-day, entry-level workshop. The Studio also provided grants for emerging aboriginal filmmakers to complete films and video projects. These initiatives assisted in the development of more than fifty film and video storytellers. The Studio developed also a database of aboriginal peoples working in the film and television sector, created an advisory board, and formed a liaison with film industry groups.

An important initiative was the Studio's involvement with the Royal Commission on Aboriginal Peoples, established by the federal government as a response to the Oka stand-off. Studio One proposed a project that would prove a key training ground for many aboriginal peoples and a document of a historic event. The project—a film to document the Commission's cross-country consultation process—was a collaboration between Studio One and the Royal Commission. Studio One recruited and trained aboriginal crews to journey from coast to coast to more than 100 communities and 40 cities listening to the stories and experiences of Métis, Inuit, and Indian people. The project spanned several years, resulting in 100 hours of archival material and an hour-long television documentary, *No Turning Back* (1996). The aboriginal people who were part of the crew later commented on the value of this experience to their professional development as filmmakers.[29]

With the departure of Carol Geddes in 1992, the Studio moved to another stage in its development.

At a Crossroads

With the appointment in 1993 of Michael Doxtater, a writer and Mohawk from Six Nations in Ontario, as the new producer, the Studio continued to develop emerging aboriginal filmmakers, undertake community awareness, and support financially the production of four documentary films: *Tlaxwesa Wa: Strength of the River; Forgotten Warriors; Picturing a People: George Johnston, Tlingit Photographer;* and *No Turning Back.* These films were the Studio's first, beginning with *Tlaxwesa Wa* (1995).

A one-hour television documentary, *Tlaxwesa Wa: Strength of the River* marked Barbara Cranmer's directorial debut. The film is a portrait of the northern British Columbia Indian fishing tradition told through the filmmaker's family story. A co-production with the private sector, the documentary was broadcast on the Discovery Channel, Knowledge Network, and Vision TV, and was described by one school as a "valuable teaching resource for the next generation of children, many of whom will want to earn their living in the fishing industry."[30]

By this time, the Studio's initial annual budget had been surpassed. The NFB maintained its commitment even though the resources to undertake activities were higher than expected. The original plan to seek resources from the private sector for an annual budget of $1.3 million had not been successful. As an evaluation of Studio One in 1995 found that

> the reasons for this include the difficulty of raising funds from the corporate sector; concerns from aboriginal organizations that their funds would be reduced if they supported government financing of Studio One; and the lack of support from Telefilm Canada and other film funding agencies to establish a specific envelope of funding for aboriginal producers which would have enabled the NFB to co-produce with aboriginal filmmakers.[31]

In 1994, the NFB submitted a brief to the Canadian Radio-television and Telecommunications Commission (CRTC) in the context of encouraging the Commission to dedicate a portion of funds for aboriginal productions from a soon-to-be established Canadian Television Fund. In their comments, the NFB called for the Commission to [set] aside $2.5 of the Fund's estimated $60 million annual base ... to be made available solely for projects initiated by aboriginal film and video producers ... to redress the underrepresentation of aboriginal productions on Canada's airwaves ... [and] to develop a viable and vibrant sector of this country's First Nations' filmmakers.[32]

The NFB also recommended that the allocation be administered by Studio One. As Canada's only national aboriginal film and video production centre, the Studio had extensive links within the community of First Nations filmmakers and had an integrated program of project development, training, and production. The NFB reminded the Commission that "what is being created for television in Canada is still someone else's interpretation of the aboriginal reality. Aboriginal people are still too often the story, and not often enough the storytellers."[33]

The need to secure funding for the Studio, and the need to expand opportunities for professional development and production, was becoming more pronounced, as expressed by AFVAA. Some aboriginal filmmakers felt the Studio was ghetto-izing filmmakers and not addressing the diversity of the aboriginal film and video community across the country.[34] The Studio had reached a crossroads.

In 1995, Michael Doxtater left the Studio and a comprehensive evaluation of Studio One was conducted. I wrote the evaluation study, *The NFB's Studio One: Future Directions*, and found that Studio One needed to be revisited. The Studio had made positive contributions to the development of filmmaking skills within the aboriginal community, but it lacked the funds to meet training needs. Most of the aboriginal filmmakers interviewed concurred that the NFB needed to create points of contact for aboriginal filmmakers across the country. The study noted that

> while there was support for the principle of having a dedicated place to give voice to aboriginal stories ... there should be many opened doors at the NFB for aboriginal directors ... [and] more focussed training opportunities for different levels of developing filmmakers.[35]

I also found that the role of the NFB through the Studio and other NFB centres was significant: filmmakers felt that their films would not have been made without the assistance of the Board. For most, the films represented their first professional directing opportunity.[36] From the perspective of Graydon McCrea, the Studio had been instrumental in creating awareness both inside and outside the NFB about the need for the Board to play a leadership role in professionally developing aboriginal filmmakers, just as Studio D had done with women filmmakers. And just as Studio D had changed the corporate culture of the NFB, so had Studio One. There was now a recognition at the NFB that "vital documentary filmmaking can only develop through strong connections beyond an institution's walls, through ... collaboration with filmmakers with diverse backgrounds and from all parts of the country."[37] This diversity needed to be reflected on and off the screen.

Based on the recommendation of the study to create a program with increased resources (using a national envelope) that would involve producers in all NFB centres across the country, the Board's English Program Branch, headed by Barbara Janes, responded by transforming Studio One into a virtual studio and renaming it the Aboriginal Filmmaking Program.

Studio One Becomes Virtual

> The [Aboriginal Filmmaking Program] is facilitating the creation of an important body of work. The films made under the Program have been innovative ... and are being invited to compete in festivals.
> —Barbara Janes

As a natural evolution of Studio One, the Aboriginal Filmmaking Program (AFP) was guided by the same vision: "to provide aboriginal filmmakers with more equitable opportunities to make films, thus ensuring a more diverse spectrum of perspectives, visions and stories in Canadian cinema."[38] The AFP received a significant increase in resources, with the NFB's English Program Branch earmarking $1 million a year to be used exclusively for productions or co-productions with independent aboriginal filmmakers across the country.

The move to make the studio virtual was a response to concerns expressed by aboriginal filmmakers who wanted opportunities to make films in their respective regions. The evaluation of Studio One had found that filmmaking opportunities for aboriginal directors and writers had, in fact, emerged from NFB centres and studios other than Studio One. As the study noted,

> since the creation of Studio One ... the NFB has [also] established ... programs which are providing aboriginal filmmakers with opportunities to enhance their filmmaking skills and direct films. Programs include the *New Initiatives in Film* Program, the *Fast Forward* Program and the *Programme de formation cinéastes autochtones.*[39]

Studio One had, in fact, helped raise awareness both inside and outside the NFB about the need to create more opportunities for aboriginal peoples to learn the craft of filmmaking. In 1995, in an study on aboriginal film images, Ted S. Palys referred to the significant role played by the NFB in assisting in the development of an aboriginal film community:

> in Canada, a series of films have given the screen to aboriginal peoples who tell their story ... more important, however, is the growing involvement of aboriginal peoples in making aboriginal film, that is, telling their own stories.[40]

The emphasis on training in all areas of filmmaking also reflected the importance of assisting the overall development of an infrastructure for an aboriginal filmmaking and television sector. This meant that, in addition to writers and directors, aboriginal people were needed in areas such as producing, sound, camera, and editing. The AFP would give preference to projects that included an apprenticeship or training position for an aboriginal person; special emphasis was to be placed on producer trainee positions. All productions required an aboriginal director.[41]

An important body of work

With the evolution of Studio One into the AFP in 1996 came the release of *Forgotten Warriors* by director Loretta Todd, the first film supported by the Studio. *Forgotten Warriors* presents the war memories of aboriginal veterans as they journey back to Europe to perform "a sacred circle of friends left behind but not forgotten in foreign grave sites." This film, first broadcast on the CBC, won the Best Short Documentary in 1996 at the American Indian Festival in San Francisco, Best Biography at the Hot Docs, and the Antoinette (Nettie) Keyski Canadian Heritage Award at the

Yorkton Festival in 1997. It was selected for screening at the prestigious Sundance Film Festival. The film weaves archival material and dramatic recreations together with interviews. Loretta Todd referred to the style of the film as unique in that it goes beyond conventional documentary: "native aesthetic, as associated with vision and dream ... propels the drama, with the documentary extending, out of native respect for the word and oral tradition."[42] This release was followed by *No Turning Back*. Directed by Greg Coyes, the production was named runner-up in the category of Best Documentary at the American Indian Film and Video Festival in Oklahoma City in 1997.

Then came *Picturing a People: George Johnston, Tlingit Photographer* directed by Carol Geddes. This documentary is a unique portrait of George Johnston, perhaps Canada's first aboriginal documentarist, who used photographs to record the history of the Tlingit nation and Yukon life between 1930 and 1945. Today, his photographs have gained international recognition. In 1997, *Picturing a People* received the Best Story Award at the American Indian Film Festival in San Francisco and was nominated for the Donald Brittain Award for Best Documentary at the Canadian Gemini awards. This film is described as "visually lyrical and very moving": "the use of voices that were really there [creates] an intimacy for viewers in a way that second-hand stories and outside experts' opinions never can." Geddes notes that the film "helps us [to] dream the future as much as to remember the past."

In 1997, *Silent Tears*, the AFP's first drama, was released. The film observes the efforts of one Cree family facing the harsh realities of life on a northern trapline. Directed by Shirley Cheechoo, the film was named the best live short subject film at the American Indian Film Festival in San Francisco in 1997 and was invited to screen at the 1998 Dreamspeakers Festival in Edmonton and at the Native Forum in the 1998 Sundance Film Festival.

Also released in 1997 was *Qatuwas—People Gathering Together*, directed by Barbara Cranmer. This hour-long film documents the rebirth of the ocean-going canoe, once a sacred vessel for First Nations, as thirty First Nations set out on a journey to Bella Bella, BC for a historic gathering. The film celebrates the healing power of tradition and marks the resurgence of Northwest Coast indigenous culture. It received the Best Documentary Feature Film Award at the American Indian Film Festival in San Francisco and won the Telefilm Canada/Television Northern Canada Award for Best Aboriginal Production.

Between 1996 and 2000, the AFP completed more than twenty films and videos. Among them are documentaries, short dramas, and feature-length docudramas. Almost all the films have aired on Canadian television and were made by filmmakers from across the country. The majority of these filmmakers made their first professional film for broadcast under the AFP; some have made second and third films. Subjects explored included horsemanship (as a vibrant part of western First Nations culture) in *The Gift of the Grandfathers*, an hour-long documentary by Doug Cuthand; and life on the edges of the medical system in a remote Ojibway community in northwestern Ontario as captured in *Band-Aid*, an hour-long documentary by Dan Prouty. Another film, *Okimah*, which won the Best of the Festival Prize at the Far North Film Festival in Yellowknife in 1998, documents the annual goose hunt, an important event for the people of Moose Factory, Ontario. In the short drama *The Strange Case of Bunny Weequod*, Steve Van Denzen blends folklore and humour with a contemporary environmental theme.

In *Singing Our Stories* (1998), Annie Frazier Henry explores the lives and historical musical roots of aboriginal women from across North America. This film is unusual for its mix of dramatic re-creation, archive, poetic imagery, storytelling, and conversation intercut with live musical performances. The film was awarded Best Musical Expression at the Dreamspeakers Festival and Best Sound Award at the Yorkton Film Festival. A more recent film by Frazier Henry is *Legends Sxwexwxiy'am: The Story of Siwash Rock,* a dramatic adaptation of an ancient Coast Salish myth about the famous Vancouver landmark Siwash Rock. Awarded the Best Dramatic Short in 1999 by the American Indian Film Festival and the First Prize Teueikan at the tenth annual Montréal First Peoples' Festival in 2000, this film was also screened at the Sundance Film Festival in 2000 in both the Native Forum and the Shorts Competition.

In an evaluation of the AFP conducted in 1999, filmmakers noted that their AFP experience was a "stepping stone and that the NFB should continue to share in the storytelling experience." Others pointed out that the AFP had allowed "more thoughtful films to be made and that a federal agency like the NFB should be leading this initiative." One filmmaker described her experience of making a film under the AFP as "having won the lottery." Overall, the AFP was seen as "much needed for the community's distinct voices to be nurtured and developed."[43]

Overall, the Program has made a significant contribution not just to the professional development of individual aboriginal filmmakers but also to the films, which convey "non-stereotyped images of Indians" and communicate the aboriginal experience in all its diversity.[44] As one filmmaker stated, the ultimate success of the Program is measured by the fact that "the stories are coming from my community and are being told by us." From the perspective of NFB producers, the AFP has introduced new talent and has afforded an opportunity to understand the unique qualities of aboriginal voices and how differently their stories are told. In 1999, the NFB's English Program Branch renewed the AFP for another three years.

More Storytelling and Stories

I believe that it is possible for people to gain a new spiritual sense of purpose and connection to old traditional values. The life lessons this story offers are as relevant now as they have been for thousands of generations past.
—Annie Frazier Henry

In 1995, the program of the Native Forum for the Sundance Festival noted that

there was [an] excellent selection of films [including films by Gil Cardinal and Gary Farmer] [which showed] the way native and aboriginal films throughout the Western hemisphere [were] moving beyond the traditional documentary form to illustrate the sociopolitical aspects of their everyday lives.

Since then, many other Canadian films made by aboriginal filmmakers have screened at the Festival, some of which have been produced by the NFB under the AFP. These include filmmakers such as Annie Henry Frazier, whose films experiment with form by merging traditional with contemporary elements of Native culture. Her films also reflect the importance of ancient traditions with today's way of life. She and others have been successful in merging the storytelling tradition with the filmmaking medium.

The role of Studio One/AFP has been instrumental in this regard, because in making their first films, these filmmakers have learned the language of filmmaking—creating a continuum for storytelling that transcends time and technology. More importantly, they now have the opportunities to document their stories for the generations to come, bearing their stamp of interpretation.

Within the broader context of the film and television industry, Studio One/AFP was the catalyst for the 1997 establishment of Telefilm Canada's Aboriginal Production Fund. Throughout the 1990s, the NFB had lobbied the CRTC and the federal government, and had sensitized agencies such as Telefilm Canada to the importance of dedicating resources specifically for aboriginal films and television programs. The combined impact of all these initiatives has resulted in the development of a vibrant aboriginal film and television sector that is producing television programs and films for distribution on conventional television networks, specialty services and, since 1999, the Aboriginal Peoples Television Network. In 1999–2000, Telefilm's fund was oversubscribed, a clear signal that storytelling by aboriginal filmmakers is flourishing.

There is little doubt that the leadership of the National Film Board, with its long history of making films about Canada's Indian, Métis, and Inuit peoples, has been instrumental in what will be seen in the future as one of the most important developments in the history of the Canadian television and film industry.

Notes

1 The terms *aboriginal, indigenous,* and *Native* are used in this article to encompass Indians, Métis, Inuit, and non-status Indians.

2 Loretta Todd, *Forgotten Warriors* proposal, 1993.

3 Cynthia Lickers, *Imagine Native: Aboriginally-Produced Film and Video* (Toronto: V-Tape and the Aboriginal Film and Video Alliance, 1998), 4.

4 Carol Geddes, memo to Graydon McCrea, National Film Board, Edmonton, 6 June 1991.

5 Paul Marchand, ed., *Our Home and Native Land: A Film and Video Resource Guide for Aboriginal Canadians* (Winnipeg: National Film Board, 1991), 1.

6 Mark Zannis, memo to Don Haig, National Film Board, Edmonton, 12 October 1995.

7 Helen Lee, "Coming Attractions: A Brief History of Canada's Nether-Cinema," *Take One* (Summer 1994): 6.

8 Lee, "Coming Attractions," 6.

9 Michael Mitchell, "Indian Education Today," *Pot Pourri* (1974), 2.

10 *Art is Never a Given: Professional Training in the Arts in Canada* (Ottawa: Minister of Supply and Services, 1991), 91.

11 Kenn Chubb, *A Survey of First Peoples Writers, Directors and Producers of Film and Television Drama in Canada* (Toronto: The Canadian Native Arts Foundation, 1993), 1.

12 Gail Valaskakis, "Preface," internal NFB document, 30 September 1991, 1.

13 See Gail Valaskakis, "Communication and Control in the Canadian North: The Potential of Interactive Satellites," *Etudes Inuit Studies* 6 (1983).

14 Valaskakis, "Preface," 2.

15 Geddes memo to McCrea.

16 Geddes memo to McCrea.

17 David Balcan, "Hearing Our Voice, Seeing Our Image," document prepared for NFB, 3.

18 NFB, "Our People ... Our Vision: An Aboriginal Studio at the National Film Board of Canada" (Edmonton: National Film Board, 1991), 2.

19 NFB, "Our People ... Our Vision," 1.

20 Lorne W. MacPherson and Wil Campbell, "The Creation of a Canadian Aboriginal Film and Video Production Fund," document prepared for the Association of Aboriginal Filmmakers of Alberta, 1991.

21 Maria De Rosa, "The NFB's Studio One: Future Directions," document prepared for the National Film Board, 1995, 1.

22 De Rosa, "The NFB's Studio One," 4.

23 National Film Board, "NFB plans Aboriginal Film Studio," press release, 9 June 1991, 2.

24 NFB, "Our People ... Our Vision," 4.

25 Geddes memo to McCrea.

26 "NFB Plans National Aboriginal Film Studio," 2.

27 National Film Board. *Studio One Newsletter,* September 1992, 1.

28 NFB, *Studio One Newsletter,* 2.

29 Maria De Rosa, *An Evaluation of the Aboriginal Filmmaking Program,* document prepared for the National Film Board, 1995, 19.

30 Hal Seybold, letter to Barbara Cranmer, 26 November 1993.

31 De Rosa, *The NFB's Studio One,* 5.

32 National Film Board, "Supplementary Comments to the CRTC," (1994), 2.

33 NFB, "Supplementary Comments to the CRTC," 2.

34 De Rosa, *The NFB's Studio One,* 18.

35 De Rosa, *The NFB's Studio One,* 24.

36 De Rosa, *The NFB's Studio One,* 20.

37 National Film Board, *National Film Board Action Plan: 1994–1997* (1994), 3.

38 De Rosa, *Evaluation of the Aboriginal Filmmaking Program,* 4.

39 De Rosa, *The NFB's Studio One,* 35. In 1991, Studio D launched the New Initiatives in Film (NIF) Program, which led aboriginal women to participate in workshops, apprenticeships, and scholarship programs. In 1994, the NFB's English Program Branch introduced the Fast Forward Program, a documentary internship program. Aboriginal filmmakers have interned under this program. In 1992, the French Program Branch established the Programme de formation cinéastes autochtones, an apprenticeship program for aboriginal filmmakers who work in French.

40 Ted Payles, "Histories of Convenience: Understanding Twentieth Century Aboriginal Film Images in Context," paper presented at Screening Culture: Constructing Image And Identity conference, York, Great Britain, 1994, 10.

41 De Rosa, *The NFB's Studio One.* Films produced or co-produced by the Aboriginal Filmmaking Program are reviewed by a programming committee composed of the Director General of the NFB's English Program Branch, three executive producers for the Documentary Program, and two aboriginal filmmakers.

42 Loretta Todd, proposal for *Forgotten Warriors*, 8.

43 De Rosa, *Evaluation of the Aboriginal Filmmaking Program*, 14–15.

44 De Rosa, *Evaluation of the Aboriginal Filmmaking Program*, 15.

In the Hands of the People
A Conversation with Marjorie Beaucage
Lynne Bell and Janice Williamson

MARJORIE BEAUCAGE IS A FILMMAKER, art teacher, and video activist whose artistic work started at age forty when she began film production studies after twenty-five years' work as an adult educator and community organizer in Manitoba. Her cultural work builds on this early commitment, creating a powerful sense of art-making as communal practice. Much of her production work is collaborative, and she has made documentary films on the participation of aboriginal women in national and international feminist and women's conferences, Native blockades, and gatherings of Saskatchewan elders and local community events. Her more personally inflected videos explore her sense of private grief, loss, and recovery in *Bingo* (1991), a heavily coded incest film, and *Good Grief* (1993), a "home movie" that explores her family's grief and mourning after the death of a young brother.

In the following interview, Marjorie Beaucage talks about the community-based video-research project *Ntapueu ... i am telling the truth* (1997). The video *Ntapueu* was developed as part of the Innu Nation's environmental-impact statement submitted to the Environmental Assessment Hearings held in December 1997 on the Inco Mining Project at Voisey's Bay. *Ntapueu* documents a year in the life of the Innu as they examine the impact of Voisey's Bay nickel mine on the land and the people.

Beaucage was invited by the Innu Nation to help them with their project based on her reputation as a video activist, in particular her video documentation of the Wiggins Bay Blockade in 1992 when the elders in northern Saskatchewan protested government clear-cutting policies. When she was first asked to come to Labrador to do this project, Beaucage said, "No. I am not Innu. But I can teach you to tell your own story." Describing herself as "a community-based film and video maker," Beaucage is committed to a practice of decolonization and self-governance in the arts which she defines as "being able to represent yourself in your own voice with your own style of storytelling."

Beaucage spent thirty-six weeks in Labrador in 1997 teaching video and research skills to a team of eight people drawn from Utshimassits and Sheshatshiu, two of the communities most affected by the mining project in that territory. In reflecting on her work with the Innu,

Beaucage speaks of many issues, including the need for a research methodology based on an Innu worldview that allows the Innu voice to be heard; the development of a hands-on teaching methodology based on the seasons; the use of storytelling as the method for passing on Innu customs, values, and history around land use; the need for a "living history" that includes the past and the future in the present moment; the significance of video for constructing a community's collective memory; and the way in which video can be used as a mirror, for the community to see itself again. Beaucage describes *Ntapueu ... i am telling the truth* as a tool for change, noting, "It is intended to empower people to have their own voice, to have control over how they get represented, and to put their stories out."

After many years working as a filmmaker in Saskatoon, where this interview took place, Marjorie Beaucage now makes her home in Jonquière, Québec.

LB: Marjorie, I watched *Ntapueu ... i am telling the truth* (1997) again this morning. It is such a marvellous example of a community-based video-research project. Can you tell us about the process of gathering footage for this video? You've talked elsewhere about how the research and production process used storytelling as the method for passing on Innu customs, values, and history around land use.

MB: Well, we had to design questions about what was important because it wasn't just storytelling. We had to do a social- and environmental-impact assessment of the mining project. Baseline research for a year [1997] in the life of the Innu at Davis Inlet, Labrador. From this material, predictions for the future, twenty years from now with this mine, can be made. It was part of the Innu Nation's environmental-impact assessment. We couldn't make just any video, we had to address the impact of the Voisey's Bay mine on the Innu land and people. And we had to decide how we were going to do that and who was going to be involved. So we designed questions with the community, and we had lots of meetings and consultations.

LB: You met with all members of the community including the children?

MB: Everybody! I have never seen a community have so many meetings and consultations about so many things.

JW: Really! This is their standard way of proceeding?

MB: Yes, everything is there for discussion and decision.

LB: Besides these community meetings and consultations, did the research team conduct individual interviews to collect material for the project?

MB: We did household surveys. We've got a big book of all the data and statistics we collected going door to door. They wanted to gather this information because it had never been done, but they didn't put it into the video. They kept it separate and submitted it to the panel hearings. We designed household surveys with the kinds of questions we needed to ask different people depending on what their issues were. We thought about what we needed to ask the kids, what we needed to ask the women, what we needed to ask the men, what we needed to ask the elders.

JW: When you say "we," who did you work with?

MB: There was a team of four video researchers from each community—four in Utshimassits and four in Sheshatshiu.

LB: How were they chosen?

MB: Well, initially, I set up some criteria I thought people should have to come into this. But it was totally unrealistic on my part. I knew that but I still did it. Anyway, there were four video researchers in each community and they were picked according to which families they belonged to, so that everybody would be represented. The organization of life is still family, no matter what, and that's one thing Indian Affairs either understood very well and intentionally used, or never understood, when they set up the band system. Because that's still the way bands run. Whichever family has the most people gets the most votes. They get the jobs and the money for three years and then the next time, whoever is chief will take care of his family and clan. That's just the way it is. That's the way it's always been, that's what comes first. So I had researchers from the four family groups which represented the Innu Nation. It didn't mean they liked each other. As a matter of fact, some never talked to each other under normal circumstances. So here we were all having to work together on our common project. It's not that they didn't talk to each other, but they only talked when they had reason to. It's a very complex system of families, but there's a lot of intermarriage as well. So that's how the researchers were chosen. Also some considerations were given to gender and age in terms of the physicality of the work. When I first thought about it, I did think that everybody would be able to learn everything and do everything.

JW: And did they?

MB: Yes and no. Everybody had different starting places so they all had different ending places.

LB: Can you tell us some more about how the research team developed the questions for the differing groups you mention—the kids, the women, the men, and the elders? I know you conducted an initial workshop with the video researchers in which you set a series of video exercises.

MB: Well, I asked the researchers what questions they wanted to address and then I sent them out to talk to the people in their communities. In the first eight-week period, I set the direction and taught the technology. Those were my two goals. I gave them tasks and assignments on a day-to-day basis to go out and get video footage and bring it back in. Then we would talk about it and figure out how it was going to be developed. It was basic community development. And then you add in the technology.

LB: Was the entire community involved in an ongoing review and analysis of the material as it came in?

MB: Eventually. The researchers would mostly go to the people they knew and were comfortable with, like their families. That's how it worked. It didn't cross over a whole lot. And then sometimes, as we got out there with the cameras and did streeters, we would put these activities on the community television station. During the first week of shooting, I insisted that we invite everybody to the community hall to watch the footage. This also gave the video researchers an opportunity to practise being in the public with the material—showing it to people and talking about it. Everything was built in that way.

JW: Doing and reflecting!

MB: Yes! Go out there and do it and then come back and talk about it. That's the only way I know, so that's what we did. I went there in January 1997 and returned once a season for a year. We wanted to document each season to follow the rhythm of life for a year in the life of the Innu—different things happen at different times of the year. The other layer of our methodology was based on the Innu or aboriginal worldview that the present contains the past and the future. We had to get those stories from the past just as much as we had to think about what they wanted for their future. It is for the next generation we are doing this. Our methodology contained both the past and the future in the moment of the present. When the mine saw that the Innu were doing way more than they had anticipated in terms of research, they got scared and hired a social scientist from the University of Manitoba to invalidate our methodology.

LB: You are kidding!

MB: No! They totally trashed our methodology. So then I knew I was on the right track! [*laughter*]

LB: How did they trash it?

MB: They said it wasn't quantitative. All those scientific terms social scientists use. It blew me away that they would go to that length to trash our methodology. But it didn't work!

LB: Did you make changes to your methodology?

MB: No! Of course not! Actually, Katie Rich, the chief at that time, asked me, "How do you want to respond to this?" And I said, "It doesn't even deserve a response. Let's just ignore it."

LB: You mentioned that you documented the activities of the seasons to show the rhythm of life. What are these activities?

MB: Well, in the winter they have the caribou and the feast; in the spring they go to the country; in the summer they have social family gatherings. There was so little time to do all the work. In January, they were also learning the camera; in the spring, they were learning sound; and in the summer, they were learning how to edit. They were also doing the surveys and streeters. They did the circles in the summer and all the interviews. The harder social issues came later in the documentary process because the researchers weren't ready to tackle them until the third round. I put the social issues forward each time, but they just didn't want to go there until the summer and fall.

LB: Can you tell me what a streeter involved in this project?

MB: Well, we'd talk to people and ask them their opinion about one thing at a time. There was one question we never did address and that was about the bingo orphans. Every Tuesday night you'd see all these people hitchhiking into town to go to bingo. And all these kids were left alone. I ended up babysitting one night. I was staying in a house with a whole bunch of kids—all of a sudden, everybody left for bingo and I was left with all these kids. That's one streeter we never did do. They just didn't want to tackle that one! But sometimes we did some fun ones. On Valentine's Day, we asked people, "Who do you love? Who is your honey?" We also did one on food. We asked people, "What did you have for breakfast? What did you have for lunch?" Diet was an important part of the household surveys.

LB: Did material from the streeters go into the video?

MB: It went mostly into the 500-page document submitted to the panel hearings along with the results of the surveys. The only streeter that went into the video is the last one when we asked the kids what they wanted to tell us about the future. That was the most discouraging one for me! But we put it in. We asked them what they saw for themselves in the future. There is nothing they see for themselves—or very little. That's how the video ends. The only jobs available are with the police, the band office, or as carpenters. These are the only role models they have. They can't be teachers, or doctors, or nurses because there is nobody in the community that is doing those things. They don't have any high-school graduates. Even though the school has been there for all these years, there has never been a high-school graduate from Davis Inlet. And you have to have official papers to teach or do social work. So they can't run their own schools, they can't run their own services, they can't do anything. Because they don't have the papers. So the kids don't see themselves as being able to do those things. They don't see anybody doing them.

JW: What was their response to having actually produced a documentary?

MB: We never thought we would get it done, to tell you the truth. And then when they realized it was finished, they saw everything they could have put in. But they are still doing it. They still have the equipment, and Christine Poker in Davis and Phillip Nuna in Sheshatshiu are really into it. They are the leaders of their teams and are continuing to do the work on their own. Christine phoned me the other day and said, "Look, if we do this piece about the impact on the water and animals and send it down to you with transla-tions, can you put the subtitles on for us because we want to present it to the hearings?" I said, "Sure!" They can't do this last part, the subtitles, on their machines. The laptop is just straight cuts, nothing fancy—no mixing, no sound, and no dissolves. When we did the fi-nal cut and edit of *Ntapueu*, Phillip and Christine came here for a week. I wanted them to see what a post-production house was like, so they wouldn't be intimidated if they wanted to do post-production work in St. John's or Toronto or wherever—they'd know what to expect and what to do.

JW: How old are the video researchers?

MB: Well, the youngest is twenty-two and the oldest are in their late fifties ... a range of ages.

JW: Who filmed the scenes of the woman drinking with her friends? Was that someone in their family?

MB: That's Sylvester's family.

LB: It must have taken tremendous courage to tell this story. I was struck by how the video keeps revealing things that would be edited out in most western family photo albums or home videos.

MB: Well, we had lots of discussions about that—the sniffing, the funeral ...

JW: ... and what was the content of that discussion? Whether to put this material in?

MB: Whether to put it in the video or not and what it has to do with the impact study. We had some sixty hours of tape to go through and it was entirely their decision as to what went in and what didn't. But the thing that became clearer and clearer as they made their choices was how important the video was in showing the people to themselves. In being that mirror. Because everybody was invisible to themselves. Everybody just walks by those kids sniffing every night. Over 130 kids sniffing and everybody just walks by them now. They don't even see them anymore. They know they are there, and no one is dealing with it. It's like you become invisible to yourself. When it becomes so painful or commonplace, when you feel so powerless, you stop seeing it, you just shut down. I walked by it too be-cause I didn't know what to do. I mean if I were in my own territory I'd know what to do. But I wasn't in my home territory. I can't tell the kids in Davis Inlet what to do. I can't go in there with that attitude, you know, it's not my responsibility. I have to keep reminding myself what I am here for, what is my responsibility. But it was still very difficult to see those kids every day. I did what any adult, or auntie, would do. I'd say, "Go home, give me your sniff bag," or "Why are you doing that stuff?" Just to let them know I saw them. But I couldn't intervene really. That was the hardest thing and that's why the chief said, "Put it in, it's your grandchildren." It was their own kids, their own grandkids, their own relations.

LB: So the video is not only addressing outside western exploitation of the area for the panel hearings, it is also addressing difficult issues in the community. It is talking to two audiences at once.

MB: Totally. But it's more for the Innu because we know it's not going to make much difference to the Voisey's Bay nickel company, or anybody else. Actually, the mine didn't think the Innu would do it. They didn't care whether we finished the video or not. As a matter of fact, they didn't expect us to finish it. And they didn't expect it to be worth anything. When they finally got it and the survey results, they did not put it in the environmental assessment they submitted to the hearings because they didn't like the way they were represented.

JW: Did they have that right to not submit?

MB: Yes.

LB: And can the Innu submit it?

MB: Yes, they can. And they will when they make their presentations.

JW: At one point in the video someone says, "I know there has been violence around here for a long time." And it sounds like they are saying there was some violence before the priest came. It's not clear to me when he's saying the violence began.

MB: What kind of violence are you talking about? Family violence?

JW: I think it was domestic violence. I thought it was about witnessing something to the community itself. That process of change that comes from seeing yourself. What was the actual effect when the video was publicly shown in the community?

MB: Well, people saw bits and pieces all along. It's not like they never saw it before. And they are all in it. It's not so much a product as a process. And it's still ongoing in that sense.

LB: In watching *Ntapueu*, I was struck by how recent the history of settlement is in Davis Inlet. It dates from the arrival of the priest in 1959. It is amazing to watch the archival footage of his arrival and the setting up of the school ...

MB: I know, that blew me away!

LB: Where did this archival footage come from?

MB: Priests, anthropologists, and eager photographers! The Oblates had a lot of photographs, and the community has collected a lot of stuff. Because it is fairly recent, the photographs are just lying around in a back room. No one is looking after them.

LB: Prior to this settlement at Davis Inlet were the Innu living in the interior?

MB: They lived in the country year-round in their tents. Not only in the interior but also on the coast. They moved their camps in the winter, summer, and spring depending upon the fish, geese, and caribou. The first building that went up in Davis Inlet was that priest's house and the school was in his house. And he said when he got there that everybody had to go to school. That's why the village was made. The priest made them build houses and stay in the village so that their kids could go to school. They had to stay in town because of their kids. Before that, they never had a permanent village with houses.

JW: And they lost their livelihood then?

MB: They lost their lifestyle. They lost what makes Innu, Innu. And that's the land.

LB: In the workshops you conducted at the outset of this research project, you set a series of video exercises designed to explore Innu culture and systems of governance. For instance, you asked the video researchers to find out what the nature of the feast was in their culture. Did you develop a lot of material around Innu customs that was not included in the video?

MB: Well, did I tell you about the creation stories? I asked them, "What are the Innu beginnings?" Everybody has origin stories, right? Every culture, every nation has some sense of how they came to be who they are. Whether it's Adam and Eve, or the Turtle, everybody has them. The Cree have them, the Ojibway have them. But everybody's stories are a little different. At first they didn't know what I was talking about when I asked, "Where do the Innu come from?" Then I found out they had Wolverine stories. Those are their teaching stories. But nobody remembered the whole thing. So I asked them to think who had told the stories to them. And to go and talk to the people who they thought would know the stories. And then they started remembering bits and pieces. Talking to each other, they started piecing it together, and they talked to the older people they thought might remember. But many had forgotten. They hadn't been told the story for so long and nobody had asked for it. You forget. And the older you get, the more you forget.

JW: This is where the videographers come in—in terms of documenting some of these narratives.

MB: Oh man, they wanted to record everything! I kept saying, "Do it later!" We had this deadline and I felt responsible for the original agenda. It was important. Of course it would have been more fun to document activities such as hunting and teach the kids how to do this, that, and the other thing. But this is not what the video was about. That's when I got onto my rant because they were giving up too easily in terms of not finding those creation stories and wanting to do all of these other things that were easier. But I also realized, after being there on my third round, why it was so hard to do this type of work. Just imagine going back to your own family and community, where you grew up, and doing that kind of work. Just think what it takes to do it! I couldn't do it!

JW: Very brave! You risk everything, really. You risk being ostracized and alienating your community.

MB: Oh, I was asking a lot. When I had my interview for this job on the phone, I told them how I would approach it and what I thought might happen based on my experiences of working in other communities. I said, "I don't want this job. I'm not Innu. But I can teach you how to tell your own story!"

JW: You talk about yourself as both a producer and mentor to the project—a double role. What did you learn from the project?

MB: I learned my limits. Not trying to change the world with every single thing I do. My agenda has always been about social change. But it's very exhausting and I expect a lot of myself in that regard. I also expect a lot of others if I'm going to join into some kind of partnership, or if I'm going to be with them for this length of time. It's too much to expect of myself or of anyone else. It's a hard price and not everybody is willing to pay it. And there is so much other stuff to deal with as well—all those suicides, burials, and family crises. Plus, the deadline of getting the job done. I mean, nobody has ever worked so hard at a job.

LB: You describe *Ntapueu ... i am telling the truth* as a community-based video project. Did you have to make shifts in your working methods as a filmmaker to work on this project?

MB: Well, it develops out of my community-based work in educational videos about change.

LB: How does it compare, for instance, to *Our Living Treasures* [1993], a video documentary you made of an elders gathering at Waden Bay in north Saskatchewan?

MB: Well, *Our Living Treasures* was an event, a situation I was recording, a moment in time. Whereas *Ntapueu* is not just an event or a moment in time, it is a tool for change. It is intended to empower people to have their own voice, to have control over how they get represented, and to put their stories out. I mean it's totally from the inside out. And I work that way too. What I'm doing in *Ntapueu* is teaching the way I work to someone else. It is about giving the tools to the people to do it themselves.

JW: When you talk about a process of disillusionment ...

MB: Disillusionment?

JW: Well, that's my interpretation. You talked about having very high demands for the video project *Ntapueu* that couldn't be met. And yet it is a project that has changed people in ways that will transform how this community perceives itself. It will have some genuinely lasting effects because the work will continue on. But is it less than you imagined?

MB: No, it's not a question of more or less—it's the price, the personal cost. I don't know how many more times I can do these types of projects without doing my own work as well. When I take on these things, it takes up all of my energy. I could not do anything else in 1997 except this. Also, sometimes I do things and they are bigger than me, they are more important, and my stuff isn't as important. I do that to myself a lot. This image of myself as an activist, it's true and I do it well. I've done it for a long time, I've been doing it all my life. So it's like, give it up already! Maybe not give it up, but give it another place. There are other places you can draw from in yourself. You don't need to live in this place all the time, you can have other dimensions.

JW: When we interviewed you the first time [published in *Tessera* 22], you talked about the impulse that made you leave a twenty-five-year career in adult education to go into film-making.

MB: Yes, I mean it's such a little seed—it's barely grown. I have only been doing this for ten years. I went to film school in 1988, right? So it's like, what do I know? And I've been doing the other way longer.

LB: I remember that in that interview, you also talked about the need to work collectively to avoid burnout and about the need to take turns going on the front lines.

MB: Totally! Totally!

Notes

This conversation was recorded in Saskatoon in 1998 and edited with some additions in July 2000. It is part of a collaborative interdisciplinary research project "West of Where? Contemporary Prairie Women's Cultures," and we are grateful to SSHRC for funding part of this research.

Cowboy Filmmaking
An Interview with Gil Cardinal
William Beard and Jerry White

DESPITE HIS QUIET DEMEANOUR and his feeling that he is not really part of the larger communities of documentary or of aboriginal filmmakers, you couldn't possibly write a history of Canadian aboriginal film making without giving Gil Cardinal an important place. Across a variety of forms—NFB documentary, episodic television drama like *North of 60*, and the TV miniseries *Big Bear* (1998, six hours)—he has forged a body of work that is closely tied to the culture of western Canada and populist in the best sense.

After making a few documentaries for the National Film Board (NFB) on a variety of subjects, Cardinal came to wide attention in 1987 with his personal documentary *Foster Child*. A quest for the identity of his biological mother forms the centre of the film, but it is also a deeply felt meditation on the meaning of family and a sometimes painful exposé of the workings of Canada's child-welfare system. It marked Cardinal as a filmmaker who knew just how emotionally powerful a pared-down, subjective documentary could be—and as a documentarian with a keen social conscience. Almost fifteen years after its production, it remains his most widely seen work and one of the best internationally known films by a Canadian aboriginal filmmaker.

This film, however, came after Cardinal's participation in the NFB's Dramalab, a program in which documentary filmmakers were paired with fiction filmmakers with a view to enabling them to expand the range of their abilities. Cardinal talks in the interview about how much he enjoyed this experience, and the films that he made around this period are indeed interesting pieces. His infrequently shown *Hotwalker* (1986) is an adaptation of a short story by Dave Billington and has a quiet, patient feel to it, evoking the coming of age of a kid who longs to train horses. *Discussion in Bioethics: The Courage of One's Convictions* (1985) is about the cultural conflict that erupts between an Indian doctor and the parents of a terminally ill young woman, who, because of their religious convictions, do not want her to get a life-saving blood transfusion. Again, the pace is slow and the literally life-or-death dilemma is evoked quietly, without melodrama. One of his best early films, *Children of Alcohol* (1984), is made up of interviews with young kids on a camping trip in the mountains, all of whom talk at length about what it is like to have alcoholic parents. None of these films have anything to do with aboriginal culture as such, but each began a pattern that can be seen throughout Cardinal's body of work: they resist emotional manipulation, have a rambling, open feel to them, and give the sense that the filmmaker is trying hard to keep his distance, to let his subjects unfold slowly and fully.

We see also this in *Big Bear*, Cardinal's most ambitious and narratively complex work. It is an adaptation of Rudy Wiebe's 1973 novel *The Temptations of Big Bear*, and Wiebe shares the writing credit with Cardinal on the miniseries adaptation. Like all of Cardinal's work, *Big Bear* is slow. Part of this is a function of its length and part is the director's unwillingness to rush or to head linearly from "high point" to "high point" in standard dramatic fashion. Equally important is his attention to detail. The lifestyle of Cree nomads at the end of the nineteenth century is lightly touched on ("We'll never find anything to eat in this bush!" Tantoo Cardinal's character laments as Big Bear's people wander around what is now Alberta and Saskatchewan trying to avoid choosing a reserve). And detail of this kind is also used to convey the highly complex politics of the Canadian west ("It's our half-brothers the Métis!" cries one of Big Bear's warriors as Gabriel Dumont approaches, a Métis sash dangling from his belt; another scene features Big Bear's son lamenting that the local buffalo population "are in Blood pots," immediately before they stage a potentially bloody raid on the local Blood campsite). Perhaps a better way of describing *Big Bear* is to say that it feels heavy: heavy with the weight of history, heavy with the sense of lost opportunities that still pervades discussions of aboriginal politics. The device (taken from Wiebe's novel) of having the Natives speak English while the whites speak some kind of Euro-gibberish works brilliantly, having a particularly salutary effect on a white Anglophone audience.

In-between these fiction films, Cardinal has produced a body of committed, thoughtful documentaries. He made a film for the BBC, *Our Home and Native Land* (1992), which tried to explain to a British audience something about the aboriginal perspective on the constitutional negotiations preceding the Charlottetown Accord. This hour-long program follows Ovide Mercredi around the country from consultations with aboriginal peoples and leaders to meetings with white political leaders in Ottawa and Québec City (there is a wonderful "documentary moment" when his delegation tries to penetrate the Québec National Assembly). He also chronicled the leadership race of the Assembly of First Nations for the CBC program *Rough Cuts* in a film called *Spirit and Intent* (1993). In 1991, he completed *Tikinagan*, an hour-long program investigating the effect of local control of child-welfare services on northwestern Ontario reserves. This film, which interviews participants and observes events in a familiar documentary fashion, nevertheless has strong qualities of its own arising not only from the vivid humanity of some of the principal subjects but from the measured pace and quiet tone that are the hallmarks of Cardinal's work. There is a similar atmosphere in *The Spirit Within* (1990, co-directed with Wil Campbell), another hour-long film, which documents the activities of Bobby Woods, a Native elder trying to bring spiritual renewal to Native prison inmates. In *David With F.A.S.* (1997), Cardinal works with low-grade video footage—including diaristic material gathered from a camera given to the subject—to investigate the problems of a young man suffering from fetal alcohol syndrome. The result in this film, as in so much of Cardinal's output, is sympathetic, moving, and quietly respectful, with no intrusiveness, preaching, or other grandstanding. The tone of Gil Cardinal's filmmaking "voice" is subtle and low-pitched, but it is unique.

WB: What led you to filmmaking? Did you have ambitions to be a filmmaker? When did it start?

GC: It just evolved. It's sort of a long history, which has to do with my foster child status, because I was not really going anywhere after high school, and I couldn't go to university, which was I think itself was an act of someone in grade nine deciding I wasn't university material. So I was just knocking around after high school, but I had a really good social worker, my last social worker, and she encouraged me to take advantage of continuing education, which the government would pay for, since I was a ward until I was twenty-one. So the only option available was the Northern Alberta Institute of Technology, so she brought me over to the education building, and an aptitude test was done, and it said that I should go into radio and TV arts or photography. And I got bumped up to the head of the waiting list for radio and TV arts. And that was fine, I enjoyed that, but I didn't really have a career path. After that I thought maybe I would be prepared to work in the industry, as a cameraman. I was quite happy behind the camera, I had no intention ... I would see these guys, these producers and directors, the high-powered ones brought in from Toronto, and they were crazy guys.

WB: Was there a time when you felt like you wanted to address issues, or when you felt like you wanted to work on particular projects?

GC: Well, now I do more consciously. Maybe the last five years or so, I've been more conscious and purposeful about being a filmmaker, about being a Native filmmaker, about using the experience and skills I have in the service of my community. But that's a relatively recent thing. And part of that is my self-identifying as Native filmmaker, as seeing that that's OK. I mean, I never resisted it that much, but a little bit. So that's a relatively recent consciousness of who I am or what I wanted to do.

WB: But *Foster Child* is more than ten years old, and *Foster Child* is clearly a passionate film. Obviously you wanted to make that film.

GC: Yeah, but that didn't mean at that time that it was the beginning of my career making Native-issue films.

JW: Because after *Foster Child*, you made a series of films that didn't have anything to do with Native life specifically, right?

GC: That's true, yeah. I just wanted to develop as a director.

JW: Were you involved in any kind of NFB training program at that time? *Foster Child* was your first film, right?

GC: Um, no, the NFB film *Children of Alcohol* was. And, yes and no. The precursor to the National Screen Institute was called Dramalab. It originated with Tom Radford at the Film Board. Even before there was such a program—and this was '82, '83—one of the things they wanted to do was put a documentary filmmaker into the drama department for four months. So I was it. And it was a fabulous, fabulous time. And that was part of the organic process of evolving this thing that became the Dramalab, which is now the National Screen Institute.

WB: Since the discussion of your coming into being as a filmmaker of different kinds has already touched indirectly on your status as a Native filmmaker, maybe we could talk about that now. At another stage you were resistant to being pigeonholed in a certain way, and since then have started to think about yourself differently as a filmmaker?

GC: I think the resistance aspect would stem not from resisting being identified as a Native person, because I very consciously chose to do that years ago. But because I had done and felt I could do any kind of film or television work ... It wasn't a big passionate deal for me. When it became OK, it just was, it's OK. If that's what I am to do, then that's OK with me. The key thing about that is that I discovered it's through that work that I have a connection to my community, that I have a relationship with those people. Because it's those films that take me into the community and allow me to interact with my people. Because if I didn't do that, I wouldn't. I mean, I don't go out to the friendship centre every weekend for round dances or go to powwows. I mean, I don't do really anything to involve myself in the Native community. It's mostly because I don't have to anymore; the work is enough to get me out there. I think that's the most important thing about it for me, about being a Native filmmaker.

WB: Just looking at your filmography, it looks like *Foster Child* was a key film in that respect, as it was in a number of ways for you. Would you say that it was a turning point bringing you more self-consciously towards Native subjects? Or was it that in the process of making the film you discovered some things you might want to follow up on?

GC: Well, the personal aspect is far more what drove that, seeking a cultural connection. But by virtue of meeting the people I did, and learning a little bit of what I did, that was the beginning of a cultural connection because until that time, I had had nothing to do with Native people. I mean, what did I do before that? Some pretty general stuff, I think.

JW: *Children of Alcohol* ...

GC: But that wasn't about Native ...

WB: No, it wasn't. But it was a kind of typically socially aware look at a problematic area of social life. But then you moved over to similar types of things in Native culture. So would you now say you have a political project as a filmmaker?

GC: No, no. I'm not a political person at all.

WB: Even though you followed Ovide Mercredi around [for *Our Home and Native Land*] for months?

GC: Yeah, but that wasn't ... [*pause*]

WB: Do you specifically address political questions in your work?

GC: I'm not conscious of it. I'm not going after that. At least not in any way I'm conscious of.

WB: So how do you find yourself doing these things?

GC: [*chuckles*] I don't know. I just let things evolve. Whatever I should be doing, I have faith that it's going to find me. Not very often do I go looking for something, that I want to do *this*. I think that I shouldn't just count on that, and I need to get more purposeful about what I'm doing. But if I get called up by CBC to comment on what I think on some hot new political issue, I won't. I don't do that, it's not me, I'm not good at it, I don't have anything to say about it. Call Loretta Todd or somebody like that; they'll give you an earful!

JW: So have you shown *Foster Child* or *Tikinagan* in Native communities?

GC: Yeah.

JW: What was the response to *Foster Child*?

GC: Well, it was a long time ago. The Film Board set up a cross-Canada tour, and certainly there were a lot of Native people who came to those, but that was in Winnipeg ...

JW: Was it shown on settlements or reserves or anything?

GC: Once that I remember. It was on a Micmac reserve. It freaked me out a little bit, because it was in a community hall, awful sound, awful everything, kids running around playing ... [*chuckles*] But people would come up afterwards and tell me that it helped in some way, that that was their story. And that happened a lot. And there was another one, not in a community but in a Native women's group. And they took me to task for having the Film Board pay for my mother's headstone. And I had to say, well no, I very clearly knew that when I found out about that, my first instinct was that I wanted to do that for her. After that, it became clear that this had to be part of the story. But that was a bit of an attack. It was aggressive.

JW: How about *Tikinagan*?

GC: Well, it was shown in Sioux Lookout, for those folks. But there were no screenings that I went to.

JW: So you mentioned that if people want an earful they should call Loretta Todd. Do you feel a kinship with Loretta Todd?

GC: Oh yeah. I mean, I don't see her very often. She knows that stuff, she can speak about it with great passion and political sense, neither of which I have.

JW: Do you feel a kinship with Alanis Obomsawin's stuff, or Marjorie Beaucage's stuff, or Loretta Todd's stuff? Or do you feel like you're just all filmmakers who are working on disparate issues?

GC: The second one. I don't follow the work and careers of my peers. When I can I watch it. But I don't actively get out there ... Because I am kind of... I'm insulated.

JW: Is that a product of geography, living in Alberta?

GC: No, it's my nature, my character.

JW: So do you think there's a cohesive community of Native filmmakers in Canada?

GC: There is.

JW: Do you feel a part of that?

GC: No. I feel I'm welcomed into the circle when I go, but I just don't participate. And it's something that bothers me a lot. Not so that I'd know what I can or should do about it. I mean, when I was at Sundance, years ago, at the Native forum, there were a lot of folks there. But I didn't feel part of their group. So it was hard to sit around at supper or at the bar and engage in whatever the talk was. I mean, it'd be better if I was in Winnipeg, or Kahnawake, or something, but mostly it's a personal thing.

WB: This does seem to go together with what you were saying about your approach to the political process, that you take the issues as you encounter them. You're not really plugged into the political process or entering into the debate about things in an active way.

GC: Well, yeah. I mean, I have my perspective on things. I mean, I was just dealing with it yesterday. I was looking at some footage, and I thought the guy was shooting such and such but he wasn't ... I want to monitor, I want to see what's going on. I don't have a great sense of what *I* want. That's why documentary is such a good fit for me. The situation is happening that I have no control over, and that's fine, I can go in there and try to access it, as opposed to saying I want this, I want that. Whatever else that drive is I don't have. I would rather be that than being too much, I don't know, a *filmmaker*, you know, this is my way, this is my vision, this is what I want. I mean, I'm a little too far the other way, and I would like to close that gap a little bit.

WB: Yeah, I would say that those kinds of qualities are visible in your work, but I wouldn't characterize them negatively. I would want to say that there is a kind of gentleness in your work. Your films are quite often about terrible stuff, about really bad situations, and various kinds of dysfunction, or about historical wrongs. And stereotypically, you might expect to see anger, something sharp in the filmmaker's response to this. I think what distinguishes your work is that there's something else instead. Does that make sense to you?

GC: It does, yeah. I mean, it's not my job to express that. You use the word *gentleness*, and I appreciate that. Because I do have that sense, that's how I go about things, the importance of letting people tell their stories. I'm the medium for that; I have the tools and the skills to allow that to happen. I have to get myself out of the way and let there be a direct connection between giver and receiver. So I would much rather act in that way, than being, you know, "A Film *by* Gil Cardinal." But that is a conflict, something I haven't resolved. And that's OK. Like I said, I should close the gap a little bit. But I don't think I'll ever become a James Cameron type [*laughs*].

WB: You must have strong feelings with respect to the people in your films, with respect to the historical situations. I mean, there's some pretty sad, some pretty awful things you're looking at. You must have feelings about this. Do you try to keep those out of it, or are you conscious of trying to channel them?

GC: I just came across this, hang on ... [*goes to get photographs*] Some old files there, I was going through. And I came across this which I had in my Great Plains office, I had a big blow-up of this [one of the subjects from *Tikinagan*]. I wanted to keep that close by me, because I wanted to remember how strongly I felt about her, and hoping and praying for her future. There was nothing I could do, I mean, I wanted to adopt her at the time. It's good for me to feel ... But that doesn't happen often enough. Like with David Diamond, from *David With F.A.S.* So yes it happens, but it's something that I keep to myself. But I would hope that some of what I feel the viewer would feel.

WB: I just have a sense that in your work there's a very particular, very personal kind of negotiation going on. There's just such a contrast with the calmness of a lot of your work in the formal sense or in terms of your own voice on the soundtrack or your presence in the film, and what is clearly a situation of great pain. That creates something unusual. I mean, there are filmmakers all over the world running around making films about terrible situations or films about things they feel need to have attention drawn to them and so on. And it's very rare that you get that feeling from those films.

GC: Well, I'm glad to hear that. I'm just not conscious of it, that's all. I'm glad to hear someone who can fertilize that ... I hope that is the case, but it's not something I'm aware of.

JW: Maybe we could turn to *Foster Child* again. I wanted to talk a little bit about this notion of the "NFB film," which is, I think, a discernible genre. I feel like *Foster Child* is pushing up against the envelope of being an NFB film and being a more personal, diaristic, almost confessional film. Did you feel a tension between institutional demands to make a certain kind of film and a personal desire to make a certain kind of film?

GC: No, not at all. It came out of talks to do an institutional kind of film, an overview of Native children and child welfare. And at the time I think I was supposed to be developing a film strip. And at some point in that, I thought maybe I would do my story as one, in addition to a girl who was going to be a subject. But it was real hands off from the Film Board. I wasn't aware at that point of any house styles or any of that; I wouldn't know if I was conforming or not!

JW: I want to talk a little bit about the part where you first meet the guy who you think is your biological dad. Do I understand that he was unaware of the camera when you met him at the veterans' march?

GC: Yeah.

JW: You can hear him pretty well, though. Was that difficult to mike?

GC: Well, we had a regular mike on me.

JW: Then you had a camera up over a hill?

GC: Across the street. But when I called him, and got confirmation that he was the guy, I found out he was at the veterans' villa, and somehow I found out that there was going to be this VE day parade, that day! So I walked over to the Film Board and got everybody together and away we went.

JW: So he had no idea he was being filmed?

GC: No, no. At some point I told him about the film, and I told him I had to have his approval. And he didn't demand anything to be taken out or anything. It was very clear to him that this would be shown on TV, and it was all fine. I had a bit of a relationship with him over a couple of years. But he was living with a real battle-axe woman, and the film came on TV again, and she saw it and hated any mention of [Cardinal's biological mother] Lucy, or his relationship with her. So she started giving him shit, and that really spoiled the relationship, and then he gave me shit, saying he didn't know it was going to be on TV, and blah blah. And that just fucked the relationship.

JW: So I have a similar set of questions about the scene where you meet your aunt and uncle. Was that the first time you had met them?

GC: Yeah, I got the information from the welfare lady there. I guess I called, and we arranged for me to come down and meet them on that day, and we sent Tom and Daryl a half-hour ahead to the house and got set up.

JW: Was that weird for them, for the first time they meet you to have a camera crew there?

GC: [laughs] No, no. They were fine with it.

JW: So do you find yourself split in *Foster Child* between making a political film and a personal film? I know you don't think of yourself as a political filmmaker, but there is a pretty discernible political critique going on in *Foster Child*.

GC: No, I mean, I was making a personal film. At the time I was not too self-conscious, I was more interested in being involved in the situations I was involved with. It was when we were editing that I had to deal with this fuckin' guy Gil Cardinal on the screen. I felt for instance, very self-conscious about when I react to my sister-in-law's in Yellowknife, where I react to the second picture of my mother and talk about how she looks like a tired Indian woman. I wanted to take that out, but I knew I couldn't, because it was an honest response, even if it makes me look like a shit. That's when I was self-conscious. But we did several hours with a psychologist, just about the process of what I was going through. But it was, I don't know, too different, too detached, too intellectual or something. But no, I never thought I was making a political film. I mean, I knew that the bit in the welfare office was political, but I wasn't trying to make a big point there. I mean, it was obvious what was going on there.

WB: I want to talk a little about *The Spirit Within*. Can you tell me how that got started as a project?

GC: Gosh, I don't remember. It was written with Wil Campbell ...

WB: Written? In what way?

GC: Well, Wil had quite a lot to do with initiating it, and I did the rest; I did the editing. But how exactly it came about, I don't know ...

WB: The specific question I wanted to ask was would you have had a film without Bobby Woods?

GC: Well, yes and no. There were other elders working in the [prison] system. Maybe not as effectively as Bobby. I mean, he's very strong. Very charismatic. And it needed that. And Wil had the relationship and the contacts with all those people. Wil was and is much more connected to all those people. We had this series, *My Partners My People*, which we did when Wil and I formed a company here. But before that in the '80s Wil was doing that show on a much smaller basis in Saskatchewan, and he did a whole lot of shows. And I think that was one of them ...

WB: With this film, and with *Tikinagan* too, I keep wanting to come back to this question of the political ... obviously Jerry and I are obsessed with this [*laughs*]. I think the film mentions, but doesn't do much more than that, about the disproportionate percentage of Native Canadians in prison. And in *Tikinagan* as well, there is a particular problem with dysfunctional families, and children who need to be placed in foster care in Native communities. And these are political questions, obviously. But you don't address yourself, in *The Spirit Within*, to the question of why these guys are there. We see a treatment with individual inmates, who sometimes will talk about what they did to get there and how they were thinking wrongly and so on, and what processes Native spirituality has done to make things more intelligible for them or show them some kind of way. But the film doesn't do that at all. Would you say that's part of your philosophy of letting things happen?

GC: Yeah. I mean, that is a strong thing in me, that I accept what I'm given. It's not often that I'll push for more than that. I don't know if it's a sin of commission or omission. But sometimes you've got to focus what the film's going to be about. Maybe it would have been better if you would have given some sort of social context for what was there. I don't know if we discussed that or not.

WB: The film is actually very well focussed. I don't feel that it's a problem with the film. I do find it a little bit curious that ...

GC: I think with Native films, or any kind of documentary, at some point you can't keep rehashing all the history. Maybe it's a bad assumption or expectation that the audience has a sense of why we're at this point and how we got from here to there. I mean, in some cases you do it and it gets cut out anyway.

WB: Do you ever feel the impulse to be analytical, as opposed to someone who's just sort of setting down what he's seeing?

GC: No, I don't think so.

JW: So do you think *Tikinagan* is a sort of continuation of stuff you started exploring in *Foster Child*? Do you see a link between those two films?

GC: Yeah, but it wasn't conscious, it wasn't purposeful. Because I was asked to participate in that series *As Long as the Rivers Flow*. I don't know if I suggested that topic or if they did. I remember how I found out about Tikinagan Child and Family Services. They may have just given me, you know, "whatever you want to do." I suspect that they suggested a topic, and then somehow I found this group.

JW: Did they look to you because of what you'd done with *Foster Child*?

GC: I don't know if it was that specific. I mean, there weren't that many Native filmmakers around, that was ten years ago now. I mean, I was aware of the parallels and the connections [between *Foster Child* and *Tikinagan*].

WB: I'm wondering what kinds of things you might be looking for when you go into a project, when it comes to finding a subject who will really come across on camera?

GC: Well, in the case of *Tikinagan*, it's not like there are going to be hundreds of people to choose from. People are very reluctant to talk about things, and to appear in a film. I think the social workers suggested a couple of possibilities. It's like with *David with F.A.S.*: his mother Mary calls me, and says that she heard I did Native film and that this was her life's work and was very important, and could there be a film done on it, a sociological overview kind of film, the NFB kind of thing you're talking about. But it became obvious in talking to her and listening of her story that the film needed to be about them, and not a social-political overview. So I didn't go off searching for who's going to be the subject of a film about fetal alcohol syndrome.

WB: Can you say anything about how you are working as an editor of your own material and what kind of pace you might be looking for?

GC: Well, I prefer a slow pace. And I've had lots of feedback that says "too slow." But I don't go into an editing room and say OK, let's make it a slow pace. I mean, I think I'm getting a little more conscious of what I'm doing.

JW: Now, *Big Bear* was commissioned by the same people who did *Canada: A People's History*, the CBC. But it's a totally different film. Why does *Big Bear* feel so much slower? I mean, they're the same form, right, a historical drama/miniseries?

GC: Well, they're not the same form. I mean, *Big Bear*, the evolution of that, it's a whole huge thing, but it's not like the CBC commissioned it and so could put its stamp on it. Certainly they had their say about actors, and scripting, but that's it. They came to see a cut, and they thought it was slow, but ... It has a very unique evolution and history.

WB: So tell us about that.

GC: When we were Great Plains Productions, we were sort of like a wing of Great North Productions. Eventually we were going to be independent. And they [Great North] had *Big Bear*, from Rudy Wiebe, so as partner companies we were developing *Big Bear*. We divorced from them much sooner than we would have thought, and a lot of it had to do with *Big Bear*, because we were kind of window-dressing aboriginal people involved with the project. So we made an issue of that, and had a separation, and part of that was to take *Big Bear* and produce it ourselves. And we came very close to having all the financing and having John N. Smith to direct, and that fell apart at the very last minute. We had an eleventh-hour meeting of the CBC, Telefilm, AMPDC, NFB, Alliance, and we were $300,000 short, and they weren't going to cover it. Because John wouldn't do it at that time, because he had just done *The Boys of St. Vincent* and was being courted by Hollywood. So we thought it was dead, because that killed the distribution deal, it killed the NFB participation. Then CBC was going to do it in-house, and Sturla Gunnarsson was going to direct. But it was too expensive for them to do in-house, so it was back to us. Our feeling about the CBC incarnation was that it wasn't really our fault. We were in a very equal partner-ship. So I took over the writing at a certain point, and then it evolved so that we thought I should direct.

WB: How did you feel about tackling a big fiction film?

GC: Well, it was something I couldn't not do. I mean, when John N. Smith quit, I said the next day, sure, I'll do it. And they had to say, very politely, that I didn't really have much experience. But in the years of continuing development, I started doing *North of 60*. I got more experience. So by this time, in 1998, I had more experience; it was credible that I could direct.

WB: Was it a major switch for you to go from documentary to fiction, or did you find that you were working with the same kinds of problems?

GC: I mean, it's different in terms of intensity. Documentary is a lot more thoughtful, it's a slow process, you let it evolve. With drama, you just get on board and hang on for dear life.

WB: There are economic pressures.

GC: Oh yeah, there's a lot to do in prep time, and it's a very intensive experience. But I seemed to get into the kismet of it, but prep is a very stressful time. But it's very immediate, it's always in your face, there's always four thousand things to deal with. With documentary, it's a much more organic process.

JW: So did you bring any of that organic approach to the process, in a way that someone who's just trained as a fiction filmmaker wouldn't? I mean, when you're doing episodes of *North of 60* or *The Rez*, you're working with guys who are trained to do television, not documentary. Did you bring something to the process that they didn't?

GC: Well, there's a thoughtfulness to that dramatic work, maybe that's the connection ...

JW: But you don't see a radical difference between you and the other guys who worked on *North of 60*?

GC: Well, my camera work would be simpler, in a documentary you don't get to do a whole lot of fancy angles.

JW: How about working with actors?

GC: I love working with actors. I think that's the thing I'm most interested in, what I worry about most, what I work at most. And that really goes back to when I did that pilot project in the drama department of the NFB for four months, and watched that amazing theatrical process. And I get a lot of good feedback sometimes from actors, that they appreciate being worked with, and not just told where to stand and that's it. It's work that I never seem to have enough time to do. I accept the confidence I get, but it's something I want to work at more and more. I was asked to do a *Mentors* episode this last summer, and when I got the script I bailed out. Because it was highly technical, involving all kinds of stuff on the river. And I just thought, this is not me, I'm interested in relationship drama, I can't do this, I'm not going to be good at it. It was very ambitious. So I made a very diffi-cult decision, that I shouldn't do this, I'm not the right person.

WB: Coming back to *Big Bear* and the question of pacing, there's no doubt that it's slow, it's slow in comparison to the average television miniseries or to most mainstream fictional filmmaking in North America. But I'm actually impressed by the way in which you didn't feel intimidated into trying to make it punchier, or make it more like something like *Canada: A People's History*. Did you strive for some kind of plainness?

GC: Yeah, I mean ... it's more what belongs to that story. I still have mixed feeling about that, I wish I could have done more as a director, given it a little more cinematic kind of style. Because it's not going to be done again, especially that one, after its fabled history in the industry. I think there's also a responsibility, especially with a historical figure like that, whose story hasn't been told in detail, or well enough, or with enough complexity for who that man really was. So I regret that, although I'm very proud of the miniseries, I'm very glad we did it, the way it is, with its pacing, or whatever else. But for whatever reason, that's what we did, as a group. But it's because of what we owe to that man, and those people, we have to tell their stories like that. I mean, it's not going to be done again. There may be a number of different versions of films on Robin Hood or whatever, but there's not going to be another Big Bear film made. So I wish it could have been more for that. I mean, the editor initially hated, *hated* the footage, and fuck, we had a big argument, and he forced the issue, and I didn't want to see it again in my life, and I wanted to quit ... but eventually he connected to something about it, and was on board one hundred percent.

WB: Can you tell us something about the reception of *Big Bear*?

GC: Well, I didn't get too much when it was broadcast. There was a terrible review, some good reviews ... probably sixty–forty, sixty negative. Especially this guy here, the *Edmonton Journal* guy. Vicious. From my point of view, you could hear him, a kind of happiness ... Did you not see it?

WB: [*laughter*] No, was it written in blood?

GC: Yeah, and there was some feedback on the language issue, some people really got it. Beyond that, not a whole lot.

WB: Do you feel some regret, not so much that you didn't get good reviews, but that there were people you didn't reach?

GC: Well, the story is meant for people. So if it didn't reach across to people, and if it didn't involve and engage people, more than it did ...

JW: Was it shown anywhere else, besides on television?

GC: It was shown at Sundance.

JW: The whole thing was shown at Sundance?

GC: Yeah.

JW: Was there much audience discussion?

GC: There was. There were two showings. The first showing was pretty good, a good discussion afterwards. The second showing was at night, and I noticed in the break between part one and part two a lot of people left. But again, for those who stayed, there was a good discussion afterwards, a real good discussion.

JW: Have you shown other stuff at Sundance?

GC: Once, I didn't go, it was four directors, *Borders*.

JW: I'm just curious, because I know Sundance has this Native Forum, and I'm interested in that aspect of Sundance, which has now become totally commercialized. But it seems to me that the Native Forum is the last gasp of the old United States Film Festival [Sundance's name until 1992]. And it's interesting that you should show *Big Bear* there, because it's made for TV, narrative, semi-commercial, something Sundance would really want to show. I mean, I can hear the Sundance programmers saying to themselves, at last!

Here's something that's not weird and didactic that we can show at the Native Forum. [*everyone laughs*] And then they get it, and they show it, and it turns out that it's not what they intended at all, that it's slow and odd. So I think there's a kind of tension in *Big Bear* that's similar to the kind of tensions that Sundance has been experiencing.

GC: Well, I don't really follow careers and I'm not very tuned into the festivals. I mean, I go to Banff [Television Festival], but I didn't know much about Sundance. The year that they invited *Borders* to go, I could have gone, but I didn't really want to go, it seemed like a lot of hoo-hah. So I knew very little about the festival when I went, but I appreciated very much the opportunity to take it there. And I think the Native Forum is a sincere thing. I mean, I had a little bit of radar up, what is this, is this some kind of "let's help our brown brothers" thing. But it was a very sincere effort.

WB: Question of language in *Big Bear*. Obviously there are lots of ironies that the Natives speak English and the whites speak gobbledygook.

GC: Well, that's Rudy, basically [the non-language spoken by the white people is also in Rudy Wiebe's book *The Temptations of Big Bear*, upon which the film is based]. I mean, we don't want four hours of subtitles, we don't want a voice-over, so what are you gonna do? And Rudy started on that track too, and came up with this jabberwocky. I mean, it's a structured language, it's not gobbledygook. What we wanted to do was we wanted the audience to be on the Cree side, to see this from the Cree point of view. We wanted them to feel that these guys were the foreigners, these guys were the contributors.

JW: Yeah, I was wondering why the English guys didn't speak Cree. I mean, Bill has a little bit of German, and when we were watching this he could pick out little bits of what the white guys were saying. That wouldn't really be the case for a Cree guy encountering English for the first time. Why didn't you just switch it, so the Cree guys speak English and the English guys speak Cree?

GC: Well, I think it would have been strange for Cree-speaking people! I mean, of course there's a lot of German influence there, but it had to be a completely new language.

JW: You followed the book really closely?

GC: Yeah, we did.

WB: There's one more film we'd like to ask you about, which is *Our Home and Native Land*. Can you say something about how you had the opportunity to be involved with the whole constitutional thing? Had you met Ovide Mercredi before? What was the background there?

GC: Well, after *Foster Child*, I was called by a producer in London, who had been in Banff the year before and had seen or heard about *Foster Child*. He was from Alberta and wanted to make a film in Canada, about a Native subject. So he called me, and we started developing a documentary, pretty simple stuff. We were going to do profiles of Native leaders. We took it to Banff, and Global Television stood up there. But Telefilm hated it, because they thought it really wasn't anything. They said look, you've got this opportunity to make a film, why don't you make something about what's really going on? That was 1992, when the constitutional negotiations were getting underway, and we re-oriented it, making it about investigating aboriginal participation in constitutional questions. So we approached BBC, and BBC has a series called *Fine Cuts*, a series of documentaries from around the world. And they thought, well, as long as it's about Canadian Indians, they didn't care what it was about. I mean, we didn't want it to be a series of news clips, it had to have a heart.

WB: Well, I think it comes over in a natural way. You've got a combination of a document about a set of circumstances regarding Native people's history in the country and where they're positioned now, and then the very specific, basically trailing Ovide Mercredi around and getting into a lot of really interesting situations. Did you think of it as being addressed to people outside of Canada?

GC: Well, yes. And I resisted having the first five minutes do the kind of background history in a very quick way. But that was necessary to do for that audience; I thought it was unnecessary or boring for a Canadian audience.

WB: Well, maybe for a Canadian audience who watches the CBC.

JW: Was it broadcast in Canada at all?

GC: Well, Global Television. They insisted on three versions, the original was 86-something, they wanted a 70-something version, and then they wanted a 48-minute version. And I think they ran the 48-minute version.

WB: Were you conscious of having to put things in a particular way for a non-Canadian audience?

GC: Just the beginning, to give the background.

WB: What was it like to follow a subject like that? Did you get attached to Ovide Mercredi as you sort of trailed him around?

GC: Well, it wasn't easy, it wasn't like we had carte blanche. We often had to beg and be patient to get access, or to get information from the media liaison. I mean, something would be going on and they wouldn't let us know until the last minute. There was one time when he was doing an interview with the *New York Times*, and he was very dynamic, and this guy from the *New York Times*, he doesn't know anything, so Ovide was giving him a lot of background, a lot of context. And thought, ah ha, that's what I should do, because if I'm just sitting there talking to him, he won't go as far as I want him to go. So Christian Langler in London, he knew a journalist with the *Manchester Guardian* who was stationed in London, and we arranged for this guy to come and interview Ovide. And that's how we got old Uncle Joe too, because all this time we were after Joe Clark too. So we arranged this interview between Ovide and the *Manchester Guardian* in Ottawa, we flew the guy out from Washington. But Ovide got delayed in Saskatchewan. He wasn't going to be back for a couple of days, and the guy had to go back to Washington. So we got drunk in the bar that night, and the next morning, eight o'clock, Joe's press secretary called up, and said OK, you're on, this morning, 9:30. I don't think Joe knew who I was, but he was a real sweetheart. So finally, in Vancouver, we arranged this again. And the guy, anyway, he interviewed Ovide about his former wife and kids, and there were all these stories about his former wife, and that was it, Ovide was mad, the interview's over, stormed out, and it took a little while to repair that. But we did. I mean, maybe I was shirking my responsibility, getting somebody out here to interview him. And I think he knew that, and I think he said something like that, really it should have been between me and him, and not some guy from the *Manchester Guardian* [*laughs*].

WB: Can you tell us something about your current project?

GC: Well, it's a documentary with the Film Board, with the aboriginal program. It's about the repatriation of a totem pole from Sweden, a Hailsa pole, from the Kitimat area. The pole was taken without real consent by the Swedish consul in the 1920s. It was located in Sweden about ten years ago, and it will be returned, but there are conditions. One of the things they offered was to carve a replacement pole, so we've been documenting that. The replacement pole is in Stockholm now, sort of lying in wait, beside the original pole. And then next summer, when the original pole comes home, the museum there wants a museum here built to house it. But the natural thing is that it just stays outside, and goes back to the earth when its time comes. But they're having to deal with raising money to deal with what will become a cultural thing. So hopefully something's going to happen there. I don't know that they'll raise six million dollars to build a cultural centre, but certainly it's going to come back as planned next summer. And I'm working on a History Channel series of one-hour dramas on chiefs—I did Poundmaker. And later I'll start another one on Joseph Brandt. Because when they approached me a few years ago, I wasn't so interested in doing what I believed were the American chiefs. I mean, of course I know the border doesn't matter, I know all that, but still in public perception, we've got ours, our own stories to tell. And everyone's heard about Geronimo and Sitting Bull and those guys, but nobody's heard of Poundmaker or Big Bear.

Alanis Obomsawin, Documentary Form, and the Canadian Nation(s)

Jerry White

WHY, ONE MIGHT REASONABLY ASK, are Alanis Obomsawin's films so important? Isn't she just an old National Film Board hand, making straightforward, sometimes pedagogical documentaries, most of which will wind up in schools and public libraries? Indeed she is, and that's precisely why her work is among the most vibrant and organically political in Canadian cinema. She is a true social filmmaker: in an age where the NFB is abandoning its traditional mission in favour of commercial film models and independent Canadian cinema looks more and more to the derivative, self-indulgent trust-fund filmmaking of the United States for inspiration, Obomsawin remains a model of commitment.

Obomsawin's films have an ambiguous relationship with the aesthetics and ideology of that most Canadian of genres, the documentary film. Formally, they appear quite utilitarian, eschewing either Errol Morris-esque flourishes or the studied objectivity of direct cinema. Ideologically, her work seems to be something of a corrective to the National Film Board of Canada's exclusion of Native subjectivity, a rejection of the Canadian film/Cinéma québécois split that has marked film north of the forty-ninth parallel. And yet, there is also a way in which Obomsawin's films embody the very essence of a Griersonian ethic of filmmaking,[1] an ethic that has been enunciated cinematically both in French and English but that has infrequently realized its promises. Further, especially in her most famous film, *Kanehsatake: 270 Years of Resistance*, Obomsawin offers a substantial, biting critique of the way in which nationhood is defined, an especially important point of dissent in a country like Canada, which prides itself on the looseness and diversity of its national identity. Overall, these are complex, critical works, which balance the needs of a utilitarian, educational cinema with the larger political project of Native self-determination; and this balance of priorities, both totally removed from a production/consumption idea of cinema, constitutes a radically revisionist film practice.

That Obomsawin's films engage so directly in a dialogue with the National Film Board (NFB) idea of filmmaking is hardly surprising give her status as staff director there. But it is also important to understand how she came to that job. In 1967, she was working as an activist in several native communities in Québec and was hired as a consultant to an NFB-produced film about just this kind of organizing. She found she liked the experience, and began making NFB filmstrips about Native life for schoolkids, eventually learning 16-mm production and moving into her own documentary film projects. She was already well known as a singer, songwriter, poet, and storyteller, and the move into filmmaking was easy for her, a new way to pursue her ongoing work. Further, the educational work in which she had been engaged as an activist could clearly be continued through her interest in filmmaking. This kind of educational work, she says, "was to reach the children and the students at the university level to talk about and tell our history and our own stories. When I was asked to come to the Film Board it was really for the same reason."[2] For Obomsawin, there is no meaningful distinction between her lives as a performer, activist, and filmmaker: they are part of the same lifelong project.

It may seem somewhat perverse to embark on an analysis of so oppositional a filmmaker as Obomsawin along Griersonian lines, given the disrepute into which his legacy has recently fallen. There has been no shortage of critiques of Grierson in recent years,[3] most of which locate him and his institutional legacy as solidly neo-conservative. Nevertheless, he enunciated very clearly, and at a very early stage in Canada's film history, an ethic that emphasized a distinctly non-commercial character for an emergent Canadian national cinema. This legacy—or, more accurately, the tragically unfulfilled possibility of what Grierson wanted to accomplish—hangs heavy over the NFB. The idealism the legacy represents must not be ignored because Grierson himself too often veered into the realm of the technocrat or élitist. The way in which he and the institutions he put in place sought to redefine the role film plays in its viewers' lives has not been forgotten by many documentarians, least of all by Obomsawin. Grierson writes, "The non-theatrical audience is today being organized on a vast scale in all progressive countries ... It represents a revolution in the film industry."[4] Cinematically, Obomsawin is a child of this revolution, having adopted a decidedly non-theatrical exhibition practice.

Indeed, both Grierson and Obomsawin clearly agree with Chuck Kleinhans' belief that "[u]nderstanding documentary as 'complete' only when seen and reacted to shifts the maker's goals from producing a perfect, whole, comprehensive work to producing a work with new values and new designs, which will make it viable, interesting and educational for a longer time."[5] Such practice was important to Grierson, and he writes approvingly that "[w]herever people are gathered together in the name of a specialized professional or social or civic or educational interest, there you have a ready-made audience for films which are devoted to their needs and interests."[6] A film's ability to meet specific social needs and affect people's lives was just as important to Grierson as any concerns about production values. Obomsawin echoes this desire for the film to have a non-theatrical life when she notes that

I was very pleased when the Alberta government bought the rights for the film [*Richard Cardinal: Cry from the Diary of a Métis Child*]. Many social workers in different departments see it now. One time I was in Edmonton for the premiere of *No Address* and a man who had been the provincial ombudsman presented me with two reports, saying that the Richard Cardinal film had helped force new policies and laws in Alberta.[7]

Speaking of changes to the welfare laws that were spurred by her film *No Address,* she notes that "[t]his is why I make these films. To go for changes."[8] This motive seems entirely consistent both with Grierson's understanding of film's possibilities to engage with civic life and with Kleinhans' insistence that a film is not finished until it is discussed and used. Obomsawin serves as a much-needed bridge between traditions of social/pedagogical and political/agitational documentary: her Griersonian sensibilities should not be downplayed simply because Grierson has fallen out of favour.

Form

Making the most of the least

> Making short films which deal with reality and are based on actual observation does not involve the same vast technical equipment, the same immense variety of skills, the same names, the same demand for big salaries. When it comes to education—and I mean education in a live and real sense which I have described—our country can be as fervent and imaginative as any other.
> —John Grierson, "A Film Policy for Canada"

One aspect of Obomsawin's cinema that quickly distinguishes it from her contemporaries' is its oddly pared-down form. Her work displays little in the way of stylistic flourish or excess, and usually features explanatory voice-overs that might remind some of dull, pedagogical (NFB?) documentaries of the 1950s. However, this apparently simple aesthetic is peppered with a pronounced subjectivity. Further, Obomsawin's work displays a tendency towards lyricism and massive narrative digressions, both techniques that shatter conventions of documentary realism. Her films should be placed in a very different cultural location than most NFB production, one that is ultimately more consistent with other aboriginal media projects than with most conventional documentary. And yet, there are even parts of this latter project that seem decidedly out of place in the Obomsawin corpus: many of her formal choices make her seem like too much of a maverick even for aboriginal media. Like her ideological concerns, Obomsawin's formal decisions are decidedly independent, refusing to parrot any predetermined formula.

Describing her style, Obomsawin has said that "I like to make it as plain as possible, so that the attention has to be on the work and what the people are saying ... I don't like to do fancy things where your attention is on other things."[9] This is especially true of her earlier work, films like *Le Patro, Le Provost* (1991) or *Poundmaker's Lodge* (1987). These portraits of institutions (*Le Patro, Le Provost* about a Montréal daycare centre, *Poundmaker's Lodge* about an alcoholic-recovery centre just outside St. Albert, Alberta) are made up mostly of images of the organizations' work accompanied by Obomsawin's explanatory voice-over, and interviews with people who run the organizations and the people who benefit from them. They look, in short, very much like countless other NFB documentaries, except they are about Native institutions run by Native people, and have Natives speaking for themselves, uninterrupted. This uninterruptedness is an especially important part of her form, because it has a way of slowing the films down. People are allowed to complete thoughts, even when they are awkwardly phrased or take a long time to get out. This minimal manipulation ends up self-consciously determining the film's pace. Even when they look straightforwardly pedagogical, Obomsawin's films break with rhetorical norms of documentary, such as focus or concision. It's clear, just as she says, that she wants your attention to be on what the people are saying: that her films feel a little slow and rambling, and formally stripped down, is a testament to how little conventional documentary really does this.

Even though she draws on a semi-minimalist form, Obomsawin's films are extremely subjective. This subjectivity is most clearly expressed by her own voice, which forms the soundtrack of almost all of her films. The voice-over is far from the voice-of-god variety that has been used to convey a false objectivity; instead, it has the effect of identifying whose eyes are seeing the action. Indeed, Peter Steven has pointed out to Obomsawin that "in all of them [her films] you are present at least in the narration, and you speak as an insider. For example, in *Poundmaker's Lodge*, you refer to 'our people,' and in *No Address* you say, 'Many of our people come to Montréal.'"[10] Her voice-overs may echo the conventions of documentary form, but their effects are the exact opposite: they assert a specific cultural identity rather than hide behind a faceless false objectivity.

No Address is an especially important example of subjectivity in Obomsawin's cinema. This film about homeless Native people in Montréal juxtaposes the stories of several men's experience with the Montréal Native Friendship Centre and the efforts on the part of a community radio station in the nearby Kahnawake to raise money for homeless relief. Obomsawin combines interviews, observational-style documentary footage (especially of the work at the radio station), and semi-documentary footage of quotidian aspects of homeless life (a lot of walking around, really). This last element is most important in terms of subjectivity: the semi-documentary sections usually have either music or Obomsawin's voice-over explaining various problems people have when they arrive in a strange city, and do very little to contribute to any kind of narrative drive (as, for example, the sections at the radio station do, most of which follow a fund drive to its conclusion). Instead, they contribute to an awareness of the filmmaker's hand, and this awareness itself helps to make clear that this is a work not simply of objective documentation but of intentional, agitational, and perhaps even propagandistic activism.

Kanehsatake: 270 Years of Resistance also makes an interesting case study in terms of subjectivity, although less so than might be expected. The film is for the most part an observational documentary, with the key players in the 1990 siege at Oka framed in long shot and hand-held camera work throughout.[11] From time to time there is an interview with one of the Native rebels, and much of the observational footage has Obomsawin's voice-over to explain and clarify, but none of this looks especially unusual from a formal point of view. Indeed, it seems an especially linear film, although the question of linearity brings some of its formal eccentricities to light.

Kanehsatake tells the story of the Oka confrontation, but it tells it *from the very beginning*, when the uprising was nothing more than a few activists blocking a dirt road, and takes it *to the very end*, with footage of the rebels being led off to jail in shackles. In between, there is an enormous amount of information, from the little arguments between the leaders of the rebels and the Canadian army units, to the details of getting food back and forth across the barricades. This level of exactitude is itself exceptional, especially given the superficial and visceral way the uprising was covered by the mainstream Canadian and Québec press. What is especially interesting from a formal point of view, though, is the way Obomsawin organizes this information. While she never abandons a sense of linearity (we learn about logistical problems with food, for instance, towards the end of the film, when the siege has begun to drag on and food becomes more of an issue), she peppers the film with fairly disruptive digressions, which she deems necessary to gain a full understanding of the problem. The most striking example of this comes when she is describing the negotiations taking place at a Trappist monastery: as some helicopters land behind a Sulpician church she notes on the voice-over that "270 years ago, this is where the trouble began," and proceeds with an illustrated, educational-film-style history lesson about French colonialism in this area and how so many of the problems of colonialism anticipate the current situation. It is a startling sequence, given the way it disrupts the linear flow of events and changes the aesthetic from hand-held, mostly observational documentary to animated, pedagogical explanation. Like the subjective elements of her other films, though, this section calls attention to the hand of the filmmaker, lest a viewer be lulled by the naturalistic, sometimes jumpy documentary aesthetic that predominates.

Gilles Marsolais takes Obomsawin to task for this sequence, among many other parts of the film, and while his critique is interesting in some ways, it misses what is so important about this moment. Writing in the second edition of his classic survey of documentary cinema *L'Aventure du cinéma direct revisitée*, he asserts that when Obomsawin turns to historical contextualization,

> Unfortunately, the analysis becomes short and spills into gross simplification in the way it short-circuits the historical periods and omits important, inglorious armed confrontations like the Lachine massacre and the genocide of the Huron nation. This is not the place to do a history course, but historians and anthropologists who are experts in this matter contest the validity of the territorial claims that have lately been made on Québec territory by Mohawks, who live on former Algonquin territory![12]

Indeed, this is not the place to enter into a history lesson, so it seems strange that Marsolais both disputes Obomsawin's version of history and fails to cite the names of "des historiens et des anthropologues experts en la matière" (he cites only a book about the Oka crisis by Robin Philipot). Leaving that aside for the time being, what seems most problematic about this line of argument is that it fails to recognize Obomsawin's entry into an area where the historical record remains highly disputed, an approach with a decidedly polemical and partisan interpretation. This is why Marsolais' failure to cite the specific historians is such a problem: in assessing the argument of Obomsawin's factuality, it would be helpful to know who her opponents are and what ideological positions they occupy. Obomsawin's ideological position is clear, and that clarity is a central part of what makes her arguments, "biased" though they may be, readable by a critical, engaged audience (as opposed to a passive audience willing to consume expert opinion wholesale, an audience Marsolais seems to assume).

This question of historical objectivity points to a larger complaint about the failure of the film to conform to a certain model of direct cinema. Marsolais summarizes his gripe against the film by writing that "Obomsawin's simplistic and demagogic approach solidifies the spectator in their prejudices, especially in the case of Québec, which is actually ahead of Canada in terms of recognizing the rights of Amerindians."[13] This is not the place to enter into a debate about the policy of Québec towards Natives: suffice it to say that the matter of Québec's policies towards Natives seems a questionable line of inquiry, since these policy matters are, by the nature of most relevant treaties, a federal matter. The real problem with this critique is that it has no teeth: *Kanehsatake* is a partisan film, and to say that it confirms the spectator's prejudices is akin to saying that the Griersonian classic *Night Mail* confirms the spectator's British patriotism. It's true, but it's not really the point. Obomsawin has said that the most important part of her making *Kanehsatake* was that "there had to be a document that came from us ... That was crucial."[14] Less than an attempt to be the definitive voice, *Kanehsatake* was a distinct voice, one among many, and one that, finally, would allow the people under siege and their compatriots to give their side of the story. Going so far as to call the film's approach demagogic shows a lack of clear understanding of the uses to which Obomsawin's subjective voice is put.

Perhaps the clearest example of subjective voice in Obomsawin's cinema is *Richard Cardinal: Cry from the Diary of a Métis Child* (1986). This film follows the story of a boy who, after being separated from his family to go into a series of horrible foster homes, commits suicide. Here

Obomsawin combines interview footage with re-enacted sequences, using actor Cory Swan to play the part of Richard Cardinal. The dramatic sequences are themselves fairly minimal and mostly lyrical (e.g., Richard playing in the woods, sitting at home), but are nevertheless striking for their violation of the codes of documentary realism. Further, the film's enormous emotional impact represents an important violation of objectivity: Obomsawin makes it quite clear, both in her choices of which interviews to include in the film and more explicitly in her voice-over, that this was a horrible tragedy that could have been prevented. It is also a self-conscious work of activism, and its activist character is perhaps best proven by the fact that the furor caused by its release was instrumental in the reform of Alberta's child welfare laws in the 1980s. This furor, however, can be at least partially ascribed to the filmmaker's formal choices: through the re-enacted sections, she gives the film the emotional impact of melodrama, an impact that, unlike the monological representation typical of Hollywood, she tempers with long sections of interview and voice-over, which attempt to provide some deep context for the emotion. This balance between clear, detailed understanding and emotional force is perhaps *the* characterizing feature of Obomsawin's aesthetic.

The meanings of the word *aesthetic* have been the subject of fierce debate in aboriginal media circles, as many activists have found film and video a useful tool in organizing, even though they may remain uninterested in more strictly formal matters. This debate itself echoes a Griersonian idea of production, given that many aboriginal media groups seem to focus on forms that privilege that Griersonian favourite, education. Further, a good deal of aboriginal media work has focussed on training people to make their own films and video by way of countering imposed representations of their lives (this is especially true of Native film and video in Canada's far north). There is certainly a way in which Obomsawin's didactic, pedagogical, and utilitarian form could be ascribed to her declarations that her aspirations are primarily educational, as opposed to aesthetic. Faye Ginsburg has summarized these points, writing about Australian aboriginal media that

> in order to open a new 'discursive space' for indigenous media that respects and understands them on their own terms, it is important to attend to the *process* of production and reception. Analysis needs to focus less on the formal qualities of film and video and more on the cultural *mediations* that occur through film and video works.[15]

Applied to Obomsawin's work, such an interpretive strategy might focus on her insistence on showing these films at public meetings and in Native communities as a stimulus to discussion; on her use of subjectivity to present a Native voice; and on her non-intrusive interview style, which allows Native people to speak clearly and at length. All of these aesthetic qualities may be violations of convention, but they make perfect sense in the context of an ongoing project to record, explain, and indeed mediate Native Canadian culture.

And yet, like understanding early NFB films (such as those of the equally celebrated and criticized B unit) solely as works of nation-building education or propaganda, there is something about this kind of analysis that feels incomplete when applied to Obomsawin's work. Many of her films, especially *Richard Cardinal* and her contributions to the *Canada Vignettes* series (a group of one-minute films that portray various aspects of quotidian Native life), display a pronounced lyrical sensibility that is at odds with a strictly pedagogical function and is closer to developments in recent experimental documentary, particularly the group of films that Bill

Nichols has identified as "performative documentary." He sums up this genre as one that "stress[es] subjective aspects of a classically objective discourse."[16] It is important to acknowledge that Nichols' examples for this form are primarily avant-garde films (such as Marlon Riggs' *Tongues Untied* or Trinh Minh-ha's *Surname Viet, Given Name Nam*), films that seem to be much more formally adventurous than Obomsawin's work. However, we can see in Obomsawin's films a refusal to acknowledge where the "documentation" ends and the "recreation" or "agitation" begins. This blurriness is on display in films as different as *Kanehsatake* (which sometimes features candid-eye moments followed by images with Obomsawin's passionate voice-over) and *No Address* (which features obviously staged moments of people hanging around the streets with actual homeless men, whom we have seen earlier in the film, on the voice-over).

The clearest illustration of Obomsawin's non-narrative, elliptical documentary ethic is visible in the films that came out of *Kanehsatake*. Obomsawin shot hundreds of hours of footage for this film, and of course found herself unable to use it all and therefore unable to tell all the stories that interested her.[17] She partially solved this problem by making two more short features, each about fifty minutes. *My Name Is Kahentiiosta* (1996) and *Spudwrench: Kahnawake Man* (1997) are both fairly in-depth portraits of Oka rebels whom we come to know in *Kanehsatake*.

Kahentiiosta is about a woman who, when she was arrested, gave her name as Kahentiiosta instead of the "Canadian name" demanded by the court. She was detained several extra days as a result. Obomsawin mixes documentary footage, interviews, court drawings, and children's drawings (a device she also used in her 1971 film *Christmas at Moose Factory*) to describe the prejudices and injustices of Canada's legal system.

Spudwrench is a very different film, diverging considerably from the topic of the Oka uprising. It is a portrait of Randy Horne (whose code name during the uprising was Spudwrench), who lives in Kahnawake, Québec as an ironworker on high bridges and buildings. The film ends up being more about the ironworking profession (practised by many Native men for several generations) and the activism and community organizing that take place as a matter of everyday life in Kahnawake. Obomsawin said she

> wanted to show more people from the community, but also I wanted to show the contribution those people have made for so many generations in terms of building bridges and buildings all around the world. It really is an important thing, since they've been at it since 1867![18]

This does not have very much to do with Oka as such, and indeed the uprising is mentioned only at the end of the film, almost in an offhand way. It was our land, Horne says, and sure, I'd do it again. Rather than a simple explanation of part of the Oka crisis, which would still be part of an essentially linear/narrative documentary form, *Spudwrench* is a complete digression from that topic but linked to *Kanehsatake*. It is an almost autonomous, non-narrative portrait of a community, a portrait sketched through the experiences of one man (which happen to include the Oka uprising); following Nichols, it stresses subjective aspects of a classically objective discourse.

Perhaps the central point of contact between Nichols and Obomsawin can be seen through a third party: French ethnographic filmmaker Jean Rouch. In discussing performative documentary, Nichols insists on the centrality of "[t]he ethnopoetics of Jean Rouch, who has consistently argued for, and embodied, a style of filmmaking that does not so much combine the subjective and objective poles of traditional ethnography as sublate them into a distinct form."[19] This distinct form that Rouch sets down could be reasonably described in the terms I have earlier used for Obomsawin: a balance between clear, detailed understanding and emotional force. A key example of this is Rouch's 1960 classic *Chronicle of a Summer*, in which he applies cine-ethnographic methods to his own community, Paris, and then shows the footage to those whom he recorded, getting their feelings about how they were represented. Obomsawin, like Rouch, wants to involve her participants in the making of the documentary, and in both filmmakers' oeuvres, the subjectivity of both filmmaker *and* subjects is centralized. This has the effect of blurring the differences between the two, complicating notions of authorship, and finally emerging as a deeply hybridized form, a form that seems equally at home and out of place in both the universe of the NFB and the world of aboriginal media (a sociocultural world that is not all that far from the NFB, given its concern with social utility and low-budget production).

Even though Obomsawin's films seem formally simple and straightforward, they represent a significant transformation of documentary aesthetics, although still essentially within the framework of a Griersonian idea of form. She takes what she finds valuable from the Canadian tradition of documentary (low-budget production, fusion of as opposed to choice between interviews, observational techniques, and voice-over) and adds what she needs for her activist project (emphasis that this is *her* speaking in the voice-over, that these films are foremost for "our people," secure in the knowledge of who that is). The mixture of forms associated with such contradictory impulses as nation-building and activism/agitation looks a little strange on first glance. But when the films are considered together, and in the context of Obomsawin's activist priority, the sheer consistency of her aesthetic mixture makes it clear that these films occupy a complex social and cultural space.

Ideology

Qu'est-ce qu'un nation?

... every year we make hundred of short films which describe the life of the nation. They describe Canada's achievements in industry and agriculture. They go into the various problems of finance and housing and labour and nutrition and child welfare. They progressively cover the whole field of civic interest: what Canadians need to know and think about if they are going to do best by Canada and by themselves.
　　—John Grierson, "A Film Policy for Canada."

Obomsawin's contribution to an analysis of Canadian nationhood is just as important as her transformation of the Canadian documentary tradition. All of her films, on a certain level, communicate an interest in working towards cohesive First Nations, as we have seen through her use of terms like "our people" in voice-overs. However, her two films that deal with confrontations with governmental forces, *Incident at Restigouche* (1984) and *Kanehsatake*, offer radical critiques of the way nationhood has been constructed by Canadian and Québec society. This critical voice is entirely organic with her hybridized documentary form: Obomsawin is not rejecting the concept of nation *per se*, but is instead insisting that *her* nation is just as legitimate and deserving of self-determination as the Canadian or Québec nations.

Benedict Anderson has famously defined a nation as an "imagined community," and this image of imagining tells us a great deal about the way Obomsawin constructs her Native community. Her films contribute, in a way that very few other films have, to an *image* of "a deep, horizontal comradeship."[20] This kind of comradeship is visualized both through the familiarity her voice-overs imply and in the way she frames her analysis. She works not through class or gender analysis, or even through a truly ethnic analysis (for she has very little to say about similar problems faced by other non-members of Canada's white élite), but instead looks at a specific ethnic group in every film. *No Address* and *Richard Cardinal* are much more about the specifics of the Native situation than they are about the way the society of the oppressor deals with its oppressed. A crucial part of the analysis of the problem in *No Address* is that many of the people who become homeless wind up that way because the shock of coming from a small, tightly knit Native community to a huge, impersonal city is overwhelming. Similarly, *Richard Cardinal*'s tragic energy comes mostly from the fact that a young boy was forcefully placed in a foster home, a life utterly alien to him. This is a part of the Canadian experience that is reasonably identified as specific to the Native community, and would not support an analysis that centralizes class or gender. Because they deal with situations that centralize the experience of a specific group of people (whose similarities may or may not be imagined, *pace* Anderson), Obomsawin's films have the thematic consistency of a national cinema. Denise Pérusse's insight that Obomsawin "makes known the customs and traditions of aboriginals, gives voice to them and puts an Amerindian gaze onto her times"[21] is arguably what distinguishes her as a filmmaker interested in constructing a nation: through a set of common signs and situations, Obomsawin makes it clear whom she is speaking about. Her films are about Natives' place in North America, in much the same way that Grierson makes it clear that his NFB will "describe Canada's place in the world."[22]

That said, what has brought Obomsawin the widest attention is her challenge to the dominant national structures, a challenge she first launched with *Incident at Restigouche*. This film follows the confrontation in 1981 between Mic'Mac warriors and the Sûreté du Québec over fishing rights. Much of the film is made up of footage of the blockades and confrontations (some of which is cut to fast-paced French folk music about the stand-off), although Obomsawin regularly breaks from this narrative momentum to show a long interview she did with Québec's Fisheries Minister. At one point, she aggressively challenges his narrow view of who has self-determination on this land, and she makes it clear that this blindness to Native sovereignty is a major problem for the separatist Parti Québécois, at that time in power and so responsible for sending in the SQ to raid what they perceived to be illegal fishing. This tense interview, rightly famous, serves as a schema for her view of the problems of the dominant nationalisms of Canada: both in Québec and in Canada, even when the concept of nation and self-determination is at the forefront of political discussion (as it certainly was in 1981, and as it always is for the PQ), the right of aboriginal people to self-determination is beyond the scope of the discourse.

This schema is given fuller realization in *Kanehsatake*, a film whose analysis is based in an illustration that much of the conflict was about different ideas of nationhood. For example, the film contains footage of a Mexican native trying to perform a ritual on one of the tanks. Obomsawin makes it clear that many of the people who came to Oka to support the rebels were from the United States. In this context, a shot of an American flag with a Native's face emblazoned upon it, a flag displayed at one of the camps for Oka supporters, takes on a very different meaning than in a conventionally "Canadian" context. For Obomsawin and those who were there supporting the rebels, it is a symbol of solidarity and pan-nationalism, as opposed to imperialism. Further, she shows an interview with Brian Mulroney, who scoffs that some of the troublemakers at Oka "are not even Canadian citizens." Including this shot has the effect of making Mulroney seem arrogant in the extreme, clearly someone who does not understand anything except the most narrow view of nation. Obomsawin also shows images of people who, resisting the brutal and often totalitarian treatment by the SQ , yell out that this shouldn't be happening here because "this is Canada!" Obomsawin shows that the violent conflict between differing definitions of "Canada" proves that the federalist myth of many nations peacefully co-existing in a benevolent Canadian state is indeed an illusion, one that can come violently unravelled given the right conditions.

That this film is a critique of *federalism* seems to me crucial: this is not always a shared assessment. Indeed, when my (mostly western Canadian) students watch *Kanehsatake*, their responses tend to run along the lines of "those nasty Québécois, they want sovereignty for themselves but not for the aboriginals; they are indeed the small-minded hypocrites we always suspected they were." There are many problems with this analysis, of course, but the primary one is that the government in power during the Oka crisis was not the PQ but the Liberals. The provincial leader who presides over the madness was not sovereigntist Jacques Parizeau but that grand old man of Québec federalism, Robert Bourassa. To say the least, this throws a wrench into the argument that this is a critique of Québec separatism (which is certainly not to say that Obomsawin isn't critical of that movement, since she castigates the PQ Fisheries Minister in *Incident at Restigouche*). Indeed, it is all too easy for English Canadians to read the film as such; understanding the film as an angry, powerful critique of the supposed solution to Québec separatism is a bitter pill to swallow.

Obomsawin continues this complication of nationhood, although in a more subtle and less fiery way, in *Spudwrench: Kahnawake Man*. The film is a detailed portrait of the ironworking trade, and Obomsawin explains at length how the jobs took these men all over Québec, Canada, and the United States. It is clear that the national identity of the people in this trade, like most of the people in Kahnawake, has little to do with any of these imagined communities. Instead, the people hold a somewhat unconventional (by English-Canadian or Québec standards) but still fully realized sense of community that can be reasonably understood as national self. Obomsawin illustrates this concept by considerable documentation of how the social fabric of Kahnawake is centred around keeping Native traditions alive and relevant. Although a fairly impressionistic, often lyrical portrait, *Spudwrench* offers just as revisionist an idea of nationhood as does *Incident at Restigouche* or *Kanehsatake*.

Following Grierson, it seems reasonable to say that Obomsawin makes films about the life of the nation. His belief that films should illustrate "what Canadians need to know and think about if they are going to do best by Canada and by themselves" is a fair summary of her project; she just has a different idea of what "Canada" is. Her films complicate the national self, and in so forcefully putting forth an imagining of a different kind of nation and demanding that it be given an equal place at the table, she disrupts some basic assumptions about Canadian life.

Grierson, Our Contemporary

Understanding Obomsawin as a seminal Griersonian filmmaker presents a delicious irony. She clearly shares his ideas about a socially useful cinema, and her practices have illustrated this idealism better than just about any other NFB production. Her films are as formally didactic and polemical as any Griersonian-era film on either side of the Atlantic: *No Address* shares a great deal with the EMB documentary *Drifters* (1929), and a fascination with industrial practices and national life can be seen in both in *Industrial Britain* (1932) and *Spudwrench*. Where she differs from Grierson's conservative view of nation is obvious, though, and her passionate advocacy of Native self-determination would have certainly troubled the respectable Scotsman. Nevertheless,

it seems imprudent to throw out the Griersonian baby with the bathwater: Grierson has his ideological problems, but he contributed a great deal to the definition of Canadian film along the line of
social rather than commercial practice. It is this definition that has allowed Obomsawin to make
her decidedly non-commercial films and remain secure at the NFB; and however else Griersonian
idealism may have failed to materialize, she serves as a potent realization of its possibilities.

Notes

1   John Grierson was the first head of the National Film Board and former head of the film units of the UK's
    Empire Marketing Board (EMB) and the General Post Office (GPO). One of his first statements on the
    possibilities of Canadian film was a manifesto called "A Film Policy for Canada," liberally quoted in this article,
    originally published in the 15 June 1944 issue of *Canadian Affairs* and reprinted in Douglas Fetherling, ed.
    Documents in Canadian Film (Peterborough: Broadview Press, 1986).

2   Interview with author, 18 February 1997.

3   See, for example, Joyce Nelson, *The Colonized Eye: Rethinking the Grierson Legend* (Toronto: Between the Lines,
    1988); Scott Forsyth, "The Failures of Nationalism and Documentary: *Grierson and Gouzenko*," *Canadian
    Journal of Film Studies* 1, no. 1 (1990); Peter Morris, "Re-thinking Grierson: The Ideology of John Grierson," in
    Dialogue: Cinema canadien et québécois/Canadian and Québec Cinema, Pierre Véronneau, Michael Dorland, and
    Seth Feldman, eds. (Montréal: Mediatexte/Cinématheque Québécois, 1986), 21–56; or Sandra Gathercole,
    "The Best Film Policy This Country Never Had," in *Take Two: A Tribute to Film in Canada*, Seth Feldman, ed.
    (Toronto: Irwin, 1984), 36–46.

4   In Fetherling, 63.

5   Chuck Kleinhans, "Forms, Politics, Makers, and Contexts: Basic Issues for a Theory of Radical Political
    Documentary," in *"Show Us Life": Towards a History and Aesthetics of the Committed Documentary*, Thomas
    Waugh, ed. (Metuchen: Scarecrow Press, 1984), 336.

6   In Fetherling, 62–63.

7   Peter Steven, *Brink of Reality: New Canadian Documentary Film and Video* (Toronto: Between the Lines, 1993),
    182.

8   Steven, *Brink of Reality*, 185.

9   Interview with author, 18 February 1997.

10 Steven, *Brink of Reality*, 184.

11 The Oka uprising occurred when Natives from Kanehsatake and neighbouring Native communities blocked a
    road in protest of a plans to build a golf course on sacred land. The conflict gradually escalated, with the
    Native protesters eventually taking up arms and the Canadian Army being called in. It concluded after a 78-
    day siege.

12 "Malheureusement, l'analyse tourne court et verse dans la simplification grossière en court-circuitant les
    époques et en omettant des faits d'armes importantes et peu glorieux, comme le massacre de Lachine et le
    génocide de la nation huronne. Ce n'est pas le lieu ici de faire un cours d'histoire, mais des historiens et des
    anthropologues experts en la matière contestent le bien-fondé des revindications territoriales des Mowhawks
    qui se sont établis tardivement sur le territoire québécois et qui habiteraient sur d'anciens territoires ...
    algonquins!" Gilles Marsolais, *L'Aventure du cinéma direct revisitée* (Laval: Les 400 Coups, 1997), 292–93. This
    translation is mine, as are all that follow.

13 "Cette approche simpliste et démagogique d'Obomsawin confirme le spectateur dans ses préjugés,
    notamment à l'endroit de Québec, alors que celui-ci est plutôt à l'avant garde au Canada pour la reconnais-
    sance des droits des Amérindiens" (Marsolais, *L'Aventure du cinéma direct revisitée*, 293).

14 Interview with author, 18 February 1997.

15 Faye Ginsburg, "Mediating Culture: Indigenous Media, Ethnographic Film, and the Production of Identity," in *Fields of Vision: Essays in Film Studies, Visual Anthropology and Photography*, Leslie Devereaux and Roger Hillman, eds. (Berkeley: University of California Press, 1996), 259.

16 Bill Nichols, *Blurred Boundaries: Questions of Meaning in Contemporary Culture* (Bloomington: Indiana University Press, 1994), 95.

17 A big part of the reason she was able to film so much footage is because the NFB allowed her almost unlimited amounts of film stock, a fairly unusual situation in documentary filmmaking. Because she has been allowed these kinds of resources, she always speaks well of the NFB, noting that "it's really the only place where you can make the type of films that I do. It would be pretty hard in the private sector to make these kinds of films" (18 February interview with author).

18 Interview with author, 12 January 1998.

19 Nichols, *Blurred Boundaries*, 103.

20 Benedict Anderson, *Imagined Communities* (London: Verso, 1991), 7.

21 "Elle fait connaître les coutumes et traditions des autochones, donne la parole aux siens et pose un regard amérindien sur son temps." Denise Pérusse, "Alanis Obomsawin," in *Le dictionnaire du cinéma québécois*, Michel Coulombe and Marcel Jean, eds. (Montréal: Boreal, 1991), 400.

22 In Fetherling, 64.

Uncommon Visions
The Films of Loretta Todd
Jason Silverman

ON A SNOWY NIGHT, when Loretta Todd was six or seven years old, she found herself alone in a motel room. Her mother had taken her and her sisters away from home during a family crisis, and then left to deal with the situation. Loretta's older sisters soon left as well. With her younger sisters asleep, Loretta turned to the television for solace. F.W. Murnau's horror classic *Nosferatu* was just beginning.

> There I was, alone at ten or eleven o'clock at night. It was terrifying for me. I couldn't move—you know how you are as a kid, too scared to even change the channel. But I was also drawn to the film, because it was so beautiful. At some point, I was shaken out of my fear by a sound outside. I pulled the curtains back, hoping somebody was there. By then, the blizzard had lifted, and there was a full moon, casting eerie shadows on the snowdrifts. At the same time, the TV was reflected in the window. In that moment, my fear abated. I saw the shadow of the film—I recognized the film as a product of light, as a shadow, in the same way the moon cast shadows on the snow. From that moment on, I was able to watch films for their craft, in a more detached way. I don't think I said, Ah ha! I'll be a filmmaker! But somehow, I began to understand that filmmakers used the tools of storytellers, which appealed to my Cree love of craft. And I also realized that filmmakers can make people feel things.[1]

That childhood incident illuminates some important aspects of Todd's career. As a young girl, she already had begun to understand the complex relationship between images, emotion, and craft, a relationship that would deeply inform her films. Like the girl in the hotel room, she refuses to indulge in self-pity or victimhood, instead drawing power from the resilience and creativity of individuals. And the recognition that occurred to the young Todd that snowy night— that cinema's magic arises from shadows and reflections—continues to shape her thoughtfully constructed films and essays.

A storyteller, imagemaker, activist, and theorist, Todd has created a rich, reflective, and uncompromising body of work. From her early experimental videos and installations through her groundbreaking documentaries of the 1990s to her feature-film-in-progress, she has demonstrated a clear and conscientious voice. Her films, videos, and essays offer a corrective to damaging stereotypes of Native peoples and cultures; and through her innovative, fluid mix of the "dramatic" and the "factual," her work points toward a less-rigid filmmaking aesthetic. Although she has been making films for less than fifteen years, Todd has already left a notable mark on Canadian cinema.

Growing Up

Todd won't disclose the date of her birth, saying only that she is "younger than Madonna and older than Janet Jackson." The child of George and Judy Todd, Loretta was born in Edmonton. Her father, a member of the Cree and Métis nations, left his community in northern Alberta and travelled from job to job, working on oil rigs, in road construction, and as a trapper. He and Judy raised their eight children in Edmonton and northern Alberta.

Loretta was the fourth of George and Judy's children. Although her family struggled with poverty and George's alcoholism, Todd remembers her childhood as being filled with storytelling and art. Her father would sometimes come home and tell her stories, drawing horses on the walls for illustration. Family gatherings were filled with aunts and uncles (George had sixteen brothers and sisters) who would dance and share stories. Judy had a lovely singing voice, and there were always beautiful objects—beadwork, paintings, embroidery—around the house.

> Even though it wasn't articulated—no one said, this is art, this is beauty—I remember being surrounded by beautiful things. The Native community, even though it was fractured, seemed to have an aesthetic sense. Everything was precise—not prissy or confined—but everything had a flair. Everything was funky—you forget that they were hip people, despite their financial constraints. The tea cozies had embroidery, everything was adorned. Beauty was always important and always there, despite the poverty.

Being in what she describes as a "rush to grow up faster," Todd left home at the age of twelve, after finishing seventh grade. Holding down a series of jobs, from waitress to bakery employee to construction worker, she grew up quickly. Pregnant while still in her early teens, Todd was soon supporting herself and an infant daughter, Kamala, while other girls her age were learning to navigate high school.

Todd managed to remain self-sufficient through these difficult years and by eighteen qualified for community college, where she discovered a gift for writing. She also began experimenting with video, turning in video essays for some of her assignments. One essay explored the works of painter and poet William Blake; another used photographs from magazines to imagine a world unspoiled by European invaders. By the time she finished school, she had gained significant videomaking skills.

Finding employment with the federal government and Native organizations, Todd supervised intervention programs, aiding Native youth in coping with drug and alcohol addiction, and helped develop and implement business projects on various reserves. She also oversaw pre-employment programs helping Native women to find jobs. At times, she used video as a tool in these jobs as well. Thus, even as an administrator, Todd's passion for storytelling, and not just as a means of entertainment or instruction, was central to her career.

If I had asked my grandparents why we tell stories, they would have laughed at me and then told me another story. But I ask that question to myself, and wonder what my grandparents might have said. Why do we tell stories? Those stories may be all you can leave—you live on through your stories. And those who don't treat the people and the land well, who lie or cheat or harm people—no one wants to tell stories about those people. They are forgotten. They may have said storytelling is a way to bring the mythical and real together, a place where they can live together. They may have told me that information just lives in the instant, but the story goes on forever.

Experimental Work

While continuing to work full time for the government, Todd began film school at Simon Fraser University in the late 1980s. Studying with professors who included theorist Kaja Silverman, experimental filmmaker Al Razutis, and cinematographer John Houtman, Todd quickly learned the basics of working with film. She described the coursework as "comprehensive," with classes in film history and film theory, and access to equipment and material; it was, she says, a "good place to make a lot of mistakes."

At the same time as Todd was creating her school projects—usually experiments in style, film language, and form—she continued to make videos for various Native organizations, often on minimal budgets. Those early videos include some of the elements used in her later work: impressionistic footage, dramatic recreations, interviews. The mix, which was then somewhat revolutionary, arose partly out of necessity and partly from political reasons, as in her video *Halfway House* (1986), about a centre for Native convicts released from prison.

> Rather than just do a straightforward portrait of the halfway house and what it does, I added some drama—a guy gets off the bus, coming out from prison, and goes to the halfway house. Part of this was practical. There were a lot of issues of confidentiality—everyone there was a parolee, and none of them could be filmed. So I cast it with friends.
>
> But I was already tired of the documentary style. I had written an article for the *Video Out* newsletter about what I called media missionaries, who would come into the Native communities and bring their gospel of the documentary. It was something I was uncomfortable with. Having grown up with documentaries from the Film Board, I knew how racist these films could be. When I was in school with white kids in the city, they would laugh and snicker at the documentary films about Native communities. So the standard documentary form always had a weight to it.

By her second year, Todd was able to scale back to part-time work and concentrate on her filmmaking (and child-rearing). She also continued to articulate her misgivings about contemporary documentary practices, fuelled in part by her study of film theory:

> I was good at the theory, if only because I grew up learning to see the meaning and subtext in things. When you are oppressed, I think you become more conscious and aware of subtext, that things aren't always as they appear.

Todd's student work was thus steeped in an activist agenda. While most of the other students were making what she called "art for art's sake," Todd was beginning to learn to use the camera to challenge the conventions of ethnographic filmmaking and to reveal some of the social inequities she had experienced. As one of the few students of colour in her class, and the only First Nations student, Todd experimented with an aesthetic that would reflect her political awareness.

By then, I was certainly conscious of the ways Native people had been depicted. With the 1960s and 1970s Canadian documentary I had grown up with, there was a lot of stationary camera work, and as a Native person, I felt that the camera was peering in at us—that the films offered a space that allowed people to laugh at us.

You have to remember that when you grow up Native, you grow up with constant inspection—checking your hair for lice, welfare workers looking in on you, the dentist yanking your teeth out. It feels like you are constantly peered at, interrogated, under surveillance. I was conscious of wanting to deconstruct that, and camera movements were a way to do that. For some reason, the moving camera allowed me to have a stronger sense of my own point of view.

Inspired in part by the films of Bernardo Bertolucci, Todd's student works explored what she called "the space between the screen and the audience." Using installation techniques, some of them quite ingenious for the era, Todd began examining some heady political issues.

Her work *Breaking Camp* (1989) included three monitors, each placed on a travois and playing a scene from *Cheyenne Autumn* (1964), John Ford's Western about the Trail of Tears, the brutal forced migration of the Cheyenne from their homelands. The scenes showed a Native woman taking down her teepee, readying to move, looped endlessly. *Breaking Camp* explores issues of displacement, Hollywood's uses of Native tragedy, and movement and mobility.

Robes of Power (1989) was created to accompany an exhibit on the value and meaning of ceremonial button blankets in Northwest Coast society. The robes, generally made by women, signify the house and status of the wearer. *Blue Neon* (1989) began as a purely abstract experiment, with Todd filming, in close-up, shots of a flashing neon sign on a used-car lot in downtown Vancouver. After she finished filming, Todd realized the footage would be appropriate to use in a work about her father's alcoholism:

The installation was to simulate one of those skid-row hotels my dad used to live in when his alcoholism was at its worst. I was imagining what it would have been like for him. So I wanted to have the neon blinking through this window frame, with one of the beat-up metal frame old beds—to try and imagine his space inside the hotel.

The installation was never fully actualized, but *The Storyteller in the City* (1989) was. This installation used footage of a storyteller (played by Len George, son of Chief Dan George) telling tales to Native urban youth. They are gathered, in Vancouver's downtown, around a fire that burns in an oil barrel. The tale is intercut with footage, shot in a studio, of Native teens telling stories they had heard as children. Monitors with looped portions of the footage were then installed on top of the oil barrels.

Perhaps Todd's most ambitious installation was set at the Museum of Anthropology at the University of British Columbia. She projected images on the pillars of the museum and, using a handmade dolly, took a long tracking shot around the museum. As the camera moved around the buildings, the pillars came alive with images of land and sky. It was Todd's attempt to "liberate" the museum (which she says has a "dead feeling") and its extensive collection of sacred Native objects. The critique of contemporary museum practice would continue in Todd's later works.

Early Professional Work

By the time Todd finished school, she had become conscious of various constraints she felt as an artist. One was what she called her "strong sense of duty to [her] community." As she turned to more ambitious projects, she also began looking to her own experiences for material.

> I thought of myself as being a means to give voice to the Native community. Because I was from somewhere else, was Cree and Métis from Alberta, and now living on the West Coast, I was conscious of being in someone else's territory, and in someone else's culture. I think my filmmaking allowed me to really respect that—the camera helped me negotiate the relationship between myself, this other territory, and these other Native cultures.
>
> But I think that sense of responsibility also made me less able to let go. I felt I had to be saying something for other people. When you are so concerned with giving voice to others, you wonder, where does my voice fit in? As I grew, I began to recognize my internal voice, my intimate voice, my personal voice. And I began to give myself the permission and freedom to be an artist. I don't always have to speak for my people. By speaking for myself, I'm engaging in an act of transformation and liberation. That's what I began bringing to my films.

Her first narrative film, the unfinished *My Dad's DTs*, was intensely personal. Told through a narrator and impressionistic imagery, the film is a visual poem about shame, guilt, and loss. Todd shot the film in northern Alberta, near her childhood home, on a deserted prairie road using an old bus. The images—the film is shot on 16-mm black and white—are the central narrative mechanism; Todd uses only sparse dialogue.

Told in flashback, *My Dad's DTs* is the story of two sisters who are riding on a bus when they see their father, who is drunk, by the side of the road. When he enters the bus, they ignore him. At the back of the bus, he sings a country song, nodding off, while the other passengers look on with disgust. The two girls are left to deal with their shame, for their father and for themselves. The narrative is framed by poetic scenes from the present, in which the camera searches the empty prairie. Todd is looking for her father—and imagining what may have been:

> This was an effort for me to resolve the grief I've carried about my father for a long time. My father loved the land, and if he had been able to live on the land, I wonder if things may have been different. My father had in some ways worked against the land—in oil fields, in road construction. But I think he wanted to restore us to the land, and he felt that he had failed.

The film marks an important aesthetic step for Todd. Moving from the cityscapes that had become the backdrop of her work to the wide-open prairies of northwest Canada, she reassessed the way she created images:

> A sense of light has always informed my relationship to the image. I can't say I lived in the traplines and the bush, but I grew up close enough that I spent a lot of time under that [prairie] sun, in the winter and the summer, and under the moon. I spent a lot of time studying the way the land was lit. I looked at the shadows, and the spaces the light created.
>
> It's much different from the way people learn to see in the city. I also spent time growing up on the hard, gritty streets of the cities, and that also informs my aesthetics—the loneliness of it. I think in the city you are divorced from relationships. But in the Native way, life is all about relationships—we say "all of our relations." That's the challenge for Native youth—is it possible for them to understand that?

Todd edited the film on video and screened it in rough cut, but, unable to fund the printing of a 16-mm copy, never completed it.

Her next project, the script *Day Glo Warrior* (1990), was produced by Omni Films for the CBC. The script explores some fascinating issues: the commodification of Native cultures and ways in which Native people are sometimes party to the exploitation. *Day Glo Warrior* follows the struggles of a Native wrestler and single father. The (ab)use of Native symbolism that has made the wrestler a success in his professional circles has left him an object of disdain in his community. Todd hoped to direct the teleplay, but the script was given to another director and broadcast, in a version starring Gary Farmer, in CBC's anthology series *Inside Stories*.

Todd also created several videos during this period. *Chronicles of Pride* (1990), commissioned by the United Native Nations Knowledge Network, explores the impact of role models in the Native community. *Eagle Run* (1990), commissioned by the Department of Physical Education and Recreation and the First Nations House of Learning, explores the cultural importance of traditional Native athletics. *Taking Care of Our Own* (1991), commissioned by the Professional Native Women Association, uses a combination of drama and interviews to promote the foster parenting of Native children by Native families.

The Learning Path

With *The Learning Path* (1991), Todd applied the aesthetic developed in her experimental and dramatic work to non-fiction filmmaking. For the hour-long documentary, she created an innovative hybrid that reflected her political and artistic intentions.

The film was commissioned as part of the series entitled *As Long as the Rivers Flow*, produced by the National Film Board (NFB) and Tamarack Productions. Each of the four films was to be created by a different director, and the film that became *The Learning Path* was initially assigned to Alanis Obomsawin, the groundbreaking Abenaki activist and filmmaker. When Obomsawin left the project to focus on her film *Kanehsatake: 270 Years of Resistance*, Todd was asked to step in and turn around a film for broadcast in less than six months.

Alanis had been everyone's hero—she had been making films for a long time, and telling very sensitive stories, and obviously was very accomplished. And the others in the series were also accomplished filmmakers. I hadn't done a major film, just some low-budget videos, and I was a woman, and was younger than all of them. All of those things could have been daunting, but I didn't have time to think about it. I just had to make the film.

Knowing that the producers chose her in part based on the footage from *My Dad's DTs*, Todd confidently departed from the conventions of documentary filmmaking. *The Learning Path* weaves together the personal stories of women who had survived Canada's often brutal residential schools with tales of educational reform and healing. The film is remarkable in its ability to recount stories of abuse, oppression, and systemic racism, perpetrated against children, while constructing a narrative about recovery. The subjects of the film include women who survived the residential schools and are today helping to recover the Native languages they once had been forbidden to speak.

I asked the women, what kind of film do you want to make? They said, we want a hopeful film, about the strength of Native women. They were tired of the victim films. And so while the film was what they had been through, it was also how they had gone beyond it, had moved beyond it. They wanted to offer a message for the people who were maybe still stuck in their pain from the past, a film that spoke to hope, and to the fact that we were all on a journey.

Essential to *The Learning Path* is Todd's use of recreations and dramatic elements. Todd inserted numerous poetic scenes into the work—including some ethereal shots of an empty boarding school—hoping these elements would transcend the stories of suffering that she feared were too powerful for audiences to digest.

So many times when non-Native people hear about aboriginal experiences, what we have had to endure, they just shut down. They say, I've heard this before. They are so hardened, I don't think they listen or pay attention. And to some extent we have repeated the stories over and over again. We repeat them because the stories are still being repeated, but also because as aboriginal people we go on automatic ourselves. "Yeah, we weren't allowed to speak our language. Yeah, we were beaten."

And as heartfelt as those stories are and as painful as the experiences are, they never go anywhere. I wanted to open up the viewers' minds and hearts, and I think that poetry and lyricism and art have a way of affecting the way people experience things. I wanted them to see these stories in ways they hadn't seen them before, experience them in ways they hadn't experienced them before.

Todd was also conscious of the ways in which the conventions of documentary film had helped marginalize the experiences of First Nations communities. In some way, *The Learning Path* reacts against the history of ethnographic films, the kind that left Todd's classmates snickering at Native people.

In one scene in *The Learning Path*, a woman returns to the residential school she had survived as a child. Recounting her painful story, she begins to cry. Todd remembers her cameraman moving in for a close-up—the standard reaction to such a situation. She instead pulled him back, asking him to move away from the woman, giving her space to mourn. It was both a respectful and inspired choice: Todd inserted some of the dramatic elements she had created into the scene, as the woman continued to tell her story. The result was a moving *and* poetic sequence.

> As a viewer, you are torn between feeling like you should witness this woman's pain and like you are invading her space. But I made the choice for them. Of course, I was conscious of the history of films that said, here is Native people's pain, being delivered up again. Here we are crying again. And as I said, I think non-Native people can shut down, or they can become vultures or cannibals of our pain.
>
> On a personal level, I'm very conscious of having been stared at—looked at but not seen. I'm trying to disrupt that, to say, you cannot own our pain. I'm saying, we won't just trot our pain out when we want to score points. You can't trot our pain out when you want to assuage your guilt ... It was an attempt to take back our emotional space— that you can't have control over our emotional landscape any more.

Among the dramatic elements Todd used in *The Learning Path* were eerie shots of a nun drifting through the hallways and rooms—faceless, haunting, frightening, and yet strangely beautiful. The shots were drawn from Todd's own childhood experiences—she had spent a year in residential schools—and represented her desire both to reclaim the histories of those who had been oppressed and to identify the perpetrators.

Although Todd's political and aesthetic motivations were clear and strong, and even radical, *The Learning Path* is a subtle, sometimes elegiac, film. Recognized with a Silver Hugo at the Chicago International Film Festival, the New Visionary Award at the Two Rivers Native Film Festival, and a Blue Ribbon at the American Film and Video Festival, the film signalled Todd's arrival as a major filmmaker. In *The Learning Path*, neither the pit of the women's suffering nor the height of their triumphs as teachers and survivors are given false emotional weight. Instead, the film moves gently, but confidently, from one crystallized moment to the next.

Hands of History

Todd's childhood hardly seems idyllic: her father's alcoholism, the institutionalized racism of the era, and frequent moves could not have made growing up easy. Nonetheless, she drew strength from her family's ability to tell stories, both verbally and through art and music.

> The family started to disintegrate after the death of my grandparents—they held the family together. Then the alcohol took over, and we ended up in the city. But before all of that, at family gatherings there really was a love of music, of the word, of the sound, a love of family, of bringing people into your sphere of influence, through story.

Todd's deep appreciation of storytelling and art are one inspiration for her second NFB production, *Hands of History* (1994). With no narration and a fluid storyline, *Hands of History* introduces four prominent female Native artists: Rena Point Bolton, a Stol'o basketweaver; Doreen Jensen, a Gitskan carver; Joanne Cardinal-Schubert, a Blood installation artist, performer, and painter; and Jane Ash Poitras, a Chippewan painter. The film begins with Jensen giving a commencement address, with words that also help explain Todd's career: "In my language there is no word for art. This is not because we are devoid of art, but because art is so powerful ... We are replete with it."

The production of *Hands of History* was difficult, with Todd and the NFB at odds over the film's style and content. Still, the finished product has a strong sense of motion. Although certainly distinct from one another, the artists are almost secondary to the movement of the film, which flows from place to place, less concerned with biography or the personalities of the artists than with the nature and role of art-making in Native communities:

> When that film was being made, there was a big debate about traditional and contemporary art, and I wanted to make a film where it was hard to distinguish between past and present. One flowing into the other, and all of it a part of a longer history.

Todd envisioned the narrative structure of the film as a storytelling circle, with each of the artists explaining her life and art. The connections between one artist and the next are subtle rather than explicit:

> One will talk for a while and then finish, and then another one will take up ... it will spark something in her mind that will take her into her own thoughts about her art, who she is and where her art comes from, and that will continue throughout the film. There's an effort to create the protocol of the circle in the construction of the film. I'm using the protocol of the circle and allowing or creating that space for them to share their stories.[2]

Hands of History is also fluent in its use of film technique. Todd varies the use of colour and stock for each artist, along with compositional and camera-movement strategies. For the segments on Poitras, perhaps the most unconventional of the artists, Todd mostly used the handheld camera. For Joanne Cardinal-Schubert, Todd chose saturated colours and a fine film stock. The distance Todd kept from Rena Point Bolton, also a legendary activist who had helped rescue the then-outlawed Potlatch ceremonies, was respectful and honouring. Todd's stylistic choices are revealing, but demonstrate great restraint. Clearly, *Hands of History* was intended to give tribute to four powerful artists rather than to showcase Todd's own art.

Todd also resists mythologizing the artists—a common strategy for films about art. Instead, she reveals her subjects as women who work and demonstrate their passion daily, whose lives and art are intertwined. Todd offers a look at the complex web of meaning that Native artists have negotiated in their art and with their lives. Their journey encompasses the spiritual and practical, the romantic and the hard lessons of history, the past, present, and future. It is a journey that Todd can understand as well, as scholar Carol Kalafatic eloquently describes:

> [Todd] and others have been taught that, as aboriginal artists, they hold an essential place on the series of interdependent circles that define community/nation. Aboriginal art—whether textile, song, film or basket—is a 'cultural record' for our living communities, rather than for museums, and provides the instructions we need for life. Our role as contemporary carriers of oral traditions that are rooted in the covenant is to examine

and acknowledge our relationships with others, between people and the universe, between the physical and the spiritual; we are story keepers who help acknowledge our peoples' collective responsibilities to fight, laugh, and tell stories in order to live.[3]

Prior to being asked to direct *The Learning Path*, Todd had submitted a detailed proposal to the NFB requesting funding for a history of First Nations World War Two veterans. Through several years of false starts and disappointments, Todd remained committed to the project, *Forgotten Warriors*, which was completed as in 1996, having taken, as Todd says, "more years to create than the war took to fight."

Nominated for a Genie Award, *Forgotten Warriors* follows the stories of several Canadian veterans who enlisted and fought alongside their non-Native countrymen during World War Two. Although they risked their lives to ensure the freedom of others, on returning home, these veterans were denied equal treatment. Land deals offered to non-Native soldiers were never announced to Native veterans, and in some cases, land seized during the war from tribes was not returned. Thus came the irony: Native soldiers defended what they considered their own land, only to find that while they were away, their land had been taken from them.

At the same time, the contribution of Native veterans was never officially recognized; their participation, Todd said, was seemingly erased from the historical record. She watched "hundreds and hundreds of rolls of film" in search of archival footage, finding only a few brief shots of First Nations soldiers, including two drinking a beer at a bar. That absence motivated her:

> Wars in any country have a way of infiltrating into the cultural memory and history. But even though the war was a part of Canada, what Canada saw itself as, these men had never been present in the consciousness and memory of Canada. I wanted to, if not make them larger than life, then certainly increase the scale in which they were present. I wanted to actually infiltrate the Canadian cultural memory, to try and implant us, to create images that were timeless, to almost create our own archive.

The most striking attempt to rewrite history comes from the film's dramatic elements, Todd's most ambitious up to that point. Several scenes follow a young man's journey from home to the war and back. The young soldier leaves his family and walks through the woods to the city; he waits at the train station; he survives the horror of modern warfare; he returns home to his girlfriend.

The inspiration for these scenes arises from a variety of sources. The sequences in the woods, Todd said, were modelled after the paintings of Cree painter Alan Sapp. The train-station scene was meant to evoke a sense of the 1940s Hollywood war films, with their romantic, off-to-war sentimentality. And the two final scenes, featuring the soldier in battle and his reunion with his girlfriend, featured some exquisite rear-screen projection images inspired by Lars von Trier's highly artificial war epic *Zentropa* (1992). The scenes, as Todd intended, have a mythic quality, along with a powerful sense of the unreality of the war years:

The sailor kissing the girl in Times Square, even if it is a faked image—that's etched in the American imagination. There are these heroic images of people coming home from the war that repeat themselves in the Canadian and American imagination. We are never in them, except in our defeat. I wanted to show us, in a sense, not as victors, but certainly as people who came home and who survived.

In pop culture, in the public imagery, we are never allowed to be ordinary and sentimental. I wanted to show this handsome man being greeted by his beautiful girlfriend. I wanted us to be heroes, to let our men be heroes.

The film also includes some remarkable interviews and, as with *The Learning Path*, a strong message about recovery. The veterans were forced to cope with both the intense psychological trauma of modern warfare and their inferior status in Canada. One soldier, who had bought a home after returning from the war, was asked to either give up his property or forfeit his affiliation with his band. Many were driven to drugs and alcohol. Decades later, the central subjects in the film had begun to come to terms with their suffering. Although *Forgotten Warriors* never shies away from documenting the mistreatment of the veterans, it also celebrates their strength and perseverance.

Chief Dan George

Todd's most recent work, the hour-long documentary *Today Is a Good Day*, is also perhaps her most straightforward. In recounting the life and influence of artist, activist, and leader Chief Dan George, *Today Is a Good Day* presents a skillful, seamless blend of Todd's storytelling elements, mixing comprehensive archival footage, strong interviews, and evocative and poetic dramatic recreations.

As she worked on the video, Todd was caring for her ailing mother, who was dying of cancer. Perhaps as a result, the film is especially perceptive in evoking a sense of death and loss. In one haunting sequence of dramatic footage, a tired old man shuffles through a deserted airport. Shot in black and white, the sequence effectively conveys George's despair after losing his wife, Amy. Set against the modern landscape, the scene also seems to mourn for our loss of connection with the natural world and our traditions.

These elegiac moments are offset by several surprisingly playful sequences. Todd shot *Today Is a Good Day* on video, and at times the bright colours are used to amusing satirical effect. One scene imagines George on stage at the Oscars, accepting an award. On screen are two pairs of feet, standing beside a podium. One pair of feet is wearing high-heeled shoes; the other, a pair of moccasins. Todd is gleefully commenting on George's impact on Hollywood, whose historically racist representations of Native peoples was challenged by Arthur Penn's *Little Big Man* (1970). (In *Today Is a Good Day*, Penn himself describes Hollywood's relationship to Native America as "genocidal.") George's character Old Lodge Skins was considered one of the first humane and three-dimensional portrayals of a Native person in a Hollywood film, and George was nominated for an Oscar for best supporting actor. George also starred in the TV series *Cariboo Country* and alongside Clint Eastwood in *The Outlaw Josey Wales*.

Today Is a Good Day was commissioned for the CBC's *Life and Times* series after George's death in 1981. In the video, the story of George's remarkable life is told largely through the words of his children, whom Todd described as "a family of storytellers":

You can't get a bad interview from those people. You'd have to be pretty inept to not make an interesting film about the family—they are so forthcoming and tell their stories so well. They hold the camera, they fill the frame, and I tried to play with that, and shot wide rather than tight. These are impressive, strong people and I wanted to give a sense of their space and scale.

Although *Today Is a Good Day* may seem less overtly political than Todd's previous films, it explores complex issues of representation. While George's talent was clearly a major part of his groundbreaking success, Todd wonders why his equally talented son Bob has had such trouble finding screen work.

I think Dan knew he was playing with some of the stereotypes. He walked the line of being the grandfatherly Indian, and there is no doubt that it was a lot easier for white America to accept a grandfatherly Indian than to accept a young powerful Indian. Bob, who was also a great actor, didn't get roles. He was a handsome young man, a powerful young man, and that made people fearful. America was more ready for a wise old Indian than a young powerful one.

Today Is a Good Day screened at numerous festivals, including the Taos Talking Picture Festival (where Todd received the Taos Mountain Award for lifetime achievement, and where I am the Artistic Director), the Sundance Film Festival, and the Vancouver Film Festival.

Other Works

Although her profile has risen, Todd continues to direct videos for Native advocacy groups. Her video *No More Secrets* (1996) uses several familiar elements—the talking circle, dramatic recreations—to help expose the problems surrounding solvent abuse in Native communities. *Voice = Life* (1995), commissioned by the Healing Our Spirit First Nations AIDS Society, challenges the preconceptions of HIV/AIDS patients (that they are to be feared, that they infect our culture, and so on). Instead, she offers portraits of people, with and without HIV, who live in a world of natural beauty and who are themselves lovely. Both films emphasize the importance of dialogue as a tool for healing.

Todd's film exploring the life of poet E. Pauline Johnson (unfinished as of this writing) included drama, recreations, and interviews. Todd left the project after creative differences with her producer. Her current project, entitled *911 Res*, is a contemporary version of a Blackfoot trickster tale, featuring a rock star who finds himself on the reserve and falls in love with a beautiful woman who is already engaged to be married. The story is framed by fictional segments documenting the making of the film, which were inspired by the real-life stories of Cliff Redcrow, a police dispatcher living on the reserve.

Todd's sphere of influence also reaches beyond her films. She produced the 1993 CBC series *The Four Directions* and has served to encourage other Native filmmakers, in part by helping to found the Aboriginal Film and Video Arts Alliance. One critic suggested Todd's example as a maverick filmmaker and her work as a mentor inspired other Canadian Native women, including Barb Cranmer, Thirza Cuthand, Dana Claxton, and Arlene Bowman, to explore and experiment with the moving image. As a result, the Vancouver area has become a locus for Native film- and videomaking.[4]

Todd also has become a thoughtful and impassioned cultural critic, having written numerous scholarly articles. In 1996, she was named a Rockefeller Fellow and spent part of the year in New York writing screenplays, giving lectures at various educational institutions, and researching the uses of multimedia in museum exhibits representing Native culture. Todd's chapter "Aboriginal Natives in Cyberspace" in the book *Immersed in Technology* calls for distance from the hype surrounding new communications technologies.[5] How will those seven generations from now be affected by new media? How do these technologies promote the divorce of humans from the natural world and from one another? What does the notion of cyberspace reveal about the differences between Western and Native thought?

Todd's essay "Decolonizing the Archival Photograph" celebrates the work of Cree artist George Littlechild.[6] Todd demonstrates the ways in which photographs of Native peoples have served to dehumanize and make irrelevant their subjects, and documents Littlechild's efforts to reclaim those archival photos. In doing so, she constructs a persuasive argument about the power of images both to corrupt history and to reinvent it. In "What More Do They Want?" Todd analyzes various ways both modern and postmodern schemas devalue the Native cosmology and describes the means by which academic discourse reduces Native experience to simple, dehumanizing terms.[7]

More so than her films, Todd's words seem intended devastate: her writing is solid, well argued, and unflinching. "Three Moments After Savage Graces" is a meditation on an exhibit of Gerald McMaster's art at the University of British Columbia's Museum of Anthropology. Returning to the scene of her earlier experimental film, Todd accuses "the collector, the cataloguer, the curator, the anthropologist" of deadly desire—a desire so deep and unhealthy that it can kill the art it caresses.[8] But the essay also demonstrates a powerful vulnerability and honesty, as Todd reaches into her own experiences to help interpret McMaster's work.

> At times my father displayed a lot of race hate—race hate toward himself—which he never identified, only internalized. When he drank, he said it was because he was Indian, but then he would act like he was a Texan. There, on the street, in a loud drunk voice, he would try to pretend he was a Texan, talking with a phony Texas accent, as if he could fool anyone.
>
> I developed a race hate for the whites who would laugh, or stare, or spit at him, or cross the street to avoid him as he stood there on the street. But I was also part white, so I internalized that hate, and then I had two hates inside me. But there was also love, so it wasn't all hate I felt. Our family had fun and tenderness. And I don't think anyone's life is completely pure red or white: there are many types of friendships, many types of alliances, many types of loves.[9]

In 1999, Todd contributed to a millennial show at the Vancouver Art Gallery, in which various curators (including writer Douglas Coupland, architect Cornelia Hahn Oberlander, and playwright Tom Cone) were asked to summarize one of the past five decades. Todd's exhibit explored the future, which seems fitting, as her work seems dedicated, in a way, to future generations:

There have only been Native film and video makers for the last 20 to 25 years in Aboriginal countries ... Are we storytellers, are we chroniclers, are we ethnographers? Who are we, and what is our role? ... I see myself in the same way as the storyteller, except my way of telling the story is different ... The storyteller, the artist, has a role to play in the health of the community. Even though there is no word for "art" and "artist" in most communities, there is a word for people who tell stories. There's a word for people who make things and help people with their dreams.

These stories, these films, are inherited by our children. The legacy that is in these films is inherited by other people, so everything I do I have to be very careful about why I do it, who I do it for, who is going to be hurt by this, who is going to gain from this. I have to think about the seven generations. I have to think about the consequences of my actions. So on the one hand, I live in this creative, imaginative world. On the other hand, I live in a world in which I am part of something, I am part of a whole, I am part of a circle. I have to make sure that I am a strong link in that circle, not a weak link in that circle.[10]

Notes

1   All unattributed quotations from Loretta Todd are from interviews with the author on 31 March, 2 June, and 15 July 2000.

2   Lawrence Abbott, "Interviews with Loretta Todd, Shelley Niro and Patricia Deadman," *Canadian Journal of Native Studies* 18, no. 2 (1998): 342.

3   Carol Kalafatic, "Keepers of the Power: Story as Covenant in the Films of Loretta Todd, Shelley Niro, and Christine Walsh," in *Gendering the Nation: Canadian Women's Cinema*, Kay Armatage, Kass Banning, Brenda Longfellow, and Janine Marchessault, eds. (Toronto: University of Toronto Press, 1999), 116.

4   Ken Eisner, "Light and Shadow," *Georgia Straight,* 15 March 1999, 15–16.

5   Loretta Todd, "Aboriginal Narratives in Cyberspace," in *Immersed in Technology: Art and Virtual Environments,* Mary Anne Moser, ed. (Cambridge: MIT Press, 1996).

6   Loretta Todd, "Decolonizing the Archival Photograph," Surrey Art Gallery exhibit catalogue, Surrey, BC, 1997.

7   Loretta Todd, "What More Do They Want?" in *Indigena,* Gerald McMaster and Lee-Ann Martin, eds. (Vancouver: Douglas & McIntyre, 1992).

8   Loretta Todd, "Three Moments After Savage Graces," *Harbour* 3, no. 1.

9   Loretta Todd, "Three Moments," 61.

10 Abbott, "Interviews with Loretta Todd," 346–47.

The Avant Garde

A Report on Canadian Experimental Film Institutions, 1980–2000

Michael Zryd

THIS ESSAY IS MEANT TO PROVIDE A SKETCH of institutions of Canadian experimental or avant-garde cinema since 1980. What is striking is the extent to which even the resources with which to write such a history are inaccessible—and as invisible as writing on Canadian experimental cinema institutions, recent or otherwise. There is no published history of Canadian experimental/avant-garde institutions, and most essays and reports that do exist are informal, anecdotal, or simply obscure. Because of the ephemeral nature of many of the institutions themselves, primary documentation is either inaccessible or does not exist.[1] This lack of resources contrasts sharply with the extensive documentation and analysis of Canadian feature-film policy that narrative and even documentary Canadian cinema has enjoyed. But before the reader thinks that this will be yet another querulous complaint from the experimental margins, so familiar in the world of the avant garde, I would note that lack of attention to experimental film institutions is endemic to almost all experimental cinema scholarship (including that of the United States and Europe) and, indeed, is structural to the variously oppositional, personal, and anti-institutional inflections of experimental film practice itself. Nonetheless, I argue that closer attention to the history of institutional structures in the experimental film world is crucial in order to save it from oblivion. This oblivion is nothing so apocalyptic as the end of experimental film; rather, the threat lies in its being lost in the exponentially multiplying image landscape of contemporary media. The massive energies of commercial film and media that continue to define the film landscape to the vast majority of Canadians may have appropriated the visual strategies of experimental film practice but retain little of its political, spiritual, or conceptual richness and complexity.

In this chapter, I will attempt to sketch a report on those institutions that have functioned or still function in the world of Canadian experimental/avant-garde film, including production co-ops, film distributors, theatres and art/film centres that exhibit experimental cinema, publications, private and public funding bodies, and universities that teach filmmakers and act as the primary market for experimental films. This report in no way proposes to be comprehensive, but should function as a starting point for further research to flesh out this tentative history. The institutions in turn are subject to more powerful economic, social, political, and historical institutions, which affect not only experimental film practice but its very definition. I will conclude by comparing two symptomatic documents that suggest the trajectory of experimental cinema in Canada over the past decade: Mike Hoolboom's 1988 essay "Artist's Film Distribution in Canada: Some Thoughts About," a report filed early in his tenure as the Experimental Film Officer of the Canadian Filmmakers Distribution Centre (CFMDC); and the 2000 catalogue for the Images Festival of Independent Film and Video in Toronto.

Before I begin, however, I must address two intertwined problems embedded in experimental film discourse. First, there is the problem of terms: what do we call this cinema? Options include *experimental, avant-garde, artist's film, underground, independent,* and *fringe,* to list just a few popular labels. Second, how do we talk about "institutions," given the self-consciously anti-institutional, oppositional, and radical stance taken in much discourse on experimental cinema? I will use the more neutral term *experimental* cinema in this essay. The CFMDC, the major national distributor of "such films," has an Experimental Film Officer; the word *experimental* is used most widely in the film community, and it has been the dominant term used in Canadian film scholarship.[2] An excursus on two viable alternatives, "avant-garde film" and "artist's film" is nonetheless illuminating.

I will for the most part sidestep discussion of "avant-garde film institutions" as, for many, the idea of an avant-garde film institution is oxymoronic or at least anathema to the avant-garde film project, whose cultural and material politics is usually grounded in acts and attitudes of subversion of dominant bourgeois society. Institutions would seem invested in a status quo, not in a revolutionary project dedicated to forging new social and cultural relations. The specific ambivalence of many filmmakers to the term *institution* is in part a holdover of the complaint that the avant garde was "institutionalized" in the wake of avant-garde film's momentary recognition by the visual-art world in the mid 1970s as "structural film" made inroads into prestigious museums (Museum of Modern Art, National Gallery of Canada, Art Gallery of Ontario, etc.) and art magazines (*Artforum, October, Canadian Art,* etc.). Yet of course, such a stance oversimplifies the relationship of artistic avant gardes to institutions, and reduces the avant garde to mere gestures intended to *épater le bourgeoisie.* Even for an artist like Al Razutis, who has persistently championed a "political" avant-garde film and media practice over three decades, institutions have their uses. On the one hand, Razutis argues for alternative cultural structures: "Alternative screenings are a necessity if the avant-garde is to resist being institutionalized by the government, grant agencies, commercial interests, etc..., including the university!"[3] On the other hand, Razutis defends his decision to return to university teaching as a way to use larger social institutions for radical purposes and in order to set up alternative institutions:

I have always (post 1977) argued for avant-gardes of disruption (of norm), ones that are dedicated to social and cultural change. So what the hell was I going to a university for? Well, I thought it would be possible to operate in this position from a university ... For a while it worked; I used university funds to bring in visitors, films, used university facilities to make my own films (after the student work was completed), encouraged the production and study of experimental and avant-garde film and worked to increase faculty numbers ... What did this mean for avant-garde film? During this time period [1978–87], a marked increase in experimental and avant-garde filmmaking occurred in Vancouver, a number of screenings were held, graffiti everywhere, publications and debates, Cineworks was created, CFDW [Canadian Filmmakers Distribution West] was created as a result of Toronto's centrist policies, and a lot of new ideas and expressions were seen ...

I'm not taking credit for everything but in all honesty must say that my strategy of turning to a university (for all its shortcomings and conservative attitudes it still has most of the $$) as a base of support was a necessary decision-move.[4]

In short, the issue of institutions and the avant garde is less one of the fact of institutional structures themselves than of their constitution, function, scope, and power. Experimental and other forms of independent film in Canada have developed a web of alternative funding, production, distribution, publicity, and exhibition structures, some short-lived, some fragile, some robust, some long-lasting. But all are in need of an account of their history, an account currently hamstrung by a lack of basic research and scholarship on the institutions that inevitably impinge upon film practice.

The term *artist's film* has the advantage of avoiding the quasi-scientific ring of experimental. Moreover, the majority of filmmakers working this milieu are trained in art schools or art departments (e.g., Ontario College of Art and Design, Simon Fraser University, Ryerson Polytechnic University, Sheridan College, and others), have their works exhibited in art spaces, and receive most review coverage in art magazines (*C, Canadian Art, Parallelogramme*, etc). However, the term ignores the extent to which the majority of experimental filmmakers are overlooked by the art establishment in Canada, and also excludes the work that emerges from regional film co-operatives like the Winnipeg Film Group (WFG), whose idiosyncratic style is often less self-identified as "artist's film." In the following quotation from *Dislocations*, a retrospective catalogue celebrating the WFG's twentieth anniversary, Gilles Hébert suggests not only how the WFG is out of the art loop, but how the division between film and video—so violent during the 1960s, '70s, and '80s—was reflected in the preference for video in the art market:

> The Winnipeg Film Group was started by a group of Manitobans with no local access to film training, equipment, or funding. Over the years, the organization has grown into one of the largest film co-operatives in the country, creating a need, developing talent, and leading the public sector into investing considerable resources in the production and dissemination of a cultural product which is ever more limited by shrinking means of dissemination. Eclipsed to a great extent by video/inter-media culture which is found in more museums and art galleries, film as a personal, independent artists' tool continues to thrive in places like the Winnipeg Film Group.[5]

Faced with the new upstart medium invariably linked to its evil twin, television, experimental film aspired to differentiate itself from video—even as the boundaries between media collapsed in other contexts—through a low-tech, anti-hip focus: film, in some contexts, would be closer to the garage than the art gallery. Film continues to celebrate a "hands-on" quality, reflected in increasing experimentation with hand-processing in the 1980s and '90s (e.g., the work of Carl Brown and Gariné Torossian, among others) more immediately difficult to achieve with video. As I will suggest later, the cessation of hostilities between film and video has contributed to a healthier, more pluralist growth of an experimental media community in which the various materialities of film (in all its gauges), analogue and digital video, Internet media, film exhibition-as-performance, and installation art can be highlighted, blurred, or synthesized. The aesthetics of experimental film have infiltrated television (music video, advertising), feature filmmaking (e.g., Kyle Cooper's title sequences), and web design in addition to more traditional spheres of art, design, theatre, and music. The question remains whether the radical political, sexual, and psycho-social energies that have driven experimental cinema through several of its avant gardes are diluted in the process.

ℱ ℱ ℱ

The 1970s saw an enormous explosion in the number of experimental film institutions, including production co-ops, distributors, publications, and exhibition sites. Of these four types of institution, the co-ops and distributors have provided the most continuity over the last two decades, while publications and exhibition sites specifically devoted to experimental cinema have varied widely in lifespan and vitality. Surviving institutions have often overlapped with other types of filmmaking; for example, Canada's largest distributor of experimental film, the CFMDC, founded in 1970, also distributes drama, documentaries, and animation, while most production co-ops allow for the production of all forms of cinema. Many alternative exhibition sites like the Pacific Cinematheque and Cinematheque Ontario program experimental cinema as a smaller subsection of other programming, often with a historical focus.

The late 1970s saw the most intense activity in the formation of film co-ops. After the formation of CFMDC in 1970 in Toronto, the Winnipeg Film Group was founded in 1975, the Saskatchewan Filmpool Collective in 1977, the Calgary Society of Independent Filmmakers (CSIF) in 1978, the Funnel in 1978 (but defunct by 1988),[6] the New Brunswick Filmmakers' Cooperative in 1979, Cineworks (Vancouver) in 1980, Main Film (Montréal) in 1982, the Liaison of Independent Filmmakers of Toronto (LIFT) in 1981 (gradually replacing the Funnel as the main Toronto film co-op), Edmonton-based FAVA (Film and Video Arts) in the late 1980s, and the Black Film and Video Network in 1988.[7] The Independent Film and Video Alliance (IFVA), "a national network linking independent film, video and electronic media producers, distributors and exhibitors from all parts of Canada," was founded in 1980, a culmination of sorts for the co-op movement. It currently includes forty-five member organizations including production co-ops and companies, festivals, distributors, and other associations.

Film co-ops provide sites for production, exhibition, and some distribution, and form a social space for the development of a film and media culture. Co-ops vary widely in their concentration on experimental film depending on shifting membership, equipment, and history. In an article for *The Independent Eye*, W. Scheff notes that "Within the context of film co-op production on the prairies, Saskatchewan films are quite distinctive in comparison with productions from Calgary and Winnipeg."[8] Scheff describes CSIF productions as "narrative-based experimental/performance films" while "the Winnipeg Film Group is developing low-budget black comedies, specifically in the work of John Paizs, Guy Maddin, and John Kozak."[9] For Scheff, "Regina seems to be defining itself as the major centre for experimental filmmaking on the prairies" and attributes the distinction to the presence of local experimental filmmakers at the University of Regina: Chris Gallagher (until 1988) and Richard Kerr (until 1999). Patricia Gruben points to a tension in film co-ops between the desires of members to make experimental or more mainstream productions, a tension that is affected by the dependence of many co-ops on government grants:

> The government wants an equitable and democratic access to the means of production, so that everyone can make work, so that people who have nothing in common can all enter, and that's the tension within the co-ops. Everyone gets to belong, but some use it

only for equipment on their way to making industrial films, while others want to work in a more artisanal fashion. These different factions are forced to work out their differences in order to gain access to equipment and funding.[10]

In some ways, the vitality and stability of regional co-ops is a testament to their necessity outside the major cities (Toronto, Montréal, Vancouver). Throughout the century, experimental film has flourished mainly in large urban centres in Europe and North America, making it an urban cultural product. In Toronto, Montréal, and Vancouver, there is little problem in finding and defining experimental cinema because there is a sufficiently large film-exhibition culture that one can differentiate mainstream venues (a Famous Players Silver City movie palace) from art or underground venues (e.g., the Blinding Light in Vancouver or the Pleasure Dome in Toronto).[11] These cities generally have a major art gallery or an alternative cinematheque with film/video screening space (and constituency). Although the Vancouver Art Gallery has been criticized for its lack of support for experimental film screenings,[12] the Art Gallery of Ontario has featured, often through its cooperative agreement with the Cinematheque Ontario, consistent programming of experimental film through the late 1980s and 1990s (especially its long-running series The Independents). In Toronto, galleries like A Space, Art Metropole, YYZ Gallery, and Power Plant/Harbourfront, while they have concentrated on video art, nonetheless exhibited experimental film over the last two decades.

Crucially, these cities all have film schools with instructors who can expose students to a tradition of experimental/avant-garde work. As Mike Hoolboom stated in his capacity as Experimental Film Officer at the CFMDC, university film rentals are "the bread and butter of the artist's film,"[13] making the university, as Razutis recognizes, one of the crucial institutions for Canadian experimental film. In Vancouver, Emily Carr College includes David Rimmer on its faculty, and during its heyday in the late 1970s and early to mid 1980s, Simon Fraser University had an impressive faculty of theorists and filmmakers including Kaja Silverman, Michael Elliot Hurst, Al Razutis, and, later, Patricia Gruben. As Hoolboom says of SFU, "a fractious faculty midwifed a new generation of fringe filmers that includes [Fumiko Kiyooka,] Valerie Tereszko, Mary Daniel, Oliver Hockenhull, Penelope Buitenhuis, and others."[14] In Toronto, Sheridan College developed perhaps the largest group of contemporary filmmakers. Richard Kerr and Rick Hancox have served as faculty, while filmmakers like Gary Popovich, Steve Sanguedolce, Phil Hoffman, and Carl Brown have emerged as students. Ross McLaren served as an important faculty member at the Ontario College of Art and Design, from which filmmakers like Annette Mangaard emerged in the late 1970s and Wrik Mead emerged in the late 1980s. Universities have also served as an important base of support from which experimental filmmakers can work, including R. Bruce Elder at Ryerson University, Richard Kerr at the University of Regina and Sheridan College, Phil Hoffman and Barbara Sternberg at York University, and Rick Hancox at Concordia University. Universities, finally, serve as *de facto* film co-ops in which students have an intellectual and social space for the production and often exhibition of experimental film, especially through university film societies. Schools like Laval, McGill, Queen's, Alberta, Montréal, Toronto, Western Ontario, and York, among others, have screened experimental films in their film and media classes, or devoted specific courses to experimental cinema.

Canadian publications are another important potential institution for Canadian experimental cinema but remain weak in comparison to Britain and the US. In 1984, Kass Banning compared the situation in Britain with that of Canada:

In this country [Canada], there exists no comparable structure of support, and most of the critical writing consists in descriptive reviews or publicity, often initiated by the filmmakers themselves. In contrast to the centralized machinery of the British academic/B.F.I./*Screen* nexus, in Canada we have been met with considerable lacunae in the circulation of information about, and analysis of, avant-garde film.[15]

In the US, semi-regular journals like *Millennium Film Journal*, *Film Culture*, and *Cinematograph* (now defunct) are devoted exclusively to experimental cinema, and there has been a relatively healthy production of recent books and catalogues on filmmakers as diverse as Stan Brakhage, George Kuchar, and Yvonne Rainer. In Canada, there are very few publications specifically devoted to experimental cinema. A few books, including film retrospective catalogues, have been published in the last two decades, including R. Bruce Elder's *Image and Identity: Reflections on Canadian Film and Culture*. The Art Gallery of Ontario has published a series of monographs on individual artists, including Michael Snow, Joyce Wieland, Rick Hancox, and David Rimmer, in addition to the catalogue for the controversial International Experimental Film Congress in 1989.[16] Cinematheque Ontario published a monograph on Joyce Wieland and is planning to publish one on Jack Chambers. The Pleasure Dome has been an active newcomer, publishing a catalogue on Wrik Mead. YYZ Gallery recently issued *Lux: A Decade of Artists' Film and Video*, a wide-ranging retrospective on the activities of the Pleasure Dome screening series since 1989, and *Plague Years: A Life in Underground Movies* by Mike Hoolboom. Pages Bookstore and Gutter Press produced Mike Hoolboom's collection of interviews with Canadian experimental filmmakers, *Inside the Pleasure Dome: Fringe Film in Canada*.

Few magazines specifically devoted to experimental film have survived long, although they serve as important documents of their period. *Opsis: The Canadian Journal of Avant-Garde and Political Cinema* published two issues in 1984 and 1985 before folding. The CFMDC published a newsletter from 1979 to 1991, *The Independent Eye*, which under Mike Hoolboom's leadership provided experimental film with a brief burst of debate and commentary from 1988 to 1991. Extreme low-budget zines included the Innis Film Society's *Spleen* (a multi-format magazine published in 1989–90 in a ziploc bag and a sealed envelope for its only two issues) and the *London Film and Video Society Magazine* (1997–2001). No doubt, many other small publications of this sort exist, but almost solely on a local or regional level, inaccessible to most readers. Some Canadian film publications have included articles on experimental cinema, including the now-defunct *Cinema Canada*, *Cine-tracts*, and *Reverse Shot* (published by the Pacific Cinematheque), and the still-active *POV*, *CineAction!*, *Canadian Journal of Film Studies*, and *Take One* (which in its revived incarnation featured a regular column by Barbara Goslawski, a CFMDC Experimental Film Officer). Many Canadian art magazines, including *Canadian Art*, *C*, *Parallelogramme*, *Fuse*, and *Public* have featured articles on experimental film. Finally, from time to time, articles on experimental film have appeared in more mainstream magazines and newspapers like *Canadian Forum* and the *Globe and Mail*.

Government arts-funding bodies continue to be crucial institutions in Canadian experimental cinema. Aside from occasional local agreements with branches of the National Film Board (NFB), arts councils are the major funders of artists and institutions like film co-ops, exhibitors, festivals, and publications. The Canada Council's Media Arts Department is the main national group, supplemented in recent years by the federal government's Department of Canadian Heritage. Provincial arts councils are the next level of government support, in some cases followed by municipal arts councils (especially in large centres like Toronto). Giving much more occasional support to experimental film are governmental film-development institutions like Telefilm Canada and provincial bodies like the Ontario Film Development Corporation. Reliance on government arts funding creates its own set of problematics for filmmakers and film culture in Canada, which deserves much more scrutiny that I can offer in this brief sketch. However, the following provocative exchange between Patricia Gruben and Mike Hoolboom succinctly captures many of the problems of self-censorship, insularity, and responsibility, as well as the economic and political context that makes arts councils so crucial to Canadian experimental film culture:

> Gruben: Nobody can afford to say "screw you" in this country because there's always the question of government money. We're always trying to figure out what the government wants us to do, and that's no way to make films. You spend your whole life going to meetings. On the other hand, film is time and time is money. I don't want to say anything derogatory towards the Canada Council or Telefilm because I grew up in a country [USA] that doesn't have anything like it, and that's much worse.
>
> ...
>
> Hoolboom: Isn't there an artificial quality to the whole of the Canadian independent film sector? Filmmakers receive production monies from Canada Council, who also support production co-ops to provide equipment access. The completed work goes into Council-supported distribution co-ops and shows in Council supported screening venues. The only people who don't get paid are the audiences.
>
> Gruben: But if you call government subsidy artificial, are you saying that the marketplace isn't? That Ellie Epp's films should go out there and compete with *Batman*, and may the best win? Without an exhibition circuit and the advertising dollars that underpin American films, the notion of a level playing field is ridiculous. I can't blame the government for giving us money. We, as filmmakers, have to take responsibility for our relationship to our money, not to assume that it's our right to get it, or that there's no other way to make work.[17]

ᘎ ᘎ ᘎ

I will conclude with a brief comparison of two documents, which might map a trajectory for Canadian experimental cinema over the last two decades. After the flurry of activity in the late 1970s leading to the formation of many pioneering Canadian production and distribution co-ops, by the late 1980s, experimental film faced a crossroads. In this period, throughout Canada and the US, many predicted the death of experimental film, and of film in general (a death knell which continues to toll despite evidence to the contrary): a rhetoric of crisis prevailed, which came to a head, and perhaps a turning point, in 1989. Mike Hoolboom's 1988 report "Artist's Film Distribution in Canada: Some Thoughts About" summarizes his bleak view of the prospects for experimental film exhibition in Canada, and suggests material reasons for the language of crisis:

> Conclusions: Festivals are nice for exposure but they cost money, materials come back damaged and often require that EXTRA print no one seems to be able to afford. Most people in the [CFMDC] collection have one print here. The most enlightened of TV pro-

grams is showing very brief excerpts, our theatres are run by Americans as well as our film press. Our major galleries are providing the substantial support we need, the artist-run centres are poor and not all that interested in film, the co-ops are mostly producing work [as opposed to exhibiting it] and mostly interested in non-experimental work anyways; our work is too difficult for the high schools who may have no $ to buy work in any event and the universities have money to rent but hardly any to buy. So where do we go from here? As it exists now the CFMDC is able to do little more than function as a kind of life support system, able to maintain the appallingly low level of distribution/visibility presently in place while being simply too short of resources to pursue other initiatives ... Given all of the above I think it's time some of us got together and decided whether the situation as it stands is acceptable or not, and if not then to what lengths we would be willing to go in order to change it.[18]

Perhaps coincidentally, Hoolboom's cry for change was answered with a series of events in the late 1980s, produced from many different and often competing positions. Most influentially, Fred Camper's 1986 article announcing the "Death of the Avant-Garde" (an aesthetic rather than institutional argument) provoked a group in the Toronto arts community to convene an International Experimental Film Congress, which took place in Toronto in 1989.[19] The event seems to have provoked a generation of filmmakers into new activist energies in exhibition, and perhaps even production, as the visibility of Canadian, American, and global experimental cinema has increased during the 1990s. However, these energies were simmering throughout the late 1980s, particularly in Toronto. The Images Festival of Independent Film and Video offered its first Showcase of Contemporary Film and Video in 1988. A major screening exhibition at the Art Gallery of Ontario, *Spirit in the Landscape* (with an accompanying catalogue by Bart Testa), toured many Canadian cities after its first run in Toronto in 1989. R. Bruce Elder's *Image and Identity* was published in 1989, serving as one of the first major scholarly texts on Canadian experimental cinema. Mike Hoolboom, meanwhile, contributed to the change he called for by publishing a series of experimental film-intensive issues of *The Independent Eye* between 1988 and 1991 (and has continued to be a major force in experimental film distribution, exhibition, and publication—in addition to his own prolific film production).

The growth of the Images Festival is one of the most optimistic signs of the health of experimental cinema. Between 1988 and 2000, it expanded from a weekend to a week-long festival, and its catalogue expanded from twenty-four to seventy-six pages. A comparison of the sponsors of the two catalogues reflects both continuities of institutions supporting experimental cinema and new developments. In 1988, sponsors (of either the festival or the catalogue) included government bodies and arts councils (Canada Council, Ontario Arts Council, Toronto Arts Council, National Film Board), distributors (CFMDC, DEC, V-Tape), co-ops and galleries (LIFT, A Space, Art Gallery of Ontario, Trinity Square Video, Art Metropole), and local media (*Fuse, CineAction!* and *Public* magazines, and CKLN, an alternative radio station). Purely commercial sponsors who took out advertisements in the catalogue included Imax Systems Corporation, the Festival Cinema group (a Toronto repertory cinema chain), Pages Bookstore, and a few other bookstores, bars, and craft shops. By 2000, Images enjoyed twenty official sponsors and its catalogue featured seventy-eight advertisers (including most of the sponsors). Government sponsorship remained constant, with the addition of new sponsors Telefilm Canada and the Toronto Film and Television Office. Sponsorship from distribution and production co-ops, galleries, and festivals increased, and new festivals (such as Desh Pardesh, Hot Docs, and Inside Out Lesbian and Gay Film and

Video Festival of Toronto) and new co-ops (such as House of Toast and Public Access) appeared. Universities and colleges formed a new category of sponsors, consisting of University of Toronto (Cinema Studies Student Union and New College), Humber College, Ryerson University, Gulf Islands Film and Television School, and Vancouver Film School. The most substantial increase in sponsorship, however, is from the private sector, especially commercial media like Alliance-Atlantis Communications (including Showcase and WTN television networks), Odeon Films (an ad for the Canadian feature narrative *New Waterford Girl*), Warner Bros. Pictures, and large-scale film production facilities like Kodak Canada, The Lab, and Medallion PFA, in addition to many more small production houses. Rounding out the other commercial sponsors are a plethora from expected sectors like alternative magazines, radio stations, bookstores, and restaurants, and some from unexpected sectors like couriers, breweries, and real-estate agents.

What is the message of this increase in sponsorship for the Images Festival? I am certainly not arguing that the recognition of Warner Brothers means that the gravy train has arrived for Canadian experimental film. On the contrary: it signals the clear presence of contemporary mainstream media and its propensity for appropriating and adapting every novelty in its path. Nor can I use one festival as a barometer of the health of experimental film culture across Canada. Moreover, many of the problems identified by Hoolboom in 1988 remain, exacerbated by new ones, like the increasing loss of 16-mm projection facilities at universities. However, significant shifts over the last decade leave some room for optimism.

First, I would argue that the success of the Images Festival is in part attributable to a move to pluralism over some of the exclusive categories that limited Canadian experimental cinema in the early 1980s. The Images Festival is not exclusively Canadian; it is international. It is not restricted to film but includes video, performance, and installations. It is not restricted to experimental work but includes narrative and documentary. And finally, the festival's curatorial practice is eclectic, including programs organized around political and cultural themes, formal issues, historical perspective, single filmmakers, and even student filmmaking. Images still focusses on largely short-format, low-budget, independent, personal media, but it avoids the self-defeating parochialisms that have embittered much experimental film discourse. Second, the new sponsors reflect the remarkable rise of the media economy (real or imaginary, it scarcely matters). With major sectors of the economy in search of "content," especially "cutting-edge" cultural media that tap into hip, urban, young-adult markets, experimental film is grist for the media mill. As cable television and the Internet hone "narrowcasting," experimental and personal media can find new avenues for distribution and exhibition.

Perhaps Canadian film institutions are faced, in the spirit of Hoolboom's 1988 challenge, with a new dilemma. Does experimental film become just one more channel in the million-channel universe of the "new media future" or can the intensely personal, critical, political, and spiritual energies of the Canadian experimental-film tradition be sustained by its collective structures of production, distribution, and exhibition? If past decades are any example, it will require both provocation and pluralist tolerance, and the spirit of integrity and adaptation.

Notes

1   One typical example: the records of the Innis Film Society, an experimental film screening group that was active in Toronto from the mid 1980s to the mid 1990s, are kept in the supply closet of an ex-executive member (mine).

2   An important exception is R. Bruce Elder's studies of Michael Snow and Jack Chambers (and to a lesser extent Ellie Epp, David Rimmer, and Joyce Wieland) in *Image and Identity: Reflections on Canadian Film and Culture*

(Waterloo: Wilfrid Laurier University Press, 1989), in which he uses the term *Canadian avant-garde*. Mike Hoolboom's anthology of interviews with filmmakers, *Inside the Pleasure Dome: Fringe Film in Canada* (Toronto: Gutter Press, 1997), proposes the term *fringe film*, but the artists themselves alternate between *experimental* and *avant-garde* (among others).

3   Mike Hoolboom et al., "Al Razutis: Under the Sign of the Beast," *The Independent Eye* 10, no. 3 (1989): 29.

4   Hoolboom et al., "Al Razutis," 29.

5   Gilles Hébert, *Dislocations: Winnipeg Film Group* (Regina: Dunlop Art Gallery, 1995), 12–13.

6   The Funnel deserves more substantial research into its rise and fall than I can provide here, for its central role in fostering experimental film (especially Super 8) in Toronto, for its locus for protest against, and capitulation to, the Ontario Censor Board, and for the polarization it helped foster in the Toronto experimental film "community" in the early to mid 1980s. Mike Hoolboom summarizes its fate:

> While the creative impetus at The Funnel was an egalitarian, anyone-can-do-it intent, its theatre screened films which were inexplicable to the uninformed and the works produced by its members clearly hailed from a modernist background. A clubhouse mentality finally prevailed, preventing the organization from opening up its membership (new members had to be approved by the board) and its complicity with the Ontario Censor Board (it continued to submit documentation to the Board while the rest of the arts community unanimously opposed any recognition of the Board's jurisdiction) led the community to abandon it. After a short-lived move to a downtown location it collapsed in debt and invective in 1988. (Hoolboom, "A History of the Canadian Avant-Garde in Film," in *The Visual Aspect: Recent Canadian Experimental Films*, Rose Lowder, ed. [Avignon: Editions des archives du film expérimental d'Avignon, 1991].)

7   Although video-only institutions are outside the scope of this chapter, it is worthwhile to note that many video production and distribution co-ops were founded in the same period, including Trinity Square Video (Toronto, 1971), Western Front (Vancouver, 1973), Satellite Video Exchange Society (Vancouver, 1973), Video Femmes (Québec City, 1974), Groupe Intervention Video (Montréal, 1975), Centre for Art Tapes (Halifax, 1978), SAW Video (Ottawa, 1980), Video Out (1980), Video Pool (Winnipeg, 1983), and EMMEDIA Gallery & Production Society (Calgary, 1983).

8   W. Scheff, "Flatland Films," *The Independent Eye* 11, no. 1 (Fall 1989): 29.

9   Scheff, "Flatland Films," 29.

10 Quoted in Hoolboom, *Inside the Pleasure Dome*, 39.

11 Because I am concentrating on English-Canadian cinema, I will bracket the complex history of experimental cinema in Québec, although I would note in passing that Montréal has had, up to now, a relatively small experimental-film scene. For a brief report, see Claude Forget, "Pour un Cinéma Libre," *The Independent Eye* 12, no. 2 (1991): 8–11.

12 See Mike Hoolboom, "Some Thoughts About Artist's Film Distribution in Canada," *The Independent Eye* 9, no. 1 (1988): 6.

13 Hoolboom, "Some Thoughts," 6.

14 Hoolboom, *Inside the Pleasure Dome*, 83.

15 Kass Banning, "RE/VISION: Reconsidering the British and Canadian Avant–Garde," in *A Commonwealth*, Lori Keating, ed. (Toronto: The Funnel, 1984).

16 For an overview of this controversy, see William Wees, "'Let's Set the Record Straight': The International Experimental Film Congress, Toronto 1989," *Canadian Journal of Film Studies* 9, no. 1 (Spring 2000): 101–16.

17 Hoolboom, *Inside the Pleasure Dome*, 39.

18. Hoolboom, "Some Thoughts," 8.

19 Fred Camper, "The End of Avant-Garde Film," *Millennium Film Journal* 16/17/18 (1986–87): 99–124.

To CELEBRATE THE TENTH ANNIVERSARY of the Toronto experimental screening venue Pleasure Dome, the author has examined a decade of largely Canadian experimental media through the lens of that organization's programming history, other Canadian venues for experimental media, and her own dreams over the same period. She finds that she has internalized the experimental film and video scene to such a degree that her unconscious accurately charts developments in the scene over the past decade. Dreams recorded over the years 1990 to 1999 uncannily reflect shifts in independent media cultures: the shift from a linguistic to a phenomenological bent; the seemingly opposed move from a visual to an information culture; changing debates in the politics of identity; the shifting interest in sexual representation. Her dreams also reflect the position of Canadian film and video in relation to an international and US-dominated art world. Above all, they celebrate the myriad of small, quirky, rebellious, anarchic—yet easily overlooked, indeed repressed—image-worlds that comprise ten years of programming at Pleasure Dome and ...

Ten Years of Dreams About Art
Laura U. Marks

All dreams guaranteed dreamed by the author.

This running excursion into Peircean semiotics is intended to help us understand aesthetic developments in experimental film and video of the 1990s in terms of the dynamic of emergence, struggle, resolution, and re-emergence. C.S. Peirce's semiotic theory, unlike the better-known Saussurean theory, allows us to think of signs as existing at different removes from the world as we experience it, some almost identical to raw experience, some quite abstract. For Peirce, the real appears to us in three modes, each at a more symbolic remove from phenomena, like layers of an onion: Firstness, Secondness, and Thirdness. Firstness, for Peirce, is a "mere quality," such as "the color of magenta, the odor of attar, the sound of a railway whistle, the taste of quinine, the quality of the emotion upon contemplating a fine mathematical demonstration, the quality of feeling of love, etc."[1] Firstness is something so emergent that it is not yet quite a sign: we can't see red itself, only something that is red. Secondness, for Peirce, is where these virtual qualities are actualized, and it is always a struggle. In the actual world, everything exists through opposition: this and not that, action–reaction, etc. Secondness is the world of brute facts. Thirdness is where signs take part in mental operations that make general statements about qualities and events: it is the realm of interpretation and symbolization. The attitudes toward the world of the three kinds of sign are perceptive, active, and reflective.

Dreams, of course, are highly condensed mental images, and thus chock full of Thirdness. But in dreams, we are immobilized and cannot physically react to the provocative signs they give us: dreams concentrate affect, or the feelings of Firstness, in our bodies.

Best musicians are three bugs

29 AUGUST 1989: I dream that the best jazz musicians in the world are three bugs. One is a spider who plays clarinet and is like Charlie Parker; one is named Habermas. They float into a huge pool on a raft and begin playing, and the audience goes wild. They are very wise and give us to think how advanced bugs can be. I knew one of them and was a little bit in love with it, and I was crying and crying, maybe because I knew the bug would be killed, maybe because of the passing of all things.

There is a handful of small programming venues worldwide, including Toronto's Pleasure Dome, that devote themselves to the most marginal and evanescent of moving-image media. Why is this kind of programming valuable from the point of view of the larger culture? Some of the works and artists will eventually be taken up by the broader art world. More important, experimental film and video is a microcosmic laboratory of the most significant developments in culture: experimental makers get to all the issues years, or decades, before mainstream media take hold of them. But finally, this work is important because it is *not* valuable from the point of view of culture at large. While it is common to say that reproducible media do not have "aura," that sense that the art object is a living being, single-print and low-circulation films and videos have an aura denied to mass-circulation media. Experimental programming venues nourish short films and videos, works in low-budget and obsolete media, filmic detritus rescued from landfills—in short, works that have aura in inverse proportion to their commercial value. Pleasure Dome revives works that are ephemeral or forgotten, films that have been censored, banned, and burned. Like bugs on a raft, they are precious because they are imperilled.

Brains or love

4 DECEMBER 1989: I dream that I am in a crowd of people, Japanese and foreigners, at the station by the My City department store in Tokyo. There's a stall where for a 9000-yen piece we can buy a new brain. There are only two of them; it's a kind of last-chance deal. A tall, young, clean-cut guy with glasses buys one immediately to go to the vending machine. I am trying to decide whether to take this rare opportunity to get this new brain. If I don't take it, my own brain would be reduced by 50 percent. I am trying to decide how important my intelligence is to me, since after all I would still have love, and love of beauty, and be more simple: I have a mental image of living in a cottage. And I don't feel I need the extra years of life the new brain would give me.

The choice between brains and love was a central struggle for filmmakers in the early 1990s. Some insisted on using their media as intellectual tools on the model of written intelligence. This is why so many works from this end of the decade are characterized by scrolling text and quotations from important scholars: purchased brains. At this period, art schools, film funders, and art magazines were telling young artists that being a "dumb artist" was no longer a viable choice: artists were now expected to issue their own considered statements and locate themselves within a verbal intellectual milieu. Work suffered as a result, although certain artists expanded the verbal imperative into an expressionist form in its own right: witness the impressive logorrhea of Istvan Kantor, in later videotapes such as *Black Flag* (1998) and *Brothers and Sisters* (1999). A few brave others accepted the apparent deterioration of their brains as a consequence of love. For example, John Porter, a Pleasure Dome regular throughout the decade, generated huge numbers of films that seemed to be produced from pure passion for the medium rather than from particular ideological or aesthetic agendas. Yet he has internalized the logic of filmmaking so profoundly that it informs even his most seemingly artless work. As a result, Porter's films, and those of others who followed this route, are fertile with ideas, even if the artists themselves are not extremely articulate in interviews.

The verbal-art phenomenon is a case of Thirdness preceding Secondness: judgements and symbolic pronouncements, such as "Film should not/should offer visual pleasure," generate a course of action. This top-heavy semiotic configuration is dangerous for artists because it tends to backfire, since Thirdness is not a stable state but generates new and unforeseen states of Secondness and Firstness. For example, numerous feminist works from the late 1980s and early '90s, in a double reaction to the pronouncement above, made "unpleasurable" works that caused audiences to howl in amusement or "pleasurable" works that made us feel we were being bullied. In contrast, work that luxuriates in Secondness, in the realm of simple action–like Porter's time-lapse films, Toy Catalogue versions, and Cinefuge versions–generates all kinds of conceptual responses in the minds of audiences.

History of cars and boats

9 JUNE 1990: I dream of an artist's book where each page is a thin wooden slab with a wood-burned picture. There are pictures of cars from five-year intervals, beginning in 1920, and pictures of boats in five-year intervals. If you flip the pages like a flip book, you can see a little animation of the evolution of car and boat design.

Postmodernism malingered into the 1990s, and with it, the disempowering notion that it was impossible for artists to produce their own new images. Many filmmakers looked to found footage and archival images as sources of fresh meaning. While any image they produced themselves seemed to arrive already encoded in the sign systems of the dominant culture, archival images had a kind of strangeness and excessiveness that resulted from their codes having been forgotten.[2] Archival images had a way of deconstructing themselves, because their codes, once implicit, were now humorously obvious. Among many archive-gleaners, Mike Hoolboom in *Escape in Canada* (1993) served up archival US propaganda about Canada with a solarized parsley garnish.

The postmodern dilemma mentioned here is that the entire Real seems to exist in the realm of Thirdness, the general idea that engulfs all particulars. According to the Baudrillardian logic by which many people were seized in this period, the meaning of everything that we perceive has already been encoded, indeed dictated in the form of what Peirce calls a *legisign*. If, as Peirce writes, the recipe for apple pie exists in the realm of Thirdness, but the particular apples used are Second, then postmodernism told us that there were no longer any apples, only recipes.[3] Thirdness can be paralyzing, but, as when these artists treat the over-symbolized old recipes as raw material, it can generate new signs, such as the arousal and nausea that are sure indicators of Firstness.

The immobilized heads of mass culture

16 APRIL 1992: I dream a friend and I are walking near a long reflecting pool, and a female reporter is speaking to the cameras from the edge of the pool, only her face visible. As we walk by, I see that her face was mounted in a shoe, a gold sandal, and in fact it is all of her there is. I am intrigued by the gimmick but also shocked. Later, my friend and I pass a dumpster and two ant-eaters walking at the edge of the road.

13 AUGUST 1992: I dream about a craft project in a women's magazine: a stiff nosegay of plastic flowers with an eyeball built into the base looking at them, lit from below by a light bulb.

Mass culture, or what the Frankfurt School theorists called "affirmative culture," is a fixed eyeball or a mounted head that can gaze in only one direction. Marginal culture is free to wander and swivel. Film and video, as industrial media, have a particular relationship to mass-produced media. Because their techniques are shared with movies and television, artists in these media are more pressured (than painters, for example) at every step of the production process to consider their relationship to mass culture. Canadian film and video in the 1990s continued its head-swivelling relationship with popular culture. In belated (as it can only be) counter-propaganda to the Gulf War, Phil Hoffman, Stephen Butson, and Heather Cook's *Technilogic Ordering* (1992–93) was a diary of television coverage of the Gulf War edited into a mosaic whose impenetrability reflected the powerlessness many Canadians felt in our complicity with the US war for oil. Screened at Pleasure Dome in 1996, AdBusters' "Uncommercials" alerted couch potatoes to the military–industrial intentions of benign-sounding sponsors like Kraft and General Electric (wait a minute, doesn't Kraft own General Electric?).

In the early 1990s, artists referred to themselves as "cultural workers" or "cultural producers" more than artists do now. This was supposed to mean that artists, as producers of culture, were responsible members of their communities, as well as to shy away from the high-art connotations of the word "artist." More work was overtly activist in the late '80s and early '90s. What happened?

Certainly, part of what happened is that less money was available for artists who wanted to make "unmarketable," i.e., truly political, work. (By contrast, "critical" art, as Gary Kibbins points out, always has a relatively ready market.[4]) But another way to understand the shift away from overtly political work that occurred in this decade is to acknowledge different ways of being political. A work that critiques popular culture reinforces its dependent relationship with popular culture. Its goal is political change at the level of language, which is collective but not deeply embodied. This relation of dependency is two-fold in Canadian critical experimental work, because it must take on all of American mass media as well as the popular in Canadian culture, if the latter can be said to exist independently.[5] By contrast, a work that is only about itself and the passion of creation offers a model of freedom from popular culture. Its goal is political change at the level of individual action—which is embodied but not collective. And of course, between these poles lay art that politicized personal, embodied experience. In short, the shift away from activist art to personal art during the 1990s can be seen as not a depoliticization but a shift in political strategies.

Yet we cannot deny that the early '90s was a lively period for work in the arguably reactive mode of identity politics. Little of this work showed up in the artist-curated programs at Pleasure Dome, in contrast to, for example, the annual Images Festival, also based in Toronto. Why?

In particular, the politics of ethnicity and nationality informed the work of many Canadian media-makers who got up to speed in the mid 1980s to the early '90s. The best of this work, such as Donna James' gentle meditation on her foremothers' Jamaican aphorisms, *Maigre Dog* (1990), and Shani Mootoo's canoe-generated rumination on Trinidadian-Canadian nationality in *A Paddle and a Compass* (1990), dissolved identity categories in favour of the fecundity of not knowing who one was; or alternatively, as in the intentionally frustrating work of Jayce Salloum, in the spirit of dissolving all predetermined bases for knowledge. While Helen Lee's critique of ethnic fetishism in *Sally's Beauty Spot* (1990) was enthusiastically received, her poetic sensibility emerged in the seemingly lighter and less-critical narrative *My Niagara* (1992), especially in the concluding shot of an Asian-Canadian latter-day Marilyn Monroe carrying a flimsy flowered suitcase and walking away from the camera in teetering heels, which suggested that presence can be prised away from identity to float precariously away—whether toward freedom or annihilation is more for the viewer to decide.

> Cultural critique tends to take place in the mode of Secondness, or reaction. It is thus doomed to a somewhat parasitic relationship with the mass media that goad it along. The best such works, however, are rich enough in their Secondness that they generate the mental connections that are the realm of Thirdness—or, more rarely, the perceptual surprises of Firstness. Identity politics, for example, when it worked, mobilized felt qualities of life into struggle (for identity, by existing in opposition to something other, is Second) and into new forms of communication. In the best cases, such work incorporated the active and reactive mode of Secondness into a journey toward the creation of mental images productive of thought, in the spirit of Thirdness.

Consciousness is no different from reality

8 FEBRUARY 1990: I dream that a bunch of us are having a political demonstration at the bottom of the stairwell in the college administration building. A tall, thin, white-haired lady from the registrar's office comes out and tells us, "For Marx, his consciousness of himself was no different from his reality." This is an absolutely huge revelation to us: the demonstration breaks up, and we are all laughing with the craziness of the enlightened. Then we go to the student lounge and,

to people's mixed delight and dismay, a woman lights a papery thing in her hand and throws it into the room, where it bursts in flowery ashes.

The relationship between reality and representation was a typically 1980s concern in art. Many works critiqued popular culture. Video artists in the '80s, in particular, eschewed the structuralist experiments of the preceding decade as being politically reactionary, and instead looked to critique the social and economic foundation of television. Hence the videos that looked like TV shows with something amiss. The critique of representation, more generally, became the air artists breathed. Saussurean semiotic theory, in turn, gave us ways to understand the world as a compendium of signs, all of which have been effectively pre-perceived for us. This gave film- and videomakers plenty of grist to grind, in the *subversion* of existing images.

But some people were uneasy with the idea that we cannot know reality directly. If their consciousness was their reality, then surely they did have direct access to some sort of reality? Less pressured to evolve with their art form than videomakers, filmmakers were somewhat freer to represent their own experience in the act of experiencing it. Politically suspect though it may have been, they gave the gift of their own perception to viewers and listeners. Ellie Epp, in *notes in origin* (1987), allowed the camera to be moved by the beating of her own heart. In *All Flesh Is Grass* (1988), Susan Oxtoby allowed luminous textures and slanting shadows to express the catharsis that comes from abandoning oneself to mourning. Zainub Verjee's gentle *Ecoute s'il pleut* (1993) allowed the viewer to experience silence, full as a drop trembling on a leaf, for eight minutes out of ordinary time. And a master of the art of gradual revelation, Barbara Sternberg retained a rich, impressionistic audiovisual texture in her work throughout the decade. These and other filmmakers remained convinced that the world is still enchanted and need only be properly recorded to enchant the viewer.

In other words, they used the medium of film as an entranced Perceiver of the world, an agent of Firstness. One might define art as a practice that cannot be subsumed in a symbolic mode. As Floyd Merrell suggests, wine-tasters, jazz musicians, and others with a non-verbal grasp of their art "know more than they can explicitly tell. A portion of their knowledge will always remain at the level of Firstness and Secondness, unmediated and unmediable by Thirdness."[6]

The pink

20 APRIL 1991: I dream I am masturbating to this commercial-looking montage of lots of women talking about "the pink," which meant masturbation, and how their men left them alone to do it.

In the 1990s, a second generation of feminist film- and videomakers came of age. While their predecessors had been into subverting patriarchal culture, the critical stance lost favour with younger artists. Constant vigilance is exhausting and not much fun. Instead, more artists, especially women queer and straight (but later in the decade gay and then straight men as well), began making work that focussed on their own sexual pleasure. Again, this work may have looked apolitical or self-indulgent, but as with the general shift from activist to personal work, it was rather a move to a politics of action rather than critique. Paula Gignac and Kathleen Pirrie Adams transcended the dyke-music-video genre in *Excess Is What I Came For* (1994), a tactile ride for the senses, thanks to the sensuous graininess of video shot in the low light of Toronto's Boom Boom Room. Queer punk movies indulged in a pleasure that was harder edged but just as sweet, in Bruce LaBruce's *I Know What It's Like to Be Dead* (1989), G.B. Jones' *Trouble Makers* (1987), and Nadia Sistonen's private performances for Super 8 camera. Kika Thorne luxuriated in female sexuality in work that had a characteristic *flou* or unwillingness to be bound by structure—although other kinds of bondage were fair game. In Thorne's *Sister* (1996), heat-seeking infrared film makes a woman's pussy (the artist's own?) glow in the throes of self-pleasure.

A glitch in the performance

17 JANUARY 1992: I dream I am at a performance in a finished-basement type place, full of metre-high slabs of crumbling gray asphalt. There are lots of male–female couples. We are scared that the performance is going to involve the wolves and dog we can hear snarling behind a door. But the artists tells each couple to put on bathing suits—we're glad it's going to be a participatory performance—and do something with water and then jump down the room. My partner is Susan Patten, and so as two women we are a glitch in the performance. But the artist says that the glitch is the point of the performance.

One area in which the critique of representation continued to be important was in queer media. Feminist film and video gave way, or opened the way (depending on your view), to queer work and the interrogation of masculinity. "Queering" Hollywood and commercial cinema was all the rage. Gender indeterminacy was hot: queer artists struggled against the imposition of definitions of gender and sexuality, as in the "Bearded Ladies" show at Pleasure Dome in spring 1993. Queer artists interrogated the bonds of language. Nelson Henricks' precisely structured *Emission* (1994) poised bodily desire against the drag of the symbolic in a quite-literal way, the frustrated lover's voice-over insisting "Turn off the TV, turn down the radio, let me take you in my arms." Canadian men of queerness produced lashings of smart, sexy, and sometimes transgressive work throughout the decade: they include, to name just a few, Richard Fung, Paul Wong, John Greyson, Steve Reinke, Robert Lee, Wrik Mead, Scott Beveridge, Dennis Day, Zachary Longboy, Ho Tam, Michael Balser, Andrew Patterson, Wayne Yung, and Kevin D'Souza. While much of this work continued to be overtly concerned with language, it also generated an audio-visual erotics of its own.

While the boys just wanted to have fun, lesbian work in the early part of the decade seemed to have more demons to battle at the level of language, only after which could they afford to be playful. A raft of political issues floated works by the performance duo Shauna Dempsey and Lorri Millan, Shani Mootoo's *Wild Woman in the Woods* (1992), Marusia Bociurkiw's films, and Michelle Mohabeer's *Coconut, Cane, and Cutlass* (1994), to name a few. Other lesbian works were overtly didactic, such as Maureen Bradley's *Safe Sex Is Hot Sex* (1992) and Kathy Daymond's *Nice Girls Don't Do It* (1990), an instructional guide to female ejaculation. The need to establish one's position and ground one's voice is well understood in terms of the politics of lesbian identity: being historically placed so far outside of language and representation, lesbian media artists need to claim them before they can transcend them. Exceptions includes some of the punky chicks from the Super 8 scene, who in the thrash 'n' burn spirit of punk were not trying to be understood but just to rebel.

In the early part of the decade, queer media was powered by struggle against the symbolic order. Secondness is the realm of "not-that," and queer work vigorously reacted to the Thirdness of received languages in both dominant culture and subcultures for what it is to be gay or lesbian. Sometimes this work remained at the level of reaction or generated its own new set of limiting languages, as in the safe-sex shorts that many activist artists produced in the early '90s. Activism around sexual activity is extremely difficult to pull off. Education is a question of the immediate perception of Firstness and the received knowledge of Thirdness converging on Secondness, or immediate response to brute facts. It is almost impossible to educate sexuality, unless a stronger motivation than desire can act like "the firm hand of the sheriff on your shoulder," as Peirce characterizes Secondness.

A hard day at the arts council

6 MARCH 1994: I dream that I had to go to an arts council jury, and it is in a building, maybe in Paris, one of those buildings that's supposed to be rationally designed, but it's a huge box divided internally into three parts with undulating inner walls. I'm trying to find Floor N, and a lady in a tiny stairwell office tells me I can't get into that room, but then she gives me a key. I have to try the key in doors on about twenty floors, but doing this I'm actually pricking my arm with a needle, all the way up the inside. I have this row of twenty neat red pricks up my arm; I put anti-biotic ointment on them.

Arts council juries have provided some of the most democratic, well-informed, and passion-ate discussions about art I've ever taken part in, and this has been at the federal, provincial, and municipal levels. The jurors' investments and expertise are different, and it's hard to make rational decisions about what kind of art deserves funding, but somehow we always reach con-sensus about which projects should get the money. Then we find out there's not enough money to fund even half of them, because of funding cuts during this decade in most of the provinces (the Ontario Arts Council was cut by 40 percent during the first premiership of Mike Harris in the early 1990s; the arts budgets of Alberta, BC, Manitoba, and Nova Scotia experienced similar cuts) and nationwide (the Canada Council lost funding and then had it restored to less than the previous level). That's where the self-mutilation comes in.

Equations for your eye

4 APRIL 1997: I have one of those dreams where I have to take a math exam, and I am all confi-dent, then I get into the exam and do terribly. I'm trying to recall trigonometry, remembering nothing. This bright-eyed young woman explains to me, "Sine and cosine are the equations for two waves that cancel each other out. Between them, they produce the equation for the shape of the lens in your eye."

Structural film and video returned to the scene in the 1990s. This was partly because the con-cern with representation diminished and artists were newly interested in medium specificity. In addition, the development of new media made it timely to re-examine the intrinsic properties of older media. Structuralism respected the internal coherence of a film or video as a physical body, with all its implied mortality. Many of John Porter's films were structured by the three-minute length of a roll of 8 mm, and this internal logic was as pleasurable to audiences as finding that the shape of one's own eye describes an equation. A rash of tapes was produced on the Pixar 2000 in the mid 1990s, and part of the pleasure of watching Pixelvision was knowing that these videos were recorded on audiotape and that the jagged black scar on the frame was the actual image of an in-camera edit. Hard-core experimental filmmakers imposed rigid structures on the most vulnerable material. Mike Cartmell used a "chiasmic" structure to explore identity and paternity in *Film in the Shape of the Letter X* (1986). In a sort of on-the-spot structuralism, Phil Hoffman's *Opening Series* (1992–) is presented in pieces to be re-organized by audiences before each screening. This kind of structuralism has the same effect as lacing a corset around a pliant torso: it allows the stuff inside to remain soft and formless. Later in the decade, it would evolve into the scratch video genre, where the ephemerality of forgettable television clips was given a loose structure by randomized commands of digital editing.

Sad classified ads

30 September 1997: I dream I am in a room full of people who are all lying on sofas and reading newspapers. People are getting all weepy reading, and the mood is very mournful, but another woman and I are catching each other's glance and grinning. It turns out everybody had placed "Sad Classified Ads": it was kind of a performance.

Like the caress of a stingray, grief immobilizes the body as it traverses it. As the AIDS epidemic continued, people succumbed to melancholy paralysis. Although the urgency of AIDS activism abated—it is hard to remain in a state of crisis indefinitely—some artists returned feeling to our numbed bodies with blazing offerings of rage and love. Sado-masochism had a profound place in this process, as in the work of Tom Chomont, for whom S/M was a way to take control of the disease in his body. During this decade, Mike Hoolboom built a flaming body of work around AIDS, whose melting saturated colours and glistening high-contrast skins, as much as the bitter poetry of their words, impelled us to cling to life even while we flailed against it.

In its power to immobilize, grief imposes a state of perpetual Firstness. According to Peirce, it is impossible to exist sempiternally in a world of Firstness, a world that "consists in nothing at all but a violet color or a stink of rotten cabbage"–or in a pure feeling, be it love or pain.[7] A changeless state of mourning, or of any emotion, is unbearable. The most powerful AIDS work of this decade transmuted the Firstness of grief into the contemplative and active states of mourning and action. In its most transformative state, Thirdness–ideas that are preconceived, verbalized, yea, published in the newspaper–still has the power to move us to emotional states that far precede discourse.

Seinfeld and the "wilderness"

9 October 1997: I dream I am in a crowded New York apartment where some show is being filmed. Jerry Seinfeld is the MC. It is very New York and we non-New Yorkers are disdained. For some reason, they need another minor celebrity to interview someone, and my mother suggests me, and Seinfeld looks at me with suspicion. I say "Yes, I'm Laura Marks" as though he should

have heard of me, and he's in a bind so he has no choice. But my lipstick has worn off. Seinfeld seems to recognize the importance of this because he offhandedly gives me some money to get some. Then I'm in the bathroom down the hall, ready to put it on. But the light switch doesn't work. The automatic sensor doesn't work, and when I press the button on the rickety old fixture the light only shines dimly for a second!

This dream is set in a big city of vast cold buildings with broad grounds. It's dark and I'm looking for free parking on the snowy streets, but I take a turn onto the highway by mistake, and the voice of eminent Canadian film critic Peter Harcourt says, "It's okay, it's just what they call the wilderness." Soon enough, I am amused to find that this circumscribed bit of land that I'm driving through is what New Yorkers call the wilderness.

For many Canadian artists, it is a political choice to remain in Toronto, the centre of the Canadian art scene, even though New York, the centre of the world art scene, deems us quaint and parochial. Pleasure Dome showed many works by New York artists, and many Canadian artists have moved to New York permanently in search of glamour and recognition. In Toronto's small media community, artists live in the light but have no lipstick: in New York, we have the lipstick but can't get the light to shine on us. A very few Canadian experimental filmmakers and videomakers, such as Donigan Cumming and Steve Reinke, do break onto the parochial New York scene, for example by having their work screened in the New York Video Festival. Other Canadian artists decamped permanently to New York, the better to maintain their Canadian identities. Perhaps the best example is Ardele Lister, who moved to New York from the Vancouver feminist media scene and proceeded to make *Conditional Love (See Under: National-ism—Canada)* (1997), a bitter reflection on the US hegemony over Canadian media and the concomitant frailty of Canadian identity.

There is a myth that funding is easier to come by for filmmakers in Canada, and therefore the work is not as strong because it does not have to compete as viciously as American art, and perhaps this is another reason that Canadians ourselves diminish Canadian work. But mostly it is because we internalize the intensely self-absorbed consciousness of the US art world, according to which we do not exist. The colonized always has to know what the colonizer is doing, but the reverse is not so: Canadian artists, programmers, and writers have to be aware of the New York/US/world film scene, but the reverse is not so. To them, we are the wilderness.

Woman ejaculates on prospective Canadian

18 MARCH 1998: I dream I am watching a video, or maybe a commercial for McDonald's, where a sensual pregnant woman is saying she loves eating hamburgers so much she makes them last for three hours. Then there is a performance in a gallery in Los Angeles, where this same pregnant woman is in a shallow pool, masturbating while watching another woman. Then she ejaculates into the face of a man standing in the pool—she shoots a good six feet! It's from my point of view, as though I were ejaculating. I am offended at the performance, though; I think it's cheap-shot (!) feminism. This poor man turns out to be a performance artist himself, probably teaches at Cal Arts. He is doing work on orgasm too: he says that in orgasm he is cultivating his plant nature. Something to do with *sisal*. I promise to mail him a Canadian magazine with a review of his work, a Canadian road map, and something else. He tries to give me money for it, but I have the impression that it's all the money he has, so I refuse to accept his payment.

Experimental cinema has almost always rejected acting as implicated in the illusionist aesthetics of commercial cinema. Plus acting is expensive to shoot. But performance, confronting the viewer with a real body enduring experience in real time, has none of the illusionism of acting. Part of the return to phenomenal experience that characterized the 1990s was the return of performance. This was often inspired by unabashedly enthusiastic performances from decades past. However, few contemporary filmmakers had not been infected in some way by the poststructuralist disease that would have us believe our own bodies are just textual objects and don't even really exist. For a while in the '90s, it was uncool to believe that a person could ever reveal the essence of himself or herself, or even that there was an essence. But in performance, you find the meaning of the body through physical, not mental, acts; the body has to be right there, not a construct. Performers sacrificed their own bodies so the rest of us could have ours back. In her 1993 series *Aberrant Motion*, Cathy Sisler spun in the streets as a proxy for our collective disequilibrium. In *Super 8 1/2* (1994) and *Hustler White* (1996), Bruce LaBruce stripped all the way down to the layer of plastic wrap covering his heart, so that we didn't have to, or we could if we wanted to. Donigan Cumming convinced non-actors to pray for a Nettie they had never met (*A Prayer for Nettie*, 1995), sacrificing their authenticity to an audience that in turn suddenly became responsible for both them and her (the deceased Nettie had been Cumming's photographic collaborator and model, but the video does not tell us that).[8]

In 1967, Godard famously responded to criticism of his gory film *Weekend*, "It's not blood, it's red," meaning that his film was meant to be taken as a sign that was already at some remove from the real world it signified. But for performers in the 1990s, it was red *and* it was blood.

In performance, the perceiving and acting body is a Peircean sign machine, quivering like a tethered string between the poles of experience and communication. Whenever one presents one's body and actions for public consumption–i.e., presents oneself consciously as a sign– the same accelerated oscillation between the three modes takes place, for one is required to act, or make relations, an operation of Secondness, and to be genuine, or to operate in the mode of Firstness, at the same time that one manages oneself as a mental image. Ejaculating or shedding blood before an audience is only one way to do this.

Divorce ritual

29 August 1998: I dream I am in Los Angeles. I exit the freeway on a ramp that is made of wood and undulates like a little roller coaster, into a hilly neighborhood that is part Chicano, part Asian, and all the houses are close together and kind of doll-like with thatched roofs. Lots of people are in the toy-like park, old Mexican men and little boys playing chess. I am going to a museum where my husband and I are supposed to have a post-divorce ritual. It looks like one of those hands-on museums that were cool in the 1970s, with lots of winding passages and purple-and-black walls. We get there, and there are several couples, presumably also divorcing, gathered around the table. I've forgotten to bring some document, and also photographs, that we're supposed to burn as part of this ritual. I'm picturing an old photograph in my head and thinking I don't want to burn it!

Later, I walk by the village again and see that the little houses with thatch roofs have been burned for acres. The whole landscape is smoking and grey. It's awful. I am embarrassed when the people from the town see me staring at the misfortune.

One of the most painfully visceral experiences you can have at the movies is when the film catches in the projector gate and burns, especially if it is a precious lone print. We have seen that in the 1990s, many artists turned to archival film for a source of images. While the images could be deftly recontextualized and critiqued, filmmakers were also sometimes struck by the material of the film itself. In this decaying surface, archival filmmaking witnessed a death, a divorce of the original meaning from the image. Rather than recontextualize the images, filmmakers held funerals for their charred remains. Gariné Torossian built up a body of work during the decade whose surfaces were thick with painstakingly collaged film fragments, their scratched and glued textures overwhelming the appropriated images on their surfaces. Carl Brown's oeuvre through-out this decade continued to be a body of self-immolating cinema, whose recorded images dissolved in the chemical conflagration on the surface of the film. Earlier in the decade, Brown collaborated with Michael Snow on *To Lavoisier, Who Died in the Reign of Terror* (1991). Through this film's scarred and crackling surface, vignettes of everyday life are just barely visible, like the charred remains of a neighbourhood.

In the 1990s, filmmakers returned to touch the material body of film at a time when the medium has been pronounced obsolete. Of course, the idea of obsolescence is meaningless to non-industrial filmmakers: when a medium has been superseded by the industry, that's when artists can finally afford it. What precipitated the divorce of images from their medium was perhaps the institution of digital filmmaking; the medium of analog video had not been the same threat to film, because the two media looked and functioned so differently. Over in the world of commercial cinema, and increasingly among independent filmmakers as well, films were edited and processed not on a Steenbeck or at a lab but in the virtual space of the Media 100. Where now was the film's body? Celluloid became just an output medium for the virtual body of the film encoded in software.

As well as these moving reflections on film's body, the end of the decade saw a surprising nostalgia for analog video. Videomakers who moved to non-linear editing swore they would never go back—yet tapes were being turned out that simulated analog interference, dropout, and generational loss!

A Peircean would note that these works of materialist cinema liberate the medium to be meaningful as a body in itself, rather than the medium for another message. While plumbing archival films for their images is an operation of Thirdness, the mourning of film's material death is First in its reaction to the film as to another body.

I forget I own art

2 FEBRUARY 1999: I dream I own a work of art I'd forgotten about, even though it's very expensive, because it's thin like a pamphlet and it's just sitting in a letter rack like the Purloined Letter.

Steve Reinke's *The Hundred Videos* appears to sum up the various concerns of the decade. The videos began with a linguistic understanding of meaning, and the use of psychoanalysis, a linguistic form of interpretation, to unravel it. They moved to interests in sexuality, desire, the body, and AIDS. Following the anti-visual turn in the arts mid decade, they questioned documentary's relation to the truth. But throughout the decade, Reinke maintained a conceptual rigour that made these slight works linger in the memory of the viewer. *The Hundred Videos* enter the mind through a tiny aperture of attention and then expand to fill all the available space. The sad ashtray, the sincere inventor of potato flakes, Neil Armstrong's tribute to his dead dog—they went by in one to three minutes but stayed with me for years. By the end of the decade, in a final rejection of linguistic signification, Reinke and his video camera were chasing dust balls under the bed (*Afternoon, March 28, 1999*).

These are theorematic videos, examples of the most fertile mode of Thirdness. By creating relations among other signs, they are mental images. Reinke brought things together: foreign films and porn films, a love letter and a yearbook photo, an over-the-top pornographic performance and a list of self-doubts. In so doing, he generated enabling new concepts and new models for thinking, such as using hand puppets to role-play your fondest desires. Reinke's work showed the generosity of Thirdness, giving audiences material (not about which, but) with which to think.

Aggressive house

18 MARCH 1999: I dream I am in the house of these radical and rich art-world people who have two young children. It is a radical house, very dark inside, claustrophobic with rough concrete walls. They all go out while I stay. I crawl under the heavy, ancient wood furniture. The floors have escalator-like treads moving through them constantly, with the angles facing up like teeth, making it fairly impossible to walk. There is something even more menacing in the floor, concealed by long shreds of carpet, but I forget what it was. I think how irresponsible to raise children in such a dangerous house. I go into the little girl's (like three years old) room and see that she's programmed her computer to organize her stuff while she is out; things are going through the air as though on an invisible conveyor belt. I am impressed and think maybe I'm the only one who's intimidated by a house like this!

At the end of the decade, we were confronted with the Peircean extremes of performance, work so obsessed with action it could barely think, and information media, work so highly encoded in symbolic form it was incapable of affect. Now that digital editing could alter voice and gesture to simulacral perfection, the apparent naïveté of appearing live before the camera's witness had a new urgency. Emily Vey Duke, Scott Beveridge, and other artists exhibited pure affect for the camera, in performances whose virtue was in being as spontaneous as the single-take exhibitionism of their 1970s forebears. Ironically, it was mostly thanks to digital editing that Hollywood movies, as always belatedly stealing ideas from independent artists, found new ways to produce affective responses in the audience.

At the extreme of Thirdness, artists moved to the small screen and concentrated information with such density that it could no longer be processed as information but only affect. This time, however, the body experiencing hot flashes was not human but silicon-based. Attacked by hell.com, jodi.org, and other online artworks, computers jittered with illegible information, sprouted rashes of windows on their faces, and crashed. Their human caretakers felt this affective rush, at most, sympathetically. Meanwhile, many Canadian media artists seized upon, or continued to develop, installation as a medium that was apparently more physical than the virtual light of single-screen projection. In works by David Rokeby, Nell Tenhaaf, and other interactive media artists, the intelligent interface embraced the visitor as though to spill its brains into our attentive bodies.

At the end of the decade, everybody was saying we had moved decisively from a visual culture to an information culture. What, then, would become the role of the audio-visual media that artists had been coddling and pummeling throughout the decade, indeed the century? Now that we had machines to see, hear, and act for us, raw experience was a more precious commodity than ever before. The processing of information and the debased notion of interactivity were behaviorist, Secondness-based modes, which besides our computers could do without us. Throughout the decade, experimental film and video artists had been pulling their media from the Secondness-based modes of narrative and critique to a Firstness that was felt only in the body, and a hyper-symbolic Thirdness that was experienced as First by the proxy bodies of our machines. We hoped that new connections, new mental images, some Third thing as yet unimagined, would come to animate our minds again.[9]

Notes

1   Charles S. Peirce, "The Categories in Detail," in *Collected Papers*, vol. 6, Charles Hartshorne and Paul Weiss, eds. (Cambridge: Harvard University Press, 1931), 150.

2   See William Wees, *Recycled Images: The Art and Politics of Found Footage Film* (New York: Anthology Film Archives, 1993), and Scott Mackenzie, "Flowers in the Dustbin: Termite Culture and Detritus Cinema," *CineAction!* 47 (September 1998).

3   Peirce, "Categories in Detail," 172–73.

4   Gary Kibbins, "Bored Bedmates: Art and Criticism at the Decade's End," *Fuse* 22, no. 2 (Spring 1999).

5   This reactive mode takes us into the footsteps of Bruce Elder, who memorably argued in *Canadian Forum* that experimental work is the quintessentially Canadian cinema; see his "The Cinema We Need," *Canadian Forum*, February 1985.

6   Floyd Merrell, *Peirce's Semiotics Now: A Primer* (Toronto: Canadian Scholars' Press, 1995), 116.

7   Peirce, "Categories in Detail," 150.

8   Sally Berger, "Beyond the Absurd, Beyond Cruelty: Donigan Cumming's Staged Realities," in *Lux: A Decade of Artists' Film and Video*, Steve Reinke and Tom Taylor, eds. (Toronto: YYZ/Pleasure Dome, 2000), 282.

9   An earlier version of this essay appears in *Lux: A Decade of Artists' Film and Video*, 15–33.

Mike Hoolboom and the Second Generation of AIDS Films in Canada

Thomas Waugh

It's not happening to us in Canada, it's happening to them ...
—*Letters from Home*

As I START TO WRITE THIS in October 2000, Canadians have been plunged into an election, but I'm more interested in the Minister of Immigration's pre-election announcement of a new policy of compulsory HIV testing for all immigration candidates. The government responds to the warnings of planetary crisis coming out of this year's Durban International AIDS Conference 2000 by ineffectually trying to block it at the border and winning an election with the same stroke. It is as if, after two decades of the longest, mostly costly and fractious—and most unnecessary—epidemic in modern Canadian history, we have learned nothing. Instead of public outrage, we go on with our lives with resigned indifference to this flagrant act of bureaucratic scapegoating and brutality. For some reason, I think immediately of Mike Hoolboom, not only because he is a child of immigrants and an artist who has done his share of raging along the way against stupidity, powerlust, and greed in Ottawa (*Kanada*, 1993; *Valentine's Day*, 1994). I think of him mostly because as an artist, infected like so many others with the retrovirus that is besieging bodies and continents, he is responsible within Canadian cinemas for unforgettable images of social otherness, corporal abjection, and psychic intensity that sum up the experience of the person living with AIDS as our society moved through the 1990s. His images summon us not only to action against state cynicism, but also to conscience, lucidity, and affect *vis-à-vis* the medico-social crisis that we allowed to happen, and to a narrative identification with the corporal and existential meltdown—and illuminations—it entails.

In this chapter, I would like to focus on Hoolboom's three principal short works of the 1990s that encompass this imagery. But first I must establish the context of other Canadian film and video confrontations with AIDS over the last generation. On accepting the assignment to write a chapter about Hoolboom for this volume, I knew immediately that this prolific and versatile artist—the focus of a substantial critical literature that has enlisted many of Canada's finest (and worst) film critics, curators, and fellow artists,[1] not to mention a prolific film writer and curator in his own right—could never receive a comprehensive treatment in such a short space and that a narrow focus and selection would be necessary. AIDS certainly does not comprise the entirety of Hoolboom's contribution as an artist, nor define him as a human being—far from it. But as he himself has put it, after his 1988 diagnosis, HIV provided "a kind of unifying locus for my identity," and without a doubt his post-diagnosis work has transformed his mission and vision as a artist.[2] It has also found him a new and expanded audience, and elevated his "national" stature within this settler territory whose history, we must not forget, was driven by overcrowded, unsanitary boatloads and planeloads of immigrants and refugees, and contoured by the propagation—both infectious and environmental, and even military—of the scurvy, smallpox, cholera, typhus, typhoid, syphilis, tuberculosis, influenza, polio, and cancer that lay in wait for those immigrants and for the land's unimmunized original inhabitants. It is as if *Plague Years*, the title of Hoolboom's collection of film writings, could serve equally as a history of Canada.

This assignment came right after I'd hosted Hoolboom at Concordia University and witnessed firsthand his extraordinary commitment and magnetism as a public intellectual/artist—a persona all too lacking in the public sphere of an English Canada mobilized around Stockwell Day, Mike Harris, and Paul Martin. I also observed the unusual power of his films, his voice, and his person to engage a non-specialist, interdisciplinary audience with no interest in experimental cinema. Hoolboom's charisma, productivity, and profile notwithstanding, I am a non-auteurist trapped in an auteurist volume: for Hoolboom's work makes sense only, he might be the first to agree, as part of that larger cultural community and trajectory focussed on and by the retrovirus in the last decades of the century. I would thus like to begin by charting the first generation of Canadian AIDS audio-visual activism, the turbulent groundwater of other oeuvres and artists from which rose to the surface Hoolboom's great AIDS triptych of the 1990s: *Frank's Cock* (1993), *Letters from Home* (1996), and *Positiv* (1997).

Part I

Because the number of the dead far outweigh the number of the living, we've divided the world into nationalities in order to mourn our dead more perfectly. And our mourning together, this must be the thing we call a country.
—*Positiv*

After its "discovery" in 1981, what is now called Human Immunodeficiency Virus (HIV) and its devastation were commonly perceived here as an "American" phenomenon, and a strictly "gay" one at that, but one mercifully lagging, epidemiologically speaking, several years behind the sky-rocketing crisis in the States. Despite the futile alarms raised by *The Body Politic*, Toronto's "national" gay-liberation journal, and others, the virus soon infiltrated the bloodstreams—but all too slowly the cultural consciousness—of Canadians. In the US by mid decade, a major counter-offensive of long and short films and video documentaries—and even porno films—about AIDS was in place, most from within the lesbian and gay "community"; the most visible mainstream cultural texts were the sanctimonious TV movie of the week *An Early Frost* and its spitting sister, Larry Kramer's pioneering Broadway play *The Normal Heart* (both 1985). Canadian media artists, initially in Toronto, then elsewhere, inaugurated around 1984 an at-first tentative trickle of cultural work about AIDS. The first Canadian documentary prophetically appeared in Toronto in 1985 (*No Sad Songs*, Sheehan, co-produced by the AIDS Committee of Toronto), a survey of gay community mobilizations intercut with dramatized fantasy vignettes and sewn together by a mournful portrait of a gay man with AIDS preparing for the end with campy humour and courage. AIDS media work picked up momentum thereafter, most community-based, but with arts networks also well represented, reaching its peak at the end of the decade.[3]

The years since *No Sad Songs*, fifteen years or so of fevers and lulls in AIDS-related cultural production, can, alas, be divided into periods and genres. As I myself have recounted,[4] the popular melodrama genre, the "tearjerker," was the first, most lasting, and most popularly effective of the cultural formats deployed in the international arena, unashamed in its aestheticization of suffering, its narrativization of loss, and its elegiac solicitation of mourning. The first cycle (*An Early Frost*, *Buddies* [Bressan, 1985], *Parting Glances* [Sherwood, 1986], and somewhat later *Longtime Companion* [René, 1990] and *Together Alone* [Castellaneta, 1991]) bounced off its brilliantly cranky German mirror opposite *A Virus Knows No Morals* (von Praunheim, 1986). The cycle culminated in the international critical and box office hits of the early 1990s, *Les nuits fauves* (Savage Nights, Collard, 1992) and *Philadelphia* (Demme, 1993), followed by a sputtering of indie latecomers, notably *Jeffrey* (Ashley, 1995), and *It's My Party* (Kleiser, 1996).

Canada's two distinctive entries into the melodrama current, both musicals, came late: Laurie Lynd's miniature narrative elegy, the crystalline *RSVP* (1991), and John Greyson's rambunctiously hybrid agit-prop feature, the comedy-romance *Zero Patience* (1993). Like many of the above works, *Zero* was eloquent in its elegiac portrait of the courage and rage of people with AIDS (PWAs), but was also close to von Praunheim in its spunky irreverence and beyond even him in its deployment of spectacle, eroticism, humour, and experimental effects adapted from art video and puppet animation. *Zero* was also both an essay on the epistemology and politics of the epidemic and a cathartic melo-engagement with two pairs of lovers challenged and ennobled by crisis and finally parted by death. A follow-up Toronto feature by Cynthia Roberts, *The Last Supper* (1994), an impressively controlled adaptation of a PWA theatre piece about the protagonist's ritualized assisted suicide, featuring real-life actor Ken McDougall performing his own final struggle, as it turned out, is unfortunately not available even on video; the Vancouver video feature *The Time Being*, by Kenneth Sherman (1997), was equally noteworthy in its achievement and even innovative in its narrativization of a gay couple's encounter with sickness, death, and mourning. Neither of these latter two titles succeeded in having an impact, and the tearjerker momentum might have seemed spent had a certain Torontonian experimentalist not come out of an unexpected direction and renewed it.

But melodrama was only one of the genres favoured in the incredible wave of artistic productivity around AIDS, and *Zero* was not Greyson's first contribution to it. "AIDS is a war," this indefatigable anti-censorship activist and wunderkind of the Toronto video and film scene had announced in 1990, summarizing the political urgency of so much AIDS media activism; "there's no time for artsy debates about formal issues." He then went on to paraphrase the contrary view that "AIDS is a war, not just of medicine and politics but of representations—we must reject dominant media discourses and forms in favour of a radical new vocabulary that deconstructs their agendas and reconstructs ours." In fact, his own prolific video work was an energetic embrace and negotiation of both positions simultaneously. Greyson must also be seen as a facilitator, critic, and impresario, working infectiously behind the scenes of the first wave of Canadian film and video production. He listed the genres of AIDS media activism and contributed to virtually all of them either through directing or offstage support: cable access; documents of performances; documentary (memorial) portraits; experimental deconstructions of mass media; educational tapes on prevention, etc., for specific audience targets; documentaries about AIDS service organizations; safer sex tapes; activist documents of demonstrations, etc.; and PWA-directed tapes on such issues as alternate treatments.[5] The Toronto video cable project that Greyson organized with PWA video artist Michael Balser encompassed most of these genres and enfranchised a diverse lineup of young artists and community voices before being shut down by Rogers Cable's ham-fisted censorship in early 1991. It could be argued that a no less palpable contribution by Greyson around the time of Montreal's V International AIDS Conference in 1989 was strictly curatorial. Affirming that the wave of in-the-streets, in-your-face community-activist video, originating mostly in New York, was on a par artistically with the more culturally prestigious and visible utterances—and in fact he didn't care whether it was or not—he compiled and circulated a cornucopia of tapes for cultural, educational, and community work. His package, called *Video Against AIDS*, co-curated with American Bill Horrigan in 1990, contained seventeen American, two British, and three Canadian videotapes, and ran the gamut from obscure art video to encyclopedic grassroots documentation assemblages and dramatized community agit-prop, enshrining the notion that alternative media were the place where the action was. *Video Against AIDS* literally changed the face of AIDS in North America.[6]

The autobiographical status of *Les nuits fauves* was unique for a feature-length work of cinematic fiction but echoed a crucial genre in both PWA literature (Hervé Guibert, Paul Monette, Michael Lynch, Ian Stephens) and fine art (David Wojnarowicz, Robert Mapplethorpe, General Idea). Yet Collard's stupendous and indulgent posthumous film had been surpassed in its epochal raw intensity by another first-person posthumous work that appeared the same year, the small-format video documentary *Silverlake Life: The View From Here* (Joslin with Friedman, 1992). The following year saw both Derek Jarman's *Blue* and Gregg Bordowitz's *Fast Trip, Long Drop*, two very different self-referential works—film and video, ascetic and carnivalesque, testamentary and "the-world's-my-oyster" respectively—that cemented the autobiographical cycle of independent non-narrative film and video as the most significant of the 1990s. (The activist wave of the late 1980s had of course had autobiographical tendencies, but submerged in its collectivist ethic any individualist sense of the maker's life as creative material.)

Canada's distinctive representation within this international convergence of autobiographical work around the beginning of the '90s had in fact preceded the above autobiographies and was manifold. In addition to the short experimental video pieces by Michael Balser and Andy Fabo in Toronto, and Zachary Longboy in Vancouver,[7] there were two principal long works. The tender and lyrical video essay *Récit d'A* by Esther Valiquette (1990), an apparently conventional PWA portrait discreetly layered over the artist's own "coming out" as infected and her reflection on the body, mortality, and landscape, announced a new voice and a new departure beyond the demographics of Canadian AIDS artwork in the 1980s (male, gay, and Anglophone[8]). The other Canadian contribution was from the West Coast. Dr. Peter Jepson-Young, a gay doctor with and for AIDS (diagnosed in 1986), began producing weekly broadcasts for the Vancouver CBC station in 1990, and a lively and inspiring series of 111 short vignettes appeared before his death in 1992. Eventually repackaged for the CBC by David Paperny as *The Broadcast Tapes of Dr. Peter*, this cumulative work preserved the broadcasts' diary format and showed, among other things, the undaunted hero, literally blinded like Jarman by an opportunistic cytomegalovirus infection, veering cheerfully down a BC ski slope. *Tapes* was less about the then-cutting-edge video activism and analysis than about giving the "general public" a brave and dignified face for the syndrome. Its Academy Award nomination and US broadcast on HBO reflected this mainstream viability. Otherwise, neither *Récit* nor *Tapes* had much impact within the international AIDS cultural vanguard, and not only for the usual factor of their "Canadianness." Valiquette's beautiful work had the disadvantage of being in French and English at once, and almost inaccessible in either language version, as well as feeling a bit literary for Anglo tastes and both dated in its political innocence and ahead of its time in its confrontation with the metaphysics and iconographies of corporal mutability. Jepson-Young's work, which went on to a book version by Daniel Gawthrop, passed virtually unnoticed by the movement's New York and London-centred gatekeepers, Douglas Crimp, Paula Treichler, Cindy Patton, and Simon Watney,[9] perhaps because of its mainstream marketing or because the image of a privileged white gay man dying of AIDS, an Anglican to boot, seemed no longer front-line.

Part II

> We didn't know back then. Nobody did.
> —*Frank's Cock*

Mike Hoolboom's 1988 diagnosis took place in the same Vancouver hospital, St. Paul's, where Dr. Peter's practice and final years were lived out. Known then as a twenty-something Toronto experimental filmmaker with a reputation for formal rigour, celluloid purism in the age of video, and film community activism, his work fluctuated between structural minimalism and excess. Having discovered the writer within, Hoolboom was increasingly pushing the "new talkie" tendency of 1980s avant-gardism to its limits, developing clear talents as raconteur, diarist, and aphorist. An ardent collaborator, then as now, Hoolboom went on at the end of the decade to quarter temporarily in Vancouver by virtue of his working and personal relationship at that time with Ann Marie Fleming, an emerging figure in that city's experimental scene. Hoolboom's critical moment of truth, later rehearsed repeatedly in his 1990s films, not only altered his life but also resituated him as an artist in the international and Canadian context I have just sketched:

> So one Saturday afternoon we trooped off together to have our juice drained [at a Red Cross blood drive] and that was that. Until a letter came for me in the mail. Saying there was a problem with my donation. My blood. That I should go see my doctor. That's when he told me I was HIV positive. He was a young guy who worked in the clinic and he handed me a bunch of pamphlets and said, "I don't really know anything about this disease, I've never talked to anyone who's had it before but read this." I didn't handle the news all that well. I kept it to myself and waited to die. Drank a lot. Phoned up a bunch of people I'd slept with and passed the word along. And began a frantic tear of short films that's lasted till now. Never wanting to make anything bigger than my head because I didn't figure I'd be around to finish it. I just didn't know.[10]

The first generation of AIDS artists, from Bressan and Valiquette to Vito Russo, and the writers and visual artists I have mentioned above, had passed or were passing the torch, almost all dead by the time of this interview (just after shooting *Frank's Cock*). With this film, Hoolboom found himself for better or worse as one of the figureheads of the second generation of the AIDS arts movement, one of the first male artists not to have emerged from gay cultures and communities. Although the era of in-the-streets activism seemed to be passing, many of the other artistic concerns I have been inventorying would be taken up and reinvented in Hoolboom's AIDS triptych: the melodramatic impulse, the recycling and reconstruction of received media images, the metaphysical thrust, the negotiation between agit-prop urgency and formal innovation, and the exploration, transgression, and affirmation of sexuality.

Vancouver had also been the site of Hoolboom's encounter with Joey, a fellow member of a PWA group, that would become dramatized in 1993 as *Frank's Cock*, the first panel in Hoolboom's AIDS triptych. Despite its risqué title, its marketing as experimental, and its consumer warning of "extremely explicit," *Frank's Cock* is basically a populist melodrama, a narration of a gay romance

and its impending end in Frank's imminent death, notable for its power of affect and identification. The narrator, played by then-unknown western Canadian actor Callum Keith Rennie, tells
of his first encounter with his lover Frank, and their mentor–novitiate relationship of ten years, a
love story embellished by feats of raconteur braggadocio. The eponymous appendage, described
not seen, signals Hoolboom's appropriation of and celebration of same-sex desire that had been
at the core of the queer arts counter-offensive for almost a decade but was relatively new within
Hoolboom's hitherto flamingly heterosexual sensibility.[11] Hoolboom's narrative format based on
a direct-address on-screen narrator and a four-way split-screen mosaic structure, visually and
narratively intricate, struck an immediate chord. The unnamed Rennie character occupies the
upper right quadrant, frontally addressing the camera in informal, voluble, confidential close-up.
After the upper left awakens with a montage of physiological microphotography (no doubt con-
noting the invading micro-organisms, or all the swimming cells that Hoolboom repeatedly tells
us in film after film die every day in the body), the lower left quadrant recycles Madonna's
banned *Erotica* video. Eventually, the lower right chimes in with close-up excerpts of anal and
oral coupling from commercial gay pornography. All three peripheral quadrants are more or less
synchronized with the ebb and flow of Renney's tale and are visualized complementarily with
Hoolboom's characteristic tinted black and white. The soundtrack includes his unabashed
appropriation of romantic if not outright sentimental music, including that of another Frank:
Sinatra. Concision is perhaps the key to the film's impact: one hardly believes that such layered
narrative complexity, visual virtuosity, and emotional wallop have all been demonstrated in only
eight minutes. Hoolboom returned to variations of this tight polyphonic formula for his subsequent two films.

If Hoolboom's breakthrough, rewarded with festival prizes and wide circulation, had come
out of an interpersonal encounter and a discovery of other sexualities, the next film was more
about a retroactive Mike-come-lately discovery of the political movement that had grown up
within the epidemic in the 1980s. A visit to an ACT UP rally in New York[12] had occasioned yet
another transformation in Hoolboom, by his account, from a living-room observer of the AIDS
crisis to a participant in a collective belonging:

> we realized that most of us—and there were thousands—were positive ... a congregation
> of those who had laid their beloveds into the ground, and come here still daring to hope.
>
> ...
>
> Vito Russo was the last to speak, and I'd never heard 20,000 people cry at the same
> time—leather giants and drag queens holding each other in the flood. Something that
> day changed for me ...[13]

Hoolboom subsequently discovered a speech that Russo had made in Albany in the summer
of 1988, which then became the core of *Letters from Home* (1996). The elements of direct address,
narrative excess, and melodramatic affect are extended from *Frank*, but this time the multi-
layered polyvocality is sequential rather than simultaneous. The narrative now migrates from
voice to voice in a multi-racial, multi-accented, multi-generational procession of protagonists
and narrators on screen and off (mostly figures from the Toronto arts scene, where Hoolboom
had by this time re-established himself). *Frank's* individually focussed simplicity was set aside;
the film now aspires in its allegorical casting beyond the gay pale to the collective universality
Hoolboom experienced that day with ACT UP. Russo's text is a narrative of his and his friends'
experience as PWAs, and an accusatory indictment of the state (ACT UP's usual target) and

society for its avoidance, indifference, and stigma. Hoolboom fleshes out the speech with his own characteristic dream narratives of a diagnosis (borrowed from Herman Hesse) plus a bodily revelation, a personal anecdote, some Canadian content, and even more high-contrast visual flair than before. The rotating first-person voice includes for the first time in this series Hoolboom himself, briefly superimposed over water images and sounds, appropriating Russo's words "As a person with AIDS" for himself. The procession finally culminates in Rennie, this time recounting a sickbed encounter between the first-person PWA he plays and a friend, incorporating the melo-tropes of flowers, embrace, and epiphany sealed in a mutual looking into eyes. All unfolds be-neath the most manipulative rendition of "Amazing Grace" imaginable (frail piano transposing into organ, swelling polyphonically under a glorious sunrise that blazes out Rennie's face). The effect of this anthem, which has migrated from the nineteenth-century abolitionist movement to the twentieth-century anti-addiction movement and now to AIDS culture, is as devastating as it is absolutely true. But that's not all: the final shot is Hoolboom, in extreme close-up, looking into the lens.

The introduction of the new multiple therapies around the time of the Vancouver Interna-tional AIDS Conference in 1996 spelled a paradigm shift of AIDS discourse, among other things what Paula Treichler has called a "transition from a concept of AIDS as a classic epidemic of acute infectious disease to that of AIDS as a chronic, potentially manageable disease"[14] (at least in the privileged and medicared pockets of the so-called developed world). This miraculous return—at least for now—of many of the sick to the ranks of the working populace, and of the arts critic from the job of necrologizing dead artists to the luxury of monitoring continuing oeuvres and maturing artists, occasioned a parallel shift in the symbolics and genres of AIDS texts. *Destroying Angel* (1998), a short film by Hoolboom's old Sheridan colleague Philip Hoffman, co-directing with American PWA Wayne Salazar, in some ways epitomized this shift. Pursuing familiar diaristic and autobiographical conventions by expanding the frame into both co-authors' "fami-lies," the film's narrative and real-world dénouement confound the AIDS mortality cliché and viewers' expectations when the PWA turns out to be a survivor mourning Hoffmann's partner, Marian McMahon, the third artist in the diaristic triangle, fallen to cancer. By 2000, the AIDS melodrama was for all intents and purposes obsolete, and a critic could welcome the pill-popping French film *Drôle de Félix* that he calls an "AIDS romance" in the following terms:

> to my knowledge at least, one of the first films with an HIV+ protagonist who is offered
> the expectation of a future, however delimited. In this charming romantic tale ... the final
> clinch between the lovers isn't a deathbed scene but the beginning of an idyllic holiday.[15]

Hoolboom's third AIDS panel *Positiv* had in fact offered the expectation of a future three years earlier, going into circulation both separately and as part of the six-film package *Panic Bodies*. With its serene image of acceptance, bliss (both carnal and spiritual), and eternity, and its presid-ing collaborator Tom Chomont, *Bodies* seemed to answer back Hoolboom's previous long work, the scandalous *House of Pain* (whose resident collaborator had been the Toronto performance artists of extreme sensation Paul Couillard and Ed Johnson). This latter film, a nightmare inferno of visual intensity, erotic extremes, and corporal abjection, part Dantesque, part Rabelaisian, had been released after *Frank's Cock* in 1994–95, put together out of four semi-autonomous shorts. It was as if *Panic Bodies'* riposte to *House of Pain* symbolically articulated the 1996 shift. Appearing as it did in 1997, *Positiv* would of course not have had the full retroactive distance to assess this paradigm shift in such explicit terms, but the film does articulate an important evolution in

Hoolboom's AIDS conception all the same, as if demonstrating and updating Russo's original ultimatum that AIDS is about living:

> Because we already know how we're going to die. What we don't know, what we're asking you now, is how we're going to live ... AIDS is a test of who we are as a people ...

Hoolboom's self-reflexive insertion into the text is now fully realized, no longer vicariously embodying "Joey" (Frank's real-life lover), Callum Keith Rennie, or Vito Russo, but maintaining a continuous presence on the screen: his own face, his own body, his own biographical trajectory, his own personal circle of family and friends. *Positiv* returns to *Frank*'s four-panel split-screen structure. Not only does he fully take over Rennie's place as the frontal on-screen narrator in the upper right; he "performs" in the other quadrants as well, recycling self-reflexive narrative fragments from earlier apparently uncompleted projects that evoke his memories of growing up and moving away (one fragment where he is decked out in angel wings on a lonely highway) and his more recent experience of medical tests and treatment (Hoolboom engaged in the prophylactic inhalation of aerosol pentamidine to ward off pneumocystis pneumonia, shots that curiously extend the orality of the earlier panels). Of this experience of medicalization, the narrator pronounces,

> There's not much the doctors can do for you, except draw [your] blood out for tests. In fact, the more your condition worsens, the more tests [they seem to need]. Your identity is clinging to these numbers, your viral loads, the ratios of enzymes and tissues that continue to betray you.[16]

At the same time, the found footage strands veer in their relation to the voice from exact synchrony (shots of detached hands matching the narrator's memories of his childhood piano efforts and conceptions of his unintegrated body parts) to delirious arbitrariness. The consistent thread through all the found footage from SF and pedagogical films alike is corporality, gleanings from pop culture's neurotic obsession with bodily transformations, from Ken Russell's *Altered States* to Fred and Ginger's *Shall We Dance*. Although not the most successful of the three works in terms of mainstream festival audience impact and prizes (at least as an autonomous short film), *Positiv* is in many ways the most challenging and original, departing from the land of melodrama and finality into its own distinctive personal territorial flux, where "I guess I'm gonna have to wait it out"—part holding-pattern, part stock-taking, part manifesto.

Part III

> ... just all of a sudden it comes to you—a new word has taken the place of your body ... the little sticker on your chest doesn't say, "Hi I'm Mike," it only says "AIDS" because you don't belong to yourself any longer, and as you get older it's not you they're talking to anymore, it's the sickness ...
> —Positiv[17]

In the final part of this chapter, I would like to revisit Mike Hoolboom's AIDS triptych and focus on his performative articulations of the sexualized, infected, abject body—in short, the *queered* body. In the 1980s, I had associated Hoolboom with a masculinist wing of Toronto experimental cinema, a certain Sheridan College-Bruce Elder cohort, approximating the network that Hoolboom himself had once termed the "escarpment" school.[18] The "Cinema We Need"[19] flurry of the mid 1980s had summed up for me many of the aspirations of the cohort, endowing a particular cultural aesthetic with imperial cultural and political pretensions on a national scale, without any serious ramifications for the rest of the cultural struggles going on elsewhere within these national borders, a *dialogue des sourds* by straight white Anglo male intellectuals living in Toronto and Ottawa. The cohort's unquestioned masculinism was of course only part of the problem, but it was the start and end of the debate for me. When Hoolboom later affectionately credited the cinematography of *Letters from Home* to his longtime collaborator Steve Sanguedolce, the "cream of the eyejocks" (with whom he had also made the pre-diagnosis road movie *Mexico*, in many ways Hoolboom's most masculinist movie[20]), he inadvertently touched my queer Montréaler's nerve that had blocked me out of the Toronto jock experimentalism of the previous decade. But the Hoolboom of *Letters* had long since moved far beyond this jockdom (despite the vestigial traces of athletic metaphors in the AIDS films, e.g., "Joey" wanting to be "Wayne Gretzky with a hard-on" in *Frank*, his fascination with the size of the titular cock, and Hoolboom's receptivity to ACT UP militarist and fire-fighting rhetoric in *Letters From Home*). At the time of his diagnosis in the late 1980s, Hoolboom was moving beyond the eyejock visual primacy and intellectualism of his earliest work. He was entering the territory of sexual iconoclasm with his heterosexual diary and performance films, where his female partners of the day, from Kika Thorne to Svetlana Lilova to Ann Marie Fleming, were offering their bodies, sexual engagements, or relationships with the filmmaker—as well as artistic input—to the camera.[21] In this territory of the body, the cracks in the machismo, its vulnerability, volatility, and relativity, seemed to be spreading.

I do not mean to overwhelm Hoolboom's frenzied productivity of the first post-diagnosis years with a teleological trajectory, all the more so since many of the short films that came out one after another had been based, like *Mexico*, on material shot earlier. Still, what is clear is that the 1993 Hoolboom of *Frank's Cock* was a vastly different species. The transformative effect of his diagnosis was repeatedly being confirmed in interviews: "Our identity hinges on our body. Now what happens to that image once you become HIV positive? ... I worked harder. Finished more films. And quite unconsciously began a series of films that take the body as its subject ...."[22] It does not require a simplistic biographical reading to recognize throughout the triptych the obsessive repetition of this diagnosis moment. One thinks of the charged use of Billy Holliday's "You've Changed" on the soundtrack or of the opening dream narrative of *Letters from Home*, punctuated by ominous flash close-up shots of a man in a surgical mask:

> as I get closer I can see a man stooped over a small set of crystals gathered on a table. He doesn't look up as I get close and I understand each of these crystals represent a part of myself ... He looks up then and for the first time I can see he's wearing a doctor's surgical mask. He says, "I'm sorry. I'm afraid you're HIV positive," pointing down at the pile, and sure enough, right in the middle of the glow, there's an off-colour stone slowing wearing down everything around it. I guess the future's not what it used to be.

This whole sequence is topped off by found footage of conflagration and catastrophe.

The spectator also repeatedly experiences variations of this trans-/per-formative pronouncement that are less medical than social, the enactment of stigma through speech or even more profoundly through the look. Reflected in the haunting look back at the lens of the speakers in *Letters*, of Hoolboom himself in *Positiv*, and in the proliferating eyes in all four quadrants as *Positiv* moves towards its end, this stigma is repeatedly recapitulated by the voice: "If I'm dying from anything, it's from the way you look when I see you with that funny kind of half smile on your face..." (*Letters*) and "you read the whole cruel truth on their faces. You watch yourself dying there..." (*Positiv*). At the same time, indissociably, there are the moments of knowing constituted by "coming out" tropes, those Foucauldian exercises in reversing and reclaiming stigmatizing discourses, once the sacrament of gay liberation, now the political ritual of the constituency of the infected. As in Bordowitz's *Fast Trip* four years earlier, the on-screen author's identity is performed repeatedly, continuously through the confession, or rather affirmation, of seropositivity and illness. Taken together, the three narrations of the triptych include about a dozen such affirmations, either enacted or narrated.

Hoolboom's performance of identity through transgressive sexuality is even more obsessive, not only spoken but also visual. This is the zone where even Cronenberg fears to tread, the zone beyond Greyson's flopping penises and anal puppets of *Zero*, the "extremely explicit" zone of throbbing indexical flesh: from the porno display and the romantic anecdote that creates worship of rimming in *Frank*, to the intensely ecstatic sequence of kissing and lovemaking by nude male couples under the shower in *Letters*, to the masturbatory frenzy, variously farcical and transcendent, of *A Boy's Life* and *Moucle's Island*, the two lusty chapters that seemingly balanced the comparatively chaste serenity of *Positiv* in the composite feature *Panic Bodies*. In this latter work, Hoolboom, the narrative and autobiographical subject with his intense eyes, earnest voice, and blistered flank, joins a processional fresco of a dozen or so other panic bodies through its six episodes. Cumulatively, the filmmaker creates equivalences between the affective intensities of mortality with the sensory frenzies of genitality, and thus questions even further the ambiguous boundaries between sex and death. Throughout, it is this obsessive play with knowledge and revelation—verbal, visual, corporal—that Eve Sedgwick identifies as having been "inexhaustibly productive of modern Western culture and history at large," "a frightening thunder [which] can also, however, be the sound of manna following."[23]

The erotic performances in *Panic Bodies* panicked more than one lazy film critic, and one of them, Odile Tremblay, did not hesitate to collapse sexual gesture into literal embodiments of authorial identity and personality, *showing* into *being*:

> How the devil could this confused film have seduced a jury [who had bestowed on *Panic* the best Canadian feature award at Montreal's 1999 Festival du nouveau cinema et des nouveaux médias], endlessly pushing its experimental side towards the land of the marginal? Excessively ambitious, this narcissistic documentary woven out of homosexual obsessions (we are forced to watch countless masturbation scenes) seems to want to demonstrate for the sake of demonstrating, upset for the sake of upsetting, provoke for the sake of provoking, without delivering any coherent message at the end of the road.[24]

Out of the mouths of homophobic incompetents, paradoxically, comes a not-far-off understanding of the artistic effect of Hoolboom's performative marshalling of sexual imagery. The performances of two discrete identities, sexual and sero-, whether verbal or gestural, are relayed separately or in tandem. Hoolboom produces or archives, looks at, shoots, shows, and speaks the gestural repertory of sexual marginality, the bodily performance of immuno-marginality. But the two identities tend to merge in their instability, all the more so within the formats of split screen, sound-image counterpoint, and narrative identification, as if together they constitute an expanded and fluid identity configuration. Beyond the post-Stonewall notion of fixed sexual essence, this is a sphere of abject stigma and otherness—in short, of queerness. Each of the three films is structured by these performative moments, where voice confronts body and sexual act, image confronts image, speech and sound confront images, and all together enact identity. *Positiv*, the final panel of the AIDS triptych, the most fully realized consummation of Hoolboom's autobiographical discourse, is the ultimate stage in his confrontation with both his body and his identities. It seems the perfect demonstration of what Annamarie Jagose has called

> the multi-directional pressures which the AIDS epidemic places on categories of identification, power and knowledge ... a radical revision of contemporary lesbian and gay politics ... a radical rethinking of the cultural psychic constitution of subjectivity itself.[25]

Hoolboom the social subject may or may not be bisexual,[26] but Hoolboom the filmmaker is here and queer.

Interestingly, Hoolboom has connected the articulations of identity, both as sexual outsider and as infected, to a general shift towards narrativity in these three works and elsewhere:

> many of those traditionally excluded from even marginal modes of expression—women, people of colour, gays—have an abiding interest in a narrative practice because their experience must be accounted for, their stories so long ignored given shape by communities of interest ... I guess I've rediscovered stories over the last few years as I've had to come to grips with my HIV status, my own imminent decline ... The time I've got. I have to make resolutions quicker, to go back and try to make explicit the patterns of dissent that have narrated my own confusions. This looking back is undertaken with the hot breath of The End on my back, and occasions my own need to tell stories again. To recount what happened and why.[27]

This movement toward narrative accompanied his general disillusionment with the avant garde through the 1990s, a contradictory development that saw him publishing *Inside the Pleasure Dome: Fringe Film in Canada*, a collection of interviews with his fellow practitioners of independent and avant-garde film/video in Canada, while at the same time pronouncing the eulogy for eyejock avant-gardism:

> The work I make and the work of others I'm interested in is very small work—not in ideas or commitment—but in terms of an economy of exchange. It lives outside the traditional menus of attention, of theatre chains and daily papers, and this marginal perspective allows it a freedom it couldn't have elsewhere. The danger in this freedom is solipsism, that "avant-garde" film becomes another genre like the western or the horror film. But without a social context. So it begins to implode. To restage its own history with a visual rhetoric that is increasingly difficult to follow by any but the most well versed of its devotees ... As I'm nearing [the close of *Fringe Film*] it's begun to take the shape of mourning, of a lament for a practice whose days are clearly numbered ... Because a real artist, someone who isn't just making work out of a recipe book, is trying to figure how to live ...[28]

The growing disenchantment with the avant garde was mutual, if the fiercely hostile, sarcastic, and *ad hominem* review of *Letters from Home* by Bart Testa, Hoolboom's erstwhile champion, is any indication. Testa taxed the "Hoolboom franchise" with a wide range of shortcomings:

"coping [sic]" techniques from experimentalists such as Bruce Elder and Bruce Connor, playing "dial-a-stylistic," "rotat[ing] personae," "the duplicity of special pleading that also uses the plea of human universalism," and in general producing "moralizing," "wordy," "arch," and ephemeral work, as well as "AIDS rhetoric" that dates badly. Even the praise is faint and begrudging: *Letters* is a "strong renter," "barely sidestepp[ing] AIDS clichés," and Hoolboom is a better "magpie montagist" than Bonnie Klein![29] Hoolboom's shortcomings are, of course, crimes against an (imagined?) avant garde of an earlier era with its doctrinaire culture and ethics of formal innovation and artistic coherence, its politics of entrenched social marginality, and its phobic fear of both sentiment and commerce. But these crimes were arguably virtues, all of them, in the postmodern '90s of multiple and crossover audiences, identities and practices, hybrid forms and influences, and queerly volatile political and cultural configurations of mainstreams and margins.

Hoolboom's affirmation of narrative as part of a new aesthetic hybridity, his embrace of autobiography and documentary, performance and eroticism, melodrama and activism, his growing detachment from the avant garde, enabled the discovery of new audiences and constituencies. The darling of both experimental and mainstream festival audiences as well as the AIDS community and educational organizations, Hoolboom was embraced, even appropriated, perhaps most enthusiastically by lesbian and gay audiences anchored in the worldwide networks of lesbian/gay/queer film and video festivals. For the copywriters at Montreal's Image et Nation festival, who offered Hoolboom a retrospective in 1998 and an update program in 2000, the Toronto filmmaker has

> a unique vision of living as a gay man with AIDS ... a revolutionary subject ... Described by some as the most important Canadian filmmaker of his generation, this adventurous and challenging experience will change the way you look at film forever.[30]

As I finish writing this during the surprisingly fierce Christmas of 2000, the election, long since over, has maintained the status quo, the policy of scapegoating silently takes its course, and Canada has increasingly become *Kanada* (with "There's No Business Like Show Business" now enshrined as the national anthem). The South African AIDS conference has made the Vancouver conference's momentary space for paradigm shifts and hope seem a distant memory, as the dimensions of the global catastrophe—and the soaring infection rates in Canadian backyards—become increasingly clear. Showing *Positiv* to various groups this year, I have found that audiences and I don't cry as we did for *Frank's Cock* and *Letters from Home*. Instead, dry-eyed but no less profoundly moved on other levels, we engage with Hoolboom's serene acceptance of the organic otherness of his body, his movement beyond the concrete particularity of seropositivity, sickness, and sexual identities, towards a generalized queerness that he performs together with his perplexed sickbed visitors and film spectators alike. Meanwhile, Hoolboom's newly deepened commitment is to writing. A novel is in progress, whose title will include some variation of the past tense of the verb "to say," the AIDS anagram he has been playing with throughout the 1990s, fascinated by how the migration of a single letter in a devastating acronym becomes the compulsion to speak, create, perform. Whether the writing extends, diverts, or problematizes Hoolboom's relationship of shared engagement with audiences and impels his continued artistic effort to "figure how to live" will depend on the changing social context as this second generation of AIDS artists, of which he is a part, plays out its mission, ceding, in turn, inevitably, to a third generation of AIDS artists. As Hoolboom said in 1993, "It used to be that we thought meaning was contained in the work but now we understand that the work is part of a social relation that is always changing. Always alive."[31]

Notes

1   Among the contributors to the often superb critical material on Hoolboom are Cameron Bailey, Michael Dorland, Peggy Gale, Marc Glassman, Noreen Golfman, Robert Everett Green, Janine Marchessault, Laura Marks, Tom McSorley, Geoff Pevere, Steve Reinke, Catherine Russell, Barbara Sternberg, William Wees, and Mike Zryd.

2   Cameron Bailey, "Interview with Mike Hoolboom," in *Lux: A Decade of Artists' Film and Video*, Steve Reinke and Tom Taylor, eds. (Toronto: YYZ/Pleasure Dome, 2000), 227.

3   For a chronology of US alternative media see Alexandra Juhasz, *AIDS TV: Identity, Community, and Alternative Video* (Durham: Duke University Press, 1995), videography by Catherine Saalfield.

4   Tom Waugh, "Erotic Self-Images in the Gay Male AIDS Melodrama," in *Fluid Exchanges: Artists and Critics in the AIDS Crisis*, James Miller, ed. (Toronto: University of Toronto Press, 1992), 122–34.

5   John Greyson, "Strategic Compromises: AIDS and Alternative Video Practices," in *Reimaging America: The Arts of Social Change*, Mark O'Brien and Craig Little, eds. (Philadelphia and Santa Cruz: New Society Publishers, 1990), 60–74. AIDS-related video works directed by Greyson in those prolific years of the late 1980s include *Moscow Doesn't Believe in Queers* (1986), *The Ads Epidemic* (1987), *Four Safer Sex Shorts* (1987), *Angry Initiatives, Defiant Strategies* (1988), *The Pink Pimpernel* (1989), *The World is Sick (Sic)* (1989). See Tom Folland, "Deregulating Identity: Video and AIDS Activism," in *Mirror Machine: Video and Identity*, Janine Marchessault, ed. (Toronto: YYZ, 1995), 227–37, for a useful contextualization of this early Toronto AIDS video activity within international theory and practice.

6   Chicago's Video Data Bank and Toronto's V-Tape were to sell up to two hundred copies of the three-cassette package to arts and educational institutions, but its impact was even wider than the sales suggest since it was often handed over free to community organizations. Data kindly provided by the two organizations, December 2000.

7   Respectively, *Survival of the Delirious* (1988) and *Choose Your Plague* (1993).

8   The lag in Québec artistic responses to the epidemic is curious. Denys Arcand and his cast put together the first mainstream Québec cinematic portrait of a PWA in 1985 in *Decline of the American Empire* (released in 1986): the "tragically" gay sex-addict art historian who pisses blood and thereby absolves/exculpates the promiscuity of his heterosexual friends. This erroneous and pernicious image figment would later be justified by actor Yves Jacques after his own coming-out a decade later by claiming that little was known at that time of AIDS—the same year that universal HIV screening was introduced into the blood-donation system in the "industrialized" worlds, Montréal AIDS community organizations were already underway, and Rock Hudson's diagnosis and death became the number-one media story! My hypothesis is that the resignation of the post-referendum arts scene, articulated in an apolitical formalism, did not spare *Decline* and, coupled with cultural insulation from the North American media's AIDS crisis of conscience, allowed Québec artists and writers to slumber on in the city with the highest infection rate in Canada until the V International Conference on HIV/AIDS in Montréal in 1989. The first Québec French-language audio-visual work of any substance, *Récit d'A*, appeared the following year: a personal masterpiece by a seropositive heterosexual woman making her first tape who nonetheless somehow felt compelled to journey to San Francisco to interview a person with AIDS.

9   *Tapes* is also ignored by Catherine Saalfield, the compiler of the videography in Juhasz' *AIDS Video*, as well as by the author herself, a surprising omission in the light of the book's aspirations to definitive historiography. However, a paragraph's attention was accorded in Rob Baker, *The Art of AIDS: From Stigma to Conscience* (New York: Continuum, 1994), 84–85.

10 Dirk de Bruyn, "What he sAID: an interview with Mike Hoolboom," *Workprint*, Spring 1993, 5.

11 Exceptionally, Hoolboom plays with drag in *Man* (1991) and *The New Man* (1992), co-directed with the feminist Fleming, and with same-sex couples in *Kanada* (1993).

12 In the company of Tom Chomont, the gay PWA experimental filmmaker from New York, a key collaborator of the 1990s, whose letter about a personal encounter with death would become the basis of *Eternity*, part of Hoolboom's *Panic Bodies* in 1998.

13 Mike Hoolboom, *Plague Years: A Life in Underground Movies*, Steve Reinke, ed. (Toronto: YYZ, 1998), 112.

14 Paula A. Treichler, *How to Have Theory in an Epidemic: Cultural Chronicles of AIDS* (Durham and London: Duke University Press, 1999), 325.

15 José Arroyo, "Review: *Drôle de Félix*," *Sight and Sound* 11, no. 1 (January 2001): 47.

16 The phrase, scored out, appears in the *Plague Years* version of the script only, while the parenthetical phrase is in the final film version. The alterations were accidental, according to Hoolboom.

17 This excerpt appears in the *Plague Years* version of the script, page 159, but not in the final film.

18 Mike Hoolboom, "A History of the Canadian Avant-Garde in Film," in *The Visual Aspect: Recent Canadian Experimental Films*, Rose Lowder, ed. (Avignon: Editions des archives du film expérimental d'Avignon, 1991), 43.

19 The principal texts in the "The Cinema We Need" debate (authored by Bruce Elder, Bart Testa, Piers Handling, Peter Harcourt, Michael Dorland, and Geoff Pevere and published in *Canadian Forum* and *Cinema Canada* in 1985) are collected in *Documents in Canadian Film*, Douglas Fetherling, ed. (Peterborough: Broadview Press, 1986), 260–336. Hoolboom also made a lesser-known contribution to the debate: "The Cinema We Have: Rumblings from Canada's Other Cinema," *Innis Herald* (November 1986) and *Splice* (newsletter of Saskatchewan Filmpool, Spring 1987).

20 *Mexico*, released in 1992 out of material shot around the time of Hoolboom's pre-Vancouver, pre-diagnosis days, was an ambitious and disturbing exploration of continental politics just as the Tories were pushing through NAFTA, but also an ambivalent immersion in the culture of the bullring and industrial landscapes.

21 Most of the sex-diary films, including *From Home* (1988), *Was* (1989), *Eat* (1989), and *Two* (1990, with Kika Thorne) have apparently—symptomatically?—been withdrawn from circulation. Still in distribution are *Man* (1991) and *The New Man* (1992), both made with Ann Marie Fleming.

22 de Bruyn, "What he sAID," 6.

23 Eve Kosofsky Sedgwick, *The Epistemology of the Closet* (Berkeley: University of California Press, 1990), 68, 78.

24 Odile Tremblay, "L'art de provoquer pour provoquer...," *Le Devoir*, 9 February 2000, B10.

25 Annamarie Jagose, *Queer Theory: An Introduction* (New York: New York University Press, 1996), 94–95.

26 Hoolboom currently does not publicly acknowledge a fixed sexual identity, but this feels more like queer fluidity than coy evasiveness; he deflected a journalist's question at Concordia as to whether it is true that he is straight with a big grin, hip motion, and "I wouldn't say *straight*," drawing out the final word in a three syllable phonetic performance of butch camp.

27 de Bruyn, "What he sAID," 2, 9.

28 de Bruyn, "What he sAID," 2.

29 Bart Testa, "Mike Hoolboom's *Letters from Home* Sidesteps AIDS Clichés," *Point of View* 32 (Summer/Fall 1997): 35–36. The critic's intemperateness is compounded by grossly presumptuous generalizations about the "banalization" of the epidemic in 1997 and the branding of those who share body fluids or needles as "moral idiots."

30 *Image & Nation: Festival international de cinéma gai & lesbien de Montréal*, catalogues 1998 and 2000, pages 49 and 25 respectively.

31 de Bruyn, "What he sAID," 4.

The Lisa Steele Tapes
Investigation and Vision
Catherine Russell

INCLUDING THE WORK OF LISA STEELE in an anthology on Canadian filmmaking is a *de facto* recognition of the interpenetration of video and film that has developed since the early years of video art. Steele herself has always worked in video, and yet over the course of twenty-five years, her tapes have evolved in ways that tend to parallel closely developments in experimental film practices. From her earliest minimalist tapes of the 1970s, to the collaborative docu-fictions produced with Kim Tomczak since 1984, Steele's trajectory moves from an intimate exploration of the medium and the self to neo-narratives, militant activism, and socio-cultural investigations of Canadian institutions and histories. A number of themes run throughout this large body of work, and I have chosen to isolate those that admittedly impinge on the practices and discourses of filmmaking and film studies. Even so, Steele's techniques of autobiography, confession, performance, narrativity, documentary, and archiveology are specific to video, which, more so than film, is always inscribed into the work as a technology of observation.

Steele's work consistently negotiates the encounter between human body and machine, in such a way that "the machine" encompasses the larger scope of social institutions. "Video" is thus not only the artist's tool and medium but also an allegory for social practices of observation, investigation, censorship, and control. Techniques of investigation and interrogation are utilized and at the same time subjected to analysis themselves, as Steele also deploys the video medium as a mode of vision and imagination, constantly finding new ways to see beyond the limits of social frames. The following is not necessarily a comprehensive survey of Steele's work, as the total oeuvre of more than twenty-one solo and seven collaborative pieces demands far more than a single chapter to be appreciated adequately. Instead, I have chosen a selection from this body of work, broken down into four overlapping stylistic and periodic stages that I have named "Involuntary memory" (1972–76), "Craving detail" (1975–78), "The performance of the other woman" (1978–82), and "Archival fictions" (1984–97).

Involuntary Memory
Autobiography and confession

Steele's work in the early 1970s was based in performance, featuring the artist's body as a site of memory; each tape practises a different method of retrieval for different kinds of confessions and stories. The tape for which she may be best known is *Birthday Suit: Scars and Defects*, a twelve-minute black-and white work made in 1972 when Steele was twenty-seven years old. This was actually her fifth tape, and its simplicity belies its conceptual richness. In honour of her birthday, Steele presents her naked body to the unblinking gaze of the camera. While the tape can be located within what Rosalind Krauss has called "the aesthetics of narcissism" that characterized the first decade of artist's video, it also provides an important counter-image to the emergent critique of the female body in narrative cinema. In fact, most commentators make this latter point the tape's main achievement. As Dot Tuer puts it: "A votive offering to the technological gaze, *Birthday Suit* ... downplays the representation of the body as a gendered subject, [and] highlights its tangible physicality as an object within an electronic medium."[1] Ranee Baert points out how "[t]he body is the ground of experience, the evidence of action: it is the guarantor of the self, the 'I.'"[2] In 1974, the tape constituted an innovative intervention into the problematic of female authorship in audio-visual media.

While these analyses provide a valuable and appropriate context for *Birthday Suit*, it is also important to realize how the feminist politics of the tape are produced not only through a discourse on the gaze but also through strategies of narrative and memory. *Birthday Suit* tells the story of Lisa Steele's body, tracing a narrative from her scars, the signs left on the surface of the body by a series of domestic and childhood accidents. Each scar stands for a memory that Steele retells in a deadpan voice as she gently rubs the mark on her body. Beyond the limited field of representation, consisting only of extreme close-ups of foot, thigh, toe, and hand, unfolds the autobiography of a tomboy. This is a little girl who fell on a bleach bottle while riding a tricycle, had a sewer pipe fall on her finger, stubbed her toe on a rock while running barefoot, fell in a parking lot while roller skating, fell off a horse, and fell on a milk bottle in the school cafeteria. The final three scars develop an increasingly dramatic narrative. In 1960, she "dropped a knife on foot while making eggs goldenrod in home economics class." Pointing to her eye, the first facial close-up in the tape, Steele continues, "Ran into branch while looking for waterfall in Banff National Park. Twenty years old." Finally, over a close-up of a scar under her right breast, the voice-over continues, "surgery for removal of benign tumour. Twenty-six years old." This final "defect" is of a completely different order of bodily trauma, indicating an abrupt shift from girl to woman. The composition of a narrative from fragments, and the rich imagery related through selective detail, gives the tape a strong poetic voice that runs up against the clinical gaze of the camera set-up.

At knee-level, the camera position is unchanging for most of *Birthday Suit*. Steele's confession is unmediated by camera person or crew, and it is performed in one unedited take as she holds her body parts up for inspection (Tuer's "votive offering"). She begins and ends the tape by walking into the background of the shot and showing her full figure to the camera. Against the back wall of the room (an apartment without furniture), she turns to show her back and left and right profiles, entering into a contract of surveillance, objectification, and scientific observation with the recording instrument. These movements create a depth of space, contrasting with the surfaces of the tight close-ups that comprise the bulk of the tape. In the shots of the scars, Steele rubs her flawed skin slowly and repetitively, making us wait, stretching out the present tense just enough for us to feel the weight of memory and the passing of time. The friction and the sense of touch likewise alert the viewer to the surface planes of the image—the mapping of the human skin onto the screen.

In this early tape, the tropes of autobiography, scientific investigation, and observation that mark Steele's subsequent practice are already at work. Likewise, her use of performance and narrativity are well developed. What will change is the documentary authenticity that *Birthday Suit* so boldly assumes. The nakedness of the videomaker, stripped down to her scars, the material evidence of her autobiography, leaves no room for doubt. This tape is a celebration of Steele's birthday, but it also celebrates the meeting of body and technology in an embrace of mutual support and entitlement. The truth of the body is laid bare, and the artist has wrestled the truth from the medium itself.

And yet there is something "in excess" of this truth, something unspoken in this tape, an intrusive "third meaning" that has always interested me. I'm speaking about Steele's bikini tan that is clearly evident when she stands in full figure in long shot. This is another kind of discourse from that of the artist's video, and another kind of "defect." The world of fashion seems so distant from this minimalist tape, and yet it enters in uninvited, unremarked upon by Steele. Her "pose" is that of the mug shot rather than that of the model, and yet the mark of her bikini clothes her nudity, compromising ever so slightly her control over the image. Before the tape ends, Steele pulls on a pair of jeans and a T-shirt and exits the room/frame, a strategy that works to reassert her domination of the image. It is thus untrue to describe the body image in this tape as "ungendered," as the bikini-tan inscribes gender onto the body over and against the tape's strategies of demystification. It tells us that the scars do not, after all, tell the "whole story" of the body, that there are other stories that this body might tell, stories of pleasure, perhaps, rather than pain.

Even in the later tapes such as *Legal Memory* (1992) and *The Blood Records* (1997), in which fact and fiction become thoroughly blurred, a utopian thrust persists in Steele's tapes. A certain faith in the image persists, even if the "visible evidence" of *Birthday Suit* is gradually replaced by a far more "visionary" technique of fabrication and a more calculated use of the medium as a tool of persuasion. Insofar as one of the key techniques that Steele deploys on her own and with Tomczak is performance, the discourse of authenticity that is so striking in *Birthday Suit* gradually disappears under layers of representation. Even Steele's subsequent 1974 tape *A Very Personal Story* begins this process of layering, introducing an element of doubt into the confessional form of the autobiography.

Once again using a single camera set-up, Steele addresses the camera directly in *Personal Story*. This time, a facial close-up remains the only composition in the tape, although for the first eleven minutes of this seventeen-minute tape, Steele holds her hands in such a way that part of her face is obscured as she twiddles her fingers nervously. Her eyes shift back and forth when we can see them behind the fingers, signalling a discomfort and awkwardness that may be entirely appropriate to the story she tells but is equally a sign of performativity. The story itself begins with a clear indication that the tape will be about storytelling rather than simply about what is told. Steele begins with "I have a story to tell you, a really, a very personal story." She pauses, then says, "It took place in December. I don't remember the date, the middle of December, 1963." She pauses again before continuing, "I'll tell you the end first. The end is about, my mother dies in the end. So there won't be any punch line. So you know that part before we start. So we can start the story now."

In a presentation in Montréal, Steele explained that *A Very Personal Story*, like most of her work from this period (e.g., *The Ballad of Dan Peoples* [1976]) and *Talking Tongues* [1982]), was unscripted. These tapes were made simply by performing for the camera in a live loop to a monitor. Other than a few false starts, there are no retakes or out-takes. In *A Very Personal Story,* the sense of unbroken time enhances the intimacy between performer and viewer; it also creates a strong impression of the present tense of the storytelling, against which the memory of the experience in 1963 is differentiated. Steele has described this tape as an attempt "to let memory become present tense."[3]

The story Steele tells is about the day she came home from school to find her mother dead of some unspecified illness in her sickbed in the living room. The details of that day include the grilled toast Steele had for breakfast, her own excellent circulation that protected her from the cold, the Shakespeare play she read at school, hanging out with her boyfriend, dawdling home, and the junk lot on the street. Some of these details have been fixed as the coordinates of that particular "regular" day; others are more vague, having been only recently retrieved; still others are offered simply for the purposes of the narrative and are less convincing, as in, "I was walking and I felt really good, probably." When she finally discovers her mother's body, she says, "And she was obviously dead." The two dogs "knew something was wrong. They knew it wasn't like it usually was. So they ... but they didn't have any answers either." At this point, Steele's hands drop to the lower part of the frame, and she goes on to describe the feeling of being a sixteen-year-old girl who finds herself alone in the world. "I'm a very dramatic person," she says, somewhat ironically, given the lack of drama in this monologue; "I felt like David Copperfield ... I would make it, you know."

A Very Personal Story concludes with the statement "I was alone in a larger way, too. Because it was a big experience in my life, and nobody really wants to hear about it, too much." But we the viewers have heard it, whether we wanted to or not. Once again, Steele plays with her control over the spectator, addressing us as interlocutor, therapist, and confessor; and then, at the last minute, she negates the viewer's presence. She has been speaking all along to a recording machine, a "nobody," and the viewer is rendered a victim of a very personal story. As an autobiographical work, this tape is also about the birth of the artist, because the "end of the story" is not, after all, the mother's death but the tape itself. The making of the tape, in accessing the unreliable recesses of memory and giving narrative form to a "big experience," also has the effect of moving beyond memory and closing off a period of time. The finality of telling this personal story is, like *Birthday Suit*, a scene of the artist stripping down and revealing herself. But she never relinquishes control, relying on the modes of performance and narrativity to mediate those inner truths and feelings. Moreover, Steele's techniques of performance and storytelling, grounded in the body of the artist, are further mediated through the video apparatus, which becomes a technology of confession.

The Ballad of Dan Peoples, an eight-minute tape made in 1976, continues her interest in storytelling, performance, and memory, although in this tape she shifts the focus slightly from autobiography to biography. Dan Peoples was Steele's grandfather on her mother's side. The end credits tell us he entered the Jackson county home for the aged (in Missouri) "early last year." As an epilogue, this statement anchors Steele's performance in history; moreover, the banal connotations of a home for the aged provide an abrupt counterpoint to the tape's otherwise spirited possession. For Steele does not simply tell Dan Peoples' story: she seems to become him, allowing his voice to come through her as if she were some kind of spirit medium. Her monologue is practically sung as she repeats phrases, moving backwards and forwards through a series of events and fragments of dialogue in the first person. She adopts a slightly Southern drawl and delivers the phrases so rapidly one has to struggle to follow the tale, which is about a boy being beaten by his father and finally "not turning back." The final words, "the most beautiful mules that you ever saw," evoke the imagery of the farm boy growing up in the harsh world of the American frontier.

Steele's physical appearance constantly changes from one tape to another. As an actress, she relies on costume and hairstyle to help create her characters. In this case, her hair is short and bluntly cut, and she wears a simple white shirt partially unbuttoned to show a flat, bare chest. Is it through this "butch" persona that she is able to "become" her grandfather? She holds his picture in her hands, but until the very end of the tape the glass reflects the light, creating a strong sense of movement throughout the monologue and preventing us from really seeing the man in the picture. When we do finally glimpse him, he looks like a cowboy. But it is not the "content" of the picture that matters, just as the "content" of the story matters less than the materiality and texture of it. Rarely does one find the glass casing of a photo used as Steele deploys it here, as more visible and tangible than the image encased within it. If the play of light lends the tape an imaginary means of "going back" and moving through the boundaries between identities, the photo itself finally registers the true otherness of Dan Peoples and the difference of Steele's performance of him.

Steele has used the concept of "involuntary memory" to describe her strategies in these performances—particularly *Dan Peoples* and *A Very Personal Story*.[4] This is the Proustian memory of the body that also plays a key role in Walter Benjamin's theorization of modernity. Steele's performance in *Dan Peoples* is a performance of memory: her memory of her grandfather's voice telling stories and his somewhat-confused memories of his childhood. Benjamin's discussion of the *mémoire involontaire* in Proust is surprisingly appropriate to this tape:

> The materials of memory no longer appear singly, as images, but tell us about a whole, amorphously and formlessly, indefinitely and weightily, in the same way as the weight of his net tells a fisherman about his catch ... And his [Proust's] sentences are the entire muscular activity of the intelligible body; they contain the whole enormous effort to raise the catch.[5]

At the end of *Dan Peoples*, when Steele's voice finally comes to rest, her hand reaches out slowly as if releasing a weight (or cueing the camera?). The sense of trance in this tape, created again as one long unedited shot, constitutes the body as a medium, making a strange alliance between body and machine. If, as Dot Tuer has suggested, Steele's video performances "signal the presence of a hybrid, a cyborg,"[6] this body-machine is created by way of memory. The enactment of involuntary memory asserts a certain veracity, a truthfulness that cannot be denied because it cannot be verified either. One is also reminded in these tapes of Benjamin's essay on "The Storyteller." Not only has Steele "borrowed her authority from death," her narratives exemplify Benjamin's claim that storytelling "sinks the thing into the life of the storyteller, in order to bring it out of him again. Thus traces of the storyteller cling to the story the way the handprints of the potter cling to the clay vessel."[7]

If for Benjamin storytelling was threatened by the bourgeois novel on one hand, and by the age of information on the other, Steele's video performances register that threat but also embrace it as the condition of the electronic age. She tells her stories to a machine, after all, and her audience—especially now, twenty-five years after the fact—is distanced once again in time. *Dan Peoples* is, on one level, simply "information": a document of her performance of Dan Peoples' memories. Moreover, as in *Birthday Suit* and *A Very Personal Story*, the artist is alone, like the novelist who, Benjamin notes, "has isolated himself."[8] Steele's storytelling is thus situated allegorically within the electronic medium of video. The memories transmitted through her body may be involuntarily accessed, randomly brought to the discursive surface of consciousness; and yet their intimacy is inevitably compromised by the distancing effects of the medium itself. *Birthday Suit* renders Steele's autobiography as a series of accidents, involuntarily etched onto her body; *A Very Personal Story* relates how a "regular day" is transformed into an exceptional day by virtue of death; and the single-take structure of these tapes registers a present tense that is as fleeting and singular as those moments of accident and death, evoking a temporality that is indeed very close to Benjamin's sense of history as the time of the now.[9]

Craving Detail

Among the many tapes that Steele produced in the 1970s are two that are linked by a number of shared themes and forms, and that are quite unlike the rest of the oeuvre. *Facing South* (1975, b&w, 22 minutes) and *Waiting for Lancelot* (1977–78, b&w, 90 minutes) both deal with issues of nature, the feminine, and the body. Compared to the confessional tapes discussed above, they are far more complex in terms of montage and narrativity. Their elliptical treatment of narrative form, authorial voice, and sexuality aligns these works with the feminist avant-garde cinema of the period, such as Sally Potter's *Thriller* (1979), Laura Mulvey and Peter Wollen's *Riddles of the Sphinx* (1977), and Patricia Gruben's *Sifted Evidence* (1982). Steele shares with these films an analytic perspective, a nascent feminist sensibility and coextensive discourse on vision, fantasy, desire, and representation. And yet these videos are also distinctive in their privileging of the close-up, appropriate to a small-screen aesthetic. They work on the level of visual detail, particularly the detail of nature—plants and insects—and the human body.

Steele appears in both *Facing South* and *Waiting for Lancelot*, not as an actor but as "the woman." Her body stands in for the female body and not for a character. This in itself signals her affinity with the feminist avant-garde cinema concerned with theoretical issues of gender and representation, relegating dramatic narrative to the margins, if not negating it altogether. These may not be as personal as the confessional tapes, but Steele's persona is still very dominant, conveyed by her distinctive voice-over. Both the cold, dry, syntactical style and the slightly high-pitched intonation become familiar traits of Steele's videos. The first-person pronoun may be a fictional, narrative device in these tapes, and yet, in conjunction with the predominance of close-ups, one still feels that these are personal tapes. Their intimacy is governed not by memory, however, but by the detail of close-ups of Steele's body, a trope introduced in *Birthday Suit*.

Facing South might be described as a diary of growing houseplants, although its tone is far more scientific than domestic. Steele holds a microscope up to begonia flowers and nasturtium sprouts, "craving detail." The discourse of observation is linked to the laws of nature, made visible by the slant of the mature nasturtiums to the sun. The title "facing south" is invoked several times in the voice-over narration, followed by "the sun moves from left to right." In the final sequence, a series of time-lapse shots of Steele's rooftop garden follows the shrinking of shadows over the course of one morning. Steele and her cat come out and sit on a chair "facing south."

In her own description of this tape, Steele says, "Here, I wanted not so much to 'record' daily life as to reflect on the unreliability of paralleling female experience which was analytic in its relation to nature." In fact, the only indication that the body in this work is a gendered body is a close-up of a vulva, which is at first out of focus, until a magnifying glass is held over it. Like all the shots in this tape, the image is disconnected, fragmented by framing and montage from its context. It is preceded by an image of Steele eating an open-face nasturtium sandwich, and succeeded by a shot of a turtle in an aquarium eating a begonia bud. The editing thus enforces an analytic perspective, refusing any discourse of continuity: in fact, the critique of the naturalization of femininity is somewhat oblique, and certainly not the strongest feature of the tape. Perhaps in 1974 the sight of female genitals would have signalled more strongly a feminist orientation, but for me, now, it contributes to the way the tape works through discourses of science and pleasure.

Steele's household becomes a site where an analytic faith in the visual field meets the sensual pleasures of taste, sexuality, and sunbathing. There is a cool irony in the opening shots of a young woman (Steele at twenty-eight looks like she's eighteen) dryly describing the colour of her begonias to the viewer of this black-and-white tape. The invisibility of their pinkness, like the invisibility of the clitoris "hidden between two folds of skin" is carefully and poetically aligned with the invisible laws of nature. The miracle of growth cannot be discovered with a magnifying glass. Moreover, the limits of the visual field are also the limits of the frame—and of course, the magnifying glass provides a frame within the frame. Steele's images are consistently well lit and formally composed with attention to diagonals and depth of field, a formalism enhanced by the stasis of the camera. The tape contains only one camera movement, tracing the line of plants from left to right on the roof at night, replacing sunlight with artificial light.

Within the banal environment of domestic space, Steele's photography produces a sublime effect obliquely linked to the laws of nature. The words "facing south" evoke that overlaying of visual beauty—the laws of aesthetic composition—with the geophysics of the natural world. The tape's real accomplishment is in the depiction of this affinity. That it does so within the domestic environment of a rather bare apartment lends the tape a further ascetic feeling. Eating a nasturtium sandwich may be an absurd activity, but it also connotes the "starving artist." I do not want to read this tape too literally, and yet it is a diary that offers only the most cryptic clues to its subject. The detail of everyday life is offered only in terms of the rhythms of the early-spring growing season and the close-up textures of the woman's plants and her body. As a "visual diary," its truthfulness and its accuracy with respect to its maker's own life are not relevant, as documentary values have begun to give way to aesthetic, analytic, and formal values of montage and composition. Even so, close-ups do not lie. The tape remains grounded in the materiality of nature and Steele's own body, while her cold, dry analysis intervenes into any process or aesthetic of naturalized affinity between the two.

If *Facing South* borrows the narrative device of the diary, *Waiting for Lancelot* takes that of mythic romance, but Steele's adherence to the conventions of narrative form is very loose. This seven-part tape is "inspired by" the Arthurian legend of Guinevere and Lancelot, but the *ménage à trois* is embedded, once again, in a visual landscape of close-up detail of nature imagery. Steele appears as "the woman" Guinevere, dressed in a white peasant dress, but her performance is restricted to a series of poses and placements within sets. This is not a story about character but about visual space and surreal effects; like *Facing South*, it draws connections between gender and nature only to invert those relations and render them strange. It is a bleaker tape than the former, as the affinities between woman and nature circulate this time around mortality, violence, and decay.

In the first segment of *Waiting for Lancelot*, "G's dream," Steele's voice-over explains, "He tied me up in the forest and left me for dead ... I dream a bug is killed." A shot of insect specimens laid out on a woman's outstretched arm begins the tape's interweaving of dramatic and scientific-analytical discourses. In the second section, "I'm having trouble with my heart," Guinevere seems to have a fantasy of open-heart surgery; in the third section, imagery of intercourse is intercut with shots of a bee moving from flower to flower. The narrator says, "Penis enters vagina with ancestral accuracy." From the fragments of narration, it is possible to follow a story of Guinevere's death in the forest; the tape concludes with "The testimony of Lancelot" in which he confesses to having killed her. And yet the elliptical, poetic narration is only "background" to the visual style of the tape, which once again frames the detailed patterns of the natural world in static compositions. For example, in section six, "At Snake Spring," the narration describes the woman's death in the first person ("I am at rest before the third repetition"), but the image-track offers only a series of static views of a tree in a small garden, littered with leaves and branches. This black-and-white tape is concerned above all with the textures and patterns of natural beauty. Captured in the video monitor, these patterns are transformed into patterns of light that offer another discourse to work against the romantic, legendary, mythic narrative. It is as if death offers the woman a means of escaping the confines of a narrative that contains her and kills her.

Waiting for Lancelot is in many ways Steele's most "difficult" tape in its multiple levels of abstraction and deconstruction. It is far less "personal" than most of her work, and yet the first-person pronoun, along with Steele's voice and body, provides an important means of locating a subjective space within the text. Guinevere's affinity with the artist may consist of little more than her gender, but Guinevere is the victim of male violence and Steele is perhaps asking us to imagine ourselves in her position, stoned to death in the forest. Instead of any depictions of violence, we are offered violent disjunctions of sound and image, banal pop music ("Love Hurts") and the fragility of insects. In section Five, "Domestication," a cat appears to "stand in" for the woman. These long sections of observing the cat are strongly reminiscent of Joyce Wieland's use of domestic animals. In fact, Steele's static framing is not unlike the distinctive camera work of structural film, and she also shares with Wieland a feminist sensibility that is less militant than discursive at this stage in her career. Like Wieland's, Steele's practice works itself out from the visual language of domestic space. *Facing South* and *Waiting for Lancelot* need to be recognized as important works of the feminist avant garde. The craving of detail is developed in these tapes as a displacement of desire from its conventional role in narrative to a desire to see more clearly, and to grow in and through the detailed textures—natural and aesthetic—of everyday life.

The Performance of the Other Woman

In 1982, Steele was invited to participate in a live satellite videocast from Toronto to Paris, an event attended by a coterie of diplomats and cultural custodians anxious for some of the cultural capital of the new high-tech art form of video to rub off on them. Steele's contribution to this international art event was not what they expected. Wearing a kerchief over stringy hair and chain-smoking throughout the monologue, Steele assumed the persona of "Beatrice Small" and gave the rambling details of raising a child on welfare, escaping a husband with a restraining order on him, and trying to hold down a job. This tape, *Talking Tongues*, along with a series of others made around this time (*The Damages* [b&w, 12 minutes, 1978] and *Makin' Strange* [b&w, 17 minutes, 1978]), was developed out of Steele's experience working at Interval House, a home for battered women and children in Toronto. The tapes constitute a new phase in her career that builds on the performative and photographic properties of the previous tapes and incorporates a critique of social institutions that continue to inform her practice and her collaborative work with Kim Tomczak in the 1980s and '90s.

The best-known tape from this period is actually a series of four "installments" called *The Gloria Tapes* (1975–80). Steele plays a welfare mother with a delinquent boyfriend in an episodic narrative structured something like a soap opera. Her shooting style is once again limited to static framings, often in close-up or medium close-up, often without any montage within scenes. The single-shot set-ups, dynamically composed with vibrant colour schemes dominated by oranges, pinks, and greens, are appropriate to a TV aesthetic. Indeed, with *The Gloria Tapes,* Steele begins to use the video medium as an anti-television vehicle, anticipating the Paper Tiger TV projects that emerged in the early 1980s in the US. In dramatizing the encounter of a welfare mother with a gamut of social institutions and discursive contexts, *The Gloria Tapes* are situated aesthetically and formally within the regime of daytime TV drama.

Most astonishing about *The Gloria Tapes* is Steele's performance as Gloria. Wearing oversized glasses, fidgeting nervously, and assuming a halting, hesitant speech pattern, Steele develops a character who is at once convincing and sympathetic; at the same time, she creates an ethnographic portrait of a welfare mother. This is not only an original mode of representation; it is also a rare feminist project that addresses issues of class directly. By taking on the role and inhabiting it, she poses implicit questions about relationships between the avant garde, social institutions, and less-educated, less-privileged members of society. Gloria is a woman with limited access to the discourses of health and the law, and over the course of the "series" she struggles to negotiate her place within the languages and institutions that constitute her social subjectivity, with the family figuring as the pivotal social formation underscoring all the others.

The four episodes of *The Gloria Tapes* introduce fragments of information about Gloria's situation, although the narrative is extremely discontinuous and episodic. Steele strenuously avoids a full-fledged narrative realism, despite her convincing performance. A gynecologist advises Gloria that she needs surgery, although Gloria is not sure why, and when she explains it to her boyfriend, he asks her for a ten-dollar loan and wonders whether they can still have sex. In the second episode, she is pregnant again and explains to her friend that she had no idea it could happen so fast after giving birth. In the supermarket, she worries desperately how to buy nutritious food on her tight budget. An incident occurs with one of her children, who is taken to the hospital. The incident itself is not shown, but Billy, the boyfriend, blames Gloria and indeed we get the sense that she may in fact have been responsible. She is asked to go to the Children's Aid Society for an interview, and although this scene is not shown, she tells her social worker that the baby ate a whole bag of chips on the bus and thus would not "perform" when Gloria was asked to demonstrate her maternal skills at the interview. Finally, she is interviewed by a judge who delves into her family background, forcing Gloria and her sister Tina to confront their abuse by their father.

The melodramatic potential of this convoluted narrative is downplayed by the tape's slow pacing and spare visual language. Gloria emerges as a woman who is confused and pressured by a father and boyfriend who take advantage of her; her abuse of her own child is thus symptomatic of a dysfunctional social system. In her article "Woman and Infanticide" (1979), Steele points out that there are important links between poverty and infanticide, "a crime in which women are the major perpetrators."[10] This statistic-laden article provides an important appendix to *The Gloria Tapes,* as it insists on the need for greater understanding of the ways that poverty and gender inequities contribute to child abuse. The tape itself replaces the academic-sociological language of Steele's article with the ethnographic and melodramatic languages of audio-visual performance.

Many of the other actors in *The Gloria Tapes* were recruited from the staff at Interval House, and the characters of the judge and the social worker, "Jenny," are benevolent, sympathetic women. These women are presumably playing "themselves" or some ideal of their roles as social-service workers. In the final scene, the judge interviews the female doctor and the social worker to determine what would be best for Gloria. Jenny announces that Gloria has decided to go back to school and give her second baby up for adoption. Gloria's "recovered memory" of her own abuse by her father is a catalyst in her transformation, but it is not depicted as any kind of revelation; Gloria even assures her father that she doesn't think anything bad will come of her telling the authorities (he's in the shower when she tells him, so there is no reaction on his part).

The recovered memory is treated more like a discursive strategy of linking Gloria's behaviour to that of her parents, not as a psychological epiphany. Nevertheless, the tape ends on an upbeat note, as Gloria tells us in voice-over that she has realized that Billy is a bad habit and Dad has gone off the booze. She says, "People can change. Look at me." This utopian finale is in keeping with Steele's tone of political advocacy in her article, which concludes with the following passage:

> Family violence, the beating, abuse and murder that occurs among husbands, wives and their children of which infanticide is a part, is a symptom of two greater maladies: the unequal distribution of this society's resources among its members and the oppression of women within this society. Is it possible to imagine a society where the 'symptomatic' relief of these sufferings is not necessary? Yes, but it cannot be a society built on the privilege of dominance that exists today.[11]

The Gloria Tapes constitutes an artist's response to this challenge to the imagination; one has to imagine the "suffering" in order to find the imagination to relieve the inequities from which such suffering derives.

Steele's performative enactment of women caught within webs of institutional discourses continues with the tape *Some Call It Bad Luck* (1982),[12] in which she plays an office worker accused of murdering a man who held her hostage. The drama of the hostage-taking, the police intervention, and the shooting is not depicted. The tape consists entirely of the police investigation of the incident, their interrogation of the woman (Donna), and their conversations between themselves—in which they discount the possibility of a veteran officer accidentally killing the gunman. Reconstructing the incident with Donna, they pry into her private life and sexuality, imagining a liaison of some kind between her and the gunman. While she insists that she was simply in the wrong place at the wrong time, they confuse the details of the incident to the point where she believes she "could have killed him." In this tape, Steele is interested above all in the techniques of police investigation and interrogation that enable them to learn only the facts that suit them best. Details of this fictional incident are drawn from various news events of the late 1970s, including the RCMP's "dirty tricks" campaign against the NDP, and from Steele's experience and observations at Interval House.

Despite the amateur acting, the low-budget sets and production values, and the limited range of most of the cast, Steele's performance is remarkable, as is her use of montage. She uses silences, gestures of smoking, and body language; she uses close-ups expertly and drops her eyes, and in this tape makes excellent use of continuity editing and film-noir lighting to develop the tensions of the interrogation sessions. This "docudrama" anticipates the documentary strategies of Errol Morris, even though it is entirely fiction; its documentary impetus stems from its analysis of authority, power, and the construction of gender roles within a system of investigation, not because of any claims to be based on a "true story." If these gender roles are somewhat overdetermined, Steele gets away with it through sociological claims to veracity and by mapping gender onto class. Donna works as a technician in a health science lab at Queen's Park. She is a single mother who only works nights to make up for days missed when her daughter is ill.

In true melodramatic fashion, *Some Call It Bad Luck* details the vulnerability and victimization of a working-class woman; and while we are never sure of the "truth" of the incident, Donna's innocence is produced by what Peter Brooks calls "the triumph of virtue" in melodramatic narrative. Steele's performance of Donna within the pervasive, invasive, persistent persecution of the authorities—a persecution veiled throughout as benevolent paternalism—is the main vehicle of this "triumph of virtue." The end credits tell us that although Donna was charged with manslaughter and possession of a firearm (she had ended up somehow with the gunman's rifle when the police arrived at the scene), when her case finally came to trial, the police officer could not recognize her and the case was dismissed. Donna ends up with no criminal record but acquires a "severe nervous disorder" in the course of her ordeal. While the truth of the events remains unclear, Steele's performance of Donna is a remarkable portrait of a woman caught within an institutional authority system in which gender is constructed in specific and unequal ways.

Archival Fictions

Steele's collaborative work with Kim Tomczak began in 1983 with a performance piece called *In the Dark,* in which the couple make love on tape, extending Steele's intimate work of the 1970s into the more public and social arena of pornography, erotica, and censorship. The collaboration has continued into their most recent tape to date, *The Blood Records.* Three tapes from the 1980s—*See Evil* (1985), *Private Eyes* (1987), and *White Dawn* (1988)—were created out of Steele and Tomczak's involvement in the Toronto arts community. These works, along with *Working the Double Shift* (1984), constitute an activist practice, directly engaged with the cultural politics of the period. *Working the Double Shift* addresses gender biases reproduced in the mass media; *See Evil* documents the anti-censorship movement in the mid 1980s when independent film exhibitors were suddenly vulnerable to indiscriminate censorship; *Private Eyes* is about the privatization of a thinly disguised Art Gallery of Ontario; and *White Dawn* deals with the protection of Canadian cultural industries in the context of the free trade debate of the late 1980s.

While for Marvisia Bociurkiw these activist tapes are "didactic," Dot Tuer has pointed out that Steele and Tomczak's method has a distinctive utopian impetus, which in each instance is developed out of their cultural critique. She argues that "they refuse to surrender the territory of the ideal to dominant representation; they refuse to capitulate to the paranoid fantasies of a dystopian future."[13] In fact, this tendency is already present in Steele's performative anti-television pieces *The Gloria Tapes* and *Some Call It Bad Luck*, in their relatively positive, upbeat endings and in her ability to appropriate the language of TV for feminist ends. The collaborative tapes add new layers to Steele's interest in performance and narrativity, including voice-overs, graphic titles, and archival footage, combined in complex architectures of docu-fictions. Through the consistent use of fictional paradigms, an imaginative and visionary element is consistently implied within the videomakers' documentary-based critique of a plethora of social institutions.

One of the best examples of the utopianism of Steele and Tomczak's videos is the "Phantasy Projection" segment of *Working the Double Shift,* which Tuer discusses. Archival footage of a parliamentary vote is accompanied by a faux-sports commentary describing a new revolutionary society being voted in by the MPs. *White Dawn* likewise develops a completely imaginary scenario in which Americans complain about the omnipresence of Canadian culture, the obliteration of their national identity, and the obscurity of their cultural heroes. *White Dawn* is loaded with statistics, which, like the archival TV footage in *Working the Double Shift,* anchors the fiction in documentary claims about historical reality. *Legal Memory* (colour and b&w, 80 minutes, 1992) and *The Blood Records* (b&w and colour, 52 minutes, 1997) take these strategies further, into feature-length tapes structured as complex architectures of historical documentation, archival memory, and narrative forms of representation. Both tapes also have personal points of departure, based on stories originating in Steele and Tomczak's own families, suggesting that the ongoing investigation of social institutions is also about identity and the network of histories that "being Canadian" can invoke.

In *Legal Memory,* Steele plays the role of a real-estate agent named Helen, a woman who introduces herself as "ordinary." She says that she "does not imagine well" because "to imagine is to remember, and I don't remember well ... I have no interior life." Over archival imagery of Queen Elizabeth visiting Canada, John Diefenbaker, the BC landscape, and naval officers on parade, this voice-over introduces one of the tape's main themes: the creative use of memory as a challenge to repression and denial. Helen is a fictional character who "investigates" events that occurred in the 1950s in Victoria; despite the lack of "hard evidence" in the form of documentation, the tape is convincing in its unveiling of these events. A gay man named Leo Mantha was executed in 1958 for the murder of a naval officer, and although Diefenbaker commuted most death sentences, Mantha was not spared. The investigation of the crime, moreover, became an RCMP witch hunt of homosexuals in the Canadian Navy. Mantha's victim was apparently a rather flamboyant gay man who kept a list of names of Naval personnel he had associated with in the various queer haunts in the region.

The details of Mantha's crime and the subsequent investigation are related via a rich texture of discursive layers, including a sensual evocation of Mantha's gay community. Played by Tomczak in black-and-white footage set in the 1950s, Mantha is associated with a big chrome-and-leather period car. Helen appears as a child in some of these flashbacks as Mantha's cousin. Her aunts, whom she has come to visit in Victoria, are of little help in reconstructing Mantha's story, which was a family scandal packed into a tightly locked trunk. So Helen "interviews" a number of men about the case, in an attempt to piece together the fragments of memory that seem to "erupt without invitation." While these interviews are introduced with titles naming each interviewee and describing their relation to the case, the interviews are in fact scripted and performed by actors. Although only the end credits confirm that they are actors and not documentary subjects, the performance style hints at their status as false documents. Even so, Steele and Tomczak use black-out edits in the interviews to mimic a documentary style, borrowing conventions of realism, perhaps to make the testimony all the more convincing.

Helen also goes to the Victoria archives, where at first she encounters the reluctance of archivists to give up their secrets in a couple of scenes that will be familiar to anyone who has done archival research. However, towards the end of *Legal Memory,* she sits down with one of the archivists, who turns out to be "Dot Smythe, archivist, [who] also records oral histories of the gay community in Victoria"—or so says the intertitle. (Smythe is played by Ruth Ann Tucker, who is clearly a lesbian.) Dot tells Helen about the many men, including Leo Mantha, who were purged from the Navy for suspected homosexual activities, many of them in the aftermath of the murder investigation. One former officer tells his first-person story of being interrogated by the RCMP and subsequently forced to resign. The actor's direct address to the camera lends an important element of persuasion to this history, which is in fact passed on to the viewer via a complicated route of "tellings" from Frank Bradley, the original officer, to the oral historian to Steele and Tomczak to the actor, Glen Lewis; and on the fictional level, the story passes from "Dot Smythe" to "Helen"/Steele to "Frank Bradley" to the viewer.

Afterward, Helen says "her tale was quite fantastic ... especially for someone like me ..." Footage of the Queen, Diefenbaker, and the naval parade evoke the period and the official histories, beyond which Mantha's story requires a leap of the imagination to be able to visualize, so deeply buried is the covert history of gay communities and their oppression. Helen seems to undergo some kind of transformation as she unveils the details of this "sordid tale," perhaps because she felt some affinity with her cousin Leo and struggles to come to terms with the tragedy precipitated by his "crime of passion." (The assistant defence council—played by Kim's father John Tomczak—suggests that Mantha's lawyer was unable to argue the case properly because it was inconceivable that a man could have such a relationship with another man at the time.) Helen even appears to have a brief, drunken, flirtation with a woman in a bar.

Legal Memory uses many documentary conventions only to undermine its own authority and insist that viewers use their imaginations to be persuaded by this tale of homophobic persecution. The fictional premise is heavily laced with autobiographical links to Steele and Tomczak's own families: Mantha was in fact a distant cousin of Tomczak's, and the tape is dedicated to his father, who, in his role as the assistant defence council, says "I'm glad this case is being reopened." Helen "remembers" her father washing dishes and being vaguely embarrassed by his effeminacy. The presence of the child in the black-and-white flashbacks, played by Steele and Tomczak's daughter Laroux Peoples, gives the imagery a feeling of home movies, situating the public drama in the context of the family.

Among the re-enacted flashback imagery are scenes of men being interrogated by RCMP officers, shot with noir-ish lighting. Many of the actors are recognizable from the 1950s "party" scene earlier in the tape. Most of them refuse to talk, one of the younger ones appears to tell all, and another one ostentatiously responds to the question "Do you associate with men from the naval base?" with "Every chance I get. I just love a man in uniform." This openly queer attitude signals the ironic cynicism possible in 1990s gay culture, an anachronistic gesture that complements the stylized setting of the interviews. One of the documentary interviewees, introduced as Derek Potts, an elderly man who was investigated in the 1950s, begins his interview by saying that he has never come out of the closet—another ironic gesture towards the status of the re-enactments and the identity of the actors/interviewees. The constant blurring of fiction and documentary, and the confusion of any possible distinction between them, is an important means by which the tape crosses the historical divide between then and now, pushing the limits of historical knowledge through the creative act of remembering.

To some extent, *Legal Memory* is another instance of the performance of "the other"—performances that strive to find an affinity with, and deeper understanding of, other constituencies of identity. Tomczak's performance as a gay man includes some scenes of light petting, but Steele and Tomczak's investigation and analysis of gay history is also premised on historical gaps and absences, and a certain unrepresentability. As Tom Waugh has pointed out, "the politics of desire and historical research [is] a contested ground of power and truth, with the archives, the media and the arts, the publishing industry and the law as its particular institutional arenas."[14] *Legal Memory* addresses censorship and homophobia by way of an exercise of the imagination, dramatizing the need to visualize that which has been excised from the historical record. It does so by inventing a fictional archive, a method of recollection in which investigation requires a certain access to the investigator's "interior"—as the character of Helen puts it—that is, to his or her own sexual identity.

The technique of constructing a fictional archive is further developed in *The Blood Records: Written and Annotated*, a tape that has been described by Mike Hoolboom as a "ghost story."[15] In this tape, set in 1944, tuberculosis figures as both a historical point of reference for Canadian health institutions and an allegorical stand-in for the AIDS pandemic. Combining archival National Film Board documentary clips from the period authoritatively describing the disease, footage of Fort San (a tuberculosis sanatorium built in 1917 in Saskatchewan), and scenes of patients and doctors "re-enacting" the routines of the institution, *The Blood Records* once again executes a fine blend of critical analysis and aesthetic delineation of a psychic territory. One of the patients, Marie, has a voice-over monologue (delivered by the video artist Vera Frankel) in which she describes not only the scenes at the sanitarium but her Francophone family persecuted by the Ku Klux Klan and isolated from the dominant Anglophone culture, and her brother who dies on the European front. The Second World War, the swearing-in of Tommy Douglas, and the first socialist government, with "a vision that included medicare," situate the story of Marie and Fort San within the texture of Canadian history.

While the first half of the tape takes up the factual narrativity of the NFB documentaries— using on-screen titles as well as voice-over explanation—at a certain point, it shifts from the "frequentive" voice of routine to the "singulative" voice of the once-only narrative event. The shift occurs with a scene of a nurse making out with a patient. Graphic titles read "12:05 pm on 4-West, door to fire escape propped open ... all night." The last two words appear in a different part of the screen, suggestively evoking the meaning of the ellipsis. Cut to Marie in bed, also at 12:05 p.m., and the beginning of her voice-over. A narrative space begins to open up within what has begun as a documentary—or rather, it erupts as a form of desire, which is then sculpted into a discursively dense space of superimpositions and digital effects. Death is described as a kind of transparency in Marie's voice-over. She says that many sick children just disappeared with no one commenting on their absence; her friend—the man whom we have seen with the nurse—seems to get thinner and thinner until he is transparent. X-ray photography is used as a discursive trope to convey the sense of medical surveillance as a technique of rendering the body ghost-like and transparent.

Colour is used in this tape only for the blood in anatomical drawings and for Marie's Catholic-inspired visions and flashbacks of Christ and the Virgin. Within the tape's dominant shadings of grey and white, these colour sequences make key links between life, the aesthetic realm, and transcendence of institutional oppression. Life in the San and the treatment of tuberculosis are depicted as the essence of clinical surveillance and institutional authoritarianism, producing boredom, apathy, and submissiveness, rather than healthy, cured patients. Marie herself concludes her narration by saying that although she survived she is still only capable of feeling "a moderate feeling of optimism ... even in moments of great joy." The sterility of the institution seems to have infiltrated her so deeply that she is released from it passionless.

Visionary transcendence of institutional oppression is suggested in *The Blood Records* through the use of landscape imagery layered over architectural forms and bodies; and to some extent, through the soundtrack, particularly the opening Leadbelly song, "TB Blues." However, it is also a profoundly melancholy tape, enhanced by the music's dominant haunting violin melodies. A cure for tuberculosis may have been discovered in 1945, but the tape makes no mention of it. Only in Steele and Tomczak's accompanying monograph by the same name are we told the history of the eventual eradication of the disease. In the tape, a doctor's prophesy, extracted from the NFB archive, that a cure for the disease might one day be found, is left unfulfilled, thereby making the parallelism with AIDS that much more urgent and provocative. The subtitle of *The Blood Records: Written and Annotated* announces the discursive level of the tape; it is very much an intellectual work. Marie cites Descartes, and the tape is clearly indebted to the work of Foucault and Sontag, even if they are not directly cited.[16]

This analytical, discursive, and intellectual dimension of *The Blood Records* distinguishes it ultimately as a video work. While digital effects enable a new kind of visual landscape and psychic territory, the superimposed titles and academic-inflected voice-over consistently inscribe the videomakers' research and socio-political commitment. This tape is dedicated to Steele and Tomczak's mothers, who were both institutionalized with tuberculosis at some point in their lives. Their "personal" investment in the issue is registered in the richness of the tape's visual textures, while the critique of health institutions and medical technologies remains hard-edged and analytical. History is once again rendered as an imaginative and flexible material, to which one may return so as to better understand and express the contemporary confrontation with disease. Hoolboom has further pointed out how *The Blood Records* invokes a history of visual technology in which video is itself deeply implicated:

> Today we are preparing for a life of complete transparency, a place where notions of the individual and the unconscious will be scrubbed away, replaced by a tribal digital consciousness ... Video artists have lent a critical edge to the project of representation, managing to preserve the ability to grieve in a society in recoil from notions of memory and history.[17]

ੴ ੴ ੴ

The story of the first twenty-five years of Lisa Steele's career is also a story of the way her chosen medium has evolved since the early 1970s. From the earliest pieces, made alone in her room with a camera and a monitor, to the latest tapes made with a partner, huge crews, and elaborate post-production effects, the tools themselves have changed dramatically. If in the 1970s, video was exhibited only in gallery spaces, now it is more likely to be projected in theatrical screening spaces or viewed privately in classrooms and living rooms. And yet, even if tapes such as *Legal Memory* and *The Blood Records* seem to converge on the terrain of cinema, sharing many of the "performative documentary" traits of contemporary independent cinema (identified by Bill Nichols in his book *Blurred Boundaries*), it is important to recognize their status as videos.

Steele's work may consistently use techniques of performance and narrativity, but the tapes always retain a sense of doubleness, an allegorical stance toward the represented world that is mediated through the electronic gaze. It is precisely because of the affinities of that gaze with institutions of mass media, surveillance, and what Janine Marchessault has called "the information order" that Steele's avant-garde practice is inevitably embedded in social history.[18] For her and her partner, social history is also personal history. Memory can be articulated in involuntary, eruptive forms, and also as a technique of investigation and analysis; but in either case, access to history is also a means of conceptualizing the future as a better place.

Notes

I would like to thank Freda Guttman for re-introducing me to the work of Lisa Steele, V-tape for providing review copies of the tapes, and Randolph Jordan for research assistance for this essay.

1   Dot Tuer, "Perspectives of the body in Canadian Video Art," *C Magazine*, Winter 1993, 32.

2   Ranee Baert, "Subjects on the Threshold: Problems with the Pronouns," *Parachute* 69 (January/February/March 1993): 16.

3   Phillip Monk, *4 Hours and 38 Minutes: Videotapes by Lisa Steele and Kim Tomczak* (Toronto: Art Gallery of Ontario, 1989), 17.

4   Clive Robertson, "Lisa Steele: The Recent Tapes," *Centerfold* 3, no. 5 (July 1979): 248.

5   Walter Benjamin, *Illuminations,* Hanna Arendt, ed., Harry Zohn, trans. (New York: Schocken Books, 1969), 214.

6   Tuer, "Perspectives of the body," 35.

7   Benjamin, *Illuminations*, 91–92.

8   Benjamin, *Illuminations*, 87.

9   Benjamin, *Illuminations*, 262.

10   Lisa Steele, "Women and Infanticide," *Centerfold* 3, no. 4 (May 1979): 155.

11   Steele, "Women and Infanticide," 162.

12   *Some Call It Bad Luck* was originally produced in colour, but has been remastered in black and white because the colour in the original had degenerated irreparably.

13   Tuer, "Perspectives of the body," 13.

14   Tom Waugh, *The Fruit Machine: Twenty Years of Writings on Queer Cinema* (Durham, NC: Duke University Press, 2000), 273–74.

15   Mike Hoolboom, "Mourning Pictures," in *Blood Records: Written and Annotated*, Vols. 1 and 2, Lisa Steele and Kim Tomczak, eds. (Oakville: Oakville Galleries, 1999).

16   Of all Steele and Tomczak's tapes, *The Blood Records* has generated some of the most informed and engaged writing. The essays by Hoolboom, Su Ditta, and Johanne Lamoureux all explore, in different ways, the tape's relation to Foucault's *Discipline and Punish* and Susan Sontag's *Illness as Metaphor*, as well as the Kantian sublime and Roland Barthes' autobiographical writings on tuberculosis.

17   Hoolboom, "Mourning Pictures," 32.

18   Janine Marchessault, "Preface," *Mirror Machine: Video and Identity* (Toronto: YYZ, 1995).

Bibliography

Abbott, Lawrence. "Interviews with Loretta Todd, Shelley Niro and Patricia Deadman." *Canadian Journal of Native Studies* 18, no. 2 (1998).

Acland, Charles R. "Popular Film in Canada: Revisiting the Absent Audience." In *A Passion for Identity: An Introduction to Canadian Studies*, third edition. David Taras and Beverly Rasporich, eds. Toronto: Nelson, 1989.

——. "Cinema-going and the Rise of the Megaplex." *Television and New Media* 1, no. 4 (2000): 375–402.

Adilman, Sid. "Famous Players hypes expansion after losing 3 Imperial screens." *Variety*, 11 June 1986.

——. "Cineplex Odeon Circuit to add 200 Canadian Screens thru '88." *Variety*, 2 July 1986.

"Alberta Movie Maker." *Maclean's*, 22 September 1986.

Allan, Blaine. "*The Grey Fox* Afoot in a Modern World." In *Canada's Greatest Features*. Gordon Collier and Gene Walz, eds. Amsterdam: Rodopi, forthcoming.

Allan, Ted and Sydney Gordon. *The Scalpel, the Sword: The Story of Dr. Norman Bethune*. Boston: Little, Brown, 1952.

Amiel, Barbara. "*The Grey Fox* is Haute NFB. *Toronto Sun*, 10 April 1983.

Anderson, Benedict. *Imagined Communities: Reflections on the Origin and Spread of Nationalism*. London: Verso, 1991.

Anderson, Elizabeth. *Pirating Feminisms: Film and the Production of Post–War Canadian Identity*. Ann Arbor: UMI, 1996.

Ang, Ien. *Watching Dallas: Soap Opera and the Melodramatic Imagination*. London: Methuen, 1982.

Angus, Ian. *A Border Within: National Identity, Cultural Plurality, and Wilderness*. Montréal: McGill-Queen's University Press, 1997.

Ansari, Renan. "Interviews with Deepa Mehta and Naseeruddin Shah." *Himal* 11/12 (December 1998): 51.

Anthony, George. "Terribly Pretty, but Pretty Terrible." *Toronto Sun*, 11 April 1983.

Appadurai, Arjun. *Modernity at Large: Cultural Dimensions of Globalization*. Minneapolis: Public Worlds, 1996.

Arendt, Hannah. *The Human Condition.* Chicago: University of Chicago Press, 1958.

Armatage, Kay, Kass Banning, Brenda Longfellow and Janine Marchessault, eds. *Gendering the Nation: Canadian Women's Cinema.* Toronto: University of Toronto Press, 1999.

Armstrong, Mary Ellen. "Expansion and Change." *Playback,* 19 May 1997.

——. i"Service, Disney Style." *Playback,* 19 May 1997.

Arroyo, José. *Drôle de Félix. Sight and Sound* 11, no. 1 (January 2001): 47.

Art is Never a Given: Professional Training in the Arts in Canada. Ottawa: Minister of Supply and Services, 1991.

"At $7.50 top, CO turns up b.o. heat." *Variety,* 14–20 June 1990.

Atkinson, Michael. "Entangling Alliances." *Village Voice,* 28 March 2000.

Atwood, Margaret. *Strange Things: The Malevolent North in Canadian Literature.* Oxford: Clarendon Press, 1995.

Augaitis, Diana George Wagner and William Wood. *Stan Douglas.* Vancouver: Vancouver Art Gallery, 1999.

Backhouse, Constance. *Colour-Coded: A Legal History of Racism in Canada, 1900–1950.* Toronto: University of Toronto Press, 1999.

Baert, Renee. "Subjects on the Threshold: Problems with the Pronouns." *Parachute* 69 (January/February/March 1993): 14–21.

Bailey, Cameron. "A Cinema of Duty: The Films of Jennifer Hodge de Silva." *CineAction!* 23 (Winter 1991): 4–21.

——. "What the Story Is: An Interview with Srinivas Krishna." *CineAction!* 28 (Spring 1992): 38–47.

——. "Fright the Power." *Fuse* 15, no. 6 (Summer 1992): 22–27.

——. "Intense Auteur Unleashes Risky Lesbian Romance." *Now,* 4–10 May 1995.

——. "Interview with Mike Hoolboom." In *Lux: A Decade of Artists' Film and Video.* Steve Reinke and Tom Taylor, eds. Toronto: YYZ/Pleasure Dome, 2000.

——. "Standing in the Kitchen All Night: A Secret History of the Toronto New Wave." *Take One* 28 (Summer 2000): 6–11.

Baker, Houston. *Blues, Ideology and African American Literature: A Vernacular Theory.* Chicago: University of Chicago Press, 1984.

Baker, Noel S. *Hard Core Road Show: A Screenwriter's Diary.* Toronto: House of Anansi Press, 1997.

Baker, Rob. *The Art of AIDS: From Stigma to Conscience.* New York: Continuum, 1994.

Bakhtin, M.M. *Art and Answerability: Early Philosophical Essays by M.M. Bakhtin.* Michael Holquist and Vadim Liapunov, eds. Vadim Liapunov, trans. Austin: University of Texas Press, 1990.

Balcan, David. "Hearing Our Voice, Seeing Our Image." National Film Board of Canada internal document, 1991.

Baldassarre, Angela. "Where do you want this killing done? Out on Highway 61." *Eye Weekly*, 13 February 1992.

Banerji, Rima. "Still on *Fire*." *Manushi* 113 (July 1999): 1821.

Banning, Kass. "RE/VISION: Reconsidering the British and Canadian Avant–Garde." In *A Commonwealth*. Lori Keating, ed. Toronto: The Funnel, 1984.

——. "Rhetorical Remarks Towards the Politics of Otherness." *CineAction!* 16 (Spring 1989): 15–19.

——. "Queerying John Greyson's *Zero Patience*." *Take One* 3 (Fall 1993): 20–23.

——. "Playing in the Light: Canadianizing Race and Nation." In *Gendering the Nation: Canadian Women's Cinema*, Kay Armatage, Kass Banning, Brenda Longfellow and Janine Marchessault, eds.

Baraka, Amira. *Blues People: Negro Music in White America*. Westport, CT: Greenwood Press, 1963.

Barker, Martin and Kate Brooks. *Knowing Audiences: Judge Dredd, Its Friends, Fans and Foes*. Luton: University of Luton Press, 1998.

Barthes, Roland. *A Lover's Discourse: Fragments*. Richard Howard, trans. New York: Hill and Wang, 1978.

Baudrillard, Jean. *Simulations*. Paul Foss, Paul Patton, and Philip Beitchman, trans. New York: Semiotext(e), 1981.

Bazin, André. *What is Cinema?* Hugh Gray, ed. and trans. Berkeley: University of California Press, 1969.

Bearchell, Chris. "A Canadian Fairytale: Chris Bearchell Talks to Patricia Rozema about Taking Her First Feature to Cannes." *Epicene*, October 1987.

Beard, William. "The Canadianness of David Cronenberg." *Mosaic* 27, no. 2 (June 1994): 113–33.

Beck, Jerry. *The 50 Greatest Cartoons*. North Dighton, MA: World Publications, 1994.

Beckett, Samuel. *Krapp's Last Tape and Other Dramatic Pieces*. New York: Grove Press, 1957.

Beggs, Mike. "McDonald road film subversive epic." *Taxi News*, May 1992.

Bell, Douglas. "Greyson's exuberantly eccentric film defies description: *Uncut*." *Globe and Mail*, 3 July 1998.

Benjamin, Walter. *Illuminations*. Hanna Arendt, ed. Harry Zohn, trans. New York: Schocken Books, 1969.

Bennett, Tony and Janet Woollacott. *Bond and Beyond: The Political Career of a Popular Hero*. New York: Methuen, 1987.

Berger, Sally. "Beyond the Absurd, Beyond Cruelty: Donigan Cumming's Staged Realities." In *Lux: A Decade of Artists' Film and Video*. Steve Reinke and Tom Taylor, eds. Toronto: YYZ Books and Pleasure Dome, 2000.

Birnbaum, Daniel. "Daily Double." *Artforum* (January 2000).

Blackhouse, Constance. *Colour-Coded: A Legal History of Racism in Canada, 1900–1950*. Toronto: Osgood Society/University of Toronto Press, 1999.

Bociurkiw, Marvisia. "Working the Double Shift: Videotape by Lisa Steele." *Video Guide* 7, no. 1 (1984): 4–5.

Bordwell, David. "The Art Film as Mode of Film Practice." *Film Criticism* 4, no. 1 (Fall 1979): 56–64.

Bouchard, Michel Marc. *Lilies or the Revival of a Romantic Drama.* Linda Gaboriau, trans. Toronto: Coach House, 1990.

Bourdieu, Pierre. *Distinction: A Social Critique of the Judgement of Taste.* Richard Nice, trans. Cambridge: Harvard University Press, 1984.

Braithwaite, Edward K. *History of the Voice: the Development of Nation Language in Anglophone Caribbean Poetry.* London: New Beacon Books, 1984.

Brand, Peggy Zeglin and Carolyn Korsmeyer, eds. *Feminism and Tradition in Aesthetics.* Pennsylvania: Pennsylvania State University Press, 1995.

Brasell, R. Bruce. "Queer Nationalism and the Musical Fag Bashing of John Greyson's *The Making of Monsters.*" *Wide Angle* 16, no. 3 (1995): 26–36.

"Briefing: Film exhibition." *Variety*, 19 November 1990.

Britton, Andrew, Richard Lippe, Tony Williams and Robin Wood. *The American Nightmare: Essays on the Horror Film.* Toronto: Festival of Festivals, 1979.

Brooks, Peter. *The Melodramatic Imagination: Balzac, Henry James, Melodrama, and the Mode of Excess.* New York: Columbia University Press, 1976.

Brunette, Peter. "'Shut up and just do it!'" *Sight and Sound* 60, no. 1 (Winter 1990–91): 55–57.

Bruno, Giuliana. *Street-Walking on a Ruined Map: Cultural Theory and the City Films of Elvira Notari.* Princeton: Princeton University Press, 1993.

de Bruyn, Dirk. "What he sAID: An interview with Mike Hoolboom." *Workprint*, Spring 1993.

Burnet, Jean. "Multiculturalism." *The Canadian Encyclopedia.* Year 2000 Edition. Toronto: McClelland and Stewart, 1999.

Burnett, Ron. "Atom Egoyan: An Interview." *CineAction!* 16 (Spring 1989): 40–44.

"Bye Bye Anne: An Edmonton Filmmaker Trades Alberta for the Coast." *Western Report*, 25 June 1990.

Cagle, Robert L. "Canadian Filmmaking in the Face of Cultural Imperialism." *Reverse Shot* 1, no. 2 (Summer 1994): 8–12.

——. "'Tell the story of my life...': The Making of Meaning, 'Monsters,' and Music in John Greyson's *Zero Patience.*" *The Velvet Light Trap* 35 (Spring 1995): 69–81.

——. "A Minority on Someone Else's Continent: Identity, Difference, and the Media in the Films of Patricia Rozema." In *Gendering the Nation: Canadian Women's Cinema*, Kay Armatage, Kass Banning, Brenda Longfellow and Janine Marchessault, eds.

"Calling the Crowds to Angel Square." *Western Report*, 14 October 1991.

Calliste, Agnes. "Car Porters in Canada: An Ethnically Submerged Labour Split Market" *Canadian Ethnic Studies* 19, no. 1 (1987): 1–20.

——. "Blacks on Canadian Railways." *Canadian Ethnic Studies* 20, no. 2 (1988): 36–52.

——. "The Struggle for Equity by Blacks on American and Canadian Railroads." *Journal of Black Studies* 25, no. 3 (January 1995): 297–317.

Camper, Fred. "The End of Avant-Garde Film." *Millennium Film Journal* 16/17/18 (1986–87): 99–124.

Canadian Heritage. *The Road to Success: Report of the Feature Film Advisory Committee.* Ottawa: Canadian Heritage, 1999.

Canadian Television Fund. *The Big Picture Behind the Small Screen: Activity Report 1998–1999.* Ottawa: Canadian Television Fund, 1999.

Cavell, Stanley. *Contesting Tears: The Hollywood Melodrama of the Unknown Woman.* Chicago and London: University of Chicago Press, 1996.

de Certeau, Michel. *The Practice of Everyday Life.* Trans. Steven F. Rendall. Berkeley: University of California Press, 1984.

Cham, Mbye B. *Ex-Iles: Essays on Caribbean Cinema.* Trenton, NJ: Africa World Press, 1992.

——. and Claire Andrade-Watkins. *Blackframes: Critical Perspectives on Black Independent Film.* Cambridge: MIT Press, 1988.

Charland, Maurice. "Technological Nationalism." *Canadian Journal of Political and Social Theory* 10, nos. 1–2 (1986): 196–220.

Chubb, Ken. *A Survey of First Peoples Writers, Directors and Producers of Film and Television Drama in Canada.* Toronto: The Canadian Native Arts Foundation, 1993.

"Cinemas need a personal touch." *Playback,* 10 November 1986.

"Cineplex empire builds." *Playback,* 10 August 1987.

"Cineplex Odeon art house re–opens with benefit fest." *Playback,* 2 May 1988.

"Cineplex Odeon hikes Canadian admissions." *Variety,* 30 May 1989.

"Cineplex Odeon ups Canada tickets to $C7." *Variety,* 31 May–7 June 1989.

"Cineplex readies Montréal fourplex." *Variety,* 26 November 1986.

"Cineplex Theater Activity." *Variety,* 26 April–2 May 1989.

Clanfield, David. *Canadian Film.* Toronto: Oxford University Press, 1987.

Clover, Carol. *Men, Women, and Chainsaws: Gender in the Modern Horror Film.* Princeton: Princeton University Press, 1993.

——. "Judging Audiences: the case of the trial movie." In *Reinventing Film Studies.* Christine Gledhill and Linda Williams, eds. New York: Oxford University Press, 2000.

"CO completes buy of 152 screens in western Canada." *Variety,* 7 February 1990.

Cole, Janis and Holly Dale. *Calling the Shots: Profiles of Women Filmmakers.* Kingston: Quarry Press, 1993.

Coldevin, Gary O. "Anik I and Isolation: Television in the Lives of Canadian Eskimos." *Journal of Communication* 27 (1977).

Coleman, Victor. "Talking Pictures with Janis Cole and Holly Dale." *The Lictor*, 4 March 1982.

Collins, Keith. "Atom Egoyan's Krapp's Last Tape." *Fox News.Com* 25 September 2000. www.foxnews.com/entertainment/092500/atom_egoyan.sml?refer=isynd, accessed 24 November 2000.

Collins, Richard. *Culture, Communication & National Identity: The Case of Canadian Television*. Toronto: University of Toronto Press, 1990.

Compton, Jim. "Indigenous Media: Building Bridges." Presented at Children and Youth Summit, Toronto, May 2000.

Cook, Pam. *The Cinema Book*. London: British Film Institute, 1994.

Crean, Susan M. *Who's Afraid of Canadian Culture?* Toronto: General, 1976.

Creed, Barbara. *The Monstrous Feminine: Film, Feminism, Psychoanalysis*. London: Routledge, 1993.

——. "The naked crunch: Cronenberg's homoerotic bodies." In *The Modern Fantastic: The Films of David Cronenberg*. Michael Grant, ed. Westport, CT: Greenwood, 2000.

Crimp, Douglas. "Randy Shilts' Miserable Failure." In *A Queer World: The Center for Lesbian and Gay Studies Reader*. Martin Duberman, ed. New York: New York University Press, 1997.

Cripps, Thomas. *Slow Fade to Black*. New York: Oxford University Press, 1993.

"*Christmas* Open, Disney OKs Next Borsos Film *Billy Buckles*. *Variety*, 27 November 1985.

Dalton, Mary. *The Time of Icicles*. St. John's: Breakwater Books, 1989.

Deleuze, Gilles. *Difference and Repetition*. Paul Patton, trans. New York: Columbia University Press, 1994.

—— and Felix Guattari. *Anti-Oedipus: Capitalism and Schizophrenia*. Robert Hurley, Mark Seem and Helen R. Lane, trans. Minneapolis: University of Minnesota Press, 1983.

Dellamora, Richard. "John Greyson's *Zero Patience* in the Canadian Firmament: Cultural Practice/Cultural Studies." *University of Toronto Quarterly* 64, no. 4 (Fall 1995): 526–35.

Dent, Gina, ed. *Black Popular Culture*. Seattle: Bay Press, 1992.

Department of Canadian Heritage. *Making Our Voices Heard: Canadian Broadcasting and Film for the 21st Century*. Ottawa: Minister of Supply and Services Canada, 1996.

de Rosa, Maria. *The nfb's Studio One: Future Directions*. 1995. Prepared for the National Film Board.

——. *An Evaluation of the Aboriginal Filmmaking Program*. 1999.

Dick, Ronald. "Regionalization of a Federal Cultural Institution: The Experience of the National Film Board of Canada 1965–1979." In *Flashback: People and Institutions in Canadian Film History*. Gene Walz, ed. Montréal: Mediatexte, 1986.

Ditta, Su. "Eyeing the Sublime: Poetic Politics in the Work of Lisa Steele and Kim Tomczak." In *Blood Records*, Lisa Steele and Kim Tomczak, eds.

Donegan, Rosemary. *Work, Weather, and the Grid: Agriculture in Saskatchewan*. Regina: Dunlop Art Gallery, 1991.

Dopp, Jamie. "Who Says That Canadian Culture is Ironic?" In *Double-Talking*, Linda Hutcheon, ed.

Dorland, Michael. *So Close to the State/s: The Emergence of Canadian Feature Film Policy*. Toronto: University of Toronto Press, 1998.

"Doubt Clouds Canada's Film Future." *Calgary Herald*, 9 September 1997.

Duggan, M.B. "Culture, Aesthetic and Obsessions: Winnipeg Film Group Films." *The Independent Eye* 11, no. 1 (1989): 24–28.

Dwyer, Rachel. "'Indian Values' and the Diaspora: Yash Chopra's Films of the 1990's." *West Coast Line* 32 (Fall 2000): 6–27.

Dwyer, Victor. "Company of Women: A Largely Female Crew Shoots a Canadian Classic *The Diviners*." *Maclean's*, 15 June 1992.

Dyer, Richard. "Stereotyping." In *Gays in Film*. Richard Dyer, ed. New York: Zoetrope, 1984.

——. *The Matter of Images*. London and New York: Routledge, 1993.

Easthope, Antony. *Literary Into Cultural Studies*. London: Routledge, 1991.

Egoyan, Atom. "Surface Tension." *Speaking Parts*. Toronto: Coach House Press, 1993.

——. "Director's Statement." *Sarabande Suite #4:Yo–Yo Ma – The Films*. Sony Classical.com, www.sonyclassical.com/releases/63203/films/direct_4.html, accessed 30 January 2002.

Ehrensetin, David. "More Than Zero." *Film Comment* 29, no. 6 (November/December 1993): 84–86.

Eichhorn, Paul. "Bruce McDonald Gets Off the Road." *The Late Harvest Journal of Creative Culture* (Winter 1994–95).

Eisner, Ken. "Light and Shadow." *Georgia Straight*, 15 March 1999.

Elder, Bruce. "The Cinema We Need." *Canadian Forum*, February 1985. Reprinted in *Documents in Canadian Film*, Douglas Fetherling, ed.

——. *Image and Identity: Reflections on Canadian Film and Culture*. Waterloo: Wilfrid Laurier University Press, 1989.

Enchin, Harvey. "Canadians Going Back to the Movies." *Globe and Mail*, 11 July 1996.

——. "Deal Creates Box Office Giant." *Globe and Mail*, 1 October 1997.

——. "Theatre deal highlights market fragmentation." *Globe and Mail*, 3 October 1997.

Evans, Gary. *In the National Interest: A Chronicle of the National Film Board of Canada 1949–1989*. Toronto: University of Toronto Press, 1991.

Evans, Jane. "Filmmakers Don't Cry? An Interview with Anne Wheeler." *NeWest Review* 15, no. 3 (February/March 1990).

Everett–Green, Robert. "Cineplex Odeon is the one trespassing." *Globe and Mail*, 1 November 1996.

——. "Not coming to a theatre near you." *Globe and Mail*, 17 January 1997.

——. "Canadian film by the numbers." *Globe and Mail*, 18 January 1997.

"Famous Players is going public; sets screen growth, pic investing." *Variety*, 25 November 1987.

"Famous Players sets $C50-million Toronto expansion." *Variety*, 18 May 1988.

"Famous Players theater chain lowers ticket prices in Canada." *Variety*, 9 March 1988.

"Famous Players ups Canadian admission to $C7." *Variety*, 17–23 May 1989.

Farrow, Jane. "Sell me down the river. Please. Courtney Love sold out. So did Bob Dylan. So what does it take for an el cheapo indie filmmaker to get on the gravy train?" *This Magazine*, March/April 1998.

Faulkner, Christopher. "Affective Identities: French National Cinema and the 1930s." *Canadian Journal of Film Studies* 3, no. 2 (Fall 1994): 3–23.

Feature Film Advisory Committee. *Report: The Road to Success*. Ottawa: Canadian Heritage, 1993.

Feldman, Seth. "The Electric Table: Aspects of the Docudrama in Canada." *Canadian Drama* 9, no. 1 (1983): 39–48.

——. ed. *Take Two: A Tribute to Film in Canada*. Toronto: Irwin/Festival of Festivals, 1984.

"Feminist Filmmaker Was a Legend." *Herizons*, Spring 1998.

Fetherling, Douglas, ed. *Documents in Canadian Film*. Peterborough: Broadview Press, 1986.

Fillion, Kate. "John Greyson's musical about AIDS won't upset fans who expect fun." *Globe and Mail*, 27 November 1993.

Fitzgerald, John. "Newfoundland Politics and Confederation Revisited: Three New Works." *Newfoundland Studies* 9, no. 1 (Spring 1993).

Folland, Tom. "Deregulating Identity: Video and AIDS Activism." In *Mirror Machine: Video and Identity*, Janine Marchessault, ed.

Forget, Claude. "Pour un Cinema Libre." *The Independent Eye* 12, no. 2 (1991): 8–11.

Fothergill, Robert. "Coward, Bully or Clown: The Dream Life of a Younger Brother." *Take One* 4, no. 3 (September 1973). Reprinted in Seth Feldman and Joyce Nelson, eds., *Canadian Film Reader*. Toronto: Peter Martin Associates, 1977.

Foucault, Michel. "What is an Author?" *Language, Counter-Memory, Practice: Selected Essays and Interviews by Michel Foucault*. Donald F. Bouchard, ed. Donald F. Bouchard and Sherry Simon, trans. Ithaca: Cornell University Press, 1977.

——. *Discipline and Punish: The Birth of the Prison*. Alan Sheridan, trans. New York: Vintage, 1979.

Francis, Daniel. *The Imaginary Indian: The Image of the Indian in Canadian Culture*. Vancouver: Arsenal Pulp Press, 1992.

Frank, David. "One Hundred Years After: Film and History in Atlantic Canada." *Acadiensis* 26, no. 2 (Spring 1997): 112–36.

Freud, Sigmund. *The Standard Edition of the Complete Psychological Works of Sigmund Freud*. XVIII. London: The Hogarth Press, 1957.

Friedrich, Otto. *Glenn Gould: A Life and Variations*. New York: Random House, 1989.

"A Frightening Time: A Film Revisits Canada's Internment Camps." *Maclean's* 7 November 1994.

Fuchs, Cynthia. "Interview with Atom Egoyan." *Pop Matters*, 24 November 2000.

Fulford, Robert [Marshall Delaney]. "You Should Know How Bad This Movie Is–You Paid For It." *Saturday Night*, September 1975.

Gale, Peggy. "Lisa Steele: Looking Very Closely." *Parachute* 2 (January/February/March 1976): 30–31.

Gasher, Mike. "Decolonizing the Imagination: Cultural Expression as Vehicle of Self-Discovery." *Canadian Journal of Film Studies* 2, no. 2 (1993): 95–106.

Gates, Henry Louis. *The Signifying Monkey: A Theory of African-American Literary Criticism.* New York: Oxford University Press, 1988.

Gawthrop, Daniel. *Affirmation: The AIDS Odyssey of Dr. Peter.* Vancouver: New Star Books, 1994.

Gilroy, Paul. *There Ain't No Black in the Union Jack.* London: Unwin Hyman, 1987.

——. "It's a Family Affair." In *Black Popular Culture*, Gina Dent, ed.

——. *The Black Atlantic: Modernity and Double Consciousness.* Cambridge: Harvard University Press, 1993.

Ginsburg, Faye. "Mediating Culture: Indigenous Media, Ethnographic Film, and the Production of Identity." In *Fields of Vision: Essays in Film Studies, Visual Anthropology and Photography.* Leslie Devereaux and Roger Hillman, eds. Berkeley: University of California Press, 1996.

Girard, Francois, and Don McKellar. *Thirty-Two Short Films About Glenn Gould.* Toronto: Coach House Press, 1995.

Glassman, Marc. "Emotional Logic." Interview with Atom Egoyan. In Atom Egoyan, *Speaking Parts.* Toronto: Coach House Press, 1993.

——. "In Search of Glenn Gould." *Take One: Film In Canada*, Winter 1994.

——. "Rockin' On the Road, The Films of Bruce McDonald." *Take One*, Summer 1995.

——. "*Last Night*: In the Year of the Don." *Take One*, Fall 1998.

——. "The Epic Sound of Melodrama: *The Red Violin* reaches the screen." *Take One*, Winter 1999.

—— and Janine Marchessault, eds. *Images 88: A Showcase of Contemporary Film & Video.* Catalogue for Images Festival, 27–30 June 1988. Toronto: Northern Visions Independent Film and Video Association, 1988.

Godwin, George. "Reclaiming the subject: A feminist reading of *I've Heard the Mermaids Singing.*" *Cinema Canada* 152 (May 1988): 23–25.

Golfman, Noreen. "Flowers for Greyson's Queer Cinema." *Canadian Forum*, November 1996.

——. "Mixed Messages; Standing in for the Hamptons." *Canadian Forum*, November 1997.

Gomery, Douglas. "Building a Movie Theatre Giant: The Rise of Cineplex Odeon." In *Hollywood in the Age of Television.* Tino Balio, ed. Boston: Unwin Hyman, 1990.

Goodden, Herman. "Reckless Coverage Spawns Copycats: News Directors Should Rein in Reporting of Tragedies." *London Free Press*, 26 April 2000.

Gopalan, Lalitha. "Avenging Women in Indian Cinema [Part 1 of 3]." *Nivedini—A Sri Lankan Feminist Journal* 5, no. 1 (June 1997): 59–67.

Graham, Bob. "*Uncut* is going to drive some people nuts." *San Francisco Chronicle,* 8 January 1999, C3.

Gravestock, Steve. "On the Road with Bruce and Don." *Innis Herald* 27, no. 1 (January 1993).

——. "The Outsiders." *Venue*, Fall 1994.

Gray, John. "Preface to *Billy Bishop Goes to War*." In *Modern Canadian Plays II*. Jerry Wasserman, ed. Vancouver: Talonbooks, 1994.

Greenbaum, Richard. "*Loyalties*." *Films in Review* 38 (December 1987): 603–08.

"Greyson, John." *1999 Canadian Encyclopedia: World Edition* [CD-ROM]. Toronto: McClelland and Stewart, 1999.

Greyson, John. "Strategic Compromises: AIDS and Alternative Video Practices." In *Reimaging America: The Arts of Social Change*. Mark O'Brien and Craig Little, eds. Philadelphia and Santa Cruz: New Society Publishers, 1990.

——. "Parma Violets for Wayland Flowers." In *Fluid Exchanges: Artist and Critics in the AIDS Crisis*. James Miller, ed. Toronto, Buffalo, and London: University of Toronto Press, 1992.

——. "Security Blankets: Sex, Video and the Police." In *Queer Looks: Perspectives on Lesbian and Gay Film and Video*. Martha Gever, Pratibha Parmar, and John Greyson, eds. New York and London: Routledge, 1993.

——. "Immigration Raids: The Toronto Black community gets top priority for police harassment—again." *Fuse* 20, no. 2 (1997): 38–39.

Grierson, John. "A Film Policy for Canada." Originally published in *Canadian Affairs*, 15 June 1944. Reprinted in *Documents in Canadian Film*, Douglas Fetherling, ed.

Grizzle, Stanley G. *My Name's Not George: The Story of the Brotherhood of Sleeping Car Porters in Canada*. Toronto: Umbrella Press, 1998.

Groen, Rick. "Stars made of pucks, and other cute things." *Globe and Mail,* 5 November 1999.

Grundmann, Roy. "Where Is This Place Called Home?" *Cinemaya* 23 (Spring 1994): 22–27.

Guibert, Hervé. *À l'ami que ne m'a pas sauvé la vie*. Paris: Gallimard, 1990. Trans. *To the Friend Who Did Not Save My Life*, New York: Macmillan, 1991.

Hall, Stuart. *Critical Dialogues in Cultural Studies*. David Morley and Kuan-Hsing Chen, eds. London: Routledge, 1996.

——. "What is this 'Black' in Black Popular Culture?" In *Black Popular Culture*, Gina Dent, ed.

Hammond, Brean S. "The Political Unconscious in Mansfield Park." *Mansfield Park*. Nigel Wood, ed. Buckingham: Open University Press, 1993.

Handling, Piers, ed. *The Shape of Rage: The Films of David Cronenberg*. Toronto: Academy of Canadian Cinema/General, 1983.

Hannant, Larry. "The Sleep Room." *Canadian Historical Review* 80, no. 4 (December 1999): 698–705.

Harcourt, Peter. "Canada: An Unfinished Text?" *Canadian Journal of Film Studies* (1993): 5–26.

——. "Imaginary Images: An Examination of Atom Egoyan's Films." *Film Quarterly* 48, no. 3 (Spring 1995): 2–14.

——. "A Conversation with Atom Egoyan." *Post Script: Essays in Film and the Humanities* 15, no. 1 (Fall 1995): 68–74.

Harkness, John. "Canada's most successful ever indie documentary soon to open in the UK." *Screen International*, 21 April 1984.

——. "Nightworld: An Interview with Janis Cole and Holly Dale." *Cinema Canada* (June 1984).

Harris, Christopher. "Famous Players makes an expansive move." *Playback*, 30 May 1988.

——. "More buys for Cineplex." *Playback*, 4 September 1989.

——. "Greyson crashes Cronenberg's party." *Globe and Mail*, 28 November 1996.

——. "Faith in Popcorn." *Globe and Mail*, 10 May 1997.

Harrison, Marion. "*Mermaids:* Singing Off Key?" *CineAction!* (Spring 1989): 25–30.

Hays, Matthew. "Film's Restricted rating appealed." *Globe and Mail*, 4 July 1998.

Hébert, Gilles, ed. *Dislocations: Winnipeg Film Group*. Regina: Dunlop Art Gallery, 1995.

Henley, Gail. "On the Record: For The Record's Ten Dramatic Years." *Cinema Canada* 117 (April 1985): 18–21.

Hibon, Danielle. *Atom Egoyan*. Paris: Galerie Nationale du Jeu de Paume, 1993.

"High–octane dance with the devil blazes trail into American Psyche." *Toronto Star*, 14 February 1992.

Hlachy, Patricia. "Lilies." *Maclean's* 11 November 1996.

Hoffman, Andy. "Cineplex deal raises multiplex of scenarios." *Playback*, 12 January 1998.

"Hold the popcorn." *Playback*, 14 December 1987.

Holden, Stephen. "*Last Night*: Stranded in the City, On Doomsday to Boot." *New York Times*, 5 November 1999.

Holquist, Michael. "Answering as Authoring." In *Bakhtin: Essays and Dialogues on His Work*. Gary Saul Morson, ed. Chicago and London: University of Chicago Press, 1981.

——. *Dialogism: Bakhtin and His World*. London and New York: Routledge, 1990.

Hoolboom, Mike. "Some Thoughts About Artist's Film Distribution in Canada." *The Independent Eye* 9, no. 1 (1988): 6–8.

——. "Mourning Pictures." In *Blood Records*, Lisa Steele and Kim Tomczak, eds.

——. "A History of the Canadian Avant-Garde in Film." In *The Visual Aspect: Recent Canadian Experimental Films*. Rose Lowder, ed. Avignon: Éditions des archives du film expérimental d'Avignon, 1991.

——. *Plague Years: A Life in Underground Movies*. Steve Reinke, ed. Toronto: YYZ Books, 1998.

——. *Inside the Pleasure Dome: Fringe Film in Canada*. Toronto: Gutter Press, 1997.

——. et al. "Al Razutis: Under the Sign of the Beast." *The Independent Eye* 10, no. 3 (1989): 26–32.

Howell, Peter. "End of the world, Canuck style." *Toronto Star*, 23 October 1998.

Howells, Coral Ann. *Private and Fictional Words: Canadian Women Novelists of the 1970s and 1980s*. London and New York: Methuen, 1987.

Hutcheon, Linda. *Splitting Images: Contemporary Canadian Ironies*. Toronto: Oxford University Press, 1991.

——. ed. *Double-Talking: Essays on Verbal and Visual Ironies in Canadian Contemporary Art and Literature*. Toronto: ECW, 1992.

Images: The 13th Annual Images Festival of Film and Video. Catalogue for Images Festival, 13–18 June 2000. Toronto: Northern Visions Independent Film and Video Association, 2000.

"International Box Office." *Variety*, 19–25 January 1998.

Irving, John. *My Movie Business: A Memoir*. Toronto: Knopf Canada, 1999.

"It's a Famous idea to drop movie prices." *Playback*, 7 March 1988.

Ivry, Bob. "Out with a Whimper—Doomsday Should Have a Little Pop." *The Record*, 5 November 1999.

Jacobowitz, Florence and Richard Lippe. "*Dead Ringers*: The Joke's on Us." *CineAction!* Spring 1989: 64–68

Jagose, Annamarie. *Queer Theory: An Introduction*. New York: New York University Press, 1996.

James, Cathy. "Kathleen Shannon: On Film, Feminism and Other Dreams." *Canadian Historical Review* 80, no. 1 (March 1999): 93–96.

James, Christine. "The Great Divide." *Boxoffice*, www.boxoffice.com/showcanada99/daily99story4.htm, accessed 3 November 1999.

James, David. "Chained to Devil Pictures: Cinema and Black Liberation in the Sixties." In *The Year Left Review* 1987, Mike Davis et al., eds.

Johnson, Brian. "Rock 'n' Roll highway." *Maclean's*, 17 February 1992: 64.

——. "Sex and the sacred girl." *Maclean's*, 8 May 1995: 93–95.

——. "Catch a rising star: cool movies and hot talent light up Toronto's film festival." *Maclean's*, 16 September 1996.

——. "A cinema of extremes: The Toronto festival's crop of Canadian movies is diverse and wildly idiosyncratic." *Maclean's*, 15 September 1997.

——. "School for celluloid: the Canadian Film Centre is a leading place to learn 'the literature of our generation'" *Maclean's*, 23 November 1998: 124–25.

Johnson, Claudia L. "Introduction." In Patricia Rozema, *Jane Austen's Mansfield Park: A Screenplay*. New York: Talk Miramax Books, 2000.

Jones, D.B. *Movies and Memoranda: An Interpretive History of the National Film Board of Canada*. Ottawa: Deneau, 1982.

——. *The Best Butler in the Business: Tom Daly of the National Film Board of Canada*. Toronto: University of Toronto Press, 1996.

Jost, François. "Proposition pour une typologie des documents audiovisuels." *Semiotica* 112 (1996): 123–40.

Juhasz, Alexandra. *AIDS TV: Identity, Community, and Alternative Video*. Videography by Catherine Saalfield. Durham: Duke University Press, 1995.

Kabir, Shameem. *Daughters of Desire: Lesbian Representation in Film*. London and Washington: Cassell, 1998.

Kalafatic, Carol. "Keepers of the Power: Story as Covenant in the Films of Loretta Todd, Shelley Niro, and Christine Walsh." In *Gendering the Nation: Canadian Women's Cinema*, Kay Armatage, Kass Banning, Brenda Longfellow and Janine Marchessault, eds.

Kamboureli, Smaro. "The Technology of Ethnicity: Canadian Multiculturalism and the Language of Law." In *Multicultural States: Rethinking Difference and Identity*. David Bennett, ed. New York: Routledge, 1989.

Kapur, Ratna. "Too Hot to Handle: The Cultural Politics of *Fire*." *Feminist Review* 64 (Spring 2000): 53–64.

Katzenbach, John. *In the Heat of the Summer*. New York: Atheneum, 1982.

Kelly, Brendan. "Major Video Chains Prepare for a Boom." *Variety*, 22 November 1993.

——. "Bigger, Better Plexes: With eight decades in business, circuit is on expansion course." *Variety*, 29 November–5 December 1999.

Kelly, Deirdre. "Cineplex apologizes to Greyson." *Globe and Mail*, 13 November 1996.

Kelly, Richard. "Last Night." *Sight and Sound* 9, no. 7 (July 1999): 44.

Kenna, Kathleen. "Land of 220 million guns." *Toronto Star*, 24 April 1999.

Kennedy, Lisa. "States of Grace." *Village Voice*, 21 November 1996.

Keohone, Kieran. "Symptoms of Canada: National Identity and the Theft of National Enjoyment." *CineAction!* 28 (Spring 1992): 20–37.

Kibbins, Gary. "Bored Bedmates: Art and Criticism at the Decade's End." *Fuse* 22, no. 2 (Spring 1999): 32–42.

Kirby, Lynne. *Parallel Tracks: The Railroad and Silent Cinema*. Durham NC: Duke University Press, 1997.

Kirkland, Bruce. "Egoyan's 'dream project.' Director thrilled to make Beckett film with John Hurt." *Toronto Sun*, 24 August 2000.

Kishwar, Madhu. "Naive Outpourings of a Self-Hating Indian: [Parts 3 and 4]." *Manushi* 109 (November 1998).

Klady, Leonard. "B.O. tastes Yank-flavored." *Variety*, 2–8 September 1996.

——. "H'wood's B.O. blast: '97 admissions highest in three decades." *Variety*, 5–11 January 1998.

Kleinhans, Chuck. "Forms, Politics, Makers, and Contexts: Basic Issues for a Theory of Radical Political Documentary." In *'Show Us Life': Towards a History and Aesthetics of the Committed Documentary*. Thomas Waugh, ed. Metuchen: Scarecrow Press, 1984.

Klinger, Barbara. *Melodrama and Meaning: History, Culture, and the Films of Douglas Sirk*. Bloomington and Indianapolis: Indiana University Press, 1994.

——. "Film history terminable and interminable: Recovering the past in reception studies." *Screen* 38, no. 2 (Summer 1997): 107–28.

Knee, Adam and Charles Musser. "William Greaves, Documentary, and the African American Experience." *Film Quarterly* 45, no. 3 (Spring 1992): 13–25.

Knelman, Martin. "Comedy, Critters, Cranko." *Toronto Life*, 1 February 1992.

——. "Sleepless in Toronto." *Toronto Life* 28, no. 1 (January 1994): 34–37.

Knight, Deborah. "Exquisite Nostalgia: Aesthetic Sensibility in the English-Canadian and Québec Cinemas." *CineAction!* 11 (Winter 1987–88): 30–37.

——. "Metafiction, Pararealism and the 'Canon' of Canadian Cinema." *Cinémas* 3, no. 1 (Fall 1992): 125–46.

Koller, George Csaba. "Street People." *Cinema Canada* 49–50.

Koller, Katherine. "Anne Wheeler: The Woman Behind the Camera." *NeWest Review* 12, no. 8 (April 1987): 18.

Korsmeyer, Carolyn. "Pleasure: Reflections on Aesthetics and Feminism." *Journal of Aesthetics and Art Criticism* 51, no. 2 (Spring 1993).

Krauss, Rosalind. "Video: The Aesthetics of Narcissism." In *Video Culture: A Critical Investigation*. John Handhardt, ed. Rochester: Visual Studies Workshop Press, 1987.

Kroker, Arthur. *Technology and the Canadian Mind: Innis/McLuhan/Grant*. Montréal: New World Perspectives, 1984.

Kuhn, Annette. *Women's Pictures*. London: Routledge & Kegan Paul, 1982.

Lacey, Liam. "John Greyson, an uncut above." *Globe and Mail*, 30 May 1997.

Laclau, Ernesto. "Politics and the Limits of Modernity." In *Postmodernism: A Reader*. Thomas Docherty, ed. New York: Columbia University Press, 1993.

Laffel, Jeff. "Bye Bye Blues." *Films in Review* 41 (November/December 1990): 558–59.

Lamoureux, Johanne. "The Blood Records: Idle Identity." In *Blood Records*, Lisa Steele and Kim Tomczak, eds.

Lane, Anthony. "The Gould variations." *The New Yorker*, 18 April 1994.

de Lauretis, Teresa. "Guerrilla in the midst: women's cinema in the 80s." *Screen* 31, no. 1 (Spring 1990): 6–25.

de Lauretis, Teresa. "Sexual Indifference and Lesbian Representation." In *The Lesbian & Gay Studies Reader*. Henry Abelove et al., eds. New York: Routledge, 1993.

Leach, Jim. "North of Pittsburgh: Genre and National Cinema from a Canadian Perspective." In *Film Genre Reader II*. Barry K. Grant, ed. Austin: University of Texas Press, 1995.

Lee, Helen. "Coming Attractions: A Brief History of Canada's Nether-Cinema." *Take One* (Summer 1994): 5–11.

Leitch, Carolyn. "Astral Considering Acquisitions: Company May Buy Small Video Distributors to Consolidate Market." *Globe and Mail*, 31 January 1997.

Lewis, Kevin. "The Journeys of Atom Egoyan." *MovieMaker* 36, www.moviemaker.com/issues/36/egoyan/36_egoyan.html, accessed 24 November 2000.

Lickers, Cynthia, ed. *Imagine Native: Aboriginally-Produced Film and Video.* Toronto: V-Tape and the Aboriginal Film and Video Alliance, 1998.

Lipset, Seymour Martin. *Continental Divide: The Values and Institutions of the United States and Canada.* New York: Routledge, 1990.

"Loews Cineplex Entertainment Announces Financial Results for Second Quarter." *Canadian NewsWire,* http://www.newswire.ca/release/October1998/08/c2008.htm, last accessed 8 May 2000.

Loiselle, André. "François Girard's Glenn Gould and The Idea of North." *Reverse Shot* 1, no. 3 (Fall 1994): 9–13.

Longfellow, Brenda. "Gender, Landscape and Colonial Allegories in *The Far Shore, Loyalties,* and *Mouvements du désir.*" In *Gendering the Nation: Canadian Women's Cinema,* Kay Armatage, Kass Banning, Brenda Longfellow and Janine Marchessault, eds.

——. "*Red Violin,* Commodity Fetishism, and Globalization." Paper given at the 1999 FSAC Conference. Forthcoming in *Canadian Journal of Film Studies.*

Lott, Eric. *Love and Theft: Blackface Minstrelsy and the American Working Class.* New York: Oxford University Press, 1993.

Lynch, Michael. *These Waves of Dying Friends: Poems.* Bowling Green, NY: Contact II Publications, 1989.

Lyotard, Jean-Francois. *The Postmodern Condition: A Report on Knowledge.* Minneapolis: University of Minnesota Press, 1984.

MacDonald, Gayle. "Onex partners launch cinema chain to show flicks to the sticks." *Globe and Mail,* 15 September 1999.

——. and John Partridge. "Cineplex executives let go: Loews merger pushes managers out door." *Globe and Mail,* 2 May 1998.

MacInnis, Craig. "Bruce and Don on the Highway to Hell." *Toronto Star,* 6 October 1991.

——. "Rozema hits nerve in unity wrangling." *Toronto Star,* 29 May 1992.

——. "AIDS: The Musical." *Toronto Star,* 10 September 1993.

——. "Patricia Rozema ... unbound." *Toronto Star,* 17 February 1995.

MacKenzie, Scott. "Flowers in the Dustbin: Termite Culture and Detritus Cinema." *CineAction!* 47 (September 1998).

Mackey, Eva. *The House of Difference.* London: Routledge, 1999.

MacPherson, Lorne W. and Wil Campbell. "The Creation of a Canadian Aboriginal Film and Video Production Fund." Prepared for the Association of Aboriginal Filmmakers of Alberta, 1991.

Magal, Uma. "Indian Cinema Fifty Years After Independence: A Cinema of Ferment." *Asian Cinema* 10, no. 1 (Fall 1998): 193–97.

Magder, Ted. *Canada's Hollywood: The Canadian State and Feature Films.* Toronto: University of Toronto Press, 1993.

Mainguy, Barbara. "Lilies: The Adaptation of Michel Marc Bouchard's Award-winning play." *Point of View* 30 (Fall 1996): 35–39.

Mandate Review Committee, CBC, NFB, Telefilm (Canada). *Making Our Voices Heard: Canadian Broadcasting and Film for the 21st Century.* [aka "The Juneau Report"] Ottawa: Minister of Supply and Services, 1996.

Marchand, Paul, ed. *Our Home and Native Land: A Film and Video Resource Guide for Aboriginal Canadians.* Winnipeg: National Film Board, 1991.

Marchessault, Janine, ed. *Mirror Machine: Video and Identity.* Toronto: YYZ Books, 1995.

Marks, Laura U. "Nice Gun You Got There: John Greyson's Critique of Masculinity." *Parachute* 66 (1992): 27–32.

Marquand, Robert. "Film Stirs Hindu Radical Rage" www.csmonitor.com/durable/2000/02/14/p13.htm.

Marshall, Bill. *Québec National Cinema.* Montréal/Kingston: McGill-Queen's University Press, 2000.

Marsolais, Gilles. *L'Aventure du cinéma direct revisitée.* Laval: Les 400 Coups, 1997.

———. "*Last Night*: Don McKellar." *24 Images* 93–94 (1998): 60–61.

Mathews, Jack. "Movie 'Angel' Could Spark Child Molesters, Critic Charges." *Vancouver Sun*, 19 December 1985.

Mazey, Steven. "AIDS given musical-comedy treatment." *Calgary Herald*, 2 May 1994.

Mazurkewich, Karen. "Film grosses far below target." *Playback*, 19 August 1991.

———. *Cartoon Capers: The History of Canadian Animators.* Toronto: McArthur and Company, 1999.

McCarthy, Shawn. "Ottawa Eyes Cineplex Merger." *Globe and Mail*, 2 October 1997.

———. "Cineplex Deal May Hinge on Sale of Unit." *Globe and Mail*, 3 October 1997.

McGregor, Gaile. *The Wacousta Syndrome: Explorations in Canadian Landscape.* Toronto: University of Toronto Press, 1986.

———. "David Cronenberg and the Ethnospecificity of Horror." *Canadian Journal of Film Studies* 2, no. 1 (1993): 43–62.

McHale, Brian. *Postmodernist Fiction.* London: Routledge, 1987.

McIntosh, David. "Memes, Genes, and Monoculture." *Money, Value, Art.* Toronto: YYZ Books, 2001.

McLuhan, Marshall. *Understanding Media.* Cambridge: MIT Press, 1995.

McMaster, Gerald. "Tenuous Lines of Descent: Indian Arts and Crafts of the Reservation Period." *Canadian Journal of Native Studies* 9, no. 2 (1989): 205–36.

——— and Lee-Ann Martin, eds. *Indigena: Contemporary Native Perspectives.* Vancouver: Douglas and McIntyre, 1992.

Merrell, Floyd. *Peirce's Semiotics Now: A Primer.* Toronto: Canadian Scholars' Press, 1995.

Miller, Mary Jane. *Turn Up the Contrast: CBC Television Drama Since 1952.* Vancouver: University of British Columbia/CBC Enterprises, 1987.

Milner, Brian. "Cineplex to Stick to Film Exhibiting: Karp Says Sell-Offs Exceed $100-million." *Globe and Mail,* 16 June 1990.

Mitchell, Jen. "New attempts to woo customers." *Playback,* 5 December 1994.

Mitchell, Michael. "Indian Education Today." *Pot Pourri,* 1974.

Mitchell, W.J.T. "Introduction." In *Landscape and Power.* W.J.T. Mitchell, ed. Chicago: University of Chicago Press, 1994.

Modleski, Tania. "The Search for Tomorrow in Today's Soap Opera: Notes on a Feminine Narrative form." *Film Quarterly* 33, no. 1 (Fall 1979): 12–21.

——. "The Terror of Pleasure: The Contemporary Horror Film and Postmodern Theory." In *Film Theory and Criticism.* Leo Braudy, Gerald Mast, and Marshall Cohen, eds. Oxford University Press, 1999.

Monette, Paul. *Borrowed Time: An AIDS Memoir.* New York: Harcourt Brace & Co., 1988.

Monk, Katherine. "Director won't undercut his Canadian focus." *Vancouver Sun,* 20 June 1998.

Monk, Phillip, ed. *4 Hours and 38 Minutes: Videotapes by Lisa Steele and Kim Tomczak.* Toronto: Art Gallery of Ontario, 1989.

Morley, David. "Bounded Realms: Household, Family, Community, and Nation." In *Home, Exile, Homeland: Film, Media, and the Politics of Place.* Hamid Naficy, ed. New York and London: Routledge, 1999.

—— and Kevin Robins. *Spaces of Identity: Global Media, Electronic Landscapes and Cultural Boundaries.* London: Routledge, 1995.

Morris, Gary. "My Penis! Where Is My Penis?: John Greyson's *Uncut.*" *Bright Lights Film Journal.* www.brightlightsfilm.com/24/uncut/html.

Morris, Peter. *Embattled Shadows: A History of Canadian Cinema, 1895–1939.* Montréal: McGill-Queen's University Press, 1978.

——. "After Grierson: The National Film Board 1945–1953." In *Take Two,* Seth Feldman, ed.

——. "In Our Own Eyes: The Canonizing of Canadian Film." *Canadian Journal of Film Studies* 3, no. 1 (Spring 1994): 27–44.

Mouat, Jeremy. "The Past of My Place: Western Canadian Artists and the Uses of History." *Prairie Forum* 17, no. 1 (Spring 1992): 79–96.

Mulvey, Laura. "Magnificent Obsession." *Parachute* 42 (1986): 6–12.

Murray, Karen. "Designing theaters around environment." *Variety,* 25–31 July 1994.

Murray, Steve. "Movies: A wacky, eloquent apocalypse unfolds." *Atlanta Journal and Constitution,* 10 December 1999.

Naficy, Hamid. "The Accented Style of the Independent Transnational Cinema: A Conversation with Atom Egoyan." *Cultural Producers in Perilous States: Editing Events, Documenting Change.* George E. Marcus, ed. Chicago: University of Chicago Press, 1997.

National Film Board. "Our People ... Our Vision: An Aboriginal Studio at the National Film Board of Canada." 1991.

——. "NFB Plans National Aboriginal Film Studio." Press release, 9 June 1991.

——. *Studio One Newsletter*. September 1992.

——. *National Film Board of Canada Action Plan: 1994–1997*. 1994.

——. *The National Film Board of Canada in the Year 2000: The Transformation Plan*. National Film Board, 12 February 1996.

——. "The Aboriginal Filmmaking Program." National Film Board, August 1997.

——. "Eight National Film Board Releases Featured at Native American Film and Video Festival." Press release, 22 October 1997.

——. *Annual Report 1997–98*. Montréal: Communication Services, 1998.

——. "NFB's Alternative Drama Program." Undated press release.

—— and Studio D. *Black on Screen: Images of Black Canadians 1950's to 1990's*. National Film Board, 1992.

Nichols, Bill. *Representing Reality: Issues and Concepts in Documentary*. Bloomington: Indiana University Press, 1991.

——. *Blurred Boundaries: Questions of Meaning in Contemporary Culture*. Bloomington: Indiana University Press, 1994.

Onodera, Midi. Interview in *Lift*. November 1992.

Orwall, Bruce. "Theatre closings possible in Cineplex-Sony merger: Draft document filed with SEC also foresees expansion." *Globe and Mail*, 4 February 1998.

Ostwald, Peter. *Glenn Gould: The Ecstasy and Tragedy of Genius*. New York: Norton, 1997.

Overton, Jim. *Making a World of Difference: Essays on Tourism, Culture, and Development in Newfoundland*. St. John's: ISER Books, 1996.

Palmieri, Giovanni. "'The Author' According to Bakhtin ... and Bakhtin the Author." In *The Contexts of Bakhtin: Philosophy, Authorship, Aesthetics*. David Shepard, ed. London: Harwood, 1998.

Palys, Ted S. *Histories of Convenience: Understanding Twentieth Century Aboriginal Film Images in Context*. New Westminster: School of Criminology, Simon Fraser University, 1995.

Paterson, Andrew J. "Private Parts in Public Places." *Fuse*, January–February 1989.

Patton, Cindy. "Tremble Hetero Swine!" *Fear of a Queer Planet: Queer Politics and Social Theory*. Michael Warner, ed. Minneapolis: University of Minnesota Press, 1983.

Peers, Martin. "Cinemark, Cineplex merge ops." *Variety*, 6–12 March 1995.

——. "Exhibs vexed by Wall St. hex on plex." *Variety*, 26 January–1 February 1998.

Peirce, Charles S. "The Categories in Detail." In *Collected Papers*, vol. 6. Charles Hartshorne and Paul Weiss, eds. Cambridge: Harvard University Press, 1931.

Pendakur, Manjunath. *Canadian Dreams and American Control: The Political Economy of the Canadian Film Industry.* Toronto: Garamond, 1990.

Pérusse, Denise. "Alanis Obomsawin." In *Le dictionnaire du cinéma québécois.* Michel Coulombe and Marcel Jean, eds. Montréal: Boreal, 1991.

Peters, Helen, ed. *The Plays of Codco.* Toronto: Peter Lang Publishing, 1993.

Peters, John Durham. "Exile, Nomadism, and Diaspora: The Stakes of Mobility in the Western Canon." In *Home, Exile, Homeland: Film, Media, and the Politics of Place.* Hamid Naficy, ed. New York: Routledge, 1999.

Pevere, Geoff. "Filmography." In Atom Egoyan, *Exotica.* Toronto: Coach House Press, 1995.

——. "Middle of Nowhere: Ontario Movies After 1980." *Post Script* 15, no. 1 (Fall 1995): 9–22. Originally published in *Les Cinémas du Canada.* Sylvain Garel and André Paquet, eds. Paris: Editions du Centre Pompidou, 1992.

—— and Greig Dymond. *Mondo Canuck: A Canadian Pop Culture Odyssey.* Scarborough: Prentice Hall Canada, 1996.

Pinedo, Isabel Cristina. *Recreational Terror: Women and the Pleasures of Horror Film Viewing.* Albany: SUNY Press, 1997.

Pollard, Velma. *Dread Talk: The Language of Rastafari.* Jamaica: Canoe Press, University of the West Indies, 1994.

Pomerance, M. and J. Sakeris, eds. *Pictures of a Generation on Hold: Selected Papers.* Toronto: Media Studies Working Group, 1996.

Porton, Richard. "Family Romances." *Cineaste* 23, no. 2 (1997): 8–15.

——. "The Politics of Denial: An Interview with Atom Egoyan." *Cineaste* 25, no. 1 (Winter 1999): 39–41.

Posner, Michael. *Canadian Dreams: The Making and Marketing of Independent Films.* Vancouver/ Toronto: Douglas & McIntyre, 1993.

Quick Canadian Facts, 1966–1967. 22nd edition. Toronto: Thorn Press, 1967.

Rainer, Yvonne. "Working round the L-word." In *Queer Looks: Perspectives on Lesbian and Gay Film and Video.* Martha Gever, John Greyson, and Pratibha Parmar, eds. New York and London: Routledge, 1993.

Ramsay, Christine. "Canadian Narrative Cinema from the Margins: 'The Nation' and Masculinity in *Goin' Down the Road.*" *Canadian Journal of Film Studies* 2, no. 2 (1993): 27–50.

Ray, Robert B. "Postmodernism." *Encyclopedia of Literature and Criticism.* Martin Coyle, Peter Garside, Malcolm Kelsall, and John Peck, eds. London: Routledge, 1990.

Rayns, Tony. "Exploitations." *Sight and Sound* 5, no. 5 (May 1995): 6–8.

——. "*Uncut.*" *Sight and Sound* 8, no. 10 (October 1998): 59–60.

Redding, Judith M. and Victoria A. Brownworth. *Film Fatales: Independent Women Directors.* Seattle: Seal Press, 1997.

Rice–Barker, Leo. "Industry Banks on New Technology, Expanded Slates." *Playback,* 6 May 1996.

Rich, B. Ruby. "When Difference Is (More Than) Skin Deep." *Queer Looks: Perspectives on Lesbian and Gay Film and Video.* Martha Gever, John Greyson, and Pratibha Parmar, eds. New York and London: Routledge, 1993. 318–39.

Richards, Jeffrey and Dorothy Sheridan, eds. *Mass-Observation at the Movies.* London and New York: Routledge and Kegan Paul, 1987.

Riche, Ed. *Rare Birds.* New York: Doubleday, 1998.

Robbins, Jim. "Drabinsky Confirms Cineplex buy of RKO Century Warner; To add 38 NY-area screens." *Variety,* 6 August 1986.

——. "Emotional crowd protests close of Regency; Cineplex Odeon mum." *Variety,* 9 September 1987.

Robertson, Clive. "Lisa Steele: The Recent Tapes." *Centerfold* 3, no. 5 (July 1979): 248–54.

Rompkey, Ronald. "The Idea of Newfoundland and Arts Policy Since Confederation." *Newfoundland Studies* 14, no. 2 (Fall 1998): 266–81.

Ross, Bob. "A *Night* to reconsider." *Tampa Tribune,* 19 November 1999.

Roth, Murray. "Cineplex boss details Chi plans; aims for 400 new U.S. screens." *Variety,* 2 April 1986.

Royer, Geneviève. "Entretien: Don McKellar." *Séquences* 200 (January–February 1998): 18–21.

——. "François Girard: Jeux sans frontières." *Séquences* 200 (January–February 1998): 36–38.

Rozema, Patricia. *Jane Austen's Mansfield Park: A Screenplay.* New York: Talk Miramax Books, 2000.

Said, Edward. "Jane Austen and Empire." *Mansfield Park and Persuasion.* Judy Simons, ed. New York: St. Martin's Press, 1997.

"St. Sebastian." Catholic Online Saints. www.saints.catholic.org/saints/stsindex, accessed 3 May 2001.

Sarris, Andrew. *The American Cinema: Directors and Directions 1929–1968.* New York: Simon & Schuster, 1973.

Saunders, Doug. "Director of *Lilies* arrested." *Globe and Mail,* 29 October 1996.

——. "Women filmmakers at the crossroads." *Globe and Mail,* 28 January 2000.

Scheff, W. "Flatland Films." *The Independent Eye,* 11, no. 1 (Fall 1989).

Schwartzberg, Shlomo. "*Highway 61.*" *Performing Arts in Canada,* 1 April 1992.

——. "In the Frame: With his second feature, *Zero Patience,* director John Greyson seems set to make his mark on the Canadian movie scene." *Performing Arts* 28, no. 4 (Spring 1994): 35.

——. "Guzzo's Gusto." *Boxoffice,* www.boxoffice.com/showcanada99/daily99story4.html, accessed 3 November 1999.

——. "Major Players." *Boxoffice,* www.boxoffice.com/showcanada99/daily99story4.html, accessed 3 November 1999.

Scott, Jay. "True Confessions." *Globe and Mail,* 24 September 1988.

Seaman, Patricia. "*The Making of Monsters* and Bodies in Trouble." *Fuse* 15, no. 15 (Winter 1992): 37–38.

Secor Group. "Canadian Government Intervention in the Film and Video Industry." 19 October 1994.

Sedgwick, Eve Kosofsky. *The Epistemology of the Closet.* Berkeley: University of California Press, 1990.

Seiler, Tamara Palmer. "Melting Pot and Mosaic: Images and Reality" In *Canada and the United States: Differences That Count.* David Thomas, ed. Peterborough: Broadview Press, 1993.

Seltzer, Mark. "Serial Killers." *Differences: A Journal of Feminist Cultural Studies* 5, no. 1 (1993): 92–128.

Sherbarth, Chris. "Why Not D? An historical look at the NFB's Woman's Studio." *Cinema Canada* 139 (March 1987): 9–13.

"Shock to silence: Exhibitors react to Drabinsky's move." *Variety,* 25 November 1987.

Siebel, Andrea. "The Ground is Always Shifting." Interview with Atom Egoyan. *Blimp* 30 (1994): 32–35.

Sidhwa, Basi. "Playing with *Fire.*" *Ms.,* November/December 1997.

Sidhwa, Bapsi. "Watching My Novel Become Her Film." *New York Times,* 5 September 1999.

Silverman, Kaja. *The Subject of Semiotics.* New York: Oxford University Press, 1983.

——. *The Acoustic Voice: The Female Voice in Psychoanalysis and Cinema.* Bloomington: Indiana University Press, 1988.

Simons, Paula. "Bye Bye Blues, Hello World: Anne Wheeler and Allarcom Go For the Big Time." *Western Report,* 22 August 1988.

Sinclair, Iain. *Crash.* London: British Film Institute, 1999.

Sineux, Michel. "*32 Short Films about Glenn Gould*: Glenn Gould revisité." *Positif* (January 1995): 36–37.

Sinker, Mark. "Thirty-Two Short Films about Glenn Gould." *Sight and Sound* 4, no. 5 (July 1994): 55–56.

Smith, Paul Julian. "*Zero Patience.*" *Sight and Sound* 4, no. 7 (September 1994): 54–55.

Smith, Valerie. "The Documentary Impulse in Contemporary U.S. African American Film." In *Black Popular Culture*, Gina Dent. ed.

Smitherson, Geneva. *Talkin and Testifyin: The Language of Black America.* Boston: Houghton Mifflin, 1977.

Smoluch, Agata. "(Con)texts of Hybrid Authorship: Canadian Cinema, Feminism, Sexual Difference and the Dialogic Films of Patricia Rozema." Unpublished master's thesis. York University, 1999.

Smythe, Dallas. *Dependency Road: Communications, Capitalism, Consciousness and Canada.* Norwood NJ: Ablex, 1981.

Sontag, Susan. *Illness as Metaphor.* New York: Vintage, 1979.

Staiger, Janet. *Interpreting Films: Studies in the Historical Reception of American Cinema.* Princeton: Princeton University Press, 1992.

Stacey, Jackie. *Star Gazing: Hollywood cinema and female spectatorship.* London and New York: Routledge, 1994.

Statistics Canada. *Film and Video, 1992–93, Culture Statistics*. Ottawa: Ministry of Industry, Science and Technology, 1995.

——. "Film and Video Distribution Survey, 1994–95." *The Daily,* 29 July 1996.

——. *Movie Theatres and Drive-ins, 1997–98: Culture Statistics*. Ottawa: Culture, Tourism and the Centre for Education Statistics, 1999.

——. "Film and Video Distribution and Wholesaling Survey, 2000." 87F0010XPE, Ottawa.

Steele, Lisa. "Women and Infanticide." *Centerfold* 3, no. 4 (May 1979): 156–62.

—— and Kim Tomczak, eds. *The Blood Records: Written and Annotated*. Vols. 1 and 2. Oakville: Oakville Galleries, 1999.

Steele, Scott. "AIDS, The Musical: *Zero Patience*." *Maclean's,* 7 March 1994.

Stephens, Ian. *Diary of a Trademark*. Ste Anne de Bellevue, Québec: The Muses' Company, 1994.

Steven, Peter. *Brink of Reality: New Canadian Documentary and Video*. Toronto: Between the Lines, 1993.

Stokes, Melvyn and Richard Maltby. *Identifying Hollywood Audiences: Cultural Identity and the Movies*. London: British Film Institute, 1999.

Stonechild, Blair and Bill Waiser. *Loyal Until Death: Indians and the North-West Rebellion*. Calgary: Fifth House Publishing, 1997.

"Summer b.o. surge posed in Canada by Famous Players." *Variety,* 15 October 1986.

Swedko, Pamela. "Theatre Executives gather for ShowCanada confab." *Playback,* 5 May 1997.

Taubin, Amy. "Pulling Punches." *Village Voice,* 29 December 1999–4 January 2000.

Taylor, Clyde. "Decolonizing the Image: New U.S. Black Cinema." *Jump Cut* 28 (1984).

——. "The Ironies of Majority–Minority Discourses." In *The Mask of Art: Breaking the Aesthetic Contract—Film and Literature*. Bloomington and Indianapolis: Indiana University Press, 1998.

Testa, Bart. "Mike Hoolboom's *Letters from Home* Sidesteps AIDS Clichés." *Point of View* 32 (Summer/Fall 1997): 35–36.

Thompson, Patricia, ed. *Film Canada Yearbook 1994*. Toronto: Cine-Communications, 1994.

"Through Women's Eyes: Female Visions Thrive in Canada." *Maclean's,* 29 March 1993.

Todd, Loretta. "What More Do They Want?" In *Indigena*, Gerald McMaster and Lee-Ann Martin, eds.

——. "Aboriginal Narratives in Cyberspace." In *Immersed in Technology: Art and Virtual Environments*. Mary Anne Moser, ed. Cambridge: MIT Press, 1996.

——. "Decolonizing the Archival Photograph." Surrey art exhibition catalogue, Surrey, BC, 1997.

——. "Three Moments After Savage Graces." *Harbour* 3, no. 1.

"Toronto CO multiplex gets liquor license." *Variety,* 17 June 1991.

Totaro, Donato and Simon Galiero. "Egoyan's Journey: An Interview with Atom Egoyan." *Hors Champ*, www.horschamp.qc.ca/new_offscreen/egoyan.html, accessed on 28 November 2000.

Treichler, Paula A. *How to Have Theory in an Epidemic: Cultural Chronicles of AIDS*. Durham and London: Duke University Press, 1999.

Tremblay, Odile. "L'art de provoquer pour provoquer..." *Le Devoir*, 9 February 2000.

Tuer, Dot. "Utopias of Resistance, Strategies of Cultural Self-Determination." In *4 Hours and 38 Minutes*, Phillip Monk, ed.

——. "The Art of Nation Building: Constructing a 'National Identity' for Post-War Canada." *Parellélogramme* 17, no. 4 (1992).

——. "Perspectives of the body in Canadian Video Art." *C Magazine* (Winter 1993): 30–36.

——. ed. *Cache Du Cinema*. Toronto: The Funnel, 1985.

Turbide, Diane. "The Sleep Room." *Maclean's*, 12 January 1998.

Tusher, Will. "Cineplex Odeon agrees to sell 57 Canadian multiplexes in fall." *Variety*, 17 August 1988.

Tyler, Carol-Anne, "Desiring Machines? Queer Re-Visions of Feminist Film Theory." In *Coming Out of Feminism?* Mandy Merck, Naomi Segal, and Elizabeth Wright, eds. Oxford and Malden, MA: Blackwell Publishers, 1998.

Valaskakis, Gail. "Communication and Control in the Canadian North: the Potential of Interactive Satellites." *Etudes Inuit Studies* 6 (1983).

Vale, Allison. "Boffo Screen Build." *Playback,* 5 May 1997.

Vermee, Alison. "Anne Wheeler and the Drama of Everyday Life." *Take One* 4, no. 9 (1995): 38–41.

Vérroneau, Pierre. *Les cinémas canadiens*. Paris: Pierre Cherminier Editeur/Montréal: Cinémathèque Québécois, 1975.

Walcott, Rinaldo. "The Politics of Reading Third Cinema: Reading the Narrative of Clement Virgo's Rude." In *Pictures of a Generation on Hold: Selected Papers*, M. Pomerance and J. Sakeris, eds.

Walsh, David. "The Case of Deepa Mehta and the Defense of Artistic Freedom." *Cinemascope* 4 (Summer 2000): 22–25.

Walz, Gene. "The PGA Connection." *Animation World Magazine* 22 (May 1997).

——. *Cartoon Charlie: The Life and Art of Animation Pioneer Charles Thorson*. Winnipeg: Great Plains Publications, 1998.

Waugh, Thomas. "Words of Command: Notes on Cultural and Political Inflections of Direct Cinema in Indian Independent Documentary." *CineAction* 23 (Winter 1990–91): 28–39.

——. "Erotic Self-Images in the Gay Male AIDS Melodrama." In *Fluid Exchanges: Artists and Critics in the Aids Crisis*. James Miller, ed. Toronto: University of Toronto Press, 1992.

——. "Cinemas, Nations, Masculinities: The Martin Walsh Memorial Lecture (1998)." *Canadian Journal of Film Studies* 8, no. 1 (Spring 1999): 8–44.

——. *The Fruit Machine: Twenty Years of Writings on Queer Cinema*. Durham: Duke University Press, 2000.

——. ed. *'Show Us Life': Toward a History and Aesthetics of the Committed Documentary*. Metuchen, NJ: Scarecrow Press, 1984.

Wees, William. *Recycled Images: The Art and Politics of Found Footage Film.* New York: Anthology Film Archives, 1993.

——. "'Let's Set the Record Straight': The International Experimental Film Congress, Toronto 1989." *Canadian Journal of Film Studies* 9, no. 1 (Spring 2000): 101–16.

Westfall, William. "On the Concept of Region in Canadian History and Literature." In *A Passion for Identity: Introduction to Canadian Studies.* Eli Mandel and David Taras, eds. Toronto: Methuen, 1987.

White, Rob. "*Lilies*." *Sight and Sound* 8, no. 1 (January 1998): 49.

Wilden, Anthony. *The Imaginary Canadian.* Vancouver: Pulp Press, 1978.

Wilkinson, Kathleen. "Filmmaker Deepa Mehta is on *Fire*." *Lesbian News* 23, no. 2 (September 1997): 38.

Wilton, Tamsin. *Immortal Invisible: Lesbians and the Moving Image.* New York and London: Routledge, 1995.

Winks, Robin. *The Blacks in Canada: A History.* Montréal and Kingston: McGill-Queen's University Press, 1997.

Winston, Brian. "Documentary: I Think We are in Trouble." In *New Challenges for Documentary.* Alan Rosenthal, ed. Berkeley: University of California Press, 1988.

Wise, Wyndham. "100 Great and Glorious Years of Canadian Cinema—The Sequel." *Take One*, Spring 1997.

——. "*Take One*'s 1998 Survey of Canadian Films in the GTA." *Take One*, Winter 1999.

Wollen, Peter. "The Auteur Theory." *Theories of Authorship: A Reader.* John Caughie, ed. London: Routledge, 1991.

Wood, Robin. *Hollywood from Vietnam to Reagan.* New York: Columbia University Press, 1986.

——. "Towards a Canadian (Inter)national Cinema: Part 2: *Loyalties* and *Life Classes*." *CineAction!* 17 (September 1989): 23–35.

Yacowar, Maurice. "The Canadian as Ethnic Minority." *Film Quarterly* (Winter 1986–87): 13–19.

Zeleke, E. Centime. "That's a Cut: Feds Close Women's Studio." *Herizons*, Summer 1996.

Zizek, Slavoj. "Multiculturalism, Or, the Cultural Logic of Multinational Captitalism." *New Left Review* 255 (1997).

Index